(M., S., & S.) Computer Law ACB

WEST'S LAW SCHOOL ADVISORY BOARD

COMPUTER LAW

Cases — Comments — Questions

By

Peter B. Maggs
Richard W. and Marie L. Corman Professor of Law
University of Illinois at Urbana-Champaign

John T. Soma
Professor of Law
University of Denver

James A. Sprowl
Senior Lecturer, School of Law
Loyola University of Chicago
Of Counsel, Fitch, Even, Tabin & Flannery
Chicago, Illinois

AMERICAN CASESBOOK SERIES®

WEST PUBLISHING CO.
ST. PAUL, MINN., 1992

610 Opperman Drive
P.O. Box 64526
St. Paul, MN 55164–0526

Printed in the United States of America

Library of Congress Cataloging-in-Publication Data

Maggs, Peter B.
Computer law : cases, comments, and questions / by Peter B. Maggs, John T. Soma, James A. Sprowl.
p. cm. — (American casebook series)
Includes index.
ISBN 0-314-92197-4
1. Computers—Law and legislation—United States—Cases.
I. Soma, John T. II. Sprowl, James A. (James Alexander), 1941–.
III. Title. IV. Series.
KF390.5.C6M34 1992
343.73'0999—dc20
[347.303999] 91–31622
CIP

ISBN 0-314-92197-4

(M., S., & S.) Computer Law ACB
1st Reprint–1997

TEXT IS PRINTED ON 10% POST CONSUMER RECYCLED PAPER

Preface

We have ventured into uncharted territory in preparing this casebook on computer law. The increasing attention of legislatures and courts to computer law issues has provided a wealth of materials from which to select. We have tried to choose cases that are both important and teachable. We have edited them to remove irrelevant issues and lengthy string citations, but have not attempted to truncate or rephrase the opinions.

We owe thanks to many who helped with this volume. Law students who provided valuable research assistance are: Mr. Vernon A. Evans, Ms. Carolyn M. Lindh, and Mr. Michael J. Santiago of the University of Denver; Mr. Royce Bedward of the University of Illinois; and Mr. Perry J. Hoffman of the University of Wisconsin. Staff members who helped greatly in preparation of the manuscript were Ms. Ma Antonieta Murphy of the University of Denver and Ms. Ruth Manint of the University of Illinois. The patent chapter was much improved by the reading and criticism of Mr. Robert J. Fox of Fitch, Even, Tabin & Flannery.

P.B.M.
J.T.S.
J.A.S.

October, 1991

*

Summary of Contents

Table of Contents

Table of Cases

The principal cases are in bold type. Cases cited or discussed in the text are roman type. References are to pages. Cases cited in principal cases and within other quoted materials are not included.

COMPUTER LAW

Cases — Comments — Questions

*

Chapter I

INTRODUCTION TO COMPUTER LAW

Is there such a subject as "computer law"? If so, what should a computer law casebook include? The answers to these questions are not obvious. Certainly there are many cases involving computers. A recent WESTLAW search for the word "COMPUTER" found 11,288 cases in the "allfeds" data base and 8,928 cases in "allstates". A similar search for "SHOE" found 15,867 Federal and 25,104 state "SHOE" cases. No one is suggesting that law students should study "shoe law" as a separate course. Students will read *Brown Shoe Co. v. United States,* 370 U.S. 294 (1962), a leading vertical merger case, in their antitrust course and may read a few more cases involving shoes in other courses. Little or nothing in these cases turns on anything peculiar about shoes. Cases involving shoes do not cite other cases involving shoes. Computer cases, in contrast, often turn on the special nature of computer software and hardware, and regularly cite other computer cases.

Why are computers "special" when shoes are not? First, computer software and hardware are the most complex and rapidly developing intellectual creations of modern man. Second, computers provide unprecedented power in accessing and manipulating data. Third, computers work in complex systems that require standardization and compatibility to function. Each of these special features has engendered one or more bodies of law. Complex intellectual creation demands comprehensive intellectual property protection. Computer technology, however, differs fundamentally from previous objects of intellectual property protection, and thus does not fit easily into traditional copyright and patent law. Courts and legislatures, consequently, have had to exert great efforts to adapt old legal forms and create new ones. The power of the computer to access and manipulate data requires new types of government regulation. Antisocial individuals may steal or destroy information in ways that involve no physical trespass on property and thus may fall outside traditional regulatory and criminal prohibitions.

Potential enemies seek access to our computers and data banks to catch up with our high technology military power. Litigators seek access to opposing parties' computer data. Tax assessors try to tax this valuable asset. Standardization is essential, but provides opportunities for companies that can set standards to exploit the public by monopolizing software and hardware markets.

These special qualities of computers have determined the scope of this casebook. The casebook opens with chapters on copyright and patent issues. These chapters serve a dual purpose. They have the utilitarian purpose of introducing an area of law that is of considerable importance in practice. But they also attempt to build an understanding of the unique features of computer technology as an intellectual creation. A chapter on computer contracts explores the issue of definition further—just what is the seller of computer hardware and software selling—pieces of metal and magnetic material or solutions to problems? The casebook then turns to ways of preventing abuses of the power of the computer—computer crimes, privacy, limits on litigation discovery, and export controls. Finally, the casebook moves on to issues of abuse of standard-setting powers, as regulated by antitrust, trademark, and misappropriation law.

Chapter II

COPYRIGHT PROTECTION OF COMPUTER SOFTWARE

A. INTRODUCTION TO COPYRIGHT CONCEPTS

Article I, sec. 8, of the United States Constitution grants Congress the power: "To promote the Progress of Science and useful Arts, by securing for limited Times to Authors and Inventors the exclusive Right to their respective Writings and Discoveries." This text needs a little explanation. In eighteenth-century English "science" meant what we today would call knowledge, while the "useful arts" meant what we would call technology. In eighteenth century style, elegance of language (one feature of which was the avoidance of repetition) prevailed over precision in legal drafting. Thus it seems likely that the word "discoveries" really means nothing other than "inventions." Finally, in another elegant stylistic feature, the drafters of the Constitution interwove the patent and copyright powers. Translated into modern English, this clause might read as follows: "To promote the progress of knowledge by securing for limited times to authors the exclusive right to their writings; and to promote the progress of technology by securing for limited times to inventors the exclusive right to their inventions." It is worth repeating the explanation of the copyright and patent power given by James Madison in *The Federalist,* No. 43:

> The utility of this power will scarcely be questioned. The copyright of authors has been solemnly adjudged, in Great Britain, to be a right of common law. The right to useful inventions seems with equal reason to belong to the inventors. The public good fully coincides in both cases with the claims of individuals. The States cannot separately make effectual provision for either of these cases. * * *

While explicitly recognizing the power of Congress to promote progress by granting copyright and patent protection, this same clause put an important restriction on the power, with the limitation that the exclusive rights be granted only for "limited times" and only for "writings and discoveries." Clearly the draftsmen had in mind some of the abuses of monopolies in England where favorites of the Crown had been granted monopolies over everyday necessities such as matches and playing cards. These monopolies provided great personal wealth at the expense of the public. The Constitutional restrictions on the copyright and patent powers reflect the basic conflict between the need to give temporary monopoly power as a reward for innovation and the general principle of free competition. Much of the work of the courts and Congress in interpreting this clause in the last two centuries has been in drawing the line this clause says must be drawn between the legitimate rewards of the innovator and the granting of monopoly power to the undeserving.

Implicit in the Commerce Clause of the Constitution is the idea that the United States should be a single economic unit linked to the world economy, rather than a collection of state economies isolated by trade barriers set up by state legislation. Madison, himself, in the passage just quoted, pointed out the inability of the states to make effectual provisions for copyrights and patents. More importantly, because the incentive for innovation is not found solely in government-created exclusive rights, but also in the rewards accruing to the first person to market a better product, it was essential that the new product markets be as broad as possible to help sustain the heavy product development costs. The work of Congress and the courts in using the Commerce power to break down state barriers to trade has provided a second essential incentive to technological progress.

Congress exercised its Constitutional power of "securing" to "authors" the "exclusive rights" to "their writings" in the Copyright Act of 1976. A 1978 Report of the National Commission on New Technological Uses of Copyrighted Works (CONTU) led Congress to amend the Act in 1980, adding provisions specifically dealing with computer programs. These provisions made it clear that computer programs were eligible for copyright protection. Because computer software and computer data are very different from traditional "writings", the courts have had an uneasy time applying copyright law to the computer area.

The structure of the copyright system is designed by three key sections of the Copyright Act, § 102, § 106, and § 109. Section 102 defines copyrightable subject matter. Section 106 defines the exclusive rights of the copyright owner. Section 109 is the most important of a group of sections listing limitations upon (exceptions to) the exclusive rights granted by § 106.

Before beginning the analysis of the scope of copyright protection for software, it is useful to consider what software is. A computer is like a tree. At the roots lie the transistor gates that support the entire tree. In theory, any system could be designed from these gates without any programming, and ultimately all hardware and software is reducible to a complex interconnection of these gates. That is the sense in which the gates support the whole tree.

Moving further up the tree, one finds the hardware level, where everything the computer can do is defined in terms of hardwired logic chips; the microcode level, where microcode sequences define all the operations the computer can perform; the machine-language level, where all of the computer's possible operations are defined in the computer's native tongue; and finally the operating system and high-level programming language level, where all the operations the computer can carry out are defined in the syntax of an English-like language. Each of these levels supports the entire tree above itself. Note that all the upper portions of the tree are supported by the high-level programming-language level. Everything the computer can do must be expressable at this level, either directly or with the help of lower-level operating system support. So the tree rests entirely upon this level just as much as it does upon the transistor gate level at the roots and the machine-language level near the base.

Above the high-level programming language level, the tree begins to branch out widely into the various disciplines. "Tailoring" types of programming are carried out at these levels, but the languages used tend to be specific to the various professional domains. Here we have left the domain of the computer scientist and entered the domain of the business man, engineer, social scientist, librarian, attorney, doctor, and "video game freak," just to name a few. System design at these high levels requires intimate knowledge of the target professional user's problems, needs, and vocabulary. For example, you will find nothing specific about designing business payroll systems in a computer science department library; for that knowledge, you must visit the business school library. An engineering system may perform the same computations as a statistician's system, but the languages used by the two professionals are so different that neither could use a system designed for the other without considerable retraining. More and more "profession-specific" systems are emerging as time passes. You can see why it is absurd to talk of a "computer expert" without specifying in precisely what part of the tree you expect the expert's expertise to reside. No computer expert knows the entire tree.

In *Apple Computer, Inc. v. Franklin Computer Corp.,* 714 F.2d 1240 (3d Cir.1983), (the leading case on software copyrightability) the court provided a helpful analysis of levels of computer language, listed some available storage media, and provided a perhaps oversimplified categorization of computer programs.

* * *

> There are three levels of computer language in which computer programs may be written. High level language, such as the commonly used BASIC or FORTRAN, uses English words and symbols, and is relatively easy to learn and understand (e.g., "GO TO 40" tells the computer to skip intervening steps and go to the step at line 40). A somewhat lower level language is assembly language, which consists of alphanumeric labels (e.g., "ADC" means "add with carry"). Statements in high level language and apparently also statements in assem-

bly language, are referred to as written in "source code." The third, or lowest level computer language, is machine language, a binary language using two symbols, 0 and 1, to indicate an open or closed switch (e.g., "01101001" means, to the Apple, add two numbers and save the result). Statements in machine language are referred to as written in "object code."

The CPU can only follow instructions written in object code. However, programs are usually written in source code which is more intelligible to humans. Programs written in source code can be converted or translated by a "compiler" program into object code for use by the computer. Programs are generally distributed only in their object code version stored on a memory device.

A computer program can be stored or fixed on a variety of memory devices, two of which are of particular relevance for this case. The ROM (Read Only Memory) is an internal permanent memory device consisting of a semi-conductor "chip" which is incorporated into the circuitry of the computer. A program in object code is embedded on a ROM before it is incorporated in the computer. Information stored on a ROM can only be read, not erased or rewritten. * * * The other device used for storing the programs at issue is a diskette or "floppy disk", an auxiliary memory device consisting of a flexible magnetic disk resembling a phonograph record, which can be inserted into the computer and from which data or instructions can be read.

Computer programs can be categorized by function as either application programs or operating system programs. Application programs usually perform a specific task for the computer user, such as word processing, checkbook balancing, or playing a game. In contrast, operating system programs generally manage the internal functions of the computer or facilitate use of application programs.

COPYRIGHT ACT OF 1976

§ 101 Definitions

* * *

A "computer program" is a set of statements or instructions to be used directly or indirectly in a computer in order to bring about a certain result.

§ 102. Subject matter of copyright: In general

(a) Copyright protection subsists, in accordance with this title, in original works of authorship fixed in any tangible medium of expression, now known or later developed, from which they can be perceived, reproduced, or otherwise communicated, either directly or with the aid of a machine or device. Works of authorship include the following categories:

(1) literary works;

(2) musical works, including any accompanying words;

(3) dramatic works, including any accompanying music;

(4) pantomimes and choreographic works;

(5) pictorial, graphic, and sculptural works;

(6) motion pictures and other audiovisual works; and

(7) sound recordings.

(b) In no case does copyright protection for an original work of authorship extend to any idea, procedure, process, system, method of operation, concept, principle, or discovery, regardless of the form in which it is described, explained, illustrated, or embodied in such work.

Notes and Questions

1. The list of categories in § 102 is not exhaustive, merely illustrative. It is now well established that computer programs are "works of authorship" protected under § 102. However, it is not completely clear that everything fixed on a computer disk is a work of authorship. Suppose a scientist buys a data recording program and uses it to record temperatures from a thermometer connected to a personal computer. Is the record of temperatures the "writing of an author"? If so, who is the author—the scientist or the company that prepared the computer program or the company that made the thermometer?

2. Many computer programs have highly utilitarian purposes, such as controlling the rate at which fuel is fed to an automobile engine. Accused infringers often argue § 102(b) precludes protection for such programs.

3. When examined closely, a computer program offers not one, but a variety of objects of copyright protection, including: source code, mnemonics, object code, microcode, "look and feel", input formats, and manuals.

B. COMPUTER-RELATED SUBJECT MATTER OF COPYRIGHT

1. SOURCE CODE

Computer programmers write in a "programming language." The program written in this language is called "source code." It is hard to find a reported copyright case concerning source code, because in most cases programmers or their employers keep the source code as a trade secret and do not distribute it. There is no doubt, however, about the availability of copyright protection for source code.

2. MNEMONICS

A significant minority of computer programs written for commercial distribution are written in "Assembly Language." This is a language which is very close to the actual instructions built into the computer's processing unit, but expressed in shorthand coined words ("mnemonics") that are easy for humans to remember. Because of the link between assembly language and the actual machine instructions, there is a different assembly language for each type of central processor or microprocessor. For each assembly language, there is a collection of mnemonics. Some are obvious and are used in many assembly languages, such as "ADD" for add or "SUB" for subtract. Others are arbitrary, such as "IMS." It is hard to find cases on point, but arguably, the collection of mnemonics that makes up an assembly language may be protected by copyright as a "compilation." Compare *Reiss v. National Quotation Bureau, Inc.*, 276 Fed. 717 (S.D.N.Y.1921) (collection of error-resistant words for telegraph code copyrightable).

3. OBJECT CODE

After a programmer writes a program in some computer language, the computer translates it into the language actually understood by the machine, "object code." Most programs are distributed in the form of object code. During the 1960s and 1970s there was some doubt about the copyrightability of object code. The following case resolved these doubts.

APPLE COMPUTER, INC. v. FRANKLIN COMPUTER CORPORATION

United States Court of Appeals, Third Circuit, 1983.
714 F.2d 1240

SLOVITER, CIRCUIT JUDGE.

I.

INTRODUCTION

Apple Computer, Inc. appeals from the district court's denial of a motion to preliminarily enjoin Franklin Computer Corp. from infringing the copyrights Apple holds on fourteen computer programs.

* * *

In this case the district court denied the preliminary injunction, *inter alia,* because it had "some doubt as to the copyrightability of the programs." *Apple Computer, Inc. v. Franklin Computer Corp.,* 545 F.Supp. 812, 812 (E.D.Pa.1982). This legal ruling is fundamental to all future proceedings in this action and, as the parties and amici curiae seem to agree, has considerable significance to the computer services industry. Because we conclude that the district court proceeded under an erroneous view of the applicable law, we reverse the denial of the preliminary injunction and remand.

II.

FACTS AND PROCEDURAL HISTORY

Apple, one of the computer industry leaders, manufactures and markets personal computers (microcomputers), related peripheral equipment such as disk drives (peripherals), and computer programs (software). It presently manufactures Apple II computers and distributes over 150 programs. Apple has sold over 400,000 Apple II computers, employs approximately 3,000 people, and had annual sales of $335,000,000 for fiscal year 1981. One of the byproducts of Apple's success is the independent development by third parties of numerous computer programs which are designed to run on the Apple II computer.

Franklin, the defendant below, manufactures and sells the ACE 100 personal computer and at the time of the hearing employed about 75 people and had sold fewer than 1,000 computers. The ACE 100 was designed to be "Apple compatible," so that peripheral equipment and software developed for use with the Apple II computer could be used in conjunction with the ACE 100. Franklin's copying of Apple's operating system computer programs in an effort to achieve such compatibility precipitated this suit.

Like all computers both the Apple II and ACE 100 have a central processing unit (CPU) which is the integrated circuit that executes programs. In lay terms, the CPU does the work it is instructed to do. Those instructions are contained on computer programs.

* * *

* * * The parties agree that the fourteen computer programs at issue in this suit are operating system programs.[4]

Apple filed suit in the United States District Court for the Eastern District of Pennsylvania pursuant to 28 U.S.C. § 1338 on May 12, 1982, alleging that Franklin was liable for copyright infringement of the fourteen computer programs, patent infringement, unfair competition, and misappropriation. Franklin's answer in respect to the copyright counts included the affirmative defense that the programs contained no copyrightable subject matter. Franklin counterclaimed for declaratory judgment that the copyright registrations were invalid and unenforceable, and sought affirmative relief on the basis of Apple's alleged misuse. Franklin also moved to dismiss eleven of the fourteen copyright infringement counts on the ground that Apple failed to comply with the procedural requirements for suit under 17 U.S.C. §§ 410, 411.

After expedited discovery, Apple moved for a preliminary injunction to restrain Franklin from using, copying, selling, or infringing Apple's copyrights. The district court held a three day evidentiary

4. The fourteen programs at issue, briefly described, are:

(1) *Autostart ROM* is sold as part of the Apple Computer and is embedded on a ROM chip. The program has also been published in source code as part of a copyrighted book, the Apple II manual. When the computer's power is turned on, Autostart ROM performs internal routines that turn on the circuits in the computer and make its physical parts (e.g. input/output devices, screen, and memory) ready for use.

(2) *Applesoft* is Apple's version of the Beginner's All-purpose Symbolic Instruction Code (BASIC) language. The program is stored in ROM and is sold as part of the computer. Applesoft translates instructions written in the higher-level BASIC language into the lower-level machine code that the computer understands.

* * *

hearing limited to the copyright infringement claims. Apple produced evidence at the hearing in the form of affidavits and testimony that programs sold by Franklin in conjunction with its ACE 100 computer were virtually identical with those covered by the fourteen Apple copyrights. The variations that did exist were minor, consisting merely of such things as deletion of reference to Apple or its copyright notice.[5] James Huston, an Apple systems programmer, concluded that the Franklin programs were "unquestionably copied from Apple and could not have been independently created." He reached this conclusion not only because it is "almost impossible for so many lines of code" to be identically written, but also because his name, which he had embedded in one program (Master Create), and the word "Applesoft", which was embedded in another (DOS 3.3), appeared on the Franklin master disk. Apple estimated the "works in suit" took 46 man-months to produce at a cost of over $740,000, not including the time or cost of creating or acquiring earlier versions of the programs or the expense of marketing the programs.

Franklin did not dispute that it copied the Apple programs. Its witness admitted copying each of the works in suit from the Apple programs. Its factual defense was directed to its contention that it was not feasible for Franklin to write its own operating system programs. David McWherter, now Franklin's vice-president of engineering, testified he spent 30–40 hours in November 1981 making a study to determine if it was feasible for Franklin to write its own Autostart ROM program and concluded it was not because "there were just too many entry points in relationship to the number of instructions in the program." Entry points at specific locations in the program can be used by programmers to mesh their application programs with the operating system program. McWherter concluded that use of the identical signals was necessary in order to ensure 100% compatibility with application programs created to run on the Apple computer. He admitted that he never attempted to rewrite Autostart ROM and conceded that some of the works in suit (*i.e.* Copy, Copy A, Master Create, and Hello) probably could have been rewritten by Franklin. Franklin made no attempt to rewrite any of the programs prior to the lawsuit except for Copy, although McWherter testified that Franklin was "in the process of redesigning" some of the Apple programs and that "[w]e had a fair degree of certainty that that would probably work." Apple introduced evidence that Franklin could have rewritten programs, including the Autostart ROM program, and that there are in existence operating programs written by third parties which are compatible with Apple II.

Franklin's principal defense at the preliminary injunction hearing and before us is primarily a legal one, directed to its contention that

5. For example, 8 bytes of memory were altered in the Autostart ROM program so that when the computer is turned on "ACE 100" appears on the screen rather than "Apple II." The Franklin DOS 3.3 program also had 16 bytes (out of 9000) that allowed use of upper and lower case.

the Apple operating system programs are not capable of copyright protection.

The district court denied the motion for preliminary injunction by order and opinion dated July 30, 1982. * * * We have jurisdiction of Apple's appeal pursuant to 28 U.S.C. § 1292(a)(1).

III.

THE DISTRICT COURT OPINION

* * *

We read the district court opinion as presenting the following legal issues: (1) whether copyright can exist in a computer program expressed in object code, (2) whether copyright can exist in a computer program embedded on a ROM, (3) whether copyright can exist in an operating system program, and (4) whether independent irreparable harm must be shown for a preliminary injunction in copyright infringement actions.

Issues

IV.

DISCUSSION

A.

Copyrightability of a Computer Program Expressed in Object Code

Certain statements by the district court suggest that programs expressed in object code, as distinguished from source code, may not be the proper subject of copyright. We find no basis in the statute for any such concern. Furthermore, our decision in *Williams Electronics, Inc. v. Artic International, Inc., supra,* laid to rest many of the doubts expressed by the district court.

In 1976, after considerable study, Congress enacted a new copyright law to replace that which had governed since 1909. Act of October 19, 1976, Pub.L. No. 94–553, 90 Stat. 2541 (*codified at* 17 U.S.C. §§ 101 *et seq.*). Under the law, two primary requirements must be satisfied in order for a work to constitute copyrightable subject matter—it must be an "original wor[k] of authorship" and must be "fixed in [a] tangible medium of expression." 17 U.S.C. § 102(a). * * *

* * *

Although section 102(a) does not expressly list computer programs as works of authorship, the legislative history suggests that programs were considered copyrightable as literary works. * * *

The 1980 amendments added a definition of a computer program:

> A "computer program" is a set of statements or instructions to be used directly or indirectly in a computer in order to bring about a certain result.

17 U.S.C. § 101. The amendments also substituted a new section 117 which provides that "it is not an infringement for the owner of a copy of a computer program to make or authorize the making of another

copy or adaptation of that computer program" when necessary to "the utilization of the computer program" or "for archival purposes only." 17 U.S.C. § 117. The parties agree that this section is not implicated in the instant lawsuit. The language of the provision, however, by carving out an exception to the normal proscriptions against copying, clearly indicates that programs are copyrightable and are otherwise afforded copyright protection.

We considered the issue of copyright protection for a computer program in *Williams Electronics, Inc. v. Artic International, Inc.,* and concluded that "the copyrightability of computer programs is firmly established after the 1980 amendment to the Copyright Act." 685 F.2d at 875. * * *

The district court here questioned whether copyright was to be limited to works "designed to be 'read' by a human reader [as distinguished from] read by an expert with a microscope and patience", 545 F.Supp. at 821. The suggestion that copyrightability depends on a communicative function to individuals stems from the early decision of *White–Smith Music Publishing Co. v. Apollo Co.,* 209 U.S. 1, 28 S.Ct. 319, 52 L.Ed. 655 (1908), which held a piano roll was not a copy of the musical composition because it was not in a form others, except perhaps for a very expert few, could perceive. *See* 1 *Nimmer on Copyright* § 2.03[B][1] (1983). However, it is clear from the language of the 1976 Act and its legislative history that it was intended to obliterate distinctions engendered by *White–Smith.* H.R.Rep. No. 1476, *supra,* at 52, *reprinted in* 1976 U.S.Code Cong. & Ad.News at 5665.

* * *

The defendant in *Williams* had also argued that a copyrightable work "must be intelligible to human beings and must be intended as a medium of communication to human beings," *id.* at 876–77. We reiterate the statement we made in *Williams* when we rejected that argument: "[t]he answer to defendant's contention is in the words of the statute itself." 685 F.2d at 877.

The district court also expressed uncertainty as to whether a computer program in object code could be classified as a "literary work." [7] However, the category of "literary works", one of the seven copyrightable categories, is not confined to literature in the nature of Hemingway's *For Whom the Bell Tolls.* The definition of "literary works" in section 101 includes expression not only in words but also "numbers, or other * * * numerical symbols or indicia", thereby ex-

7. The district court stated that a programmer working directly in object code appears to think more as a mathematician or engineer, that the process of constructing a chip is less a work of authorship than the product of engineering knowledge, and that it may be more apt to describe an encoded ROM as a pictorial three-dimensional object than as a literary work. 545 F.Supp. at 821–22. The district court's remarks relied in part on a quotation about "microcode", *see id.* at 821 n. 14; Apple introduced testimony that none of the works in suit contain "microcode." Moreover, Apple does not seek to protect the ROM's architecture but only the program encoded upon it.

panding the common usage of "literary works." Thus a computer program, whether in object code or source code, is a "literary work" and is protected from unauthorized copying, whether from its object or source code version.

B.

Copyrightability of a Computer Program Embedded on a ROM

* * * In *Williams* we rejected the argument that "a computer program is not infringed when the program is loaded into electronic memory devices (ROMs) and used to control the activity of machines." 685 F.2d at 876. Defendant there had argued that there can be no copyright protection for the ROMs because they are utilitarian objects or machine parts. We held that the statutory requirement of "fixation", the manner in which the issue arises, is satisfied through the embodiment of the expression in the ROM devices. Therefore we reaffirm that a computer program in object code embedded in a ROM chip is an appropriate subject of copyright.

C.

Copyrightability of Computer Operating System Programs

We turn to the heart of Franklin's position on appeal which is that computer operating system programs, as distinguished from application programs, are not the proper subject of copyright "regardless of the language or medium in which they are fixed." Brief of Appellee at 15 (emphasis deleted). Apple suggests that this issue too is foreclosed by our *Williams* decision because some portion of the program at issue there was in effect an operating system program. Franklin is correct that this was not an issue raised by the parties in *Williams* and it was not considered by the court. Thus we consider it as a matter of first impression.

Franklin contends that operating system programs are *per se* excluded from copyright protection under the express terms of section 102(b) of the Copyright Act, and under the precedent and underlying principles of *Baker v. Selden,* 101 U.S. 99, 25 L.Ed. 841 (1879). These separate grounds have substantial analytic overlap.

In *Baker v. Selden,* plaintiff's testator held a copyright on a book explaining a bookkeeping system which included blank forms with ruled lines and headings designed for use with that system. Plaintiff sued for copyright infringement on the basis of defendant's publication of a book containing a different arrangement of the columns and different headings, but which used a similar plan so far as results were concerned. The Court, in reversing the decree for the plaintiff, concluded that blank account-books were not the subject of copyright and that "the mere copyright of Selden's book did not confer upon him the exclusive right to make and use account-books, ruled and arranged as designated by him and described and illustrated in said book." *Id.* at 107. The Court stated that copyright of the books did not give the plaintiff the exclusive right to use the system explained in the books, noting, for example, that "copyright of a work on mathematical science cannot give to the author an exclusive right to the methods of operation which he propounds." *Id.* at 103.

Franklin reads *Baker v. Selden* as "stand[ing] for several fundamental principles, each presenting * * * an insuperable obstacle to the copyrightability of Apple's operating systems." It states:

> *First, Baker* teaches that use of a system itself does not infringe a copyright on the description of the system. *Second, Baker* enunciates the rule that copyright does not extend to purely utilitarian works. *Finally, Baker* emphasizes that the copyright laws may not be used to obtain and hold a monopoly over an idea. In so doing, *Baker* highlights the principal difference between the copyright and patent laws—a difference that is highly pertinent in this case.

Brief of Appellee at 22.

Section 102(b) of the Copyright Act, the other ground on which Franklin relies, appeared first in the 1976 version, long after the decision in *Baker v. Selden.* It provides:

> In no case does copyright protection for an original work of authorship extend to any idea, procedure, process, system, method of operation, concept, principle, or discovery, regardless of the form in which it is described, explained, illustrated, or embodied in such work.

It is apparent that section 102(b) codifies a substantial part of the holding and dictum of *Baker v. Selden. See* 1 *Nimmer on Copyright* § 2.18[D], at 2–207.

We turn to consider the two principal points of Franklin's argument.

1. "Process", "System" or "Method of Operation"

Franklin argues that an operating system program is either a "process", "system", or "method of operation" and hence uncopyrightable. Franklin correctly notes that underlying section 102(b) and many of the statements for which *Baker v. Selden* is cited is the distinction which must be made between property subject to the patent law, which protects discoveries, and that subject to copyright law, which protects the writings describing such discoveries. However, Franklin's argument misapplies that distinction in this case. Apple does not seek to copyright the method which instructs the computer to perform its operating functions but only the instructions themselves. The method would be protected, if at all, by the patent law, an issue as yet unresolved. *See Diamond v. Diehr,* 450 U.S. 175, 101 S.Ct. 1048, 67 L.Ed.2d 155 (1981).

Franklin's attack on operating system programs as "methods" or "processes" seems inconsistent with its concession that application programs are an appropriate subject of copyright. Both types of programs instruct the computer to do something. Therefore, it should make no difference for purposes of section 102(b) whether these instructions tell the computer to help prepare an income tax return (the task of an application program) or to translate a high level language program from source code into its binary language object code form (the task of an operating system program such as "Applesoft", *see* note 4 *supra*). Since it is only the instructions which are protected, a "process" is no more involved because the instructions in an operating system program may be used to activate the operation of the computer than it would be if instructions were written in ordinary English in a manual which described the necessary steps to activate an intricate complicated machine. There is, therefore, no reason to afford any less copyright protection to the instructions in an operating system program than to the instructions in an application program.

Franklin's argument, receptively treated by the district court, that an operating system program is part of a machine mistakenly focuses on the physical characteristics of the instructions. But the medium is not the message. We have already considered and rejected aspects of this contention in the discussion of object code and ROM. The mere fact that the operating system program may be etched on a ROM does not make the program either a machine, part of a machine or its equivalent. Furthermore, as one of Franklin's witnesses testified, an operating system does not have to be permanently in the machine in ROM, but it may be on some other medium, such as a diskette or magnetic tape, where it could be readily transferred into the temporary memory space of the computer. In fact, some of the operating systems at issue were on diskette. * * *

* * *

Although a literal construction of this language could support Franklin's reading that precludes copyrightability if the copyright work is put to a utilitarian use, that interpretation has been rejected by a later Supreme Court decision. In *Mazer v. Stein,* 347 U.S. 201, 218, 74 S.Ct. 460, 471, 98 L.Ed. 630 (1954), the Court stated: "We find nothing in the copyright statute to support the argument that the intended use or use in industry of an article eligible for copyright bars or invalidates its registration. We do not read such a limitation into the copyright law." *Id.* at 218, 74 S.Ct. at 471. * * *

Perhaps the most convincing item leading us to reject Franklin's argument is that the statutory definition of a computer program as a set of instructions to be used in a computer in order to bring about a certain result, 17 U.S.C. § 101, makes no distinction between application programs and operating programs. Franklin can point to no decision which adopts the distinction it seeks to make. In the one other reported case to have considered it, *Apple Computer, Inc. v. Formula International, Inc.,* 562 F.Supp. 775 (C.D.Cal.1983), the court reached the same conclusion which we do, *i.e.* that an operating system program is not *per se* precluded from copyright. It stated, "There is nothing in any of the statutory terms which suggest a different result for different types of computer programs based upon the function they serve within the machine." *Id.* at 780. Other courts have also upheld the copyrightability of operating programs without discussion of this issue. *See Tandy Corp. v. Personal Micro Computers, Inc.,* 524 F.Supp. at 173 (input-output routine stored in ROM which translated input into machine language in a similar fashion as Applesoft and Apple Integer Basic proper subject of copyright); *GCA Corp. v. Chance,* 217 U.S.P.Q. at 719–20 (object code version of registered source code version of operating programs is the same work and protected).

2. *Idea/Expression Dichotomy*

Franklin's other challenge to copyright of operating system programs relies on the line which is drawn between ideas and their expression. *Baker v. Selden* remains a benchmark in the law of copyright for the reading given it in *Mazer v. Stein, supra,* where the Court stated, "Unlike a patent, a copyright gives no exclusive right to the art disclosed; protection is given only to the expression of the idea—not the idea itself." 347 U.S. at 217, 74 S.Ct. at 470 (footnote omitted).

The expression/idea dichotomy is now expressly recognized in section 102(b) which precludes copyright for "any idea." This provision was not intended to enlarge or contract the scope of copyright protection but "to restate * * * that the basic dichotomy between expression and idea remains unchanged." H.R.Rep. No. 1476, *supra,* at 57, *reprinted in* 1976 U.S.Code Cong. & Ad.News at 5670. The legislative history indicates that section 102(b) was intended "to make clear that the expression adopted by the programmer is the copyrightable element in a computer program, and that the actual processes or methods embodied in the program are not within the scope of the copyright law." *Id.*

Many of the courts which have sought to draw the line between an idea and expression have found difficulty in articulating where it falls. *See, e.g., Nichols v. Universal Pictures Corp.,* 45 F.2d 119, 121 (2d Cir.1930) (L. Hand, J.); *see* discussion in 3 *Nimmer on Copyright* § 13.03[A]. We believe that in the context before us, a program for an operating system, the line must be a pragmatic one, which also keeps in consideration "the preservation of the balance between competition and protection reflected in the patent and copyright laws". *Herbert Rosenthal Jewelry Corp. v. Kalpakian,* 446 F.2d 738, 742 (9th Cir.1971).

* * * If other programs can be written or created which perform the same function as an Apple's operating system program, then that program is an expression of the idea and hence copyrightable. In essence, this inquiry is no different than that made to determine whether the expression and idea have merged, which has been stated to occur where there are no or few other ways of expressing a particular idea.

The district court made no findings as to whether some or all of Apple's operating programs represent the only means of expression of the idea underlying them. Although there seems to be a concession by Franklin that at least some of the programs can be rewritten, we do not believe that the record on that issue is so clear that it can be decided at the appellate level. Therefore, if the issue is pressed on remand, the necessary finding can be made at that time.

Franklin claims that whether or not the programs can be rewritten, there are a limited "number of ways to arrange operating systems to enable a computer to run the vast body of Apple-compatible software", Brief of Appellee at 20. This claim has no pertinence to either the idea/expression dichotomy or merger. The idea which may merge with the expression, thus making the copyright unavailable, is the idea which is the subject of the expression. The idea of one of the operating system programs is, for example, how to translate source code into object code. If other methods of expressing that idea are not foreclosed as a practical matter, then there is no merger. Franklin may wish to achieve total compatibility with independently developed application programs written for the Apple II, but that is a commercial and competitive objective which does not enter into the somewhat metaphysical issue of whether particular ideas and expressions have merged.

In summary, Franklin's contentions that operating system programs are *per se* not copyrightable is unpersuasive. The other courts before whom this issue has been raised have rejected the distinction. Neither the CONTU majority nor Congress made a distinction between operating and application programs. We believe that the 1980 amendments reflect Congress' receptivity to new technology and its desire to encourage, through the copyright laws, continued imagination and creativity in computer programming. Since we believe that the district court's decision on the preliminary injunction was, to a large part, influenced by an erroneous view of the availability of copyright for operating system programs and unnecessary concerns about object code and ROMs, we must reverse the denial of the preliminary injunction and remand for reconsideration.

* * *

V.

For the reasons set forth in this opinion, we will reverse the denial of the preliminary injunction and remand to the district court for further proceedings in accordance herewith.

Notes and Questions

1. Obviously the authors of the Constitution did not have computer programs in mind when they drafted the patent and copyright clause. The courts, however, have always interpreted the clause broadly to incorporate new technology. In *Reiss v. National Quotation Bureau, Inc.,* 276 Fed. 717 (S.D.N.Y.1921), the distinguished Judge Learned Hand held that the Constitution's "grants of power to Congress comprise, not only what was then known, but what the ingenuity of men should devise thereafter. Of course, the new subject-matter must have some relation to the grant; but we

interpret it by the general practices of civilized peoples in similar fields, for it is not a strait-jacket, but a charter for a living people."

2. The United States Supreme Court has never decided a case involving the eligibility of "object code" or "operating system programs" for copyright protection. Thus, although *Apple v. Franklin* is merely an appellate court case, it is the leading case on these issues.

3. Was Franklin's argument against copyrightability of "operating system programs" as weak as the court seems to indicate? Increasingly, computer software performs functions previously performed by machine parts. One of the reasons for Apple's success was that its developers found ways to use software instead of hardware to control disk drives, allowing them to dramatically reduce the number of hardware components needed so as to produce a lighter-weight, cheaper, and more reliable personal computer. Competitors' disk drive controller hardware certainly was ineligible for copyright protection. Why should Apple's software, which performed exactly the same function, receive protection? Why should an automobile manufacturer who makes a computer-controlled fuel injection system receive intellectual property protection when a manufacturer of a mechanical fuel injection system does not?

4. MICROCODE

"Microcode" is object code incorporated in a central processor or microprocessor. Typically the processor performs a simple set of functions, such as addition and subtraction; the microcode combines these functions to perform more complex functions, such as multiplication and division. This approach speeds product development, since it is much simpler to correct errors in microcode than in hardware designs. It also makes the product cheaper, since microcode uses fewer elements than the hardware it replaces. Programmers typically are unaware of which functions are implemented in hardware and which are in microcode. For this reason, the argument against copyright protection is somewhat stronger than that in *Apple v. Franklin,* where programmers and sophisticated users, at least, knew that the "operating systems" programs were software.

NEC CORP. AND NEC ELECTRONICS, INC. v. INTEL CORP.

United States District Court, Northern District of California, 1989.
1989 Copr.L.Dec. ¶ 26,379, 1989 WL 67434.

GRAY, DISTRICT JUDGE: In this action, NEC seeks a declaration that Intel's copyrights on its 8086 and 8088 microcodes * are invalid and/or are not infringed by NEC. Intel has filed a counterclaim for infringement of its copyrights on those microcodes.

* Except as otherwise noted herein, the 8086 and 8088 microcodes may be considered to be identical for purposes of this action, and will be referred to in the singular as the "8086/88 microcode".

* * *

I. THE COPYRIGHTABILITY OF INTEL'S MICROCODE

A microcode consists of a series of instructions that tell a microprocessor which of its thousands of transistors to actuate in order to perform the tasks directed by the macroinstruction set. As such, it comes squarely within the definition of a "computer program," which Congress added to the Copyright Act in 1980, namely, "a set of statements or instructions to be used directly or indirectly in a computer in order to bring about a certain result." 17 U.S.C. § 101.

A computer program, even though articulated in object code, is afforded copyright protection as a "literary work" under Section 101, which includes works "expressed in words, numbers, or other verbal or numerical symbols or indicia, regardless of the nature of the material objects * * * in which they are embodied." *See Apple Computer, Inc. v. Franklin Computer Corp.*, 714 F.2d 1240, 1249 (3d Cir.1983); 17 U.S.C. § 101. For a particular literary work to be copyrightable, two requirements must be satisfied: the work must be "fixed in any tangible medium of expression," and it must be "original." *See* 17 U.S.C. § 102(a). It is undisputed that Intel's microcode is fixed in a tangible medium of expression. However, NEC challenges the originality of Intel's microcode, and urges two other bases for denying copyright protection.

A. Originality.

NEC contends that many of Intel's microsequences are not copyrightable because they consist only of a few obvious steps and thus lack the originality required for copyright protection. * * * NEC seeks to have such a ruling applied to several of the microsequences in the Intel microcode that are very short, involve only a few steps, and are handled almost identically in NEC's accused microcode and by Mr. Davidian in the "Clean Room" microcode (which will be discussed later).

It well may be that, considered alone, several of the microsequences in Intel's microcode consist of "forms of expression directed solely by functional considerations" lacking even "minimal creativity." But these examples are only small segments of the copyrighted microcode. As Intel points out, any copyrighted work, be it a poem, novel or computer program, can be chopped into parts that could be said to have very few creative steps.

However, for purposes of copyrightability, "[o]riginality means only that the work owes its origin to the author, i.e., is independently created, and not copied from other works," and that the work contains a modicum of originality, i.e., "exceeds that required for a fragmentary work or short phrase." 1 M. Nimmer, *Nimmer on Copyright* § 2.01[A] at 2–8, § 2.01[B] at 2–15. The Intel microcode fully meets this test. There is no evidence that Intel's microcode was other than an independent effort and, overall, Intel's microcode exceeds the required modicum of originality.

B. Microcode As Part Of The Computer.

As stated above, the Copyright Act defines a computer program as "a set of statements or instructions to be used * * * *in* a computer." 17 U.S.C. § 101 (emphasis added). NEC contends that Intel's microcode is a defining element of the computer itself. According to NEC, Intel's microcode does not come within the definition of a computer program because it cannot be used *in* a computer and also be a defining part of the computer. But, as stated at the outset, Intel's microcode is within the statutory definition of a "computer program," and NEC's semi-semantical argument runs counter to the authority cited by Intel: "There is nothing in any of the statutory terms which suggest a different result [concerning copyrightability] for different types of computer programs based upon the function they serve within the machine." *Apple Computer, Inc. v. Franklin Computer Corp.,* 714 F.2d 1240, 1252 (3d Cir.1983) (quoting *Apple Computer, Inc. v. Formula Intern, Inc.,* 562 F.Supp. 775, 780 (C.D.Cal.1983)). See also National Commission on New Technological Uses of Copyright Works, Final Report at 21, which asserted that "[p]rograms should no more be considered machine parts than videotapes should be considered parts of projectors or phonorecords parts of sound reproduction equipment. * * * That the words of a program are used ultimately in the implementation of a process should in no way affect their copyrightability."

C. Idea v. Expression.

It is an axiom of copyright law that only the expression of an idea is copyrightable, not the idea, itself. This doctrine was announced in *Baker v. Selden,* 101 U.S. 99, 103 (1879), and a substantial portion has been codified in 17 U.S.C. § 102(b). *See Apple Computer, Inc. v. Franklin Computer Corp.,* 714 F.2d 1240, 1250 (3d Cir.1983). Stemming from *Baker v. Selden* is the related doctrine of "merger", which was well stated by Judge Browning in *Herbert Rosenthal Jewelry Corp. v. Kalpakian,* 446 F.2d 738, 742 (9th Cir.1971):

> When the "idea" and its "expression" are thus inseparable, copying the "expression" will not be barred, since protecting the "expression" would confer a monopoly of the "idea" upon the copyright owner free of the conditions and limitations imposed by the patent law.

NEC contends that if substantial similarities do exist between its accused microroutines and those of Intel, they are because of constraints that severely limit the ways in which the "ideas" therein contained can be expressed. NEC therefore urges that such merger of idea and expression forestalls copyrightability, and relies basically upon *Morrissey v. Procter & Gamble Co.,* 379 F.2d 675 (1st Cir.1967), which so held.

However, Mr. Nimmer suggests the appropriate rule to be that the "merger" of idea and expression "will preclude a finding of substantial similarity", thus forestalling a finding of infringement, and he criticized *Morrissey* as "a questionable extension of this principle." 3 M. Nimmer, *Nimmer on Copyright,* § 13.03[A] at 13–33 to 13–34.

Although Ninth Circuit cases have not specifically discussed this issue raised by NEC, they appear uniformly to treat the "merger" issue as a question of whether or not there is infringement rather than copyrightability.

It also seems to me that, as a matter of practicality, the issue of a limited number of ways to express an idea is relevant to infringement, but should not be the basis for denying the initial copyright. The Register of Copyrights will not know about the presence or absence of constraints that limit ways to express an idea. The burden of showing such constraints should be left to the alleged infringer. Accordingly, in the absence of Ninth Circuit authority to the contrary, it is concluded that the relationship between "idea" and "expression" will not be considered on the issue of copyrightability, but will be deferred to the discussion of infringement.

It is the view of this court that NEC's above mentioned objections to the copyrightability of Intel's microcode are not persuasive. On the contrary, the statutory references discussed at the outset of this section on copyrightability, and particularly the specific definition of "computer program" that Congress enacted in 1980, "reflect Congress' receptivity to new technology and its desire to encourage, through the copyright laws, continued imagination and creativity in computer programming." *Apple Computer, Inc. v. Franklin Computer Corp.,* 714 F.2d 1240, 1254 (3d Cir.1983). In light of the foregoing, it is concluded that Intel's microcode was a proper subject for copyright protection and that the copyright registrations contained thereon were initially valid.

* * *

NEC's Challenged V20 and V30 Microcodes As "Improvements" Upon Its uPD 8086 and uPD 8088.

On February 23, 1983, Intel granted a license authorizing NEC to copy Intel's 8086/88 microcode in NEC's uPD 8086 and uPD 8088 microprocessors, "including improvements thereon developed by NEC." A memorandum of understanding mutually executed on September 27, 1984, set the royalties to be paid by NEC.

In this litigation, as an alternative argument, NEC asserts that the V20 and V30 microprocessors are "improvements" upon the uPD 8086 and uPD 8088 and that they therefore are covered by the above mentioned license. It is the position of this court that this issue is rendered moot by the above announced decision with respect to forfeiture and noninfringement. However, for purposes of completeness, it will be considered here.

It often is very difficult for a court to determine whether a writing or a physical creation is no more than an improvement over its predecessors, and thus covered by a license, or is an independent item. However, the task becomes much easier if the intent of the parties, particularly the licensee, can be ascertained. * * *

* * *

In this case, the responsible officers of NEC never did consider the V20 and V30 to be simply improvements of the 8086 and 8088. This is shown by the testimony of NEC's principal license negotiator, Shigeo Yamamoto, and of NEC's Engineer Manager of Advanced Microprocessors, Tadashi Izumi. Certainly NEC did not pay any royalties under the license based upon its sales of the V20 and V30. It seems evident that NEC's contention of "improvement" was conceived after this litigation began, and it is rejected.

CONCLUSION

For reasons hereinabove set forth, judgment will be entered holding that:

1. The Intel microcode for its 8086 and 8088 microprocessors were proper subjects for protection under United States copyright laws.

* * *

3. The microcodes that NEC produced for its V20, V30, V40 and V50 microprocessors do not infringe the Intel copyrights for its 8086 and 8088 microcodes.

4. NEC's V20 and V30 microprocessors are not simply "improvements" upon its uPD 8086 and uPD 8088 microprocessors, which were licensed by Intel under its copyrights.

This memorandum shall constitute findings of fact and conclusions of law, pursuant to Federal Rule of Civil Procedure 52(a).

Notes and Questions

1. The fact Intel held a valid copyright and that NEC's microcode performed the same functions as Intel's did not mean that NEC had infringed upon Intel's copyright. To show infringement, Intel had to prove copying. The portion of this case dealing with infringement is printed below, in the section on "Infringement".

2. Intellectual property exists to provide encouragement for intellectual effort—as the Constitution says, "To promote the Progress of Science and useful Arts". In a splendid book, *The Soul of a New Machine* (1981), Tracy Kidder provides a gripping account of the extraordinary efforts involved in writing microcode for a new computer.

5. COPYRIGHT-LIKE PROTECTION FOR SEMICONDUCTOR CHIP DESIGNS

If one accepts the principle that software and hardware implementations of microprocessors should have the same level of intellectual property protection, this does not necessarily mean that software should be denied protection. Perhaps the answer lies in increasing the protection of hardware components. Congress sought to provide just such protection in the Semiconductor Chip Protection Act of 1984, 17 U.S.C.A. §§ 901–914.

The Semiconductor Chip Act of 1984 was implemented to protect the masks used to create computer chips. The enactors believed that the copyright and patent laws did not adequately protect semiconductor chips, and thus a special statute was needed. The design and manufacture of semiconductor chips is extremely complex, and thus a detailed explanation is beyond the scope of this text. A very basic overview, however, of chip design and manufacture will be helpful in understanding the 1984 Semiconductor Chip Act.

A semiconductor foundry has sophisticated hardware and software tools used to create a computer-aided design (CAD) program which forms the basis of the design of the semiconductor chip. It is important to note that the software tools and the resulting computer program that is created can each individually be copyrighted. The foundry software and hardware tools then design a mask. The mask in essence is a picture of the circuit created by the software program. Through a complicated series of steps, the mask is then used to create a chip. This "mask" is what is protected under The Chip Act of 1984, which is why the Act is sometimes called the "Mask Work Act."

The reasons for the Chip Act are numerous. The scope of protection for chips under copyrights and patents is uncertain and in some areas, severely limited. Chips are useful articles, so courts might be hesistant to protect them under the Copyright Act. Patent protection is also not an attractive mode of protection because many extremely successful chips are not original nor novel according to patent law, and thus not patentable. The Chip Act supporters hoped that the Act would bridge the gap between patent and copyright protection.

Relevant sections of the Act follow.

SEMICONDUCTOR CHIP PROTECTION ACT OF 1984 17 U.S.C.A. §§ 901–914

§ 901. Definitions

(a) As used in this chapter—

(1) a "semiconductor chip product" is the final or intermediate form of any product—

(A) having two or more layers of metallic, insulating, or semi-conductor material, deposited or otherwise placed on, or etched away or otherwise removed from, a piece of semiconductor material in accordance with a predetermined pattern; and

(B) intended to perform electronic circuitry functions;

(2) a "mask work" is a series of related images, however fixed or encoded—

(A) having or representing the predetermined, three-dimensional pattern of metallic, insulating, or semiconductor material present or removed from the layers of a semiconductor chip product; and

(B) in which series the relation of the images to one another is that each image has the pattern of the surface of one form of the semiconductor chip product;

(3) a mask work is "fixed" in a semiconductor chip product when its embodiment in the product is sufficiently permanent or stable to permit the mask work to be perceived or reproduced from the product for a period of more than transitory duration;

(4) to "distribute" means to sell, or to lease, bail, or otherwise transfer, or to offer to sell, lease, bail, or otherwise transfer;

(5) to "commercially exploit" a mask work is to distribute to the public for commercial purposes a semiconductor chip product embodying the mask work; except that such term includes an offer to sell or transfer a semiconductor chip product only when the offer is in writing and occurs after the mask work is fixed in the semiconductor chip product;

(6) the "owner" of a mask work is the person who created the mask work, the legal representative of that person if that person is deceased or under a legal incapacity, or a party to whom all the rights under this chapter of such person or representative are transferred in accordance with section 903(b); except that, in the case of a work made within the scope of a person's employment, the owner is the employer for whom the person created the mask work or a party to whom all the rights under this chapter of the employer are transferred in accordance with section 903(b);

(7) an "innocent purchaser" is a person who purchases a semiconductor chip product in good faith and without having notice of protection with respect to the semiconductor chip product;

(8) having "notice of protection" means having actual knowledge that, or reasonable grounds to believe that, a mask work is protected under this chapter; and

(9) an "infringing semiconductor chip product" is a semiconductor chip product which is made, imported, or distributed in violation of the exclusive rights of the owner of a mask work under this chapter.

(b) For purposes of this chapter, the distribution or importation of a product incorporating a semiconductor chip product as a part thereof is a distribution or importation of that semiconductor chip product.

§ 902. Subject matter of protection

(a)(1) Subject to the provisions of subsection (b), a mask work fixed in a semiconductor chip product, by or under the authority of the owner of the mask work, is eligible for protection under this chapter if—

(A) on the date on which the mask work is registered under section 908, or is first commercially exploited anywhere in the world, whichever occurs first, the owner of the mask work is (i) a national or domiciliary of the United States, (ii) a national, domiciliary, or sovereign authority of a foreign nation that is a party to a treaty affording protection to mask works to which the United

States is also a party, or (iii) a stateless person, wherever that person may be domiciled;

(B) the mask work is first commercially exploited in the United States; or

(C) the mask work comes within the scope of a Presidential proclamation issued under paragraph (2).

(2) Whenever the President finds that a foreign nation extends, to mask works of owners who are nationals or domiciliaries of the United States protection (A) on substantially the same basis as that on which the foreign nation extends protection to mask works of its own nationals and domiciliaries and mask works first commercially exploited in that nation, or (B) on substantially the same basis as provided in this chapter, the President may by proclamation extend protection under this chapter to mask works (i) of owners who are, on the date on which the mask works are registered under section 908, or the date on which the mask works are first commercially exploited anywhere in the world, whichever occurs first, nationals, domiciliaries, or sovereign authorities of that nation, or (ii) which are first commercially exploited in that nation. The President may revise, suspend, or revoke any such proclamation or impose any conditions or limitations on protection extended under any such proclamation.

(b) Protection under this chapter shall not be available for a mask work that—

(1) is not original; or

(2) consists of designs that are staple, commonplace, or familiar in the semiconductor industry, or variations of such designs, combined in a way that, considered as a whole, is not original.

(c) In no case does protection under this chapter for a mask work extend to any idea, procedure, process, system, method of operation, concept, principle, or discovery, regardless of the form in which it is described, explained, illustrated, or embodied in such work.

§ 903. Ownership, transfer, licensing, and recordation

(a) The exclusive rights in a mask work subject to protection under this chapter belong to the owner of the mask work.

(b) The owner of the exclusive rights in a mask work may transfer all of those rights, or license all or less than all of those rights, by any written instrument signed by such owner or a duly authorized agent of the owner. Such rights may be transferred or licensed by operation of law, may be bequeathed by will, and may pass as personal property by the applicable laws of intestate succession.

(c)(1) Any document pertaining to a mask work may be recorded in the Copyright Office if the document filed for recordation bears the actual signature of the person who executed it, or if it is accompanied by a sworn or official certification that it is a true copy of the original, signed document. The Register of Copyrights shall, upon receipt of the document and the fee specified pursuant to section 908(d), record the document and return it with a certificate of recordation. The recordation of any transfer or license under this paragraph gives all persons constructive notice of the facts stated in the recorded document concerning the transfer or license.

(2) In any case in which conflicting transfers of the exclusive rights in a mask work are made, the transfer first executed shall be void as against a subsequent transfer which is made for a valuable consideration and without notice of the first transfer, unless the first transfer is recorded in accordance with paragraph (1) within three months after the date on which it is executed, but in no case later than the day before the date of such subsequent transfer.

(d) Mask works prepared by an officer or employee of the United States Government as part of that person's official duties are not protected under this chapter, but the United States Government is not precluded from receiving and holding exclusive rights in mask works transferred to the Government under subsection (b).

§ 904. Duration of protection

(a) The protection provided for a mask work under this chapter shall commence on the date on which the mask work is registered under section 908, or the date on which the mask work is first commercially exploited anywhere in the world, whichever occurs first.

(b) Subject to subsection (c) and the provisions of this chapter, the protection provided under this chapter to a mask work shall end ten years after the date on which such protection commences under subsection (a).

(c) All terms of protection provided in this section shall run to the end of the calendar year in which they would otherwise expire.

§ 905. Exclusive rights in mask works

The owner of a mask work provided protection under this chapter has the exclusive rights to do and to authorize any of the following:

(1) to reproduce the mask work by optical, electronic, or any other means;

(2) to import or distribute a semiconductor chip product in which the mask work is embodied; and

(3) to induce or knowingly to cause another person to do any of the acts described in paragraphs (1) and (2).

§ 906. Limitation on exclusive rights: reverse engineering; first sale

(a) Notwithstanding the provisions of section 905, it is not an infringement of the exclusive rights of the owner of a mask work for—

(1) a person to reproduce the mask work solely for the purpose of teaching, analyzing, or evaluating the concepts or techniques embodied in the mask work or the circuitry, logic flow, or organization of components used in the mask work; or

(2) a person who performs the analysis or evaluation described in paragraph (1) to incorporate the results of such conduct in an original mask work which is made to be distributed.

(b) Notwithstanding the provisions of section 905(2), the owner of a particular semiconductor chip product made by the owner of the mask work, or by any person authorized by the owner of the mask work, may import, distribute, or otherwise dispose of or use, but not reproduce, that particular semiconductor chip product without the authority of the owner of the mask work.

§ 907. Limitation on exclusive rights: innocent infringement

(a) Notwithstanding any other provision of this chapter, an innocent purchaser of an infringing semiconductor chip product—

(1) shall incur no liability under this chapter with respect to the importation or distribution of units of the infringing semiconductor chip product that occurs before the innocent purchaser has notice of protection with respect to the mask work embodied in the semiconductor chip product; and

(2) shall be liable only for a reasonable royalty on each unit of the infringing semiconductor chip product that the innocent purchaser imports or distributes after having notice of protection with respect to the mask work embodied in the semiconductor chip product.

(b) The amount of the royalty referred to in subsection (a)(2) shall be determined by the court in a civil action for infringement unless the parties resolve the issue by voluntary negotiation, mediation, or binding arbitration.

(c) The immunity of an innocent purchaser from liability referred to in subsection (a)(1) and the limitation of remedies with respect to an innocent purchaser referred to in subsection (a)(2) shall extend to any person who directly or indirectly purchases an infringing semiconductor chip product from an innocent purchaser.

(d) The provisions of subsections (a), (b), and (c) apply only with respect to those units of an infringing semiconductor chip product that an innocent purchaser purchased before having notice of protection with respect to the mask work embodied in the semiconductor chip product.

§ 908. Registration of claims of protection

(a) The owner of a mask work may apply to the Register of Copyrights for registration of a claim of protection in a mask work. Protection of a mask work under this chapter shall terminate if application for registration of a claim of protection in the mask work is not made as provided in this chapter within two years after the date on which the mask work is first commercially exploited anywhere in the world.

* * *

§ 909. Mask work notice

(a) The owner of a mask work provided protection under this chapter may affix notice to the mask work, and to masks and semiconductor chip products embodying the mask work, in such manner and location as to give reasonable notice of such protection. * * * The affixation of such notice is not a condition of protection under this chapter, but shall constitute prima facie evidence of notice of protection.

(b) The notice referred to in subsection (a) shall consist of—

(1) the words "mask [work]", the [symbol] *M*, or the symbol Ⓜ (the letter M in a circle); and

(2) the name of the owner or owners of the mask work or an abbreviation by which the name is recognized or is generally known.

§ 910. Enforcement of exclusive rights

(a) Except as otherwise provided in this chapter, any person who violates any of the exclusive rights of the owner of a mask work under this chapter, by conduct in or affecting commerce, shall be liable as an infringer of such rights.

* * *

Note on Registrations Under the Act

Since enactment in 1984, registrations under the Act have been as follows:

1985—1,263 registrations

1986— 859 registrations

1987—1,122 registrations

1988—1,047 registrations

1989—1,229 registrations

Total 5,520

The pattern at present appears to be an ebb and flow. Some observers think the numbers may increase as a result of the inclusion of foreign registrations in the United States. The low numbers of registrations may be due in part to the newness of the Act, as well as the fact that the option exists to copyright the underlying computer program, which the chip represents in electrical form. In addition, one chip program may be used to produce multiple masks.

BROOKTREE CORPORATION v. ADVANCED MICRO DEVICES, INC.

United States District Court, Southern District of California, 1988.
705 F.Supp. 491.

ENRIGHT, DISTRICT JUDGE.

* * *

FACTUAL BACKGROUND

Brooktree is a California corporation in the business of designing, manufacturing, and selling semiconductor chip products used in computer graphic displays.

Defendant Advanced Micro Devices, Inc. ("AMD") is a competitor in the same business. It is one of the five largest manufacturers of chip products in the United States, with sales almost 30 times that of Brooktree.

Brooktree alleges that between 1981 and 1986 it invested approximately $3.8 million in developing integrated circuit chips that convert digital graphics image information to analog information at high frequencies for display on very high resolution computer video screens. It further claims that its chip has captured this niche market previously dominated by AMD.

Brooktree alleges that AMD has introduced pirated chips at lower prices in an attempt to recapture its lost market. These pirated chips are allegedly copies of two of Brooktree's chips.

The two Brooktree chips that are allegedly being copied represent 40% of Brooktree's sales. Brooktree alleges that AMD's unlawful conduct has caused irreparable injury, including damages of over $2,753,000 in the last six months, lost sales, and lost ability to expand or go public due to lost profits. It further alleges that its total $30 million investment since 1981 is in jeopardy as the firm has only recently reached profitability and thus does not have the strength to weather the loss of sales due to AMD's conduct. Finally, Brooktree alleges that AMD's pirating is damaging Brooktree's other products as Brooktree is being forced to cut the cost of all its chips in order to keep its cost structure in line.

* * *

I.

MASK WORK ACT

This case was brought under the Mask Work Act, 17 U.S.C. §§ 901–914. Because both copyright and patent protection were inadequate, the Mask Work Act was passed in an effort to protect the original layout of a semiconductor chip from piracy. (S.Rep. 98–425, p. 6–7). However, the Mask Work Act is not *sui generis* legislation; it is based upon concepts derived from copyright laws. (130 Cong.Rec. § 12924). * * *

* * *

Discussion

In the instant action, Brooktree alleges that AMD misappropriated two mask works from its Bt451 and Bt458 chips. The mask works are: (1) the location and configuration of the active areas in the Static Ram cells and (2) the location and path of the polysilicon lines in the Static Ram cells. * * *

Brooktree alleges that these two masks allow its Bt451 chip to: (1) utilize a low power technology—"CMOS"—which operates at very high frequencies without the need of a special supply of negative voltage; (2) change the colors in the color palette without disrupting the selection of particular colors from the palette for display on a video screen, and (3) simultaneously read information from, and write information to, the RAM without synchronizing the read and write operations while operating at very high frequencies.

Brooktree's allegations against AMD are twofold. First, Brooktree alleges that the mask works at issue in AMD's chips are substantially identical and/or substantially similar to those in Brooktree's own chips. Second, that this resemblance is not the result of extensive reverse engineering, but rather the result of simple copying.

A. *Identical/Similar*

The parties agree that if the defendant can produce a paper trail establishing reverse engineering, the appropriate standard is substantially identical rather than substantially similar. The court finds that defendant has produced a sufficient paper trail to require the plaintiff to prove that the alleged pirated chip is substantially identical to the original chip.

AMD argues that while the layout of the mask works at issue may be similar, they are not substantially identical. AMD also argues that this type of layout is the result of functional requirements, or, in other words, that it is essentially the only way of laying out the Static Ram circuit.

In response, Brooktree offers exhibits of two alternative designs developed by two separate individuals with limited knowledge of Brooktree's own layout. * * * However, rather than prove that there are a wide variety of potential layouts, these two new layouts, at best, merely confuse the issue, and, at worst, confirm AMD's position that functionally there is little room for diversity.

The two new designs do not utilize the same donut and pyramid shapes that Brooktree refers to in describing its own layout, but they do have the same basic clusters of components as the original designs. Also, the two new layouts were admittedly developed in a matter of hours. It is possible that if these designs had undergone testing to determine whether they would perform in the desired manner, they would have been modified and eventually appear more similar to the original layouts.

William Plants, the designer of AMD's chips, states in his declaration that the shape of the various regions in his layout was dictated by the functions of the regions. He also states that although his layout is similar to Brooktree's, there are substantial differences between specific aspects of the active regions of the two layouts.

Finally, AMD argues that even if the layouts were identical, these two cells do not comprise enough of the chips in question to support an allegation of misappropriation of a mask work. They argue that although the cells are repeated many times in the chip, they compromise only approximately 27–35% of the chip area. Brooktree counters this argument by stating that the cells compromise approximately 80% of the transistors in the chip, and that the transistors are the heart and soul of the chip.

B. Reverse Engineering

AMD argues that Plants discovered his layout through reverse engineering, and that reverse engineering is specifically allowed under the Mask Work Act. AMD has presented evidence of a paper trail showing the various stages of Plants' discovery process. AMD maintains that it has invested an equal or greater amount of funds in developing its chips, and that the Mask Work Act was directed at minimal investment piracy rather than the type of long-term research and reverse engineering it performed.

Brooktree argues that what the paper trail actually establishes is that Plants was incapable of discovering the layout on his own. According to Brooktree, Plants had no experience in designing CMOS chips and spent over one year attempting to design a layout utilizing first six and then eight transistors as compared to Brooktree's layout which utilizes ten transistors. During this one-year period, [P]lants studied Brooktree's Bt451 chip under a microscope and was unable to discover all ten of the transistors.

Brooktree alleges that Plants did not discover the ten transistors on his own but rather was shown a copy of Brooktree's ten transistor static RAM circuit by an employee of another competitor of Brooktree (Integrated Device Technology Corporation) which had supposedly copied Brooktree's Bt451 chip. After Plant was shown the ten transistor design, he allegedly went back to the microscope and studied the Bt451 chip to confirm the number of transistors and to determine their location and function in the design.

Brooktree maintains that the fact that Plant was able to finish his work on the layout in less than three months after being shown the ten transistor design is significant. Accordingly, Brooktree argues that the only paper trail that is relevant is what was created after Plant was shown the ten transistor design. Because the paper trail for the last three months is minimal, Brooktree argues that AMD has failed to offer sufficient facts to establish that AMD discovered the layout of the mask work at issue through reverse engineering.

AMD responds by arguing that the entire paper trail must be reviewed, and that the paper trail shows that Plant gradually discovered the correct layout. Plant states in his declaration that he started with six transistors as that is the minimum number possible, and that designers always begin at the minimum and work up. He states that the amount of time he spent working on six and eight transistor layouts demonstrates that he did not simply copy the Bt451. Plant admits to analyzing the Bt451 chip through a microscope, but maintains that only stripping the chip down chemically layer by layer and photographing each layer is prohibited by the Mask Work Act.

Based upon the above discussion, the court finds that Brooktree has failed to make a showing of a strong likelihood of success on the merits.
* * *

* * *

IV.

CONCLUSION

Upon due consideration of the parties' memoranda and exhibits, the arguments advanced at hearing, and for the reasons set forth above, the court hereby denies plaintiff's motion for preliminary injunction.

Notes and Questions

1. *Brooktree* has been criticized due to the extremely conservative "substantially identical" standard adopted by the parties and accepted by the court. It held that if a defendant can produce a paper trail demonstrating reverse engineering, then the burden of proof is on the plaintiff to show that the copying was substantially identical. Does the decision signal the beginning and ending of the enforcement of the Act, except in the most extreme piracy cases?

2. Under § 910, the owner of the mask work, or the exclusive licensee of the mask work, is entitled to civil remedies. These remedies in § 911 include temporary restraining orders, preliminary injunctions, permanent injunctions, actual damages, and the infringer's profits which are not taken into account in the actual damage award. Statutory damages may also be awarded, and can be as high as $250,000 per infringement.

3. Under § 914 of the Act, other nations are encouraged to enact similar legislation. To date, most important industrial nations have chosen to enact some type of legal protection for masks.

4. Where did Congress get the power to enact the Silicon Chip Protection Act? The Act is a hybrid of patent and copyright law. The legislative history shows that Congress considered a "Mask Work" to be a "Writing" protectable under the Patent and Copyright Clause of the Constitution. However, to provide further Constitutional support, Congress also relied upon the Commerce Clause, by limiting the proscriptions

of the Act to conduct "in or affecting commerce." Kastenmeier and Remington, "The Semiconductor Chip Protection Act of 1984: A Swamp or Firm Ground," 70 Minn.L.Rev. 417 (1985).

6. SCREEN DISPLAYS

Users of computers interact not with source code, object code, or microcode, but with the screen displays. The importance of screen displays varies from program to program. They may be relatively unimportant in the case of word processing programs that present a virtually blank screen. They are very important in video games. The following case settled the question of copyrightability of screen displays.

WILLIAMS ELECTRONICS, INC. v. ARTIC INTERNATIONAL, INC.

United States Court of Appeals, Third Circuit, 1982.
685 F.2d 870.

SLOVITER, CIRCUIT JUDGE.

Defendant Artic International, Inc. appeals from the district court's entry of a final injunction order permanently restraining and enjoining it from infringing plaintiff's copyrights on audiovisual works and a computer program relating to the electronic video game DEFENDER. The district court severed plaintiff's demand for injunctive relief from its demand for monetary damages, and further severed plaintiff's claims of copyright infringement from its claims of trademark infringement and unfair competition. App. at 210a. These latter claims have not yet been adjudicated. However, because the injunction granted by the district court goes to the merits of the dispute and has "serious, perhaps irreparable, consequences", the order can be considered a "routine interlocutory injunctive order" and appealable under 28 U.S.C. § 1292(a)(1).

Plaintiff-appellee Williams Electronics, Inc. manufactures and sells coin-operated electronic video games. A video game machine consists of a cabinet containing, *inter alia,* a cathode ray tube (CRT), a sound system, hand controls for the player, and electronic circuit boards. The electronic circuitry includes a microprocessor and memory devices, called ROMs (*R* ead *O* nly *M* emory), which are tiny computer "chips" containing thousands of data locations which store the instructions and data of a computer program. The microprocessor executes the computer program to cause the game to operate. Judge Newman of the Second Circuit described a similar type of memory device as follows: * * *

In approximately October 1979 Williams began to design a new video game, ultimately called DEFENDER, which incorporated various original and unique audiovisual features. The DEFENDER game was introduced to the industry at a trade show in 1980 and has since achieved great success in the marketplace. One of the attractions of video games contributing to their phenomenal popularity is apparently their use of unrealistic fantasy creatures, a fad also observed in the popularity of certain current films. In the DEFENDER game, there are symbols of a spaceship and aliens who do battle with symbols of human figures. The player operates the flight of and weapons on the spaceship, and has the mission of preventing invading aliens from kidnapping the humans from a ground plane.

Williams obtained three copyright registrations relating to its DEFENDER game: one covering the computer program, Registration No. TX 654–755, effective date December 11, 1980; the second covering the audiovisual effects displayed during the game's "attract mode",[2] Registration No. PA 97–373, effective date March 3, 1981; and the third covering the audiovisual effects displayed during the game's "play mode",[3] Registration No. PA 94–718, effective date March 11, 1981. Readily visible copyright notices for the DEFENDER game were placed on the game cabinet, appeared on the CRT screen during the attract mode and at the beginning of the play mode, and were placed on labels which were attached to the outer case of each memory device (ROM). In addition, the Williams program provided that the words "Copyright 1980—Williams Electronics" in code were to be stored in the memory devices, but were not to be displayed on the CRT at any time.

Defendant-appellant Artic International, Inc. is a seller of electronic components for video games in competition with Williams. The district court made the following relevant findings which are not disputed on this appeal. Artic has sold circuit boards, manufactured by others, which contain electronic circuits including a microprocessor and memory devices (ROMs). These memory devices incorporate a computer program which is virtually identical to Williams' program for its DEFENDER game. The result is a circuit board "kit" which is sold by Artic to others and which, when connected to a cathode ray tube, produces audiovisual effects and a game almost identical to the Williams DEFENDER game including both the attract mode and the play mode. The play mode and actual play of Artic's game, entitled "DEFENSE COMMAND", is virtually identical to that of the Williams game, i.e., the characters displayed on the cathode ray tube including the player's spaceship are identical in shape, size, color, manner of movement and interaction with other symbols. Also, the attract mode of the Artic game is substantially identical to that of Williams' game, with minor exceptions such as the absence of the Williams name and the substitution of the terms "DEFENSE" and/or "DEFENSE COMMAND" for the term "DEFENDER" in its display. Based on the evidence before it, the district court found that the defendant Artic had

2. The "attract mode" refers to the audiovisual effects displayed before a coin is inserted into the game. It repeatedly shows the name of the game, the game symbols in typical motion and interaction patterns, and the initials of previous players who have achieved high scores.

3. The "play mode" refers to the audiovisual effects displayed during the actual play of the game, when the game symbols move and interact on the screen, and the player controls the movement of one of the symbols (*e.g.,* a spaceship).

infringed the plaintiff's computer program copyright for the DEFENDER game by selling kits which contain a computer program which is a copy of plaintiff's computer program, and that the defendant had infringed both of the plaintiff's audiovisual copyrights for the DEFENDER game by selling copies of those audiovisual works.

In the appeal before us, defendant does not dispute the findings with respect to copying but instead challenges the conclusions of the district court with respect to copyright infringement and the validity and scope of plaintiff's copyrights. The recent market interest in electronic audiovisual games has created an active market for original work, and as frequently happens, has also spawned copies, many of which have been the subject of a flurry of recent opinions.

In the case before us, the parties agreed at the district court level that the only issues to be decided on the injunction were legal ones. Essentially, defendant Artic attacks the validity and the scope of the copyrights which it has been found by the district court to have infringed. Plaintiff possesses certificates of registration issued by the Copyright Office. Under the Copyright Act, these certificates constitute *prima facie* evidence of the validity of plaintiff's copyright. 17 U.S.C. § 410(c). Defendant, therefore, has the burden of overcoming this presumption of validity.

With respect to the plaintiff's two audiovisual copyrights, defendant contends that there can be no copyright protection for the DEFENDER game's attract mode and play mode because these works fail to meet the statutory requirement of "fixation." Section 101 of the 1976 Copyright Act, 17 U.S.C. § 102, provides in part:

> (a) Copyright protection subsists ... in original works of authorship *fixed in any tangible medium of expression,* now known or later developed, from which they can be perceived, reproduced, or otherwise communicated, either directly or with the aid of a machine or device. Works of authorship include the following categories:
>
> (1) literary works;
>
> ....
>
> (6) motion pictures and other audiovisual works;
>
> ....

(emphasis added). The fixation requirement is defined in section 101 in relevant part as follows:

> A work is "fixed" in a tangible medium of expression when its embodiment in a copy or phonorecord, by or under the authority of the author, is sufficiently permanent or stable to permit it to be perceived, reproduced, or otherwise communicated for a period of more than transitory duration.

Defendant claims that the images in the plaintiff's audiovisual game are transient, and cannot be "fixed." Specifically, it contends that there is a lack of "fixation" because the video game generates or creates "new" images each time the attract mode or play mode is displayed, notwithstanding the fact that the new images are identical or substantially identical to the earlier ones.

We reject this contention. The fixation requirement is met whenever the work is "sufficiently permanent or stable to permit it to be . . . reproduced, or otherwise communicated" for more than a transitory period. Here the original audiovisual features of the DEFENDER game repeat themselves over and over. The identical contention was previously made by this defendant and rejected by the court in *Midway Manufacturing Co. v. Artic International, Inc., supra,* slip op. at 16–18. * * *

* * *

Defendant also apparently contends that the player's participation withdraws the game's audiovisual work from copyright eligibility because there is no set or fixed performance and the player becomes a coauthor of what appears on the screen. Although there is player interaction with the machine during the play mode which causes the audiovisual presentation to change in some respects from one game to the next in response to the player's varying participation, there is always a repetitive sequence of a substantial portion of the sights and sounds of the game, and many aspects of the display remain constant from game to game regardless of how the player operates the controls. *See Stern Electronics, Inc. v. Kaufman,* 669 F.2d at 855–56. Furthermore, there is no player participation in the attract mode which is displayed repetitively without change.

* * *

For the above reasons, the district court's order granting the injunction will be affirmed except for Conclusion of Law No. 8 finding that the infringement was willful and deliberate. The case will be remanded for further proceedings consistent with this opinion.

Notes and Questions

1. Williams Electronics obtained three separate copyright registrations, one for the computer program, one for the "attract mode," and one for the "play mode." A more recent Copyright Office regulation, discussed in a later section of this casebook, allows video game authors to make a single registration covering both a computer program and the related displays. This change in formalities in no way affects the force of *Williams Electronics* as a precedent.

2. A coauthor of a work protected by copyright has the right to publish the work without the permission of the other coauthor. Could a video game expert legally publish a videotape called "How to Win at the DEFENDER," featuring detailed replays of the expert playing DEFENDER? Consider the implications of *Edward B. Marks Music Corp. v. Jerry Vogel Music Co.,* 140 F.2d 266 (2d Cir.1944) and *Shapiro, Bernstein & Co. v. Jerry Vogel Music Co.,* 161 F.2d 406 (2d Cir.1946) ("Melancholy Baby"), which held that the coauthor's identity need not be determined at the time the first author wrote.

7. "LOOK AND FEEL"

There is now no doubt that actual computer programs and the artistic design of screen displays are proper subjects for copyright. Computer software has another aspect, which differentiates it to a large extent from other copyrightable subject matter. This is "look and feel." Using a familiar software program, for instance a word processor, is like riding one's own bicycle or driving one's own car—there is some intangible combination of the screen displays and key functions that is immediately familiar.

It is perfectly legal to copy the look and feel of consumer products. Business writers praised the brilliance of Toshiko Hirai, designer for Mazda, who "recorded exhaust sounds of classic sports cars," listened to them, and created, for the Mazda Miata, "a throaty growl somewhere between an MG's and a Bugatti's." Woodruff, Miller, Armstrong, and Peterson, "A New Era for Auto Quality," Business Week, October 22, 1990, p. 84. Should it be legal to copy the look and feel of LOTUS 1–2–3?

Arguably, forbidding copying of "look and feel" gives the first program to dominate a field an unfair advantage, since users are reluctant to shift to unfamiliar products. However, is this advantage really any different from the advantage Ian Fleming got by writing the "James Bond" series of spy-adventure thrillers and getting them turned into a series of major motion pictures?

WHELAN ASSOCIATES, INC. v. JASLOW DENTAL LABORATORY, INC.

United States Court of Appeals, Third Circuit, 1986.
797 F.2d 1222.

BECKER, CIRCUIT JUDGE.

This appeal involves a computer program for the operation of a dental laboratory, and calls upon us to apply the principles underlying our venerable copyright laws to the relatively new field of computer technology to determine the scope of copyright protection of a computer program. More particularly, in this case of first impression in the courts of appeals, we must determine whether the structure (or sequence and organization)[1] of a computer program is protectible by copyright, or whether the protection of the copyright law extends only as far as the literal computer code. The district court found that the copyright law covered these non-literal elements of the program, and we agree. This conclusion in turn requires us to consider whether there was sufficient evidence of substantial similarity between the structures of the two programs at issue in this case to uphold the

1. We use the terms "structure," "sequence," and "organization" interchangeably when referring to computer programs, and we intend them to be synonymous in this opinion.

district court's finding of copyright infringement. Because we find that there was enough evidence, we affirm.

I. FACTUAL BACKGROUND

Appellant Jaslow Dental Laboratory, Inc. ("Jaslow Lab") is a Pennsylvania corporation in the business of manufacturing dental prosthetics and devices. Appellant Dentcom, Inc. ("Dentcom") is a Pennsylvania corporation in the business of developing and marketing computer programs for use by dental laboratories. Dentcom was formed out of the events that gave rise to this suit, and its history will be recounted below. Individual appellants Edward Jaslow and his son Rand Jaslow are officers and shareholders in both Jaslow Lab and Dentcom. Appellants were defendants in the district court. Plaintiff-appellee Whelan Associates, Inc. ("Whelan Associates") is also a Pennsylvania corporation, engaged in the business of developing and marketing custom computer programs.

Jaslow Lab, like any other small-or medium-sized business of moderate complexity, has significant bookkeeping and administrative tasks. Each order for equipment must be registered and processed; inventory must be maintained; customer lists must be continually updated; invoicing, billing, and accounts receivable, must be dealt with. While many of these functions are common to all businesses, the nature of the dental prosthetics business apparently requires some variations on the basic theme.

Although Rand Jaslow had not had extensive experience with computers, he believed that the business operations of Jaslow Lab could be made more efficient if they were computerized. In early 1978, he therefore bought a small personal computer and tried to teach himself how to program it so that it would be of use to Jaslow Lab. Although he wrote a program for the computer, he was ultimately not successful, limited by both his lack of expertise and the relatively small capacity of his particular computer.

A few months later, stymied by his own lack of success but still confident that Jaslow Lab would profit from computerization, Rand Jaslow hired the Strohl Systems Group, Inc. ("Strohl"), a small corporation that developed custom-made software to develop a program that would run on Jaslow Lab's new IBM Series One computer and take care of the Lab's business needs. Jaslow Lab and Strohl entered into an agreement providing that Strohl would design a system for Jaslow Lab's needs and that after Strohl had installed the system Strohl could market it to other dental laboratories. Jaslow Lab would receive a 10% royalty on all such sales. The person at Strohl responsible for the Jaslow Lab account was Elaine Whelan, an experienced programmer who was an officer and half-owner of Strohl.

Ms. Whelan's first step was to visit Jaslow Lab and interview Rand Jaslow and others to learn how the laboratory worked and what its needs were. She also visited other dental laboratories and interviewed people there, so that she would better understand the layout, workflow, and administration of dental laboratories generally. After this education into the ways of dental laboratories, and Jaslow Lab, in particular, Ms. Whelan wrote a program called Dentalab for Jaslow Lab. Dentalab was written in a computer language known as EDL (Event Driven Language), so that it would work with IBM Series One machines. The program was completed and was operative at Jaslow Lab around March 1979.

Presumably with an eye towards exploiting the economic potential of the Dentalab program, Ms. Whelan left Strohl in November, 1979, to form her own business, Whelan Associates, Inc., which acquired Strohl's interest in the Dentalab program. Shortly thereafter, Whelan Associates entered into negotiations with Jaslow Lab for Jaslow Lab to be Whelan Associates' sales representative for the Dentalab program. Whelan Associates and Jaslow Lab entered into an agreement on July 30, 1980, according to which Jaslow Lab agreed to use its "best efforts and to act diligently in the marketing of the Dentalab package," and Whelan Associates agreed to "use its best efforts and to act diligently to improve and augment the previously successfully designed Dentalab package." * * *

The parties' business relationship worked successfully for two years. During this time, as Rand Jaslow became more familiar with computer programming, he realized that because Dentalab was written in EDL it could not be used on computers that many of the smaller dental prosthetics firms were using, for which EDL had not been implemented. Sensing that there might be a market for a program that served essentially the same function as Dentalab but that could be used more widely, Rand Jaslow began in May or June of 1982 to develop in his spare time a program in the BASIC language for such computers. That program, when completed, became the alleged copyright infringer in this suit; it was called the Dentcom PC program ("Dentcom program").

It appears that Rand Jaslow was sanguine about the prospects of his program for smaller computers. After approximately a year of work, on May 31, 1983, his attorney sent a letter to Whelan Associates giving one month notice of termination of the agreement between Whelan Associates and Jaslow Lab. The letter stated that Jaslow Lab considered itself to be the exclusive marketer of the Dentalab program which, the letter stated, "contains valuable trade secrets of Jaslow Dental Laboratory." The letter concluded with a thinly veiled threat to Whelan Associates: "I * * * look for your immediate response confirming that you will respect the rights of Jaslow and not use or disclose to others the trade secrets of Jaslow." App. at 1221.

Approximately two months later, on about August 1, Edward and Rand Jaslow, Paul Mohr, and Joseph Cerra formed defendant-appellant Dentcom to sell the Dentcom program. At about the same time, Rand Jaslow and Jaslow Lab employed a professional computer programmer,

Jonathan Novak, to complete the Dentcom program. The program was soon finished, and Dentcom proceeded to sell it to dental prosthetics companies that had personal computers. Dentcom sold both the Dentalab and Dentcom programs, and advertised the Dentcom program as "a new version of the Dentlab computer system." App. at 178; 1567–73; 1766–69.

Despite Jaslow Lab's May 31 letter warning Whelan Associates not to sell the Dentalab program, Whelan Associates continued to market Dentalab. This precipitated the present litigation.

II. Procedural History

On June 30, 1983, Jaslow Lab filed suit in the Court of Common Pleas of Montgomery County (Pennsylvania), alleging that Whelan Associates had misappropriated its trade secrets. Whelan Associates responded by filing the instant suit in the United States District Court for the Eastern District of Pennsylvania on September 21, 1983. As set forth in its amended complaint, Whelan Associates alleged that Dentcom's licensing of the Dentalab and Dentcom programs infringed Whelan Associates' copyright in Dentalab, App. at 452–53; that Dentcom's use of the terms "Dentlab" or "Dentalab," violated Pennsylvania common law and 15 U.S.C. § 1125(a) (Lanham Trademark Act of 1946) (false designation of origin), App. at 454–57; and that Dentcom's activities violated various other federal and state laws pertaining to unfair competition and tortious interference with contractual relations, App. at 457–63. Whelan Associates sought injunctive relief, as well as compensatory and punitive damages. App. at 464–69.

Jaslow Lab and its co-defendants answered, denying all liability. They claimed that Whelan Associates' copyright was invalid for two reasons. First, they said that although he had not been listed in the copyright registration, Rand Jaslow had been a co-author (with Elaine Whelan) of the Dentalab program. The omission of Rand Jaslow from the registration form, defendants averred, rendered the copyright defective. App. at 506–09. Second, the defendants maintained that even if Rand Jaslow had not co-authored the program, he owned the copyright because the program had been written by someone employed by him. App. at 507. Defendants also averred that Rand Jaslow had developed the Dentcom system independently, and therefore could not have violated Whelan Associate's copyright, even if the copyright were valid.[7] Finally, defendants claimed that their use of "Dentalab" or "Dentlab" violated neither federal nor state law, for, *inter alia,* those terms are merely general descriptions of goods and services, not names of particular products. App. at 504. Defendants counterclaimed that Whelan

7. 17 U.S.C. § 106 (1982), which prescribes copyright holders' exclusive rights, forbids the copying of copyrighted works. The independent creation of even identical works is therefore not a copyright infringement, and independent creation is a complete defense to a claim of copyright infringement. *See also Fred Fisher, Inc. v. Dillingham,* 298 F. 145, 147 (S.D.N.Y.1924) (L. Hand, J.) ("the law imposes no prohibition upon those who, without copying, independently arrive at the precise combination of words or notes which have been copyrighted.").

Associates had usurped defendants' copyright and that by continuing to sell Dentalab, Whelan Associates was engaging in unfair competition. App. at 505–11. By agreement of the parties, the trade secret action was removed from the Court of Common Pleas to the district court and became a counterclaim. App. at 509–12.

* * *

The district court ruled for Whelan Associates on all grounds. *Whelan Associates v. Jaslow Dental Laboratory,* 609 F.Supp. 1307 (E.D.Pa.1985). It found that Elaine Whelan was the sole author of the Dentalab system (and, hence, that Rand Jaslow was not a co-author) and that the contract between Strohl and Rand Jaslow, *see supra* n. 2, made clear that Strohl would retain full ownership over the software. *Whelan Associates v. Jaslow Dental Laboratory,* 609 F.Supp. at 1318–19. The court thus concluded that Whelan Associates' copyright in the Dentalab System was valid, and that Dentcom's sales of the Dentalab program were violations of that copyright. *Id.* at 1320.

The court also found that Rand Jaslow had not created the Dentcom system independently, and that the Dentcom system, although written in a different computer language from the Dentalab, and although not a direct transliteration of Dentalab, was substantially similar to Dentalab because its structure and overall organization were substantially similar. *Id.* at 1321–22. (The district court's opinion on this point is described *infra* at 1238–39). This substantial similarity, in conjunction with Rand Jaslow's acknowledged access to the Dentalab system, led the district court to conclude that each sale of the Dentcom program by Dentcom violated Whelan Associates' copyright on the Dentalab system. The court therefore awarded Whelan Associates damages for these copyright infringements, and enjoined Dentcom from selling any more copies of the Dentalab or Dentcom programs. *Whelan Associates v. Jaslow Dental Laboratory,* 609 F.Supp. at 1322–23. The court also held that plaintiffs had exclusive use of the term "Dentalab," and enjoined defendants from using either "Dentalab" or "Dentlab" in their business. *Id.* at 1324–25.

* * * On appeal, [defendants] raise a single issue: whether the district court erred in its finding that the Dentcom program infringes the copyright of plaintiffs' Dentalab system.

III. Technological Background

We begin with a brief description of computer programs and an explanation of how they are written. This introduction is necessary to our analysis of the issue in this case.

A computer program is a set of instructions to the computer. * * *

* * *

As the programmer learns more about the problem, she or he may begin to outline a solution. The outline can take the form of a flowchart, which will break down the solution into a series of smaller units called "subroutines" or "modules," each of which deals with elements of the larger problem. * * *

As the program structure is refined, the programmer must make decisions about what data are needed, where along the program's operations the data should be introduced, how the data should be inputted, and how it should be combined with other data. The arrangement of the data is accomplished by means of data files, discussed *infra* at 1242–44, and is affected by the details of the program's subroutines and modules, for different arrangements of subroutines and modules may require data in different forms. Once again, there are numerous ways the programmer can solve the data-organization problems she or he faces. Each solution may have particular characteristics—efficiencies or inefficiencies, conveniences or quirks—that differentiate it from other solutions and make the overall program more or less desirable. Because the Dentalab program was intended to handle all of the business-related aspects of a dental laboratory, it had to accommodate and interrelate many different pieces and types of data including patients' names, dentists' names, inventory, accounts receivable, accounts payable, and payroll.

Once the detailed design of the program is completed, the coding begins. Each of the steps identified in the design must be turned into a language that the computer can understand. This translation process in itself requires two steps. The programmer first writes in a "source code," which may be in one of several languages, such as COBOL, BASIC, FORTRAN, or EDL. The choice of language depends upon which computers the programmer intends the program to be used by, for some computers can read only certain languages. Once the program is written in source code, it is translated into "object code," which is a binary code, simply a concatenation of "0"s and "1"s. In every program, it is the object code, not the source code, that directs the computer to perform functions. The object code is therefore the final instruction to the computer.[20]

As this brief summary demonstrates, the coding process is a comparatively small part of programming. By far the larger portion of the expense and difficulty in creating computer programs is attributable to the development of the structure and logic of the program, and to debugging, documentation and maintenance, rather than to the coding. * * * The evidence in this case shows that Ms. Whelan spent a tremendous amount of time studying Jaslow Labs, organizing the modules and subroutines for the Dentalab program, and working out the data arrangements, and a comparatively small amount of time actually coding the Dentalab program.

20. The discussion assumes that the program is "compiled" or "assembled." If a program is "interpreted," then the source and object codes are joined in a single step. Whether a program is compiled or interpreted depends on the program and the machine on which it is run. The difference is not important in this case.

IV. LEGAL BACKGROUND

A. *The elements of a copyright infringement action*—To prove that its copyright has been infringed, Whelan Associates must show two things: that it owned the copyright on Dentalab, and that Rand Jaslow copied Dentalab in making the Dentacom program. *Sid & Marty Krofft Television Prods., Inc. v. McDonald's Corp.*, 562 F.2d 1157, 1162 (9th Cir.1977); *Reyher v. Children's Television Workshop,* 533 F.2d 87, 90 (2d Cir.), *cert. denied,* 429 U.S. 980, 97 S.Ct. 492, 50 L.Ed.2d 588 (1976); 3 *Nimmer On Copyright* § 13.01 (1985) [referred to hereinafter as "Nimmer"]. Although it was disputed below, *see supra* 1228, the district court determined, and it is not challenged here, that Whelan Associates owned the copyright to the Dentalab program. We are thus concerned only with whether it has been shown that Rand Jaslow copied the Dentalab program.

As it is rarely possible to prove copying through direct evidence, *Roth Greeting Cards v. United Card Co.,* 429 F.2d 1106, 1110 (9th Cir.1970), copying may be proved inferentially by showing that the defendant had access to the allegedly infringed copyrighted work and that the allegedly infringing work is substantially similar to the copyrighted work. The district court found, and here it is uncontested, that Rand Jaslow had access to the Dentalab program, both because Dentalab was the program used in Jaslow Labs and because Rand Jaslow acted as a sales representative for Whelan Associates. *See Whelan Associates v. Jaslow Dental Laboratory,* 609 F.Supp. at 1314. Thus, the sole question is whether there was substantial similarity between the Dentcom and Dentalab programs.

B. *The appropriate test for substantial similarity in computer program cases*—* * *

* * *

* * * We * * * join the growing number of courts which do not apply the ordinary observer test in copyright cases involving exceptionally difficult materials, like computer programs, but instead adopt a single substantial similarity inquiry according to which both lay and expert testimony would be admissible. * * *

C. *The arguments on appeal*—On appeal, the defendants attack on two grounds the district court's holding that there was sufficient evidence of substantial similarity. First, the defendants argue that because the district court did not find any similarity between the "literal" elements (source and object code) of the programs, but only similarity in their overall structures, its finding of substantial similarity was incorrect, for the copyright covers only the literal elements of computer programs, not their overall structures. Defendants' second argument is that even if the protection of copyright law extends to "non-literal" elements such as the structure of computer programs, there was not sufficient evidence of substantial similarity to sustain the district court's holding in this case. We consider these arguments in turn.

V. The Scope of Copyright Protection of Computer Programs

It is well, though recently, established that copyright protection extends to a program's source and object codes. In this case, however, the district court did not find any copying of the source or object codes, nor did the plaintiff allege such copying. Rather, the district court held that the Dentalab copyright was infringed because the *overall structure* of Dentcom was substantially similar to the overall structure of Dentalab. *Whelan Associates v. Jaslow Dental Laboratory,* 609 F.Supp. at 1321–22. The question therefore arises whether mere similarity in the overall structure of programs can be the basis for a copyright infringement, or, put differently, whether a program's copyright protection covers the structure of the program or only the program's literal elements, *i.e.,* its source and object codes.

Title 17 U.S.C. § 102(a)(1) extends copyright protection to "literary works," and computer programs are classified as literary works for the purposes of copyright. *See* H.R.Rep. No. 1476, 94th Cong., 2d Sess. 54, *reprinted in* 1976 U.S.Code Cong. & Ad.News 5659, 5667. The copyrights of other literary works can be infringed even when there is no substantial similarity between the works' literal elements. One can violate the copyright of a play or book by copying its plot or plot devices. *See, e.g., Twentieth Century–Fox Film Corp. v. MCA, Inc.,* 715 F.2d 1327, 1329 (9th Cir.1983) (13 alleged distinctive plot similarities between *Battlestar Galactica* and *Star Wars* may be basis for a finding of copyright violation); *Sid & Marty Krofft Television Productions, Inc.,* 562 F.2d at 1167 (similarities between McDonaldland characters and H.R. Pufnstuf characters can be established by " 'total concept and feel' " of the two productions (quoting *Roth Greeting Cards v. United Card Co.,* 429 F.2d 1106, 1110 (9th Cir.1970)); *Sheldon v. Metro–Goldwyn Pictures Corp.,* 81 F.2d 49, 54–55 (2nd Cir.1936); *Nichols v. Universal Pictures Corp.,* 45 F.2d 119, 121 (2d Cir.1930) (copyright "cannot be limited literally to the text, else a plagiarist would escape by immaterial variations"). By analogy to other literary works, it would thus appear that the copyrights of computer programs can be infringed even absent copying of the literal elements of the program. Defendants contend, however, that what is true of other literary works is not true of computer programs. They assert two principal reasons, which we consider in turn.

A. *Section 102(b) and the dichotomy between idea and expression*— It is axiomatic that copyright does not protect ideas, but only expressions of ideas. This rule, first enunciated in *Baker v. Selden,* 101 U.S. (11 Otto) 99, 25 L.Ed. 841 (1879), has been repeated in numerous cases. The rule has also been embodied in statute. Title 17 U.S.C. § 102(b) (1982) states:

> In no case does copyright protection for an original work of authorship extend to any idea, procedure, process, system, method of operation, concept, principle, or discovery, regardless of the form in which it is described, explained, illustrated, or embodied in such work.

The legislative history of this section, adopted in 1976, makes clear that § 102(b) was intended to express the idea-expression dichotomy. *See* H.R.Rep. No. 1476 at 57, *reprinted in* 1976 U.S.Code Cong. & Ad.News at 5670 (§ 102(b) is intended to "restate * * * that the basic dichotomy between expression and idea remains unchanged.") *See also Apple Computer, supra,* 714 F.2d at 1252.

Defendants argue that the structure of a computer program is, by definition, the idea and not the expression of the idea, and therefore that the structure cannot be protected by the program copyright. Under the defendants' approach, any other decision would be contrary to § 102(b). We divide our consideration of this argument into two parts. First, we examine the caselaw concerning the distinction between idea and expression, and derive from it a rule for distinguishing idea from expression in the context of computer programs. We then apply that rule to the facts of this case.

1. *A rule for distinguishing idea from expression in computer programs*—It is frequently difficult to distinguish the idea from the expression thereof. No less an authority than Learned Hand, after a career that included writing some of the leading copyright opinions, concluded that the distinction will "inevitably be *ad hoc.*" *Peter Pan Fabrics, Inc. v. Martin Weiner Corp.,* 274 F.2d 487, 489 (2d Cir.1960). Although we acknowledge the wisdom of Judge Hand's remark, we feel that a review of relevant copyright precedent will enable us to formulate a rule applicable in this case. In addition, precisely because the line between idea and expression is elusive, we must pay particular attention to the pragmatic considerations that underlie the distinction and copyright law generally. In this regard, we must remember that the purpose of the copyright law is to create the most efficient and productive balance between protection (incentive) and dissemination of information, to promote learning, culture and development. *See* U.S. Const. Art. I, § 8, cl. 8 (Copyright Clause) (giving Congress the power to "promote the Progress of Science * * * by securing for limited Times to Authors * * * the exclusive Right to their respective Writings".)

We begin our analysis with the case of *Baker v. Selden,* which, in addition to being a seminal case in the law of copyright generally, is particularly relevant here because, like the instant case, it involved a utilitarian work, rather than an artistic or fictional one. In *Baker v. Selden,* the plaintiff Selden obtained a copyright on his book, "Selden's Condensed Ledger, or Bookkeeping Simplified," which described a new, simplified system of accounting. Included in the book were certain "blank forms," pages with ruled lines and headings, for use in Selden's accounting system. Selden alleged that Baker had infringed Selden's copyright by making and selling accounting books that used substantially the same system as Selden's and that reproduced Selden's blank forms. No one disputed that Baker had the right to use and promulgate Selden's system of accounting, for all parties agreed that the system could not be copyrighted, although the Court opined that it might be patentable. *Id.,* 101 U.S. at 102. Nor did the parties dispute that the text of Baker's book on accounting did not infringe Selden's copyright. The dispute centered on whether Selden's blank forms were part of the method (idea) of Selden's book, and hence non-copyrightable, or part of the copyrightable text (expression). *Id.* at 101.

In deciding this point, the Court distinguished what was protectible from what was not protectible as follows:

> [W]here the art [*i.e.,* the method of accounting] it teaches cannot be used without employing the methods and diagrams used to illustrate the book, or such as are similar to them, such methods and diagrams are to be considered as necessary incidents to the art, and given to the public.

Id. at 103. Applying this test, the Court held that the blank forms were necessary incidents to Selden's method of accounting, and hence were not entitled to any copyright protection. *Id.* at 104.

The Court's test in *Baker v. Selden* suggests a way to distinguish idea from expression. Just as *Baker v. Selden* focused on the end sought to be achieved by Selden's book, the line between idea and expression may be drawn with reference to the end sought to be achieved by the work in question. In other words, *the purpose or function of a utilitarian work would be the work's idea, and everything that is not necessary to that purpose or function would be part of the expression of the idea.* Where there are various means of achieving the desired purpose, then the particular means chosen is not necessary to the purpose; hence, there is expression, not idea.[28]

Consideration of copyright doctrines related to *scenes a faire* and fact-intensive works supports our formulation, for they reflect the same underlying principle. *Scenes a faire* are "incidents, characters or settings which are as a practical matter indispensable * * * in the treatment of a given topic." *Atari, Inc. v. North American Philips Consumer Elecs. Corp.,* 672 F.2d 607, 616 (7th Cir.), *cert. denied,* 459 U.S. 880, 103 S.Ct. 176, 74 L.Ed.2d 145 (1982). *See also See v. Durang,* 711 F.2d 141, 143 (9th Cir.1983). It is well-settled doctrine that *scenes a faire* are afforded no copyright protection.

Scenes a faire are afforded no protection because the subject matter represented can be expressed in no other way than through the particular *scene a faire.* Therefore, granting a copyright "would give the first author a monopoly on the commonplace ideas behind the *scenes a faire.*" *Landsberg v. Scrabble Crossword Game Players, Inc.,* 736 F.2d at 489. This is merely a restatement of the hypothesis advanced above,

28. This test is necessarily difficult to state, and it may be difficult to understand in the abstract. It will become more clear as we discuss and explain it in the textual discussion that follows this footnote. *See also infra* at 1242–44 (discussion of the copyrightability of file structures that raise many of the issues considered here). As will be seen, *see infra* at 1238–39, the idea of the Dentalab program was the efficient management of a dental laboratory (which presumably has significantly different requirements from those of other businesses). Because that idea could be accomplished in a number of different ways with a number of different structures, the structure of the Dentalab program is part of the program's expression, not its idea.

that the purpose or function of a work or literary device is part of that device's "idea" (unprotectible portion). It follows that anything necessary to effecting that function is also, necessarily, part of the idea, too.

Fact intensive works are given similarly limited copyright coverage. Once again, the reason appears to be that there are only a limited number of ways to express factual material, and therefore the purpose of the literary work—telling a truthful story—can be accomplished only by employing one of a limited number of devices. *Landsberg,* 736 F.2d at 488. Those devices therefore belong to the idea, not the expression, of the historical or factual work.

Although the economic implications of this rule are necessarily somewhat speculative, we nevertheless believe that the rule would advance the basic purpose underlying the idea/expression distinction, "the preservation of the balance between competition and protection reflected in the patent and copyright laws." *Herbert Rosenthal Jewelry Corp. v. Kalpakian,* 446 F.2d 738, 742 (9th Cir.1971). As we stated above, *see supra* at 1231, among the more significant costs in computer programming are those attributable to developing the structure and logic of the program. The rule proposed here, which allows copyright protection beyond the literal computer code, would provide the proper incentive for programmers by protecting their most valuable efforts, while not giving them a stranglehold over the development of new computer devices that accomplish the same end.

The principal economic argument used against this position—used, that is, in support of the position that programs' literal elements are the only parts of the programs protected by the copyright law—is that computer programs are so intricate, each step so dependent on all of the other steps, that they are almost impossible to copy except literally, and that anyone who attempts to copy the structure of a program without copying its literal elements must expend a tremendous amount of effort and creativity. * * * A further argument against our position is not economic but jurisprudential; another commentator argues that the concept of structure in computer programs is too vague to be useful in copyright cases. * * *

Neither of the two arguments just described is persuasive. The first argument fails for two reasons. In the first place, it is simply not true that "approximation" of a program short of perfect reproduction is valueless. To the contrary, one can approximate a program and thereby gain a significant advantage over competitors even though additional work is needed to complete the program. Second, the fact that it will take a great deal of effort to copy a copyrighted work does not mean that the copier is not a copyright infringer. The issue in a copyrighted case is simply whether the copyright holder's expression has been copied, not how difficult it was to do the copying. Whether an alleged infringer spent significant time and effort to copy an original work is therefore irrelevant to whether he has pirated the expression of an original work.

As to the second argument, it is surely true that limiting copyright protection to computers' literal codes would be simpler and would yield more definite answers than does our answer here. Ease of application is not, however, a sufficient counterweight to the considerations we have adduced on behalf of our position.

* * *

We are not convinced that progress in computer technology or technique is qualitatively different from progress in other areas of science or the arts. In balancing protection and dissemination the copyright law has always recognized and tried to accommodate the fact that all intellectual pioneers build on the work of their predecessors.[33] Thus, copyright principles derived from other areas are applicable in the field of computer programs.

2. *Application of the general rule to this case*—The rule proposed here is certainly not problem-free. The rule has its greatest force in the analysis of utilitarian or "functional" works, for the purpose of such works is easily stated and identified. By contrast, in cases involving works of literature or "non-functional" visual representations, defining the purpose of the work may be difficult. Since it may be impossible to discuss the purpose or function of a novel, poem, sculpture or painting, the rule may have little or no application to cases involving such works. The present case presents no such difficulties, for it is clear that the purpose of the utilitarian Dentalab program was to aid in the business operations of a dental laboratory.[34] *See supra* 1225. It is equally clear that the structure of the program was not essential to that task: there are other programs on the market, competitors of Dentalab and Dentcom, that perform the same functions but have different structures and designs.

* * *

* * * The conclusion is thus inescapable that the detailed structure of the Dentalab program is part of the expression, not the idea, of that program.

* * *

The Copyright Act of 1976 provides further support, for it indicates that Congress intended that the structure and organization of a literary work could be part of its expression protectible by copyright. Title 17

33. Long before the first computer, Sir Issac Newton humbly explained that "if [he] had seen farther than other men, it was because [he] had stood on the shoulders of giants."

34. We do not mean to imply that the idea or purpose behind *every* utilitarian or functional work will be precisely what it accomplishes, and that structure and organization will therefore always be part of the expression of such works. The idea or purpose behind a utilitarian work may be to accomplish a certain function *in a certain way, see, e.g., Baker v. Selden,* 101 U.S. at 100 (referring to Selden's book as explaining "a peculiar system of book-keeping"), and the structure or function of a program might be essential to that task. There is no suggestion in the record, however, that the purpose of the Dentalab program was anything so refined; it was simply to run a dental laboratory in an efficient way.

U.S.C. § 103 (1982) specifically extends copyright protection to compilations and derivative works. Title 17 U.S.C. § 101, defines "compilation" as "a work formed by the collection and *assembling* of preexisting materials or of data that are selected, *coordinated, or arranged* in such a way that the resulting work as a whole constitutes an original work of authorship," and it defines "derivative work," as one "based upon one or more preexisting works, such as * * * *abridgement, condensation,* or any other form in which a work may be *recast,* transformed, or adapted." (emphasis added). Although the Code does not use the terms "sequence," "order" or "structure," it is clear from the definition of compilations and derivative works, and the protection afforded them, that Congress was aware of the fact that the sequencing and ordering of materials could be copyrighted, *i.e.,* that the sequence and order could be parts of the expression, not the idea, of a work.

Our solution may put us at odds with Judge Patrick Higginbotham's scholarly opinion in *Synercom Technology, Inc. v. University Computing Co.,* 462 F.Supp. 1003 (N.D.Tex.1978), which dealt with the question whether the "input formats" of a computer program—the configurations and collations of the information entered into the program—were idea or expression. The court held that the input formats were ideas, not expressions, and thus not protectible. *Synercom* did not deal with precisely the materials at issue here—input formats are structurally simple as compared to full programs—and it may therefore be distinguishable. However, insofar as the input formats are devices for the organization of data into forms useful for computers, they are *similar* to programs; thus, *Synercom* is relevant and we must come to grips with it.

Central to Judge Higginbotham's analysis was his conviction that the organization and structure of the input formats was inseparable from the idea underlying the formats. Although the court acknowledged that in some cases structure and sequence might be part of expression, not idea, *see id.* at 1014, it stated that in the case of input formats, structure and organization were inherently part of the idea. The court put its position in the form of a powerful rhetorical question: "if sequencing and ordering [are] expression, what separable idea is being expressed?" *Id.* at 1013.

To the extent that *Synercom* rested on the premise that there was a difference between the copyrightability of sequence and form in the computer context and in any other context, we think that it is incorrect. As just noted, the Copyright Act of 1976 demonstrates that Congress intended sequencing and ordering to be protectible in the appropriate circumstances * * * and the computer field is not an exception to this general rule. Although Congress was aware that computer programs posed a novel set of issues and problems for the copyright law, Congress did not then make, and has not since made, any special provision for ordering and sequencing in the context of computer programs. There is thus no statutory basis for treating computer programs differently from other literary works in this regard.

Despite the fact that copyright protection extends to sequence and form in the computer context, unless we are able to answer Judge Higginbotham's powerful rhetorical question—"if sequencing and ordering [are] expression, what separable idea is being expressed?"—in our own case, we would have to hold that the structure of the Dentalab program is part of its idea and is thus not protectible by copyright. Our answer has already been given, however: the idea is the efficient organization of a dental laboratory (presumably, this poses different problems from the efficient organization of some other kinds of laboratories or businesses). Because there are a variety of program structures through which that idea can be expressed, the structure is not a necessary incident to that idea.[36] * * *

* * *

VI. Evidence of Substantial Similarity

Defendants' second argument is that even if copyright protection is not limited to computer programs' literal elements as a matter of law, there is insufficient evidence of substantial similarity presented in this case to support a finding of copyright infringement. * * *

A. *File structures*—* * * Defendants analogize files to blank forms, which contain no information but merely collect and organize information that is entered from another source. They argue, relying on *Baker v. Selden,* that, as a matter of law, blank forms cannot be copyrighted. Thus, they conclude, neither can file structures be part of the copyright of a program.

Defendants' description of the file structures is indeed correct. Dr. Moore himself described a computer's file as "a storage place for data, and it's really no different in a computer than it is in a file drawer, it's like a manila folder that contains all the data on a particular subject category in a computer." App. at 682. (Another analogy, particularly accessible to lawyers, is to a very complex cataloguing structure like the structure of Lexis or Westlaw without any entries yet made.) Defendants' legal conclusion is not correct, however. Although some courts have stated that the meaning of *Baker v. Selden* is that blank forms cannot be copyrighted, this circuit, like the majority of courts that have considered the issue, has rejected this position and instead have held that blank forms may be copyrighted if they are sufficiently innovative that their arrangement of information is itself informative.

This is not to say that *all* blank forms or computer files are copyrightable. Only those that by their arrangement and organization convey some information can be copyrighted. * * * Defendants do not

36. It is not clear whether the end sought to be accomplished by the input formats involved in *Synercom* could be accomplished with different sequences and orders. *Compare* 462 F.Supp. at 1013 ("there are many * * * possible choices of computer formats, and the decision among them [is] arbitrary") *with id.* at 1014 ("The 'idea or principle' behind the forms in question, and the 'method or system' involved in them, [are] no more or less than the formats."). Moreover, as noted above, the input formats involved in *Synercom* are not identical to the structures of computer programs that concern us here.

contend, however, that the file structures convey no information, and it appears to us that the structures are sufficiently complex and detailed that such an argument would not succeed. As we have noted, *supra* at 1239, there are many ways in which the same goal—the organization of the business aspects of a dental laboratory—might be accomplished, and several of these approaches might use significantly different file structures.[43] The file structures in the Dentalab and Dentcom systems require certain information and order that information in a particular fashion. Other programs might require different information or might use the same information differently. When we compare the comprehensiveness and complexity of the file structures at issue here with the "blank forms" at issue in the cases mentioned above, we have no doubt that these file structures are sufficiently informative to deserve copyright protection.

B. *Screen outputs*—Defendants' second line of argument is slightly confusing. Defendants appear to argue that to the extent that the district court relied upon the similarity of the screen outputs of Dentalab and Dentcom its finding of substantial similarity was erroneous because (1) the screen outputs are covered by a different copyright from the program's, and/or (2) the screen outputs bear no relation to the programs that produce them. Although these arguments are not always clearly distinguished, Appellants' Br. at 38–41; Reply Br. at 8–10, the distinction is important because whereas the first argument is weak, we feel that the second is more persuasive.

It is true that screen outputs are considered audio-visual works under the copyright code, *see Williams Electronics,* 685 F.2d at 874; *Midway Manufacturing Co.,* 564 F.Supp. at 749 (distinguishing audiovisual copyright in display of videogame from copyright in program that creates the audiovisual display), and are thus covered by a different copyright than are programs, which are literary works, *see supra* at 1233. It is also true that Whelan Associates asserts no claim of copyright infringement with respect to the screen outputs. But the conclusion to be drawn from this is not, as defendants would have it, that screen outputs are completely irrelevant to the question whether the copyright in the program has been infringed. Rather, the only conclusion to be drawn from the fact of the different copyrights is that the screen output cannot be *direct* evidence of copyright infringement. There is no reason, however, why material falling under one copyright category could not be indirect, inferential evidence of the nature of material covered by another copyright.

43. Defendants' expert, Mr. Ness, testified that, given the problem to be solved, there were in fact few possible, efficient, file structures, and that the similarity in the programs' file structures was therefore neither surprising nor probative. *See* App. at 834–37. The district court apparently did not find Mr. Ness persuasive on this point, however, and we defer to the court's assessment. Had the defendants offered more evidence to support their position, our answer might have been different. It is true that for certain tasks there are only a very limited number of file structures available, and in such cases the structures might not be copyrightable and similarity of file structures might not be strongly probative of similarity of the program as a whole. We are simply not convinced that this is such a case.

Thus, the question is whether the screen outputs have probative value concerning the nature of the programs that render them sufficient to clear the hurdles of Fed.R.Evid. 401 and 403. The defendants argue that the screen outputs have *no* probative value with respect to the programs because many different programs can create the same screen output. Defendants rely on *Stern Electronics Inc. v. Kaufman,* 669 F.2d at 855 ("many different computer programs can produce the same 'results,' whether those results are an analysis of financial records or a sequence of images and sounds."), and *Midway Manufacturing Co.,* 564 F.Supp. at 749 ("it is quite possible to design a game that would infringe Midway's audiovisual copyright but would use an entirely different computer program."). Neither court, however, was presented with the question that faces us today, the evidentiary value of screen outputs in a suit for infringement of the underlying program.

Insofar as everything that a computer does, including its screen outputs, is related to the program that operates it, there is necessarily a causal relationship between the program and the screen outputs. The screen outputs must bear *some* relation to the underlying programs, and therefore they have some probative value. The evidence about the screen outputs therefore passes the low admissibility threshold of Fed.R.Evid. 401.

* * *

C. *The five subroutines*—With respect to the final piece of evidence, Dr. Moore's testimony about the five subroutines found in Dentalab and Dentcom, defendants state that they "fail to understand how a substantial similarity in *structure* can be established by a comparison of only a small fraction of the two works." Appellants' Brief at 43, *see also* Reply Br. at 12. The premise underlying this declaration is that one cannot prove substantial similarity of two works without comparing the entirety, or at least the greater part, of the works. We take this premise to be the defendants' argument.

The premise does not apply in other areas of copyright infringement. There is no general requirement that most of each of two works be compared before a court can conclude that they are substantially similar. In the cases of literary works—novels, movies, or plays, for example—it is often impossible to speak of "most" of the work. The substantial similarity inquiry cannot be simply quantified in such instances. Instead, the court must make a qualitative, not quantitative, judgment about the character of the work as a whole and the importance of the substantially similar portions of the work.

* * * Because all steps of a computer program are not of equal importance, the relevant inquiry cannot therefore be the purely mechanical one of whether most of the programs' steps are similar. Rather, because we are concerned with the overall similarities between the programs, we must ask whether the most significant steps of the programs are similar. *See Midway Mfg. Co. v. Strohon, supra,* 564

F.Supp. at 753. This is precisely what Dr. Moore did. He testified as follows:

> What I decided to do was to look at the programs that had the primary, or let's say most important, tasks of the system, and also ones which manipulate files, because there are a lot of programs that simply print lists, or answer a question when you ask him it, but I thought that the programs which actually showed the flow of information, through the system, would be the ones that would illustrate the system back.

App. at 704. Dr. Moore's testimony was thus in accord with general principles of copyright law. As we hold today that these principles apply as well to computer programs, we therefore reject the defendants' argument on this point.

D. *Sufficiency of the evidence*—Defendants' final argument is that the district court erred in evaluating the testimony of Dr. Moore and Mr. Ness. They contend that, properly evaluated, Mr. Ness' testimony was sufficiently strong and Dr. Moore's sufficiently weak, that there was not sufficient evidence of substantial similarity for plaintiff to prevail.

* * *

* * * Determinations of credibility and the relative weight to be given expert witnesses are, of course, left primarily to the discretion of the district court. Our review of the record convinces us that the district court's analysis of the two experts' opinions was far from being erroneous. * * *

In addition, we believe, on re-reading the trial transcript, that although Mr. Ness' testimony was quite competent, Dr. Moore's was more persuasive on the issues relevant to this appeal. Whereas the greater part of Mr. Ness' testimony was concerned with the dissimilarities between the two programs' source and object codes, *see, e.g.,* App. at 824–32, Dr. Moore discussed the crucial issue in this case, the similarities and differences in the programs' *structures.* * * *

* * *

> Q. Do you have any comment about the invoicing?
>
> A. *[Dr. Moore] Well, I think it should be clear, it was clear to me from going through these programs that there is a very marke[d] similarity between the two, that they, item by item, are doing pretty much the same thing with the same fields in the same files, and accomplishing roughly the same results.*
>
> *So there was quite a match, line by line, between these two, flow in these two.*
>
> Q. What do you conclude from that?
>
> A. [Dr. Moore] Well, back together with the file's structure, sort of set up with the—how the programs have to proceed. I would think that

the person who designed or constructed the Dentalab system must have been thoroughly familiar with the Dentcom system.

The person who constructed the Dentcom system must have been familiar with the series one system, because the same file structure and same program steps are followed, same overall flow takes place in both systems.

App. at 710–12 (emphasis added). Dr. Moore's testimony about Dentcom's and Dentalab's month-end subroutines also demonstrates the structural comparisons in which he engaged:

Q. What did you find in month-end?

A. Okay. Month-end, the calling program in Dentcom, this obviously is done at the end of each month.

In the Dentcom system there is a program called MOEND, which chains all these other programs, that is, MOEND calls MOPRDL, and after that program runs, goes back to MEEND, calls the print sale and so on.

In the Dentalab system there is a supervisory program also called MOEND, and that system calls or runs a series of programs doing various functions.

Now *if we look at the functions done by the programs in order, we find that they are the same except for a flipping of the order in the first two things.*

The Dentcom system, it first prints product group report, and then prints the monthly customer sales analysis.

In Dentalab, just reverses, prints sales analysis first, product group report second.

After that, both systems do the same thing in the same order.

They now do accounts receivable aging, since a month has gone by they have to update all the 30 days, 60 days, et cetera, calculate service charges. Then they print the monthly AR reports that had to do with service charges, only those that involve service charges, they both do that. Then they both print the age file balance, balance report, and following that they print the month and accounts receivable report. That's the total accounts receivable rport [*sic*].

Then they both go through and look for accounts that are not active that month, and print a list of these accounts, accounts not serviced, an account that doesn't have any access.

The final thing that the Dentcom system does is to calculate the new AR total for the entire lab, which I mentioned is contained in the company file.

Dentalab doesn't keep that total, so that's the last item, that is not as far as I can tell, done by Dentalab. I may have said—did I say Dentcom keeps that total? Dentalab does not. That's the only difference.

App. at 716–18 (emphasis added). * * *

VII. Conclusion

We hold that (1) copyright protection of computer programs may extend beyond the programs' literal code to their structure, sequence, and organization, and (2) the district court's finding of substantial similarity between the Dentalab and Dentcom programs was not clearly erroneous. The judgment of the district court will therefore be affirmed.

APPENDIX A

ORDER ENTRY PROGRAMS

Dentcom PC Systems	*Dentalab System*
Primary Menu, choose [1] Production MENU	Primary Menu, choose [1] Production SCHEDULING
Production menu choose [1] ORDER ENTRY ORDER ENTRY program	Production Menu, choose [1] ORDER ENTRY DL1000 program (Order entry)
"ENTER ACCOUNT NAME KEY: ____________	"ENTER ACCOUNT OR NAMEKEY"
Check CUSTMAST for valid customer. If valid, read CUSTMAST file for this customer.	"Check CUSTMAST for valid customer. Read CUSTMAST file on this customer.
If yes, increment order # in ORDERS	Increment sequential order no. in ORDERS. Display customer name, address.
Display entry screen, patient shade, mould, remake, call Dr.?	Display entry screen (6.6), patient shade, remake, call
Dr.?	
case/span #, Drs. request date, final case statut T, F, B, R.	Pan #, Dr's. request date.
IS THIS SCREEN CORRECT?	
If yes ask for first department number. Display dept. order screen (P10) (list of item in this dept. from ITEMMAST)	Ask for first department number. Display dept. order screen (6.8–6.11) (list of items in this dept. from ITEMMAST)
User entry choices	User entry choices
System adds days in dept. from COMPANY to present date to find due out date. Time is of AM. "Noon" or PM. System accumulates case load by product of item load factor × quantity.	System adds days in dept. [DAYVAL] to present date to find due out date. System computes workload for dept/day out by product of load factor × quantity.
ITEMMAST	ITEMMAST
Adds this to load already in DEPTLOAD for date out.	Add this to load already in DAYVAL for date out.

LOTUS DEVELOPMENT CORPORATION v. PAPERBACK SOFTWARE INTERNATIONAL

United States District Court, District of Massachusetts, 1990.
740 F.Supp. 37.

Keeton, District Judge.

The expression of an idea is copyrightable. The idea itself is not. When applying these two settled rules of law, how can a decisionmaker distinguish between an idea and its expression?

Answering this riddle is the first step—but only the first—toward disposition of this case in which the court must decide, among other issues, (1) whether and to what extent plaintiff's computer spreadsheet program, Lotus 1–2–3, is copyrightable, (2) whether defendants' VP–Planner was, on undisputable facts, an infringing work containing elements substantially similar to copyrightable elements of 1–2–3, and (3) whether defendants' proffered jurisdictional and equitable defenses are meritorious.

* * *

I. A Background Statement About Computers, Computer Programs, and Copyrightability

Though their influence in our society is already pervasive, digital computers—along with computer "programs" and "user interfaces"—are relatively new to the market, and newer still to litigation over "works" protected by intellectual property law.

* * *

This case concerns two competing application programs—Lotus 1–2–3 and VP–Planner—which are primarily spreadsheet programs, but which also support other tasks such as limited database management and graphics creation. Programs such as these, because they can perform several different kinds of tasks, are called "integrated" application programs.

* * *

National Commission on New Technological Uses of Copyrighted Works, *Final Report and Recommendations* 43 (1978) (hereinafter "*Final Report*"). * * *

Defendants vigorously dispute, however, the copyrightability of any nonliteral elements of computer programs. That is, defendants assert that only literal manifestations of computer programs are copyrightable. Plaintiff, on the other hand, maintains that copyright protection extends to all elements of computer programs that embody original expression, whether literal or non-literal, including any original expression embodied in a program's "user interface."

* * *

3. *Relevant Aspects of the Whole Law of Copyright*

a. *"Nonliteral" Expression*

With respect to such things as musical, dramatic, and motion picture works, and works of "literature" (as contrasted with "literary" works in the broader statutory sense, it is crystal clear that, to the extent original, the literal manifestations of such works are protected by copyright. Thus, during a period of copyright protection, one cannot copy an author's book, score, or script without authorization in law or in fact. It is also well settled that a copyright in a musical, dramatic, or motion picture work, or a work of literature, may be infringed even if the infringer has not copied the literal aspects of the work. That is, even if an infringer does not copy the words or dialogue of a book or play, or the score of a musical work, infringement may be found if there is copying of the work's expression of setting, characters, or plot with a resulting substantial similarity.

This type of copying of nonliteral expression, if sufficiently extensive, has never been upheld as permissible copying; rather, it has always been viewed as copying of elements of an expression of creative originality.

b. "Useful Articles"

A "useful article" is defined by the Copyright Act as

> an article having an intrinsic utilitarian function that is not merely to portray the appearance of the article or to convey information. An article that is normally a part of a useful article is considered a "useful article."

17 U.S.C. § 101 (1988). Such articles—or more accurately, the utilitarian aspects of such articles—are not works of authorship in which copyright can subsist. * * *

* * *

4. The Objects and Policies of Copyright Law

The court's final task in divining the statutory mandates is to look to the "object and policy" of the copyright law. * * *

Copyright monopolies are not granted for the purpose of rewarding authors. Rather, Congress has granted copyright monopolies to serve the public welfare by encouraging authors (broadly defined) to generate new ideas and disclose them to the public, being free to do so in any uniquely expressed way they may choose. * * *

* * *

B. The Idea–Expression and Useful–Expressive Distinctions

Although the statutory mandates are ambiguous in some critical respects, one point on which they are clear (one marker of the boundary line) is this: at least some, but clearly not all, aspects of computer programs, if original, are "works of authorship" in which copyright can subsist. 17 U.S.C. § 102(a)(1); House Report at 54, reprinted at 5667; CONTU, *Final Report* at 21. How can a court determine which aspects are copyrightable?

The interplay between sections 102(a) and 102(b), illumined by the related legislative history, manifests that the statute extends copyright protection to expressive elements of computer programs, but not to the ideas, processes, and methods embodied in computer programs. House Report at 54, 57, *reprinted at* 5667, 5670. This dichotomy—which is often referred to as the "idea-expression distinction," and which embraces also the process-expression, method-expression, and useful-expressive distinctions, *see* Note, *Determining the Scope of Copyright*

Protection of Computer Program Structure, 88 Mich.L.Rev. at 866–67—has long been a fundamental part of our copyright law. *Baker v. Selden,* 101 U.S. 99, 25 L.Ed. 841 (1879). In that seminal case, the Court held that the text of a book describing a special method of double-entry accounting on paper spreadsheets—the now almost universal T-accounts system—was copyrightable *expression,* but that the method itself, which embodied the *idea* of this particular kind of double-entry bookkeeping, was not. The Court thus concluded that Baker did not infringe Selden's copyright when Baker wrote his own treatise, in his own words, describing the special double-entry method of bookkeeping.

* * *

I conclude that, with the Copyright Act of 1976 and the 1980 amendments to that Act, Congress manifested an intention to use the idea-expression distinction as part of the test of copyrightability for computer programs. * * *

* * *

IV. The Legal Test for Copyrightability Applicable to This Case

A. Functionality, Useful Articles, and the Useful–Expressive Distinction

Defendants suggest that the user interface of Lotus 1–2–3 is a useful, "function[al]" object like the functional layout of gears in an "H" pattern on a standard transmission, the functional assignment of letters to keys on a standard QWERTY keyboard, and the functional configuration of controls on a musical instrument (*e.g.,* keys of a piano). Lewis Affdvt. ¶¶ 52–54. These "functional" "useful articles," defendants contend, are not entitled to copyright protection.

A similar analogy was made in *Synercom* where the court concluded that a sequence of data inputs for a statistical analysis program was like the "figure-H" pattern of a standard transmission. 462 F.Supp. at 1013. *Synercom,* though, was published less than a month after the publication of the CONTU report (which it never cites) and well before the 1980 amendments. Since then, congressional and judicial development of the law of copyrightability of computer programs has advanced considerably, and *Synercom's* central proposition—that the expression of nonliteral sequence and order is inseparable from the idea and accordingly is not copyrightable—has been explicitly rejected by several courts. In any event, *Synercom's* input formats are quite different from, and distinguishable from, the nonliteral aspects of 1–2–3 at issue in this case.

* * *

* * * Elements of expression, even if embodied in useful articles, are copyrightable if capable of identification and recognition independently of the functional ideas that make the article useful. This mandate may be viewed as a corollary of the central distinction of

copyright law between idea and expression, which is explored further immediately below.

B. The Idea–Expression Riddle: Four Additional Concepts

It is by now plain that an idea is not copyrightable and an expression may be. It does not follow, though, that every expression of an idea is copyrightable. To begin to get an understanding of the legally significant contrasts among an idea, non-copyrightable expressions of the idea, and a copyrightable expression, we must take account of four more concepts.

Earlier parts of this Opinion refer to two of these four—"originality" and "functionality." * * *

The third concept is "obviousness." When a particular expression goes no farther than the obvious, it is inseparable from the idea itself. Protecting an expression of this limited kind would effectively amount to protection of the idea, a result inconsistent with the plain meaning of the statute.

It is only a slight extension of the idea of "obviousness"—and one supported by precedent—to reach the fourth concept: "merger." If a particular expression is one of a quite limited number of the possible ways of expressing an idea, then, under this fourth concept, the expression is not copyrightable:

* * *

C. Elements of the Legal Test for Copyrightability

* * *

FIRST

* * *

As Learned Hand recognized in a 1930 case concerning the alleged infringement of the copyright of a play:

> Upon any work, and especially upon a play, a great number of patterns of increasing generality will fit equally well, as more and more of the incident is left out. The last may perhaps be no more than the most general statement of what the play is about, and at times might consist only of its title; but there is a point in this series of abstractions where they are no longer protected, since otherwise the playwright could prevent the use of his "ideas," to which, apart from their expression, his property is never extended. Nobody has ever been able to fix that boundary, and nobody ever can.

Nichols, 45 F.2d at 121 (citations omitted). * * *

* * *

In addition to taking account of the distinction between generality and specificity, to make use of Hand's abstraction scale for applying the idea-expression distinction we need to identify and distinguish between essential and nonessential details of expressing the idea. Some, but of course not all, details, are so essential that their omission would result in a failure to express *that* idea, or in the expression of only a different and *more general* idea. Accordingly, two more elements in the legal test for copyrightability are:

> SECOND, the decisionmaker must focus upon whether an alleged expression of the idea is limited to elements essential to expression of *that* idea (or is one of only a few ways of expressing the idea) or instead includes identifiable elements of expression not essential to every expression of that idea.
>
> THIRD, having identified elements of expression not essential to every expression of the idea, the decisionmaker must focus on whether those elements are a substantial part of the allegedly copyrightable "work."

In addressing this third element of the test for copyrightability, the decisionmaker is measuring "substantiality" not merely on a quantum scale but by a test that is qualitative as well. *SAS Institute,* 605 F.Supp. at 829–30 ("the piracy of even a quantitatively small fragment ('a rose by any other name would smell as sweet') may be qualitatively substantial").

* * *

V. Application of the Legal Test to Lotus 1–2–3

A. *"Look and Feel"*

In musical, dramatic, and motion picture works, and works of literature, nonliteral elements that are copyrightable have sometimes been described as the "total concept and feel" of a work, *Roth Greeting Cards,* 429 F.2d at 1110. In the context of computer programs, nonliteral elements have often been referred to as the "look and feel" of a program, * * *.

Despite its widespread use in public discourse on the copyrightability of nonliteral elements of computer programs, I have not found the "look and feel" concept, standing alone, to be significantly helpful in distinguishing between nonliteral elements of a computer program that are copyrightable and those that are not.

C. *Elements of the User Interface as Expression*

Applying to 1–2–3 the legal test stated in Part IV(C), *supra,* I consider first where along the scale of abstraction to conceive the "idea" for the purpose of distinguishing between the idea and its expression.

At the most general level of Hand's abstractions scale, *Nichols,* 45 F.2d at 121—the computer programs at issue in this case, and other computer programs that have been considered during the course of trial, are expressions of the idea of a computer program for an electronic spreadsheet. Defendants are quite correct, then, in asserting that the idea of developing an electronic spreadsheet is not copyrightable—that the core idea of such a spreadsheet is both functional and obvious, even to computer users who claim no technical competence. Thus, even though programs like VisiCalc, 1–2–3, Multiplan, SuperCalc4, and Excel are very different in their structure, appearance, and method of operation, each is, at the most basic level, just a different way of expressing the same idea: the electronic spreadsheet. It does not follow, however, that every possible method of designing a metaphorical spreadsheet is obvious, or that no form of expressing the idea of the spreadsheet metaphor can possibly have such originality in pressing beyond the obvious as is required for copyrightability, or that no special form of metaphorical spreadsheet can possibly be a distinctive expression of a particular method of preparing financial information.

The idea for a two-line moving cursor menu is also functional and obvious, and, indeed, is used in a wide variety of computer programs including spreadsheet programs. Nevertheless, it does not follow that every possible method of designing a menu system that includes a two-line moving cursor is non-copyrightable.

Of course, if a particular expression of the idea of an electronic spreadsheet communicates no details beyond those essential to stating the idea itself, then that expression would not be copyrightable. The issue here is whether Lotus 1–2–3 does go beyond those details essential to any expression of the idea, and includes substantial elements of expression, distinctive and original, which are thus copyrightable.

* * *

Just as 1–2–3 expressed the idea of an electronic spreadsheet differently from VisiCalc, so did Microsoft's Excel. Originally written for the Apple Macintosh computer, it exploits the enhanced graphics capabilities of the Macintosh, as well as the mouse input device that is standard with the Macintosh. Excel has pull-down bar menus rather than a two-line moving-cursor menu, and a very different menu-command hierarchy. Tr. Ex. 79.

As already noted, these three products—VisiCalc, 1–2–3, and Excel—share the general idea of an electronic spreadsheet but have expressed the idea in substantially different ways. These products also share some elements, however, at a somewhat more detailed or specific point along the abstractions scale. One element shared by these and many other programs is the basic spreadsheet screen display that resembles a rotated "L." Although Excel uses a different basic spreadsheet screen display that more closely resembles a paper spreadsheet, there is a rather low limit, as a factual matter, on the number of ways of making a computer screen resemble a spreadsheet. Accordingly, this aspect of electronic spreadsheet computer programs, if not present in every expression of such a program, is present in most expressions. Thus the second element of the legal test weighs heavily against treating the rotated "L" screen display as a copyrightable element of a computer program.

Another expressive element that merges with the idea of an electronic spreadsheet—that is, that is an essential detail present in most if not all expressions of an electronic spreadsheet—is the designation of a particular key that, when pressed, will invoke the menu command system. The number of keys available for this designation is limited for two reasons. First, because most of the keys on the keyboard relate either to values (*e.g.,* the number keys and mathematical operation keys) or labels (*e.g.,* the letter keys), only a few keys are left that can be used, as a practical matter, to invoke the menu command system. Without something more, the programmed computer would interpret the activation of one of these keys as an attempt by the user to enter a value or label into a cell. Second, because users need to invoke the command system frequently, the key designated for this purpose must be easily accessible. For example, the user should not be required to press two keys at the same time (such as "Shift," "Alt," or "Ctrl" along with another key).

As just noted, when all the letter, number, and arithmetic keys are eliminated from consideration, the number of keys remaining that could be used to invoke the menu command system is quite limited. They include the slash key ("/") and the semi-colon key (";"). The choice of the creators of VisiCalc to designate the slash ("/") key to invoke the menu command system is not surprising. It is one of very few practical options. Thus the second element of the legal test weighs heavily against copyrightability of this aspect of VisiCalc—and of 1–2–3. This expression merges with the idea of having a readily available method of invoking the menu command system.

Other elements of expression a decisionmaker may regard as either essential to every expression of an electronic spreadsheet, or at least "obvious" if not essential, include the use of the "+" key to indicate addition, the "−" key to indicate subtraction, the " *" key to indicate multiplication, the "/" key within formulas to indicate division, and the "enter" key to place keystroke entries into the cells. *See* Dauphinais Affidavit, ¶ 78.

Each of the elements just described is present in, if not all, at least most expressions of an electronic spreadsheet computer program. Other aspects of these programs, however, need not be present in every expression of an electronic spreadsheet. An example of distinctive details of expression is the precise "structure, sequence, and organization," *Whelan,* 797 F.2d at 1248, of the menu command system.

* * *

I conclude that a menu command structure is capable of being expressed in many if not an unlimited number of ways, and that the command structure of 1–2–3 is an original and nonobvious way of expressing a command structure. Emery Decl. ¶ 15. Accordingly, the menu structure, taken as a whole—including the choice of command terms, the structure and order of those terms, their presentation on the screen, and the long prompts—is an aspect of 1–2–3 that is not present in every expression of an electronic spreadsheet. It meets the requirements of the second element of the legal test for copyrightability.

Finally, I consider the third element of the legal test—whether the structure, sequence, and organization of the menu command system is a substantial part of the alleged copyrighted work—here Lotus 1–2–3. That the answer to this question is "yes" is incontrovertible. The user interface of 1–2–3 is its most unique element, and is the aspect that has made 1–2–3 so popular. That defendants went to such trouble to copy that element is a testament to its substantiality. Accordingly, evaluation of the third element of the legal test weighs heavily in favor of Lotus.

Taking account of all three elements of the legal test, I determine that copyrightability of the user interface of 1–2–3 is established.

VI. Copying of Lotus 1–2–3

As noted at the beginning of this Opinion, the parties' stipulation regulating this first phase of trial reserved for a later, jury phase, any issues of fact requiring jury determination with respect to any alleged copying of Lotus 1–2–3. If in this first phase the court had rejected Lotus' claim of copyrightability of nonliteral elements of the user interface, a jury phase would plainly have been required under that stipulation to determine whether any copying of source code or object code had occurred. Because, however, the court has decided instead that Lotus prevails on this issue, the court must next consider whether any issue remains that must be submitted to a jury before the court considers whether defendants are liable for infringement of Lotus' copyright in 1–2–3.

For the reasons stated below, the answer to that inquiry must be "no." Not only is the copying in this case so "overwhelming and pervasive" as to preclude, as a matter of law, any assertion of independent creation, *see Midway Manufacturing Co. v. Bandai–America, Inc.*, 546 F.Supp. 125, 141 n. 11, 149 (D.N.J.1982) ("overwhelming and pervasive" copying can preclude, as a matter of law, finding of independent creation, and can support grant of summary judgment for plaintiff, but such virtual identity not shown in this case), but also, defendants in this case have *admitted* that they copied these elements of protected expression.

* * *

Order

For the reasons explained in this Opinion and on the findings and conclusions stated, it is hereby ordered:

(1) Liability for infringement by defendants' is established.

(2) Any party wishing an explicit ruling on any reserved evidentiary objection may so move on or before July 19, 1990, identifying specifically each objection on which a more explicit ruling is requested with references, if available, to specific pages in the transcript of the first phase of this trial.

(3) A conference with respect to further proceedings will be held as specified in the Joint Procedural Order of this date.

TELEMARKETING RESOURCES v. SYMANTEC CORP.

United States District Court, Northern District of California, 1989.
1990 Copr.L.Dec. ¶ 26,514, 12 U.S.P.Q.2d 1991, 1989 WL 200350.

AGUILAR, J.

AMENDED ORDER GRANTING SUMMARY JUDGMENT MOTION

I.

The Court is called upon to decide whether the "look and feel" of the screen displays in defendants' computer outlining program are substantially dissimilar from plaintiffs' copyrighted program so as to justify a grant of summary judgment. Towards this end, the Court must decide which elements of the computer program are ideas and which are protected expressions.

In addition to the briefs and supplemental papers filed on the summary judgment motion, the Court entertained an in-court demonstration of the two programs and has carefully reviewed submitted copies of relevant outlining programs. Good cause appearing therefor, the Court HEREBY GRANTS the motion for summary judgment for the reasons set out below.

II. FACTUAL BACKGROUND

A. Computer Outlining Programs

In 1983, Living Videotext, now a division of defendant Symantec, developed one of the premier computer outlining programs—"Think-Tank." Like most computer adaptations of everyday tasks, a computer outliner allows a user to create, revise, expand and reorganize an outline more quickly and easily than can be done on paper. The program has two components—the computer code and the resulting displays on the computer screen.

Since 1983, Symantec has published several enhanced versions of ThinkTank and a series of increasingly more powerful outlining programs—"Ready!", "More" and "Grandview."

* * *

Plaintiffs allege that Grandview is substantially similar to PC–Outline and actually an infringing derivative work of the copyrighted program. Defendants contend that the alleged infringing features are unprotected ideas, not expressions.

* * *

Copyright protection applies to the user interface, or overall structure and organization of a computer program, including its audiovisual displays, or screen "look and feel." *Whelan Associates, Inc. v. Jaslow*

Dental Laboratory, Inc., 797 F.2d 1222, 1234 [230 USPQ 481, 488–89] (3d Cir.1986); *Broderbund Software v. Unison World,* 648 F.Supp. 1127 [231 USPQ 700] (N.D.Cal.1986). In this case, defendants do not contest the copyrightability of computer screens in general, but argue that the functions which plaintiffs point to as evidence of copying are ideas and hence not protected. * * *

[T]he classic distinction between an idea and an expression serves to limit the scope of a copyright. "No one infringes, unless he descends so far into what is concrete as to invade ... [its] expression." *Sid and Marty Kroft,* 562 F.2d at 1163. In addition, the courts have developed what is known as the merger doctrine, if an idea is indistinguishable or inseparable from, or limited by, its expression, "copying the expression will not be barred." *Herbert Rosenthal Jewelry v. Kalpakian,* 446 F.2d 738, 742. *See also Morrisey v. Procter & Gamble Co.,* 379 F.2d 675 [154 USPQ 193] (1st Cir.1967).

Furthermore, if the underlying idea is subject to a limited range of expression, copyright protection would apply only "against virtually identical copying." *Frybarger v. IBM,* 812 F.2d at 530.

Finally, copyright protection is not "afforded to elements of expression that necessarily follow from an idea" and are " 'as a practical matter, indispensable or at least standard in the treatment of a given [idea].' " *Data East v. Epyx,* 862 F.2d at 208.

Substantial similarity is established by first applying an "extrinsic" test to determine whether two ideas are similar. "This is an objective test which rests upon specific criteria that can be listed and analyzed." *Data East v. Epyx,* 862 F.2d at 208. If the ideas are similar, the expression of the idea is compared under an intrinsic, subjective test "which depends on the response of the ordinary reasonable person." *Data East,* 862 F.2d at 208.

IV. A Comparison of the Two Programs

The idea of a computer run outlining program is undisputedly identical in both Grandview and PC–Outline. However, defendants also describe many of the features which plaintiff seeks to protect as ideas inherent within a computer outlining program.

* * *

"Analytic dissection" of plaintiffs' alleged similarities may be performed to determine if the similarities result from unprotectable expression. *Data East,* 862 F.2d at 208.

Inherent in the idea of an outlining program is the need to access existing files, edit the work, and print the work. These concepts are fundamental to a host of computer programs. Nevertheless, plaintiffs assert that the presence of these four options in the menu screen demonstrates substantial similarity of expression. This expression is unprotectable.

Plaintiff similarly asserts that the nine functions listed in the menu bar, and virtually all of the functions of the PC–Outline program, can be performed by Grandview, even though they may be called something different and accessed differently. However, these functions constitute the idea of the outlining program, for example, Grandview has a "Reorganize" menu and PC–Outline has an "Outline" menu. Both menus perform similar functions associated with reorganizing the outline. In addition, PC–Outline allows you to delete and create new entries when in the "Outline" menu. As a comparison, Grandview offers four move functions compared to the single move function available in this menu on PC–Outline.

A review of the various nine menus available in each of the programs leads to the conclusion that the features/functions on PC–Outline and Grandview are similar in their essence, but quite different in their complementary features. The expression of the ideas inherent in the features are accordingly distinct.

Apparently, plaintiff is also asserting the use of pull down windows as a similarity. This idea is employed in a number of computer programs, including MORE! and ThinkTank. Plaintiffs may not claim copyright protection of an idea and expression that is, if not standard, then commonplace in the computer software industry. Plaintiff's copyright validly covers only "original works of authorship." 17 U.S.C. § 102(a). Originality, although not defined by statute, requires independent creation, it means "only that the work owes its origin to the author, i.e. is independently created." Nimmer on Copyright, 2–8.1 § 2.01[A]. Although a presumption of originality attaches to a valid copyright registration, defendants have rebutted this presumption in this case. John L. Friend testified that he based his PC–Outline on ThinkTank. In light of the use of pull-downs in previous programs, plaintiff has failed to show that the pull down windows were original and independently created for PC–Outline.

* * *

Plaintiff cites the similarity of using the main editing screen to enter and edit data. The need to have a screen from which a user can perform editing functions is essential to the very idea of a computer outline program. BrownBag points to the expression of that concept as similar inasmuch as the color shading is identical. Plaintiff admits that fewer than 10 of the 44 default color selections in the grandview program are the same as the default color selections in the PC–Outline program. Nevertheless, plaintiff asserts that the choice of the blue background infringes on the PC–Outline copyright. Defendant submitted declarations from an expert describing the functional role of the blue background "relating to the physiology of the human eye, the characteristics of the computer video displays and the connotations of the color blue for financial and corporate institutions." The Rules of the Copyright Office also specifically exclude from copyright registration "typographic ornamentation, lettering or coloring." 37 C.F.R.

§ 202.1. Finally, the limited number of background colors for computer programs precludes copyright protection for such choices.

* * *

The Court's "analytic dissection" of plaintiff's alleged similarities shows that the majority of the alleged similarities pertain to features that are not protected under the copyright. However, plaintiff also spent considerable time pointing out the similarities between the two programs' opening menus, beginning with the title, "opening menu." The use of an opening menu, named an opening menu, is itself an idea and not protectable. Nevertheless, once the ideas are found to be similar, the Court must review the expression of that idea on the screen.

At first glance, the screen's announcements are quite distinct. Grandview's name is portrayed in large, block letters at the top of the screen. "Welcome to PC–Outline" is modestly placed at the top of plaintiff's program. The list of the opening menu options are quite distinct. Grandview offers seven options, PC–Outline offers four. Some of the functions are the same, opening or starting a new outline, accessing an existing outline, accessing the directory and quitting the program altogether. Nevertheless, these functions are inherent in the idea of a computer outlining program and are not protected under the copyright. The description of these functions is different. Additionally, Grandview allows the user to access the functions by hitting a key letter or by highlighting the function.

* * *

Pursuant to its Order Granting Summary Judgment * * *, Judgment is HEREBY ENTERED for defendants.

* * *

Notes and Question

1. Readers who have not seen "Lotus 1–2–3" in action should try to get someone to demonstrate the software and try to identify the "non-literal elements" that Judge Keeton found to be protected by copyright.

2. As Judge Keeton points out, there is no "bright line" test that can decide the question of the copyrightability of screen displays. For this reason there is sure to be continual litigation on this topic.

3. Does the decision for the defendant in *Symantec* reflect a different test from *Lotus,* a different fact situation, or the inherent uncertainty of drawing the line between what is protected and unprotected by copyright?

8. INPUT FORMATS

Before the days of highly interactive computer software, programs often demanded that data be presented on punched cards or tapes in a very rigid, predetermined format. Copyright protection for such a format could make it difficult for competitors to enter a field, since users would have all their data in a single format.

SYNERCOM TECHNOLOGY, INC. v. UNIVERSITY COMPUTING COMPANY AND ENGINEERING DYNAMICS, INC.

United States District Court, Northern District of Texas, 1978.
462 F.Supp. 1003.

PATRICK E. HIGGINBOTHAM, DISTRICT JUDGE.

This case presents claims of copyright infringement of instruction manuals and input formats used with a computer program designed to solve engineering problems incident to the analysis of structures.

* * *

INPUT FORMATS

EDI and UCC here contend that the formats are mere forms not intended to convey information and are not subject to copyright. That these ciphers bear the computer world name of formats is unfortunate because it suggests that they are formats as that term is used in copyright law; they are not.

Certainly blank forms are not the subject of copyright. *See Baker v. Selden,* 101 U.S. 99, 25 L.Ed. 841 (1879); *Aldrich v. Remington Rand, Inc.,* 52 F.Supp. 732 (N.D.Tex.1942). However "forms" which communicate information can be the subject of copyright. And code books have received protection. * * *

* * *

The litmus seems to be whether the material proffered for copyright undertakes to express. At first glance these input formats are simply devices for the assistance of the user to facilitate his task—forms. On reflection, however, one must conclude that they indeed express ideas. The usage by EDI of the formats (which it contends is not infringing) undercuts its argument that the input formats are not expression. EDI does not furnish card formats to the customer for use; instead it expects the customer to use an 80–column paper, common to the industry. However, in its manual used to instruct users of its SACS II program, it used mirror images of the forms themselves. Their usage only buttresses the reality that these input formats express to the user the sequencing of data for simplified access to the computer programs. The formats by their placement of lines, shaded art, and words tell the user what data to place where and how to do it. It communicates the selection arrangements and the sequence. That was the usage EDI made of it. It follows that the formats are copyrightable if the ideas they express are separable from their expression. This issue is focused by examining the companion question of infringement.

INFRINGEMENT

A. Formats

Closely related to the contention that the formats do not contain expression is the defensive argument that EDI has only used any ideas expressed by the formats. The argument continues that stopping EDI's usage would give the formats patent, not copyright protection.

EDI was free to "read" Synercom's formats and employ their teaching; it was not free to "copy" the formats and contends that it did not. Thus the issue is whether EDI copied expressed ideas or their expression. EDI put forward an alternative argument that because use of the idea required substantial duplication of Synercom's arrangements and sequencing, copyright protection ought not be allowed.

One can argue that inseparability of idea and expression is here an antinomy. The argument asks if the idea and the usage are not separable, what is the expression?

EDI argues that it did not "copy" the formats, pointing out that it did not even use preprinted formats. EDI instead wrote a preprocessor program to accept Synercom's exact formats. The FORTRAN statements in its preprocessor program are derived directly and precisely from the copyrighted manual card formats. This was not accidental. Independent and coincidentally exact duplication was a statistical improbability. By varying only the order constituent of the format instruction, the manner of communicating with the computer may be expressed in ten factorial (10–9–8–7–6–5–4–3–2–1); that is 3,628,800 expressions. It is true that the common engineering problem and common discipline of users would reduce the number of practical variances; regardless before trial ended defendant had conceded that they had indeed done what they set out to do—exactly duplicate. But critically, EDI in doing so, has only appropriated the idea expressed by the formats; that it was deliberate is immaterial.

Title 17 § 1 grants to the copyright owner the exclusive right " * * * (b) to translate the copyrighted work into other language or dialects, or make any other version thereof, if it be a literary work. * * *" Synercom urges that EDI's preprocessor program infringes because it does no more than translate the expression of the formats to a different computer language, unless the subject matter here is not classed as a literary work. The copyright office so classified it although its decision is not determinative.

* * *

* * * The difficult question is whether EDI plagiarized Synercom's idea or its expression. If the idea is the sequence and ordering of data, there was no infringement. If sequencing and ordering of data was, however, expression, it follows that EDI's preprocessor program infringed. As earlier suggested and as will be demonstrated, Synercom's argument is double-edged. If sequencing and ordering is expression, what separable idea is expressed?

A hypothetical, oversimplified, may serve to illuminate the idea versus expression controversy. The familiar "figure-H" pattern of an automobile stick is chosen arbitrarily by an auto manufacturer. Several different patterns may be imagined, some more convenient for the driver or easier to manufacture than others, but all representing possible configurations. The pattern chosen is arbitrary, but once chosen, it is the only pattern which will work in a particular model. The pattern (analogous to the computer "format") may be expressed in several different ways: by a prose description in a driver's manual, through a diagram, photograph, or driver training film, or otherwise. Each of these expressions may presumably be protected through copyright. But the copyright protects copying of the particular expressions of the pattern, and does not prohibit another manufacturer from marketing a car using the same pattern. Use of the same pattern might be socially desirable, as it would reduce the retraining of drivers. Likewise, the second manufacturer is free to use its own prose descriptions, photographs, diagrams, or the like, so long as these materials take the form of original expressions of the copied idea (however similar they may be to the first manufacturer's materials) rather than copies of the expressions themselves. Admittedly, there are many more possible choices of computer formats, and the decision among them more arbitrary, but this does not detract from the force of the analogy.

Synercom's argument that the order and sequence of data was the expression, not the idea, has been rejected. Its acceptance, although answering EDI's claim of noninfringement, would result in a finding that the formats are not proper subjects for copyright protection.

B. Format Copyrightability Revisited

As noted "in cases of literary or artistic works, and works of similar character, in which the form, arrangement, or combination of ideas represents the product of labor and skilled effort *separate and apart from that entailed in the development of the intellectual conception ivolved,"* copyright protection is available. *Long v. Jordan,* 29 F.Supp. 287, 288 (N.D.Cal.1939) (emphasis supplied). Here if order and sequence is the expression, the skilled effort is not separable, for the form, arrangement, and combination is itself the intellectual conception involved. It would follow that only to the extent the expressions involve stylistic creativity *above and beyond* the bare expression of sequence and arrangement, should they be protected. As Mooers states:

> Also included in the "expression" is the sequence, choice, and arrangement of descriptive elements * * *. Calvin N. Mooers, *Computer Software and Copyright, Computing Surveys,* Vol. 7, No. 1, March 1975 at p. 50.

This is because in the usual case sequence, choice, and arrangement have only stylistic significance, rather than constituting as they would here, the essence of the expression. Finally, Copyright Circular 32 states "Thus, there is no way to secure copyright protection for the idea or principle behind a blank form or similar work, or for any of the methods or systems involved in it." The "idea or principle" behind the forms in question, and the "method or system" involved in them, would be no more or less than the formats. The manuals are copyrightable, but the formats would not be. In sum, if the court is wrong in its finding that order and sequence are expressed ideas, not expressions, its alternative holding is that the formats are not copyrightable.

* * *

9. MANUALS

There is an old saying among computer users, "if all else fails, read the manual." Likewise, lawyers seeking to protect computer software should not forget that the manuals are, of course, covered by copyright.

SYNERCOM TECHNOLOGY, INC. v. UNIVERSITY COMPUTING COMPANY AND ENGINEERING DYNAMICS, INC.

United States District Court, Northern District of Texas, 1978.
462 F.Supp. 1003.

PATRICK E. HIGGINBOTHAM, DISTRICT JUDGE.

This case presents claims of copyright infringement of instruction manuals and input formats used with a computer program designed to solve engineering problems incident to the analysis of structures.

[Plaintiff Synercom alleged that defendants University Computing Company (UCC) and Engineering Dynamics, Inc. (EDI) had copied the manuals for Synercom's structural analysis program.]

MANUALS

In the summer of 1975 EDI had distributed its EDI Manual without copyright or other proprietary notice to its customers and potential customers. EDI did not furnish format cards, but its instruction manual which contained mirror images of some of the input cards and instructions effectively enabled a customer to use the STRAN input format. The EDI Manual contained no page numbers and no reference to UCC, but before publication of the EDI Manual, EDI had access to the STRAN User's Manual, Third Edition.

In the latter part of 1976 and after distribution by Synercom of its STRAN User's Manual, Third Edition with copyright notice, EDI published user's manuals for its SACS II program entitled "SACS II CODING INSTRUCTIONS" ("EDI Manual"). Also in the latter part of 1976 UCC distributed user's manuals for EDI SACS II program (hereafter referred to as the "UCC Manual"). The UCC Manual contains on its title page the names and addresses of both UCC and EDI, UCC's designation "UCC 3581" and the publication date of "8–76", *i.e.,* August, 1976. The UCC Manual was published without copyright or other proprietary notice and was distributed by both UCC and EDI to customers and potential customers. The UCC Manual contains page numbers and was physically produced in Texas by UCC from a master provided to it by EDI. Other than for differences in the title pages and the addition of pagination, the UCC Manual is a copy of the EDI Manual. Before publication of the UCC Manual, UCC had access to the STRAN User's Manual, Third Edition.

These facts present four ultimate questions. First, does Synercom hold valid copyrights on its manuals and input cards. Second, has EDI and UCC infringed any of these copyrights. Third, what relief is available. And fourth, have EDI and UCC competed unfairly.

Validity of Copyrights

The attack of EDI and UCC at trial was upon "originality" of the manuals and with lesser emphasis they urged that Synercom published without notice before any claim to proprietary rights. Extensive evidence demonstrated that parts of the STRAN manuals contained paragraphs virtually identical to manuals earlier published by McAuto, FRAN, and others. Indisputably parts of the STRAN manual (first edition and brought forward through succeeding editions) were in no sense of the word original with Synercom; but equally undisputed was that substantial parts of all Synercom manuals were original in every sense of the word.

Although originality is judicially imposed gloss upon the copyright statute, its legal force and definition are settled. As stated by Judge Friendly:

> Although "[t]he Copyright Act nowhere expressly invokes the requirement of originality," courts have uniformly inferred this from the constitutional and statutory condition of authorship. * * * However, originality has been considered to mean "only that the work owes its origin to the author, i.e., is independently created and not copied from other works." *Puddu v. Buonamici Statuary, Inc.,* 450 F.2d 401, 171 U.S.P.Q. 709 (2d Cir.1971).

Continuing, the court related:

> Originality sufficient for copyright protection exists if the "author" has introduced *any* element of novelty as contrasted with the material previously known to him." (Emphasis added) *Puddu v. Buonamici Statuary, Inc.,* 450 F.2d 401, 171 U.S.P.Q. 709 (2d Cir.1971).

EDI's and UCC's effort to defeat proof of originality is confronted by the fact that at least 70% of the prose found in Synercom's manuals is indeed original to Synercom. Although proof of prior art is familiar to patent law, under copyright law the 30% nonoriginal content does not void the copyright as to the 70% *or* even the 30%, at least as an integrated part of a product whose whole is original. This is not to infer that Synercom's copyright removed the nonoriginal material from the public domain. It is to say that if an assembly of parts—old and new—results in original expression, the whole is protected. In the case at hand, with only approximately 21% of the material in Synercom's STRAN User's Manual, Third Edition being based upon prior material and the remaining 79% being *entirely* original, Synercom has contributed something "recognizably its own" to prior treatments of the same subject. Its copyright is not invalid because some parts of the whole were not independently conceived. Unlike the patent law, originality is not first idea but independent conception. As L. Hand stated it:

> [T]he law imposes no prohibition upon those who, without copying, independently arrive at the precise combination of words or notes which have been copyrighted. *Fred Fisher, Inc. v. Dillingham,* 298 F. 145, 147 (S.D.N.Y.1924).

The requirement of originality is an *a priori* result of protecting expression only by forbidding copying. That is, because the grant of exclusivity to the copyright holder is only of the right to copy the expression, originality can require no more than independent work. But requiring the work to be independent does not deny the role of synergism in protectable expression. * * *

* * *

It follows that the copyright registrations for Synercom's first and second editions which contain only slightly less new matter than the third edition are also valid.

* * *

INFRINGEMENT

* * *

C. Manuals

There is little question but that EDI and UCC have infringed Synercom's manuals. EDI and UCC have (since the commencement of trial) not seriously contended that its use of the Synercom manuals would not be an infringing use. The battle here was over the validity of the manual's copyrights. Substantial portions of EDI's (and UCC's) manuals are verbatim from the Synercom manual. Some of the Synercom material copied had been in turn copied by Synercom. Nonetheless, some material by UCC and EDI had not been. This question, unlike the others, presents little subtlety.

* * *

Prefatory to a consideration of relief, the following explicit facts are found:

EDI knew before entering the market with its SACS II program that Synercom's STRAN User's Manuals were copyrighted by Synercom.

The infringements by UCC and EDI were willful, deliberate, and for profit. * * *

* * *

Order

Synercom is now entitled to injunctive relief and further discovery regarding other possible relief. It is ORDERED that the defendants, their agents, servants, officers, and employees, privies, successors, and assigns, and all holding by, through or under them or any of them be and the same are hereby perpetually ENJOINED and RESTRAINED as follows:

All "printed infringing materials" shall mean all printed material derived, directly or indirectly, from Synercom's copyrighted materials, and shall include all user's manuals and other instructional literature for the SACS II program, whether the "UCC Manual" or the "EDI Manual", preliminary draft versions or later versions or copies, abridgments or translations.

1. Defendants EDI and UCC shall hereafter produce no printed infringing materials;

2. Defendants EDI and UCC shall, separately, and within 20 days of the filing of this memorandum and order, account under oath for the production of all printed infringing materials and deliver to Synercom's attorney a list of all entities to which any printed infringing materials have been delivered, and, also recall by written request all printed infringing material and provide Synercom's attorney with copies of all written requests for recall; and

3. Defendants EDI and UCC shall return to Synercom's attorney all recalled printed infringing materials. Defendants shall complete the recall within 60 days of the filing of this order.

Attorney Fees

Synercom shall have and recover from defendants EDI and UCC the costs of this suit and a reasonable attorney's fee, in an amount to be determined later.

Discovery

The parties may proceed with such discovery as shall be necessary to establish the amount of damages, profits, and other awards as may be proper in the accounting phase of this case.

* * *

Note

Some video game programs require users to answer a bizarre question (selected by the program at random from dozens of such questions) at the start of each playing session. If the user gives the wrong answer, the program will not run. The manual gives a list of all possible questions and answers. The copyright owner not only is protected by the copyright in the manual, but also by the fact that copying and distributing printed material is substantially more expensive than copying and distributing software.

C. GENERAL STANDARDS OF COPYRIGHTABILITY

FEIST PUBLICATIONS, INC. v. RURAL TELEPHONE SERVICE COMPANY, INC.

Supreme Court of the United States, 1991.
___ U.S. ___, 111 S.Ct. 1282, 113 L.Ed.2d 358.

JUSTICE O'CONNOR delivered the opinion of the Court.

This case requires us to clarify the extent of copyright protection available to telephone directory white pages.

I

Rural Telephone Service Company is a certified public utility that provides telephone service to several communities in northwest Kansas. It is subject to a state regulation that requires all telephone companies operating in Kansas to issue annually an updated telephone directory. Accordingly, as a condition of its monopoly franchise, Rural publishes a typical telephone directory, consisting of white pages and yellow pages. The white pages list in alphabetical order the names of Rural's subscribers, together with their towns and telephone numbers. The yellow pages list Rural's business subscribers alphabetically by category and feature classified advertisements of various sizes. Rural distributes its directory free of charge to its subscribers, but earns revenue by selling yellow pages advertisements.

Feist Publications, Inc., is a publishing company that specializes in area-wide telephone directories. Unlike a typical directory, which covers only a particular calling area, Feist's area-wide directories cover a much larger geographical range, reducing the need to call directory assistance or consult multiple directories. The Feist directory that is the subject of this litigation covers 11 different telephone service areas in 15 counties and contains 46,878 white pages listings—compared to Rural's approximately 7,700 listings. Like Rural's directory, Feist's is distributed free of charge and includes both white pages and yellow pages. Feist and Rural compete vigorously for yellow pages advertising.

As the sole provider of telephone service in its service area, Rural obtains subscriber information quite easily. Persons desiring telephone service must apply to Rural and provide their names and addresses; Rural then assigns them a telephone number. Feist is not a telephone company, let alone one with monopoly status, and therefore lacks independent access to any subscriber information. To obtain white pages listings for its area-wide directory, Feist approached each of the 11 telephone companies operating in northwest Kansas and offered to pay for the right to use its white pages listings.

Of the 11 telephone companies, only Rural refused to license its listings to Feist. Rural's refusal created a problem for Feist, as omitting these listings would have left a gaping hole in its area-wide directory, rendering it less attractive to potential yellow pages advertisers. In a decision subsequent to that which we review here, the District Court determined that this was precisely the reason Rural refused to license its listings. The refusal was motivated by an unlawful purpose "to extend its monopoly in telephone service to a monopoly in yellow pages advertising." *Rural Telephone Service Co. v. Feist Publications, Inc.*, 737 F.Supp. 610, 622 (Kan.1990).

Unable to license Rural's white pages listings, Feist used them without Rural's consent. Feist began by removing several thousand listings that fell outside the geographic range of its area-wide directory, then hired personnel to investigate the 4,935 that remained. These employees verified the data reported by Rural and sought to obtain additional information. As a result, a typical Feist listing includes the individual's street address; most of Rural's listings do not. Notwithstanding these additions, however, 1,309 of the 46,878 listings in Feist's 1983 directory were identical to listings in Rural's 1982–1983 white pages. App. 54 (¶ 15–16), 57. Four of these were fictitious listings that Rural had inserted into its directory to detect copying.

Rural sued for copyright infringement in the District Court for the District of Kansas taking the position that Feist, in compiling its own directory, could not use the information contained in Rural's white pages. Rural asserted that Feist's employees were obliged to travel door-to-door or conduct a telephone survey to discover the same information for themselves. Feist responded that such efforts were economically impractical and, in any event, unnecessary because the information copied was beyond the scope of copyright protection. The District Court granted summary judgment to Rural, explaining that "[c]ourts have consistently held that telephone directories are copyrightable" and citing a string of lower court decisions. 663 F.Supp. 214, 218 (1987). In an unpublished opinion, the Court of Appeals for the Tenth Circuit affirmed "for substantially the reasons given by the district court." App. to Pet. for Cert. 4a, judgt. order reported at 916 F.2d 718 (1990). We granted certiorari, 498 U.S. ___, 111 S.Ct. 40, 112 L.Ed.2d 17 (1990), to determine whether the copyright in Rural's directory protects the names, towns, and telephone numbers copied by Feist.

II

A

This case concerns the interaction of two well-established propositions. The first is that facts are not copyrightable; the other, that compilations of facts generally are. Each of these propositions possesses an impeccable pedigree. That there can be no valid copyright in facts is universally understood. The most fundamental axiom of copyright law is that "[n]o author may copyright his ideas or the facts he narrates." *Harper & Row, Publishers, Inc. v. Nation Enterprises*, 471 U.S. 539, 556, 105 S.Ct. 2218, 2228, 85 L.Ed.2d 588 (1985). Rural wisely concedes this point, noting in its brief that "[f]acts and discoveries, of course, are not themselves subject to copyright protection." Brief for Respondent 24. At the same time, however, it is beyond dispute that compilations of facts are within the subject matter of copyright. Compilations were expressly mentioned in the Copyright Act of 1909, and again in the Copyright Act of 1976.

There is an undeniable tension between these two propositions. Many compilations consist of nothing but raw data—*i.e.,* wholly factual information not accompanied by any original written expression. On what basis may one claim a copyright in such a work? Common sense tells us that 100 uncopyrightable facts do not magically change their status when gathered together in one place. Yet copyright law seems to contemplate that compilations that consist exclusively of facts are potentially within its scope.

The key to resolving the tension lies in understanding why facts are not copyrightable. The *sine qua non* of copyright is originality. To qualify for copyright protection, a work must be original to the author. See *Harper & Row, supra,* at 547–549, 105 S.Ct., at 2223–2224. Original, as the term is used in copyright, means only that the work was independently created by the author (as opposed to copied from other works), and that it possesses at least some minimal degree of creativity. 1 M. Nimmer & D. Nimmer, Copyright §§ 2.01[A], [B] (1990) (hereinafter Nimmer). To be sure, the requisite level of creativity is extremely low; even a slight amount will suffice. The vast majority of works make the grade quite easily, as they possess some creative spark, "no matter how crude, humble or obvious" it might be. *Id.,* § 1.08[C][1]. Originality does not signify novelty; a work may be original even though it closely resembles other works so long as the similarity is fortuitous, not the result of copying. To illustrate, assume that two poets, each ignorant of the other, compose identical poems. Neither work is novel, yet both are original and, hence, copyrightable. See *Sheldon v. Metro–Goldwyn Pictures Corp.,* 81 F.2d 49, 54 (CA2 1936).

Originality is a constitutional requirement. The source of Congress' power to enact copyright laws is Article I, § 8, cl. 8, of the Constitution, which authorizes Congress to "secur[e] for limited Times to Authors * * * the exclusive Right to their respective Writings." In two decisions from the late 19th Century—*The Trade–Mark Cases,* 100 U.S. 82, 25 L.Ed. 550 (1879); and *Burrow–Giles Lithographic Co. v. Sarony,* 111 U.S. 53, 4 S.Ct. 279, 28 L.Ed. 349 (1884)—this Court defined the crucial terms "authors" and "writings." In so doing, the Court made it unmistakably clear that these terms presuppose a degree of originality.

In *The Trade–Mark Cases,* the Court addressed the constitutional scope of "writings." For a particular work to be classified "under the head of writings of authors," the Court determined, "originality is required." 100 U.S., at 94. The Court explained that originality requires independent creation plus a modicum of creativity: "[W]hile the word *writings* may be liberally construed, as it has been, to include original designs for engraving, prints, &c., it is only such as are *original,* and are founded in the creative powers of the mind. The writings which are to be protected are *the fruits of intellectual labor,* embodied in the form of books, prints, engravings, and the like." *Ibid.* (emphasis in original).

In *Burrow–Giles,* the Court distilled the same requirement from the Constitution's use of the word "authors." The Court defined "author," in a constitutional sense, to mean "he to whom anything owes its origin; originator; maker." 111 U.S., at 58, 4 S.Ct., at 281 (internal quotations omitted). As in *The Trade–Mark Cases,* the Court emphasized the creative component of originality. It described copyright as being limited to "original intellectual conceptions of the author," *ibid.,* and stressed the importance of requiring an author who accuses another of infringement to prove "the existence of those facts of originality, of intellectual production, of thought, and conception." *Id.,* 111 U.S., at 59–60, 4 S.Ct., at 281–282.

The originality requirement articulated in *The Trade–Mark Cases* and *Burrow–Giles* remains the touchstone of copyright protection today. See *Goldstein v. California,* 412 U.S. 546, 561–562, 93 S.Ct. 2303, 2312, 37 L.Ed.2d 163 (1973). It is the very "premise of copyright law." *Miller v. Universal City Studios, Inc.,* 650 F.2d 1365, 1368 (CA5 1981). Leading scholars agree on this point. As one pair of commentators succinctly puts it: "The originality requirement is *constitutionally mandated* for all works." Patterson & Joyce, Monopolizing the Law: The Scope of Copyright Protection for Law Reports and Statutory Compilations, 36 UCLA L.Rev. 719, 763, n. 155 (1989) (emphasis in original) (hereinafter Patterson & Joyce). Accord *id.,* at 759–760, and n. 140; Nimmer § 1.06[A] ("originality is a statutory as well as a constitutional requirement"); *id.,* § 1.08[C][1] ("a modicum of intellectual labor * * * clearly constitutes an essential constitutional element").

It is this bedrock principle of copyright that mandates the law's seemingly disparate treatment of facts and factual compilations. "No one may claim originality as to facts." *Id.,* § 2.11[A], p. 2–157. This is because facts do not owe their origin to an act of authorship. The distinction is one between creation and discovery: the first person to find and report a particular fact has not created the fact; he or she has merely discovered its existence. To borrow from *Burrow–Giles,* one who discovers a fact is not its "maker" or "originator." 111 U.S., at 58, 4 S.Ct., at 281. "The discoverer merely finds and records." Nimmer § 2.03[E]. Census-takers, for example, do not "create" the population figures that emerge from their efforts; in a sense, they copy these figures from the world around them. Denicola, Copyright in Collections of Facts: A Theory for the Protection of Nonfiction Literary Works, 81 Colum.L.Rev. 516, 525 (1981) (hereinafter Denicola). Census data therefore do not trigger copyright because these data are not "original" in the constitutional sense. Nimmer § 2.03[E]. The same is true of all facts—scientific, historical, biographical, and news of the day. "[T]hey may not be copyrighted and are part of the public domain available to every person." *Miller, supra,* at 1369.

Factual compilations, on the other hand, may possess the requisite originality. The compilation author typically chooses which facts to include, in what order to place them, and how to arrange the collected data so that they may be used effectively by readers. These choices as to selection and arrangement, so long as they are made independently by the compiler and entail a minimal degree of creativity, are sufficiently original that Congress may protect such compilations through the copyright laws. Nimmer §§ 2.11[D], 3.03; Denicola 523, n. 38. Thus, even a directory that contains absolutely no protectible written expression, only facts, meets the constitutional minimum for copyright protection if it features an original selection or arrangement. See *Harper & Row,* 471 U.S., at 547, 105 S.Ct., at 2223. Accord Nimmer § 3.03.

This protection is subject to an important limitation. The mere fact that a work is copyrighted does not mean that every element of the work may be protected. Originality remains the *sine qua non* of copyright; accordingly, copyright protection may extend only to those components of a work that are original to the author. Patterson & Joyce 800–802; Ginsburg, Creation and Commercial Value: Copyright Protection of Works of Information, 90 Colum.L.Rev. 1865, 1868, and n. 12 (1990) (hereinafter Ginsburg). Thus, if the compilation author clothes facts with an original collocation of words, he or she may be able to claim a copyright in this written expression. Others may copy the underlying facts from the publication, but not the precise words used to present them. In *Harper & Row,* for example, we explained that President Ford could not prevent others from copying bare historical facts from his autobiography, see 471 U.S., at 556–557, 105 S.Ct., at 2228–2229, but that he could prevent others from copying his "subjective descriptions and portraits of public figures." *Id.,* at 563, 105 S.Ct., at 2232. Where the compilation author adds no written expression but rather lets the facts speak for themselves, the expressive element is more elusive. The only conceivable expression is the manner in which the compiler has selected and arranged the facts. Thus, if the selection and arrangement are original, these elements of the work are eligible for copyright protection. See Patry, Copyright in Compilations of Facts (or Why the "White Pages" Are Not Copyrightable), 12 Com. & Law 37, 64 (Dec.1990) (hereinafter Patry). No matter how original the format, however, the facts themselves do not become original through association. See Patterson & Joyce 776.

This inevitably means that the copyright in a factual compilation is thin. Notwithstanding a valid copyright, a subsequent compiler remains free to use the facts contained in another's publication to aid in preparing a competing work, so long as the competing work does not feature the same selection and arrangement. As one commentator explains it: "[N]o matter how much original authorship the work displays, the facts and ideas it exposes are free for the taking. * * *

[T]he very same facts and ideas may be divorced from the context imposed by the author, and restated or reshuffled by second comers, even if the author was the first to discover the facts or to propose the ideas." Ginsburg 1868.

It may seem unfair that much of the fruit of the compiler's labor may be used by others without compensation. As Justice Brennan has correctly observed, however, this is not "some unforeseen byproduct of a statutory scheme." *Harper & Row,* 471 U.S., at 589, 105 S.Ct., at 2245 (dissenting opinion). It is, rather, "the essence of copyright," *ibid.,* and a constitutional requirement. The primary objective of copyright is not to reward the labor of authors, but "[t]o promote the Progress of Science and useful Arts." Art. I, § 8, cl. 8. Accord *Twentieth Century Music Corp. v. Aiken,* 422 U.S. 151, 156, 95 S.Ct. 2040, 2044, 45 L.Ed.2d 84 (1975). To this end, copyright assures authors the right to their original expression, but encourages others to build freely upon the ideas and information conveyed by a work. *Harper & Row, supra,* 471 U.S., at 556–557, 105 S.Ct., at 2228–2229. This principle, known as the idea/expression or fact/expression dichotomy, applies to all works of authorship. As applied to a factual compilation, assuming the absence of original written expression, only the compiler's selection and arrangement may be protected; the raw facts may be copied at will. This result is neither unfair nor unfortunate. It is the means by which copyright advances the progress of science and art.

This Court has long recognized that the fact/expression dichotomy limits severely the scope of protection in fact-based works. More than a century ago, the Court observed: "The very object of publishing a book on science or the useful arts is to communicate to the world the useful knowledge which it contains. But this object would be frustrated if the knowledge could not be used without incurring the guilt of piracy of the book." *Baker v. Selden,* 101 U.S. 99, 103, 25 L.Ed. 841 (1880). We reiterated this point in *Harper & Row:*

> "[N]o author may copyright facts or ideas. The copyright is limited to those aspects of the work—termed 'expression'—that display the stamp of the author's originality.
>
> "[C]opyright does not prevent subsequent users from copying from a prior author's work those constituent elements that are not original—for example * * * facts, or materials in the public domain—as long as such use does not unfairly appropriate the author's original contributions." 471 U.S., at 547–548, 105 S.Ct., at 2223–2224 (citation omitted).

This, then, resolves the doctrinal tension: Copyright treats facts and factual compilations in a wholly consistent manner. Facts, whether alone or as part of a compilation, are not original and therefore may not be copyrighted. A factual compilation is eligible for copyright if it features an original selection or arrangement of facts, but the copyright is limited to the particular selection or arrangement. In no event may copyright extend to the facts themselves.

B

As we have explained, originality is a constitutionally mandated prerequisite for copyright protection. The Court's decisions announcing this rule predate the Copyright Act of 1909, but ambiguous language in the 1909 Act caused some lower courts temporarily to lose sight of this requirement.

* * *

Making matters worse, these courts developed a new theory to justify the protection of factual compilations. Known alternatively as "sweat of the brow" or "industrious collection," the underlying notion was that copyright was a reward for the hard work that went into compiling facts. * * *

* * *

The "sweat of the brow" doctrine had numerous flaws, the most glaring being that it extended copyright protection in a compilation beyond selection and arrangement—the compiler's original contributions—to the facts themselves. * * *

Decisions of this Court applying the 1909 Act make clear that the statute did not permit the "sweat of the brow" approach. The best example is *International News Service v. Associated Press,* 248 U.S. 215, 39 S.Ct. 68, 63 L.Ed. 211 (1918). In that decision, the Court stated unambiguously that the 1909 Act conferred copyright protection only on those elements of a work that were original to the author. * * *

* * *

[T]he originality requirement is not particularly stringent. A compiler may settle upon a selection or arrangement that others have used; novelty is not required. Originality requires only that the author make the selection or arrangement independently (*i.e.,* without copying that selection or arrangement from another work), and that it display some minimal level of creativity. Presumably, the vast majority of compilations will pass this test, but not all will. There remains a narrow category of works in which the creative spark is utterly lacking or so trivial as to be virtually nonexistent. See generally *Bleistein v. Donaldson Lithographing Co.,* 188 U.S. 239, 251, 23 S.Ct. 298, 300, 47 L.Ed. 460 (1903) (referring to "the narrowest and most obvious limits"). Such works are incapable of sustaining a valid copyright. Nimmer § 2.01[B].

Even if a work qualifies as a copyrightable compilation, it receives only limited protection. This is the point of § 103 of the Act. Section 103 explains that "[t]he subject matter of copyright * * * includes compilations," § 103(a), but that copyright protects only the author's original contributions—not the facts or information conveyed:

"The copyright in a compilation * * * extends only to the material contributed by the author of such work, as distinguished from the preexisting material employed in the work, and does not imply any exclusive right in the preexisting material." § 103(b).

* * *

In summary, the 1976 revisions to the Copyright Act leave no doubt that originality, not "sweat of the brow," is the touchstone of copyright protection in directories and other fact-based works. Nor is there any doubt that the same was true under the 1909 Act. The 1976 revisions were a direct response to the Copyright Office's concern that many lower courts had misconstrued this basic principle, and Congress emphasized repeatedly that the purpose of the revisions was to clarify, not change, existing law. The revisions explain with painstaking clarity that copyright requires originality, § 102(a); that facts are never original, § 102(b); that the copyright in a compilation does not extend to the facts it contains, § 103(b); and that a compilation is copyrightable only to the extent that it features an original selection, coordination, or arrangement, § 101.

* * *

III

There is no doubt that Feist took from the white pages of Rural's directory a substantial amount of factual information. At a minimum, Feist copied the names, towns, and telephone numbers of 1,309 of Rural's subscribers. Not all copying, however, is copyright infringement. To establish infringement, two elements must be proven: (1) ownership of a valid copyright, and (2) copying of constituent elements of the work that are original. See *Harper & Row,* 471 U.S., at 548, 105 S.Ct., at 2224. The first element is not at issue here; Feist appears to concede that Rural's directory, considered as a whole, is subject to a valid copyright because it contains some foreword text, as well as original material in its yellow pages advertisements. See Brief for Petitioner 18; Pet. for Cert. 9.

The question is whether Rural has proved the second element. In other words, did Feist, by taking 1,309 names, towns, and telephone numbers from Rural's white pages, copy anything that was "original" to Rural? Certainly, the raw data does not satisfy the originality requirement. Rural may have been the first to discover and report the names, towns, and telephone numbers of its subscribers, but this data does not " 'ow[e] its origin' " to Rural. *Burrow–Giles,* 111 U.S., at 58, 4 S.Ct., at 281. Rather, these bits of information are uncopyrightable facts; they existed before Rural reported them and would have continued to exist if Rural had never published a telephone directory. The originality requirement "rule[s] out protecting * * * names, addresses, and telephone numbers of which the plaintiff by no stretch of the imagination could be called the author." Patterson & Joyce 776.

Rural essentially concedes the point by referring to the names, towns, and telephone numbers as "preexisting material." Brief for Respondent 17. Section 103(b) states explicitly that the copyright in a compilation does not extend to "the preexisting material employed in the work."

The question that remains is whether Rural selected, coordinated, or arranged these uncopyrightable facts in an original way. As mentioned, originality is not a stringent standard; it does not require that facts be presented in an innovative or surprising way. It is equally true, however, that the selection and arrangement of facts cannot be so mechanical or routine as to require no creativity whatsoever. The standard of originality is low, but it does exist. See Patterson & Joyce 760, n. 144 ("While this requirement is sometimes characterized as modest, or a low threshold, it is not without effect") (internal quotations omitted; citations omitted). As this Court has explained, the Constitution mandates some minimal degree of creativity, see *The Trade–Mark Cases,* 100 U.S., at 94; and an author who claims infringement must prove "the existence of * * * intellectual production, of thought, and conception." *Burrow–Giles, supra,* 111 U.S., at 59–60, 4 S.Ct., at 281–282.

The selection, coordination, and arrangement of Rural's white pages do not satisfy the minimum constitutional standards for copyright protection. As mentioned at the outset, Rural's white pages are entirely typical. Persons desiring telephone service in Rural's service area fill out an application and Rural issues them a telephone number. In preparing its white pages, Rural simply takes the data provided by its subscribers and lists it alphabetically by surname. The end product is a garden-variety white pages directory, devoid of even the slightest trace of creativity.

Rural's selection of listings could not be more obvious: it publishes the most basic information—name, town, and telephone number—about each person who applies to it for telephone service. This is "selection" of a sort, but it lacks the modicum of creativity necessary to transform mere selection into copyrightable expression. Rural expended sufficient effort to make the white pages directory useful, but insufficient creativity to make it original.

We note in passing that the selection featured in Rural's white pages may also fail the originality requirement for another reason. Feist points out that Rural did not truly "select" to publish the names and telephone numbers of its subscribers; rather, it was required to do so by the Kansas Corporation Commission as part of its monopoly franchise. See 737 F.Supp., at 612. Accordingly, one could plausibly conclude that this selection was dictated by state law, not by Rural.

Nor can Rural claim originality in its coordination and arrangement of facts. The white pages do nothing more than list Rural's subscribers in alphabetical order. This arrangement may, technically speaking, owe its origin to Rural; no one disputes that Rural undertook the task of alphabetizing the names itself. But there is nothing remotely creative about arranging names alphabetically in a white pages directory. It is an age-old practice, firmly rooted in tradition and so commonplace that it has come to be expected as a matter of course. See Brief for Information Industry Association et al. as *Amici Curiae* 10 (alphabetical arrangement "is universally observed in directories published by local exchange telephone companies"). It is not only unoriginal, it is practically inevitable. This time-honored tradition does not possess the minimal creative spark required by the Copyright Act and the Constitution.

We conclude that the names, towns, and telephone numbers copied by Feist were not original to Rural and therefore were not protected by the copyright in Rural's combined white and yellow pages directory. As a constitutional matter, copyright protects only those constituent elements of a work that possess more than a *de minimis* quantum of creativity. Rural's white pages, limited to basic subscriber information and arranged alphabetically, fall short of the mark. As a statutory matter, 17 U.S.C. § 101 does not afford protection from copying to a collection of facts that are selected, coordinated, and arranged in a way that utterly lacks originality. Given that some works must fail, we cannot imagine a more likely candidate. Indeed, were we to hold that Rural's white pages pass muster, it is hard to believe that any collection of facts could fail.

Because Rural's white pages lack the requisite originality, Feist's use of the listings cannot constitute infringement. This decision should not be construed as demeaning Rural's efforts in compiling its directory, but rather as making clear that copyright rewards originality, not effort. As this Court noted more than a century ago, " 'great praise may be due to the plaintiffs for their industry and enterprise in publishing this paper, yet the law does not contemplate their being rewarded in this way.' " *Baker v. Selden,* 101 U.S., at 105.

The judgment of the Court of Appeals is reversed.

JUSTICE BLACKMUN concurs in the judgment.

Notes and Question

1. The plaintiff, Rural Telephone Service Co., sought protection for a directory which it created by computer. This fact does not appear from the Supreme Court opinion, but it is clear from the record and briefs.

2. The process that Rural used was explained in Defendant's brief:

> In preparing to publish its directory, RTSC does not do a door to door canvass of its telephone service area either. (J.A. 89). Nor does it do any phone dialing survey before compiling its directory. (J.A. 90). Rather, it receives information automatically from subscribers. Phone customers come to RTSC for telephone service and "make application" to RTSC by providing their names and addresses. (J.A. 89). RTSC then assigns them a number and updates its records kept in computer data base form. That information becomes a white page listing—

name, address, and telephone number—which RTSC maintains to identify the subscriber.

2. The process that Defendant Feist used was also explained in Defendant's brief:

Q. (Mr. Knobbe) Okay, go ahead, move on to Exhibit D.

A. Okay. This is an alphabetical list of our base, the directory we used the year before. The computer had to alphabetize it by town in order for us to do some editing on it, updating it from notes that we had.

* * *

A. G is a preparation—well, I am not certain what G is.

Q. Identified as a computer printout interlocking?

A. It is supposed to be phone order directory that we send to the verifiers. In other words, we—our computer lists these—

Q. Excuse me, isn't G—this says we sent that to Data Graphics for key. Are you down the line? H is the verifiers?

A. Okay, that went through our computer vendor in Phoenix, Arizona. When it comes back to us, it is in phone order sequence which means the smallest number first going down to the largest. We do this for two different reasons. * * *

* * *

These corrections and updating changes are computer keyed to combine these sources and computer sort the material into two initially edited print outs. One which interlocks alphabetically all listings regardless of town [Exhibit (G)] is sent to a computer service vendor in Arizona for merger into the rest of the Feist directory, which covers a much wider area than only plaintiff's listings [Affidavit, Tom Feist, paragraph 7].

* * *

When the directory proof is received from Feist's Arizona computer service vendor, it is proofread for errors, all data compiled from verifiers' research is added and the corrected proof is returned to the Arizona computer service vendor. A final repro (paste up pages) [Exhibit (M)] of the directory is finally proofed and updated and sent to a printer for printing of the directory.

4. In *Feist,* the Supreme Court seems to hold that the computerized alphabetization does not meet the requirements of creativity necessary to support a valid copyright. Suppose a telephone company uses a computer program that employs an elaborate formula to design the Yellow Pages to maximize the eye-appeal of the placement of different sizes of advertisements. Is the resulting arrangement copyrightable? If so, who owns the copyright, the telephone company or the owner of the copyright in the computer software?

WEST PUBLISHING COMPANY v. MEAD DATA CENTRAL, INC.

United States Court of Appeals, Eighth Circuit, 1986.
799 F.2d 1219.

ARNOLD, CIRCUIT JUDGE.

Mead Data Central, Inc. (MDC) appeals from a preliminary injunction issued by the District Court for the District of Minnesota in a copyright-infringement action brought by West Publishing Company (West). West's claim is based upon MDC's proposed introduction of "star pagination," keyed to West's case reports, into the LEXIS system of computer-assisted legal research.

For more than a century, West has been compiling and reporting opinions of state and federal courts. West publishes these opinions in a series of books known as the "National Reporter System." Before it publishes an opinion, West checks the accuracy of case and statutory citations in the opinion and adds parallel citations, prepares headnotes and a synopsis for the opinion, and arranges the opinion in West's style and format. West then assigns its report of each opinion to one of the individual series in the National Reporter System, such as *Federal Reporter, Second Series* or *Bankruptcy Reporter;* this assignment is based on the court and/or the subject matter of the opinion. Next, West assigns the case to a volume in the series, further categorizes and arranges the cases within the volume, and prepares additional materials, such as indices and tables of cases, for each volume. Volumes and pages are numbered sequentially to facilitate precise reference to West reports; citing the proper volume number, series name, and page number communicates the exact location of a West report, or a portion thereof, within the National Reporter System. West represents that upon completion of each volume, it registers a copyright claim with the Register of Copyrights and receives a Certificate of Registration for the volume.

MDC developed, owns, and operates LEXIS, a computer-assisted, on-line legal-research service first marketed in 1973. LEXIS, like West's National Reporter System, reports the decisions of state and federal courts. Since LEXIS's inception, MDC has included on the first computer screen of each LEXIS case report the citation to the first page of West's report of the opinion. West concedes that citation to the first page of its reports is a noninfringing "fair use" under 17 U.S.C. § 107, so these citations are not at issue here.

On June 24, 1985, MDC announced that it planned to add "star pagination" to the text of opinions stored in the LEXIS database. This new service, named the LEXIS Star Pagination Feature, was to be available to LEXIS users by September or October of 1985. This feature would insert page numbers from West's National Reporter System publications into the body of LEXIS reports, providing "jump" or "pinpoint" citations to the location in West's reporter of the material viewed on LEXIS. Thus, with the LEXIS Star Pagination Feature, LEXIS users would be able to determine the West page number corresponding to the portion of an opinion viewed on LEXIS without ever physically referring to the West publication in which the opinion appears.

In response to MDC's announcement, West brought this action, claiming, *inter alia,* that the LEXIS Star Pagination Feature is an appropriation of West's comprehensive arrangement of case reports in violation of the Copyright Act of 1976, 17 U.S.C. §§ 101–810. West sought, and was granted, a preliminary injunction. * * *

ANALYSIS

* * *

I.

MDC's principal contention here is that there is no likelihood that West will succeed on the merits of its copyright claim. MDC readily concedes that portions of West's National Reporter System publications that are not at issue here, such as headnotes prepared by West, merit copyright protection.[2] Yet, MDC maintains that any aspects of West's reporters affected by the LEXIS Star Pagination Feature are not copyrightable. The dominant chord of MDC's argument is that West claims copyright in mere page numbers. MDC adds that in any event, whether West claims copyright in its case arrangement or simply in its pagination, West's claim must fail because neither case arrangement nor pagination can ever qualify as the original work of an author. Even were this possible, MDC goes on, West's case arrangement and pagination do not in fact meet this standard. Finally, MDC contends that even were West's arrangement of cases protected by copyright, the proposed use of West's page numbers in LEXIS reports would not constitute infringement.

We do not agree with MDC that West's claim here is simply one for copyright in its page numbers. Instead, we concur in the District Court's conclusion that West's arrangement is a copyrightable aspect of its compilation of cases, that the pagination of West's volumes reflects and expresses West's arrangement, and that MDC's intended use of West's page numbers infringes West's copyright in the arrangement.

A. Copyright Protection

The Copyright Act provides copyright protection for "original works of authorship fixed in any tangible medium of expression." 17 U.S.C. § 102(a). The standard for "originality" is minimal. It is not necessary that the work be novel or unique, but only that the work have its origin with the author—that it be independently created.

2. West does not and could not claim any copyright in the judicial opinions themselves. See *Wheaton v. Peters,* 8 Pet. 591, 668, 33 U.S. 591, 8 L.Ed. 1055 (1834) ("no reporter * * * can have any copyright in the written opinions delivered by this court").

Hutchinson Telephone Co. v. Fronteer Directory Co., 770 F.2d 128, 131 (8th Cir.1985). * * *

* * *

West publishes opinions not from just one court, but from every state and all the federal courts in the United States. As it collects these opinions, West separates the decisions of state courts from federal-court decisions. West further divides the federal opinions and the state opinions and then assigns them to the appropriate West reporter series. State court decisions are divided by geographic region and assigned to West's corresponding regional reporter. Federal decisions are first divided by the level of the court they come from into district court decisions, court of appeals decisions, and Supreme Court decisions; Court of Claims and military court decisions are also separated out. Before being assigned to a reporter, district court decisions are subdivided according to subject matter into bankruptcy decisions, federal rules decisions, and decisions on other topics. After an opinion is assigned to a reporter, it is assigned to a volume of the reporter and then arranged within the volume. Federal court of appeals decisions, for example, are arranged according to circuit within each volume of West's *Federal Reporter, Second Series,* though there may be more than one group of each circuit's opinions in each volume.

We conclude, as did the District Court, that the arrangement West produces through this process is the result of considerable labor, talent, and judgment. As discussed above, *supra* pp. 1223–1224, to meet intellectual-creation requirements a work need only be the product of a modicum of intellectual labor; West's case arrangements easily meet this standard. Further, since there is no allegation that West copies its case arrangements from some other source, the requirement of originality poses no obstacle to copyrighting the arrangements. In the end, MDC's position must stand or fall on its insistence that all West seeks to protect is numbers on pages. If this is a correct characterization, MDC wins: two always comes after one, and no one can copyright the mere sequence of Arabic numbers. As MDC points out, the specific goal of this suit is to protect some of West's page numbers, those occurring within the body of individual court opinions. But protection for the numbers is not sought for their own sake. It is sought, rather, because access to these particular numbers—the "jump cites"—would give users of LEXIS a large part of what West has spent so much labor and industry in compiling, and would *pro tanto* reduce anyone's need to buy West's books. The key to this case, then, is not whether numbers are copyrightable, but whether the copyright on the books as a whole is infringed by the unauthorized appropriation of these particular numbers. On the record before us (and subject to reconsideration if materially new evidence comes in at the plenary trial on the merits), the District Court's findings of fact relevant to this issue are supportable. We therefore hold (again subject to reexamination after the record has closed) that West's case arrangements, an important part of which is internal page citations, are original works of authorship entitled to copyright protection.

* * *

Affirmed.

OLIVER, SENIOR DISTRICT JUDGE, concurring in part and dissenting in part.

* * *

The fact that the sequential numbering of the pages of any volume, including a volume of law reports, is an important part of the volume, does not support a finding of fact that such a part of the whole of a particular volume of West's publications is subject to copyright. Nor, in my judgment, does such a fact support a finding of fact that West's arrangement of cases is subject to copyright. All parts of a copyrighted volume may not be automatically considered a subject to copyright simply because a publisher claims a copyright on the whole volume.

* * *

The record in this case does not indicate in any way how or by whom West's page numbers are, in fact, created. West's affidavits do not identify any person as the "author" of any of the page numbers. The only thing the record in this case shows, as I read it, is that West's bound volumes carry the same volume numbers and the same page numbers as West's advance sheets. How those page numbers are assigned West's advance sheets is a total mystery so far as the record is concerned.

Judicial notice may be taken of the fact that the original page numbers that appear on a slip opinion submitted by a judge for publication never appear in any West advance sheet. There is indeed substantial doubt whether those page numbers could be considered part of the judge's work of authorship. For the pagination of a judge's slip opinion is, at best, the work of a judge's secretary or, in this day of advanced technology, the work of the secretary's word processor in electronic response to the secretary's punch of a button on a machine.[27]

Thus, the factual question in regard to how or by what process, electronic or otherwise, West assigns a completely new set of page numbers to a judge's slip opinion is an open factual question that can only be determined on a trial of the merits. It is my view that West's probability of success on the merits simply cannot be measured on a record that does not provide any information in regard to whether West's new advance sheet pagination, like a judge's secretary's original pagination of his slip opinion, is nothing more than an electronic response to a direction given a machine or whether, as a matter of fact,

27. This is also true where the judge drafts his opinion in long hand and "authors" the page numbers on his legal pad. For his secretary does not copy the judge's page numbers when the judge's long hand draft is transcribed; the secretary or the word processor, rather than the judge, is the "author" of the page numbers on the slip opinion in its typewritten form.

West's new pagination may be considered an original work of authorship.

* * *

Notes and Question

1. West and Mead eventually settled both this case and a related antitrust case. Mead Data Central (owner of the LEXIS/NEXIS computer service) had sued West Publishing Co. claiming that West has monopolized important areas of legal publishing. The antitrust case got only as far as a preliminary skirmish over venue—each team wanted to play on its home court. *Mead Data Central, Inc. v. West Publishing Co.,* 679 F.Supp. 1455 (S.D.Ohio 1987). According to a newspaper report, the parties then settled both the copyright and the antitrust cases, with Mead agreeing to pay a licensing fee to West. Linda Greenhouse, "Progress Spawns Question: Who owns the Law?," *New York Times,* Feb. 16, 1990, Sec. B, p. 7, col. 3.

2. If a situation like that in *Mead Data Central, Inc. v. West Publishing Co.* arose today, what impact, if any, would the Supreme Court decision in *Feist Publications v. Rural Telephone Service Co.* have?

ATARI GAMES CORPORATION v. OMAN

United States Court of Appeals, District of Columbia Circuit, 1989.
888 F.2d 878.

RUTH BADER GINSBURG, CIRCUIT JUDGE:

By letter dated December 7, 1987, the Copyright Office reported its final action refusing to register a claim to copyright in the video game BREAKOUT, an audiovisual work created in 1975 by Atari, Inc., the predecessor of plaintiff-appellant Atari Games Corporation (Atari). The December 1987 letter, written on behalf of the United States Register of Copyrights (Register), stated that the video game in question "does not contain sufficient original visual or musical authorship to warrant registration." Invoking the judicial review prescriptions of the Administrative Procedure Act, 5 U.S.C. §§ 701–706, Atari unsuccessfully challenged the agency's determination in the district court as "arbitrary, capricious, an abuse of discretion, or otherwise not in accordance with law." 5 U.S.C. § 706(2)(A).

In this appeal from the district court's entry of summary judgment for the Register, we hold that the Copyright Office did not intelligibly account for its ruling. Because we are unable to determine on the current record whether the Register's action comports with the demand of reasoned decisionmaking, we vacate the district court's judgment and remand the case to that court with instructions to return the matter to the Copyright Office for further consideration consistent with this opinion.

I. BACKGROUND AND PRIOR PROCEEDINGS

BREAKOUT, the audiovisual work that is the subject of this dispute, is a coin-operated, ball and paddle video game created in 1975 and successfully marketed by Atari in the following years. BREAKOUT's audiovisual display features a wall formed by red, amber, green, and blue layers of rectangles representing bricks. A player maneuvers a control knob that causes a rectangular-shaped representation of a paddle to hit a square-shaped representation of a ball against the brick wall. When the ball hits a brick, that brick disappears from its row, the player scores points, and a brick on a higher row becomes exposed. A "breakout" occurs when the ball penetrates through all rows of bricks and moves into the space between the wall and the top of the screen; the ball then ricochets in a zig-zag pattern off the sides of the screen and the top layer of the wall, removing bricks upon contact and adding more points to the player's score. Various tones sound as the ball touches different objects or places on the screen. The size of the paddle diminishes and the motion of the ball accelerates as the game is played.

By letter dated February 5, 1987, Atari sought expedited registration of a copyright claim in the audiovisual work embodied in BREAKOUT. Atari asserted an "urgent need for special handling because of prospective litigation in which [Atari] would be acting as plaintiff." The Copyright Office responded promptly, but unfavorably. By letter dated February 13, 1987, Copyright Examiner Carmen Martorana declared the work not copyrightable. She reasoned that "[t]o be considered an audiovisual work for registration purposes, the work must contain related pictorial or graphic images, and at least one of those images must be copyrightable." BREAKOUT did not qualify, she wrote, because neither the "[c]ommon geometric shapes * * * contained in th[e] work" nor "the coloring of th[o]se shapes" constituted copyrightable subject matter. Similarly, she stated, "[t]here is not enough original authorship to register a claim in the sounds." She further said that the "images * * * created by playing the video game * * * are also not registrable since they are created randomly by the player and not by the author of the video game."

By letter dated May 22, 1987, Shirley B. Wendell of the Examining Division denied reconsideration. She repeated that the common geometric shapes contained in BREAKOUT are not copyrightable, that adding color did not render the work copyrightable, and that "[t]he individual tones or sounds are not copyrightable."

By letter dated December 7, 1987, Harriet L. Oler, Chief of the Examining Division, denied further reconsideration and announced the agency's final action on the claim. She initially stated that the Register views the work "as a whole" to determine whether registration is warranted. However, to explain her conclusion that BREAKOUT "does not contain sufficient original visual or musical authorship to warrant registration," she separately treated the work's several parts:

> [T]he use of a symbol for a wall drawn in a familiar tile type design is not copyrightable. The same is true of the image of a rectangle used

> in place of a paddle, a circle [sic] for a ball, and a common four colored stripe embellishing the wall.

The game's sounds, she added, "the three tones used before the ball, and the string of double tones used after it," do not "constitute any copyrightable audio authorship." She further stated that the arrangement of the "stationary screen display" contains no copyrightable authorship because "so few items" appear on the screen and "the arrangement is basically dictated by the functional requirements of this or similar backboard type games." Finally, she noted, Atari was not precluded "from registering a claim in the computer program."

Atari sought court review of the agency's final action. On cross-motions for summary judgment, the district court concluded that the Register reasonably applied controlling law to the facts before him. Describing the three letters from the Copyright Office as "thoughtful and well-orchestrated" expositions of the "pertinent considerations," the court held that the Register did not abuse his discretion in treating BREAKOUT as one of the "rare" instances of expressive value so slight as to be insufficient for copyright purposes. *Atari Games Corp. v. Oman,* 693 F.Supp. 1204, 1206, 1207 (D.D.C.1988).

* * *

III. Appellate Measurement of the Register's Action

Regarding the district court, our review stance in this case is not deferential:

> Because an award of summary judgment reflects "a determination of law rather than fact," we do not defer to the District Court's conclusions but consider the matter de novo.

Nepera Chem., Inc. v. Sea–Land Serv., Inc., 794 F.2d 688, 699 (D.C.Cir. 1986) (quoting *Liberty Lobby v. Anderson,* 746 F.2d 1563, 1572 (D.C.Cir. 1984), *vacated on other grounds,* 477 U.S. 242, 106 S.Ct. 2505, 91 L.Ed.2d 202 (1986)). We accord due respect, however, to decisions made by the Copyright Office pursuant to authority vested in the Register by Congress. Accordingly, we review the Register's decision under an "abuse of discretion" standard. For the reasons stated below, we are unable to discern from the final agency action disqualifying BREAKOUT for registration just how the Register is applying the relevant statutory prescriptions. We therefore return the case for the requisite rational explanation.

We initially summarize our concerns; then, to facilitate the Register's further consideration, and guard against rudderless administrative pronouncements, we develop those concerns more fully. *See Pacific Northwest Newspaper Guild v. NLRB,* 877 F.2d 998, 1003 (D.C.Cir. 1989) ("core concern" of court, when petitioned to check against arbitrary and capricious administrative action, is to assure that executive agencies hew to principled "legal theory" and do not indulge in "ad hocery"); *Kamargo Corp. v. FERC,* 852 F.2d 1392, 1398 (D.C.Cir.1988) (denial of permit is arbitrary and capricious unless the Commission has "acceptable legal support under its authorizing statute"). First, we note the Copyright Act's definition of "audiovisual works" as "a series of related images * * * intrinsically intended to be shown by the use of * * * devices such as * * * electronic equipment, together with accompanying sounds, if any, regardless of the nature of the material objects * * * in which the works are embodied." 17 U.S.C. § 101 (definitions). Although the Act uses the phrase "a series of related images," the Copyright Office, even in its final action, emphasized the non-copyrightability of the work's several parts—the wall, paddle, ball, and tones—and also treated "the stationary screen display." *See supra* p. 880. We are at a loss to understand why the Register did not more solidly link the final decision to the Act's apparent recognition that the whole—the "series of related images"—may be greater than the sum of its several or stationary parts.

Second, we do not grasp the standard of creativity the Copyright Office employed in determining whether to register BREAKOUT as an audiovisual work. Was it the normal standard under which a very modest degree of intellectual labor will suffice? *See, e.g., West Publishing Co. v. Mead Data Cent., Inc.,* 799 F.2d 1219, 1223 (8th Cir.1986), *cert. denied,* 479 U.S. 1070, 107 S.Ct. 962, 93 L.Ed.2d 1010 (1987); 1 M. NIMMER & D. NIMMER, NIMMER ON COPYRIGHT § 1.08[C][1] (1989). Or did the Office test BREAKOUT against a higher standard, one resembling the "substantial creativity" measuring rod sometimes used to judge derivative works? *See* 17 U.S.C. § 103; *Chamberlin v. Uris Sales Corp.,* 150 F.2d 512, 513 (2d Cir.1945) (compilations or other derivative works must contain "some substantial, not merely trivial, originality"). And if an elevated creativity requirement was employed, what justified use of a heightened standard?

Third, the cryptic character of the final agency decision leaves us uncertain whether the action regarding BREAKOUT is consistent with earlier and later pronouncements of the Copyright Office and courts. Put more particularly, we are concerned that the Register may have confused or blended in this case the analytically and operationally separate questions: (1) is a work registrable as one constituting "copyrightable subject matter," *see* 17 U.S.C. § 410(a), (b); and (2) what is the extent of copyright protection—solid or thin—due a given "original work of authorship." The first question relates to the *existence* of copyright, the second, to the *scope* of protection.

V. COPYRIGHTABLE SUBJECT MATTER

"Copyright protection subsists * * * in original works of authorship" including, among several categories of copyrightable subject matter, "audiovisual works." 17 U.S.C. § 102(a)(6). Video games, case law confirms, rank as "audiovisual works" that may qualify for copyright protection.

This court and others have defined the word "original" in the Copyright Act's term "original works of authorship," 17 U.S.C. § 102(a), to mean "only that the work 'owes its origin to the author'—*i.e.,* that the work is independently created, rather than copied from other works." *Reader's Digest Ass'n v. Conservative Digest, Inc.,* 821 F.2d 800, 806 (D.C.Cir.1987) (quoting *Alfred Bell & Co. v. Catalda Fine Arts, Inc.,* 191 F.2d 99, 102 (2d Cir.1951)). As the district court stated, "[t]here is no dispute in this case, and the Register expressly recognized, that BREAKOUT originated with or was independently created by Atari." *Atari Games Corp.,* 693 F.Supp. at 1205.

While the Register concedes that BREAKOUT is an independent creation, he concluded that the game is not a "work of authorship" within the meaning of the statute. To constitute a "work of authorship," the material deposited with the Register must pass a "creativity" threshold, *i.e.,* it must embody "some modest amount of intellectual labor." *Baltimore Orioles, Inc. v. Major League Baseball Players Ass'n,* 805 F.2d 663, 668 n. 6 (7th Cir.1986) (distinguishing the concepts "originality," "creativity," and "novelty," and observing that "[f]or a work to be copyrightable, it must be original and creative, but need not be novel"), *cert. denied,* 480 U.S. 941, 107 S.Ct. 1593, 94 L.Ed.2d 782 (1987).

A. The focus of inquiry

The Register subjected BREAKOUT to a component-by-component analysis, and considered in the aggregate "the stationary screen display." The Act, however, uses the definitional term "series of related images," 17 U.S.C. § 101, and the case law correspondingly indicates that the Register's focus, even if initially concentrated on discrete parts, *ultimately* should be on the audiovisual work as a whole, *i.e.,* the total sequence of images displayed as the game is played.

In the clarification forthcoming on reconsideration by the Copyright Office, we anticipate that the Register will take careful account of our recent opinion in *Reader's Digest,* 821 F.2d at 806, in which we observed:

> None of the individual elements of the Reader's Digest cover—ordinary lines, typefaces, and colors—qualifies for copyright protection. But the distinctive arrangement and layout of those elements is entitled to protection as a graphic work. * * * Reader's Digest has combined and arranged common forms to create a unique graphic design and layout. This design is entitled to protection under the Copyright Act as a graphic work.

See also Apple Barrel Prods., Inc. v. Beard, 730 F.2d 384, 388 (5th Cir.1984) (component parts "neither original to the plaintiff nor copyrightable" may, in combination, create a "separate entity [that] is both original and copyrightable"); *Roth Greeting Cards v. United Card Co.,* 429 F.2d 1106, 1109 (9th Cir.1970) (greeting cards held to be copyrightable although textual matter standing alone was not copyrightable; "all elements of each card, including text, art work, and association between art work and text, [must] be considered as a whole").

B. The creativity threshold

The level of creativity necessary and sufficient for copyrightability has been described as "very slight," "minimal," "modest." *See, e.g., West Publishing Co.,* 799 F.2d at 1223; *Thomas Wilson & Co. v. Irving J. Dorfman Co.,* 433 F.2d 409, 411 (2d Cir.1970), *cert. denied,* 401 U.S. 977, 91 S.Ct. 1200, 28 L.Ed.2d 326 (1971); 1 M. NIMMER & D. NIMMER, NIMMER ON COPYRIGHT §§ 1.08[C][1], 2.01[B][1] (1989). In defense of the judgment that BREAKOUT does not pass the "modest" creativity threshold, appellate counsel for the Register pointed to the Copyright Office regulation providing that "familiar symbols or designs" and "mere variations of typographic ornamentation, lettering or coloring" are not subject to copyright. 37 C.F.R. § 202.1. Again, we are concerned that the Register's attention may have trained dominantly on components, not on the work as a whole—the full "series of related images." 17 U.S.C. § 101 (defining "audiovisual works"); *see supra* pp. 879–880, 882–883.

Furthermore, we note that simple shapes, when selected or combined in a distinctive manner indicating some ingenuity, have been accorded copyright protection both by the Register and in court. We are thus uncertain whether or how the Register's decision on BREAKOUT harmonizes with prior Copyright Office actions and court rulings on the creativity threshold.

In its brief on appeal, the Copyright Office compared Atari's claim for protection of its work "as a whole," to the protection copyright law affords to compilations and other derivative works. Brief for Appellee at 14. Derivative works, several decisions state, to be copyrightable, must meet a test of "substantial," not merely "minimal," creativity. To our knowledge, however, neither the Copyright Office nor any court has ranked as "derivative" a video game that, like the BREAKOUT game Atari produced in 1975, is not based on prior models.

C. "Idea" or "expression," scènes à faire, *and the distinction between registrability and scope of copyright protection*

Copyright protection extends only to "expression," not to "ideas." 17 U.S.C. § 102(b); *Mazer v. Stein,* 347 U.S. 201, 217, 74 S.Ct. 460, 470, 98 L.Ed. 630 (1954). The Register sees the two as merged in the BREAKOUT game. BREAKOUT contains no expression, he maintains, separable from the game itself, and therefore does not qualify as copyrightable subject matter. Eleven months prior to the final agency action in this case, the Fourth Circuit declared "untenable" lump categorization of video games as "idea" rather than "expression." *M. Kramer Mfg. Co.,* 783 F.2d at 436–37.

The Fourth Circuit, in *M. Kramer Mfg. Co.,* acknowledged and distinguished precedent holding that when the subject matter allows for only a very limited manner of expression, the idea and its expression remain a unit, so that there is no copyrightable material. *Morrissey v. Procter & Gamble,* 379 F.2d 675, 678–79 (1st Cir.1967) (copyright does not extend to rules for "sweepstakes" type sales promotion contest).[7] But works in the computer's domain generally have not fit that bill, the *M. Kramer Mfg. Co.* panel observed. Instead, the variety of ways to perform the same function sustains the classification of such works as "expression."

In this light, we do not follow the Register's thought in describing BREAKOUT's arrangement as dictated by "functional requirements." *See supra* p. 880. Atari demonstrated that a large variety of "arrangements" or designs might have been devised in lieu of those featured in BREAKOUT, *i.e.,* in place of the objects represented (multi-colored brick wall, square ball, and shrinkable rectangular paddle), the sounds employed (their tones and duration), and the speed and artificial direction of the ball's movement.

* * *

Nor can it convincingly be maintained that audiovisual display and computer program are so linked that it is necessary or sufficient for Atari to register a claim in the computer program. *Cf. supra* p. 880. Registering a claim in the program would not securely protect "the series of related images," 17 U.S.C. § 101, for which Atari seeks an "original work of authorship" copyright seal. "[M]any different computer programs can produce the same 'results,' whether those results are an analysis of financial records or a sequence of images and sounds." *Stern Elecs.,* 669 F.2d at 855. "[W]riting a new program to replicate the play of [a video game] requires a sophisticated effort, but it is a manageable task." *Id.; see* Patry, 31 J. Copr. Soc'y at 5 ("A knock-off manufacturer could * * * write a computer program which would exactly replicate the audiovisual display but which would not replicate the underlying computer program. In such an event, the registration of the computer program * * * would be ineffective since it is the audiovisual display which is sought to be protected.").

Even if BREAKOUT contains "expression," the Register additionally suggests, the symbols displayed are so ordinary and commonplace as to fail under *scènes à faire* analysis. The term *scènes à faire* refers to stereotyped expressions, "incidents, characters or settings which are as a practical matter indispensable, or at least standard, in the treatment of a given topic." *Alexander v. Haley,* 460 F.Supp. 40, 45 (S.D.N.Y.1978). In *Atari, Inc. v. North Am. Phillips Consumer Elecs. Corp.,* 672 F.2d 607 (7th Cir.), *cert. denied,* 459 U.S. 880, 103 S.Ct. 176, 74 L.Ed.2d 145 (1982), the court placed "[c]ertain expressive matter" in

7. *But cf. NEC Corp. v. Intel Corp.,* 10 U.S.P.Q.2d 1177, 1179, 1989 WL 67434 (N.D.Cal.1989):

> [A]s a matter of practicality, the issue of a limited number of ways to express an idea is relevant to infringement, but should not be the basis for denying the initial copyright. The Register of Copyrights will not know about the presence or absence of constraints that limit ways to express an idea. The burden of showing such constraints should be left to the alleged infringer. Accordingly, in the absence of Ninth Circuit authority to the contrary, it is concluded that the relationship between "idea" and "expression" will not be considered on the issue of copyrightability, but will be deferred to the discussion of infringement.

the video game PAC–MAN in a *scènes à faire* compartment. 672 F.2d at 616–17. But the panel in that case ultimately did not conclude that the expressions it treated as *scènes à faire* gained no copyright protection. Instead, the panel said that the items in question (maze, scoring table, tunnel exits, dots) should "receive protection only from virtually identical copying." *Id.* at 617. That statement indicates that "the *scènes à faire* doctrine limits only the scope of a given material's protection, not its copyrightability." *Nash v. CBS, Inc.,* 691 F.Supp. 140, 144 (N.D.Ill.1988).

We are unable to detect from the final decision before us the standard the Register is using to differentiate material that cannot constitute copyrightable subject matter and therefore should not be registered, from material that may be copyrightable, although perhaps meriting only "thin" protection when the character of its "expression" is tested in an infringement suit. Because neither the idea/expression dichotomy nor the *scènes à faire* doctrine, under the prevailing case law, reveals to us why BREAKOUT should rank as a work in which no copyright can exist, we are currently unable to approve the Register's decision under those rubrics.

CONCLUSION

For the reasons stated, we reverse the summary judgment entered by the district court. We remand this case to that court with instructions to return the matter of Atari's application to the Register for renewed consideration consistent with this opinion.

It is so ordered.

* * *

Notes

1. As this case shows, copyright in a computer program with an important audiovisual component is easier for judges to handle, because there are numerous relevant precedents outside the computer field. The main different issue which might arise is how copyright should relate to the fact that the sequence of images in a video game is different every time it is played.

2. In *Lotus,* Paperback Software had argued that the menu structure of Lotus 1–2–3 was not protected because it did not originate with Lotus, but was copied from an earlier spreadsheet, VisiCalc. However, in the excerpt quoted above, Judge Keeton found against Lotus on this issue. Keeton wrote:

> It is plain that plaintiff did not impermissibly copy copyrighted elements of VisiCalc. Lotus 1–2–3 uses a very different menu structure. In contrast with VisiCalc's one-line main menu that reads "Command: BCDEFGIMPRSTVW–", the main menu of Lotus 1–2–3,

which uses a two-line moving cursor menu system, reads: "Worksheet Range Copy Move File Graph Data Quit". * * *

3. The "originality" required for copyright protection includes the requirement that the writing "originate" with the author, not with some-one else. The development of computer software is like that of other applied sciences. New programs build on what has been learned in making and testing older programs. As a result, computer software is particularly vulnerable to charges of lack of original authorship.

4. If Lotus had copied elements of VisiCalc, would it matter, as between Lotus and Paperback, whether VisiCalc was protected by copyright or was in the public domain?

5. The examiners at the Copyright Office examine works for copyrightability. Like the freshman English instructors trying to catch students submitting plagiarized term papers, the examiners have great difficulty detecting non-original works, because they lack the staff or means to compare works submitted for registration with the vast body of existing published and unpublished material. Therefore they must rely on the statements made on the registration application form. Jurisprudential theory suggests that the harder it is to detect an infraction, the more severe the punishment must be in order to deter potential violators. In *Ashton–Tate Corp. v. Fox Software,* 760 F.Supp. 831 (C.D.Cal.1990), the court found "Ashton–Tate, when it filed its original applications for copyright, repeatedly failed to disclose material information to the United States Copyright Office—that the dBase line of computer software programs was derived from JPLDIS, a public domain computer software program developed by the Jet Propulsion Laboratory, and that dBase III was derived from dBase II." The court further found "Ashton–Tate's repeated failure to disclose such material information was done knowingly and with an intent to deceive." On the basis of these findings, the court applied a severe sanction, invalidating the copyright and dismissing the case. Then the District Judge rescinded his order. Ashton–Tate, however, already had appealed to the Ninth Circuit, perhaps thereby depriving the District Judge of jurisdiction. PC Week, April 29, 1991, p. 127. Was the judge right the first time or the second time?

D. EXCLUSIVE RIGHTS

1. THE BASIC RIGHTS

COPYRIGHT ACT OF 1976

§ 106. Exclusive rights in copyrighted works

Subject to sections 107 through 118, the owner of copyright under this title has the exclusive rights to do and to authorize any of the following:

(1) to reproduce the copyrighted work in copies or phonorecords;

(2) to prepare derivative works based upon the copyrighted work;

(3) to distribute copies or phonorecords of the copyrighted work to the public by sale or other transfer of ownership, or by rental, lease, or lending;

(4) in the case of literary, musical, dramatic, and choreographic works, pantomimes, and motion pictures and other audiovisual works, to perform the copyrighted work publicly; and

(5) in the case of literary, musical, dramatic, and choreographic works, pantomimes, and pictorial, graphic, or sculptural works, including the individual images of a motion picture or other audiovisual work, to display the copyrighted work publicly.

* * *

MIDWAY MFG. CO. v. ARTIC INTERNATIONAL, INC.

United States Court of Appeals, Seventh Circuit, 1983.
704 F.2d 1009.

CUMMINGS, CHIEF JUDGE.

This appeal involves questions regarding the scope of protection video games enjoyed under the 1976 Copyright Act, 90 Stat. 254, 17 U.S.C. § 101 *et seq.*

Plaintiff manufactures video game machines. Inside these machines are printed circuit boards capable of causing images to appear on a television picture screen and sounds to emanate from a speaker when an electric current is passed through them. On the outside of each machine are a picture screen, sound speaker, and a lever or button that allows a person using the machine to alter the images appearing on the machine's picture screen and the sounds emanating from its speaker. Each machine can produce a large number of related images and sounds. These sounds and images are stored on the machine's circuit boards—how the circuits are arranged and connected determines the set of sounds and images the machine is capable of making. When a person touches the control lever or button on the outside of the machine he sends a signal to the circuit boards inside the machine which causes them to retrieve and display one of the sounds and images stored in them. Playing a video game involves manipulating the controls on the machine so that some of the images stored in the machine's circuitry appear on its picture screen and some of its sounds emanate from its speaker.

Defendant sells printed circuit boards for use inside video game machines. One of the circuit boards defendant sells speeds up the rate of play—how fast the sounds and images change—of "Galaxian," one of plaintiff's video games, when inserted in place of one of the "Galaxian" machine's circuit boards. Another of defendant's circuit boards stores a set of images and sounds almost identical to that stored in the circuit boards of plaintiff's "Pac-Man" video game machine so that the video game people play on machines containing defendant's circuit board looks and sounds virtually the same as plaintiff's "Pac–Man" game.

Plaintiff sued defendant alleging that defendant's sale of these two circuit boards infringes its copyrights in its "Galaxian" and "Pac–Man" video games. In a memorandum opinion and order reported at 547 F.Supp. 999 (N.D.Ill.1982), the district court granted plaintiff's motion for a preliminary injunction and denied defendant's motion for summary judgment. The district court's order enjoins defendant from manufacturing or distributing circuit boards that can be used to play video games substantially similar to those protected by plaintiff's copyrights. Defendant appeals from that order on the ground that plaintiff has not shown a likelihood of succeeding on the merits of its claim of copyright infringement. We affirm for the reasons that follow.

* * *

The final argument of defendant's that we address is that selling plaintiff's licensees circuit boards that speed up the rate of play of plaintiff's video games is not an infringement of plaintiff's copyrights. Speeding up the rate of play of a video game is a little like playing at 45 or 78 revolutions per minute ("RPM's") a phonograph record recorded at 33 RPM's. If a discotheque licensee did that, it would probably not be an infringement of the record company's copyright in the record. One might argue by analogy that it is not a copyright infringement for video game licensees to speed up the rate of play of video games, and that it is not a contributory infringement for the defendant to sell licensees circuit boards that enable them to do that.

There is this critical difference between playing records at a faster than recorded speed and playing video games at a faster than manufactured rate: there is an enormous demand for speeded-up video games but there is little if any demand for speeded-up records. Not many people want to hear 33 RPM records played at 45 and 78 RPM's so that record licensors would not care if their licensees play them at that speed. But there is a big demand for speeded-up video games. Speeding up a video game's action makes the game more challenging and exciting and increases the licensee's revenue per game. Speeded-up games end sooner than normal games and consequently if players are willing to pay an additional price-per-minute in exchange for the challenge and excitement of a faster game, licensees will take in greater total revenues. Video game copyright owners would undoubtedly like to lay their hands on some of that extra revenue and therefore it cannot be assumed that licensees are implicitly authorized to use speeded-up circuit boards in the machines plaintiff supplies.

Among a copyright owner's exclusive rights is the right "to prepare derivative works based upon the copyrighted work." 17 U.S.C. § 106(2). If, as we hold, the speeded-up "Galaxian" game that a licensee creates with a circuit board supplied by the defendant is a derivative work based upon "Galaxian," a licensee who lacks the plaintiff's authorization to create a derivative work is a direct infringer and the defendant is a contributory infringer through its sale of the speeded-up circuit board.

Section 101 of the 1976 Copyright Act defines a derivative work as "a work based upon one or more preexisting works, such as a translation, musical arrangement, dramatization, fictionalization, motion picture version, sound recording, art reproduction, abridgment, condensation, or any other form in which a work may be recast, transformed, or adapted." It is not obvious from this language whether a speeded-up video game is a derivative work. A speeded-up phonograph record probably is not. Cf. *Shapiro, Bernstein & Co. v. Jerry Vogel Music Co.*, 73 F.Supp. 165, 167 (S.D.N.Y.1947) ("The change in time of the added chorus, and the slight variation in the base of the accompaniment, there being no change in the tune or lyrics, would not be 'new work' "); 1 Nimmer on Copyright § 3.03 (1982). But that is because the additional value to the copyright owner of having the right to market separately the speeded-up version of the recorded performance is too trivial to warrant legal protection for that right. A speeded-up video game is a substantially different product from the original game. As noted, it is more exciting to play and it requires some creative effort to produce. For that reason, the owner of the copyright on the game should be entitled to monopolize it on the same theory that he is entitled to monopolize the derivative works specifically listed in Section 101. The current rage for video games was not anticipated in 1976, and like any new technology the video game does not fit with complete ease the definition of derivative work in Section 101 of the 1976 Act. But the amount by which the language of Section 101 must be stretched to accommodate speeded-up video games is, we believe, within the limits within which Congress wanted the new Act to operate.

Defendant raises other arguments on appeal, all of which we reject for the reasons set forth in District Judge Decker's exhaustive opinion. See 547 F.Supp. at 1005–1012.

Affirmed.

LEWIS GALOOB TOYS, INC. v. NINTENDO OF AMERICA, INC.

United States District Court, Northern District of California, 1991.
___ F.Supp. ___, 1991 WL 149826.

MEMORANDUM OF DECISION

FERN M. SMITH, DISTRICT JUDGE.

INTRODUCTION

These two consolidated suits test the scope of copyright protection for audio-visual games (video games). Nintendo of America, Inc. ("Nintendo") markets and sells home video games hardware systems and compatible video game cartridges. The audio-visual portions of the game cartridges in suit are protected by registered copyrights held by Nintendo.

Lewis Galoob Toys, Inc. ("Galoob") markets and sells toy products. Galoob has a license to market a video game accessory known as the Game Genie Video Game Enhancer ("Game Genie"), which attaches to a video game cartridge and allows the player to temporarily alter certain attributes of the video game. It is sold for personal consumer use only, not for video game arcades. The Game Genie does not create a separate copy of the original video game, does not make permanent changes to the original game work, and can only be used when attached to the original game.

Nintendo contends that the Game Genie creates a derivative work as defined in 17 U.S.C. § 101, and that Galoob is therefore either a direct or contributory infringer of Nintendo's copyrights in the original video games in suit.

For the reasons set forth below, the Court finds to the contrary and vacates the pending preliminary injunction forthwith.

Summary of Rulings

This case has included one and one-half years of litigation, a two-week trial, and extensive briefing of all issues, both pre- and post-trial. After careful consideration of the evidence and briefing submitted by both sides, and for the reasons set forth below, this Court rules as follows:

(1) Use of the Game Genie by consumers to temporarily alter copyrighted video games for their own enjoyment does not create a derivative work under 17 U.S.C. § 101. Because the consumers are not direct infringers, Galoob is not a contributory infringer.

(2) In the alternative, even if the Game Genie did create a derivative product, the doctrine of "fair use" enables consumers to use the Game Genie for their personal enjoyment, 17 U.S.C. § 107, and therefore allows Galoob to sell it.

(3) Galoob's use of copyrighted video games for purposes of testing or marketing the Game Genie does not violate any of Nintendo's rights under the Copyright Act.

(4) On this record, injunctive relief is not appropriate for either side.

* * *

Findings of Fact and Conclusions of Law

I. Products

This suit involves the interplay of three products, the Nintendo Entertainment System, Nintendo copyrighted video games and the Game Genie.

Nintendo markets and sells video game hardware systems. The system is known as the Nintendo Entertainment System ("NES") and is designed for playing video games in the home. Nintendo has sold in excess of 25,000,000 of these systems in the United States. Nintendo also markets and sells video game cartridges, and licenses third parties to market and sell video games which are compatible with Nintendo's hardware. The video games are displayed on a home television.

The NES includes a microprocessor-based console, the "control deck," which houses two processing units: the central processing unit ("CPU"), which controls the overall operation of the system, and the picture processing unit ("PPU"), which generates the pictures for display on the television. The control deck is connected to the television.

B. Video Games

The video games which may be played on the NES control deck are both audio-visual works and computer programs. The audio-visual works and game programs are permanently stored on ROMs (i.e., Read Only Memory chips) contained in game cartridges.

Nintendo owns valid and subsisting registered copyrights in the audio-visual programs contained in many of its video games, including those in suit.

Each game typically has a theme and a goal. For example, a game might consist of the main character's attempt to obtain a certain level of points before he is defeated by hostile forces.[1] In an attempt to reach that point goal, he has a certain number of chances ("lives") in which to overcome obstacles, battle adversaries, and travel through various levels ("worlds"). Each time he overcomes an obstacle or reaches a new world, additional points are added to the score. On the other hand, each time he is defeated by a villain and/or obstacle, he loses a chance or life. If he loses all of his lives before obtaining a certain number of points, the game ends, and he must start again.

More than 500 different video games have been produced and offered for sale for use with the NES Control Deck. In addition to those owned and copyrighted directly by Nintendo, hundreds of games have been produced by some 71 other companies. Sixty-three of the non-Nintendo producers of video games have licenses from Nintendo, and an additional eight do not.

Players can buy various devices ("interactive devices") which connect to the NES control deck and allow the player to influence various aspects of the game being played. Changes include speeding up certain aspects of the game, skipping one or more levels of play, etc. Interactive devices which may be used with the NES control deck include devices marketed as the "Control Pad," "NES Advantage," "Power Glove," "NES Max," and "Turbo Blaster." Light guns may also be used by players for playing certain games. Nintendo markets and sells, or licenses others to sell, such interactive devices for use with the NES control deck.

1. For reasons that remain obscure, the protagonists are generally male.

The NES video game cartridges contain two separate memories: one memory (the "program memory") is connected to the CPU when the game cartridge is physically inserted into the control deck; the other memory (the "character memory") is connected to the PPU when the game cartridge is physically inserted into the control deck.

In order to play an NES video game, the player inserts a game cartridge into the control deck. The player begins game play and interacts with the video game by manipulating buttons on the standard controller, which is sold with the NES and which attaches to the control deck.

The game's action is performed on the television screen. Players use the controller (which contains a four-way control pad, for directional control, and four other buttons labeled "start," "select," "A" and "B") to guide the actions of "their" character in an attempt to reach the game's goal, as described earlier.

The copyrights allegedly infringed in this suit are for the audiovisual portion of the video game cartridges manufactured by Nintendo. The games are only compatible for play on the NES; they have a retail list price of approximately $40 to $50 each.

C. *The Game Genie*

Galoob is in the business of marketing and selling toy products in the United States. Galoob obtained a license to market the Game Genie from Codemasters Software Co., Ltd., a United Kingdom corporation, and Camerica, Ltd., a Canadian corporation. The Game Genie, the accused product, allows players to alter certain attributes of video games, in ways similar to the interactive devices and published codes described supra at 7–8 and infra at 35.

The Game Genie can function in combination with any NES-compatible game cartridge. Six licensed producers of copyrighted Nintendo-compatible games, as well as Nintendo itself, are known to object to the use of the Game Genie with their copyrighted games. It is not known whether the nontestifying Nintendo- licensees or the eight nonlicensed producers of NES-compatible games object or consent to the use of the Game Genie with their copyrighted games, nor is it known how many of the games of Nintendo licensees or nonlicensee producers have registered copyrights.

At this time, the Game Genie is configured both electronically and physically to plug into NES control decks and NES-compatible video game cartridges only; it has no other use.

The Game Genie is designed to fit between the NES control deck and NES- compatible video game cartridges. When a Game Genie is used (i.e., when a game cartridge has been attached to a Game Genie and the Game Genie is then inserted into a control deck), it has two modes of operation: a programming or "set-up" mode, and a game play mode.

If the game cartridge is detached from the Game Genie during operation, all audio-visual displays of the game cease. Likewise, if a game cartridge inserted into a control deck without the Game Genie is removed from the control deck, all game audio-visual displays cease. The Game Genie cannot be used unless it is physically attached to a video game cartridge and then inserted into an NES control deck.

During the Game Genie's set-up mode, a display appears on the television screen and the player is presented with the choice of entering from one to three codes into the Game Genie. Each code can be six to eight letters in length, and each letter may be chosen from among sixteen available letters of the alphabet. Although there are billions of possible codes, a maximum of three codes can be entered for any single play of a game. When code selection is complete, the player presses the "select" button on the controller, the set- up mode screens display disappears, and the Game Genie shifts into its "game play mode." In this mode, the game begins, and the player plays the game with the alterations allowed by the Game Genie codes the player has entered. If no code has been entered, the Game Genie has no influence on game play, and the game plays exactly as it would if no Game Genie were attached.[2]

If the game player inputs one, two, or three codes into the Game Genie, each entered code causes the CPU to receive different data than it would if the Game Genie were not attached and activated by the game player.

Galoob has prepared a booklet intended to be distributed with the Game Genie entitled "Programming Manual and Code Book" ("Code Book"). The Game Genie Code Book instructions expressly encourage players to alter listed codes and to create various effects by programming their own codes. The effects of all codes, whether devised by Galoob or by the players themselves, are temporary in nature, and will last only until the player unplugs the game or resets in order to start a new game.

There are approximately 1,660 listed codes in the Game Genie Code Book, allowing various categories of temporary changes to be created with the use of the Game Genie. Some permit the player to choose where to begin the game, i.e. at a higher level of the game rather than

2. The Game Genie interprets each of the codes a player selects to refer to a particular "address" in the game cartridge program ROM, and the data that are stored there. As the game proceeds, the CPU inquiries that are directed to the game cartridge's program ROM pass through the Game Genie.

If an inquiry is directed to an address that matches one of the codes the player has selected, the Game Genie substitutes the data it has stored for the data that the game cartridge would otherwise transmit to the CPU. (For example, assume the CPU asks for the initial number of lives and the game cartridge has the number "three" at the address corresponding to initial "lives." If the player has selected a code for six lives, the Game Genie would substitute data signifying six lives and send that data to the CPU.)

Each Game Genie code can substitute only a single byte of data at a single address. Thus, of the million or so inquiries per second that the CPU directs to the game cartridge, the Game Genie can interrupt and change relatively few.

at the beginning. Other codes allow the player to increase or decrease the number of chances the player has to complete the game or the amount of time in which those chances can be exercised. Others allow a player to advance more quickly through the game by skipping certain obstacles.

The Game Genie cannot be used to play or do anything unless a separate game cartridge is also used. It can neither substitute for an NES game cartridge, nor can it reproduce or copy an independent version of the game. The effects of the Game Genie last only for the temporal period in which a particular sequence of play continues. Its effects vanish as the player ends a sequence of play by disconnecting the power to the game or by resetting and starting over. The Game Genie codes cannot change the plot, theme, or characters of any game. The vast majority of the Game Genie codes alter the rules of the game or method of play. See infra at 18–19.

The Game Genie is marketed for use by consumers as an accessory to their home video system. It is not intended to be used in connection with any public performance of a video game, e.g. in an arcade setting. Cf. *Midway Mfg. Co. v. Artic Int'l, Inc.,* 704 F.2d 1009 (7th Cir.1983), cert. denied, 464 U.S. 823, 104 S.Ct. 90, 78 L.Ed.2d 98 (1983). No evidence was presented of any such actual or potential public performance.

II. Scope of Copyright Protection

* * *

A. Derivative Works

The Copyright Act gives the holder exclusive rights to use and authorize the use of the work in five qualified ways, including the preparation of derivative works based upon the copyrighted work. 17 U.S.C. § 106(2). Nintendo alleges that the Game Genie is a derivative work. This Court does not agree.

Section 101 of the 1976 Copyright Act defines a derivative work as "a work based upon one or more preexisting works such as a translation, musical arrangement, dramatization, fictionalization, motion picture version, sound recording, art reproduction, abridgement, condensation, or any other form in which a work may be recast, transformed, or adapted" (emphasis added).

Nintendo relies heavily on *Midway Mfg. Co. v. Artic Int'l., Inc.,* 704 F.2d 1009 (7th Cir.1983), *cert. denied,* 464 U.S. 823, 104 S.Ct. 90, 78 L.Ed.2d 98 (1983) in claiming that the Game Genie is a derivative work. That reliance is misplaced. As Midway noted, "It is not obvious from [the language of section 101] whether a speeded up video game is a derivative work." Id. at 1014. If it was doubtful as to whether or not the product in that case was a derivative work, the uncertainty is far greater regarding the Game Genie. In Midway, the allegedly infringing product was a printed circuit board which could be used to speed up the rate of play—how fast the sounds and images changed—of one of plaintiff's video games ("Galaxian"), licensed for use in a play-for-pay arcade setting. Under those circumstances, the Seventh Circuit found that speeding up that specific game increased the licensee's revenue by making the game more challenging and decreasing the time it took to complete a game, i.e., more games could be played in a given time period, generating more income for the licensee. Acknowledging that the copyright owners of that video game would be anxious to obtain that extra revenue, the court found that commercial licensees were not implicitly authorized to use the speeded up circuit boards; therefore, the suppliers of those circuit boards contributorily infringed because the speeded version of the game was a derivative work. 704 F.2d at 1014.

Based on those facts, Midway held that the "amount by which the language of section 101 must be stretched to accommodate speeded up video games is . . . within the limits with which Congress wanted the new act to operate." Id., (emphasis added). The result appeared to be based on the equities of that situation. Under those facts, the court was willing to "stretch" the acceptable definition of a derivative work. Midway's result, if not its analysis, appears to have turned on the fact that the licensee arcade owner, not the copyright holder, was making money from the public performance of the altered game, a violation of section 106(4) (copyright holder has exclusive right "to perform the copyrighted work publicly").[4]

The alleged infringer in this case is not a commercial licensee, but rather a consumer utilizing the Game Genie for noncommercial, private enjoyment. Such use neither generates a fixed transferable copy of the work, nor exhibits or performs the work for commercial gain. See §§ 102, 106(4).

Whether or not video games modified by the Game Genie constitute derivative works is a difficult question. Viewing the Copyright Act as a whole, however, and considering the policies behind that Act, this Court concludes that inherent in the concept of a "derivative work" is the ability for that work to exist on its own, fixed and transferable from the original work, i.e., having a separate "form". See § 101 (derivative work definition). The Game Genie does not meet that definition.

As explained supra, a Game Genie allows a player to choose one to three modifications in the rules of a game, during a limited sequence of play. Once the Game Genie and its attached game cartridge are disconnected from the NES, or the power is turned off, those changes disappear and the video game reverts to its original form. No independent, fixed work is created.

In construing the phrase "derivative work" in light of technological change which has rendered its literal meaning ambiguous, the Court looks to the "basic purpose" of the Copyright Act—balancing a fair

4. This Court expresses no view as to whether commercial arcade use of the Game Genie would be an unauthorized showing under section 106.

return on an author's creative labor against the need for "broad public availability of literature, music, and the other arts." *Twentieth Century Music Corp. v. Aiken,* 422 U.S. 151, 156, 95 S.Ct. 2040, 2043, 45 L.Ed.2d 84 (1975). The Game Genie is a tool by which the consumer may temporarily modify the way in which to play a video game, legally obtained at market price. Any modification is for the consumer's own enjoyment in the privacy of the home. Such a process is analogous in purpose, if not in technology, to skipping portions of a book, learning to speed read, fast-forwarding a video tape one has purchased in order to skip portions one chooses not to see, or using slow motion for the opposite reasons. None of those practices permanently modifies or alters the original work, none produces a separate work which can then be transferred in any way, none replaces the original work, and none deprives the copyright holder of current or expected revenue.

Both parties agree that it is acceptable, under the copyright laws, for a noncopyright holder to publish a book of instructions on how to modify the rules and/or method of play of a copyrighted game. Once having purchased, for example, a copyrighted board game, a consumer is free to take the board home and modify the game in any way the consumer chooses, whether or not the method used comports with the copyright holder's intent. The copyright holder, having received expected value, has no further control over the consumer's private enjoyment of that game.

Because of the technology involved, owners of video games are less able to experiment with or change the method of play, absent an electronic accessory such as the Game Genie. This should not mean that holders of copyrighted video games are entitled to broader protections or monopoly rights than holders of other types of copyrighted games, simply because a more sophisticated technology is involved. Having paid Nintendo a fair return, the consumer may experiment with the product and create new variations of play, for personal enjoyment, without creating a derivative work. Cf. Midway, 704 F.2d at 1013–14 (arcade use is a derivative work, because "[v]ideo game copyright owners would like to lay their hands on some of that extra revenue").

For these reasons, this Court finds that the Game Genie does not create a derivative work protected by the copyright laws.

B. Fair Use

Had the Court found that the Game Genie was a derivative work, Galoob would still be exempt from liability under the doctrine of "fair use." In making this finding, the Court has relied extensively on *Sony v. Universal* [464 U.S. 417, 104 S.Ct. 774, 78 L.Ed.2d 574 (1984)] as well as the trial court's opinion in that matter.

As the Supreme Court stated in Sony, "[a]ny individual may reproduce a copyrighted work for a 'fair use'; the copyright owner does not possess the exclusive right to such a use." 464 U.S. at 433, 104

S.Ct. at 784. "The doctrine of fair use allows a holder of the privilege to use copyrighted material in a reasonable manner without the consent of the copyright owner." *Narell v. Freeman,* 872 F.2d 907, 913 (9th Cir.1989). Determination of fair use requires analysis under an "equitable rule of reason." *Sony,* at 464 U.S. at 448, 104 S.Ct. at 792 (quoting H.R.Rep. No. 94–1476, reprinted in 1976 U.S.Code Cong. & Admin.News at 5679). "The copyright law, like the patent statutes, makes reward to the owner a secondary consideration." *Sony,* 464 U.S. at 429, 104 S.Ct. at 782 (quoting *Fox Film Corp. v. Doyal,* 286 U.S. 123, 127, 52 S.Ct. 546, ___, 76 L.Ed. 1010 (1932)).

Sony—the only pronouncement by the Supreme Court on fair use in the contributory infringement context—involved facts analogous to those here. In *Sony,* holders of copyrights for certain television programs sued the manufacturer of the Betamax video tape recorder (video cassette recorder, or VCR) for contributory infringement. Those copyright holders (like Nintendo) sought to enjoin Sony (like Galoob) from manufacturing and selling an electronic device, claiming that purchasers of that device were using it to infringe copyrights. One use of the device was recording unauthorized copies of copyrighted television programs to "time shift" on-the-air broadcasts. The Supreme Court found the consumers' use of Sony's product for time shifting purposes to be a "fair use" of the copyrighted programs.

Fair use is a privilege against a direct infringement claim (17 U.S.C. § 107), and is a privilege held in the first instance by the alleged direct infringer—i.e., by the person playing the video game. Just as application of the fair use doctrine in Sony resulted in substantial economic gain for Sony and other VCR manufacturers, the fair use doctrine applied to this case will benefit Galoob. Sony makes clear, however, that it is the fairness of the family's use of its video game, not some evaluation of the commercial "fairness" of Galoob's product, that must guide the Court's analysis.

In examining the fairness of the family's use, the Court is guided statutorily by 17 U.S.C. § 107, through which Congress, in 1976, codified the common law doctrine of fair use. Section 107 enumerates four non-exclusive "factors to be considered" in assessing fair use; they are intended to guide but not to limit analysis. H.R.Rep. No. 94–1476 at 5680; see also Harper & Row Publishers, 471 U.S. 539, 560, 105 S.Ct. 2218, 2230, 85 L.Ed.2d 588 (1985) (four factors "not meant to be exclusive"). In determining whether the use made of a work in any particular case is a fair use, the factors to be considered shall include:

(1) the purpose and character of the use, including whether such use is of a commercial nature or is for nonprofit educational purposes;

(2) the nature of the copyrighted work;

(3) the amount and substantiality of the portion used in relation to the copyrighted work as a whole; and

(4) the effect of the use upon the potential market for or value of the copyrighted work.

The first factor is "the purpose and character of the use, including whether such use is of a commercial nature or is for nonprofit purposes." 17 U.S.C. § 107(1). If the consumer were making a commercial or profit-making use of the copyrighted work, that use would be presumptively unfair. *Sony,* 464 U.S. at 449, 104 S.Ct. at 792. "The contrary presumption is appropriate here, however, * * * because time-shifting for private home use must be characterized as a non-commercial, nonprofit activity." *Sony,* 464 U.S. at 449, 104 S.Ct. at 792. Likewise, a family's use of a Game Genie for private home enjoyment must be characterized as a non-commercial, nonprofit activity. The game owner is simply playing the game purchased for personal enjoyment, not exploiting the game in some commercial venture. The first factor therefore establishes a presumption of fair use, which could be overcome only by Nintendo's direct proof of injury.[6]

The Midway decision does not analyze the commercial use of such products vis-a-vis private home use. By contrast, this Court finds a convincing and persuasive analogy in the trial court's analysis of legislative intent in *Universal City Studios v. Sony Corp. of America,* 480 F.Supp. 429 (C.D.Cal.1979). That court, in discussing whether or not home recording of copyrighted works violated the Copyright Act, quoted the following from the House Report accompanying the 1971 Amendment:

> "Specifically, it is not the intention of the Committee to restrain the home recording, from broadcasts or from tapes or records, of recorded performances, where the home recording is for private use and with no purpose of reproducing or otherwise capitalizing commercially on it." H.R.Rep. No. 487, 92nd Cong., First Sess. 7, reprinted in 1971 U.S.Code Cong. & Admin.News at 1566–1572.

Further citations to the Congressional Record acknowledged a reluctance to interpret or enforce the Copyright Act by carrying copyright protection into the home or by banning devices for off-the-air recording. Id., at 445, 104 S.Ct. at 790. While the Game Genie is a different device than a video home recorder, it involves the same policy decision, i.e., whether Congress wishes to carry copyright enforcement into the home.

2. The Second Factor: The Published "Nature" Of Video Games Supports Fair Use.

The second factor considers "the nature of the copyrighted work." 17 U.S.C. § 107(2). The courts have traditionally inquired whether the

6. Although Nintendo emphasized the "productive use" doctrine, Sony minimized the importance of that doctrine by reversing the Ninth Circuit's conclusion that time-shifting "was not a fair use because it was not a 'productive use.'" *Sony* 464 U.S. at 427, 104 S.Ct. at 781; see also Fisher, Reconstructing The Fair Use Doctrine, 101 Harv.L.Rev. 1661, 1684 (1988) ("The most dramatic change wrought by Sony and Harper & Row in the fair use doctrine was the subordination of the idea of productivity").

work is published, with unpublished works gaining more protection. 3 Nimmer § 13.05[A][2], at 13–75 to 13–79. "The fact that a work is unpublished is a critical element of its 'nature'" suggesting that pre-publication exploitation of the work would be unfair. Harper & Row, 471 U.S. at 564, 105 S.Ct. at 2232 (unfair to scoop key excerpts of unpublished manuscript without author's consent). By contrast, Nintendo has already published millions of copies of its games to anyone willing to pay the purchase price. Only after acquiring a published copy of the game may its owner use it in combination with the Game Genie. The works' published nature supports the fairness of the use.

3. The Third Factor: Because Game Owners Have The Right To Use The Games They Purchase, Their Use Does Not Weigh Against Fair Use.

The third factor in the fair use analysis is the "amount and substantiality of the portion used in relation to the copyrighted work as a whole." 17 U.S.C. § 107(3). Again, the *Sony* decision is dispositive. Sony recognized that the reproduction of an entire work ordinarily weighs against the claim of fair use. 464 U.S. at 450, 104 S.Ct. at 792. In Sony, however, because the VCR owner "had been invited to witness [the television program] in its entirety free of charge, the fact that the entire work is reproduced does not have its ordinary effect of militating against a finding of fair use." Id. at 449, 104 S.Ct. at 792. Likewise, in this action a game owner who has fairly acquired a Nintendo game has a right to use the entire work. The game owner's rights are equal to, if not greater than, those of the user in *Sony,* who did not pay for the product being used. Because the game owner is entitled to use the entire work, no matter what the "amount and substantiality" of his use, the third factor cannot assist Nintendo in overcoming the presumption of fair use.

4. The Fourth Factor: Nintendo Has Not Proven Harm.

The last and "undoubtedly the single most important" factor is the "effect of the use upon the potential market for or value of the copyrighted work." *Harper & Row,* 471 U.S. at 566, 105 S.Ct. at 2233; 17 U.S.C. § 107(4). To defeat fair use under this factor "requires proof either that the particular use is harmful, or that if it should become widespread, it would adversely affect the potential market for the copyrighted work." *Sony,* 464 U.S. at 451, 104 S.Ct. at 793.

Nintendo bears the burden of proving that these particular uses will have an adverse effect on the market for the copyrighted Nintendo games. *Sony,* 464 U.S. at 451, 104 S.Ct. at 793. It has not met that burden, for the reasons explained below.

a. Nintendo Has Not Shown That The Game Genie Supplants, Rather Than Suppresses, The Market For The Copyrighted Works.

The fourth fair use factor looks primarily to whether a use "supplants any part of the normal market for a copyrighted work."

H.R.Rep. No. 83, 90th Congress, 1st Sess. 33, 35 (1967), as quoted in *Marcus v. Rowley,* 695 F.2d 1171, 1177 (9th Cir.1983). Nintendo cannot demonstrate that use of the Game Genie "fulfills the demand for the original" of the copyrighted games at issue. *Fisher v. Dees,* 794 F.2d 432, 438 (9th Cir.1986) (emphasis in original). Widespread use of the Game Genie cannot supplant the market for the games in suit. The Game Genie cannot operate without a game cartridge. Significantly, Nintendo does not contend that families will buy fewer new games because they are using their Game Genie with old ones. The Game Genie does not compete for sales with the original copyrighted works for which Nintendo claims infringement.

Nintendo's claim is that the Game Genie will indirectly harm its overall market because it will make people enjoy their games less, and thereby generally reduce demand for Nintendo's copyrighted games. Nintendo had the burden of proof on that issue and failed to meet it.

A fair use will frequently suppress demand for a work, but as long as it does so without supplanting demand, the indirect detrimental effect on the market is not the subject of copyright protection. An obvious example is an unfavorable book or movie review containing quotations from the copyrighted work, along with criticism which may suppress demand. This capacity to injure does not impede a finding of fair use. See *Fisher v. Dees,* 794 F.2d at 438. Another example is a parody, which "may quite legitimately aim at garroting the original, destroying it commercially as well as artistically." Id. at 437. As the Ninth Circuit holds, however, "the economic effect of [the use] with which we are concerned is not its potential to destroy or diminish the market for the original—any bad review can have that effect—but rather whether it fulfills the demand for the original. Biting criticism suppresses demand; copyright infringement usurps it." Id. at 438 (emphasis in original).

The Second Circuit applied this principle in *Consumers Union of U.S. Inc. v. General Signal Corp.,* 724 F.2d 1044 (2d Cir.1983), cert. denied 469 U.S. 823, 105 S.Ct. 100, 83 L.Ed.2d 45 (1984). There, defendant's advertisements quoted the favorable rating of its product by Consumer Reports, a copyrighted magazine. In an argument reminiscent of Nintendo's claim that it will lose "goodwill" as a result of the Game Genie, Consumer Reports alleged that the value of its magazine was diminished because its reputation for independence would suffer as a result of being perceived as endorsing defendant's product. The Second Circuit rejected plaintiff's argument in no uncertain terms:

> The Copyright Act was not designed to prevent such indirect negative effects of copying. The fourth factor is aimed at the copier who attempts to usurp the demand for the original work. The copyright laws are intended to prevent copiers from taking the owner's intellectual property, and are not aimed at recompensing damages which may flow indirectly from copying.

Nintendo argues that its market may be affected by suppression of demand rather than supplanting of it. That injury, even if it were likely, does not defeat fair use.

b. Nintendo Has Not Shown Any Injury to the Relevant Market for the Copyrighted Works.

Nintendo has likewise failed to prove an adverse effect on the relevant market for the copyrighted works at issue. Most of Nintendo's original copyrighted works are no longer on the market, including the vast majority for which the Galoob Code Book lists codes. The Game Genie cannot affect sales of products no longer available.[7]

Nintendo also seeks relief for harm that may occur in the future, on the grounds that the Game Genie may decrease demand for sequels or slightly altered versions of Nintendo games. Nintendo has not, to date, issued or considered issuing altered versions of existing games. Nintendo argues, however, that should such a market develop within the copyright period, it is entitled to decide if such games are appropriate and to reap the resulting revenues. In theory, Nintendo is correct; however, it has failed to show the reasonable likelihood of such a market. Nintendo's video games are expensive toys; each retails in the $40 to $50 range. There is neither evidence nor reason to believe that a consumer who owns the original game would invest a similar amount in a slight variation thereof.

In addition, Nintendo's assertion that it may wish to re-release altered versions of the games in suit 10, 20 or 30 years from now (much as Parker Brothers recently did with "Monopoly") is at odds with the position taken by Nintendo in various other lawsuits pending before this Court. In those actions, Nintendo opposes antitrust claims by using the vagaries of the video game industry to rebut the impact and permanence of its market control, if any. Having indoctrinated this Court as to the fast pace and instability of the video game industry, Nintendo may not now, without any data, redefine that market in its request for the extraordinary remedy sought herein. Nintendo has failed to show any harm to the present market for its copyrighted games and has failed to establish the reasonable likelihood of a potential market for slightly altered versions of the games at suit. While good board games may never die, good video games are mortal.

c. Nintendo Has Not Shown That Any Uses of the Game Genie Would Have a Deleterious Effect On Sales.

The only empirical evidence of market reaction to the Game Genie is the Canadian study, which indicates that the Game Genie will enhance not detract from, Nintendo's sales. See *Sony,* 464 U.S. at 423–24, 452–53 n. 36–37, 104 S.Ct. at 779–80, 793–94 n. 36–37 (relying on consumer survey to determine market impact). During February of this year, 6 months after introduction of the Genie in Canada, a market

7. Furthermore, even if the Game Genie published code books for up-to-the-minute games, Nintendo has not shown that consumers would be less likely to buy the games simply because code books for current games were available.

research firm polled 300 Canadian owners of the Game Genie, aged 8 or older. The survey failed to reveal any detrimental effect to the Nintendo market.[8]

Nintendo objected to the survey on various grounds, including the fact that Canadians, not Americans, were polled. Nintendo's criticisms go to the weight of the survey, not its admissibility. Nintendo offered no meaningful evidence that consumer research in the United States is performed differently from that conducted in Canada, or that consumers who play video games in the United States have different tastes or attitudes than do video game players in Canada. Nintendo has access to its own sales data for the nine months Game Genie has been on sale in Canada. Nevertheless, it produced neither statistical evidence of lost sales nor any Canadian retailer testimony of adverse impact from Game Genie on the demand for Nintendo games. The Court is influenced by Nintendo's failure to proffer any empirical evidence of a negative market impact or potential impact from the Game Genie. The only reasonable inference for the trier of fact is that no such impact exists.

Nintendo failed to take advantage of other opportunities to show lost sales. For instance, Nintendo uses ongoing focus groups as part of its continuing marketing and quality control. It could have used those groups to test the effect of Game Genie use on attitudes about Nintendo games. It did not. Since Nintendo had the incentive, opportunity and ability to proffer such evidence, its failure to do so gives rise to the contrary inference, i.e., that there are no material differences between the Canadian and American markets, and that the Game Genie has had no detrimental impact on Nintendo's sales in Canada.

Galoob's evidence on sales was persuasive. In addition to the survey data, Galoob proffered expert testimony from Glenn Rubenstein, a member of Nintendo's "target" market (males between 8 and 14 years old). He has been a serious player of video games for several years and spends as many as 30 hours per week with this avocation. He has written numerous magazine and newspaper articles critiquing various video games, including Nintendo's. Rubenstein's opinion is that the Game Genie would encourage rather than discourage enthusiasm over video games in general, because it allows players to explore new ways of playing a game, thereby making the game more accessible to players of differing abilities. This would likely increase the use of a video game in a multi-player family, providing more value per consumer dollar. The Court found his testimony more convincing than that of Nintendo's employees and experts.

8. 72% of the respondents believe that the Game Genie makes video games more fun. 45% enjoy playing their games more than before they had a Game Genie, 53% enjoy their games the same, only 2% enjoy their games less. 52% are more interested in buying new video games since they have had the Game Genie, and only 2% are less interested. 29% of the respondents play their Nintendo games more often than before they had a Game Genie, 67% play their games the same amount, and only 4% play their games less often.

For these reasons, the Court is unconvinced that the Game Genie will decrease Nintendo's sales.

d. Harm to the Nintendo Culture Is Not Cognizable Under Copyright Law.

Nintendo's main objection to and claimed damage from the Game Genie is the potential detriment to the "Nintendo Culture," a concept discussed at length by Nintendo's attorneys and witnesses. This culture, the apex of Nintendo's marketing strategy, is a mind-set intentionally created by Nintendo in its consumers. Like most cults, fads or addictions, it thrives when fueled by constant peer pressure. Nintendo fears that, by allowing users to change the rules of Nintendo games, the Game Genie will upset the inculturation process that Nintendo has designed into its products, thereby lessening the value of membership in "the culture" and reducing product loyalty. Having rescued the video game industry from the shambles of the early 1980s, Nintendo argues that it is now entitled to decide how its games should be enjoyed, by whom, and under what circumstances, even after the consumer has paid full price.

According to Nintendo, the Game Genie will harm the Nintendo culture in two distinct ways. First, it argues that the use of the Game Genie allows players to modify Nintendo's carefully crafted games in such a way that ultimate user satisfaction will be diminished, leading to an over-all decline in the video game industry. Nintendo called several witnesses, including its own game designers and two behavior modification psychologists, each of whom opined that 1) Nintendo's games are designed to provide ultimate satisfaction; 2) tampering with Nintendo's design in any way thwarts the "challenge of the game", or its "playability", thereby resulting in lesser enthusiasm for video games in general, and Nintendo games in particular; and 3) this reduced enjoyment may lead to the drastic decline in the video game market similar to that which occurred in the early 1980s, even if it does not diminish revenue for the particular games in suit.[9] Neither the Nintendo employees nor the behavioralists provided empirical data upon which to support the claim that Nintendo is better able to judge when a player is having fun than is the player herself.

9. For instance, Nintendo's expert Professor Gregory Loftus declared:

> The majority of Nintendo's players belong to a loose social confederation that might collectively be called the 'Nintendo culture.' This culture includes talking about Nintendo video games with friends, comparing scores and achievements, * * * and getting high scores published. The operation of the Nintendo culture rests entirely on the games being challenging * * *.
>
> Being part of the Nintendo culture would no longer be enjoyable or meaningful, and sales of Nintendo video games would decline * * *. Were Game Genie use to become prevalent, the photographing of a particular screen [to show a high score] would not be indicative of any skill or achievement, and this socially-reinforcing practice would fall by the wayside.

G. Loftus narr. stmnt at 3; see also P. Main narr. stmnt at 3; H. Lincoln narr. stmnt at 17; H. Phillips narr. stmnt at 6.

There is no doubt that Nintendo revitalized the video game industry, nor is there any doubt that it produces a carefully controlled and well-made product which is impressively marketed. Nevertheless, those achievements do not give Nintendo a right to expand its copyright protection beyond that granted under the copyright laws.

Moreover, Nintendo's argument that any device that makes game play easier will injure its market for video games is undermined by its own behavior. It is significant that Nintendo markets publications and devices that make similar modifications available. For example, Nintendo publishes "passwords" enabling game owners to start game play at different levels or worlds and with different powers. Nintendo Power magazine [10] contains "secret" codes which allow game owners to skip to portions of games they enjoy, or to gain additional lives. Nintendo also markets an interactive device called the "NES Advantage," which can substitute for the controller included with the standard Nintendo system. Among the advantages that NES Advantage provides are the options of slow motion play and extra fire power to make game play easier. These are similar to options that Game Genie makes available to players. The fact that Nintendo offers consumers the ability to temporarily alter the images of their games undercuts Nintendo's arguments that such alterations are likely to create disincentive for the purchase of additional video games. If Nintendo believed this, it would not market accessories which it feared would lead to the demise of its multibillion dollar share of the video game industry.[11]

Nintendo has attempted to achieve in this litigation what it could not achieve in the market—the "exclusive right to modify game play as it alone sees fit and to maintain game play in its original state." Nintendo's Reply Memo. In Supp.Prelim.Injunc. at 17–18. This Court does not interpret the Copyright Act as bestowing such broad monopoly powers. The Copyright Act protects authorship, not market psychology.

5. Fair use summarized

To summarize the four fair use factors, then, the non-commercial nature of the player's home use of the Game Genie creates a presumption of fair use under Sony. The published nature of video games supports the fairness of a consumer's transitory alterations of those

10. The magazine is copyrighted by Nintendo of America.

11. Indeed, Nintendo's chief marketing officer, Peter Main, contradicts the theory that Nintendo asserts in this case. In the analysis he presented at a 1989 Nintendo sales meeting, Mr. Main stated:

> Let's not forget that key category called accessories. Good accessories are important for several reasons including * * * because they give added value to our software by giving an NES player a whole new experience and sense of game play when he replays a piece of software with one of the accessor[ies]. And all that adds up to increased consumer satisfaction which brings them back for more. Two of the strongest performers in this regard are the Max and Advantage controllers * * *.

Text of speech delivered at the 1989 SCES sales meeting, June 2, 1989, Ex. G–364 (emphasis added).

images. Because the game owner has the indisputable right to use his or her entire game, the amount of his or her use cannot weigh against fairness. Further, Nintendo has failed, in three respects, to carry its burden to prove injury: It has not shown that any use supplants demand for its works, that any actual or reasonably likely market is injured, or that use of the Game Genie in ways that arguably infringe Nintendo's copyrights would diminish the overall demand for Nintendo games. Lacking proof that either actual or likely markets for the copyrighted works are liable to be affected, Nintendo has failed to satisfy the fourth fair use factor.

In short, even were the Court to find that the use of the Game Genie allows players to produce a derivative work, the shield of fair use is available and would provide a complete defense to any claim of direct infringement against the game players. Absent direct infringement, there is no contributory infringement.

III. Direct Infringement

Because the Game Genie does not create a derivative work when used in conjunction with a copyrighted video game, Galoob does not "authorize the use of a copyrighted work without actual authority from the copyright owner." Sony, 464 U.S. at 435 n. 17. All of the cases Nintendo cites on this point deal with unauthorized public performances for profit, § 106(4), not private, non-commercial use. Further, Galoob is not liable as a direct infringer for testing, demonstrating, and marketing the Game Genie, or for developing codes for use with the Game Genie.

IV. Injunctive Relief

Even had this Court found that the Game Genie infringes Nintendo's copyrights, a permanent injunction in favor of Nintendo would not be the appropriate remedy because:

(1) Any presumption of immediate and irreparable harm resulting from the alleged infringement was rebutted;

(2) The presence of the Game Genie in the market benefits the public by expanding personal consumer utilization of purchased games; and

(3) Assuming infringement, adequate remedies exist at law.

Conclusion

For the reasons stated above, the Court orders declaratory relief as follows: (1) the use of a Game Genie by consumers, for non-commercial use, does not violate Nintendo's rights under the Copyright Act of 1976; and (2) Galoob is neither a contributory nor a direct infringer.

* * *

E. LIMITATIONS ON THE EXCLUSIVE RIGHTS

COPYRIGHT ACT OF 1976

§ 109. Limitations on exclusive rights: Effect of transfer of particular copy or phonorecord

(a) Notwithstanding the provisions of section 106(3), the owner of a particular copy or phonorecord lawfully made under this title, or any person authorized by such owner, is entitled, without the authority of the copyright owner, to sell or otherwise dispose of the possession of that copy or phonorecord.

(b)(1)(A) Notwithstanding the provisions of subsection (a), unless authorized by the owners of copyright in the sound recording or the owner of copyright in a computer program (including any tape, disk, or other medium embodying such program), and in the case of a sound recording in the musical works embodied therein, neither the owner of a particular phonorecord nor any person in possession of a particular copy of a computer program (including any tape, disk, or other medium embodying such program), may, for the purposes of direct or indirect commercial advantage, dispose of, or authorize the disposal of, the possession of that phonorecord or computer program (including any tape, disk, or other medium embodying such program) by rental, lease, or lending, or by any other act or practice in the nature of rental, lease, or lending. Nothing in the preceding sentence shall apply to the rental, lease, or lending of a phonorecord for nonprofit purposes by a nonprofit library or nonprofit educational institution. The transfer of possession of a lawfully made copy of a computer program by a nonprofit educational institution to another nonprofit educational institution or to faculty, staff, and students does not constitute rental, lease, or lending for direct or indirect commercial purposes under this subsection.

(B) This subsection does not apply to—

(i) a computer program which is embodied in a machine or product and which cannot be copied during the ordinary operation or use of the machine or product; or

(ii) a computer program embodied in or used in conjunction with a limited purpose computer that is designed for playing video games and may be designed for other purposes.

(C) Nothing in this subsection affects any provision of chapter 9 of this title.

(2)(A) Nothing in this subsection shall apply to the lending of a computer program for nonprofit purposes by a nonprofit library, if each copy of a computer program which is lent by such library has affixed to the packaging containing the program a warning of copyright in accordance with requirements that the Register of Copyrights shall prescribe by regulation.

(B) Not later than three years after the date of the enactment of the computer Software Rental Amendments Act of 1990, and at such times thereafter as the Register of Copyright considers appropriate, the Register of Copyrights, after consultation with representatives of copyright owners and librarians, shall submit to the Congress a report stating whether this paragraph has achieved its intended purpose of maintaining the integrity of the copyright system while providing nonprofit libraries the capability to fulfill their function. Such report shall advise the Congress as to any information or recommendations that the Register of Copyrights considers necessary to carry out the purposes of this subsection."; and

(3) Nothing in this subsection shall affect any provision of the antitrust laws. For purposes of the preceding sentence, 'antitrust laws' has the meaning given that term in the first section of the Clayton Act and includes section 5 of the Federal Trade Commission Act to the extent that section relates to unfair methods of competition.

(4) Any person who distributes a phonorecord or a copy of a computer program (including any tape, disk, or other medium embodying such program) in violation of paragraph (1) is an infringer of copyright under section 501 of this title and is subject to the remedies set forth in sections 502, 503, 504, 505, and 509. Such violation shall not be a criminal offense under section 506 or cause such person to be subject to the criminal penalties set forth in section 2319 of title 18.

(c) Notwithstanding the provisions of section 106(5), the owner of a particular copy lawfully made under this title, or any person authorized by such owner, is entitled, without the authority of the copyright owner, to display that copy publicly, either directly or by the projection of no more than one image at a time, to viewers present at the place where the copy is located.

(d) The privileges prescribed by subsections (a) and (c) do not, unless authorized by the copyright owner, extend to any person who has acquired possession of the copy or phonorecord from the copyright owner, by rental, lease, loan, or otherwise, without acquiring ownership of it.

(e) Notwithstanding the provisions of sections 106(4) and 106(5), in the case of an electronic audiovisual game intended for use in coin-operated equipment, the owner of a particular copy of such a game lawfully made under this title, is entitled, without the authority of the copyright owner of the game, to publicly perform or display that game in coin-operated equipment, except that this subsection shall not apply to any work of authorship embodied in the audiovisual game if the copyright owner of the electronic audiovisual game is not also the copyright owner of the work of authorship.

Notes and Questions

1. Section 109 of the Copyright Act gives the lawful owner of a copy of a copyrighted work extensive rights with respect to that copy. In particular the owner has the right to rent the copy to others. Three groups, the audio, video, and software industries, lobbied for exceptions to rental rights. The audio and software lobbies easily succeeded in persuading Congress that many people were renting their products so as to make illegal copies. The video industry was less successful, because the vast majority of people who rent video cassettes do not make copies. Congress added the prohibitions against audio and software rentals in 1990 amendments to the Copyright Act.

2. Video rental stores won the continued right to rent out video games. The stores argued that it is virtually impossible for the average renter to copy video games made for home video game machines.

3. The anti-rental amendments incorporated an exception to allow computer hardware rental. All personal computers contain some software built into the machine to handle the interface between computer programs and the machine hardware. This software is usually stored on ROMs, which are difficult to copy. Congress exempted this type of software to avoid burdening the computer rental business. The continued existence of the computer rental business, however, creates a continued need for software rental. Businesses that rent computers also need to rent software with the computers. What sort of arrangements can software companies and rental organizations now make to meet these legitimate needs while avoiding the risk of illegal copying?

4. Ownership of a copyrighted work does not give the right of public display. You may have a legal copy of the movie "Casablanca" in your home collection of videos. The copyright law lets you watch it with your family and friends. However, § 106 of the copyright act requires permission of the copyright owner before you can "publicly" display an "audiovisual work." So you may not show your copy of "Casablanca" to the public in a movie theater unless you have permission from the copyright owner. In *Red Baron–Franklin Park, Inc. v. Taito Corp.*, 883 F.2d 275 (4th Cir. 1989), the court held that video game emporia were engaged in public display of copyrighted works and so were violating the rights of the owners of the copyrights in the games. Congress nullified this holding in revised § 109(e). Copyright lawyers therefore call § 109(e) the "anti-Red-Baron" provision.

COPYRIGHT ACT OF 1976

§ 117. Limitations on exclusive rights: Computer programs

Notwithstanding the provisions of section 106, it is not an infringement for the owner of a copy of a computer program to make or authorize the making of another copy or adaptation of that computer program provided:

(1) that such a new copy or adaptation is created as an essential step in the utilization of the computer program in conjunction with a machine and that it is used in no other manner, or

(2) that such new copy or adaptation is for archival purposes only and that all archival copies are destroyed in the event that continued possession of the computer program should cease to be rightful.

Any exact copies prepared in accordance with the provisions of this section may be leased, sold, or otherwise transferred, along with the copy from which such copies were prepared, only as part of the lease, sale, or other transfer of all rights in the program. Adaptations so prepared may be transferred only with the authorization of the copyright owner.

ATARI, INC. v. JS & A GROUP, INC.

United States District Court, Northern District of Illinois, 1983.
597 F.Supp. 5.

DECKER, DISTRICT JUDGE.

This is a suit for declaratory and injunctive relief and for damages for contributory copyright infringement, patent infringement, unfair competition, and various state law torts. The plaintiff, Atari, Inc. ("Atari"), brought this suit because the defendant, JS & A, Inc., ("JS & A") sells and advertises a device called the "PROM BLASTER". The case is before the court on plaintiff's motion for a preliminary injunction on the copyright infringement claim.

FACTUAL BACKGROUND

Atari manufactures and sells a home computer video game system, the "2600", and game cartridges such as "CENTIPEDE" and "PAC–MAN" for use in the 2600. In order to play the games at home, the consumer connects the Atari computer to a television set and plugs his controls, or "joysticks", into the computer. A game cartridge, which is usually purchased separately, is then inserted into the computer. The computer program in the cartridge causes the audiovisual aspects of the game to emanate from the television. The 2600 has been a resounding commercial success.

The various game cartridges consist of a heavy plastic housing which contains an electronic circuit, or "chip", which in turn contains the game's computer program. The chips in Atari 2600 game cartridges are "Ready Only Memory", or "ROM", chips. The parties have stipulated that a ROM can neither be reprogrammed nor erased. The game cartridges sell for as much as $40 apiece.

Atari has copyrighted its video games as audiovisual works. In addition, it is seeking to register a copyright of the computer program for the CENTIPEDE game. Plaintiff's Exhibit D.

JS & A is a retailer of electronic products. It began this fall an effort to market its PROM BLASTER, a device for the duplication of those video games which are compatible with the Atari 2600 home computer. The machine has two slots, one for a 2600–compatible cartridge and one for a blank cartridge sold by JS & A for $10. In the words of JS & A's advertisements, "[y]ou simply plug in your Atari© or Activision© cartridge in one slot and a blank cartridge in another, press a button and three minutes later you've created an exact duplicate." Plaintiff's Exhibit A. The PROM BLASTER sells for $119, and JS & A currently has $12,000 in inventory on hand. The defendant agreed not to fill any orders for the product pending the disposition of this motion.

JS & A markets the PROM BLASTER primarily as a means of making "back-up" copies of 2600–compatible games. The advertisements urge the consumer to protect his investment in video game cartridges which "can easily be ruined." Plaintiff's Exhibit A. The advertisements assure the public that this copying does not violate the copyright laws because "[i]n 1980, Congress passed an amendment to the copyright act that clearly permitted consumers to duplicate their cartridges" but warn that "[y]ou can't sell, lease or give away a duplicate cartridge produced from a copyrighted original that you own." *Id.* A related selling point for the PROM BLASTER is that the buyer "can make copies for [his] friends who wish to own archival copies of their favorite games and charge them for the service." *Id.*

JS & A also sells nine 2600–compatible video games of its own. JS & A grants the purchaser of a PROM BLASTER the right to copy the games, and even to sell the copies, without any limitation.

Atari alleges that any copying of its video games infringes its copyrights, even if the consumer does it for "archival purposes." Atari also contends that "[t]he purpose and effect of JS & A's acts are actively to induce, cause, and materially contribute to the making of infringing copies of ATARI's copyrighted home video games." Complaint at ¶ 5. Atari seeks a preliminary injunction against JS & A to prevent the use, advertising, offering for sale, and the sale of the PROM BLASTER and the blank cartridges.

Discussion

To establish its right to a preliminary injunction, Atari must show that it is likely to prevail on the merits, that it will suffer irreparable harm if the injunction does not issue, that the balance of hardships is in its favor, and that granting the injunction is in the public interest.

1. Likelihood of Success on the Merits

Atari's copyright claim against JS & A is for contributory infringement. "[O]ne who, with knowledge of the infringing activity, induces, causes or materially contributes to the infringing conduct of another, may be held liable as a 'contributory' infringer." *Gershwin Publishing Corp. v. Columbia Artists Management, Inc.*, 443 F.2d 1159, 1162 (2d Cir.1971) (footnote omitted). JS & A raises no issue as to its knowledge or encouragement of the use of the PROM BLASTER to copy copyrighted Atari and other 2600–compatible video games. The defendant argues instead that the copying of those games is legal and, even if it is not, the court may not enjoin the sale of the PROM BLASTER because it has other, legal uses.

Whether the copying of others' video games is an infringing activity is an issue the court discusses in detail below. Here, it must be noted that if JS & A is wrong, and such copying does infringe, its misinterpretation of the Copyright Act is no defense to a charge of contributory infringement. *Universal City Studios v. Sony Corp. of America,* 659 F.2d 963, 975 (9th Cir.1981), *cert. granted,* 457 U.S. 1116, 102 S.Ct. 2926, 73 L.Ed.2d 1328 (1982). Furthermore, it is not enough for JS & A to establish that the PROM BLASTER has *a* legal use. The machine must have a *substantial* noninfringing use to preclude an injunction against its sale.

The PROM BLASTER can perform only two functions: copy others' video games or duplicate JS & A's own games. JS & A argues that the later use, which is of course noninfringing, is enough. This argument fails because that use is not substantial. JS & A markets only nine games. Since they evidently went on the market with the PROM BLASTER, quite recently, no one knows if consumers want to play these games, much less copy them. Furthermore, PROM BLASTERS sell for $119. It strains credulity to assert that consumers would spend that much for a machine that could only copy JS & A's games. This capability of the PROM BLASTER is by itself insufficient to make its sale legal.

JS & A's liability as a contributory infringer thus turns ultimately on the legality of the primary use of the machine, that which JS & A encourages with its advertisements, the duplication of others' video games. This is the machine's only substantial use, and if it is an infringing use the PROM BLASTER is fatally limited.

Section 106 of the Copyright Act details the exclusive rights of copyright owners, and it states in relevant part:

> "Subject to sections 107 through 118, the owner of copyright under this title has the exclusive right to do and to authorize any of the following:
>
> (1) To reproduce the copyrighted work in copies. * * * "

17 U.S.C. § 106. Absent an exception, therefore, the duplication of Atari's copyrighted games is an infringement of its rights. Atari is likely to prevail unless JS & A can establish that an exception applies. JS & A has the burden because it "claims the benefits of an exception to the prohibition of a statute." *United States v. First City National Bank,* 386 U.S. 361, 366, 87 S.Ct. 1088, 18 L.Ed.2d 151 (1966); *accord, Federal Trade Commission v. Morton Salt Co.,* 334 U.S. 37, 44–45, 68 S.Ct. 822, 827, 92 L.Ed. 1196 (1948).

The exception on which JS & A seeks to rely is the new § 117 of the Copyright Act, which was enacted in 1980 to replace the original § 117. That provision states in relevant part:

> "Notwithstanding the provisions of section 106, it is not an infringement for the owner of a copy of a computer program to make or

> authorize the making of another copy or adaptation of that computer program provided:
>
> * * *
>
> "(2) that any such new copy or adaptation is for archival purposes only and that all archival copies are destroyed in the event that the continued possession of the computer program should cease to be rightful."

17 U.S.C. § 117. This "archival exception," according to JS & A, legalizes the PROM BLASTER and its use in making back-up copies.

Apparently, no other court has interpreted § 117, and the legislative history is scant. Congress' only statement is that the section "embodies the recommendations of the Commission on New Technological Works ["the Commission"] with respect to clarifying the law of copyright of computer software." H.R.Rep. No. 96–1307 (Part I), *reprinted in* 1980 U.S.Code Congressional and Administrative News 6460, 6482.

Congress created the Commission in 1974 to study copyright problems with respect to computers and photocopying and to make recommendations for statutory changes. The Final Report of the Commission ("CONTU Report") sets forth and explains those recommendations, which Congress in 1980 adopted. * * *

The CONTU Report does provide some guidance in that it explains the limited purpose of the archival exception:

> "One who rightfully possesses a copy of a program, therefore, should be provided with a legal right to copy it to that extent which will permit its use by that possessor. This would include the right to load it into a computer and *to prepare archival copies of it to guard against destruction or damage by mechanical or electrical failure.* But this permission would not extend to other copies of the program."

CONTU Report at 31 (emphasis added). The purpose of the exception is to protect the use of a copy against a particular type of risk: "destruction or damage by mechanical or electrical failure." The parties accept that this is the purpose of the exception. They disagree, however, as to the applicability of the exception to computer programs embodied in ROMs.

Computer programs are stored in a wide variety of media. Not all of these are subject to the same risks, and not all are subject to mechanical or electrical failure. For example, the instructions of the program can be printed on paper in a human-readable form. CONTU report at 55. That piece of paper could be burned or shredded, yet it could not be destroyed by mechanical or electrical failure. The medium of storage must, therefore, determine whether the archival exception applies. Where, and only where, a medium may be destroyed by mechanical or electrical failure, the archival exception protects the owners of programs stored in that medium by granting them the right to make backup copies.

The parties stipulated at the December 1 hearing in this case that the programs in ROMs can be neither reprogrammed nor erased. Atari concludes from this that the programs are not susceptible to destruction or damage through mechanical or electrical failure. JS & A disagrees, and argues that ROMs can be destroyed "as a result of a wire becoming disconnected, liquid spillage, crushing, etc." Defendant's Brief at 3. In support of its argument, JS & A offered Exhibit 1, a letter from a customer who wrote that four of his cartridges "died." Defendant's Exhibit 1 at 2. The customer did not, however, specify the cause of death. This is the only evidence JS & A presented as to the nature of the danger to the ROMs, despite the court's invitation on December 1 to present expert or other testimony on this point.

The court concludes that JS & A has not met its burden of bringing itself within the § 117 exception. The dangers to ROMs presented by JS & A are *physical* dangers not unlike the risk that a handwritten computer program will be shredded accidentally. Virtually every copy of a copyrighted work, be it a book, a phonograph record, or a videotape, faces that kind of risk. Yet Congress did not enact a general rule that making back-up copies of copyrighted works would not infringe. Rather, according to the CONTU report, it limited its exception to computer programs which are subject to "destruction or damage by mechanical or electrical failure." Some media must be especially susceptible to this danger. JS & A has simply offered no evidence that a ROM in a 2600–compatible video game cartridge is such a medium.

In sum, the PROM BLASTER would have a substantial noninfringing use only if it could legally be used to make archival copies of copyrighted 2600–compatible video games. That use is legal only if the § 117 exception applies, and JS & A has the burden of showing that it does. JS & A has not done so. The court must conclude, therefore, that Atari is likely to prevail on its arguments that the exception does not apply, that the PROM BLASTER has no substantial noninfringing use, and that its sale should be enjoined.

2. *Irreparable Harm*

In seeking a preliminary injunction on its copyright infringement claim, Atari's burden to show irreparable harm is "very light." *Midway Mfg. Co. v. Artic International Co.,* 547 F.Supp. at 1014. "In fact, if the plaintiff can show probable success on the merits, the requisite irreparable injury is normally presumed." *Id.* (citations omitted).

Atari has amply demonstrated that it will suffer irreparable harm if this injunction does not issue. The development, production and marketing of its copyrighted 2600–compatible video games represents an investment by Atari of "hundreds of millions of dollars." Second Aff. of Charles S. Paul at 2. JS & A markets the PROM BLASTER primarily as a means of copying those video games, and Atari has shown that such copying is likely an infringement of its copyrights. If JS & A sells the PROM BLASTER and the buyers put it to its intended and encouraged use, it is at least a fair inference that Atari will lose some sales, even if the copies thus made merely replace damaged copies. Because consumers do the copying, Atari can never know the extent of the copying or the extent of its loss. Those lost sales constitute immediate, irreparable harm sufficient to support the issuance of a preliminary injunction.

3. Balance of Hardships

The balance of hardships tips in Atari's favor. Against its investment of hundreds of millions of dollars in its video games, JS & A can offer only its $12,000 investment in inventory and potential sales in an undetermined amount. Atari stands to lose much more than JS & A could hope to gain if this injunction does not issue.

4. Public Interest

The public interest in the protection of Atari's copyrights is the reward and encouragement of creative expression. If the defendant could legally infringe Atari's right to make and distribute copies, Atari and other producers of copyrightable material would hesitate to invest in its creation and development. The public interest in preserving the rewards for such investment and thereby encouraging it will be served by issuing this injunction to protect Atari's exclusive § 106 rights under the Copyright Act.

Conclusion

For the reasons stated above, the court grants plaintiff's motion for a preliminary injunction. Defendant JS & A and its agents and servants will be preliminarily enjoined from selling, marketing, distributing or otherwise disposing of PROM BLASTERS. Plaintiff will prepare an appropriate order to submit to the court, and at that time bond will be fixed.

MICRO–SPARC, INC. v. AMTYPE CORP.

United States District Court, District of Massachusetts, 1984.
592 F.Supp. 33.

Garrity, District Judge.

In what may be a case of first impression, we are called upon to decide whether copyrighted computer programs that appear in a magazine published by the copyright owner may be put on disks, duplicated and sold to purchasers of the magazine by a third party.

Plaintiff, Micro–SPARC, Inc., publishes Nibble, a monthly magazine aimed at users of Apple brand computers. Each issue of Nibble, which sells for $3.25, contains twelve to fifteen computer programs that readers may type into their Apple computers and then use. Plaintiff owns the copyrights to these programs, which also are offered for sale on disks to those who choose not to type in the programs themselves, a task that may entail up to 30 hours of tedious work for a single program. The programs on disks are sold by plaintiff for between $20.00 and $30.00 per program.

Defendant, Amtype Corporation, offers a "typing service" to purchasers of Nibble and other similar publications.[3] For a fee of between $7.50 and $10.00 defendant will put on one disk all the programs that appear in an issue of any of these computer magazines. As will become clear, the technique defendant uses to perform its service is significant. The programs from the magazine first are typed into a computer and then are transferred onto a "master disk." Next the programs are copied from the master disk onto blank disks, which then are sent to defendant's customers. By utilizing a master disk, defendant needs to type in each program only once.

Plaintiff claims that defendant's "typing service" constitutes a copyright infringement and seeks injunctive relief and damages. Defendant responds that a recently enacted amendment to the copyright laws, 17 U.S.C. § 117, legalizes its activities. Before us now are cross-motions for summary judgment.[5] We heard oral argument and received comprehensive briefs.

The amendment on which defendant relies states in pertinent part:

> Notwithstanding the provisions of section 106, it is not an infringement for the owner of a copy of a computer program to make or authorize the making of another copy or adaptation of that computer program provided:
>
> (1) that such a new copy [or adaptation] is created as an essential step in the utilization of the computer program in conjunction with a machine and that it is used in no other manner, or
>
> (2) that such copy [or adaptation] is for archival purpose only. * * *

17 U.S.C. § 117.

Both parties agree that a Nibble purchaser is "the owner of a copy of a computer program" appearing in the magazine. The issue is whether he may "authorize the making of another copy" by the defendant under either subsection (1) or (2).

Subsection (1) permits the creation of a copy for a strictly limited purpose: "as an essential step in the utilization of the computer program in conjunction with a machine." Apparently, no other court has interpreted this provision. In our opinion, it refers to the placement of a program into a computer—or, in the jargon of the trade, the "inputting" of it. Inputting a computer program entails the preparation of a copy. 2 *Nimmer on Copyright* ¶ 8.08.[6] Because one must input

3. Defendant maintains, and plaintiff does not seem to contest, that its "typing service" is provided only to purchasers of the magazines. Defendant's sales literature says as much. Defendant also requires its customers to sign a declaration that they have purchased the magazine in which the ordered programs appear. Furthermore, defendant does not supply any instructions with the programs, so its customers need the magazines, which contain the instructions, to use the programs.

5. The court previously denied plaintiff's motions for a temporary restraining order and a preliminary injunction.

6. To illustrate why inputting a program creates a copy, suppose a Nibble program is either typed in manually from the

a program in order to use it, each use constitutes a potential copyright violation. The legislative history of § 117 indicates to us that subsection (1) was enacted simply to permit the rightful possessor of a program to input and use it:

> [T]he placement of a work into a computer is the preparation of a copy. * * * One who rightfully possesses a copy of a program, therefore, should be provided with a legal right to copy it *to that extent which will permit its use* by that possessor. This would include the right to load it into a computer. * * *

Final Report of the National Commission on New Technological Uses of Copyrighted Works ("CONTU Report") at 31 (emphasis added). For example, subsection (1) permits an owner of Nibble programs, whether in the magazine or on disks, to input and use them, by either manually typing in the programs from the magazine or electronically transferring them in from the disks.

The permission to copy stated in subsection (1) is strictly limited to inputting programs. That is the import of the phrase "essential step in the utilization of the computer program" that appears in the statute and the phrase "to that extent which will permit its use" that appears in the CONTU Report. Subsection (1) does not permit a Nibble purchaser to authorize the defendant to put the programs on a disk for him. In so doing the defendant does not input the programs. It instead creates a disk copy that the *purchaser* then uses to input the programs. Subsection (1) permits the second "input copy" created by the purchaser, not the first disk copy created by the defendant.

In the alternative, defendant relies on the "archival exception" in subsection (2), the purpose of which is "to protect the use of a copy against a particular type of risk: 'destruction or damage by mechanical or electrical failure.'" *Atari, Inc. v. JS & A Group, Inc.*, 597 F.Supp. 5, 9 (N.D.Ill.1983), quoting CONTU Report at 31. Subsection (2) thus permits a Nibble purchaser who, under subsection (1), types in the programs himself to create a disk copy. This is because the typed-in program, which is contained in the computer's memory, is subject to "destruction or damage by mechanical or electrical failure." [8] Subsection (2) does not, however, permit the purchaser to authorize the defendant to put Nibble programs on disks for archival purposes. This is because the purchaser has not first created a "destructable" or "damageable" copy. When a Nibble purchaser orders a disk from the defendant, he possesses the programs as they appear in the magazine.

magazine or transferred in electronically from a disk. After the input is complete, the user has two copies of the program. One is contained in either the magazine or the disk; the other is contained in the computer's memory. This second copy can be displayed on the computer's screen, printed on its typewriter, or transferred onto a blank disk.

8. We need not decide whether one who purchases a program disk from the plaintiff also may make archival copies. Because the program is stored on a disk instead of in the computer's memory, it is less susceptible to destruction or damage by mechanical or electrical failure; however, it is not completely immune from such a mishap.

In this printed form, the programs are susceptible only to physical dangers, such as accidental shredding. However, "virtually every copy of a copyrighted work, be it a book, a phonograph record, or a videotape, faces that kind of risk. Yet Congress did not enact a general rule that making back-up copies of copyrighted works would not infringe. Rather, according to the CONTU Report, it limited its exception to computer programs which are subject to 'destruction or damage by mechanical or electrical failure.'" *Atari, supra* at 10.

Because defendant's activities do not fall within the exceptions provided in § 117(1) and (2), we hold that defendant's copying of the programs appearing in Nibble infringes upon plaintiff's copyright. Plaintiff's motion for summary judgment therefore is allowed and defendant's denied. Defendant, its officers, agents, servants and employees are hereby enjoined from copying, publishing, selling and distributing all or a part of the contents, including computer programs, contained in Volume V, Issues 2 and 3 of Nibble magazine.

* * *

Notes

1. There is no practical way for sellers of inexpensive, mass-marketed software to negotiate licenses with purchasers of the software. Thus § 117 determines the rights of such purchasers. Sellers of expensive software to limited markets do negotiate licenses providing more explicit restrictions on archival copies and program alteration. The terms of these licenses would normally prevail over those of § 117.

2. Among the specific terms found in negotiated licenses are terms forbidding use of reverse engineering techniques to analyze the software. These techniques include "disassembling" and "reverse compiling," both of which are attempts to reconstruct something like the original source code of the program from the object code that the purchaser receives. Presumably § 117 allows use of these techniques where they are necessary for modification of the program. The doctrine of "fair use" may allow students to disassemble or reverse compile programs to see how they work. It may also be "fair use" to disassemble or reverse compile portions of a program in order to gain the information needed to write software which is not competitive, but is compatible. The negotiated terms forbidding disassembly and reverse compiling prevail over the rights that the copyright law would otherwise give the owner of the program, unless the licensee can show copyright misuse by the licensor. See *Lasercomb America, Inc. v. Reynolds,* 911 F.2d 970 (4th Cir.1990).

F. COPYRIGHT FORMALITIES

1. NOTICE

COPYRIGHT ACT OF 1976, § 401

§ 401. Notice of copyright: Visually perceptible copies

(a) General Provisions.—Whenever a work protected under this title is published in the United States or elsewhere by authority of the copyright owner, a notice of copyright as provided by this section may be placed on publicly distributed copies from which the work can be visually perceived, either directly or with the aid of a machine or device.

(b) Form of Notice.—If a notice appears on the copies, it shall consist of the following three elements:

(1) the symbol © (the letter C in a circle), or the word "Copyright", or the abbreviation "Copr."; and

(2) the year of first publication of the work; in the case of compilations or derivative works incorporating previously published material, the year date of first publication of the compilation or derivative work is sufficient. The year date may be omitted where a pictorial, graphic, or sculptural work, with accompanying text matter, if any, is reproduced in or on greeting cards, postcards, stationery, jewelry, dolls, toys, or any useful articles; and

(3) the name of the owner of copyright in the work, or an abbreviation by which the name can be recognized, or a generally known alternative designation of the owner.

(c) Position of Notice.—The notice shall be affixed to the copies in such manner and location as to give reasonable notice of the claim of copyright. The Register of Copyrights shall prescribe by regulation, as examples, specific methods of affixation and positions of the notice on various types of works that will satisfy this requirement, but these specifications shall not be considered exhaustive.

(d) Evidentiary Weight of Notice.—If a notice of copyright in the form and position specified by this section appears on the published copy or copies to which a defendant in a copyright infringement suit had access, then no weight shall be given to such a defendant's interposition of a defense based on innocent infringement in mitigation of actual or statutory damages, except as provided in the last sentence of section 504(c)(2).

CODE OF FEDERAL REGULATIONS, 37 CFR § 201.20(g)

* * *

(g) *Works reproduced in machine-readable copies.* For works reproduced in machine-readable copies (such as magnetic tapes or disks, punched cards, or the like, from which the work cannot ordinarily be visually perceived except with the aid of a machine or device,[1] each of the following constitute examples of acceptable methods of affixation and position of notice:

1. Works published in a form requiring the use of a machine or device for purposes of optical enlargement (such as film, filmstrips, slide films, and works published in any variety of microform) and works published in visually perceptible form but used in connection with optical scanning devices, are not within this category.

(1) A notice embodied in the copies in machine-readable form in such a manner that on visually perceptible printouts it appears either with or near the title, or at the end of the work;

(2) A notice that is displayed at the user's terminal at sign on;

(3) A notice that is continuously on terminal display; or

(4) A legible notice reproduced durably, so as to withstand normal use, on a gummed or other label securely affixed to the copies or to a box, reel, cartridge, cassette, or other container used as a permanent receptacle for the copies.

Note

As a condition of joining the Berne Copyright Convention, the United States eliminated the former requirement that published works bear a copyright notice. It is still important to put a copyright notice on published computer software for two reasons. First, the notice may deter infringers. Second, under § 401(d) of the Copyright Act, the notice will prevent an "innocent infringement" defense. Section 401(d) refers to "the last sentence of section 504(c)(2)." This sentence relieves certain employees of non-profit institutions of liability for statutory damages, if the employees had reasonable ground for believing that they were engaged in "fair use."

2. REGISTRATION AND DEPOSIT

COPYRIGHT ACT OF 1976

§ 408. Copyright registration in general

(a) Registration Permissive.—At any time during the subsistence of copyright in any published or unpublished work, the owner of copyright or of any exclusive right in the work may obtain registration of the copyright claim by delivering to the Copyright Office the deposit specified by this section, together with the application and fee specified by sections 409 and 708. Such registration is not a condition of copyright protection.

(b) Deposit for Copyright Registration.—Except as provided by subsection (c), the material deposited for registration shall include—

(1) in the case of an unpublished work, one complete copy or phonorecord;

(2) in the case of the published work, two complete copies or phonorecords of the best edition;

(3) in the case of a work first published outside the United States, one complete copy or phonorecord as so published;

(4) in the case of a contribution to a collective work, one complete copy or phonorecord of the best edition of the collective work.

Copies or phonorecords deposited for the Library of Congress under section 407 may be used to satisfy the deposit provisions of this section, if they are accompanied by the prescribed application and fee, and by any additional identifying material that the Register may, by regulation, require. The Register shall also prescribe regulations establishing requirements under which copies or phonorecords acquired for the Library of Congress under subsection (e) of section 407, otherwise than by deposit, may be used to satisfy the deposit provisions of this section.

(c) Administrative Classification and Optional Deposit.—

(1) The Register of Copyrights is authorized to specify by regulation the administrative classes into which works are to be placed for purposes of deposit and registration, and the nature of the copies or phonorecords to be deposited in the various classes specified. The regulations may require or permit, for particular classes, the deposit of identifying material instead of copies or phonorecords, the deposit of only one copy or phonorecord where two would normally be required, or a single registration for a group of related works. This administrative classification of works has no significance with respect to the subject matter of copyright or the exclusive rights provided by this title.

* * *

REGULATIONS, ON SOFTWARE COPYRIGHT DEPOSITS 37 CFR § 202.20(a)(vii)–(ix)

* * *

(vii) *Computer programs and databases embodied in machine-readable copies.* In cases where a computer program, database, compilation, statistical compendium or the like, if unpublished is fixed, or if published is published only in the form of machine-readable copies (such as magnetic tape or disks, punched cards, semiconductor chip products, or the like) from which the work cannot ordinarily be perceived except with the aid of a machine or device, the deposit shall consist of:

(A) For published or unpublished computer programs, one copy of identifying portions of the program, reproduced in a form visually perceptible without the aid of a machine or device, either on paper or in microform. For these purposes "identifying portions" shall mean one of the following:

(*1*) The first and last 25 pages or equivalent units of the source code if reproduced on paper, or at least the first and last 25 pages or equivalent units of the source code if reproduced in microform, together with the page or equivalent unit containing the copyright notice, if any. If the program is 50 pages or less, the required deposit will be the entire source code. In the case of revised versions of computer programs, if the revisions occur throughout the entire program, the deposit of the page containing the copyright notice and the first and last 25 pages of source code will suffice; if the revisions do not occur in the first and last 25 pages, the deposit should consist of the page containing the copyright notice and any 50 pages of source code representative of the revised material; or

(*2*) Where the program contains trade secret material, the page or equivalent unit containing the copyright notice, if any, plus one of the following: the first and last 25 pages or equivalent units of source code with portions of the source code containing trade secrets blocked-out, provided that the blocked-out portions are proportionately less than the material remaining, and the deposit reveals an appreciable amount of original computer code; or the first and last 10 pages or equivalent units of source code alone with no blocked-out portions; or the first and last 25 pages of object code, together with any 10 or more consecutive pages of source code with no blocked-out portions; or for programs consisting of or less than 25 pages or equivalent units, source code with the trade secret portions blocked-out, provided that the blocked-out portions are proportionately less than the material remaining, and the remaining portion reveals an appreciable amount of original computer code. If the copyright claim is in a revision not contained in the first and last 25 pages, the deposit shall consist of either 20 pages of source code representative of the revised material with no blocked-out portions, or any 50 pages of source code representative of the revised material with portions of the source code containing trade secrets blocked-out, provided that the blocked-out portions are proportionately less than the material remaining and the deposit reveals an appreciable amount of original computer code. Whatever method is used to block out trade secret material, at least an appreciable amount of original computer code must remain visible.

(B) Where registration of a program containing trade secrets is made on the basis of an object code deposit the Copyright Office will make registration under its rule of doubt and warn that no determination has been made concerning the existence of copyrightable authorship.

(C) Where the application to claim copyright in a computer program includes a specific claim in related computer screen displays, the deposit, in addition to the identifying portions specified in paragraph (c)(2)(vii)(A) of this section, shall consist of:

(*1*) Visual reproductions of the copyrightable expression in the form of printouts, photographs, or drawings no smaller than 3 × 3 inches and no larger than 9 × 12 inches; or

(*2*) If the authorship in the work is predominantly audiovisual, a one-half inch VHS format videotape reproducing the copyrightable expression, except that printouts, photographs, or drawings no smaller than 3 × 3 inches and no larger than 9 × 12 inches must be deposited in lieu of videotape where the computer screen material simply constitutes a demonstration of the functioning of the computer program.

(D) For published and unpublished automated databases, compilations, statistical compendia, and the like, so fixed or published, one copy of identifying portions of the work, reproduced in a form visually perceptible without the aid of a machine or device, either on paper or in microform. For these purposes:

(*1*) "Identifying portions" shall generally mean either the first and last 25 or equivalent units of the work if reproduced on paper or in microform.

(*2*) "Datafile" and "file" shall mean a group of data records pertaining to a common subject matter regardless of their size or the number of data items in them.

(*3*) In the case of individual registration of a revised version of the works identified in this paragraph (c)(2)(vii)(D), the identifying portions deposited shall contain 50 representative pages or data records which have been added or modified.

(*4*) If the work is an automated database comprising multiple separate or distinct data files, "identifying portions" shall instead consist of 50 complete data records from each data file or the entire data file, whichever is less, and the descriptive statement required by paragraph (c)(2)(vii)(D)(5).

(*5*) In the case of group registration for revised or updated versions of a database, the claimant shall deposit identifying portions that contain 50 representative pages or equivalent units, or representative data records which have been marked to disclose (or do in fact disclose solely) the new material added on one representative publication date if published, or on one representative creation date, if unpublished, and shall also deposit a brief typed or printed descriptive statement containing the notice of copyright information required under "(*6*)" or "(*7*)" immediately below, if the work bears a notice, and;

(*i*) The title of the database;

(*ii*) A subtitle, date of creation or publication, or other information, to distinguish any separate or distinct data files for cataloging purposes;

(*iii*) The name and address of the copyright claimant;

(*iv*) For each separate file, its name and content, including its subject, the origin(s) of the data, and the approximate number of data records it contains; and

(*v*) In the case of revised or updated versions of an automated database, information as to the nature and frequency of changes in the database and some identification of the location within the database or the separate data files of the revisions.

(*6*) For a copyright notice embodied in machine-readable form, the statement shall describe exactly the visually perceptible content of the notice which appears in or with the database, and the manner and frequency with which it is displayed (e.g., at user's terminal only at sign-on, or continuously on terminal display, or on printouts, etc.).

(7) If a visually perceptible copyright notice is placed on any copies of the work (or on magnetic tape reels or containers therefor), a sample of such notice must also accompany the statement.

(viii) *Machine-readable copies of works other than computer programs and databases.* Where a literary, musical, pictorial, graphic, or audiovisual work, or a sound recording, except for literary works which are computer programs, databases, compilations, statistical compendia or the like, if unpublished has been fixed or, if published, has been published only in machine-readable form, the deposit must consist of identifying material. The type of identifying material submitted should generally be appropriate to the type of work embodied in machine-readable form, but in all cases should be that which best represents the copyrightable content of the work. In all cases the identifying material must include the title of the work. A synopsis may also be requested in addition to the other deposit materials as appropriate in the discretion of the Copyright Office. In the case of any published work subject to this section, the identifying material must include a representation of the copyright notice, if one exists. Identifying material requirements for certain types of works are specified below. In the case of the types of works listed below, the requirements specified shall apply except that, in any case where the specific requirements are not appropriate for a given work the form of the identifying material required will be determined by the Copyright Office in consultation with the applicant, but the Copyright Office will make the final determination of the acceptability of the identifying material.

(A) For pictorial or graphic works, the deposit shall consist of identifying material in compliance with § 202.21 of these regulations;

(B) For audiovisual works, the deposit shall consist of either a videotape of the work depicting representative portions of the copyrightable content, or a series of photographs or drawings, depicting representative portions of the work, plus in all cases a separate synopsis of the work;

(C) For musical compositions, the deposit shall consist of a transcription of the entire work such as a score, or a reproduction of the entire work on an audiocassette or other phonorecord;

(D) For sound recordings, the deposit shall consist of a reproduction of the entire work on an audiocassette or other phonorecord;

(E) For literary works, the deposit shall consist of a transcription of representative portions of the work including the first and last 25 pages or equivalent units, and five or more pages indicative of the remainder.

(ix) *Copies containing both visually-perceptible and machine-readable material.* Where a published literary work is embodied in copies containing both visually-perceptible and machine-readable material, the deposit shall consist of the visually-perceptible material and identifying portions of the machine-readable material.

§ 411. Registration and infringement actions

(a) Except for actions for infringement of copyright in Berne Convention works whose country of origin is not the United States, and subject to the provisions of subsection (b), no action for infringement of the copyright in any work shall be instituted until registration of the copyright claim has been made in accordance with this title. In any case, however, where the deposit, application, and fee required for registration have been delivered to the Copyright Office in proper form and registration has been refused, the applicant is entitled to institute an action for infringement if notice thereof, with a copy of the complaint, is served on the Register of Copyrights. The Register may, at his or her option, become a party to the action with respect to the issue of registrability of the copyright claim by entering an appearance within sixty days after such service, but the Register's failure to become a party shall not deprive the court of jurisdiction to determine that issue.

* * *

§ 412. Registration as prerequisite to certain remedies for infringement

In any action under this title, other than an action instituted under section 411(b), no award of statutory damages or of attorney's fees, as provided by sections 504 and 505, shall be made for—

(1) any infringement of copyright in an unpublished work commenced before the effective date of its registration; or

(2) any infringement of copyright commenced after first publication of the work and before the effective date of its registration, unless such registration is made within three months after the first publication of the work.

Notes

1. The creator of a copyrightable work obtains copyright protection automatically and immediately upon creation of a work. Thus statements such as, "I copyrighted my computer program," show an incorrect understanding of the law. It is important, however, for two reasons to register computer software and other machine-readable material. Under § 411, registration is a prerequisite to an infringement action. Under § 412, delay in registration causes loss of the chance to recover statutory damages and attorney's fees. Because it is often difficult to prove actual damages, it is crucial to have the right to statutory damages, which the Copyright Act grants even in the absence of a showing of actual damages. Copyright litigation is often complex, so attorney's fees can be high.

2. The vast majority of owners of program copyrights wish to keep their source code as a trade secret. This desire potentially conflicts with

the provision of § 408(b)(2) requiring a deposit of the "best edition" of a published work. 33 CFR § 220.20(a)(vii)–(ix) is an attempt to resolve this conflict in favor of the copyright owners.

3. The deposit requirements would be impossibly burdensome for the owners of the copyright in a large data base, such as that of the WESTLAW system. 33 CFR § 220.20(a)(vii) provides a practical means for deposit of a reasonable quantity of identifying material rather than the whole data base.

3. RECORDATION OF SHAREWARE

JUDICIAL IMPROVEMENT ACT OF 1990
PL 101–650

§ 805. Recordation of Shareware

(a) In General.—The Register of Copyrights is authorized, upon receipt of any document designated as pertaining to computer shareware and the fee prescribed by section 708 of title 17, United States Code, to record the document and return it with a certificate of recordation.

(b) Maintenance of Records; Publication of Information.—The Register of Copyrights is authorized to maintain current, separate records relating to the recordation of documents under subsection (a), and to compile and publish at periodic intervals information relating to such recordations. Such publications shall be offered for sale to the public at prices based on the cost of reproduction and distribution.

(c) Deposit of Copies in Library of Congress.—In the case of public domain computer software, at the election of the person recording a document under subsection (a), 2 complete copies of the best edition (as defined in section 101 of title 17, United States Code) of the computer software as embodied in machine-readable form may be deposited for the benefit of the Machine–Readable Collections Reading Room of the Library of Congress.

(d) Regulations.—The Register of Copyrights is authorized to establish regulations not inconsistent with law for the administration of the functions of the Register under this section. All regulations established by the Register are subject to the approval of the Librarian of Congress.

G. INFRINGEMENT

1. PROOF OF INFRINGEMENT BY ACCESS AND SIMILARITY

E.F. JOHNSON CO. v. UNIDEN CORPORATION OF AMERICA.

United States District Court, District of Minnesota, 1985.
623 F.Supp. 1485.

MACLAUGHLIN, DISTRICT JUDGE.

This matter is before the Court on plaintiff's motion for a preliminary injunction. Plaintiff seeks an order of the Court enjoining defendant from publishing, selling, marketing, or otherwise disposing of any copies of defendant's LTR–compatible radio program in any form, and impounding during the pendency of this action and destruction upon conclusion thereof any materials, programs, or other articles of information by means of which plaintiff's copyrighted computer software has been or may be produced by defendant. The Court heard testimony and arguments on plaintiff's motion September 9–10, 1985. Plaintiff's motion will be granted. This order incorporates the findings of fact and conclusions of law required by Federal Rule of Civil Procedure 52.

I. FACTS

A. Parties

Plaintiff E.F. Johnson Co. (EFJ) is a Minnesota corporation engaged in the business of manufacturing and selling two-way land-based communications systems. EFJ's principal place of business is in Waseca, Minnesota. Defendant Uniden Corporation of America (Uniden) is an Indiana corporation, a subsidiary of Uniden Corporation of Japan. Uniden imports and distributes electronic equipment including land-based communications systems.

B. Background

In the spring of 1980 EFJ introduced into the market its newly developed "Clearchannel LTR" logic trunked radio system (LTR). A logic trunked radio system is one consisting of mobile radio units, typically installed in motor vehicles such as taxis, police cars, delivery trucks, etc., and "repeaters," base stations which receive and transmit signals to and from the mobile radio units. The heart of the EFJ LTR system is computer software contained in the mobile radios and repeaters. The computer software, independently developed by EFJ engineers Mervin Grindahl, Keith Barnes, and Phillip Keefer, allows the LTR system to pool radio frequency channels, thereby making all assigned radio channels accessible to all system users, at a significant gain in operational efficiency. The software contained in the EFJ 8700 series mobile radio units are subject to copyright.

In April, 1985, defendant Uniden introduced into the market its model FTS 250T two-way 800 MHZ FM trunked mobile radio compatible with LTR-system radios and repeaters. The Uniden mobile radio also contains computer software, which allows it to receive and transmit messages from and to EFJ's LTR–system radios.

Shortly after the Uniden FTS 250T radios came onto the market EFJ engineers subjected one of the radios to scrutiny at their Waseca laboratories. Concluding that the software contained in the FTS 250T radio is identical to software contained in EFJ radios, EFJ commenced the instant litigation, claiming copyright infringement, 17 U.S.C. § 501 *et seq.*, and seeking preliminary injunctive relief.

* * *

D. EFJ's Development of the LTR–System Radio

EFJ engineers first conceived the idea of a trunked mobile radio system in late summer, 1977. At that time no trunked radio systems were on the market. EFJ engineer Mervin Grindahl was assigned the task of developing the LTR code. In pursuit of this objective, Grindahl first developed signal methods for sending data transmissions over radio waves to direct mobile radios. Grindahl then developed a system architecture which permitted use of the signalling method, and signalling protocols to implement the system architecture. Finally, Grindahl created the algorithms necessary to development of the LTR computer software.

At this point the baton was passed to Keith Barnes, another EFJ engineer, who wrote the LTR software program from specifications detailed in the Grindahl algorithms. Barnes completed the detailed program sometime in 1978. Following an extensive period of "debugging" and program modification, the LTR system was ready for public unveiling in April, 1980.

The LTR mobile radio introduced into the market in 1980 was the model 8800 radio. The model 8800 radio contains a computer software program authored by Grindahl and Barnes. The Grindahl–Barnes EFJ LTR software is the subject of a valid copyright, Registration No. TX 957–037, registered June 30, 1982.

* * *

Sales of EFJ's LTR–system radios since their introduction have been brisk. EFJ's annual sales volume of trunked radios is approximately $25 million factory net, $40 million retail. Approximately 30 percent of EFJ's total sales are of mobile trunked radios. The national retail market for mobile trunked radios is on the order of $200–$250 million per year. Of 500 authorized EFJ retail dealers, 150 carry trunked mobile radios.

E. Logic Trunked Radio Systems

The concept of "trunking" had its genesis in the telephone industry. As the Court understands it, the "trunking" of frequency channels permits the system to afford all system users automatic access to all channels for maximum efficiency. Rather than assigning each user a discrete channel, the trunked system, through the use of sophisticated computer software, patches together unutilized airwave "spaces" to create an uninterrupted channel of communication. The net result is that the system can accommodate more users than it has frequency channels available.

EFJ's clearchannel LTR system is composed of two elements: (1) repeaters, which control access to the system and receive and retransmit signals from mobile radio units; and (2) mobile radio and control units. The system works in the following manner. Each mobile radio is assigned to a repeater. Repeaters are analogous to radio station transmitters. The mobile radios send signals—high speed digital data bursts at sub-audible frequencies—to the repeater, which identifies the sending unit and which retransmits and amplifies the signal so that it can be received by the appropriate mobile unit. The "trunked logic" aspect of the system comes into play in the system's selection of open frequency channels. The FCC has assigned certain radio frequencies for use by trunked radio systems. Dealers who sell repeaters are licensed by the FCC to operate a trunked system on an assigned frequency. In addition, any purchaser of a mobile radio or radios must purchase the right to use the repeater from the licensed dealer or system operator and must also obtain an FCC license for the radios. Thus, the universe of potential utilizers of trunked radios is finite, as constrained by the number of frequency channels assigned by the FCC for trunked radio use. A "fully loaded" trunked radio channel will support between 100 and 500 mobile radios. Hence, the market for mobile radios is much larger than the market for repeaters.

EFJ manufactures both repeaters and mobile radios. The heart of the LTR system, as mentioned above, is the copyrighted computer software found in both repeaters and mobile radios. EFJ's software is mounted on a Read–Only Memory (ROM) microchip. EFJ's mobile radios use an Intel 8049 microprocessor.

Currently, there are four major manufacturers of mobile trunked radio systems in the United States: General Electric, Motorola, Tac–Tel, and EFJ. Three companies manufacture mobile radios compatible with LTR–system repeaters and radios: Standard Communications, Regency, and Uniden.

F. Uniden Enters the Fray

Uniden commenced development of a mobile radio compatible with EFJ's LTR radios and repeaters sometime in 1984. In the course of developing an LTR–compatible radio, Uniden engineer S. Katsukura disassembled the software found in EFJ's model 8855 and 8800 radios. Disassembly of a computer program is done by translating the machine or object code into humanly-readable assembly language. Having disassembled the EFJ software program, Uniden engineers Katsukura and S. Uwabe prepared and studied flow charts of the EFJ program. Uniden engineers also studied EFJ hardware and service manuals in developing the FTS 250T software.

When through industry sources EFJ learned of Uniden's plans to market an LTR–compatible radio, EFJ in letters dated January 24, 1984 and March 5, 1984, advised Uniden that the software in the LTR mobile radios was copyrighted, and that any attempt by competitors to infringe the EFJ copyrights would be vigorously contested. Uniden unveiled its model FTS 250T 800 MHZ trunked mobile radio at the Expo West industry trade show in Las Vegas, Nevada on April 23–26, 1985. EFJ engineer Phillip A. Keefer attended Expo West, visually examined the Uniden radio and obtained Uniden promotional literature.

Thereafter EFJ engineers obtained a Uniden model FTS 250T radio and subjected it to scrutiny at EFJ's Waseca laboratories. EFJ engineers Grindahl and Keefer first checked to see if the Uniden radio was in fact compatible with LTR repeaters. Finding that it was, Keefer removed from the Uniden radio the Eraseable Programmable Read–Only Memory microchip (EPROM) on which the Uniden software was stored. Keefer and Grindahl "dumped" the Uniden program or "code" from the EPROM, using for this purpose a PROM programmer, before "uploading" it into an EFJ computer for purposes of making a comparison of the Uniden and EFJ programs.

EFJ engineers Grindahl and Keefer first compared the "data tables" contained in the Uniden and EFJ software programs. They came to the conclusion that the data tables were identical.

Grindahl then wrote a disassembly program—one which converts machine language code into humanly-readable assembly language. Grindahl made a brief comparison of the Uniden and EFJ codes in assembly language, and when he found evidence of copying, instructed Keefer to conduct a more thorough examination. Keefer did a line-by-line comparison of the codes. As a consequence of their comparisons, Grindahl and Keefer came to the conclusion that the EFJ software had been copied by Uniden.

The Uniden model FTS 250T radio utilizes a Hitachi HD63B05X2P microprocessor. Uniden manufactures its FTS 250T radios in Taiwan and distributes them throughout the United States. Many of the same dealers who carry EFJ mobile trunked radios also carry Uniden FTS 250T radios. Retail prices for Uniden's radios are some 31–39 percent less than the retail price of EFJ radios.

II. Discussion

Plaintiff has moved the Court for an order enjoining the defendant from publishing, selling, marketing, or otherwise disposing of any copies of defendant's LTR–compatible radio program, and is further seeking impoundment of any and all materials, programs, and other articles and information by means of which plaintiff's copyright has been or is being produced by defendant. * * *

* * *

A. Likelihood of Success on the Merits

1. Copyright Ownership

In order to establish a claim of copyright infringement, plaintiff must prove its ownership of a valid copyright, and copying, or infringement, of the copyrighted work by the defendant. Plaintiff has introduced into evidence Certificate of U.S. Copyright Registration No. TX1–568–701, dated June 4, 1985 issued to E.F. Johnson. This registration is prima facie evidence of the validity of the copyright and the facts stated in the certificate, including ownership. 17 U.S.C. § 410(c).

* * *

a. Access

The Court finds that defendant had access to EFJ's copyrighted software program. By their own admission, Uniden engineers removed the ROM on which the EFJ program is mounted from EFJ model 8800 and 8855 radios, dumped the EFJ programs, disassembled the EFJ programs, and analyzed and flow charted the EFJ programs in the course of developing the software for Uniden's radio.

b. Substantial Similarity

The test of substantial similarity in the Eighth Circuit is "whether the work is recognizable by an ordinary observer as having been taken from the copyrighted source." *Wihtol v. Crow,* 309 F.2d 777, 780 (8th Cir.1962), *quoting Bradbury v. Columbia Broadcasting System, Inc.,* 287 F.2d 478 (9th Cir.1961). The ordinary observer test has proven "one of the most difficult questions in copyright law, and one which is the least susceptible of helpful generalization." 3 *Nimmer on Copyright,* § 13.-03[A]. Under any formulation it is clear that "[s]light differences and variations will not serve as a defense," *Wihtol,* 309 F.2d at 780, and that there is substantial similarity where "enough 'material of substance and value' has been taken so that an ordinary observer would recognize that there is 'borrowing' from the original." *Animal Fair,* at 188, *quoting Atari, Inc.,* 672 F.2d at 614. The copying need not be slavishly detailed, *Comptone Co. v. Rayex Corp.,* 251 F.2d 487, 488 (2d Cir.1958) (per curiam) so long as the accused work has captured the "total concept and feel" of the copyrighted work.[5]

Because a copyrighted computer program is stored on a computer chip or disc well-hidden from public view, application of the ordinary observer test in a computer software context has proven problematical.

5. The substantial similarity test had its genesis in the opinion of Judge Learned Hand in *Nichols v. Universal Pictures Corp.,* 45 F.2d 119 (2d Cir.1930). In *Harold Lloyd Corp. v. Witwer,* 65 F.2d 1 (9th Cir. 1933) the United States Court of Appeals for the Ninth Circuit gauged substantial similarity from the standpoint of the "ordinary observer." *Witwer,* 65 F.2d at 19. * * * The test was later modified to include the requirement of "access," defined generally as opportunity to view the copyrighted work. In the absence of access, courts have required a showing of "striking similarity" sufficient to "preclude the possibility of independent creation." *See Ferguson v. National Broadcasting Co.,* 584 F.2d 111, 113 (5th Cir.1978); 3 *Nimmer on Copyright* at 13.01[A].

The absence of an easily perceived general aura or feeling emanating from a silicon chip has led some commentators to suggest an "iterative" approach to substantial similarity. The iterative approach requires proof (1) that the defendant "used" the copyrighted work in preparing the alleged copy, which may be established by proof of access and similarity sufficient to reasonably infer use of the copyrighted work; and (2) that the defendant's work is an iterative reproduction, that is, one produced by iterative or exact duplication of substantial portions of the copyrighted work. Under the iterative approach, adopted in form if not name by several courts, the factfinder's focus shifts from the hypothetical ordinary observer's impressions of the "total concept and feel" of the copyrighted and allegedly infringing works to an analysis of the "quantitative and qualitative evidence of similarities" as gauged by the Court's evaluation of expert testimony. The fiction of the lay observer is thus abandoned in favor of an analysis of similarities and differences in the copyrighted and allegedly offending computer programs.

Under either the traditional "ordinary observer" or the contemporary "iterative" test of substantial similarity, it is clear that the software program found in Uniden's FTS 250T mobile trunked radio is substantially similar to EFJ's copyrighted version 3.0 software program.

The indicia of substantial similarity may perhaps most usefully be set forth in tabular form:

(1) Barker Code

Due to the fact that Uniden designed its radio to be compatible with EFJ's LTR system, both parties acknowledge that some similarities in software design were inevitable. The Court finds that in order to make its radios compatible with LTR repeaters Uniden was required to copy the "Barker code" found in the copyrighted EFJ program. A "Barker code" is a pattern of ones and zeroes alternated in a prepatterned sequence. Both the sending and receiving units must identify the Barker code in order for communication to be established. The EFJ Barker code is numerically depicted as 1011000. In order to make its radios compatible, Uniden was required to and did copy this aspect of the EFJ program.

The matter does not end there, however. In the LTR scheme of transmission identification, synchronization is achieved by a comparison of incoming streams of data with the seven-bit Barker code. By counting the number of matches and nonmatches, and by comparing the number of nonmatches or "errors" to the "sample error" data table contained in the EFJ program, the Intel microprocessor is able to determine if an incoming stream of data is in fact the 1011000 Barker word, in which event the number of errors is nil, or whether it is something else, in which event the number of errors is very high. Only when a certain threshold of matches is achieved has synchronization word detection occurred. This is known in the parlance as the shifting correlator scheme for detection.

In order to make this comparison of incoming data with the Barker code the LTR system takes eight "samples" of seven bits each and compares the 56 bits with an internal table, called the "sample error" or "lookup" table. The significance of the 56 bit sampling technique is threefold.

First, EFJ engineers chose to sample 56 bits at a time because the Intel microprocessor is incapable of sampling at a greater rate. By sampling at a 56 bit rate the EFJ program utilizes 96 percent of the Intel microprocessor's top speed. In contrast, the Hitachi microprocessor used by Uniden in its radios is capable of sampling bits at a much higher rate of speed. Sampling at a rate in excess of 56 bits is preferable because, as admitted by Uniden engineers, the error detection capability increases exponentially with increases in the number of bits sampled. Nevertheless, Uniden chose to sample incoming data streams in exactly the same manner as EFJ—eight samples of seven bits each. This coincidence of sampling rates indicates inferentially that Uniden engineers copied the EFJ code verbatim without considering the utility which the greater speed of the Hitachi microprocessor afforded them.

Second, the sample error table found in the EFJ program has its exact duplicate in the Uniden program. The duplication is not necessary to compatability, in that other methods of counting errors exist, as, for example, by counting the number of errors in the cross-correlation word by shifting the word one bit at a time and counting the number of bits that have ones. Further, Uniden's choice of the sample-error method of detecting errors is contrary to logic, in light of design differences in the Intel and Hitachi microprocessors. The sample error table works particularly well with an Intel microprocessor because of the availability in the Intel microprocessor of a "swap command," one that allows the program to swap bits four at a time. In the Hitachi microprocessor, in contrast, bits must be swapped one at a time, at a corresponding loss of efficiency.[8] Hence, Uniden's use of a sample error table technique identical to EFJ's when more efficient methods were available raises an inference of copying.

Third, as originally conceived, the EFJ "error threshold" was set at eight. Synchronization was deemed to have occurred when eight or fewer errors were detected. Later experimentation by Phillip Keefer revealed that better synchronization could be achieved by setting the threshold at six errors, which is the threshold incorporated in later

8. Uniden engineer Uwabe contended in an unsworn declaration filed in the case that the swap command was not necessary to four bit sampling, and that the same result could be achieved with a sequence of four shift right operations. Considerable doubt was cast upon this assertion by the testimony of EFJ engineer Keefer, however. The Court finds that Uniden's duplication of EFJ's sampling technique is evidence of copying, and that use of the sample error table in a microprocessor without a swap command is contrary to logic.

versions of the EFJ code. Defendant's code retains the eight error threshold copied from version 3.0, at a corresponding loss of efficiency.

(2) H–Matrix

The Court finds that in order to make its radios compatible with the LTR system Uniden was required to include an H–Matrix table in its software program. An H–Matrix is a series of ones and zeroes arranged in rows and columns in a matrix format. An H–Matrix is used in the LTR system to detect errors in transmission, once communication has been established by matching of Barker codes. To make its radios compatible with the LTR system, Uniden was required to and did employ *some form* of H–matrix in its software program, as EFJ's experts admitted in their testimony.

In fact, Uniden's H-matrix is *identical* to the H–matrix found in the EFJ program. This exact duplication was not necessary, in that the H-matrix can be configured any of 32 different ways. The fact that Uniden configured its H-matrix in precisely the same manner as EFJ is evidence of copying.

In addition, Uniden's program includes an inverse H-matrix identical to the inverse H-matrix found in the EFJ program. The EFJ inverse H-matrix is, as the name implies, an H-matrix in which the rows of the matrix have been interchanged. The inverse H-matrix is used in conjunction with the H-matrix to detect transmission errors and is found in both repeaters and radios. The inverse H-matrix in the Uniden program serves the same purpose. The significance of an inverse H-matrix for present purposes lies in the fact that it is almost completely superfluous to the LTR system's operation. The inverse H-matrix was included in the EFJ program solely due to a miscommunication between EFJ engineers Grindahl, who designed the LTR algorithms, and Barnes, who reduced the algorithms to computer program form. The end result, transmission error detection, could have been achieved through use of the H-matrix solely. Nevertheless, Uniden's program includes an inverse H-matrix identical to the inverse H-matrix mistakenly included in the EFJ program.

Finally, the EFJ H-matrix was loaded into the software code in reverse order. The reason for this apparent anamoly is that the Intel microprocessor more efficiently decrements (subtracts) than increments (adds) resulting in system efficiencies with a reverse-loaded matrix. In contrast, the Hitachi microprocessor is equally efficient at incrementing and decrementing. Nevertheless, the Uniden H-matrix is loaded in reverse order.

(3) Duplex Function Instructions

The EFJ software program contains three lines of code which are completely unnecessary to operation of the LTR system. The unnecessary instructions are found in the "transmit audio" subroutine. The instructions were originally written into the code by EFJ engineer Barnes to accommodate a "duplex feature"—one which would allow a system user speaking over the LTR radio to simultaneously hear transmissions directed to the user from other radios. When it was determined that duplex transmission was not feasible, that part of the code was removed, with the exception of the offending three instructions, which Barnes left in the code by mistake.

Precisely the same three superfluous instructions are found in the Uniden program, in precisely the same location, the "transmit audio" subroutine. Uniden engineer S. Uwabe acknowledged the presence of the unnecessary instructions. Uwabe contended that the surplusage was written into the code purposely to accommodate a duplex feature in the event that Uniden determined to add such a feature to their radio at some future date. The Court has difficulty comprehending how Uniden engineers could have independently determined to include precisely the same unnecessary instruction at precisely the same location in the program without having in fact copied the program. The more likely explanation, and the one the Court finds to be credible, is that Uniden unwittingly copied the unnecessary instructions when translating the EFJ code virtually verbatim from Intel to Hitachi code.

The existence of the identical unnecessary instructions in both codes is strong proof of substantial similarity. In *SAS Industries, Inc. v. S & H Computer Systems, Inc.,* 605 F.Supp. 816 (M.D.Tenn.1985), in finding that a copyrighted program had been pirated the court found probative the presence of "totally functionless" instructions in both the copyrighted and infringing codes. *SAS Industries,* 605 F.Supp. at 824. In that case the court stated "[t]he only conceivable explanation is that [the defendant] copied this non-functional feature from the [plaintiff's] source code." *Id.*

(4) Select Call Prohibit

The select call prohibit feature of the EFJ radio prevents LTR system users from attempting to communicate with the "dispatcher" or system operator when the dispatcher is transmitting to another user. Essentially, the select call prohibit causes a "busy signal" to be communicated. In version 3.0 of the LTR software program an error in the select call prohibit feature was written into the program. In brief, the error causes transmissions to be blocked to all dispatchers aligned with a particular repeater when in fact only one dispatcher is transmitting. In later versions of the EFJ code the error has been corrected.

The Uniden select call prohibit feature incorporates the same error found in version 3.0 of the EFJ software. For this comity of errors the Court can conceive of only two plausible explanations: one, that EFJ and Uniden engineers independently committed the same inadvertences; or two, that Uniden engineers unknowingly wrote the error into their code when copying the EFJ code. The Court finds the latter explanation to be the likelier one.

The presence of identical errors in copyrighted and infringing computer programs was held to be evidence of copying in *Williams*

Electronics, Inc. v. Arctic International, Inc., 685 F.2d 870, 876 (3d Cir.1982). In assessing the similarities between video game software programs the Third Circuit noted:

> There is overwhelming evidence in the present case that the [plaintiff's] computer program has been copied in some form. The following facts, among others, manifest the similarities between the [plaintiff's] program and that stored in the [defendant's] memory devices:
>
> (1) The game created by the [defendant's] circuit boards contained an error which was present in early versions of the [defendant's] computer program—it displays the wrong score value for destroying a particular alien symbol[.]

Williams, 685 F.2d at 876 n. 6.

(5) Other Evidence of Substantial Similarity

Other, miscellaneous evidence of copying abounds. One of the unnecessary lines of code is a "counter" set arbitrarily by EFJ engineers at 20 code cycles. The Uniden counter is also set at 20 code cycles. The EFJ "receive executive" routine, as modified by Phillip Keefer, is "neat," in the sense of concise, while the "transmit executive" routine is rambling. In the Uniden code the receive executive routine is neat and the transmit executive routine is rambling. Further, EFJ's experts testified that 38 of 44 subroutines found in its version 3.0 code are duplicated in the Uniden code. * * *

In sum, the Court finds that the similarities between the EFJ program and the Uniden program are substantial. Both programs achieve Barker word synchronization in precisely the same manner, despite the fact that alternative techniques are available. Both programs "sample" incoming bits at precisely the same speed, despite the fact that Uniden's Hitachi microprocessor is capable of sampling at a higher speed. Both programs utilize identical sample error tables, H-matrices and inverse H-matrices. Perhaps most tellingly, both programs contain precisely the same superfluous instructions and precisely the same select call prohibit error. The duplicative tables and errors, the identity of 38 out of 44 subroutines and the marked similarity in overall design lead the Court to conclude that the programs are substantially similar.

Defendant has introduced into evidence an exhibit consisting of a line-by-line, side-by-side comparison of the EFJ and Uniden codes, both translated into Hitachi language. While it is obvious at a glance that the programs thus depicted are not line-by-line duplications, the Court finds the comparison on the whole unconvincing. Because of differences in addressing features of the Intel and Hitachi microprocessors a given step may take a differing number of commands depending on whether the instructions are set forth in Intel or Hitachi language. Thus, literal translation of plaintiff's Intel instructions into Hitachi language necessarily involves a skewing of the program such that line-by-line comparison becomes meaningless. * * *

* * *

Against the Court's finding of substantial similarity, the defendant raises two somewhat related defenses: (1) preexisting material, and (2) the idea/expression dichotomy.

(i) Preexisting Material

Originality is widely recognized as the *sine qua non* of copyrightability. * * *

Defendant argues that plaintiff's version 3.0 software program is not copyrightable because derived in large part from preexisting material in the public domain. Specifically, defendant contends that the H-matrices, Barker word, error look-up tables and Barker correlation tables have long been in general scientific use and are not original with EFJ.

The Court finds that while some aspects of the EFJ program are taken from the public domain, the degree of originality contributed by plaintiff to version 3.0 is far from "trivial." For example, Mervin Grindahl testified that the EFJ Barker word is a unique permutation of the textbook Barker. EFJ engineers turned the "classic" Barker end for end and inverted all the bits, changing ones to zeroes and zeroes to ones, for the purpose of eliminating inter-symbol interference produced by the textbook Barker word. Further, EFJ engineers "rolled" or inverted the ones on each corner of the Barker digits to accommodate the Intel hardware and changed the textbook Barker correlation table from seven to 56 bits. In addition, the Barker correlation table found in the EFJ code was empirically derived by Grindahl using data streams and an emulator. Thus, while the concept of a Barker word and Barker correlation table is not original with EFJ, the particular word and particular configuration of that table found in version 3.0 is.

Further, the Court finds that the H-matrix found in the EFJ code is not a "classic" matrix taken from textbooks, but rather one created by Grindahl through the use of a computer program which generated a number of pseudorandom six bit sequences which were in turn compiled to form the H-matrix table.

In sum, the Court finds that EFJ has contributed something "recognizeably its own" to the compilation of standardized programming techniques and innovative EFJ–generated instructions.

* * *

III. Conclusion

The plaintiff has demonstrated a substantial likelihood of success on the merits of its copyright claim. Plaintiff has also established the remaining equitable prerequisites for injunctive relief set forth in *Dataphase Systems, Inc. v. CL Systems, Inc.*, 640 F.2d 109 (8th Cir.1981). A preliminary injunction restraining the defendant from publishing, selling, marketing, or otherwise disposing of any copies of its LTR–

compatible radio program in any form is therefore warranted in this case.

Based on the foregoing, IT IS ORDERED that:

1. defendant, its officers, employees, agents, servants, and all those in active concert or participation with defendant in the manufacture, promotion, distribution, or sale of its LTR-compatible radio program are hereby preliminarily enjoined and restrained from infringing, in any manner, plaintiff's copyrighted LTR-system computer programs and from publishing, selling, marketing, or otherwise disposing of any copies of defendant's LTR-compatible radio program in any form, pending the final judgment after trial on the merits of this action;

2. defendant is to take all reasonable steps to make its officers, agents, servants, employees, attorneys and those in active concert and participation with it aware of the existence and terms of this preliminary injunction order, as well as their duty to abide by said order;

3. the parties shall confer and advise the Court if agreement can be reached as to the amount of bond to be posted by the plaintiff, and if no agreement can be reached, each side shall submit to the Court within 21 days of the date of this order briefs detailing a proposed bond amount.

ATARI, INC. v. NORTH AMERICAN PHILIPS CONSUMER ELECTRONICS CORP.

United States Court of Appeals, Seventh Circuit, 1982.
672 F.2d 607.

HARLINGTON WOOD JR., CIRCUIT JUDGE.

Plaintiffs-appellants Midway Manufacturing Co. ("Midway") and Atari, Inc. ("Atari") instituted this action against defendants-appellees North American Philips Consumer Electronics Corp. ("North American") and Park Magnavox Home Entertainment Center ("Park") for copyright infringement of and unfair competition against their audiovisual game "PAC–MAN." The district court denied plaintiffs' motion for a preliminary injunction, and this appeal followed, 28 U.S.C. § 1292(a)(1).

I. FACTS

Atari and Midway own the exclusive United States rights in PAC–MAN under the registered copyright for the "PAC–MAN audiovisual work." Midway sells the popular coin-operated arcade version, and Atari recently began to market the home video version. As part of its Odyssey line of home video games, North American developed a game called "K.C. Munchkin" which Park sells at the retail level. Plaintiffs filed this suit alleging that K.C. Munchkin infringes their copyright in PAC–MAN in violation of 17 U.S.C. §§ 106, 501 (Supp. I 1977), and that North American's conduct in marketing K.C. Munchkin constitutes unfair competition in violation of the Illinois Uniform Deceptive Trade

Practices Act, Ill.Rev.Stat. Ch. 121½, §§ 311–17 (1980), and the common law. The district court denied plaintiffs' motion for a preliminary injunction, ruling that plaintiffs failed to show likelihood of success on the merits of either claim.

Because this appeal requires us to make an ocular comparison of the two works, we describe both games in some detail.

A. The Copyrighted Work

The copyrighted version of PAC–MAN is an electronic arcade maze-chase game. Very basically, the game "board," which appears on a television-like screen, consists of a fixed maze, a central character (expressed as a "gobbler"), four pursuit characters (expressed as "ghost monsters"), several hundred evenly spaced pink dots which line the pathways of the maze, four enlarged pink dots ("power capsules") approximately located in each of the maze's four corners, and various colored fruit symbols which appear near the middle of the maze during the play of the game.

Using a "joy stick," the player guides the gobbler through the maze, consuming pink dots along the way. The monsters, which roam independently within the maze, chase the gobbler. Each play ends when a monster catches the gobbler, and after three plays, the game is over. If the gobbler consumes a power capsule, the roles reverse temporarily: the gobbler turns into the hunter, and the monsters become vulnerable. The object of the game is to score as many points as possible by gobbling dots, power capsules, fruit symbols, and monsters.

The PAC–MAN maze has a slightly vertical rectangular shape, and its geometric configuration is drawn in bright blue double lines. Centrally located on the left and right sides of the maze is a tunnel opening. To evade capture by a pursuing monster, the player can cause the central character to exit through one opening and re-enter through the other on the opposite side. In video game parlance this concept is called a "wraparound." In the middle is a rectangular box ("corral") which has a small opening on the upper side. A scoring table, located across the top of the maze, displays in white the first player's score on the left, the high score to date in the middle, and the second player's score on the right. If a player successfully consumes all of the dots, the entire maze flashes alternately blue and white in victory, and a new maze, replenished with dots, appears on the screen. When the game ends a bright red "game over" sign appears below the corral.

At the start of the game, the gobbler character is located centrally near the bottom of the maze. That figure is expressed as a simple yellow dot, somewhat larger than the power capsules, with a V-shaped aperture which opens and closes in mechanical fashion like a mouth as it travels the maze. Distinctive "gobbling" noises accompany this action. If fate (or a slight miscalculation) causes the gobbler to fall prey to one of the monsters, the action freezes, and the gobbler is deflated, folding back on itself, making a sympathetic whining sound, and disappearing with a star-burst.

The four monster characters are identical except that one is red, one blue, one turquoise, and one orange. They are about equal in size to the gobbler, but are shaped like bell jars. The bottom of each figure is contoured to stimulate three short appendages which move as the monster travels about the maze. Their most distinctive feature is their highly animated eyes, which appear as large white circles with blue irises and which "look" in the direction the monster is moving. At the start of each play, the monsters are located side-by-side in the corral, bouncing back and forth until each leaves through the opening. Unlike the gobbler, they do not consume the dots, but move in a prearranged pattern about the maze at a speed approximately equal to that of the gobbler. When the gobbler consumes a power capsule and the roles reverse, the monsters panic: a siren-like alarm sounds, they turn blue, their eyes contract into small pink dots, a wrinkled "mouth" appears, and they immediately reverse direction (moving at a reduced speed). When this period of vulnerability is about to end, the monsters warn the player by flashing alternately blue and white before returning to their original colors. But if a monster is caught during this time, its body disappears, and its original eyes reappear and race back to the corral. Once in the corral, the monster quickly regenerates and reenters the maze to resume its pursuit of the gobbler.

Throughout the play of PAC–MAN, a variety of distinctive musical sounds comprise the audio component of the game. Those sounds coincide with the various character movements and events occurring during the game and add to the excitement of the play.

B. The Accused Work

North American's K.C. Munchkin is also a maze-chase game that employs a player-controlled central character (also expressed as a "gobbler"), pursuit characters (also expressed as "ghost monsters"), dots, and power capsules. The basic play of K.C. Munchkin parallels that of PAC–MAN: the player directs the gobbler through the maze consuming dots and avoiding capture by the monsters; by gobbling a power capsule, the player can reverse the roles; and the ultimate goal is to accumulate the most points by gobbling dots and monsters.

K.C. Munchkin's maze also is rectangular, has two tunnel exits and a centrally located corral, and flashes different colors after the gobbler consumes all of the dots. But the maze, drawn in single, subdued purple lines, is more simple in overall appearance. Because it appears on a home television screen, the maze looks broader than it is tall. Unlike that in PAC–MAN, the maze has one dead-end passageway, which adds an element of risk and strategy. The corral is square rather than rectangular and rotates ninety degrees every two or three seconds, but serves the same purpose as the corral in PAC–MAN. The scoring table is located below the maze and, as in PAC–MAN, has places on the left and right for scores for two players. But instead of simply registering the high score in the middle, the K.C. Munchkin game displays in flashing pink and orange a row of question marks where the high scorer can register his or her name.

The gobbler in K.C. Munchkin initially faces the viewer and appears as a round blue-green figure with horns and eyes. The gobbler normally has an impish smile, but when a monster attacks it, its smile appropriately turns to a frown. As it moves about the maze, the gobbler shows a somewhat diamond-shaped profile with a V-shaped mouth which rapidly opens and closes in a manner similar to PAC–MAN's gobbler. A distinctive "gobbling" noise also accompanies this movement. When the gobbler stops, it turns around to face the viewer with another grin. If captured by a monster, the gobbler also folds back and disappears in a star-burst. At the start of each play, this character is located immediately above the corral. If successful in consuming the last dot, the munchkin turns to the viewer and chuckles.

K.C. Munchkin's three ghost monsters appear similar in shape and movement to their PAC–MAN counterparts. They have round bodies (approximately equal in size to the gobbler) with two short horns or antennae, eyes, and three appendages on the bottom. The eyes are not as detailed as those of the PAC–MAN monsters, but they are uniquely similar in that they also "look" in the direction in which the monster is moving. Although slightly longer, the "legs" also move in a centipede-like manner as the monster roams about the maze. The similarity becomes even more pronounced when the monsters move vertically because their antennae disappear and their bodies assume the more bell jar-like shape of the PAC–MAN monsters. Moreover, the monsters are initially stationed inside the corral (albeit in a piggyback rather than a side-by-side arrangement) and exit into the maze as soon as play commences.

K.C. Munchkin's expression of the role reversal also parallels that in PAC–MAN. When the gobbler consumes one of the power capsules, the vulnerable monsters turn purple and reverse direction, moving at a slightly slower speed. If caught by the gobbler, a monster "vanishes": its body disappears and only white "eyes" and "feet" remain to indicate its presence. Instead of returning directly to the corral to regenerate, the ghost-like figure continues to wander about the maze, but does not affect the play. Only if the rotating corral happens to open up toward the monster as it travels one of the adjacent passageways will the monster re-enter the corral to be regenerated. This delay in regeneration allows the gobbler more time to clear the maze of dots. When the period of vulnerability is about to end, each monster flashes its original color as a warning.

There are only twelve dots in K.C. Munchkin as opposed to over two hundred dots in PAC–MAN. Eight of those dots are white; the other four are power capsules, distinguished by their constantly changing color and the manner in which they blink. In K.C. Munchkin, the dots are randomly spaced, whereas in PAC–MAN, the dots are uniformly spaced. Furthermore, in K.C. Munchkin, the dots are rectangular and are always moving. As the gobbler munches more dots, the speed of the remaining dots progressively increases, and the last dot moves at the same speed as the gobbler. In the words of the district court, "the last dot * * * cannot be caught by overtaking it; it must be munched by strategy." At least initially, one power capsule is located in each of the maze's four corners, as in PAC–MAN.

Finally, K.C. Munchkin has a set of sounds accompanying it which are distinctive to the whole line of Odyssey home video games. Many of these sounds are dissimilar to the sounds which are played in the arcade form of PAC–MAN.

C. The Creation and Promotion of the Accused Work

Ed Averett, an independent contractor, created K.C. Munchkin for North American. He had previously developed approximately twenty-one video games, including other maze-chase games. He and Mr. Staup, who is in charge of North American's home video game development, first viewed PAC–MAN in an airport arcade. Later, after discussing the strengths and weaknesses of the PAC–MAN game and its increasing popularity, they decided to commence development of a modified version to add to North American's Odyssey line of home video games. Mr. Averett also played PAC–MAN at least once before beginning work on K.C. Munchkin.

Mr. Staup and Mr. Averett agreed, however, that the PAC–MAN game, as is, could become popular as a home video game, but only if marketed under the "PAC–MAN" name. Thus, as Mr. Averett worked on K.C. Munchkin, North American sought to obtain from Midway a license under the PAC–MAN copyright and trademark. Mr. Staup later learned that the license was not available and so informed Mr. Averett. At that time, Mr. Averett had not yet completed K.C. Munchkin.

When Mr. Averett finished the project, North American examined the game and concluded that it was "totally different" from PAC–MAN. To avoid any potential claim of confusion, however, Mr. Averett was told to make further changes in the game characters. As a result, the color of the gobbler was changed from yellow to its present bluish color. North American also adopted the dissimilar name "K.C. Munchkin" and issued internal instructions not to refer to PAC–MAN in promoting K.C. Munchkin.

An independent retailer in the Chicago area nonetheless ran advertisements in the *Chicago Sun–Times* and the *Chicago Tribune,* describing K.C. Munchkin as "a Pac–Man type game" and "as challenging as Pac–Man." Another printed advertisement referred to K.C. Munchkin as "a PAC–MAN game." Plaintiffs also sent investigators to various stores to purchase a K.C. Munchkin game. In response to specific inquiries, sales persons in two stores, one being the aforementioned independent retailer, described the Odyssey game as "like PAC–MAN" and as "Odyssey's PAC–MAN."

* * *

III. Copyright Infringement

To establish infringement a plaintiff must prove ownership of a valid copyright and "copying" by the defendant. Because direct evidence of copying often is unavailable, copying may be inferred where the defendant had access to the copyrighted work and the accused work is substantially similar to the copyrighted work. The parties stipulated to the validity of plaintiffs' copyright and to access; the district court's ruling turned solely on the question of substantial similarity.

Some courts have expressed the test of substantial similarity in two parts: (1) whether the defendant copied from the plaintiff's work and (2) whether the copying, if proven, went so far as to constitute an improper appropriation. Our analysis focuses on the second part of that test and the response of the "ordinary observer." *See Ideal Toy Corp. v. Fab–Lu Ltd. (Inc.),* 360 F.2d 1021, 1023 n.2 (2d Cir.1966). Specifically, the test is whether the accused work is so similar to the plaintiff's work that an ordinary reasonable person would conclude that the defendant unlawfully appropriated the plaintiff's protectible expression by taking material of substance and value. *Krofft,* 562 F.2d at 1164. Judge Learned Hand, in finding infringement, once stated that "the ordinary observer, unless he set out to detect the disparities, would be disposed to overlook them, and regard their aesthetic appeal as the same." *Peter Pan Fabrics, Inc. v. Martin Weiner Corp.,* 274 F.2d 487, 489 (2d Cir.1960). It has been said that this test does not involve "analytic dissection and expert testimony," *Arnstein,* 154 F.2d at 468, but depends on whether the accused work has captured the "total concept and feel" of the copyrighted work, *Roth Greeting Cards v. United Card Co.,* 429 F.2d 1106, 1110 (9th Cir.1970).

While dissection is generally disfavored, the ordinary observer test, in application, must take into account that the copyright laws preclude appropriation of only those elements of the work that are protected by the copyright. * * *

* * *This appeal requires us to address the * * * question of the *scope* of copyright protection to be afforded audiovisual games such as PAC–MAN. To do so, we must first attempt to distill the protectible forms of expression in PAC–MAN from the game itself. *See, e.g., Durham,* 630 F.2d at 914–15.

There is no litmus paper test by which to apply the idea-expression distinction; the determination is necessarily subjective. As Judge Learned Hand said, "Obviously, no principle can be stated as to when an imitator has gone beyond copying the 'idea,' and has borrowed its 'expression.' Decisions must therefore inevitably be *ad hoc.*" *Peter Pan Fabrics,* 274 F.2d at 489. Courts and commentators nevertheless have developed a few helpful approaches. In *Nichols v. Universal*

Pictures Corp., 45 F.2d 119, 121 (2d Cir.1930), *cert. denied*, 282 U.S. 902, 51 S.Ct. 216, 75 L.Ed. 795 (1931), Judge Hand articulated what is now known as the "abstractions test":

> Upon any work * * * a great number of patterns of increasing generality will fit equally well, as more and more of the incident is left out. * * * [T]here is a point in this series of abstractions where they are no longer protected, since otherwise the playwright could prevent the use of his "ideas," to which, apart from their expression, his property is never extended. Nobody has ever been able to fix that boundary, and nobody ever can. * * * As respects plays, the controversy chiefly centers upon the characters and sequence of incident, these being the substance.

(citations omitted). This "test" has proven useful in analyzing dramatic works, literary works, and motion pictures, where the recurring patterns can readily be abstracted into very general themes.

A related concept is that of idea-expression unity: where idea and expression are indistinguishable, the copyright will protect against only identical copying. * * *

In the context of literary works, some courts have adopted a similar *scenes a faire* approach. *Scenes a faire* refers to "incidents, characters or settings which are as a practical matter indispensable, or at least standard, in the treatment of a given topic." *Alexander v. Haley*, 460 F.Supp. 40, 45 (S.D.N.Y.1978). Such stock literary devices are not protectible by copyright. *Reyher*, 533 F.2d at 91. Thus, "similarity of expression, whether literal or nonliteral, which necessarily results from the fact that the common idea is only capable of expression in more or less stereotyped form will preclude a finding of actionable similarity." 3 Nimmer § 13.03[A][1], at 13–28. Courts have applied this concept to written game rules, *see, e.g., Morrissey v. Procter & Gamble Co.*, 379 F.2d 675, 678 (1st Cir.1967). * * *

* * *

* * * In applying the abstractions test, we find that plaintiffs' game can be described accurately in fairly abstract terms, much in the same way as one would articulate the rules to such a game. *Cf. Morrissey* (no infringement of written game rules). PAC–MAN is a maze-chase game in which the player scores points by guiding a central figure through various passageways of a maze and at the same time avoiding collision with certain opponents or pursuit figures which move independently about the maze. Under certain conditions, the central figure may temporarily become empowered to chase and overtake the opponents, thereby scoring bonus points. The audio component and the concrete details of the visual presentation constitute the copyrightable expression of that game "idea."

Certain expressive matter in the PAC–MAN work, however, should be treated as *scenes a faire* and receive protection only from virtually identical copying. The maze and scoring table are standard game devices, and the tunnel exits are nothing more than the commonly used "wrap around" concept adapted to a maze-chase game. Similarly, the use of dots provides a means by which a player's performance can be gauged and rewarded with the appropriate number of points, and by which to inform the player of his or her progress. Given their close connection with the underlying game, K.C. Munchkin's maze design, scoring table, and "dots" are sufficiently different to preclude a finding of infringement on that basis alone.

Rather, it is the substantial appropriation of the PAC–MAN characters that requires reversal of the district court. The expression of the central figure as a "gobbler" and the pursuit figures as "ghost monsters" distinguishes PAC–MAN from conceptually similar video games. Other games, such as "Rally–X" (described in *Dirkschneider*) and North American's own "Take the Money and Run," illustrate different ways in which a basic maze-chase game can be expressed. *See also Durham,* 630 F.2d at 914–15. PAC–MAN's particular artistic interpretation of the game was designed to create a certain impression which would appeal to a nonviolent player personality. The game as such, however, does not dictate the use of a "gobbler" and "ghost monsters." Those characters are wholly fanciful creations, without reference to the real world.[11]

North American not only adopted the same basic characters but also portrayed them in a manner which made K.C. Munchkin appear substantially similar to PAC–MAN. The K.C. Munchkin gobbler has several blatantly similar features, including the relative size and shape of the "body," the V-shaped "mouth," its distinctive gobbling action (with appropriate sounds), and especially the way in which it disappears upon being captured. An examination of the K.C. Munchkin ghost monsters reveals even more significant visual similarities. In size, shape, and manner of movement, they are virtually identical to their PAC–MAN counterparts. K.C. Munchkin's monsters, for example, exhibit the same peculiar "eye" and "leg" movement. Both games, moreover, express the role reversal and "regeneration" process with such great similarity that an ordinary observer could conclude only that North American copied plaintiffs' PAC–MAN.

Defendants point to a laundry list of specific differences—particularly the concept of moving dots, the variations in mazes, and certain changes in facial features and colors of the characters—which they contend, and the district court apparently agreed, shows lack of substantial similarity. Although numerous differences may influence the impressions of the ordinary observer, "slight differences between a protected work and an accused work will not preclude a finding of infringement" where the works are substantially similar in other respects. *Durham,* 630 F.2d at 913. Exact reproduction or near identity is not necessary to establish infringement. * * * In comparing

11. With each video game, the line of demarcation between idea and expression and the extent to which certain expressions may constitute *scenes a faire* will vary.

the two works, the district court focused on certain differences in detail and seemingly ignored (or at least failed to articulate) the more obvious similarities. The *sine qua non* of the ordinary observer test, however, is the overall similarities rather than the minute differences between the two works. The nature of the alterations on which North American relies only tends to emphasize the extent to which it deliberately copied from the plaintiffs' work. * * * When analyzing two works to determine whether they are substantially similar, courts should be careful not to lose sight of the forest for the trees.[12]

To assess the impact of certain differences, one factor to consider is the nature of the protected material and the setting in which it appears. *Universal Athletic Sales,* 511 F.2d at 908. Video games, unlike an artist's painting or even other audiovisual works, appeal to an audience that is fairly undiscriminating insofar as their concern about more subtle differences in artistic expression. The main attraction of a game such as PAC–MAN lies in the stimulation provided by the intensity of the competition. A person who is entranced by the play of the game "would be disposed to overlook" many of the minor differences in detail and "regard their aesthetic appeal as the same." *Cf. Krofft,* 562 F.2d at 1166–67 (children would view accused characters as substantially similar to the protected characters despite differences in detail).

The defendants and the district court order stress that K.C. Munchkin *plays* differently because of the moving dots and the variety of maze configurations from which the player can choose. The focus in a copyright infringement action, however, is on the similarities in protectible *expression.* Even to the extent that those differences alter the visual impression of K.C. Munchkin, they are insufficient to preclude a finding of infringement. * * * It is irrelevant that K.C. Munchkin has other game modes which employ various maze configurations. The only mode that concerns this court is the one that uses a display most similar to the one in PAC–MAN. Other cases similarly have separated the "attract" mode from the "play" mode in comparing two audiovisual games. Moreover, PAC–MAN's distinctive characters alone may constitute material of substantial value. *Cf. Walt Disney; Krofft* (cartoon characters).

12. Many of the differences, such as North American's inability to duplicate some of the more distinctive features of PAC–MAN's monsters, may be due to the lesser capacity of the home video medium. That a work is transferred into a different medium is not itself a bar to recovery. *Universal Pictures,* 162 F.2d at 360; 2 Nimmer § 8.01[B], at 8–13. An author has the exclusive right to produce derivative works based on the original work, 17 U.S.C. § 106(2), and that right often can be more valuable than the right to the original work itself. Although dissection and expert testimony is not favored, the judicially created ordinary observer test should not deprive authors of this significant statutory grant merely because the technical requirements of a different medium *dictate* certain differences in expression. Without deciding the question, we note that in some cases it may be important to educate the trier of fact as to such considerations in order to preserve the author's rights under the Copyright Act. *See* 3 Nimmer § 13.03[E], at 13–45. We do not, however, propose that wholly *voluntary* changes in expression be given any less weight by the trier of fact.

While not necessarily conclusive, other extrinsic evidence additionally suggests that plaintiffs are likely to succeed on their copyright claim. In promoting K.C. Munchkin, several retailers and sales clerks described that game by referring to PAC–MAN. Comments that K.C. Munchkin is "Odyssey's PAC–MAN" or "a PAC–MAN game" especially reflect that at least some lay observers view the games as similar. Furthermore, North American's direction to Mr. Averett that he make certain superficial changes in the gobbler figure may be viewed as an attempt to disguise an intentional appropriation of PAC–MAN's expression.

Based on an ocular comparison of the two works, we conclude that plaintiffs clearly showed likelihood of success. Although not "virtually identical" to PAC–MAN, K.C. Munchkin captures the "total concept and feel" of and is substantially similar to PAC–MAN. This case is a far cry from those in which the defendant appropriated only the game idea, but adopted its own unique form of expression, *see Durham,* 630 F.2d at 914–15, or where minor variations or differences were sufficient to avoid liability because the form of expression was inextricably tied to the game itself.

* * *

V. Conclusion

The district court's conclusion that the two works are not substantially similar is clearly erroneous, and its refusal to issue a preliminary injunction constitutes an abuse of discretion. Since this is an interlocutory appeal, however, we are mindful that our holding does not constitute a conclusive adjudication of the merits of plaintiffs' claim. The ordinary observer test should not be applied in a judicial vacuum. Further development of the facts at trial may command a different conclusion.

For the foregoing reasons, we reverse the district court's denial of plaintiffs' motion for a preliminary injunction and direct the district court to enter a preliminary injunction against continued infringement of plaintiffs' copyright.

DATA EAST USA, INC. v. EPYX, INC.

United States Court of Appeals, Ninth Circuit, 1988.
862 F.2d 204.

Trott, Circuit Judge:

Plaintiff-appellee Data East USA, Inc., brought this action against defendant-appellant Epyx, Inc. for copyright, trademark, and trade dress infringement. The district court found a copyright infringement and issued a permanent injunction and impoundment. Epyx appeals the grant of the permanent injunction.

Epyx contends (1) the district court erred in granting the injunction because Epyx never had access to Data East's copyrighted work, (2) the district court erred in finding substantial similarity, and (3) the district court's injunction was impermissibly vague and overbroad. We reverse.

I. Facts

Data East is a California corporation engaged in the design, manufacture, and sale of audio-visual works embodied in video games for coin-operated and home computer use. In July 1984, Data East commenced distribution in Japan of an arcade game entitled "Karate Champ" ("Arcade # 1"). In September 1984, Data East commenced distribution in Japan and later in the United States and Europe of an updated version of "Karate Champ" ("Arcade # 2" or more generally as "arcade game"). Finally, on October 12, 1985, Data East commenced distribution in the United States of a home computer game version of "Karate Champ" ("home game"). Data East applied for and received audio-visual copyright certificates for each game.

In November of 1985, System III Software, Ltd., an English company, commenced distribution in England of a home computer game entitled "International Karate." Epyx, a California corporation engaged in the development and distribution of audio-visual works for use on home computers, obtained a license agreement with System III and commenced distribution in the United States on April 30, 1986 of a Commodore-compatible version of "International Karate" under the name "World Karate Championship."

Each competing product, "Karate Champ" and "World Karate Championship," consists of the audio-visual depiction of a karate match or matches conducted by two combatants, one clad in a typical white outfit and the other in red. Successive phases of combat are conducted against varying stationary background images depicting localities or geographic scenes. The match is supervised by a referee who directs the beginning and end of each phase of combat and announces the winning combatant of each phase by means of a cartoon-style speech balloon. Each game has a bonus round where the karate combatant breaks bricks and dodges objects. Similarities also exist in the moves used by the combatants and the scoring method.

* * *

II. Discussion

A district court's determination of findings of fact is subject to the clearly erroneous standard of review. The issues of access and substantial similarity are findings of fact reviewable for clear error. *McCulloch,* 823 F.2d at 318. Under the clearly erroneously standard of review, an appellate court must accept the lower court's findings of fact unless upon review the appellate court is left with the definite and firm conviction that a mistake has been committed.

* * *

B. Substantial Similarity

"To show that two works are substantially similar, plaintiff must demonstrate that the works are substantially similar in both *ideas* and *expression.*" *Frybarger v. International Business Machines Corp.,* 812 F.2d 525, 529 (9th Cir.1987). Although plaintiff must first show that the ideas are substantially similar, the ideas themselves are not protected by copyright and therefore, cannot be infringed. It is an axiom of copyright law that copyright protects only an author's expression of an idea, not the idea itself. There is a strong public policy corollary to this axiom permitting all to use freely ideas contained in a copyrightable work, so long as the protected expression itself is not appropriated. Thus, to the extent the similarities between plaintiff's and defendant's works are confined to ideas and general concepts, these similarities are noninfringing.

The Ninth Circuit has developed a two-step test for the purposes of determining substantial similarity. First, an "extrinsic" test is used to determine whether two ideas are substantially similar. This is an objective test which rests upon specific criteria that can be listed and analyzed. *Krofft, id.* Second, an "intrinsic" test is used to compare forms of expression. This is a subjective test which depends on the response of the ordinary reasonable person. *Id.*

In applying the extrinsic test, the district court found that the *idea* expressed in plaintiff's game and in defendant's game is identical. The *idea* of the games was described by the court as follows:

> "* * * a martial arts karate combat game conducted between two combatants, and presided over by a referee, all of which are represented by visual images, and providing a method of scoring accomplished by full and half point scores for each player, and utilizing dots to depict full point scores and half point scores."

The district court further found that:

> "In each of the games, the phases of martial arts combat are conducted against still background images purporting to depict geographic or locality situses and located at the top of the screen as the game is viewed. The action of the combatants in each of the games takes place in the lower portion of the screen as the game is viewed, and is against a one color background in that portion of the screen as the game is viewed."

Once an idea is found to be similar or identical, as in this case, the second or intrinsic step is applied to determine whether similarity of the expression of the idea occurs. This exists when the "total concept and feel of the works" is substantially similar. *Aliotti v. R. Dakin & Co.,* 831 F.2d 898 (9th Cir.1987). Analytic dissection of the dissimilarities as opposed to the similarities is not appropriate under this test because it distracts a reasonable observer from a comparison of the total concept and feel of the works. *Id.*

The rule in the Ninth Circuit, however, is that "[n]o substantial similarity of expression will be found when 'the idea and its expression are * * * inseparable,' given that 'protecting the expression in such circumstances would confer a monopoly of the *idea* upon the copyright owner.'" *Id.* (quoting *Herbert Rosenthal Jewelry Corp. v. Kalpakian,* 446 F.2d 738, 742 (9th Cir.1971)) (emphasis added).

Nor can copyright protection be afforded to elements of expression that necessarily follow from an idea, or to "scenes a faire," i.e., expressions that are "as a practical matter, indispensable or at least standard in the treatment of a given [idea]." *Aliotti,* 831 F.2d at 901 (quoting *Atari, Inc. v. North American Phillips Consumer Elecs Corp.,* 672 F.2d 607, 616 (7th Cir.1982), *cert. denied,* 459 U.S. 880, 103 S.Ct. 176, 74 L.Ed.2d 145 (1982)).

To determine whether similarities result from unprotectable expression, analytic dissection of *similarities* may be performed. If this demonstrates that all similarities in expression arise from use of common ideas, then no substantial similarity can be found. *Id.*

The district court performed what can be described as an analytic dissection of similarities in its findings of fact and stated: Plaintiff's and defendant's games each encompass the idea of depicting the performance of karate martial arts combat in each of the following respects:

A. Each game has fourteen moves.

B. Each game has a two-player option.

C. Each game has a one-player option.

D. Each game has forward and backward somersault moves and about-face moves.

E. Each game has a squatting reverse punch wherein the heel is not on the ground.

F. Each game has an upper-lunge punch.

G. Each game has a back-foot sweep.

H. Each game has a jumping sidekick.

I. Each game has low kick.

J. Each game has a walk-backwards position.

K. Each game has changing background scenes.

L. Each game has 30–second countdown rounds.

M. Each game uses one referee.

N. In each game the referee says "begin," "stop," "white," "red," which is depicted by a cartoon-style speech balloon.

O. Each game has a provision for 100 bonus points per remaining second.

The district court found that the visual depiction of karate matches is subject to the constraints inherent in the sport of karate itself. The number of combatants, the stance employed by the combatants, established and recognized moves and motions regularly employed in the sport of karate, the regulation of the match by at least one referee or judge, and the manner of scoring by points and half points are among the constraints inherent in the sport of karate. Because of these constraints, karate is not susceptible of a wholly fanciful presentation. Furthermore, the use of the Commodore computer for a karate game intended for home consumption is subject to various constraints inherent in the use of that computer. Among the constraints are the use of sprites,[5] and a somewhat limited access to color, together with limitations upon the use of multiple colors in one visual image.

The fifteen features listed by the court "encompass the idea of karate." These features, which consist of the game procedure, common karate moves, the idea of background scenes, a time element, a referee, computer graphics, and bonus points, result from either constraints inherent in the sport of karate or computer restraints. After careful consideration and viewing of these features, we find that they necessarily follow from the *idea* of a martial arts karate combat game, or are inseparable from, indispensable to, or even standard treatment of the *idea* of the karate sport. As such, they are not protectable. "When idea and expression coincide, there will be protection against nothing other than identical copying." *Krofft,* 562 F.2d at 1168. A comparison of the works in this case demonstrates that identical copying is not an issue.

Accordingly, we hold that the court did not give the appropriate weight and import to its findings which support Epyx's argument that the similarities result from unprotectable expression. Consequently, it was clear error for the district court to determine that protectable substantial similarity existed based upon these facts.

The lower court erred by not limiting the scope of Data East's copyright protection to the author's contribution—the scoreboard and background scenes. In actuality, however, the backgrounds are quite dissimilar and the method of scorekeeping, though similar, is inconsequential. Based upon these two features, a discerning 17.5 year-old boy [6] could not regard the works as substantially similar. Accordingly, Data East's copyright was not infringed on this basis either.

Because we reverse in its entirety the district court's finding of copyright infringement, it follows that the injunction was improvident-

5. A "sprite" involves the use of a special technique for creating mobile graphic images on a computer screen that is appropriate for animation. An increase in sophistication of sprite techniques used in the computer program will increase the graphic quality of the game's animation.

6. The district court found that the average age of individuals purchasing "Karate Champ" is 17.5 years, that the purchasers are predominantly male, and comprise a knowledgeable, critical, and discerning group.

ly granted. Accordingly, we remand to the district court to lift the injunction.

Each party is to bear its own costs.

Reversed and Remanded.

Notes

1. Great efforts were expended by Johnson to show that defendant copied. When advising a potential software copyright plaintiff, the lawyer must warn of the enormous resources that the plaintiff must devote to the litigation.

2. The existence of three "superfluous instructions" helped persuade the court in *Johnson* that there had been illicit copying. Software developers can improve their chances of proving copying by a software pirate by inserting such superflous instructions in their programs.

3. Note the detailed analysis the court performed in comparing PAC–MAN and K.C. Munchkin in *Atari.* What advice would you have given to the North American Phillips software designers if they had approached you before beginning their development of K.C. Munchkin?

4. Given the *Data East* decision, do developers of "clone" game software, have great latitude in using basic game rules?

2. AVOIDING INFRINGEMENT BY THE "CLEAN ROOM" APPROACH

In the manufacture of computer chips, the physical environment must be exceptionally clean, because the least speck of dust will ruin a computer chip. Chip assembly takes place in special "clean rooms". Developers of "clone" software use what their lawyers call "clean rooms" to avoid infringement. Because copyright protects only against copying, the "clone" maker has a complete defense if it can prove it developed its product independently. The technique uses two teams. The first is a "spec" or "dirty" team that has access to the competing product to be cloned and its associated documentation. The second, "clean" team works in a "clean room" where there are no copies of the competitor's product or documentation. Only employees who are unfamiliar with the competitor's product serve on the clean team. The spec team communicates with the clean team by sending it formal written specifications. (Clean team members do not have informal conversations with spec team members.) A typical specification, for instance, might indicate a subroutine located at a particular memory location should have the function of erasing the computer screen. Clerical employees keep a complete record of all communications and all steps in software development. When the clean team has completed a draft program it sends it back to the spec team (or to a separate testing team). After testing, the clean team receives a test report with an indication of ways in which the program fails to perform as specified.

There are many variations on the "clean room" technique. A company may use an outside consulting firm for the clean team. It may videotape the clean room operations to have further proof of independent program development. Problems with clean room techniques include the difficulty of finding good programmers that have never seen the competing product and the risk that the clean team will "cheat" to meet programming deadlines. If the specifications describe the "look and feel" of the competing program, the program written in the clean room may infringe by duplicating that look and feel, even though the duplication was done indirectly.

NEC CORPORATION AND NEC ELECTRONICS, INC. v. INTEL CORPORATION.

United States District Court, Northern District of California, 1989.
1989 Copr.L.Dec. ¶ 26,379; 10 U.S.P.Q. 1177; 1989 WL 67434.

GRAY, DISTRICT JUDGE: In this action, NEC seeks a declaration that Intel's copyrights on its 8086 and 8088 microcodes * are invalid and/or are not infringed by NEC. Intel has filed a counterclaim for infringement of its copyrights on those microcodes. This case was tried without a jury for eighteen days between April 25 and July 18, 1988. Post-trial briefs were filed, final arguments were heard on July 29, 1988, and the case then was submitted for decision. The issues to be determined and the decision that the court now renders on each are as follows:

* * *

3. Do the microcodes that NEC produced for its V20, V30, V40 and V50 microprocessors infringe the Intel copyrights for its 8086 and 8088 microcodes? NEC's microcodes do not so infringe.

4. Are NEC's V20 and V30 microprocessors no more than "improvements" upon its uPD 8086 and uPD 8088 microprocessors, which were licensed by Intel under its copyrights? NEC's V20 and V30 microprocessors are not simply "improvements" upon its uPD 8086 and uPD 8088 microprocessors.

The reasons for the foregoing decision are contained in the following discussion:

* * *

III. THE NONINFRINGEMENT BY NEC'S MICROCODE

A. The Issue Of Substantial Similarity

In order to make a prima facie case of infringement, Intel must have a valid copyright, which it did obtain as noted above, establish access by NEC to the copyrighted microcode, which is admitted, and show substantial similarity between the latter and the accused microcode of NEC. In seeking to resolve the issue of substantial similarity, I have given careful consideration to the testimony and the conflicting conclusions of the two eminent experts, Dr. Patterson and Dr. Frieder,

* Except as otherwise noted herein, the 8086 and 8088 microcodes may be considered to be identical for purposes of this action, and will be referred to in the singular as the "8086/88 microcode".

and I have also taken into account my own impressions upon comparing the respective microcodes in light of the other testimony and the exhibits in the case. In pursuing this study, I have sought to adhere to the admonition that

> [i]n deciding whether there is substantial similarity between the copyrighted work and the accused work, courts do not allow the accused work to be dissected into pieces, and the pieces isolated, as if each stood alone. Where the accused work reflects an accumulation of similarities, the totality of the taking is to be considered: "When analyzing two works to determine whether they are substantially similar, courts should be careful not to lose sight of the forest for the trees." ** In programming infringement cases involving comprehensive nonliteral similarity, the "trees" are the individual lines of codes, and the "forest" is the detailed design.

Clapes, Lynch & Steinberg, *Silicon Epics and Binary Bards: Determining the Proper Scope of Copyright Protection For Computer Programs,* 34 UCLA L.Rev. 1493, 1570 (1987). Having pondered all of these matters, it is my conclusion that the NEC microcode (Rev. 2), when considered as a whole, is not substantially similar to the Intel microcode within the meaning of the copyright laws.

In the first place, none of the approximately ninety microroutines in the accused microcode are identical to Intel's copyrighted microcode. Some of the shorter ones are, indeed substantially similar. * * * But most of these involve simple, straightforward operations in which close similarity in approach is not surprising. On the other hand, others of the shorter microroutines of the NEC microcode are substantially different from the comparable Intel items. * * *

Most of the approximately forty NEC microroutines that Intel acknowledges not to be substantially similar are much longer than the accused NEC items and are quite different from the comparable Intel items in the manner in which the instructions are expressed.

As I have pondered upon the testimony of the experts and studied the exhibits, I have developed a sympathetic understanding of what Judge Learned Hand meant when he observed in a relevant situation that "the more the court is led into the intricacies of dramatic craftsmanship, the less likely it is to stand upon the firmer, if more naive, ground of its considered impressions upon its own perusal." *Nichols v. Universal Pictures Corp.,* 45 F.2d 119, 123 (2d Cir.1930). Also, Intel has proposed a finding and has cited valid authority to the effect that "[t]he test for infringement or substantial similarity is whether the work is recognized by an ordinary observer as having been taken from the copyrighted source." Intel's Proposed Conclusions Of Law, ¶ 5. For the reasons set forth above, this court concludes, based upon its own perusal, as well as upon the conflicting testimony of the experts, that

** Citing *Atari, Inc. v. North American Phillips Consumer Elec. Corp.,* 672 F.2d 607, 618 (7th Cir.1982).

the ordinary observer, considering the accused microcode as a whole, would not recognize it as having been taken from the copyrighted source.

I believe that the foregoing conclusion comes close to resolving the issue of infringement. However, as pointed out, several of the shorter accused microroutines are substantially similar to Intel's corresponding items, and it is my obligation to "make a qualitative, not quantitative, judgment about the character of the work as a whole and the importance of the substantially similar portions of the work." *Whelan Assoc. v. Jaslow Dental Laboratory,* 797 F.2d 1222, 1245 (3d Cir.1986). Some of these similar microroutines may be very important, and if they result from copying of protected expressions their use by NEC may be enjoined, irrespective of the general lack of similarity between the two microcodes. Accordingly, we shall discuss what the evidence indicates as to whether or not actionable copying is responsible for the similarities that do exist in some of the microroutines.

B. The Evidence Regarding Copying.

In preparing this portion of this memorandum, I am assuming that it will be of particular interest only to Intel and NEC and their respective counsel, and therefore that anyone who reads it will be familiar with the facts. Accordingly, I shall refrain from the extremely arduous and lengthy task of describing or explaining the background circumstances involving the specific issues.

Intel urges several bases for its contention that Mr. Kaneko created NEC's microcode for its V20/V30 microprocessors by copying substantial portions of Intel's 8086/88 microcode. These arguments are found not to be compelling.

1. Assessment Of Mr. Kaneko's Expertise.

Intel contends that the indications are that Mr. Kaneko must have copied because of his relative inexperience with microprograms, the arduous schedule imposed upon him within which to write the microprograms and the specifications for the hardware, and the fact that he made relatively few notes as compared to his work on other microprograms. The record shows Mr. Kaneko to have been a very talented young man with an outstanding academic record that is highly relevant to microprocessors, and he previously had completed a substantial assembly language compiler program. Mr. Kaneko testified very creditably that he did not feel himself to have been under great pressure to complete his assignment and that he easily was able to accomplish it in two months, well within the time requested of him. The court also accepts Mr. Kaneko's testimony that the lack of notes stemmed from his conclusion that the task was relatively simple and that he was working alone, as compared with other assignments in which the participation of others made greater note taking more appropriate.

Mr. Kaneko testified in a straightforward manner and displayed considerable technical knowledge in explaining the decisions that he made in the creation of the V20/V30 microcode. He did not contend that he had not been influenced by his experience in previously having disassembled the 8086/88 microcode. Such experience inevitably became part of his expertise, and the acquired knowledge of how Mr. McKevitt created instructions to be executed by the 8086/88 microcode very well may have been a source of ideas that Mr. Kaneko utilized in preparing a microcode for the V20/V30. However, he testified creditably that he did not undertake to copy the 8086/88 microcode, and, as is noted herein, the other evidence received in the trial of this action by no means impels a contrary conclusion.

* * *

C. The Constraints.

1. The Hardware, Architecture And Specifications.

In seeking to show that there were many alternate ways in which Mr. Kaneko's various microprograms could have been written, and therefore that the substantial similarities to Intel's microcode that did exist stemmed from copying, Intel declined to take into consideration the constraints that limited Mr. Kaneko's choices. Intel contends that NEC could have created a microprocessor compatible with Intel's 8086/88 by using "different hardware, different architecture, different specifications and a different microinstruction format." Intel's Memorandum for the Trial Court, dated June 7, 1988, page 18. However, NEC had a license from Intel to duplicate the 8086/88 microprocessor hardware to the extent comprehended by the Intel patents. Both Dr. Patterson and Dr. Frieder acknowledged that the use of such hardware limited substantially the choices available to Mr. Kaneko in creating the microcode for the V-series. Having granted to NEC a license to duplicate the hardware of its 8086/88 to the extent comprehended by the Intel patents, and having conceded at trial that NEC had a right to duplicate the hardware of the 8086/88 because it was not otherwise protected by Intel, Intel is in no position to challenge NEC's right to use the aspects of Intel's microcode that are mandated by such hardware.

2. The Storage Space.

Intel also asserts that if NEC had utilized all of the storage area (ROM) available to it on its microprocessor, which would have been double the storage space that was available to Intel, any constraint imposed by size would have been removed and a different and better microcode would have resulted. Intel's Memorandum for the Trial Court, dated June 7, 1988, page 18. NEC elected to use part of the ROM space existing on the V-series, in order to accommodate microcode for additional macroinstructions on the same ROM. This also was a legitimate constraint; NEC was not obliged to avoid the similarity that other constraints imposed by creating a larger microcode.

3. The Clean Room.

The Clean Room microcode constitutes compelling evidence that the similarities between the NEC microcode and the Intel microcode resulted from constraints. The Clean Room microcode was governed by the same constraints of hardware, architecture and specifications as applied to the NEC microcode, and copying clearly was not involved. Mr. McKevitt, who created the 8086 microcode for Intel, readily acknowledged that the microarchitecture of the 8086 microprocessor affected the manner in which he created his microcode, and that he would expect that another independently created microcode for the 8086 would have some similarities to his. (See Tr.Vol. 8 1358: 10–24). Accordingly, the similarities between the Clean Room microcode and the Intel microcode must be attributable largely to the above mentioned constraints. But the similarities between the Clean Room microcode and Rev. 2 are at least as great as are the similarities between the latter and the Intel microcode. This is made evident by an examination of Exhibit 705. The strong likelihood follows that these similarities, also resulted from the same constraints.

Mr. McKevitt also acknowledged that he would expect that independently created microcode for the 8086 would have fewer similarities in the longer sequences than in the shorter sequences because "there is more opportunity for the longer sequences to be expressed differently." (Tr.Vol. 8 1359: 5–10). This is exactly what occurred here; the longer sequences in Rev. 2 and Intel's microcode are not nearly so much alike as are the shorter sequences.

In light of the foregoing, it is reasonable to conclude that the same constraints, rather than copying, were responsible for the principal similarities between Rev. 2 and the Intel microcode.

D. Idea v. Expression.

As concluded above, overall, and particularly with respect to the longer microroutines, NEC's microcode is not substantially similar to Intel's; but some of the shorter, simpler microroutines resemble Intel's. None, however, are identical. As to these shorter, simpler microroutines, if their underlying ideas are capable of only a limited range of expression, they "may be protected only against virtually identical copying." Frybarger v. International Business Machines, Inc., 812 F.2d 525, 530 (9th Cir.1987).

In determining an idea's range of expression, constraints are relevant factors to consider. In this case, the expression of NEC's microcode was constrained by the use of the macroinstruction set and hardware of the 8086/88. Mr. McKevitt so testified (Tr.Vol. 8 1358: 10–24), Dr. Patterson initially expressed the same opinion (Exhibit R, pages 7598 and 7601), and the close similarities of the Clean Room microcode to Intel's and NEC's microcodes emphatically concur.

Mr. Davidian and Dr. Frieder testified that, in light of these constraints, the shorter, simpler microroutines can be expressed only in a few limited ways, and I agree. (Davidian Tr.Vol. 18 3092: 18–3093:

13; Frieder as cited in NEC's Supplemented and Annotated Findings of Fact and Conclusions of Law ¶ 75). These include those microroutines identified as similar in Section A, pages 20–21 above. A good illustration is "ESCAPE". The Clean Room and NEC's version are identical, which is evidence of its constrained nature. Further, Dr. Frieder testified that "ESCAPE" was highly constrained given the existing hardware. (Tr.Vol. 14 2479: 10–2480:1).

Accordingly, it is the conclusion of this court that the expression of the ideas underlying the shorter, simpler microroutines (including those identified earlier as substantially similar) may be protected only against virtually identical copying, and that NEC properly used the underlying ideas, without virtually identically copying their limited expression.

* * *

CONCLUSION

For reasons hereinabove set forth, judgment will be entered holding that:

1. The Intel microcode for its 8086 and 8088 microprocessors were proper subjects for protection under United States copyright laws.

2. Intel did forfeit the copyrights that it had obtained for its 8086 and 8088 microcodes because more than a relatively small number of copies of product distributed by its authority did not contain the copyright notice prescribed by 17 U.S.C. § 401, because it failed to make a reasonable effort to cause such notice to be added to those copies after the omission had been discovered, within the meaning of 17 U.S.C. § 405, and because those copies were distributed at times when no express requirement in writing, within the meaning of 17 U.S.C. § 405, mandated such marking.

3. The microcodes that NEC produced for its V20, V30, V40 and V50 microprocessors do not infringe the Intel copyrights for its 8086 and 8088 microcodes.

4. NEC's V20 and V30 microprocessors are not simply "improvements" upon its uPD 8086 and uPD 8088 microprocessors, which were licensed by Intel under its copyrights.

This memorandum shall constitute findings of fact and conclusions of law, pursuant to Federal Rule of Civil Procedure 52(a).

BROOKTREE CORPORATION v. ADVANCED MICRO DEVICES, INC.

United States District Court, Southern District of California, 1988.
705 F.Supp. 491.

ENRIGHT, DISTRICT JUDGE.

INTRODUCTION

* * *

Brooktree alleges that AMD has introduced pirated chips at lower prices in an attempt to recapture its lost market. These pirated chips are allegedly copies of two of Brooktree's chips.

* * *

MASK WORK ACT

This case was brought under the Mask Work Act, 17 U.S.C. §§ 901–914.

* * *

B. Reverse Engineering

AMD argues that Plants discovered his layout through reverse engineering, and that reverse engineering is specifically allowed under the Mask Work Act. AMD has presented evidence of a paper trail showing the various stages of Plants' discovery process. AMD maintains that it has invested an equal or greater amount of funds in developing its chips, and that the Mask Work Act was directed at minimal investment piracy rather than the type of long-term research and reverse engineering it performed.

Brooktree argues that what the paper trail actually establishes is that Plants was incapable of discovering the layout on his own. According to Brooktree, Plants had no experience in designing CMOS chips and spent over one year attempting to design a layout utilizing first six and then eight transistors as compared to Brooktree's layout which utilizes ten transistors. During this one-year period, plants studied Brooktree's Bt451 chip under a microscope and was unable to discover all ten of the transistors.

Brooktree alleges that Plants did not discover the ten transistors on his own but rather was shown a copy of Brooktree's ten transistor static RAM circuit by an employee of another competitor of Brooktree (Integrated Device Technology Corporation) which had supposedly copied Brooktree's Bt451 chip. After Plant was shown the ten transistor design, he allegedly went back to the microscope and studied the Bt451 chip to confirm the number of transistors and to determine their location and function in the design.

Brooktree maintains that the fact that Plant was able to finish his work on the layout in less than three months after being shown the ten transistor design is significant. Accordingly, Brooktree argues that the only paper trail that is relevant is what was created after Plant was shown the ten transistor design. Because the paper trail for the last three months is minimal, Brooktree argues that AMD has failed to offer sufficient facts to establish that AMD discovered the layout of the mask work at issue through reverse engineering.

AMD responds by arguing that the entire paper trail must be reviewed, and that the paper trail shows that Plant gradually discovered the correct layout. Plant states in his declaration that he started with six transistors as that is the minimum number possible, and that designers always begin at the minimum and work up. He states that the amount of time he spent working on six and eight transistor layouts demonstrates that he did not simply copy the Bt451. Plant admits to analyzing the Bt451 chip through a microscope, but maintains that only stripping the chip down chemically layer by layer and photographing each layer is prohibited by the Mask Work Act.

Based upon the above discussion, the court finds that Brooktree has failed to make a showing of a strong likelihood of success on the merits. Therefore, the degree of irreparable harm that Brooktree must establish is high. In the Ninth Circuit, the formulations applied to determine the appropriateness of a preliminary injunction "represent two points on a sliding scale in which the required degree of irreparable harm increases as the probability of success decreases." Arcamuzi, 819 F.2d at 937, citing Oakland Tribune, Inc. v. Chronicle Publishing Co., 762 F.2d 1374, 1376 (9th Cir.1985).

* * *

IV.

CONCLUSION

Upon due consideration of the parties' memoranda and exhibits, the arguments advanced at hearing, and for the reasons set forth above, the court hereby denies plaintiff's motion for preliminary injunction.

Note and Question

The *Brooktree* court looked favorably on the extensive paper trail the defendant had created. Will software developers' combination of using a clean room and creating an extensive paper trail during the use of the clean room virtually guarantee a finding of no software copyright infringement?

3. CONTRIBUTORY INFRINGEMENT

IN RE CERTAIN PERSONAL COMPUTERS AND COMPONENTS THEREOF

U.S. International Trade Commission, 1984.
224 U.S.P.Q. 270.

VIEWS OF THE COMMISSION

On January 20, 1984, the Commission determined to review the initial determination (ID) of the administrative law judge (ALJ) in Certain Personal computers and Components Thereof, Inv. No. 337–TA–140. The ALJ issued the ID on December 9, 1983, and determined that there was a violation of section 337 of the Tariff Act of 1930 on the basis that: (1) the patents and copyrights involved are valid, enforceable and infringed; (2) there is an "industry, efficiently and economically operated, in the United States," within the meaning of section 337; and (3) the importation of the subject articles has the tendency to substantially injure that industry.

We concur in the finding of a violation of section 337 on the basis that (1) the patents and copyrights involved are valid, enforceable, and infringed; (2) there is an "industry, efficiently and economically operated, in the United States;" and (3) the importation of the subject articles has the tendency to substantially injure that industry. However, we have modified the ID in accordance with the standards adopted for review in our rules. We have found some conclusions of material fact clearly erroneous and some legal conclusions erroneous. Additionally, we have provided more complete reasoning in some instances where we have concurred in the finding of the ALJ.

Procedural History

On January 31, 1983, Apple Computer Inc. (Apple) filed a complaint with the Commission under section 337 of the Tariff Act of 1930. On the basis of that complaint, the Commission instituted this investigation on March 2, 1983. The notice of investigation defined its scope as the determination of whether there is a violation of section 337 in the importation of certain personal computers and components thereof into the United States, or in their sale, by reason of alleged:

(1) Infringement of the claims of U.S. Letters Patent 4,136,359;

(2) Infringement of the claims of U.S. Letters Patent 4,278,972;

(3) Direct or contributory infringement of U.S. Copyright Reg. No. TX 873–203 and U.S. Copyright Reg. No. TX 886–569; and

(4) Misappropriation of trade dress;

the effect or tendency of which is to destroy or substantially injure an industry, efficiently and economically operated, in the United States.

* * *

Copyrights Involved

1. Registration No. TX 873–203

The copyright which is the subject of this registration is for a work entitled "Autostart ROM," a computer program. The deposit copy, which was introduced into evidence, is a hard copy printout in hexadecimal-coded machine language, i.e., each byte is represented as two hexadecimal numbers. The program is 2048 bytes long, filling the hexadecimal-coded memory addresses F800 to FFFF.

The Autostart ROM program is an operating system program, as opposed to a translator or applications program. It is a relatively short program and, indeed, is actually a collection of about 70 shorter programs which are referred to as "subroutines." These subroutines or groups of these subroutines instruct the microprocessor to perform certain housekeeping functions. Like all operating system programs, the Autostart ROM program is used every time the computer is used, no matter what applications program is being run. For this reason, like many other operating system programs, it is permanently stored in "read-only memory," referred to as ROM. The machine language in which the Autostart ROM program is written is that used by the 6502 microprocessor; it cannot be used on any other type of microprocessor. ROM is incorporated in a ROM chip, of which there may be several in a given computer. The Autostart ROM program is stored on such a ROM chip, known as an F8 ROM, since for the 6502 microprocessor, it must be located in that area of memory, i.e., beginning at memory address F8, i.e., F800. In the Apple II + the F8 ROM chip is located at approximately location F3 on the printed circuit board (PCB) or motherboard.

* * *

Products Involved

Complainant Apple

Apple's products subject to this investigation are all complete personal computers: the Apple II, Apple II +, Apple IIe and Apple III. The Apple II and Apple II + are no longer being manufactured, however. The Apple II, Apple II +, and Apple IIe incorporate the patented inventions and have ROM chips incorporating the Applesoft and Autostart ROM programs. The Apple III incorporates the patented inventions, but does not incorporate the Applesoft and Autostart ROM programs.

Copyright Validity

The copyrights, including the Apple II System Monitor copyright, were registered within five years of publication of the copyrighted works and are thus presumed valid. Their ability is not disputed here.

* * *

Contributory Copyright Infringement

The ALJ found contributory copyright infringement with regard to ROMless computers and motherboards which Apple had established were associated with parallel importations of infringing ROM chips. However, the ALJ found that for all other ROMless computers and motherboards, contributory copyright infringement could not be found because of the availability of non-infringing copies of the Applesoft or Autostart ROM programs from Apple or other suppliers. We agree with the ALJ's former finding, but find the latter clearly erroneous, for the reasons discussed below.

In Sony Corporation of America v. Universal City Studios, Inc., — U.S. —, 220 USPQ 665 (1984), slip opinion at 17, the Supreme Court stated that contributory copyright infringement "is merely as species of the broader problem of identifying the circumstances in which it is just to hold one individual accountable for the actions of another." As a general rule, a contributory infringer is one who with knowledge of the infringing activity, induces, causes or materially contributes to the infringing conduct of another. Knowledge includes reason to have knowledge. However, where the contributory infringement is alleged to lie in the sale or distribution of an article, it will not be found it [sic] that article is capable of commercially significant non-infringing uses.

Of course, there must first be a finding that direct copyright infringement is occurring.

Dr. Hulina testified with regard to several ROMless computers and motherboards. Among these were the ROMless Guan Haur Golden II computer and the ROMless NAR MIND II computer. Dr. Hulina testified that the motherboards for these computers, which apparently are identical to Apple II series motherboards, had room for socket for six ordinary ROM chips, but had sockets for 3 large 2732 EPROM chips. Dr. Hulina testified that these EPROM chips contain twice as much information as ordinary ROM chips, and their use as a substitute is a well-known expedient. He also testified that other than the Apple programs, he knew of no presently available programs which could be placed in those ROM chips to make these computers, or computers like them, useful. Dr. Hulina testified similarly with regard to the Formula/Leader motherboard. The foregoing evidence is sufficient to imply the existence of direct copyright infringement by at least third parties, i.e., copying of the copyrighted programs onto ROM chips and their insertion into the ROMless computers and motherboards. Persons who import or sell ROMless computers or components with identical motherboards have reason to know that activity which results in such direct infringement is occurring or will occur.

Finally, such ROMless computers and components are not capable of a commercially significant non-infringing use. The Commission investigative attorney argues that the availability of the Applesoft program on disk from Apple or others indicates that at least with regard to the Applesoft program, ROMless computers and components in general have a substantial non-infringing use. Guan Haur would go even further and include the Autostart ROM program as well, which is still available as part of one or more card inserts formerly manufactured by Apple and still available from inventory of some distributors and retailers. The mere availability of these programs, however, does not avoid contributory copyright infringement; it does not provide sufficient probative evidence of any commercially significant use of these Apple program cards or disks in conjunction with an imported unstuffed motherboard or ROMless computer to make a fully operational computer.

Apple argues that in addition to finding that ROMless computers and components having identical motherboards contributorily infringe the copyrights, the Commission should also find that ROMless computers and components having motherboards which are not identical to the Apple motherboard contributorily infringe the copyrights. We have found no expert testimony in the record with regard to this and no such ROMless computers or motherboards have been placed in the record. We therefore decline to make such a finding.

* * *

VAULT CORP. v. QUAID SOFTWARE LTD.

United States Court of Appeals, Fifth Circuit, 1988.
847 F.2d 255.

REAVLEY, CIRCUIT JUDGE:

Vault brought this copyright infringement action against Quaid seeking damages and preliminary and permanent injunctions. The district court denied Vault's motion for a preliminary injunction, holding that Vault did not have a reasonable probability of success on the merits. *Vault Corp. v. Quaid Software Ltd.*, 655 F.Supp. 750 (E.D.La. 1987). By stipulation of the parties, this ruling was made final and judgment was entered accordingly. We affirm.

I

Vault produces computer diskettes under the registered trademark "PROLOK" which are designed to prevent the unauthorized duplication of programs placed on them by software computer companies, Vault's customers. Floppy diskettes serve as a medium upon which computer companies place their software programs. To use a program, a purchaser loads the diskette into the disk drive of a computer, thereby allowing the computer to read the program into its memory. The purchaser can then remove the diskette from the disk drive and operate the program from the computer's memory. This process is repeated each time a program is used.

The protective device placed on a PROLOK diskette by Vault is comprised of two parts: a "fingerprint" and a software program ("Vault's program").[1] The "fingerprint" is a small mark physically placed on the magnetic surface of each PROLOK diskette which contains certain information that cannot be altered or erased. Vault's program is a set of instructions to the computer which interact with the "fingerprint" to prevent the computer from operating the program recorded on a PROLOK diskette (by one of Vault's customers) unless the computer verifies that the *original* PROLOK diskette, as identified by the "fingerprint," is in the computer's disk drive. While a purchaser can copy a PROLOK protected program onto another diskette, the computer will not read the program into its memory from the copy unless the original PROLOK diskette is also in one of the computer's disk drives. The fact that a fully functional copy of a program cannot be made from a PROLOK diskette prevents purchasers from buying a single program and making unauthorized copies for distribution to others.

1. A PROLOK diskette contains two programs, the program placed on the diskette by a software company (e.g, word processing) and the program placed on the diskette by Vault which interacts with the "fingerprint" to prevent the unauthorized duplication of the software company's program. We use the term "software program" or "program" to refer to the program placed on the diskette by one of Vault's customers (a computer company) and "Vault's program" to refer to the program placed on the diskette by Vault as part of the protective device. We collectively refer to the "fingerprint" and Vault's program as the "protective device."

Vault produced PROLOK in three stages. The original commercial versions, designated as versions 1.01, 1.02, 1.03, 1.04 and 1.06 ("version 1.0") were produced in 1983. Vault then incorporated improvements into the system and produced version 1.07 in 1984. The third major revision occurred in August and September of 1985 and was designated as versions 2.0 and 2.01 ("version 2.0"). Each version of PROLOK has been copyrighted and Vault includes a license agreement with every PROLOK package that specifically prohibits the copying, modification, translation, decompilation or disassembly of Vault's program.[2] Beginning with version 2.0 in September 1985, Vault's license agreement contained a choice of law clause adopting Louisiana law.[3]

Quaid's product, a diskette called "CopyWrite," contains a feature called "RAMKEY" which unlocks the PROLOK protective device and facilitates the creation of a fully functional copy of a program placed on a PROLOK diskette. The process is performed simply by copying the contents of the PROLOK diskette onto the CopyWrite diskette which can then be used to run the software program *without* the original PROLOK diskette in a computer disk drive. RAMKEY interacts with Vault's program to make it appear to the computer that the CopyWrite diskette contains the "fingerprint," thereby making the computer function as if the original PROLOK diskette is in its disk drive. A copy of a

2. The license agreement refers to the program placed on the diskette by Vault, not the software program placed on the diskette by Vault's customers. *See supra* note 1 for terminology. The companies that place their software programs on PROLOK diskettes, not Vault, own the copyright to their programs and may include a license agreement covering their programs in the package for sale to the public.

Vault's license agreement reads:

IMPORTANT! VAULT IS PROVIDING THE ENCLOSED MATERIALS TO YOU ON THE EXPRESS CONDITION THAT YOU ASSENT TO THIS SOFTWARE LICENSE. BY USING ANY OF THE ENCLOSED DISKETTE(S), YOU AGREE TO THE FOLLOWING PROVISIONS. IF YOU DO NOT AGREE WITH THESE LICENSE PROVISIONS, RETURN THESE MATERIALS TO YOUR DEALER, IN ORIGINAL PACKAGING WITHIN 3 DAYS FROM RECEIPT, FOR A REFUND.

1. This copy of the PROLOK Software Protection System and this PROLOK Software Protection Diskette (the "Licensed Software") are licensed to you, the end-user, for your own internal use. Title to the Licensed Software and all copyrights and proprietary rights in the Licensed Software shall remain with VAULT. You may not transfer, sublicense, rent, lease, convey, copy, modify, translate, convert to another programming language, decompile or disassemble the Licensed Software for any purpose without VAULT's prior written consent.

2. THE LICENSED SOFTWARE IS PROVIDED "AS–IS". VAULT DISCLAIMS ALL WARRANTIES AND REPRESENTATIONS OF ANY KIND WITH REGARD TO THE LICENSED SOFTWARE, INCLUDING THE IMPLIED WARRANTIES OF MERCHANTABILITY AND FITNESS FOR A PARTICULAR PURPOSE. UNDER NO CIRCUMSTANCES WILL VAULT BE LIABLE FOR ANY CONSEQUENTIAL, INCIDENTAL, SPECIAL OR EXEMPLARY DAMAGES EVEN IF VAULT IS APPRISED OF THE LIKELIHOOD OF SUCH DAMAGES OCCURRING. SOME STATES DO NOT ALLOW THE LIMITATION OR EXCLUSION OF LIABILITY FOR INCIDENTAL OR CONSEQUENTIAL DAMAGES, SO THE ABOVE LIMITATION OR EXCLUSION MAY MAY NOT APPLY TO YOU.

3. The license agreement included the following language beginning with version 2.0:

To the extent the laws of the United States of America are not applicable, this license agreement shall be governed by the laws of the State of Louisiana.

program placed on a CopyWrite diskette can be used without the original, and an unlimited number of fully functional copies can be made in this manner from the program originally placed on the PROLOK diskette.

Quaid first developed RAMKEY in September 1983 in response to PROLOK version 1.0. In order to develop this version of RAMKEY, Quaid copied Vault's program into the memory of its computer and analyzed the manner in which the program operated. When Vault developed version 1.07, Quaid adapted RAMKEY in 1984 to defeat this new version. The adapted version of RAMKEY contained a sequence of approximately 30 characters found in Vault's program and was discontinued in July 1984. Quaid then developed the current version of RAMKEY which also operates to defeat PROLOK version 1.07, but does not contain the sequence of characters used in the discontinued version. Quaid has not yet modified RAMKEY to defeat PROLOK version 2.0, and has agreed not to modify RAMKEY pending the outcome of this suit. Robert McQuaid, the sole owner of Quaid, testified in his deposition that while a CopyWrite diskette can be used to duplicate programs placed on all diskettes, whether copy-protected or not, the only purpose served by RAMKEY is to facilitate the duplication of programs placed on copy-protected diskettes. He also stated that without the RAMKEY feature, CopyWrite would have no commercial value.

II

Vault brought this action against Quaid seeking preliminary and permanent injunctions to prevent Quaid from advertising and selling RAMKEY, an order impounding all of Quaid's copies of CopyWrite which contain the RAMKEY feature, and monetary damages in the amount of $100,000,000. Vault asserted three copyright infringement claims cognizable under federal law, 17 U.S.C. § 101 *et seq.* (1977 & Supp.1988) (the "Copyright Act"), which included: (1) that Quaid violated 17 U.S.C. §§ 501(a) & 106(1) by copying Vault's program into its computer's memory for the purpose of developing a program (RAMKEY) designed to defeat the function of Vault's program; (2) that Quaid, through RAMKEY, contributes to the infringement of Vault's copyright and the copyrights of its customers in violation of the Copyright Act as interpreted by the Supreme Court in *Sony Corp. of Am. v. Universal City Studios,* 464 U.S. 417, 104 S.Ct. 774, 78 L.Ed.2d 574 (1984); and (3) that the second version of RAMKEY, which contained approximately thirty characters from PROLOK version 1.07, and the latest version of RAMKEY, constitute "derivative works" of Vault's program in violation of 17 U.S.C. §§ 501(a) & 106(2). Vault also asserted two claims based on Louisiana law, contending that Quaid breached its license agreement by decompiling or disassembling Vault's program in violation of the Louisiana Software License Enforcement Act, La.Rev.Stat.Ann. § 51:1961 *et seq.* (West 1987), and that Quaid misappropriated Vault's program in violation of the Louisiana Uniform Trade Secrets Act, La.Rev.Stat.Ann. § 51:1431 *et seq.* (West 1987).

The district court originally dismissed Vault's complaint for lack of in personam jurisdiction. This court reversed the district court's order of dismissal and remanded the case for further proceedings. *Vault Corp. v. Quaid Software Ltd.,* 775 F.2d 638 (5th Cir.1985). On remand, the district court, after a three-day bench trial, denied Vault's motion for a preliminary injunction holding that Vault had not established a reasonable probability of success on the merits. *Vault,* 655 F.Supp. at 763. Subsequently, the parties agreed to submit the case for final decision based on the evidence adduced at the preliminary injunction trial. On July 31, 1987 the district court entered final judgment in accordance with its decision on the preliminary injunction.

Vault now contends that the district court improperly disposed of each of its claims.

III. Vault's Federal Claims

An owner of a copyrighted work has the exclusive right to reproduce the work in copies, to prepare derivative works based on the copyrighted work, to distribute copies of the work to the public, and, in the case of certain types of works, to perform and display the work publicly. 17 U.S.C. § 106. Sections 107 through 118 of the Copyright Act limit an owner's exclusive rights, and section 501(a) provides that "[a]nyone who violates any of the exclusive rights of the copyright owner as provided by sections 106 through 118 * * * is an infringer of the copyright."

It is not disputed that Vault owns the copyright to the program it places on PROLOK diskettes and is thus an "owner of copyright" under § 106. Therefore, Vault has, subject to the exceptions contained in sections 107 through 118, the exclusive right to reproduce its program in copies and to prepare derivative works based on its program. Vault claims that Quaid infringed its copyright under § 501(a) by: (1) directly copying Vault's program into the memory of Quaid's computer; (2) contributing to the unauthorized copying of Vault's program and the programs Vault's customers place on PROLOK diskettes; and (3) preparing derivative works of Vault's program.

Section 117 of the Copyright Act limits a copyright owner's exclusive rights under § 106 by permitting an owner of a computer program to make certain copies of that program without obtaining permission from the program's copyright owner. With respect to Vault's first two claims of copyright infringement, Quaid contends that its activities fall within the § 117 exceptions and that it has, therefore, not infringed Vault's exclusive rights under § 501(a). To appreciate the arguments of the parties, we examine the legislative history of § 117.

* * *

C. Contributory Infringement

Vault contends that, because purchasers of programs placed on PROLOK diskettes use the RAMKEY feature of CopyWrite to make unauthorized copies, Quaid's advertisement and sale of CopyWrite diskettes with the RAMKEY feature violate the Copyright Act by contributing to the infringement of Vault's copyright and the copyrights owned by Vault's customers. Vault asserts that it lost customers and substantial revenue as a result of Quaid's contributory infringement because software companies which previously relied on PROLOK diskettes to protect their programs from unauthorized copying have discontinued their use.

While a purchaser of a program on a PROLOK diskette violates sections 106(1) and 501(a) by making and distributing unauthorized copies of the program, the Copyright Act "does not expressly render anyone liable for the infringement committed by another." *Sony,* 464 U.S. at 434, 104 S.Ct. at 785. The Supreme Court in *Sony,* after examining the express provision in the Patent Act which imposes liability on an individual who "actively induces infringement of a patent," 35 U.S.C. § 271(b) & (c), and noting the similarity between the Patent and Copyright Acts, recognized the availability, under the Copyright Act, of vicarious liability against one who sells a product that is used to make unauthorized copies of copyrighted material. *Id.* at 434–42, 104 S.Ct. at 785–89. The Court held that liability based on contributory infringement could be imposed only where the seller had constructive knowledge of the fact that its product was used to make unauthorized copies of copyrighted material, *id.* at 339, 104 S.Ct. at 787, and that the sale of a product "does not constitute contributory infringement if the product is widely used for legitimate, unobjectionable purposes. Indeed, it need merely be capable of substantial noninfringing uses." *Id.* at 442, 104 S.Ct. at 789.

While Quaid concedes that it has actual knowledge that its product is used to make unauthorized copies of copyrighted material, it contends that the RAMKEY portion of its CopyWrite diskettes serves a substantial noninfringing use by allowing purchasers of programs on PROLOK diskettes to make archival copies as permitted under 17 U.S.C. § 117(2), and thus that it is not liable for contributory infringement. The district court held that Vault lacked standing to raise a contributory infringement claim because "it is not Vault, but the customers of Vault who place their programs on PROLOK disks, who may assert such claims. Clearly the copyright rights to these underlying programs belong to their publishers, not Vault." *Vault,* 655 F.Supp. at 759. Alternatively the court held that CopyWrite is capable of "commercially significant noninfringing uses" because the RAMKEY feature permits the making of archival copies of copy-protected software, and CopyWrite diskettes (without the RAMKEY feature) are used to make copies of unprotected software and as a diagnostic tool to analyze the quality of new computer programs. *Id.* Therefore, the court held that the sale of CopyWrite did not constitute contributory infringement.

While we hold that Vault has standing to assert its contributory infringement claim, we find that RAMKEY is capable of substantial noninfringing uses and thus reject Vault's contention that the advertisement and sale of CopyWrite diskettes with RAMKEY constitute contributory infringement.

1. Standing

The Copyright Act provides that the "legal or beneficial owner of an exclusive right under a copyright is entitled, subject to the requirements of sections 205(d) and 411 [concerning the recordation and registration of copyrights], to institute an action for any infringement of that particular right committed while he or she is the owner of it." 17 U.S.C. § 501(b). The Supreme Court in *Sony* noted that it was the taping of plaintiff's "own copyrighted programs that provides them with standing to charge Sony with contributory infringement." 464 U.S. at 434, 104 S.Ct. at 785.

The focus of Vault's allegation of contributory infringement in its amended complaint is that CopyWrite, through RAMKEY, enables purchasers of PROLOK protected programs to infringe the copyrights of Vault's customers and that, as a result, Vault has suffered damages due to its loss of customers. While Vault does not own the copyrights to its customer's programs, it does own the copyright to the program it places on each PROLOK diskette. This program operates in conjunction with the "fingerprint" to prevent the duplication of Vault's customer's programs. Uncontroverted testimony established that both Vault's protective program and its customer's program are copied onto a CopyWrite diskette when an individual executes a computer's "copy" function in order to duplicate the customer's program from a PROLOK diskette onto a CopyWrite diskette, and that RAMKEY then interacts with Vault's program to defeat its protective function and to make the computer operate as if the original PROLOK diskette was in one of its disk drives.[14] Therefore, CopyWrite diskettes, through RAMKEY, facilitate not only the copying of Vault's customer's software programs but also the copying of Vault's protective program, and, in addition, RAMKEY interacts with Vault's program to destroy its purpose.

Quaid does not take issue with the validity of Vault's copyright under § 501(b) but instead contends that Vault lacks standing because it failed to allege contributory infringement based on the copying of its program, as opposed to the programs of its customers. Vault responds that its pleadings should be broadly construed to include its contributory infringement claim based on the copying of its program, and that even if its pleadings are narrowly construed, they were amended, pursuant to Fed.R.Civ.P. 15(b), to include this claim by trial testimony which established that Quaid's product contributes to the unauthorized copying of Vault's program.

14. The latest version of RAMKEY, developed in response to PROLOK version 1.07, operates by intercepting service calls made by Vault's program to the computer. By this process, RAMKEY is able to make the computer operate as if the original PROLOK diskette, rather than the CopyWrite diskette with RAMKEY, is in the computer's disk drive. *See* McQuaid Deposition at 68–72. In order for RAMKEY to perform this function, Vault's protective program, as well as Vault's customer's program, must be copied onto the CopyWrite diskette.

Rule 15(b) provides that "[w]hen issues not raised by the pleadings are tried by express or implied consent of the parties, they shall be treated in all respects as if they had been raised in the pleadings." While Vault's pleadings do not allege contributory infringement based on the copying of its copyrighted program, Quaid's consent to this claim is evidenced by a pretrial memorandum, signed by counsel for both Vault and Quaid, which listed as a contested issue of law "[w]hether Quaid has contributorily infringed *Vault's* and Vault's customer copyrights" (emphasis added). Quaid does not contend that it has been unfairly prejudiced by Vault's contention of contributory infringement based on the copying of its own program, *see Mason v. Hunter,* 534 F.2d 822, 825 (8th Cir.1976), nor does Quaid contend that it had inadequate notice of the nature of Vault's claim or an inadequate opportunity to fully and fairly respond, *see Henry v. Coahoma County Bd. of Educ.,* 246 F.Supp. 517, 519 (N.D.Miss.1963), *aff'd,* 353 F.2d 648 (5th Cir.1965), *cert. denied,* 384 U.S. 962, 86 S.Ct. 1586, 16 L.Ed.2d 674 (1966). Vault's proposed interpretation or amendment of its pleadings in no way changes the character of the case. *See id.* at 518. It is beyond dispute that RAMKEY destroys the commercial value of PROLOK diskettes, and while the extent of Vault's damages were not fully developed at trial, the evidence indicated that Vault sustained substantial injuries as a result of RAMKEY and thus has a significant personal stake in the outcome of this litigation. Under these circumstances, we hold that, pursuant to Fed.R.Civ.P. 15(b), Vault has fairly alleged contributory infringement of its copyrighted program and has standing to pursue this claim.

2. Substantial Noninfringing Uses of RAMKEY

Vault's allegation of contributory infringement focuses on the RAMKEY feature of CopyWrite diskettes, not on the non-RAMKEY portions of these diskettes. Vault has no objection to the advertising and marketing of CopyWrite diskettes without the RAMKEY feature, and this feature is separable from the underlying diskette upon which it is placed. Therefore, in determining whether Quaid engaged in contributory infringement, we do not focus on the substantial noninfringing uses of CopyWrite, as opposed to the RAMKEY feature itself. *See Vault,* 655 F.Supp. at 759. The issue properly presented is whether the RAMKEY feature has substantial noninfringing uses.

The starting point for our analysis is with *Sony.* The plaintiffs in *Sony,* owners of copyrighted television programs, sought to enjoin the manufacture and marketing of Betamax video tape recorders ("VTR's"), contending that VTR's contributed to the infringement of their copyrights by permitting the unauthorized copying of their programs. 464 U.S. at 419–20, 104 S.Ct. at 777. After noting that plaintiffs' market share of television programming was less than 10%, and that copyright holders of a significant quantity of television broadcasting authorized the copying of their programs, the Court held that VTR's serve the legitimate and substantially noninfringing purpose of recording these programs, as well as plaintiffs' programs, for future viewing (authorized and unauthorized time-shifting respectively), and therefore rejected plaintiffs' contributory infringement claim. *Id.* at 442–55, 104 S.Ct. at 789–95.

Quaid asserts that RAMKEY serves the legitimate purpose of permitting purchasers of programs recorded on PROLOK diskettes to make archival copies under § 117(2) and that this purpose constitutes a substantial noninfringing use. At trial, witnesses for Quaid testified that software programs placed on floppy diskettes are subject to damage by *physical and human mishap* and that RAMKEY protects a purchaser's investment by providing a fully functional archival copy that can be used if the original program on the PROLOK protected diskette, or the diskette itself, is destroyed. Quaid contends that an archival copy of a PROLOK protected program, made without RAMKEY, does not serve to protect against these forms of damage because a computer will not read the program into its memory from the copy unless the PROLOK diskette containing the original undamaged program is also in one of its disk drives, which is impossible if the PROLOK diskette, or the program placed thereon, has been destroyed due to physical or human mishap.

Computer programs can be stored on a variety of mediums, including floppy diskettes, hard disks, non-erasable read only memory ("ROM") chips, and a computer's random access memory, and may appear only as printed instructions on a sheet of paper. Vault contends that the archival exception was designed to permit *only* the copying of programs which are subject to "destruction or damage by *mechanical or electrical failure.*" CONTU Report at 31 (emphasis added). While programs stored on all mediums may be subject to damage due to physical abuse or human error, programs stored on certain mediums are not subject to damage by mechanical or electrical failure. Therefore, Vault argues, the medium of storage determines whether the archival exception applies, thus providing only owners of programs, placed on mediums of storage which subject them to damage by mechanical or electrical failure, the right to make back-up copies. To support its construction of § 117(2), Vault notes that one court has held that the archival exception does not apply to the copying of programs stored on ROM chips where there was no evidence that programs stored on this medium were subject to damage by mechanical or electrical failure, *Atari,* 597 F.Supp. at 9–10, and another court has likewise held that the archival exception does not apply to the copying of programs which appear only in the form of printed instructions in a magazine, *Micro–Sparc,* 592 F.Supp. at 35–36.

Vault contends that the district court's finding that programs stored on floppy diskettes are subject to damage by mechanical or electrical failure is erroneous because there was insufficient evidence presented at trial to support it, and, based on this contention, Vault asserts that the archival exception does not apply to permit the unauthorized copying of these programs. Vault performed a trial demonstration to prove that even if a program on an original PROLOK diskette, and Vault's protective program, were completely erased from this diskette, these programs could be restored on the original diskette using a copy made *without* RAMKEY. Therefore, Vault argues that even if a program recorded on a PROLOK diskette is subject to damage by mechanical or electrical failure, the non-operational copy of a PROLOK protected program made without RAMKEY is sufficient to protect against this type of damage. Vault concludes that, in light of the fact that RAMKEY facilitates the making of unauthorized copies and owners of PROLOK protected programs can make copies to protect against damage by mechanical and electrical failure without RAMKEY, the RAMKEY feature is not capable of substantial noninfringing uses.

The narrow construction of the archival exception, advanced by Vault and accepted in the *Atari* and *Micro–Sparc* decisions, has undeniable appeal. This construction would leave the owner of a protected software program free to make back-up copies of the software to guard against erasures, which is probably the primary concern of owners as well as the drafters of the CONTU Report. Software producers should perhaps be entitled to protect their product from improper duplication, and Vault's PROLOK may satisfy producers and most purchasers on this score—*if* PROLOK cannot be copied by the purchaser onto a CopyWrite diskette without infringing the PROLOK copyright. That result does have appeal, but we believe it is an appeal that must be made to Congress. "[I]t is not our job to apply laws that have not yet been written." *Sony,* 464 U.S. at 456, 104 S.Ct. at 796. We read the statute as it is now written to authorize the owner of the PROLOK diskette to copy both the PROLOK program and the software program for any reason so long as the owner uses the copy for archival purposes only and not for an unauthorized transfer.

The CONTU Report's words of "mechanical or electrical failure" are contained in a paragraph quoted in the footnote. We read the stated causes of damage to be illustrative only, and not exclusive. Similarly, the statement follows with the prohibited use of the archival copies which does not include a prohibition against copying for purposes other than to protect against "mechanical or electrical failure." The Report, or Congress, could have easily limited the scope of § 117(2) to authorize the making of archival copies of programs subject to damage, and to guard against, only mechanical or electrical failure. CONTU did not recommend that language, nor did Congress enact it. Congress, following CONTU's advice, provided that an owner of a computer program may make a copy of that program provided that "such new copy * * * is for archival purposes only." 17 U.S.C. § 117(2). Congress did not choose to spell out detailed restrictions on the copying as was done in sections 108 and 112. Congress imposed no restriction upon the purpose or reason of the owner in making the archival copy; only the use made of that copy is restricted. *See* CONTU Report at 31 ("one could not, for example, make archival copies of a program and later sell some to another while retaining some for use"). An owner of a program is entitled, under § 117(2), to make an archival copy of that program in order to guard against *all* types of risks, including physical and human mishap as well as mechanical and electrical failure.

A copy of a PROLOK protected program made with RAMKEY protects an owner from all types of damage to the original program, while a copy made without RAMKEY only serves the limited function of protecting against damage to the original program by mechanical and electrical failure. Because § 117(2) permits the making of fully functional archival copies, it follows that RAMKEY is capable of substantial noninfringing uses. Quaid's advertisement and sale of CopyWrite diskettes with the RAMKEY feature does not constitute contributory infringement.

* * *

V. CONCLUSION

We hold that: (1) Quaid did not infringe Vault's exclusive right to reproduce its program in copies under § 106(1); (2) Quaid's advertisement and sale of RAMKEY does not constitute contributory infringement; (3) RAMKEY does not constitute a derivative work of Vault's program under § 106(2); and (4) the provision in Vault's license agreement, which prohibits the decompilation or disassembly of its program, is unenforceable.

The judgment of the district court is Affirmed.

Note and Question

1. With the spread of hard disks in personal computers, software suppliers largely stopped using copy protection techniques. Techniques that required the user to keep a floppy disk in the computer whenever using the program caused the computer user the inconvenience of flipping disks when moving from program to program. Techniques that involved manipulating data on the hard disks themselves terrorized users, who feared loss of data integrity and inability to make backups.

2. Under what circumstances does the court in *Vault* hold that the owner of copyrighted software may disassemble software to examine and use the ideas contained in the software?

Chapter III

THE PATENTABILITY OF COMPUTER PROGRAMS AND PROGRAMMED COMPUTERS

A. INTRODUCTION

In the early days of computers, the programs did little more than solve mathematical equations. Since mathematical equations are traditionally not patentable, initially the Patent Office and the Courts refused to grant patents on computer programs or on programmed computers. Starting in 1969, the Court of Customs and Patent Appeals [C.C.P.A.], a Federal appellate tribunal which had supervisory jurisdiction over the Patent Office, began to reverse the patent examiners and the Patent Office's Board of Patent Appeals and to compel the issuance of software patents. Accordingly, the U.S. Patent Office was forced to issue computer program patents from 1969 until 1972. In 1972, the United States Supreme Court, at the request of the Patent Office, reversed the C.C.P.A. and blocked the issuance of a patent directed to a method of converting one form of number into another. *Gottschalk v. Benson,* 409 U.S. 63 (1972).

The C.C.P.A. reacted to this Supreme Court decision with hostility, construing *Benson* as narrowly as possible. But even so, the Patent Office issued very few computer program or programmed computer patents between 1972 and 1981 (when the Supreme Court again ruled on programmed computer patents). Between 1972 and 1981 most attorneys advised their clients not to file patents directed to software. Many fundamental software inventions, (for example, the spreadsheet program) were not patented. Attorneys advised their clients to utilize copyright and trade secret protection as substitutes for software patent protection. The World Intellectual Property Organization (WIPO) even proposed a new form of intellectual property protection designed especially for computer programs. Europe, taking its lead from the United States Supreme Court, enacted statutes prohibiting the patenting of computer programs. The United Kingdom Patents Act of 1977, for example, contains the following language: "(2) It is hereby declared that the following (among other things) are not inventions for the purposes of this Act, that is to say, anything which consists of—* * * a program for a computer * * *." In both Europe and the United States, however, attorneys for proprietors of software inventions tried to circumvent the restrictions on patenting programs by seeking patents for programmed computers.

In *Diamond v. Diehr,* 450 U.S. 175 (1981), the Supreme Court authorized the grant of a software-hardware patent. This decision opened the door to the patentability of programmed computers, but did not overrule the earlier Supreme Court precedents holding some computer programs unpatentable. Most programmed computer inventions are now patentable. However, a "black hole" of unpatentability, centered about *Benson,* remains. The patentability of a pure "computer program" has yet to be addressed by the Supreme Court.

The C.C.P.A.'s appellate jurisdiction was limited to appeals from the Patent and Trademark Office and several other federal agencies. Prior to 1980 patent holders had to file patent infringement suits in the Federal district courts. Appeals of these suits went to the individual Circuit Courts of Appeals, as in other "federal question" matters. Perceived nonuniformity in the appellate decisions produced considerable "forum shopping", since some circuits were considered more "pro-patent" than others. The 8th Circuit, for example, was reputed to be extremely "anti-patent" a charge which that Court itself denied. Conflicting Circuit Court decisions created considerable uncertainty. In 1980 the C.C.P.A. was expanded, renamed the "United States Court of Appeals For The Federal Circuit," and given exclusive appellate jurisdiction over all patent-related appeals, even in cases where there are other non-patent issues.

The creation of this new appellate court has eliminated conflicts between Circuits in patent law and has reduced the need for Supreme Court certiorari supervision. Because lawyers perceive the court as "pro-patent," they now more readily advise clients to get patents and sue infringers. This new court has also increased the importance of prior C.C.P.A. decisions, particularly since several of the former C.C.P.A. judges were appointed to this new court and write many of its patent decisions. Judge Rich, in particular, is regarded as highly by many patent attorneys as the late Judge Learned Hand is by copyright attorneys. The debate between Judge Rich and Supreme Court Justice Stevens over the relationship between Sections 101, 102 and 103 of the Patent Act is set forth below. This debate lies at the heart of the legal problem of defining what types of software inventions are now patentable under the law.

The cases generally assume, without proof, that software inventions must be treated differently than mechanical and other types of inventions. Since virtually any programmed computer can be transformed into an electronic circuit that is functionally identical to the programmed computer, it appears that the particular way in which a machine is constructed (hardwired circuitry versus programmed computer) can affect its patentability.

The present authors question the wisdom of permitting the way in which an engineer chooses to express inventive ideas to affect the patentability of those ideas. Does it make sense, as a matter of policy, to grant a patent to the inventor of a mechanical device that uses cams and levers to adjust alarm limits in a petrochemical factory but not to grant a patent to the inventor of a computer program that does the same thing? See *Parker v. Flook,* 437 U.S. 584 (1978). What if a patent issued on the mechanical device? Could a functionally equivalent computer program infringe the patent?

Is there some way to interpret the cases presented below that applies the law uniformly to all inventions, regardless of whether or not they contain computer programs? The Benson invention, as claimed, is a "reentrant shift register"—could this be a hardware device? Arguably, a reentrant shift register could even be a piece of paper bearing pencil marks—clearly an incursion into the heretofore unpatentable domain of mathematical equations. As you read these cases, think about how one can differentiate between patentable and unpatentable computer programs and programmed computers. Consider if these cases, properly construed, hold even some mechanical, chemical and electrical inventions that utilize no software at all to be unpatentable as well as some software inventions.

An analogy to nuclear power generation may be appropriate. We now routinely condemn nuclear power plants that give off too much "heat pollution." Having done so, consistency requires that we condemn those coal-burning power plants that generate just as much heat pollution as nuclear plants. Similarly, having recognized in *Benson* that some computer program inventions may be unpatentable, does not consistency require us to treat similar non-program inventions in the same way?

B. ORGANIZATION OF THIS CHAPTER

This chapter has two goals: First, to present the law of patents as it relates to computer programs and programmed computers; secondly, to present an introduction to patent law. The cases that follow are set forth essentially in historical order. Interspersed between some of the cases are brief historical summaries of other relevant cases. These summaries are taken from Justice Stevens' dissenting opinion in *Diamond v. Diehr,* the landmark Supreme Court case on the patentability of computer programs, the remainder of which is set forth at a later point.

The cases focus heavily upon 35 U.S.C.A. § 101, the section of the patent statute that defines what is patentable. Most cases consider the patentability of computer programs, but two related cases on the patentability of living organisms under § 101 are included. These are the Supreme Court decision in *Chakrabarty,* and the C.C.P.A. decision in *Application of Bergy and Application of Chakrabarty,* which the Supreme Court's *Chakrabarty* case affirmed.

The C.C.P.A.'s *Bergy/Chakrabarty* decision is included for two additional reasons. First, it presents an excellent introduction to patent law, particularly §§ 101, 102 and 103 of Title 35, exploring the general requirements for patentability (utility, novelty, non-obviousness) in considerable detail. Secondly, it sets forth C.C.P.A. Judge Rich's strong criticism of Supreme Court Justice Stevens' majority opinion in *Flook.* The background of the Rich/Stevens debate is essential to a full understanding of Justice Stevens' later dissenting opinion in Diehr. Since *Flook* and *Diehr* appear to reach exactly contrary results and since *Diehr* purports to be consistent with *Flook* and *Bergy,* all three cases warrant very careful study.

A series of additional C.C.P.A. and Federal Circuit opinions are set forth to explain, in more detail, the practical "rules of thumb" which have evolved for determining the patentability of programmed computer and computer program inventions. Relevant Patent and Trademark Office guidelines are also set forth at the end of this chapter. The last few cases, also from the Federal Circuit, provide additional details on patent law, particularly with regard to the use of "means for" terminology which is frequently included in claims to define the metes and bounds of software inventions.

C. A SOFTWARE PATENT

This patent defines *both* a mechanical invention—a "mouse" pointer device for a computer—and a related software invention. We have reproduced the entire patent to give an idea of what a patent is like, but the reader need not study all the details of the "mechanical" invention. Rather, the reader should focus upon the "software" invention portions of this patent. The parts of this patent that define the "software" invention are:

Figures 14 and 15;

Text, column 1 line 14 through column 2 line 34;

Text, column 6 line 4 through column 7 line 25; and

Claims 9, 11, 12, and 13 (columns 8, 9, and 10).

United States Patent [19]

Atkinson

[11] E **Patent Number: Re. 32,632**

[45] **Reissued Date of Patent: Mar. 29, 1988**

[54] **DISPLAY SYSTEM**

[75] Inventor: **William D. Atkinson,** Los Gatos, Calif.

[73] Assignee: **Apple Computer, Inc.,** Cupertino, Calif.

[21] Appl. No.: **811,372**

[22] Filed: **Dec. 20, 1985**

Related U.S. Patent Documents

Reissue of:

[64] Patent No.: **4,464,652**
Issued: **Aug. 7, 1984**
Appl. No.: **399,704**
Filed: **Jul. 19, 1982**

U.S. Applications:

[62] Division of Ser. No. 399,704, Jul. 19, 1982, Pat. No. 4,464,652.

[51] **Int. Cl.**[4] **G09G 1/16**

[52] **U.S. Cl.** **340/709**; 340/710; 340/706; 340/721

[58] **Field of Search** .... 340/706, 709, 710, 711, 340/712, 809, 810, 716, 870.28, 870.29; 178/18, 19; 74/471 XY; 358/183

[56] **References Cited**

U.S. PATENT DOCUMENTS

3,395,589	8/1968	Gersten	74/198
3,541,541	11/1970	Englebart	340/710
3,625,083	12/1971	Bose	74/471 XY
3,835,464	9/1974	Kider	340/710
3,987,685	10/1976	Opocensky	340/710
4,232,311	11/1980	Agneta	340/709
4,245,244	1/1981	Lijewski et al.	358/183
4,310,839	1/1982	Schwerdt	340/709
4,369,439	1/1983	Broos	340/710
4,404,865	9/1983	Kim	74/471 XY
4,451,895	5/1984	Sliwkowski	340/707

FOREIGN PATENT DOCUMENTS

1526428	9/1978	United Kingdom	340/710

OTHER PUBLICATIONS

"The Smalltalk Environment", BYTE, Aug. 1981, p. 90, Larry Teslor.
"A Display Oriented Programmer's Assistant", *Int. J. Man-Machine Studies*, 1979, Teitleman.
"A Tour Through Cedar", *IEEE Software*, Apr., 1984, Teitleman.
"Xerox's 'Star'", *Seybold Report*, vol. 10, No. 16, Apr. 27, 1981.
"Star Graphics: An Object Oriented Implementation", *Computer Graphics*, Jul., 1982, Lipkie et al.

Primary Examiner—Gerald L. Brigance
Attorney, Agent, or Firm—Blakely, Sokoloff, Taylor & Zafman

[57] **ABSTRACT**

A cursor control device having particular application to a computer display system is disclosed. The cursor control includes a unitary frame, having a domed portion substantially surrounding and retaining a ball which is free to rotate. X-Y position indicating means are provided, such that rotation of the ball provides signals indicative of X-Y positions on the display system. The ball is free to "float" in the vertical direction within the dome, and thereby maintain good surface contact. X-Y positions are established by movement of the control device over a surface. A display system and method is disclosed for use in conjunction with the cursor control device, which permits a user to select command options simply by movement of the displayed cursor over a "pull-down" menu bar.

4 Claims, 15 Drawing Figures

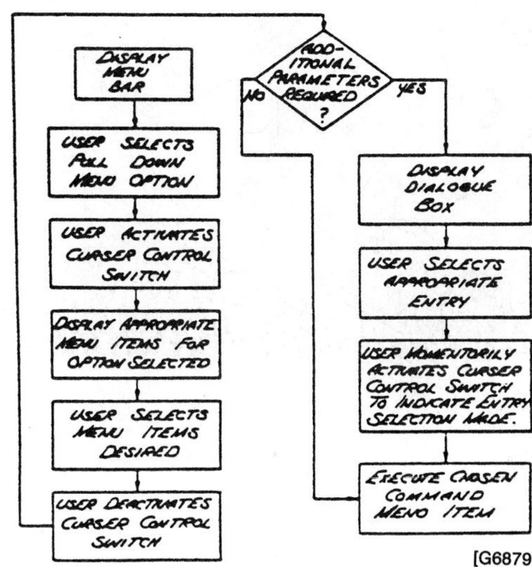

[G6879]

U.S. Patent Mar. 29, 1988 Sheet 1 of 8 **Re.32,632**

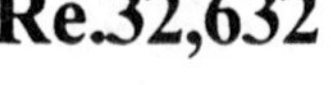

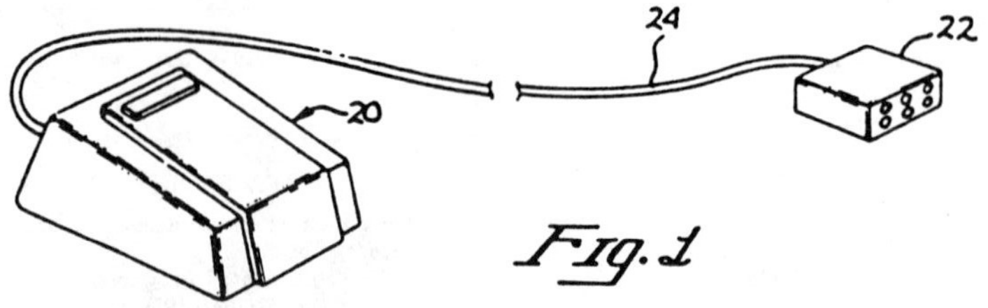

24

22

20

Fig. 1

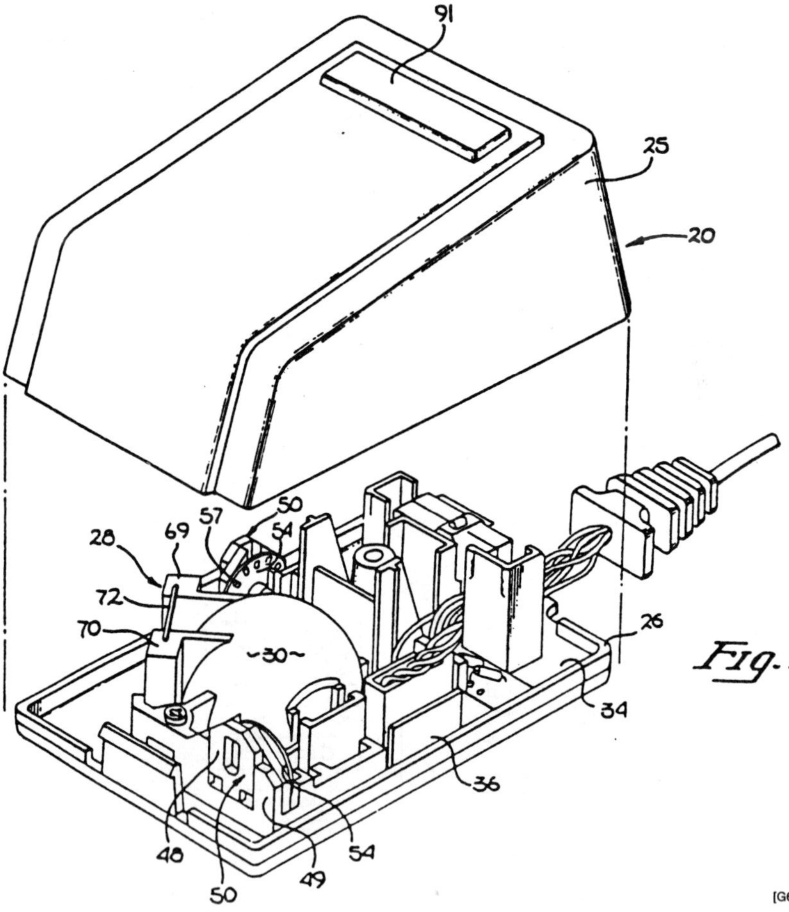

91

25

20

28

69

57

50

54

72

70

~30~

26

Fig. 2

34

36

48

50

49

54

[G6880]

U.S. Patent Mar. 29, 1988 Sheet 2 of 8 Re.32,632

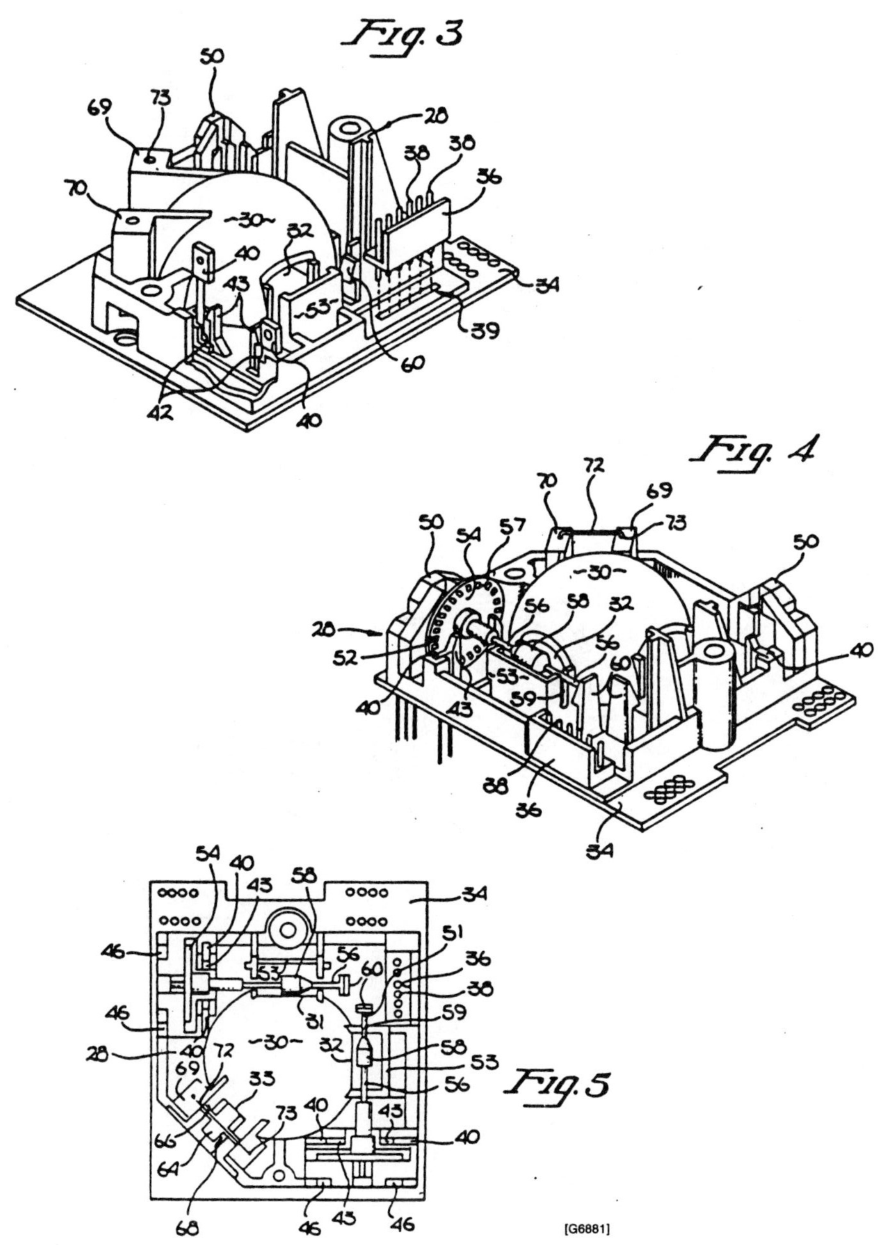

[G6881]

U.S. Patent Mar. 29, 1988 Sheet 3 of 8 **Re.32,632**

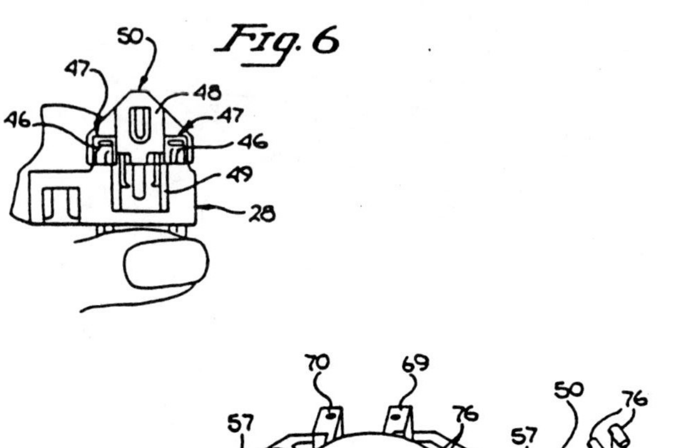

Fig. 6

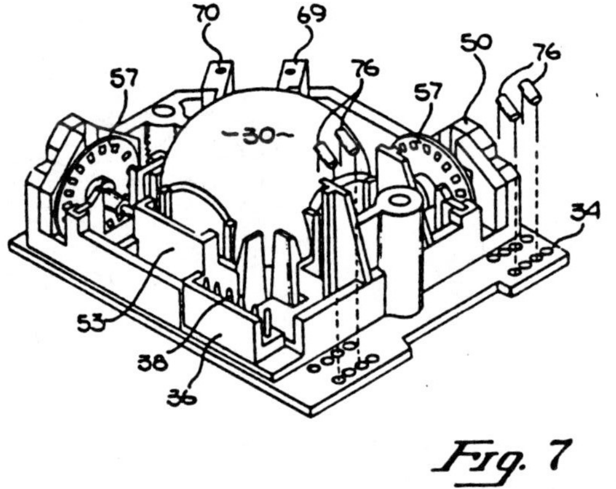

Fig. 7

[G6882]

U.S. Patent Mar. 29, 1988 Sheet 4 of 8 Re.32,632

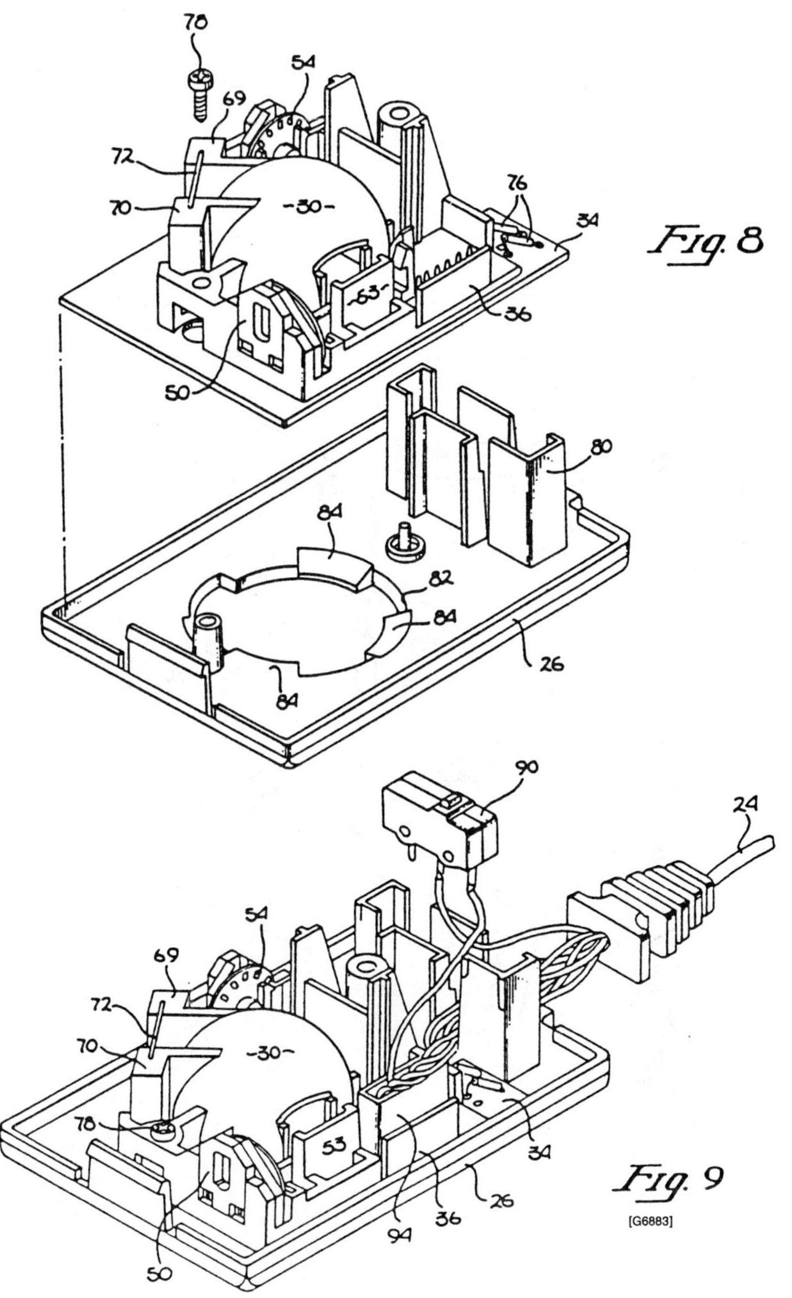

Fig. 8

Fig. 9

[G6883]

U.S. Patent Mar. 29, 1988 Sheet 5 of 8 Re.32,632

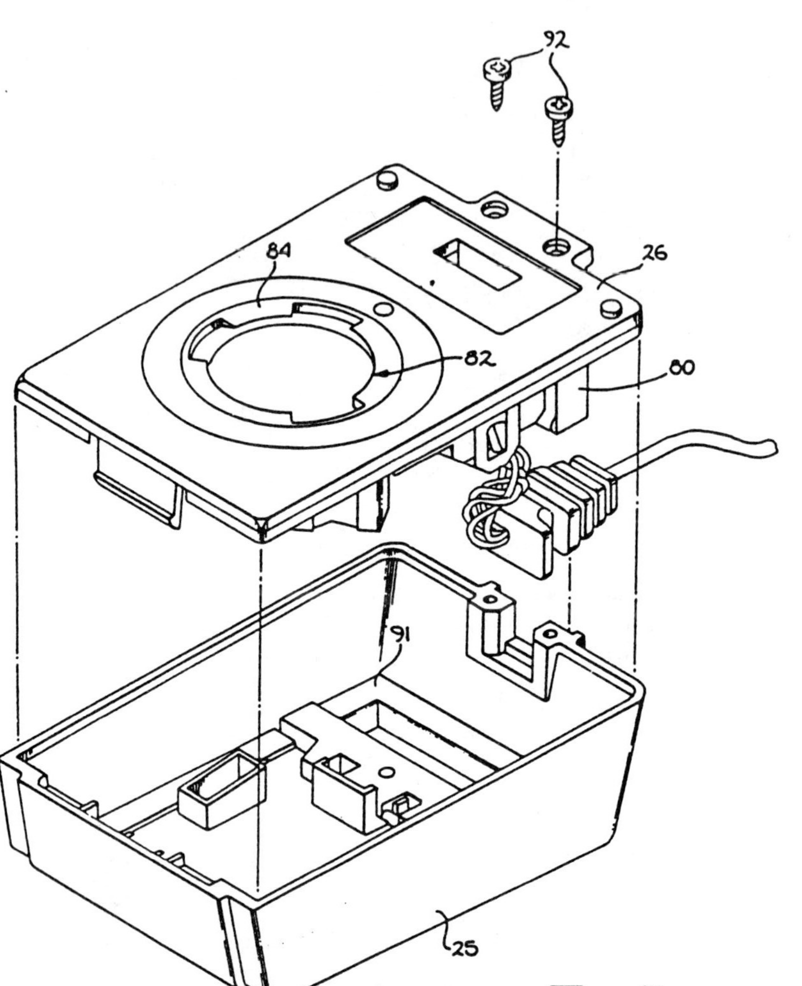

Fig. 10

[G6884]

U.S. Patent Mar. 29, 1988 Sheet 6 of 8 Re.32,632

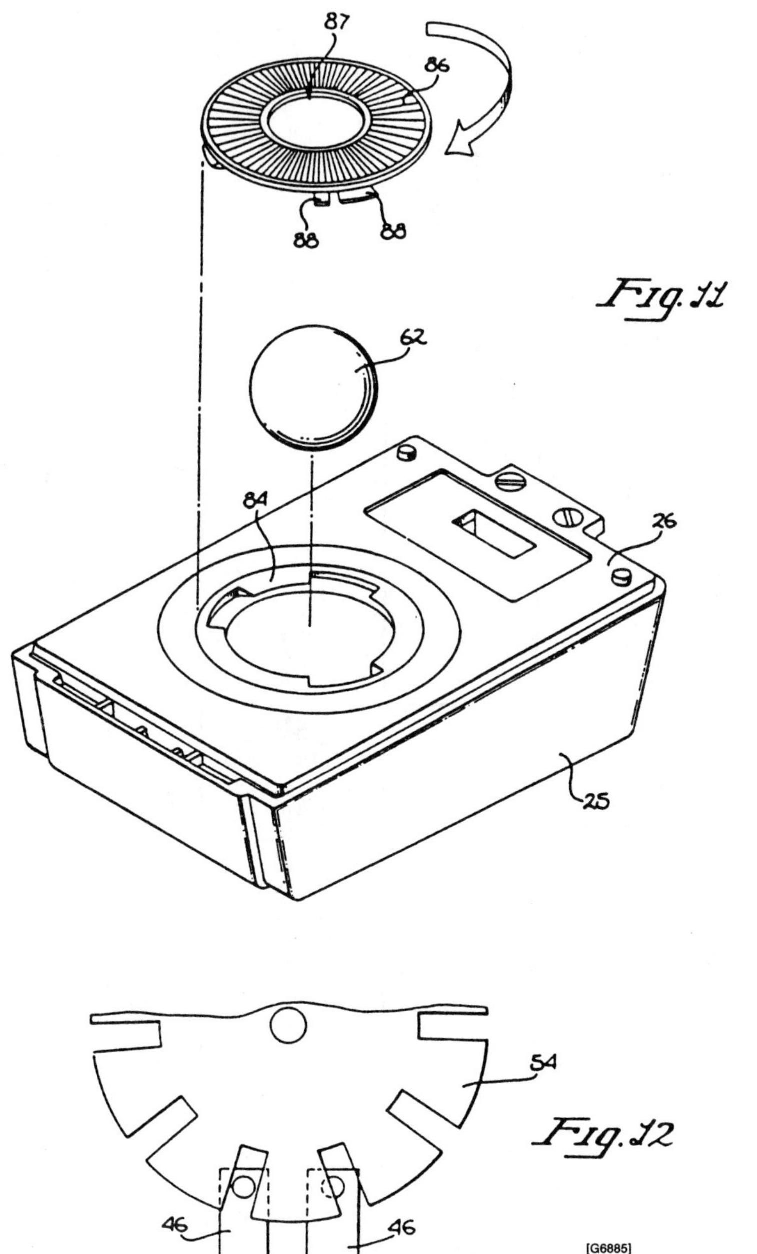

U.S. Patent Mar. 29, 1988 Sheet 7 of 8 Re.32,632

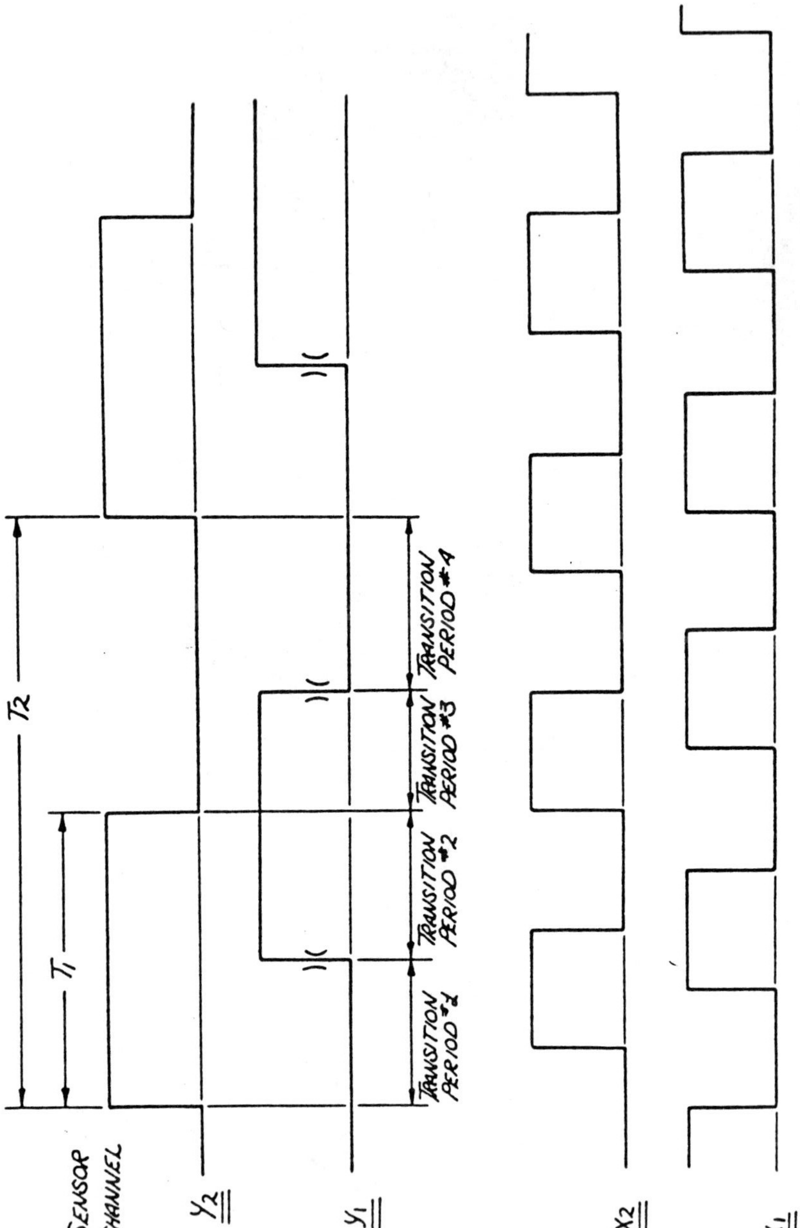

SENSOR CHANNEL
Y_2
Y_1
X_2
X_1
T_1
T_2
TRANSITION PERIOD #1
TRANSITION PERIOD #2
TRANSITION PERIOD #3
TRANSITION PERIOD #4
OUTPUT SIGNAL TIMING

Fig. 13

[G6886]

U.S. Patent Mar. 29, 1988 Sheet 8 of 8 Re.32,632

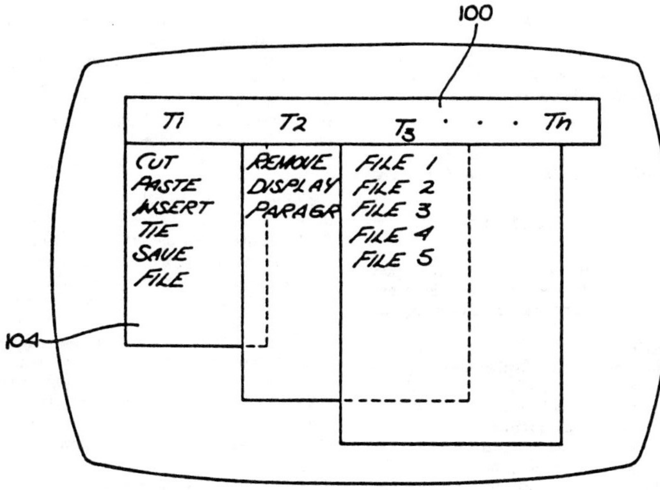

100

T1 T2 T3 . . . Tn

CUT
PASTE
INSERT
TIE
SAVE
FILE

REMOVE
DISPLAY
PARAGR

FILE 1
FILE 2
FILE 3
FILE 4
FILE 5

104

Fig. 14

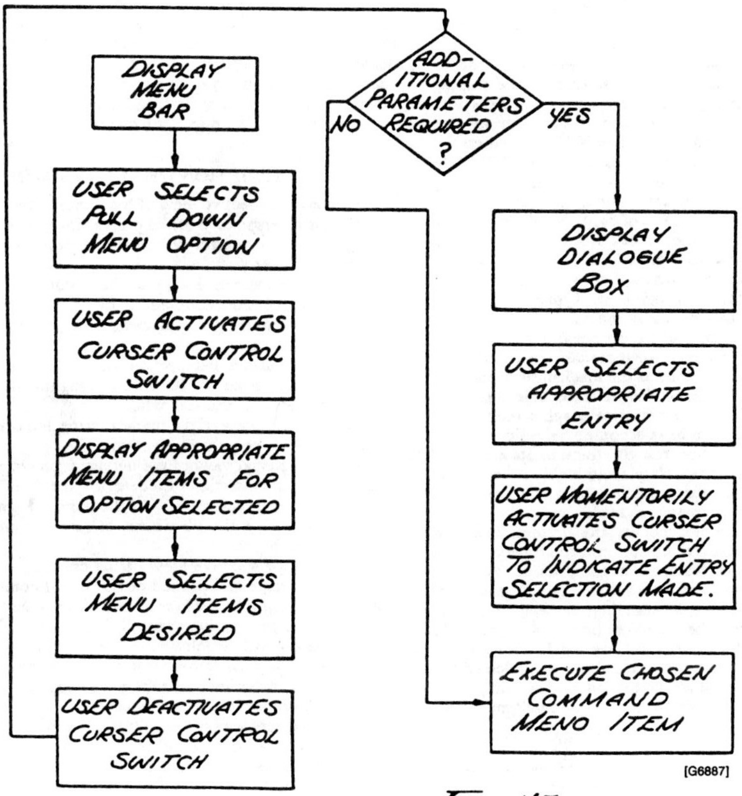

DISPLAY MENU BAR

USER SELECTS PULL DOWN MENU OPTION

USER ACTIVATES CURSER CONTROL SWITCH

DISPLAY APPROPRIATE MENU ITEMS FOR OPTION SELECTED

USER SELECTS MENU ITEMS DESIRED

USER DEACTIVATES CURSER CONTROL SWITCH

ADDITIONAL PARAMETERS REQUIRED ?

NO

YES

DISPLAY DIALOGUE BOX

USER SELECTS APPROPRIATE ENTRY

USER MOMENTORILY ACTIVATES CURSER CONTROL SWITCH TO INDICATE ENTRY SELECTION MADE.

EXECUTE CHOSEN COMMAND MENO ITEM

[G6887]

Fig. 15

Re. 32,632

1

DISPLAY SYSTEM

Matter enclosed in heavy brackets [ ] appears in the original patent but forms no part of this reissue specification; matter printed in italics indicates the additions made by reissue.

This application is a divisional reissue of application Ser. No. 06/399704, filed Jul. 19, 1982, now U.S. Pat. No. 4,464,652.

BACKGROUND OF THE INVENTION

1. Field

The present invention relates to the field of display systems, and more particularly to devices which can position a cursor over selected locations on a computer controlled display.

2. Art Background

In many computer controlled display systems, it is desirable to allow the user to control the position of a cursor or the like by means which are external from the main computer keyboard. For example, a user may be required to repetitively choose software options displayed on a cathode ray tube (CRT), or may desire to input data in a diagram format into the computer system. In such situations traditional keyboard input systems are not as effective as a cursor control device commonly referred to as a "mouse".

In a typical "mouse" system, a hand-held transducer provides positional movement signals to the display system. Traditionally, the movement of wheels within the cursor control device are coupled to potentiometers to provide signals indicative of an X-Y position on the display screen (see U.S. Pat. Nos. 3,541,541; 3,269,190; and 3,835,464). Other mouse systems utilize rotating balls on wheels which are in turn coupled to rotate apertures interrupting beams of light, thereby providing positional signals to the display system (see U.S. Pat. Nos. 3,892,963 and 3,541,521).

One common disadvantage of cursor control devices found in the prior art is their cost. Typically, prior art cursor controls include costly mechanical parts which require precise alignment for proper operation. Moreover, it is not uncommon for these devices to exhibit a loss in accuracy over time as the mechanism wears. As computer display capabilities have become more advanced in terms of user real-time graphic interaction, cursor control devices have become a necessity in many computer systems. Accordingly, there exists a need to provide a cost effective, simple and highly reliable cursor control device for providing signals indicative of X-Y positions on a computer display system.

As will be disclosed below, the present invention provides an improved cursor control device which overcomes the disadvantages of the prior art by utilizing a unitary frame structure for accurate alignment of all elements and simple assembly, as well as photo-optics to provide the required positional signals. In addition, a display system and method is disclosed for use in association with the cursor control device which permits a user to select command options simply by movement of the cursor over a "pull-down" menu bar.

SUMMARY OF THE INVENTION

A cursor control device having particular application to computer display systems is disclosed. The cursor control includes a unitary frame having a domed portion which houses a ball which is free to rotate. Two encoder disc assemblies are provided, which include roller shafts disposed substantially 90 degrees relative to one another and in contact with the ball. Each roller shaft is coupled to an encoder disc having a plurality of slots disposed radially around the disc periphery. These slots interrupt light beams which are provided by photo-emitters and directed at photo-detectors. Each slotted disc interrupts two light beams which are arranged such that when one beam is fully transmitted, the other is partially blocked. Beam interruptions produce signal pulses representing increments of motion, while the order in which the light beams are interrupted indicates the direction of motion, thereby resulting in an X-Y position on a display system. The ball is maintained in contact with the roller shafts by a spring biased idler wheel. The ball is free to "float" in the vertical direction within the dome, and thereby maintain good surface contact. Moreover, the ball may be easily removed for cleaning to insure that any build up of lint or the like does not prevent the ball from rotating smoothly. A switch is provided within the cursor control housing in order to signal the display system that a desired X-Y location on the display screen has been selected. In operation, a user may selectively position a cursor or the like on a display system by simply moving the cursor control device over a surface, such as a desk, until the desired cursor position is shown on the display device. A display system and method is disclosed for use in conjunction with the cursor control device, which permits user to select command options simply by movement of the displayed cursor over a "menu bar".

BRIEF DESCRIPTION OF THE DRAWINGS

FIG. 1 is a perspective view of the present invention.

FIG. 2 is a perspective of the present invention illustrating the cursor control device as it appears without the housing cover.

FIG. 3 is a perspective view of the unitary frame of the present invention coupled to the printed circuit board base, illustrating the placement of photo-detectors and the coupling connector.

FIG. 4 is a further perspective view of the unitary frame and circuit boad of FIG. 3 illustrating the position of a roller shaft and encoder wheel.

FIG. 5 is a top view of the unitary frame and printed circuit board of the present invention.

FIG. 6 is a partial view of the unitary frame in FIG. 3, illustrating the insertion of a detector aperture.

FIG. 7 is a perspective view of the unitary frame of FIG. 3, illustrating the placement of resistors on the printed circuit board.

FIG. 8 is a perspective view of the coupling of the unitary frame cage and printed circuit board combination to the housing base of the present invention.

FIG. 9 is a perspective view illustrating the placement of the control switch within the housing base.

FIG. 10 is the perspective view of the final assembly of the present invention illustrating the coupling of the cover and base portions of the housing.

FIG. 11 is a perspective view illustrating the insertion or removal of the floating and rotating ball.

FIG. 12 is a diagrammatical illustration of the alignment of the photo-emitters in relation to each encoder disc.

[G6888]

FIG. 13 is a diagrammatical illustration of a sample quadrature output of the present invention indicative of X-Y locations on display system.

FIG. 14 is a diagrammatical illustration of a "pull down" menu bar display.

FIG. 15 is a block diagram illustrating the sequence of steps utilized by the present invention to display options and associated commands on a "pull-down" menu bar display.

DETAILED DESCRIPTION OF THE INVENTION

A cursor control device having particular application for use in conjunction with a computer display system is disclosed. In the following description for purposes of explanation, specific numbers, materials and configurations are set forth in order to provide a thorough understanding of the present invention. However, it will be apparent to one skilled in the art that the present invention may be practiced without the specific details. In other instances, well known systems are shown in diagrammatical or block diagram form in order not to obscure the present invention unnecessarily.

Referring now to FIG. 1, the present invention includes a hand held cursor control unit 20 which is coupled to a plug 22 by means of a cable 24. As best illustrated in FIG. 2, cursor control unit 20 includes a cover 25 and a base 26 upon which the internal workings of the present invention are disposed. As will be apparent from the discussion which follows, cursor control unit 20 is designed with ease of assembly in mind, while providing very close tolerances and high X-Y position location accuracy.

With reference to FIGS. 3, 4 and 5, a premolded unitary frame 28 is provided which includes a domed housing 30 presently having three cut-out locations 31, 32 and 33. As illustrated, cut-outs 31 and 32 are disposed substantially at 90 degrees with respect to one another, with cut-out 33 being oriented generally symmetrically opposite the other cut-outs. In addition, frame 28 includes a plurality of bosses, slots and shaped stems of material which when pertinent will be discussed in this specification. In the presently preferred embodiment, the frame 28 is comprised of a plastic material (e.g. polycarbonate) which is impregnated with a lubricant (e.g. teflon). Thus, during operation and throughout its useful life, cursor control unit 20 does not require the addition of either wet or dry lubricants. Frame 28 is mounted on a printed circuit board 34 to facilitate electrical connection between the various electrical elements within the unit. Electrical connector header 36 is mounted as shown (see FIG. 3) to the unitary frame 28 such that connector pins 38 pass through a rectangular slot 39 through the frame to the circuit board below. As will be discussed, cable 24 is electrically coupled to the cursor control unit 20 through connector 36.

As illustrated in FIG. 3, photo-emitters 40 are inserted into slots 42 such that the emitter portion is facing away from the dome 30 (note that one emitter 40 is shown in FIG. 3 partially inserted). Upwardly extending clips 43 are snapped over portions of each emitter 40, as shown, to prevent them from being dislodged. Similarly, two photo-detectors 46 are inserted facing the emitters 40 into slots 47 in each of two detector apertures 50. As shown in FIG. 6, an outwardly extending portion 48 of each detector aperture 50 is aligned with guides 49 formed integrally with the frame 28, and the aperture is then snapped downward into place.

Thus, each detector aperture 50 houses two detectors 46 which face two emitters 40, respectively. In the presently preferred embodiment, the emitter/detector combination operates within the infrared region. However, it will be appreciated that any suitable wavelength may be used in a particular application. In addition, presently, the detectors 46 incorporate integral Schmitt triggers to provide detector outputs which more closely approximate a digital signal.

Two encoder disc assemblies are provided to convert, as will be described, the movement of the cursor control unit 20 into signals indicative of X-Y locations defined on the display system. Each encoder assembly 52 includes an encoder disc 54 axially coupled to a roller shaft 56. In addition, each encoder disc 54 is provided with a plurality of radially disposed slots 57 which interrupt the light beams generated by the photo-emitters 40. A cylindrical contact member 58 surrounds each roller shaft 56 at each respective cut out location, as illustrated. Each encoder disc assembly 52 is mounted on the unitary frame 28 by inserting the encoder disc 54 between the detector aperture 50 and emitters 40 and snapping an end clip 60 over the opposite end of the roller shaft 56 (see FIGS. 4, 5 and 7), thereby allowing rotation of the roller shaft and encoder disc with a minimum of friction. As illustrated, each shaft 56 is slipped into and carried by a "U" shaped guide 59 formed from upwardly extending alignment bosses 53 to maintain each roller shaft 56 in proper orientation. End 51 of the shaft 56 is carried for rotation within a hollow portion of the detector aperture 50, such that encoder disk 54 is disposed in close proximity to the aperture 50. The present invention's use of integral lubrication within the frame material, permits each shaft 56 to freely rotate about its longitudinal axis.

As a result of the above described configuration, the radially disposed slots 57 of each encoder disc interrupt two light beams from photo-emitters 40. The position of the emitter/detector combination and encoder disc is such that when one beam is fully transmitted, the other is partially blocked by a slit on the encoder disc. As will be discussed, in operation a ball 62 is disposed within the dome 30 of the frame, and retained such that it is maintained in contact with both cylindrical contact members 58. The rotation of the ball 62 within the dome 30 in turn causes the rotation of each roller shaft 56 and its respective encoder disc. As will be discussed, the beam interruptions from the rotation of each encoder disc 54 produce signal pulses representing increments of motion, while the order in which the light beams are interrupted indicates the direction of motion of the cursor control unit.

Ball 62 is retained against the cylindrical contact members 58 by an idler wheel for rotation on a fixed shaft 66, as best shown in FIG. 5. The idler wheel 64 and shaft 66 are inserted within a slot 68 formed by rectangular bosses 69 and 70 extending upwardly from the frame's base. Wheel 64 extends through cut-out 33 into the interior of the dome 30. The legs of a staple shaped idler spring 72 are inserted through passages 73 passing perpendicular to the horizontal plane of the frame 28 and circuit board 34, thereby retaining the shaft 66 within the slot 68.

Referring now to FIG. 7, resistors 76, which are required by the specific electronics of the emitter/detector combination of the present invention, are inserted into the printed circuit board 34. The resistors 76 and associated leads from the connector 36, photo-emitters

40, and photo-detectors 46 are then electrically connected and soldered in place as is conventionally done in the art.

With reference now to FIGS. 8, 9 and 10, the assembled frame 28 and circuit assembly is mounted on the base 26 by means of a screw 78. As illustrated, base 26 includes an upwardly extending switch retaining portion 80 and a generally circular cut-out orifice 82. As best shown in FIGS. 8, 10 and 11, circular orifice 82 is disposed substantially below the opening of dome 30, and includes outwardly extending locking ridges 84 which are designed to accommodate a lock cap 86 (See FIG. 11), such that ball 62 may be retained within the dome 30. Lock cap 86 includes outwardly extending tabs 88 arranged to interleaf with ridges 84. In operation, a user desiring to insert or remove ball 62 from the cursor control unit 20, may unlock and remove the lock cap 86 from the orifice 82 by simply rotating the cap such that the tabs 88 and ridges 84 no longer interleaf.

As illustrated, lock cap 86 generally has a toroidal form having a central orifice 87 of smaller diameter than cutout orifice 82. It will be apparent, that once ball 62 is inserted and retained by lock cap 86, Thus, ball 62 contacts the surface below the cursor control unit 20 and rotates in response to the movement of the unit on the surface.

As shown in FIG. 9, cable 24 is coupled to cursor control 20 through a female connector 94 which is inserted over pins 38. A switch 90 is coupled to the cable 24 through electrical connector 36, and is inserted within the retaining portion 80. A switch cap 91 forms part of the cover 25 (see FIG. 1), and is disposed above switch 90 such that the depression of the switch cap 91 forces switch 90 to electrically close, and thereby signal the computer display system that an appropriate X-Y location has been selected. As shown in FIG. 10, base 26 and cover 25 are coupled by securing both sections to one another using screws 92. Once the cover and base have been joined, ball 62 is inserted and lock cap 86 is attached as discussed above to retain the ball within the dome portion 30.

With reference to FIGS. 12 and 13, a sample quadrature output of the cursor control unit 20 is illustrated. As previously described, photo-detectors 46 are disposed such that if one detector is fully exposed by a slot of the encoder disc 54, the other detector is only partially exposed. Thus, in addition to the increments of motion of the cursor control over a surface, the direction of motion may also be determined. Assume for sake of example that the cursor control 20 is moved. As illustrated in FIG. 13, a substantially digital output signal is generated by each photo-emitter/detector combination associated with each encoder assembly. In the example shown, cursor control 20 would provide a regularly spaced output from the X channel detectors if the control 20 is moved over a surface at a constant speed along the X-axis. Similarly, if there is little movement of the control unit along the Y axis, little change will occur on the Y channels inasmuch as the Y encoder disk is not being rotated significantly (see FIG. 13). The computer display system is provided with appropriate software or hardware, for example edge detectors, to detect signal state transitions. Thus, the signals from each pair of channels may be decoded such that the X-Y direction of motion may be determined for the particular order of transition changes from each channel along an axis. Inasmuch as the particular circiutry and software used for decoding the various signals and positioning the cursor or the like on a display system will be apparent to one skilled in the art, the details of such will not be recited herein.

Referring now to FIGS. 14 and 15, a display system and method for use in conjunction with the cursor control device 20 will be described. As previously discussed, control 20 is coupled to a display system which is controlled by a computer or other equivalent circuitry. Appropriate programming of the computer is provided such that a "menu" bar 100 comprising a variety of command options indicated by titles (for example, T_1, T_2, $T_3 \ldots T_n$), is displayed across the CRT screen or the like as shown in FIG. 14. If a particular title (for example T_1) is selected, one or more sub-command items 104 are displayed by the computer system below the primary menu title. As illustrated, the sub-command items appear to the user to be "pulled down" from the main menu bar 100. The user then selects a desired item for execution by the computer by appropriate movement of a cursor control, as will be described. Although the list of items 104 are shown for illustration below menu title options T_1, T_2, and T_3, in the present embodiment only one menu option may be pulled down and displayed at a time.

The sequence of operations executed by the computer system to permit the user to select a particular menu title and sub-command item is shown in FIG. 15. The computer initially displays menu bar 100 on the display system as shown in FIG. 14. A user desiring to select a particular title moves cursor control unit 20 over a surface, thereby rotating ball 62 within dome 30 and sending signals indicative of X-Y locations to the display system for corresponding movement of a cursor or the like on the display screen. Once the cursor is positioned over (or in proximity with) the chosen menu title selection, the user depresses switch cap 91 on cursor control 20, thereby activating switch 90, and signaling the computer system that the particular title has been selected. The computer display system then either executes the menu title if it is an immediate command, or displays a set of sub-command items for user selection. If items are displayed, the user continues to depress switch cap 91, and once again moves the cursor control over the surface until the displayed cursor lies over or in proximity with the item to be executed. The user then removes pressure from the switch cap 91 thereby deactivating switch 90, and indicating to the computer which item is to be executed.

The computer system then determines if further parameters are required to be specified by the user. If no further data is required, the computer executes the item indicated by the cursor position on the display screen. However, if parameters must be specified by the user prior to execution a "dialogue box" is defined on the display system which displays the various data selections which are required. For example, a user may be required to select page formats, specify numerical values, etc. In the present embodiment, a user inputs the desired data selections by positioning the cursor over the selection, in for example a multiple choice format, and momentarily activates the switch 90 on the cursor control unit. Once the required selections are made, the computer proceeds to execute the chosen menu item.

Accordingly, it is possible for a user to select and execute a variety of commands without the necessity of inputting characters on a keyboard, as is commonly required in the art. Rather, the present invention permits fast entry and execution of commands, such as for

Re. 32,632

7

example in a word processing system or the like, wherein large blocks of text or other data may be manipulated or operated upon simply by movement of the cursor control 20 over a surface and the appropriate depression of switch 90.

Thus, an improved cursor control and display system has been described. The present invention permits a user to select desired menu titles on a menu bar by movement of a cursor control over a surface. Sub-command items may be specified for execution by the computer control display system in the same manner, such that the operator need not enter command characters on a keyboard or the like in order to access and execute most system functions.

Although the present invention has been described with reference to FIGS. 1–15 and with emphasis on a "pull down" type display system, it should be understood that the figures are for illustration only and should not be taken as limitations upon the invention. It is contemplated that many changes and modifications may be made, by one of ordinary skill in the art, to the materials and arrangements of the elements of the invention without department from the spirit and scope of the invention as disclosed above.

What is claimed is:

[1. A device for providing signals indicative of X-Y locations on a display system or the like, comprising:

a housing including a base having an opening for the passage of a rotatable ball;

a unitary frame disposed on said base including:

a domed portion integrally formed with said frame substantially surrounding and retaining said rotatable ball;

said domed portion having first and second cut-outs through said dome disposed substantially at 90 degrees with respect to one another, and a third cut-out disposed at an angle with respect to said first and second cut-outs;

X-Y position indicating means passing through said first and second cut-outs, for converting the rotation of said ball into signals indicative of X-Y positions on said display system;

biasing means passing through said third cut-out, for biasing said ball against said X-Y position indicating means;

means for removing said ball from said domed portion through said opening in said base, such that said ball and the interior or said dome may be serviced, said means for removing comprising:

outwardly extending lock ridges integrally formed with said opening in said base;

a lock cap having a second opening of smaller diameter then said base opening to permit only a portion of said ball to pass therethrough and contact said surface;

said lock cap further including outwardly extending lock tabs to interleaf with said lock ridges, such that rotation of said cap interleafs with said tabs and ridges thereby locking said cap onto said base;

whereby movement of said device over a surface such that a portion of said ball is maintained in contact with said surface results in X-Y positions defined on said display system.]

[2. The device as defined by claim 1, wherein said biasing means comprises a wheel carried by a shaft, said shaft being biased such that said wheel is maintained in contact with said ball.]

8

[3. The device as defined by claim 2, wherein said third cut-out is disposed generally at 45 degrees with respect to said first and second cut-outs.]

[4. The device as defined by claim 3, wherein said X-Y position indicating means includes a roller shaft coupled to an encoder disc having a plurality of radially disposed slots, said disc being disposed between a photo-emitter and photo-detector.]

[5. The device as defined by claim 4, wherein said photo-detector is diposed within a detector aperture, said aperture being retained on said unitary frame to form an integral unit.]

[6. The device as defined by claim 5, further including a circuit board disposed between said frame and said base.]

[7. The device as defined by claim 6, further including a switch coupled to said circuit board to specify selected X-Y positions on said display system.]

[8. The device as defined by claim 7, said device being coupled to a computer controlled display system wherein menu commands are displayed and selected by a user through movement of said device.]

9. A computer controlled display system having a display wherein a plurality of command options are displayed along a menu bar and sub-command items corresponding to each option are displayed once said option has been selected, comprising:

first display means coupled to said computer for generating and displaying said menu bar comprising said plurality of command options;

cursor control means coupled to said display system for selectively positioning a cursor on said display, said cursor control means including a cursor control device for movement over a surface, the movement of said cursor control device over said surface by a user resulting in a corresponding movement of said cursor on said display;

signal generation means including a switch having a first and second position coupled to said display system for signalling said computer of an option choice once said cursor is positioned over a first predetermined area on said display corresponding to an option to be selected, said user placing said switch in said second position while moving said cursor control device over said surface such that said cursor is over said first predetermined area;

second display means coupled to said computer for generating and displaying said sub-command items corresponding to said selected option;

said switch being placed in said first position by said user once said user has positioned said cursor over a second predetermined area corresponding to a sub-command item to be selected;

whereby an option and a sub-command item is selected and executed by said computer.

[10. The display system of claim 9 wherein said cursor control device comprises:

a housing including a base having an opening for the passage of a rotatable ball;

a unitary frame disposed on said base including:

a domed portion integrally formed with said frame substantially surrounding and retaining said rotatable ball;

said domed portion having first and second cut-outs through said dome disposed substantially at 90 degrees with respect to one another, and a third cut-out disposed at an angle with respect to said first and second cut-outs;

[G6891]

X-Y position indicating means passing through said first and second cut-outs, for converting the rotation of said ball into signals indicative of X-Y positions on said display system;

biasing means passing through said third cut-out, for biasing said ball against said X-Y position indicating means;

means for removing said ball from said domed portion through said opening in said base, such that said ball and the interior of said dome may be serviced, said means for removing said ball comprising:

outwardly extending lock ridges integrally formed with said opening in said base;

a lock cap having a second opening of smaller diameter then said base opening to permit only a portion of said ball to pass therethrough and contact said surface;

said lock cap further including outwardly extending lock tabs to interleaf with said lock ridges, such that rotation of said cap interleafs with said tabs and ridges thereby locking said cap onto said base;

whereby said option and sub-command item may be selected by movement of said cursor control means over a surface such that a portion of said ball is in contact with said surface.]

11. In a computer controlled display system having a display wherein a plurality of command options are displayed along a menu bar and sub-command items corresponding to each option are displayed once said option has been selected, a method for selecting an option and an item, comprising the steps of:

(a) generating and displaying said menu bar comprising said plurality of command options;

(b) positioning a cursor on said display using a cursor control device for movement over a surface, the movement of said cursor control device over said surface by a user resulting in a corresponding movement of said cursor on said display;

(c) signalling said computer of an option choice once said cursor is positioned over a first predetermined area on said display corresponding to an option to be selected, said user signalling said computer by placing a switch coupled to said display system in a second position while moving said cursor control device over said surface such that said cursor is over said first predetermined area;

(d) generating and displaying said sub-command items corresponding to said selected option;

(e) positioning said cursor over a second predetermined area corresponding to a sub-command item to be selected, said switch being maintained in said second position until said cursor is positioned over said second predetermined area;

(f) placing said switch in a first position once said user has positioned said cursor over said second predetermined area;

whereby an option and an item associated with said option is selected.

12. The method as defined by claim **11**, wherein said switch is disposed on said cursor control device.

13. The method as defined by claim **12**, where said computer displays said sub-command items generally below said optiion on said menu bar.

* * * * *

[G6892]

Notes on the "Atkinson" Patent

1. A patent begins by summarizing what the inventor knows about the "prior art"—the work of others that relates to the invention. It then continues with a brief summary of the invention. A completely detailed description of the preferred embodiment of the invention then follows. A precise definition of the invention itself (not to be confused with the "preferred embodiment") is set forth in one or more "claims" that are appended to the very end of the patent. 35 U.S.C.A. §§ 111, 112. Each "claim" defines a unique invention. Drawings disclosing all the individual elements of the claims are required. 35 U.S.C.A. § 113; 37 CFR § 1.83(a).

2. There is no "typical" software patent. The inventions defined by Atkinson patent claims 9, 11, 12, and 13 are "pure software" in the sense that the inventions are implementable on a general-purpose computer having no new or novel elements other than the software with a mouse. Note that only a very simple "flow diagram" of the program is defined by one or more of these claims. There is no detailed program listing, and the description in Figure 15 (column 6 line 4 to column 7 line 25) is simple and brief. In cases where hardware or software elements are novel, they must be disclosed. Sometimes complete or partial program listings are essential, and they may be submitted on microfiche or printed as part of the patent. Section 112 of the Patent Act requires "a written description of the invention and of the manner and process of making and using it, in such full, clear, concise, and exact terms as to enable any person skilled in the art to which it pertains, or with which it is most nearly connected, to make and use the same, and shall set forth the best mode contemplated by the inventor of carrying out his invention." 35 U.S.C.A. § 119 requires "such full and complete disclosure of the preferred embodiment of the invention as enables one skilled in the art to make it without undue experimentation". How well have Apple's attorneys explained this invention?

3. This is a "reissue" patent. That means the patent, as originally issued, contained some defects. It was "reissued" by the Patent and Trademark Office with portions (enclosed in square brackets) deleted and possibly with additions and corrections. The effect of this particular reissue is to split one patent into two "divisions"—one patent for the inventor Atkinson that focuses upon a "software" invention, and a separate patent (not shown) for a different set of inventors that focuses upon a "mechanical" mouse. See 35 U.S.C.A. § 25 *et seq.* Prior to a 1984 amendment to 35 U.S.C. 116, a patent could be invalidated if all the named inventors did not jointly contribute to and invent *all* of the inventions claimed. Apple cured this technical defect in its patent by reissuing the single patent as two divisional patents having different inventors.

4. "Reissue" proceedings (35 U.S.C.A. § 251 *et seq.*) are used to correct defects in a patent. "Reexamination" proceedings (35 U.S.C.A. § 301 *et seq.*) are used to present additional "prior art" to the Patent Examiner and to have the patent's validity reaffirmed by the Patent and Trademark Office, reestablishing the presumption of validity (35 U.S.C.A. § 282).

5. Note that the date when the patent was applied for appears in the patent along with an application serial number. Once approved by the

Patent Examiner, a patent is assigned a unique patent number and a date of issuance. Once issued, a patent grants the inventors, or their assignee, a monopoly on making, using and selling the invention that lasts for seventeen years from the date of issuance (35 U.S.C.A. § 154). A reissuance or reexamination of a patent does not extend the seventeen year monopoly.

6. If the patent number is marked upon the patented goods sold, everyone is presumed to know about the patent, and up to six years worth of back damages may be obtained. (See if Apple is marking its patent number upon the Macintosh). If not, then damages commence on the date of formal notice of infringement (35 U.S.C.A. § 287).

7. Note the list of "prior art" references on the first page of the patent. These patents and articles were examined by the Patent Examiner, and the patent is presumed to be valid over these references (35 U.S.C.A. § 282). The applicant has an ethical duty to send copies of relevant prior art references to the Examiner, and failure to do so may constitute fraud and may also invalidate the patent (37 CFR § 1.56), with the defendant possibly recovering its attorney's fees (35 U.S.C.A. § 285).

8. The process of applying for and obtaining a patent is called the "prosecution" of a patent. Individual inventors may "prosecute" their own patents (usually a very unwise approach), or they may be represented by a "registered" patent attorney or patent agent. To register one must meet educational requirements in science and engineering (or have equivalent experience) and also pass a rigorous examination on patent procedure. 37 CFR § 107. The examination covers Title 35, the Rules of Practice set forth in 37 CFR Chapter 1, and the Manual of Patent Examining Procedure, or M.P.E.P. (a set of two bulky three-ring binders containing numerous additional rules of practice). In addition, the examination includes writing sample patent claims of various types. Nonregistered attorneys may not practice before the patent section of the Patent and Trademark Office. They may practice before the Trademark section, however. See 37 CFR § 10.14.

9. Large corporations usually require employees to sign contracts agreeing to assign their inventions to the corporation. If the corporation decides that the benefits of a potential patent outweigh the costs of the application procedure, it will pay patent attorneys to prosecute the patent application. The inventor here, William Atkinson, assigned his patent to Apple Computer, Inc., which then hired the firm of Blakely, Sokoloff, Taylor & Zafman to represent it. Assignments of patents must be recorded in the Patent and Trademark Office. 35 U.S.C.A. § 261. An assignment is void as against a subsequent purchaser for value if not recorded within three months or prior to the subsequent assignment. If there is more than one owner of a patent, each owns the whole in the sense that each joint owner may grant licenses and collect royalties, and there is no obligation to account to the other joint owners (35 U.S.C.A. § 262) unlike the case with joint owners of a copyright (see NIMMER ON COPYRIGHT, 6.12[A]). Accordingly, an agreement on ownership, licensing and distribution of royalties is essential.

10. Each claim appended to the end of a patent, for instance each of the 13 claims of the "Atkinson" patent, defines a unique invention. The

Patent Examiner studies the "prior art" and then negotiates with the inventor's patent attorney or agent over the precise wording of the patent claims. Initially, the Examiner typically rejects all of the claims, sends the "prior art" to the applicant's attorney or agent, and awaits a response. The applicant's attorney or agent responds with an "amendment" to the claims, typically narrowing the inventions defined by the claims. The patent may then issue, or negotiations may continue for years, with the patent application refiled several times as a "continuation" of the original, claiming the benefit of the original application's filing date under 35 U.S.C. § 120. An adverse decision of the Examiner may be appealed first to the Board of Patent Appeals and Interferences within the Patent and Trademark Office (35 U.S.C.A. § 134) and then to the Court of Appeals for the Federal Circuit (35 U.S.C.A. § 141). Alternatively, the Commissioner of Patents may be sued in the United States District Court for the District of Columbia (35 U.S.C.A. § 145), but that is not a particularly favorable forum for inventors.

11. Prior to the issuance of a patent, and if no patent issues, the application is preserved in secrecy. 35 U.S.C.A. § 122. Hence, trade secrets are preserved until a patent issues. The issuance of a patent can destroy trade secrets disclosed in the application. See *Conmar Products Corp. v. Universal Slide Fastener Co.,* 172 F.2d 150, 155–156 (2d Cir.1949). But compare *Smith v. Dravo Corp.,* 203 F.2d 369 and 208 F.2d 388 (7th Cir.1953), where disclosure of trade secrets in patents and in sold articles did not destroy the secrets where there was a wrongful taking.

12. While not reproduced here, the original patent application, plus all correspondence between the applicant and the Examiner, is open to public inspection once the patent issues, with copies available at nominal cost. It is stored in a large manilla folder called a "file wrapper". Statements made by the applicant during "prosecution" of the patent before the Examiner are frequently used later by the Courts in construing the meaning of the "claim" language and thus the scope of the invention. These statements can give rise to a "file wrapper estoppel." If an applicant has interpreted a claim narrowly to get the examiner to issue a patent, the patent-holder is "estopped" to argue later for a broader interpretation of the same claim. Accordingly, it is essential to review the file wrapper of a patent before rendering an opinion on patent validity or patent infringement.

13. The process of suing a patent infringer before a United States District Court is called "litigation". Any attorney admitted to practice may "litigate" a patent. The trend in recent years is toward more jury trials in patent cases. Patent infringement is for the trier of fact to determine, as are damages. The patent claims, such as claims 1–13 in the "Atkinson" patent, define the scope of the patent for the purpose of determining infringement. (In some instances, the claims may be interpreted to cover "equivalents" outside the scope of their literal language.) The successful litigant may receive actual damages or, if greater, a "reasonable royalty", typically 3 to 5 percent of the sale price of the invention as claimed in the patent claims. 35 U.S.C.A. § 284. Compare this to copyright damages, which include actual damages plus defendant's profits not included in actual damages, (17 U.S.C.A. § 504(b)) or, in the alternative,

"statutory damages" set by the judge (17 U.S.C.A. § 504(c)). Injunction against further infringement is also available under 35 U.S.C.A. § 283 (patent) and 17 U.S.C.A. § 502 (copyright).

D. ELIGIBILITY FOR PATENT PROTECTION

In general, an invention must be "useful" and "patentable" under § 101, "novel" under § 102, "nonobvious" under § 103, and meet "procedural requirements" set forth in § 102(b), § 112 and other sections for the Patent and Trademark Office to issue a valid patent.

The issue of whether or not a patent application meets the requirements of the Patent Act may arise before the Patent and Trademark Office. This happens when, as is usually the case, the patent examiner rejects the application and the applicant contests the rejection. The issue of validity may also be raised by the defendant in patent infringement litigation, who may (and usually does) argue that the Patent and Trademark Office erred in issuing a patent because the applicant has failed to meet the statutory standards. (The defendant usually will also argue in the alternative, that if the patent is valid, the defendant has not infringed it because the defendant's process or product does not fall within the claims of the patent.)

PATENT ACT
35 U.S.C.A. §§ 101–103, 112

§ 101. Inventions patentable

Whoever invents or discovers any new and useful process, machine, manufacture, or composition of matter, or any new and useful improvement thereof, may obtain a patent therefor, subject to the conditions and requirements of this title.

§ 102. Conditions for patentability; novelty and loss of right to patent

A person shall be entitled to a patent unless—

(a) the invention was known or used by others in this country, or patented or described in a printed publication in this or a foreign country, before the invention thereof by the applicant for patent, or

(b) the invention was patented or described in a printed publication in this or a foreign country or in public use or on sale in this country, more than one year prior to the date of the application for patent in the United States, or

(c) he has abandoned the invention, or

(d) the invention was first patented or caused to be patented, or was the subject of an inventor's certificate, by the applicant or his legal representatives or assigns in a foreign country prior to the date of the application for patent in this country on an application for patent or inventor's certificate filed more than twelve months before the filing of the application in the United States, or

(e) the invention was described in a patent granted on an application for patent by another filed in the United States before the invention thereof by the applicant for patent, or on an international application by another who has fulfilled the requirements of paragraphs (1), (2), and (4) of section 371(c) of this title before the invention thereof by the applicant for patent, or

(f) he did not himself invent the subject matter sought to be patented, or

(g) before the applicant's invention thereof the invention was made in this country by another who had not abandoned, suppressed, or concealed it. In determining priority of invention there shall be considered not only the respective dates of conception and reduction to practice of the invention, but also the reasonable diligence of one who was first to conceive and last to reduce to practice, from a time prior to conception by the other.

§ 103. Conditions for patentability; non-obvious subject matter

A patent may not be obtained though the invention is not identically disclosed or described as set forth in section 102 of this title, if the differences between the subject matter sought to be patented and the prior art are such that the subject matter as a whole would have been obvious at the time the invention was made to a person having ordinary skill in the art to which said subject matter pertains.

Patentability shall not be negatived by the manner in which the invention was made. Subject matter developed by another person, which qualifies as prior art only under subsection (f) or (g) of section 102 of this title, shall not preclude patentability under this section where the subject matter and the claimed invention were, at the time the invention was made, owned by the same person or subject to an obligation of assignment to the same person.

§ 112. Specification

The specification shall contain a written description of the invention, and of the manner and process of making and using it, in such full, clear, concise, and exact terms as to enable any person skilled in the art to which it pertains, or with which it is most nearly connected, to make and use the same, and shall set forth the best mode contemplated by the inventor of carrying out his invention.

The specification shall conclude with one or more claims particularly pointing out and distinctly claiming the subject matter which the applicant regards as his invention.

A claim may be written in independent or, if the nature of the case admits, in dependent or multiple dependent form.

Subject to the following paragraph, a claim in dependent form shall contain a reference to a claim previously set forth and then specify a further limitation of the subject matter claimed. A claim in dependent form shall be construed to incorporate by reference all the limitations of the claim to which it refers.

A claim in multiple dependent form shall contain a reference, in the alternative only, to more than one claim previously set forth and then specify a further limitation of the subject matter claimed. A multiple dependent claim shall not serve as a basis for any other multiple dependent claim. A multiple dependent claim shall be construed to incorporate by reference all the limitations of the particular claim in relation to which it is being considered.

An element in a claim for a combination may be expressed as a means or step for performing a specified function without the recital of structure, material, or acts in support thereof, and such claim shall be construed to cover the corresponding structure, material, or acts described in the specification and equivalents thereof.

* * *

Notes

1. In general, § 101 issues arise rather rarely in non-computer cases. Applicants do not waste time and money on applying, unless they think their inventions are new and useful. The typical invention, for instance the proverbial "better mousetrap," clearly falls into the category of a process, machine, manufacture, or composition of matter. Computer programs, however, have had to overcome precedents to the effect that "mental steps," mathematical equations, and ways of doing business are not patentable inventions under § 101.

2. Section 102 defines what is meant by "novelty"—the requirement that an invention be new. Under 35 U.S.C.A. § 102(a), the applicant for a patent must have invented it prior to its sale or use in this country and also prior to the appearance of its description in a printed publication anywhere in the world.

Note that "public use" of an invention can be completely private and secret so long as the use is not an experimental use. Private use of a corset for ten years was held to be "public use". *Egbert v. Lippmann,* 104 U.S. 333 (1881). Likewise secret use of a process was held to be "public use", *Metallizing Engineering Co. v. Kenyon Bearing & Auto Parts Co.,* 153 F.2d 516 (2d Cir.1946), and market testing has been held to be "public use," not experimental use. *Western Marine Electronics, Inc. v. Furuno Electric Co., Ltd.,* 764 F.2d 840 (Fed.Cir.1985). When developing software, it is important to document "bug" reports and fixes to establish proof of experimental use that is product testing and not market testing. "Beta testing," the testing of new software by friendly users, is essential in software development. It is important to monitor Beta testing to avoid unintended "public use."

A "printed publication" can be ten to twenty handouts at a show, a microfilm in a public library, or a newspaper article printed in Mongolia in Mongolian.

3. Under 35 U.S.C.A. § 102(b), the applicant must file no later than 12 months after the first "sale" or "public use" of the invention in the United States or "publication" of a description of the invention anywhere in the world. In virtually all countries other than the United States, the applicant must file *before* the invention is disclosed publicly in any way. If foreign patents are desired, the initial U.S. filing must precede public disclosure of the invention (an exception is made for disclosure at certain designated World Fairs). To protect foreign rights, it is important to have employees and outside organizations that test the programs sign and obey trade secret agreements. These are "procedural" requirements—the inventor loses his or her right to an invention if the application for a patent is not filed promptly enough.

The "filing date" of an application has important legal effects, although the United States (unlike most foreign countries) does not have a system that gives the patent to the "first to file" when two persons invent the same invention independently. Foreign inventors may claim the priority of their foreign filing dates if they file in the United States within twelve months. 35 U.S.C.A. § 119. Likewise, U.S. citizens, by treaty, may claim the priority of their U.S. filing date before a foreign Patent Office, if they file in the foreign country within twelve months. The Patent Act, 35 U.S.C.A. § 35, also provides for the filing of an "International Application" under the Patent Cooperation Treaty which may be effective in many countries. A "national" phase of patent prosecution in each designated country follows an initial search of the "prior art" conducted by the United States Patent and Trademark Office acting as an "international searching authority" under the treaty.

An invention normally cannot be "on sale" before it is built, but it can be "on sale" if it is offered to buyers when the specifications have been worked out in such full detail that implementation will be straightforward.

4. "Novel" means that nothing identical to the invention is to be found in a single item of prior art, such as a published article. If two separately published articles must be combined to reveal all the claimed elements of an invention, then the invention is "novel", since it is not fully revealed in a single published article. Patentability is not barred for "novel" inventions under § 102, since § 102 applies only where "*the* invention" appears in the prior art. The invention, however, may still be attacked as "obvious" under § 103.

5. Although § 103 speaks of "nonobviousness" "at the time the invention was made", case precedents hold any public use or sale in this country or any publication anywhere occurring after the invention was made but more than one year prior to the application filing date may be included in the "prior art" that one "skilled in the art" is presumed to have known. This fiction means, in practical effect, that all public uses, sales and publications occurring:

(a) more than a year before a patent's filing date; or

(b) prior to the date of invention

are part of what the courts call the "prior art" that is used in testing the invention not only for novelty under § 102, but also for nonobviousness under § 103.

6. To test an invention for patentability, you first assemble the "prior art" as defined above. If all the elements of a patent claim (which defines an invention) can be found in a single item of "prior art" (a single article, for example), then the invention is not "novel", and § 102 blocks its patentability. If the novelty test is passed, the invention is "new", and one moves on to the § 103 test. If all the elements of a patent claim (which defines an invention) can be found in two or more items of "prior art" (two or more articles or patents, for example), and if a hypothetical individual "skilled in the art" and familiar with these items of "prior art" would find the invention to be "obvious", then § 103 blocks patentability.

The cryptic language of § 103 provides little guidance to the application of the "nonobviousness" test in practice. The Supreme Court has offered some suggestions in the leading case of *Graham v. John Deere.*

GRAHAM v. JOHN DEERE CO.

Supreme Court of the United States, 1966.
383 U.S. 1, 86 S.Ct. 684, 15 L.Ed.2d 545.

* * *

While the ultimate question of patent validity is one of law, Great A. & P. Tea Co. v. Supermarket Equipment Corp., supra, 340 U.S. at 155, 71 S.Ct. at 131, the § 103 condition, which is but one of three conditions, each of which must be satisfied, lends itself to several basic factual inquiries. Under § 103, the scope and content of the prior art are to be determined; differences between the prior art and the claims at issue are to be ascertained; and the level of ordinary skill in the pertinent art resolved. Against this background, the obviousness or nonobviousness of the subject matter is determined. Such secondary considerations as commercial success, long felt but unsolved needs, failure of others, etc., might be utilized to give light to the circumstances surrounding the origin of the subject matter sought to be patented. As indicia of obviousness or nonobviousness, these inquiries may have relevancy. See Note, Subtests of "Nonobviousness": A Nontechnical Approach to Patent Validity, 112 U.Pa.L.Rev. 1169 (1964).

This is not to say, however, that there will not be difficulties in applying the nonobviousness test. What is obvious is not a question upon which there is likely to be uniformity of thought in every given factual context. The difficulties, however, are comparable to those encountered daily by the courts in such frames of reference as negligence and scienter, and should be amenable to a case-by-case development. We believe that strict observance of the requirements laid down here will result in that uniformity and definiteness which Congress called for in the 1952 Act.

* * *

E. HISTORICAL DEVELOPMENT OF COMPUTER PROGRAM PATENT LAW

The dissent in *Diamond v. Diehr* contains an excellent summary of the pre–1981 history of computer program patent law. As you read the following excerpt from the dissent, do not worry, for the moment, about the holding and implications of *Diamond v. Diehr*—concentrate on the history that led up to the case.

DIAMOND v. DIEHR

Supreme Court of the United States, 1981.
450 U.S. 175, 101 S.Ct. 1048, 67 L.Ed.2d 155.

JUSTICE STEVENS, with whom JUSTICE BRENNAN, JUSTICE MARSHALL, and JUSTICE BLACKMUN join, dissenting.

* * *

Prior to 1968, well-established principles of patent law probably would have prevented the issuance of a valid patent on almost any conceivable computer program. Under the "mental steps" doctrine, processes involving mental operations were considered unpatentable. The mental-steps doctrine was based upon the familiar principle that a scientific concept or mere idea cannot be the subject of a valid patent. The doctrine was regularly invoked to deny patents to inventions consisting primarily of mathematical formulae or methods of computation. It was also applied against patent claims in which a mental operation or mathematical computation was the sole novel element or inventive contribution; it was clear that patentability could not be predicated upon a mental step. Under the "function of a machine" doctrine, a process which amounted to nothing more than a description of the function of a machine was unpatentable. This doctrine had its origin in several 19th–century decisions of this Court,[8] and it had been consistently followed thereafter by the lower federal courts. Finally, the definition of "process" announced by this Court in *Cochrane v. Deener,* 94 U.S. 780, 787–788, 24 L.Ed. 139 (1877), seemed to indicate that a patentable process must cause a physical transformation in the materials to which the process is applied. See *ante,* at 1054–1055.

Concern with the patent system's ability to deal with rapidly changing technology in the computer and other fields led to the formation in 1965 of the President's Commission on the Patent System. After studying the question of computer program patentability, the

8. The "function of a machine" doctrine is generally traced to *Corning v. Burden,* 15 How. 252, 268 (1854), in which the Court stated: "[I]t is well settled that a man cannot have a patent for the function or abstract effect of a machine, but only for the machine which produces it." The doctrine was subsequently reaffirmed on several occasions.

Commission recommended that computer programs be expressly excluded from the coverage of the patent laws; this recommendation was based primarily upon the Patent Office's inability to deal with the administrative burden of examining program applications.[10] At approximately the time that the Commission issued its report, the Patent Office published notice of its intention to prescribe guidelines for the examination of applications for patents on computer programs. See 829 Off.Gaz.Pat.Off. 865 (Aug. 16, 1966). Under the proposed guidelines, a computer program, whether claimed as an apparatus or as a process, was unpatentable.[11] The Patent Office indicated, however, that a programmed computer could be a component of a patentable process if combined with unobvious elements to produce a physical result. The Patent Office formally adopted the guidelines in 1968. See 33 Fed.Reg. 15609 (1968).

The new guidelines were to have a short life. Beginning with two decisions in 1968, a dramatic change in the law as understood by the Court of Customs and Patent Appeals took place. By repudiating the well-settled "function of a machine" and "mental steps" doctrines, that court reinterpreted § 101 of the Patent Code to enlarge drastically the categories of patentable subject matter. This reinterpretation would lead to the conclusion that computer programs were within the categories of inventions to which Congress intended to extend patent protection.

In *In re Tarczy–Hornoch,* 397 F.2d 856, 55 CCPA (Pat.) 1441 (1968), a divided Court of Customs and Patent Appeals overruled the line of cases developing and applying the "function of a machine" doctrine. The majority acknowledged that the doctrine had originated with decisions of this Court and that the lower federal courts, including the Court of Customs and Patent Appeals, had consistently adhered to it during the preceding 70 years. Nonetheless, the court concluded that the doctrine rested on a misinterpretation of the precedents and that it was contrary to "the basic purposes of the patent system and productive of a range of undesirable results from the harshly inequitable to the silly." *Id.,* at 867, 55 CCPA (Pat.), at 1454. Shortly thereafter, a similar fate befell the "mental steps" doctrine. In *In re Prater,* 415 F.2d 1378, 56 CCPA (Pat.) 1360 (1968), modified on rehearing, 415 F.2d 1393, 56 CCPA (Pat.) 1381 (1969), the court found that the precedents

10. The Commission's report contained the following evaluation of the current state of the law with respect to computer program patentability:

"Uncertainty now exists as to whether the statute permits a valid patent to be granted on programs. Direct attempts to patent programs have been rejected on the ground of nonstatutory subject matter. Indirect attempts to obtain patents and avoid the rejection, by drafting claims as a process, or a machine or components thereof programmed in a given manner, rather than as a program itself, have confused the issue further and should not be permitted." Report of the President's Commission on the Patent System, "To Promote the Progress of * * * Useful Arts" in an Age of Exploding Technology 14 (1966).

11. The Patent Office guidelines were based primarily upon the mental-steps doctrine and the *Cochrane v. Deener,* 94 U.S. 780, 24 L.Ed. 139 (1877), definition of "process." See 829 Off.Gaz.Pat.Off. 865 (Aug. 16, 1966); 33 Fed.Reg. 15609 (1968).

on which that doctrine was based either were poorly reasoned or had been misinterpreted over the years. 415 F.2d, at 1382–1387, 56 CCPA (Pat.), at 1366–1372. The court concluded that the fact that a process may be performed mentally should not foreclose patentability if the claims reveal that the process also may be performed without mental operations. *Id.,* at 1389, 56 CCPA (Pat.), at 1374–1375. This aspect of the original *Prater* opinion was substantially undisturbed by the opinion issued after rehearing. However, the second *Prater* opinion clearly indicated that patent claims broad enough to encompass the operation of a programmed computer would not be rejected for lack of patentable subject matter. 415 F.2d, at 1403, n. 29, 56 CCPA (Pat.), at 1394, n. 29.

The Court of Customs and Patent Appeals soon replaced the overruled doctrines with more expansive principles formulated with computer technology in mind. In *In re Bernhart,* 417 F.2d 1395, 57 CCPA (Pat.) 737 (1969), the court reaffirmed *Prater,* and indicated that all that remained of the mental-steps doctrine was a prohibition on the granting of a patent that would confer a monopoly on all uses of a scientific principle or mathematical equation. *Id.,* at 1399, 57 CCPA (Pat.), at 743. The court also announced that a computer programmed with a new and unobvious program was physically different from the same computer without that program; the programmed computer was a new machine or at least a new improvement over the unprogrammed computer. *Id.,* at 1400, 57 CCPA (Pat.), at 744. Therefore, patent protection could be obtained for new computer programs if the patent claims were drafted in apparatus form.

The Court of Customs and Patent Appeals turned its attention to process claims encompassing computer programs in *In re Musgrave,* 431 F.2d 882, 57 CCPA (Pat.) 1352 (1970). In that case, the court emphasized the fact that *Prater* had done away with the mental-steps doctrine; in particular, the court rejected the Patent Office's continued reliance upon the "point of novelty" approach to claim analysis. *Id.,* at 889, 57 CCPA (Pat.), at 1362.[15] The court also announced a new standard for evaluating process claims under § 101: any sequence of operational steps was a patentable process under § 101 as long as it was within the "technological arts." *Id.,* at 893, 57 CCPA (Pat.), at 1366–1367. This standard effectively disposed of any vestiges of the mental-steps doctrine remaining after *Prater* and *Bernhart.*[16] The "technological arts"

15. Under the "point of novelty" approach, if the novelty or advancement in the art claimed by the inventor resided solely in a step of the process embodying a mental operation or other unpatentable element, the claim was rejected under § 101 as being directed to nonstatutory subject matter. See Blumenthal & Riter, Statutory or Non-Statutory?: An Analysis of the Patentability of Computer Related Inventions, 62 J.Pat.Off.Soc. 454, 457, 461, 470 (1980).

16. The author of the second *Prater* opinion, Judge Baldwin, disagreed with the *Musgrave* "technological arts" standard for process claims. He described that standard as "a major and radical shift in this area of the law." 431 F.2d, at 893–894, 57 CCPA (Pat.), at 1367. As Judge Baldwin read the majority opinion, claims drawn solely to purely mental processes were now entitled to patent protection. *Id.,* at 895–896, 57 CCPA (Pat.), at 1369. Judge Baldwin's understanding of *Musgrave* seems to have been confirmed in *In re Foster,* 438

standard was refined in *In re Benson,* 441 F.2d 682, 58 CCPA (Pat.) 1134 (1971), in which the court held that computers, regardless of the uses to which they are put, are within the technological arts for purposes of § 101. *Id.,* at 688, 58 CCPA (Pat.), at 1142.

* * *

Notes

1. The original Court of Customs and Patent Appeals decision holding software patentable, *In re Prater,* involved an "analog computer," not a "digital computer." An analog computer is a mechanical device whose action mimics action in the real world. Therefore, there was no computer program in the usual sense. The opinion was by Judge Smith, who in earlier years made great contributions to the legal profession as a very distinguished member of the patent bar, lecturer at the University of Michigan College of Law, and casebook author. This opinion, however, fell far short of the quality of his earlier work. The opinion of his colleagues upon rehearing is also not particularly lucid, since they lacked Judge Smith's technical credentials. We suggest that you not attempt to read either of the *In re Prater* decisions.

2. The evident hostility expressed by Justice Stevens toward the C.C.P.A. will be explained at a later point.

3. The President's Commission on the Patent System, whose report opposing the patentability of software is cited by Stevens (note 10), was chaired by an I.B.M. executive. At the time, I.B.M. "bundled" software with its hardware and did not charge for the software. Following the *Prater* decision in 1968, assertions were made that some of this bundled I.B.M. software infringed patents. I.B.M., when notified of such allegations of infringement, agreed to hold its customers harmless. What better way to protect its customers than to get Court implementation of a Presidential Commission's recommendation that software be unpatentable? In the later *Benson* case, the Supreme Court also relies heavily upon this same report as a basis for its holding that mathematical algorithms are unpatentable.

The Patent Office was opposed to software patents at the time the President's Commission met. Previously the patent office had been overwhelmed with voluminous hardware logic patents that defied classification, since each patent contained hundreds of inventions. These were all placed in Class 340, Subclass 172.5, which quickly grew to the point where it was unsearchable. (In patent libraries, patents are—or should be—arranged for searching by Class and Subclass.) The real problem was that integrated circuit designers were highly prolific inventors and software designers were ever so much more prolific at invention. The Patent Office was simply overwhelmed by the number and complexity of the hardware and software inventions that occurred during the 1960s. As is noted in the *Benson* case, below, this inability of the Patent Office to process software inventions was a major reason why the Commission Report opposed software patent protection.

F.2d 1011, 1014–1015, 58 CCPA (Pat.) 1001, 1004–1005 (1971).

GOTTSCHALK v. BENSON

Supreme Court of the United States, 1972.
409 U.S. 63, 93 S.Ct. 253, 34 L.Ed.2d 273.

MR. JUSTICE DOUGLAS delivered the opinion of the Court.

Respondents filed in the Patent Office an application for an invention which was described as being related "to the processing of data by program and more particularly to the programmed conversion of numerical information" in general-purpose digital computers. They claimed a method for converting binary-coded decimal (BCD) numerals into pure binary numerals. The claims were not limited to any particular art or technology, to any particular apparatus or machinery, or to any particular end use. They purported to cover any use of the claimed method in a general-purpose digital computer of any type. Claims 8 and 13 [1] were rejected by the Patent Office but sustained by the Court of Customs and Patent Appeals, 441 F.2d 682. The case is here on a petition for a writ of certiorari. Gottschalk v. Benson, 405 U.S. 915, 92 S.Ct. 934, 30 L.Ed.2d 784.

The question is whether the method described and claimed is a "process" within the meaning of the Patent Act.

A digital computer, as distinguished from an analog computer, operates on data expressed in digits, solving a problem by doing arithmetic as a person would do it by head and hand. Some of the digits are stored as components of the computer. Others are introduced into the computer in a form which it is designed to recognize. The computer operates then upon both new and previously stored data. The general-purpose computer is designed to perform operations under many different programs.

* * *

The patent sought is on a method of programming a general-purpose digital computer to convert signals from binary-coded decimal form into pure binary form. A procedure for solving a given type of mathematical problem is known as an "algorithm." The procedures set forth in the present claims are of that kind; that is to say, they are a generalized formulation for programs to solve mathematical problems of converting one form of numerical representation to another. From the generic formulation, programs may be developed as specific applications.

The decimal system uses as digits the 10 symbols 0, 1, 2, 3, 4, 5, 6, 7, 8, and 9. The value represented by any digit depends, as it does in any positional system of notation, both on its individual value and on its relative position in the numeral. Decimal numerals are written by placing digits in the appropriate positions or columns of the numerical sequence, *i.e.,* "unit" (10^0), "tens" (10^1), "hundreds" (10^2), "thousands"

1. They are set forth in the Appendix to this opinion.

(10^3), etc. Accordingly, the numeral 1492 signifies $(1 \times 10^3) + (4 \times 10^2) + (9 \times 10^1) + (2 \times 10^0)$.

The pure binary system of positional notation uses two symbols as digits—0 and 1, placed in a numerical sequence with values based on consecutively ascending powers of 2. In pure binary notation, what would be the tens position is the twos position; what would be hundreds position is the fours position; what would be the thousands position is the eights. Any decimal number from 0 to 10 can be represented in the binary system with four digits or positions as indicated in the following table.

		Shown as the sum of powers of 2								
		2^3		2^2		2^1		2^0		
Decimal		(8)		(4)		(2)		(1)		Pure Binary
0	=	0	+	0	+	0	+	0	=	0000
1	=	0	+	0	+	0	+	2^0	=	0001
2	=	0	+	0	+	2^1	+	0	=	0010
3	=	0	+	0	+	2^1	+	2^0	=	0011
4	=	0	+	2^2	+	0	+	0	=	0100
5	=	0	+	2^2	+	0	+	2^0	=	0101
6	=	0	+	2^2	+	2^1	+	0	=	0110
7	=	0	+	2^2	+	2^1	+	2^0	=	0111
8	=	2^3	+	0	+	0	+	0	=	1000
9	=	2^3	+	0	+	0	+	2^0	=	1001
10	=	2^3	+	0	+	2^1	+	0	=	1010

The BCD system using decimal numerals replaces the character for each component decimal digit in the decimal numeral with the corresponding four-digit binary numeral, shown in the right-hand column of the table. Thus decimal 53 is represented as 0101 0011 in BCD, because decimal 5 is equal to binary 0101 and decimal 3 is equivalent to binary 0011. In pure binary notation, however, decimal 53 equals binary 110101. The conversion of BCD numerals to pure binary numerals can be done mentally through use of the foregoing table. The method sought to be patented varies the ordinary arithmetic steps a human would use by changing the order of the steps, changing the symbolism for writing the multiplier used in some steps, and by taking subtotals after each successive operation. The mathematical procedures can be carried out in existing computers long in use, no new machinery being necessary. And, as noted, they can also be performed without a computer.

The Court stated in Mackay Co. v. Radio Corp., 306 U.S. 86, 94, 59 S.Ct. 427, 431, 83 L.Ed. 506 that "[w]hile a scientific truth, or the mathematical expression of it, is not patentable invention, a novel and useful structure created with the aid of knowledge of scientific truth may be." That statement followed the longstanding rule that "[a]n idea of itself is not patentable." Rubber–Tip Pencil Co. v. Howard, 20 Wall. (87 U.S.) 498, 507, 22 L.Ed. 410. "A principle, in the abstract, is a fundamental truth; an original cause; a motive; these cannot be patented, as no one can claim in either of them an exclusive right." Le Roy v. Tatham, 14 How. (55 U.S.) 156, 175, 14 L.Ed. 367. Phenomena of nature, though just discovered, mental processes, and abstract intellectual concepts are not patentable, as they are the basic tools of scientific and technological work. As we stated in Funk Bros. Seed Co. v. Kalo Co., 333 U.S. 127, 130, 68 S.Ct. 440, 441, 92 L.Ed. 588, "He who discovers a hitherto unknown phenomenon of nature has no claim to a monopoly of it which the law recognizes. If there is to be invention from such a discovery, it must come from the application of the law of nature to a new and useful end." We dealt there with a "product" claim, while the present case deals with a "process" claim. But we think the same principle applies.

Here the "process" claim is so abstract and sweeping as to cover both known and unknown uses of the BCD to pure binary conversion. The end use may (1) vary from the operation of a train to verification of drivers' licenses to researching the law books for precedents and (2) be performed through any existing machinery or future-devised machinery or without any apparatus.

In O'Reilly v. Morse, 15 How. (56 U.S.) 62, 14 L.Ed. 601, Morse was allowed a patent for a process of using electromagnetism to produce distinguishable signs for telegraphy. *Id.,* at 111, 14 L.Ed. 601. But the Court denied the eighth claim in which Morse claimed the use of "electromagnetism, however developed for marking or printing intelligible characters, signs, or letters, at any distances." *Id.,* at 112. The Court in disallowing that claim said, "If this claim can be maintained, it matters not by what process or machinery the result is accomplished. For aught that we now know, some future inventor, in the onward march of science, may discover a mode of writing or printing at a distance by means of the electric or galvanic current, without using any part of the process or combination set forth in the plaintiff's specification. His invention may be less complicated—less liable to get out of order—less expensive in construction, and in its operation. But yet, if it is covered by this patent, the inventor could not use it, nor the public have the benefit of it, without the permission of this patentee." *Id.,* at 113, 14 L.Ed. 601.

* * *

It is argued that a process patent must either be tied to a particular machine or apparatus or must operate to change articles or materials to a "different state or thing." We do not hold that no process patent could ever qualify if it did not meet the requirements of our prior precedents. It is said that the decision precludes a patent for any program servicing a computer. We do not so hold. It is said that we have before us a program for a digital computer but extend our holding to programs for analog computers. We have, however, made clear from the start that we deal with a program only for digital computers. It is said we freeze process patents to old technologies, leaving no room for the revelations of the new, onrushing technology. Such is not our purpose. What we come down to in a nutshell is the following.

It is conceded that one may not patent an idea. But in practical effect that would be the result if the formula for converting BCD numerals to pure binary numerals were patented in this case. The mathematical formula involved here has no substantial practical application except in connection with a digital computer, which means that if the judgment below is affirmed, the patent would wholly pre-empt the mathematical formula and in practical effect would be a patent on the algorithm itself.

It may be that the patent laws should be extended to cover these programs, a policy matter to which we are not competent to speak.

* * *

If these programs are to be patentable, considerable problems are raised which only committees of Congress can manage, for broad powers of investigation are needed, including hearings which canvass the wide variety of views which those operating in this field entertain. The technological problems tendered in the many briefs before us indicate to us that considered action by the Congress is needed.

Reversed.

Mr. Justice Stewart, Mr. Justice Blackmun, and Mr. Justice Powell took no part in the consideration or decision of this case.

Appendix to Opinion of the Court

Claim 8 reads:

"The method of converting signals from binary coded decimal form into binary which comprises the steps of

"(1) storing the binary coded decimal signals in a reentrant shift register,

"(2) shifting the signals to the right by at least three places, until there is a binary '1' in the second position of said register,

"(3) masking out said binary '1' in said second position of said register,

"(4) adding a binary '1' to the first position of said register,

"(5) shifting the signals to the left by two positions,

"(6) adding a '1' to said first position, and

"(7) shifting the signals to the right by at least three positions in preparation for a succeeding binary '1' in the second position of said register."

Claim 13 reads:

"A data processing method for converting binary coded decimal number representations into binary number representations comprising the steps of

"(1) testing each binary digit position '1,' beginning with the least significant binary digit position, of the most significant decimal digit representation for a binary '0' or a binary '1';

"(2) if a binary '0' is detected, repeating step (1) for the next least significant binary digit position of said most significant decimal digit representation;

"(3) if a binary '1' is detected, adding a binary '1' at the (i + 1)th and (i + 3)th least significant binary digit positions of the next lesser significant decimal digit representation, and repeating step (1) for the next least significant binary digit position of said most significant decimal digit representation;

"(4) upon exhausting the binary digit positions of said most significant decimal digit representation, repeating steps (1) through (3) for the next lesser significant decimal digit representation as modified by the previous execution of steps (1) through (3); and

"(5) repeating steps (1) through (4) until the second least significant decimal digit representation has been so processed."

DIAMOND v. DIEHR

Supreme Court of the United States, 1981.
450 U.S. 175, 101 S.Ct. 1048, 67 L.Ed.2d 155.

JUSTICE STEVENS, with whom JUSTICE BRENNAN, JUSTICE MARSHALL, and JUSTICE BLACKMUN join, dissenting.

[This is the second of a number of excerpts from *Diamond v. Diehr,* which the casebook authors have included not for the legal arguments they make but for the historical information they contain.]

* * *

The Court of Customs and Patent Appeals had its first opportunity to interpret *Benson* in *In re Christensen,* 478 F.2d 1392 (1973). In *Christensen,* the claimed invention was a method in which the only novel element was a mathematical formula. The court resurrected the point-of-novelty approach abandoned in *Musgrave* and held that a process claim in which the point of novelty was a mathematical equation to be solved as the final step of the process did not define patentable subject matter after *Benson.* 478 F.2d, at 1394. Accordingly, the court affirmed the Patent Office Board of Appeals' rejection of the claims under § 101.

The Court of Customs and Patent Appeals in subsequent cases began to narrow its interpretation of *Benson.* In *In re Johnston,* 502 F.2d 765 (1974), the court held that a recordkeeping machine system which comprised a programmed digital computer was patentable subject matter under § 101. *Id.,* at 771. The majority dismissed *Benson* with the observation that *Benson* involved only process, not apparatus claims. 502 F.2d, at 771. Judge Rich dissented, arguing that to limit *Benson* only to process claims would make patentability turn upon the form in which a program invention was claimed. 502 F.2d, at 773–774.[19] The court again construed *Benson* as limited only to process claims in *In re Noll,* 545 F.2d 141 (1976), cert. denied, 434 U.S. 875, 98 S.Ct. 226, 54 L.Ed.2d 155 (1977); apparatus claims were governed by the court's pre-*Benson* conclusion that a programmed computer was structurally different from the same computer without that particular program. 545 F.2d, at 148. In dissent, Judge Lane, joined by Judge Rich, argued that *Benson* should be read as a general proscription of the patenting of computer programs regardless of the form of the claims. 545 F.2d, at 151–152. Judge Lane's interpretation of *Benson* was rejected by the majority in *In re Chatfield,* 545 F.2d 152 (1976), cert. denied, 434 U.S. 875, 98 S.Ct. 226, 54 L.Ed.2d 155 (1977), decided on the same day as *Noll.* In that case, the court construed *Benson* to preclude the patenting of program inventions claimed as processes only where the claims would pre-empt all uses of an algorithm or mathematical formula. 545 F.2d, at 156, 158–159.[20] The dissenting judges argued, as they had in *Noll,* that *Benson* held that programs for general-purpose digital computers are not patentable subject matter. 545 F.2d, at 161.

Following *Noll* and *Chatfield,* the Court of Customs and Patent Appeals consistently interpreted *Benson* to preclude the patenting of a program-related process invention only when the claims, if allowed, would wholly pre-empt the algorithm itself. One of the cases adopting this view was *In re Flook,* 559 F.2d 21 (1977), which was reversed in *Parker v. Flook,* 437 U.S. 584, 98 S.Ct. 2522, 57 L.Ed.2d 451 (1978). Before this Court decided *Flook,* however, the lower court developed a two-step procedure for analyzing program-related inventions in light of *Benson.* In *In re Freeman,* 573 F.2d 1237 (1978), the court held that such inventions must first be examined to determine whether a mathematical algorithm is directly or indirectly claimed; if an algorithm is recited, the court must then determine whether the claim would wholly preempt that algorithm. Only if a claim satisfied both inquiries was *Benson* considered applicable. 573 F.2d, at 1245. See also *In re Toma,* 575 F.2d 872, 877 (Cust. & Pat.App.1978).

In *Flook,* this Court clarified *Benson* in three significant respects. First, *Flook* held that the *Benson* rule of unpatentable subject matter was not limited, as the lower court believed, to claims which wholly preempted an algorithm or amounted to a patent on the algorithm itself. 437 U.S., at 589–590, 98 S.Ct., at 2525–2526. Second, the Court made it clear that an improved method of calculation, even when

19. The decision of the Court of Customs and Patent Appeals was reversed by this Court on other grounds in *Dann v. Johnston,* 425 U.S. 219, 96 S.Ct. 1393, 47 L.Ed.2d 692 (1976).

20. In addition to interpreting *Benson,* the majority also maintained that *Christensen,* despite its point-of-novelty language, had not signalled a return to that form of claim analysis. 545 F.2d, at 158. The court would reaffirm this proposition consistently thereafter. See, *e.g., In re de Castelet,* 562 F.2d 1236, 1240 (1977); *In re Richman,* 563 F.2d 1026, 1029–1030 (1977); *In re Freeman,* 573 F.2d 1237, 1243–1244 (1978); *In re Toma,* 575 F.2d 872, 876 (1978); *In re Walter,* 618 F.2d 758, 766–767 (1980).

employed as part of a physical process, is not patentable subject matter under § 101. *Id.,* at 595, n. 18, 98 S.Ct., at 2528. Finally, the Court explained the correct procedure for analyzing a patent claim employing a mathematical algorithm. Under this procedure, the algorithm is treated for § 101 purposes as though it were a familiar part of the prior art; the claim is then examined to determine whether it discloses "some other inventive concept." *Id.,* at 591–595, 98 S.Ct., at 2526–2528.[22]

Notes

1. *In re Christensen* was the first case to reach the C.C.P.A. following the Supreme Court's *Benson* decision. The claims in *Christensen* contained an equation describing a filtering technique useful in seismic echo surveying for oil deposits. Without understanding the equation, the C.C.P.A. held the claims to be unpatentable. If one's claims contain an equation, one is likely to find them rejected as unpatentable under *Benson.* Moral: Do not use claims that contain an equation—define the invention verbally, not mathematically.

Can one always convert a patent claim that contains a mathematical equation into a patent claim that is verbal and that is patentable? Try writing a patent claim covering the method of performing long division.

2. *Dann v. Johnston,* 425 U.S. 219 (1976) was the second Supreme Court decision involving software patentability. The invention was a bank computer system that permitted one to indicate on a check whether it was "deductible", "nondeductible", "charitable", etc. At the end of the year, the bank would then produce a financial statement useful in the preparation of a tax return. The "patentability of a computer program" issue occupied the attention of the Board of Patent Appeals and the C.C.P.A. The Supreme Court ruled that the invention was "obvious" to one skilled in the art and therefore unpatentable under 35 U.S.C.A. § 103. (One of the casebook authors heard a story that a Supreme Court "in-house" programmer suggested to clerks of the Supreme Court that the program was obvious, but we cannot vouch for the accuracy of this story.)

3. Note particularly that a "two-step procedure" for analyzing program-related inventions in light of *Benson* was introduced in *In re Freeman,* 573 F.2d 1237, 197 U.S.P.Q. 464 (C.C.P.A.1978). This test is the law currently applied by the Court of Appeals for the Federal Circuit.

4. In the preceeding excerpt from his dissent in *Diamond v. Diehr,* Justice Stevens carried forward the history of software patentability, ending with his reasons for opposing patentability in *Parker v. Flook.* The main body of Justice Stevens' opinion in *Parker v. Flook* follows.

22. This form of claim analysis did not originate with *Flook.* Rather, the Court derived it from the landmark decision of *O'Reilly v. Morse,* 15 How. 62, 115, 14 L.Ed. 601 (1854). In addition, this analysis is functionally the same as the point-of-novelty analysis used in conjunction with the mental-steps doctrine. In fact, the Patent Office in the past occasionally phrased its mental-steps rejections in essentially the terms later employed in Flook. * * *

PARKER v. FLOOK

Supreme Court of the United States, 1978.
437 U.S. 584, 98 S.Ct. 2522, 57 L.Ed.2d 451.

MR. JUSTICE STEVENS delivered the opinion of the Court.

Respondent applied for a patent on a "Method for Updating Alarm Limits." The only novel feature of the method is a mathematical formula. In *Gottschalk v. Benson,* 409 U.S. 63, 93 S.Ct. 253, 34 L.Ed.2d 273, we held that the discovery of a novel and useful mathematical formula may not be patented. The question in this case is whether the identification of a limited category of useful, though conventional, post-solution applications of such a formula makes respondent's method eligible for patent protection.

I.

An "alarm limit" is a number. During catalytic conversion processes, operating conditions such as temperature, pressure, and flow rates are constantly monitored. When any of these "process variables" exceeds a predetermined "alarm limit," an alarm may signal the presence of an abnormal condition indicating either inefficiency or perhaps danger. Fixed alarm limits may be appropriate for a steady operation, but during transient operating situations, such as start-up, it may be necessary to "update" the alarm limits periodically.

Respondent's patent application describes a method of updating alarm limits. In essence, the method consists of three steps: an initial step which merely measures the present value of the process variable (*e.g.,* the temperature); an intermediate step which uses an algorithm [1] to calculate an updated alarm-limit value; and a final step in which the actual alarm limit is adjusted to the updated value.[2] The only difference between the conventional methods of changing alarm limits and that described in respondent's application rests in the second step—the mathematical algorithm or formula. Using the formula, an operator can calculate an updated alarm limit once he knows the original alarm base, the appropriate margin of safety, the time interval that should elapse between each updating, the current temperature (or other process variable), and the appropriate weighting factor to be used to average the original alarm base and the current temperature.

The patent application does not purport to explain how to select the appropriate margin of safety, the weighting factor, or any of the other variables. Nor does it purport to contain any disclosure relating to the chemical processes at work, the monitoring of process variables, or the means of setting off an alarm or adjusting an alarm system. All that it provides is a formula for computing an updated alarm limit. Although the computations can be made by pencil and paper calculations, the abstract of disclosure makes it clear that the formula is

1. We use the word "algorithm" in this case, as we did in *Gottschalk v. Benson,* 409 U.S. 63, 65, 93 S.Ct. 253, 254, 34 L.Ed.2d 273, to mean "[a] procedure for solving a given type of mathematical problem * * *."

2. Claim 1 of the patent is set forth in the appendix to this opinion. * * *

primarily useful for computerized calculations producing automatic adjustments in alarm settings.

The patent claims cover any use of respondent's formula for updating the value of an alarm limit on any process variable involved in a process comprising the catalytic chemical conversion of hydrocarbons. Since there are numerous processes of that kind in the petrochemical and oil-refining industries,[4] the claims cover a broad range of potential uses of the method. They do not, however, cover every conceivable application of the formula.

II

* * *

III

This case turns entirely on the proper construction of § 101 of the Patent Act, which describes the subject matter that is eligible for patent protection. It does not involve the familiar issues of novelty and obviousness that routinely arise under §§ 102 and 103 when the validity of a patent is challenged. For the purpose of our analysis, we assume that respondent's formula is novel and useful and that he discovered it. We also assume, since respondent does not challenge the examiner's finding, that the formula is the only novel feature of respondent's method. The question is whether the discovery of this feature makes an otherwise conventional method eligible for patent protection.

The plain language of § 101 does not answer the question. It is true, as respondent argues, that his method is a "process" in the ordinary sense of the word. But that was also true of the algorithm, which described a method for converting binary-coded decimal numerals into pure binary numerals, that was involved in *Gottschalk v. Benson.* The holding that the discovery of that method could not be patented as a "process" forecloses a purely literal reading of § 101. Reasoning that an algorithm, or mathematical formula, is like a law of nature, *Benson* applied the established rule that a law of nature cannot be the subject of a patent. * * *

* * *

The line between a patentable "process" and an unpatentable "principle" is not always clear. Both are "conception[s] of the mind, seen only by [their] effects when being executed or performed." *Tilghman v. Proctor,* 102 U.S. 707, 728, 26 L.Ed. 279. In *Benson* we concluded that the process application in fact sought to patent an idea, noting that

4. Examples mentioned in the abstract of disclosure include naphtha reforming, petroleum distillate and petroleum residuum cracking, hydrocracking and desulfurization, aromatic hydrocarbon and paraffin isomerization and disproportionation, paraffin-olefin alkylation, and the like.

> "[t]he mathematical formula involved here has no substantial practical application except in connection with a digital computer, which means that if the judgment below is affirmed, the patent would wholly preempt the mathematical formula and in practical effect would be a patent on the algorithm itself." 409 U.S. at 71–72, 93 S.Ct., at 257.

Respondent correctly points out that this language does not apply to his claims. He does not seek to "wholly preempt the mathematical formula," since there are uses of his formula outside the petrochemical and oil-refining industries that remain in the public domain. And he argues that the presence of specific "post-solution" activity—the adjustment of the alarm limit to the figure computed according to the formula—distinguishes this case from *Benson* and makes his process patentable. We cannot agree.

The notion that post-solution activity, no matter how conventional or obvious in itself, can transform an unpatentable principle into a patentable process exalts form over substance. A competent draftsman could attach some form of post-solution activity to almost any mathematical formula; the Pythagorean theorem would not have been patentable, or partially patentable, because a patent application contained a final step indicating that the formula, when solved, could be usefully applied to existing surveying techniques. The concept of patentable subject matter under § 101 is not "like a nose of wax which may be turned and twisted in any direction * * *." *White v. Dunbar,* 119 U.S. 47, 51, 7 S.Ct. 72, 74, 30 L.Ed. 303.

Yet it is equally clear that a process is not unpatentable simply because it contains a law of nature or a mathematical algorithm. * * * For instance, in *Mackay Radio & Telegraph Co. v. Radio Corp. of America,* 306 U.S. 86, 59 S.Ct. 427, 83 L.Ed. 506, the applicant sought a patent on a directional antenna system in which the wire arrangement was determined by the logical application of a mathematical formula. Putting the question of patentability to one side as a preface to his analysis of the infringement issue, Mr. Justice Stone, writing for the Court, explained:

> "While a scientific truth, or the mathematical expression of it, is not patentable invention, a novel and useful structure created with the aid of knowledge of scientific truth may be." *Id.,* at 94, 59 S.Ct., at 431.

* * *

Mackay Radio * * * point[s] to the proper analysis for this case: The process itself, not merely the mathematical algorithm, must be new and useful. Indeed, the novelty of the mathematical algorithm is not a determining factor at all. Whether the algorithm was in fact known or unknown at the time of the claimed invention, as one of the "basic tools of scientific and technological work," see *Gottschalk v. Benson,* 409 U.S., at 67, 93 S.Ct., at 255, it is treated as though it were a familiar part of the prior art.

This is also the teaching of our landmark decision in *O'Reilly v. Morse,* 15 How. 62. In that case the Court rejected Samuel Morse's broad claim covering any use of electromagnetism for printing intelligible signs, characters, or letters at a distance. *Id.,* at 112–121. * * *

* * *

We think this case must also be considered as if the principle or mathematical formula were well known.

Respondent argues that this approach improperly imports into § 101 the considerations of "inventiveness" which are the proper concerns of §§ 102 and 103. This argument is based on two fundamental misconceptions.

First, respondent incorrectly assumes that if a process application implements a principle in some specific fashion, it automatically falls within the patentable subject matter of § 101 and the substantive patentability of the particular process can then be determined by the conditions of §§ 102 and 103. This assumption is based on respondent's narrow reading of *Benson,* and is as untenable in the context of § 101 as it is in the context of that case. It would make the determination of patentable subject matter depend simply on the draftsman's art and would ill serve the principles underlying the prohibition against patents for "ideas" or phenomena of nature. The rule that the discovery of a law of nature cannot be patented rests, not on the notion that natural phenomena are not processes, but rather on the more fundamental understanding that they are not the kind of "discoveries" that the statute was enacted to protect. The obligation to determine what type of discovery is sought to be patented must precede the determination of whether that discovery is, in fact, new or obvious.

Second, respondent assumes that the fatal objection to his application is the fact that one of its components—the mathematical formula—consists of unpatentable subject matter. In countering this supposed objection, respondent relies on opinions by the Court of Customs and Patent Appeals which reject the notion "that a claim may be dissected, the claim components searched in the prior art, and, if the only component found novel is outside the statutory classes of invention, the claim may be rejected under 35 U.S.C. § 101." *In re Chatfield,* 545 F.2d 152, 158 (Cust. & Pat.App.1976). Our approach to respondent's application is, however, not at all inconsistent with the view that a patent claim must be considered as a whole. Respondent's process is unpatentable under § 101, not because it contains a mathematical algorithm as one component, but because once that algorithm is assumed to be within the prior art, the application, considered as a whole, contains no patentable invention. Even though a phenomenon of nature or mathematical formula may be well known, an inventive application of the principle may be patented. Conversely, the discovery of such a phenomenon cannot support a patent unless there is some other inventive concept in its application.

Here it is absolutely clear that respondent's application contains no claim of patentable invention. The chemical processes involved in catalytic conversion of hydrocarbons are well known, as are the practice of monitoring the chemical process variables, the use of alarm limits to trigger alarms, the notion that alarm limit values must be recomputed and readjusted, and the use of computers for "automatic monitoring-alarming." Respondent's application simply provides a new and presumably better method for calculating alarm limit values. If we assume that that method was also known, as we must under the reasoning in *Morse*, then respondent's claim is, in effect, comparable to a claim that the formula 2 r can be usefully applied in determining the circumference of a wheel. As the Court of Customs and Patent Appeals has explained, "if a claim is directed essentially to a method of calculating, using a mathematical formula, even if the solution is for a specific purpose, the claimed method is nonstatutory." *In re Richman,* 563 F.2d 1026, 1030 (1977).

* * *

The judgment of the Court of Customs and Patent Appeals is reversed.

APPENDIX TO OPINION OF THE COURT

Claim 1 of the patent describes the method as follows:

"1. A method for updating the value of at least one alarm limit on at least one process variable involved in a process comprising the catalytic chemical conversion of hydrocarbons wherein said alarm limit has a current value of

$$Bo + K$$

"wherein Bo is the current alarm base and K is a predetermined alarm offset which comprises:

"(1) Determining the present value of said process variable, said present value being defined as PVL;

"(2) Determining a new alarm base B_1, using the following equation:

$$B_1 = Bo(1.0—F) + PVL(F)$$

"where F is a predetermined number greater than zero and less than 1.0;

"(3) Determining an updated alarm limit which is defined as B_1 + K; and thereafter

"(4) Adjusting said alarm limit to said updated alarm limit value." App. 63A.

* * *

MR. JUSTICE STEWART, with whom THE CHIEF JUSTICE and MR. JUSTICE REHNQUIST join, dissenting.

* * *

The issue here is whether a claimed process loses its status of subject-matter patentability simply because *one step* in the process would not be patentable subject matter if considered in isolation. The Court of Customs and Patent Appeals held that the process is patentable subject matter, *Benson* being inapplicable since "[t]he present claims do not preempt the formula or algorithm contained therein, because solution of the algorithm, per se, would not infringe the claims." *In re Flock,* 559 F.2d 21, 23.

That decision seems to me wholly in conformity with basic principles of patent law. Indeed, I suppose that thousands of processes and combinations have been patented that contained one or more steps or elements that themselves would have been unpatentable subject matter. *Eibel Process Co. v. Minnesota & Ontario Paper Co.,* 261 U.S. 45, 43 S.Ct. 322, 67 L.Ed. 523, is a case in point. There the Court upheld the validity of an improvement patent that made use of the law of gravity, which by itself was clearly unpatentable. * * *

The Court today says it does not turn its back on these well-settled precedents, *ante,* at 2527–2528, but it strikes what seems to me an equally damaging blow at basic principles of patent law by importing into its inquiry under 35 U.S.C. § 101 the criteria of novelty and inventiveness. Section 101 is concerned only with subject-matter patentability. Whether a patent will actually *issue* depends upon the criteria of §§ 102 and 103, which include novelty and inventiveness, among many others. It may well be that under the criteria of §§ 102 and 103 no patent should issue on the process claimed in this case, because of anticipation, abandonment, obviousness, or for some other reason. But in my view the claimed process clearly meets the standards of subject-matter patentability of § 101.

* * *

Note

Justice Stevens' rationale in *Flook* is strongly criticized by the Court of Customs and Patent Appeals in the following *Bergy* case, which relates to the patentability of life forms. *Bergy* also contains an excellent tutorial on patent law.

APPLICATION OF BERGY

APPLICATION OF CHAKRABARTY

United States Court of Customs and Patent Appeals, 1979.
596 F.2d 952.

RICH, JUDGE.

[The casebook authors have included the *Bergy* court tutorial on patent law and criticism of Stevens' rationale below. Those portions of *Bergy* which focus upon the patentability of life forms are omitted in view of the full discussion of that topic which is set forth more authoritatively in the Supreme Court's *Chakrabarty* decision which follows.]

Introduction

These appeals are from decisions of the Board of Appeals (board) of the United States Patent and Trademark Office (PTO) under 35 U.S.C. § 141 by dissatisfied applicants for patents. We reverse.

These two cases come before us for the second time under the circumstances hereinafter detailed. Since our first decisions, they have been to the United States Supreme Court and back without any decision by that Court. They are separate appeals, not formally consolidated, but on this second round they were heard together on November 6, 1978, and are now decided together because, as will appear, they involve only the same single question of law.

The question before us is a limited one of statutory construction, not whether appellants have made and disclosed *patentable* inventions. The PTO has already determined that both applicants are entitled to patents; in technical patent law terms, unappealed claims to their respective inventions have been allowed to each appellant and, whatever the final disposition of these appeals, patents will issue if the applicants choose to pay their fees and take them out.

* * *

The real question before us is whether appellants are to be allowed to define their inventions—already determined to be patentable—in a certain way in "claims" pursuant to 35 U.S.C. § 112, second paragraph. This question, which is the same in each case, involves the construction and application of 35 U.S.C. § 101, more particularly the meaning to be given to the words "manufacture" and "composition of matter" in that section, which reads:

> Whoever invents or discovers any new and useful process, machine, *manufacture,* or *composition of matter,* or any new and useful improvement thereof, may obtain a patent therefor, subject to the conditions and requirements of this title. [Emphasis ours.]

The PTO has raised no issue in either case, as to any aspect of the inventions, about compliance with the "conditions and requirements of this title," that is to say the basic Title 35 requirements for patentability, which are utility, novelty, and nonobviousness (35 U.S.C. §§ 101, 102, and 103), or any other statutory condition or requirement such as adequacy of disclosure (35 U.S.C. § 112, first paragraph). The sole issue, as the PTO chooses to view it, is whether an invention, otherwise patentable under the statute, is excluded from the categories of subject matter which may be patented, set forth in § 101, because it is "alive." * * *

* * *

Clearly, our assigned task is first to determine the bearing of *Flook,* if any, on these two appeals. This requires, as we see it, consideration not only of what was *decided* in *Flook* but examination of everything that was said in the opinion. Preliminary to that consideration, however, and laying the groundwork therefor, we will examine the Constitutional basis for the patent system and the anatomy of the statutes Congress has enacted insofar as they are relevant to the problem before us.

The Constitution

The grant of power to Congress to establish a patent system is in these familiar words of Article I, section 8, clauses 8 and 18:

> [The Congress shall have Power] * * *
>
> [8] To promote the Progress of Science and useful Arts, by securing for limited Times to Authors and Inventors the exclusive Right to their respective Writings and Discoveries; * * * [And]
>
> [18] To make all Laws which shall be necessary and proper for carrying into Execution the foregoing Powers * * *.

Scholars who have studied this provision, its origins, and its subsequent history, have, from time to time, pointed out that it is really two grants of power rolled into one; first, to establish a copyright system and, second, to establish a patent system. Their conclusions have been that the constitutionally-stated purpose of granting patent rights to inventors for their discoveries is the promotion of progress in the "useful Arts," rather than in science. * * *

* * *

It is to be observed that the Constitutional clause under consideration neither gave to nor preserved in inventors (or authors) any rights and set no standards for the patentability of individual inventions; it merely empowered Congress, if it elected to do so, to secure to inventors an "exclusive right" for an unstated "limited" time for the stated purpose of promoting useful arts. We have previously pointed out that the present day equivalent of the term "useful arts" employed by the Founding Fathers is "technological arts."

We turn now to a consideration of how Congress has implemented the power delegated to it.

Anatomy of the Patent Statute

The reason for our consideration of the statutory scheme in relation to its Constitutional purpose is that we have been directed to review our prior decisions in the light of *Flook* and we find in *Flook* an unfortunate and apparently unconscious, though clear, commingling of distinct statutory provisions which are conceptually unrelated, namely, those pertaining to the *categories* of inventions in § 101 which *may* be patentable and to the *conditions* for patentability demanded by the statute for inventions within the statutory categories, particularly the nonobviousness condition of § 103. The confusion creeps in through such phrases as "eligible for patent protection," "patentable process," "new and useful," "inventive application," "inventive concept," and "patentable invention." The last-mentioned term is perhaps one of the most difficult to deal with unless it is used *exclusively* with reference to an invention which complies with *every* condition of the patent statutes so that a valid patent may be issued on it.

The problem of accurate, unambiguous expression is exacerbated by the fact that prior to the Patent Act of 1952 the words "invention," "inventive," and "invent" had distinct legal implications related to the concept of patentability which they have not had for the past quarter century. Prior to 1952, and for some time thereafter, they were used by courts as imputing *patentability*. Statements in the older cases must be handled with care lest the terms used in their reasoning clash with the reformed terminology of the present statute; lack of meticulous care may lead to distorted legal conclusions.

* * *

All of the statutory law relevant to the present cases is found in four of the five sections in Chapter 10, the first chapter of Part II:

Sec. 100 Definitions

Sec. 101 Inventions patentable [if they qualify]

Sec. 102 Conditions for patentability; novelty and loss of right to patent

Sec. 103 Conditions for patentability; non-obvious subject matter

More strictly speaking, these cases involve only § 101, as did *Flook*. Achieving the ultimate goal of a patent under those statutory provisions involves, to use an analogy, having the separate keys to open in succession the three doors of sections 101, 102, and 103, the last two guarding the public interest by assuring that patents are not granted which would take from the public that which it already enjoys (matters already within its knowledge whether in actual use or not) or *potentially* enjoys by reason of obviousness from knowledge which it already has.

Inventors of patentable inventions, as a class, are those who bridge the chasm between the known and the obvious on the one side and that which promotes progress in useful arts or technology on the other.

The first door which must be opened on the difficult path to patentability is § 101 (augmented by the § 100 definitions), * * *. The person approaching that door is *an inventor,* whether his invention is patentable or not. There is always an inventor; being an inventor might be regarded as a preliminary legal requirement, for if he has not invented something, if he comes with something he knows was invented by someone else, he has no right even to approach the door. Thus, section 101 begins with the words "Whoever invents or discovers," and since 1790 the patent statutes have always said substantially that. Being an inventor or having an invention, however, is no guarantee of opening even the first door. What *kind* of an invention or discovery is it? In dealing with the question of kind, as distinguished from the qualitative conditions which make the invention patentable, § 101 is broad and general; its language is: "any * * * process, machine, manufacture, or composition of matter, or any * * * improvement thereof." Section 100(b) further expands "process" to include "art or method, and * * * a new use of a known process, machine, manufacture, composition of matter, or material." If the invention, as the inventor defines it in his claims (pursuant to § 112, second paragraph), falls into any one of the named categories, he is allowed to pass through to the second door, which is § 102; "novelty and loss of right to patent" is the sign on it. Notwithstanding the words "new and useful" in § 101, the invention is not examined under that statute for novelty because that is not the statutory scheme of things or the long-established administrative practice.

Section 101 *states* three requirements: novelty, utility, and statutory subject matter. The understanding that these three requirements are *separate* and *distinct* is long-standing and has been universally accepted. The text writers are all in accord and treat these requirements under separate chapters and headings. Thus, the questions of whether a particular invention is *novel* or *useful* are questions wholly apart from whether the invention falls into a category of *statutory subject matter.* Of the three requirements *stated* in § 101, only two, utility and statutory subject matter, are *applied* under § 101. As we shall show, in 1952 Congress voiced its intent to consider the novelty of an invention under § 102 where it is first made clear what the statute means by "new", notwithstanding the fact that this requirement is first *named* in § 101.

The PTO, in administering the patent laws, has, for the most part, consistently applied § 102 in making rejections for lack of novelty. To provide the option of making such a rejection under either § 101 or § 102 is confusing and therefore bad law. Our research has disclosed only two instances in which rejections for lack of novelty were made by the PTO under § 101, *In re Bergstrom,* 427 F.2d 1394, 57 CCPA 1240, 166 USPQ 256 (1970); *In re Seaborg,* 328 F.2d 996, 51 CCPA 1109, 140 USPQ 662 (1964). In *In re Bergstrom* we in effect treated the rejection as if it had been made under § 102, observing in the process that "The word 'new' in § 101 is defined and is to be construed in accordance with the provisions of § 102." 427 F.2d at 1401, 57 CCPA at 1249, 166 USPQ at 262.

When § 101 was enacted, the accompanying Reviser's Note stated (inserts and emphasis ours):

> The corresponding section of the existing statute [R.S. § 4886] is split into two sections, section 101 relating to the *subject matter* for which patents *may* be obtained ["subject to the conditions and requirements of this title"], and section 102 defining statutory novelty and stating other conditions for patentability.

H.R.Rep. No. 1923, supra at 6, U.S.Code Cong. & Admin.News 1952, p. 2409, another contemporaneous document, states (emphasis ours):

> Part II relates patentability of inventions and the grant of patents.
>
> Referring first to section 101, this section specifies *the type of material* which can be the subject matter of a patent.

* * *

> Section 101 sets forth the *subject matter* that can be patented "subject to the conditions and requirements of this title." *The conditions* under which a patent may be obtained *follow,* and section 102 covers the conditions relating to novelty.
>
> A person may have "invented" a machine or a manufacture, which may include anything under the sun that is made by man, *but it is not necessarily patentable* under section 101 unless the conditions of the title are fulfilled.
>
> Section 102 in paragraphs (a), (b), and (c) repeats the conditions in the existing law relating to novelty.

The Senate report, No. 1979, makes the identical statement.

The second door then, as we have already seen, is § 102 pursuant to which the inventor's claims are examined for novelty, requiring, for the first time in the examination process, comparison with the prior art which, up to this point, has therefore been irrelevant.

Section 102 also contains other conditions under the heading "loss of right" which need not be considered here. An *invention* may be in a statutory category and not patentable for want of *novelty,* or it may be novel and still not be patentable because it must meet yet another condition existing in the law since 1850 when *Hotchkiss v. Greenwood,* 11 How. 248, 13 L.Ed. 683, was decided. This condition developed in the ensuing century into the "*requirement for invention.*"

The third door, under the 1952 Act, is § 103 which was enacted *to take the place of the requirement for "invention."* We need not examine this requirement in detail for it is not involved in the present appeals, and was not involved in *Flook.* It will suffice to quote what the House and Senate reports, cited supra—"signals" from Congress—say about the third requirement, from which it will be seen that, again, the claimed invention for which a patent is sought must be compared with the prior art. * * *

* * *

If the inventor holds the three different keys to the three doors, his *invention* (here assumed to be "useful") qualifies for a patent, otherwise not; but he, as *inventor,* must meet still other statutory requirements in the preparation and prosecution of his patent application. We need not here consider the latter because appellants have not been faulted by the PTO in their paperwork or behavior. * * *

We have observed with regret that the briefs filed by the Solicitor General for Acting Commissioner Parker in *Parker v. Flook,* a case which, as the Court noted, "turns entirely on the proper construction of § 101," badly, and with a seeming sense of purpose, confuse the statutory-categories requirement of § 101 with a requirement for the existence of "invention." This they do by basing argument on the opening words of § 101, "Whoever invents or discovers," thereby importing into the discussion of compliance with § 101 a requirement for "invention" in a patentability sense. But there has not been a requirement for "invention" in the patentability sense in the laws since 1952—the requirement was replaced by the § 103 requirement for nonobviousness. *Graham v. John Deere Co.,* supra. Furthermore, when one has only compliance with § 101 to consider, the sole question, aside from utility, is whether the invention falls into a named category, not whether it is *patentable.* Falling into a category, does not involve considerations of novelty or nonobviousness and *only* those two considerations involve comparison with prior art or inquiry as to whether all or any part of the invention is or is not in, or assumed to be in, the prior art or the public domain. *Prior art is irrelevant to the determination of statutory subject matter under § 101.* An invention can be statutory subject matter and be 100% old, devoid of any utility, or entirely obvious. This is our understanding of the statute and the basis on which we proceed to the further consideration of these appeals.

* * *

IN LIGHT OF PARKER V. FLOOK

We are redeciding these appeals, as directed, "in light of *Parker v. Flook.*" The parties were given the opportunity in briefs and oral argument to tell us what bearing *Flook* has on these appeals. As might have been foreseen, the results are not helpful.

* * *

The only thing we see in common in these appeals and in *Flook* is that they all involve § 101. *Flook* was a review of one of the many appeals we have heard involving the general theme of the patentability of computer programs. The only way to claim a program is as a programmed "machine" or as a "process" or "method." The *Flook* invention was claimed as a "process" under § 101. That was the second case of its kind from this court reviewed by the Supreme Court, the first being *Gottschalk v. Benson,* 409 U.S. 63, 93 S.Ct. 253, 34 L.Ed.2d 273 (1972), which involved two method claims. Method and process claims are equivalents. *Flook* appears to have been decided on the authority of *Benson.* No method or process claim is here involved. In fact, the PTO has *allowed* (all three doors, §§ 101–2–3, passed) Bergy's method claims 1 through 4 and Chakrabarty's process claims 27 through 29, thereby holding that the process aspects of their inventions are not only *subject matter* within § 101 but also new and unobvious under § 102 and § 103, therefore patentable. *Flook* was concerned only with the question of what is a "process" under § 101, in the context of computer program protection. No such issue is presented in either of these appeals.

There is no better authority on what the Supreme Court has decided in a case than the Court itself and we are fortunate to have its own summary of what it decided in *Flook.* It appears at the end of footnote 18, 437 U.S. at 595, 98 S.Ct. at 2528, as follows:

> Very simply, our holding today is that a claim for an improved method of calculation, even when tied to a specific end use, is unpatentable subject matter under § 101.

We do not venture to elaborate. The appeals here involve no method of calculation, and the *Flook holding* appears to have no bearing.

As indicated earlier, we deem it our duty to seek whatever additional light there may be in the Court's opinion on the meaning of § 101, without restricting ourselves to the holding. It is stated to be well established in patent law that the following are not within the statutory categories of subject matter enumerated in § 101 and its predecessor statutes as interpreted through the years: principles, laws of nature, mental processes, intellectual concepts, ideas, natural phenomena, mathematical formulae, methods of calculation, fundamental truths, original causes, motives, the Pythagorean theorem, and the computer-implementable method claims of Benson and Tabbot. The present appeals do not involve an attempt to patent any of these things and the Court's review of this hornbook law is, therefore, inapplicable to the issue before us, which involves only the construction of the terms "manufacture, or composition of matter."

Another principle stated in *Flook* is that a "mathematical algorithm" or formula is like a law of nature in that it is one of the " 'basic tools of scientific and technological work' " and as such must be *deemed* to be "a familiar part of the prior art," even when it was not familiar, was not prior, was discovered by the applicant for patent, was novel at the time he discovered it, and was useful. This gives to the term "prior art," which is a *very* important term of art in patent law, particularly in the application of § 103, an entirely new dimension with consequences of unforeseeable magnitude.

Insofar as the present appeals are concerned, the foregoing novel principle has no applicability whatever since, as we have said no formula, algorithm, or law of nature is involved, and there has been no rejection on prior art of any kind in either application. In each, both the examiner and the Board of Appeals expressly stated that no references evidencing prior art have been relied on or applied.

Insofar as the general patent law is concerned, however, the above-stated novel *Flook* doctrine may have an unintended impact in putting an untimely and unjustifiable end to the long-standing proposition of law that patentability may be predicated on discovering the cause of a problem even though, once that *cause* is known, the solution is brought about by obvious means. Such causes may often be classed as laws of nature or their effects. The potential for great harm to the incentives of the patent system is apparent.

It is one thing to say that a principle, natural cause, or formula, *per se,* is not within the categories of § 101, but quite another to say it is "prior art" in determining the nonobviousness of an invention predicated on it even though the inventor discovered it.

* * *

To conclude on the light *Flook* sheds on these cases, very simply, for the reasons we have stated, we find none.

* * *

[Judge Rich then went on to find that both Bergy's and Chakrabarty's claims, directed to living products of genetic engineering, defined subject matter that falls within the categories named in § 101. Judge Baldwin concurred, disagreeing with Rich on the relevancy of *Parker v. Flook.* Judge Miller dissented.]

Notes

1. The Supreme Court later affirmed the *Chakrabarty* portion of this decision in *Diamond v. Chakrabarty,* which is set forth below.

2. Needless to say, Justice Stevens, the author of the majority opinion in *Parker v. Flook,* was less than pleased with Judge Rich's highly critical remarks. In his dissenting opinion in *Diamond v. Diehr,* Justice Stevens wrote:

> Although the Court of Customs and Patent Appeals in several post-*Flook* decisions held that program-related inventions were not patentable subject matter under § 101, see *e.g., In re Sarkar,* 588 F.2d 1330 (1978); *In re Gelnovatch,* 595 F.2d 32 (1979), in general *Flook* was not enthusiastically received by that court. In *In re Bergy,* 596 F.2d 952 (1979), the majority engaged in an extensive critique of *Flook,* concluding that this Court had erroneously commingled "distinct statutory provisions which are conceptually unrelated." 596 F.2d, at 959. In subsequent cases, the court construed *Flook* as resting on nothing more than the way in which the patent claims had been drafted, and it expressly declined to use the method of claim analysis spelled out in that decision. The Court of Customs and Patent Appeals has taken the position that, if an application is drafted in a way that discloses an entire process as novel, it defines patentable subject matter even if the only novel element that the inventor claims to have discovered is a new computer program. The court interpreted *Flook* in this manner in its opinion in this case. See *In re Diehr,* 602 F.2d 982, 986–989 (1979). In my judgment, this reading of *Flook*—although entirely consistent with the lower court's expansive approach to § 101 during the past 12 years—trivializes the holding in *Flook,* the principle that underlies *Benson,* and the settled line of authority reviewed in those opinions.

* * *

DIAMOND v. CHAKRABARTY

Supreme Court of the United States, 1980.
447 U.S. 303, 100 S.Ct. 2204, 65 L.Ed.2d 144.

MR. CHIEF JUSTICE BURGER delivered the opinion of the Court.

We granted certiorari to determine whether a live, human-made micro-organism is patentable subject matter under 35 U.S.C. § 101.

[The casebook authors have included this non-computer case because it is a leading case on the application of § 101 to new technology]

I

In 1972, respondent Chakrabarty, a microbiologist, filed a patent application, assigned to the General Electric Co. The application asserted 36 claims related to Chakrabarty's invention of "a bacterium from the genus *Pseudomonas* containing therein at least two stable energy-generating plasmids, each of said plasmids providing a separate hydrocarbon degradative pathway."[1] This human-made, genetically engineered bacterium is capable of breaking down multiple components of crude oil. Because of this property, which is possessed by no naturally occurring bacteria, Chakrabarty's invention is believed to have significant value for the treatment of oil spills.

Chakrabarty's patent claims were of three types: first, process claims for the method of producing the bacteria; second, claims for an inoculum comprised of a carrier material floating on water, such as straw, and the new bacteria; and third, claims to the bacteria themselves. The patent examiner allowed the claims falling into the first two categories, but rejected claims for the bacteria. His decision rested on two grounds: (1) that micro-organisms are "products of nature," and (2) that as living things they are not patentable subject matter under 35 U.S.C. § 101.

Chakrabarty appealed the rejection of these claims to the Patent Office Board of Appeals, and the Board affirmed the Examiner on the second ground. Relying on the legislative history of the 1930 Plant Patent Act, in which Congress extended patent protection to certain asexually reproduced plants, the Board concluded that § 101 was not intended to cover living things such as these laboratory created micro-organisms.

The Court of Customs and Patent Appeals, by a divided vote, reversed on the authority of its prior decision in *In re Bergy,* 563 F.2d 1031, 1038 (1977), which held that "the fact that microorganisms * * * are alive * * * [is] without legal significance" for purposes of the patent law. Subsequently, we granted the Acting Commissioner of Patents and Trademarks' petition for certiorari in *Bergy,* vacated the judgment, and remanded the case "for further consideration in light of *Parker v. Flook,* 437 U.S. 584, [98 S.Ct. 2522, 57 L.Ed.2d 451] (1978)." 438 U.S. 902, 98 S.Ct. 3119, 57 L.Ed.2d 1145 (1978). The Court of Customs and Patent Appeals then vacated its judgment in *Chakrabarty* and consolidated the case with *Bergy* for reconsideration. After re-examining both cases in the light of our holding in *Flook,* that court, with one dissent, reaffirmed its earlier judgments. 596 F.2d 952 (1979).

1. Plasmids are hereditary units physically separate from the chromosomes of the cell. * * *

The Commissioner of Patents and Trademarks again sought certiorari, and we granted the writ as to both *Bergy* and *Chakrabarty.* 444 U.S. 924, 100 S.Ct. 261, 62 L.Ed.2d 180 (1979). Since then, *Bergy* has been dismissed as moot, 444 U.S. 1028, 100 S.Ct. 696, 62 L.Ed.2d 664 (1980), leaving only *Chakrabarty* for decision.

* * *

The question before us in this case is a narrow one of statutory interpretation requiring us to construe 35 U.S.C. § 101, which provides:

> "Whoever invents or discovers any new and useful process, machine, manufacture, or composition of matter, or any new and useful improvement thereof, may obtain a patent therefor, subject to the conditions and requirements of this title."

Specifically, we must determine whether respondent's micro-organism constitutes a "manufacture" or "composition of matter" within the meaning of the statute.

III

In cases of statutory construction we begin, of course, with the language of the statute. * * *

Guided by these canons of construction, this Court has read the term "manufacture" in § 101 in accordance with its dictionary definition to mean "the production of articles for use from raw or prepared materials by giving to these materials new forms, qualities, properties, or combinations, whether by hand-labor or by machinery." *American Fruit Growers, Inc. v. Brogdex Co.,* 283 U.S. 1, 11, 51 S.Ct. 328, 330, 75 L.Ed. 801 (1931). Similarly, "composition of matter" has been construed consistent with its common usage to include "all compositions of two or more substances and * * * all composite articles, whether they be the results of chemical union, or of mechanical mixture, or whether they be gases, fluids, powders or solids." *Shell Development Co. v. Watson,* 149 F.Supp. 279, 280 (D.C.1957) (citing 1 A. Deller, Walker on Patents § 14, p. 55 (1st ed. 1937)). In choosing such expansive terms as "manufacture" and "composition of matter," modified by the comprehensive "any," Congress plainly contemplated that the patent laws would be given wide scope.

The relevant legislative history also supports a broad construction. The Patent Act of 1793, authored by Thomas Jefferson, defined statutory subject matter as "any new and useful art, machine, manufacture, or composition of matter, or any new or useful improvement [thereof]." Act of Feb. 21, 1793, § 1, 1 Stat. 319. The Act embodied Jefferson's philosophy that "ingenuity should receive a liberal encouragement." 5 Writings of Thomas Jefferson 75–76 (Washington ed. 1871). See *Graham v. John Deere Co.,* 383 U.S. 1, 7–10, 86 S.Ct. 684, 688–690, 15 L.Ed.2d 545 (1966). Subsequent patent statutes in 1836, 1870, and 1874 employed this same broad language. In 1952, when the patent laws were recodified, Congress replaced the word "art" with "process," but otherwise left Jefferson's language intact. The Committee Reports accompanying the 1952 Act inform us that Congress intended statutory subject matter to "include anything under the sun that is made by man." S.Rep. No. 1979, 82d Cong., 2d Sess., 5 (1952); H.R.Rep. No. 1923, 82d Cong., 2d Sess., 6 (1952).[6]

This is not to suggest that § 101 has no limits or that it embraces every discovery. The laws of nature, physical phenomena, and abstract ideas have been held not patentable. Thus, a new mineral discovered in the earth or a new plant found in the wild is not patentable subject matter. Likewise, Einstein could not patent his celebrated law that $E = mc^2$; nor could Newton have patented the law of gravity. Such discoveries are "manifestations of * * * nature, free to all men and reserved exclusively to none." *Funk, supra,* 333 U.S., at 130, 68 S.Ct., at 441.

Judged in this light, respondent's micro-organism plainly qualifies as patentable subject matter. His claim is not to a hitherto unknown natural phenomenon, but to a nonnaturally occurring manufacture or composition of matter—a product of human ingenuity "having a distinctive name, character [and] use." *Hartranft v. Wiegmann,* 121 U.S. 609, 615, 7 S.Ct. 1240, 1243, 30 L.Ed. 1012 (1887). * * *

* * *

Here, by contrast, the patentee has produced a new bacterium with markedly different characteristics from any found in nature and one having the potential for significant utility. His discovery is not nature's handiwork, but his own; accordingly it is patentable subject matter under § 101.

IV

Two contrary arguments are advanced, neither of which we find persuasive.

(A)

The petitioner's first argument rests on the enactment of the 1930 Plant Patent Act, which afforded patent protection to certain asexually reproduced plants, and the 1970 Plant Variety Protection Act, which authorized protection for certain sexually reproduced plants but excluded bacteria from its protection. In the petitioner's view, the passage of these Acts evidences congressional understanding that the terms "manufacture" or "composition of matter" do not include living things; if they did, the petitioner argues, neither Act would have been necessary.

We reject this argument. Prior to 1930, two factors were thought to remove plants from patent protection. The first was the belief that

6. This same language was employed by P.J. Federico, a principal draftsman of the 1952 recodification, in his testimony regarding that legislation: "[U]nder section 101 a person may have invented a machine or a manufacture, which may include anything under the sun that is made by man. * * *" Hearings on H.R. 3760 before Subcommittee No. 3 of the House Committee on the Judiciary, 82d Cong., 1st Sess., 37 (1951).

plants, even those artificially bred, were products of nature for purposes of the patent law. * * *

* * *

Nor does the passage of the 1970 Plant Variety Protection Act support the Government's position. As the Government acknowledges, sexually reproduced plants were not included under the 1930 Act because new varieties could not be reproduced true-to-type through seedlings. Brief for Petitioner 27, n. 31. By 1970, however, it was generally recognized that true-to-type reproduction was possible and that plant patent protection was therefore appropriate. The 1970 Act extended that protection. There is nothing in its language or history to suggest that it was enacted because § 101 did not include living things.

In particular, we find nothing in the exclusion of bacteria from plant variety protection to support the petitioner's position. See n. 7, *supra.* The legislative history gives no reason for this exclusion. As the Court of Customs and Patent Appeals suggested, it may simply reflect congressional agreement with the result reached by that court in deciding *In re Arzberger,* 27 C.C.P.A. (Pat.) 1315, 112 F.2d 834 (1940), which held that bacteria were not plants for the purposes of the 1930 Act. Or it may reflect the fact that prior to 1970 the Patent Office had issued patents for bacteria under § 101. In any event, absent some clear indication that Congress "focused on [the] issues * * * directly related to the one presently before the Court," *SEC v. Sloan,* 436 U.S. 103, 120–121, 98 S.Ct. 1702, 1713, 56 L.Ed.2d 148 (1978), there is no basis for reading into its actions an intent to modify the plain meaning of the words found in § 101.

(B)

The petitioner's second argument is that micro-organisms cannot qualify as patentable subject matter until Congress expressly authorizes such protection. His position rests on the fact that genetic technology was unforeseen when Congress enacted § 101. From this it is argued that resolution of the patentability of inventions such as respondent's should be left to Congress. The legislative process, the petitioner argues, is best equipped to weigh the competing economic, social, and scientific considerations involved, and to determine whether living organisms produced by genetic engineering should receive patent protection. In support of this position, the petitioner relies on our recent holding in *Parker v. Flook,* 437 U.S. 584, 98 S.Ct. 2522, 57 L.Ed.2d 451 (1978), and the statement that the judiciary "must proceed cautiously when * * * asked to extend patent rights into areas wholly unforeseen by Congress." *Id.,* at 596, 98 S.Ct. at 2529.

It is, of course, correct that Congress, not the courts, must define the limits of patentability; but it is equally true that once Congress has spoken it is "the province and duty of the judicial department to say what the law is." *Marbury v. Madison,* 1 Cranch 137, 177, 2 L.Ed. 60 (1803). Congress has performed its constitutional role in defining patentable subject matter in § 101; we perform ours in construing the language Congress has employed. In so doing, our obligation is to take statutes as we find them, guided, if ambiguity appears, by the legislative history and statutory purpose. Here, we perceive no ambiguity. The subject-matter provisions of the patent law have been cast in broad terms to fulfill the constitutional and statutory goal of promoting "the Progress of Science and the useful Arts" with all that means for the social and economic benefits envisioned by Jefferson. Broad general language is not necessarily ambiguous when congressional objectives require broad terms.

Nothing in *Flook* is to the contrary. That case applied our prior precedents to determine that a "claim for an improved method of calculation, even when tied to a specific end use, is unpatentable subject matter under § 101." 437 U.S., at 595, n. 18, 98 S.Ct., at 2528, n. 18. The Court carefully scrutinized the claim at issue to determine whether it was precluded from patent protection under "the principles underlying the prohibition against patents for 'ideas' or phenomena of nature." *Id.*, at 593, 98 S.Ct. at 2527. We have done that here. *Flook* did not announce a new principle that inventions in areas not contemplated by Congress when the patent laws were enacted are unpatentable *per se.*

To read that concept into *Flook* would frustrate the purposes of the patent law. This Court frequently has observed that a statute is not to be confined to the "particular application[s] * * * contemplated by the legislators." *Barr v. United States,* 324 U.S. 83, 90, 65 S.Ct. 522, 525, 89 L.Ed. 765 (1945). This is especially true in the field of patent law. A rule that unanticipated inventions are without protection would conflict with the core concept of the patent law that anticipation undermines patentability. * * *

* * *

We have emphasized in the recent past that "[o]ur individual appraisal of the wisdom or unwisdom of a particular [legislative] course * * * is to be put aside in the process of interpreting a statute." *TVA v. Hill,* 437 U.S., at 194, 98 S.Ct., at 2302. Our task, rather, is the narrow one of determining what Congress meant by the words it used in the statute; once that is done our powers are exhausted. Congress is free to amend § 101 so as to exclude from patent protection organisms produced by genetic engineering. Cf. 42 U.S.C. § 2181(a), exempting from patent protection inventions "useful solely in the utilization of special nuclear material or atomic energy in an atomic weapon." Or it may chose to craft a statute specifically designed for such living things. But, until Congress takes such action, this Court must construe the language of § 101 as it is. The language of that section fairly embraces respondent's invention.

Accordingly, the judgment of the Court of Customs and Patent Appeals is affirmed.

MR. JUSTICE BRENNAN, with whom MR. JUSTICE WHITE, MR. JUSTICE MARSHALL, and MR. JUSTICE POWELL join, dissenting.

* * *

Notes and Questions

1. The Patent and Trademark Office prospered under Reagan, when budgets were generally tight. Why is the patent system typically favored by "conservative" politics?

2. Does this decision undercut the rationale of *Benson?* Why not apply *Benson* and wait for Congress to decide that living things should be patentable before granting patent protection to them?

3. In the *Diehr* case which follows, the most conservative justices favored the patentability of a programmed computer, while the more liberal justices (including Stevens) opposed it. Note how the Court split in *Chakrabarty?* Why?

DIAMOND v. DIEHR

Supreme Court of the United States, 1981.
450 U.S. 175, 101 S.Ct. 1048, 67 L.Ed.2d 155.

JUSTICE REHNQUIST delivered the opinion of the Court.

We granted certiorari to determine whether a process for curing synthetic rubber which includes in several of its steps the use of a mathematical formula and a programmed digital computer is patentable subject matter under 35 U.S.C. § 101.

I

The patent application at issue was filed by the respondents on August 6, 1975. The claimed invention is a process for molding raw, uncured synthetic rubber into cured precision products. The process uses a mold for precisely shaping the uncured material under heat and pressure and then curing the synthetic rubber in the mold so that the product will retain its shape and be functionally operative after the molding is completed.[1]

Respondents claim that their process ensures the production of molded articles which are properly cured. Achieving the perfect cure depends upon several factors including the thickness of the article to be molded, the temperature of the molding process, and the amount of time that the article is allowed to remain in the press. It is possible using well-known time, temperature, and cure relationships to calculate by means of the Arrhenius equation[2] when to open the press and

1. A "cure" is obtained by mixing curing agents into the uncured polymer in advance of molding and then applying heat over a period of time. If the synthetic rubber is cured for the right length of time at the right temperature, it becomes a usable product.

2. The equation is named after its discoverer Svante Arrhenius and has long been used to calculate the cure time in rubber-molding presses. The equation can be expressed as follows:

$$\ln v = CZ + x$$

remove the cured product. Nonetheless, according to the respondents, the industry has not been able to obtain uniformly accurate cures because the temperature of the molding press could not be precisely measured, thus making it difficult to do the necessary computations to determine cure time.[3] Because the temperature *inside* the press has heretofore been viewed as an uncontrollable variable, the conventional industry practice has been to calculate the cure time as the shortest time in which all parts of the product will definitely be cured, assuming a reasonable amount of mold-opening time during loading and unloading. But the shortcoming of this practice is that operating with an uncontrollable variable inevitably led in some instances to overestimating the mold-opening time and overcuring the rubber, and in other instances to underestimating that time and undercuring the product.

Respondents characterize their contribution to the art to reside in the process of constantly measuring the actual temperature inside the mold. These temperature measurements are then automatically fed into a computer which repeatedly recalculates the cure time by use of the Arrhenius equation. When the recalculated time equals the actual time that has elapsed since the press was closed, the computer signals a device to open the press. According to the respondents, the continuous measuring of the temperature inside the mold cavity, the feeding of this information to a digital computer which constantly recalculates the cure time, and the signaling by the computer to open the press, are all new in the art.

The patent examiner rejected the respondents' claims on the sole ground that they were drawn to nonstatutory subject matter under 35 U.S.C. § 101.[5] He determined that those steps in respondents' claims

wherein In v is the natural logarithm of v, the total required cure time; C is the activation constant, a unique figure for each batch of each compound being molded, determined in accordance with rheometer measurements of each batch; Z is the temperature in the mold; and x is a constant dependent on the geometry of the particular mold in the press. A rheometer is an instrument to measure flow of viscous substances.

3. During the time a press is open for loading, it will cool. The longer it is open, the cooler it becomes and the longer it takes to reheat the press to the desired temperature range. Thus, the time necessary to raise the mold temperature to curing temperature is an unpredictable variable. The respondents claim to have overcome this problem by continuously measuring the actual temperature in the closed press through the use of a thermocouple.

5. Respondents' application contained 11 different claims. Three examples are claims 1, 2, and 11 which provide:

"1. A method of operating a rubber-molding press for precision molded compounds with the aid of a digital computer, comprising:

"providing said computer with a data base for said press including at least,

"natural logarithm conversion data (ln),

"the activation energy constant (C) unique to each batch of said compound being molded, and

"a constant (x) dependent upon the geometry of the particular mold of the press,

"initiating an interval timer in said computer upon the closure of the press for monitoring the elapsed time of said closure,

"constantly determining the temperature (Z) of the mold at a location closely adjacent to the mold cavity in the press during molding,

"constantly providing the computer with the temperature (Z),

"repetitively calculating in the computer, at frequent intervals during each cure,

that are carried out by a computer under control of a stored program constituted nonstatutory subject matter under this Court's decision in *Gottschalk v. Benson,* 409 U.S. 63, 93 S.Ct. 253, 34 L.Ed.2d 273 (1972). The remaining steps—installing rubber in the press and the subsequent closing of the press—were "conventional and necessary to the process and cannot be the basis of patentability." The examiner concluded that respondents' claims defined and sought protection of a computer program for operating a rubber-molding press.

The Patent and Trademark Office Board of Appeals agreed with the examiner, but the Court of Customs and Patent Appeals reversed. *In re Diehr,* 602 F.2d 982 (1979). The court noted that a claim drawn to subject matter otherwise statutory does not become nonstatutory because a computer is involved. The respondents' claims were not directed to a mathematical algorithm or an improved method of calculation but rather recited an improved process for molding rubber articles by solving a practical problem which had risen in the molding of rubber products.

The Commission of Patents and Trademarks sought certiorari arguing that the decision of the Court of Customs and Patent Appeals was inconsistent with prior decisions of this Court. Because of the importance of the question presented, we granted the writ. 445 U.S. 926, 100 S.Ct. 1311, 63 L.Ed.2d 758 (1980).

II

Last Term in *Diamond v. Chakrabarty,* 447 U.S. 303, 100 S.Ct. 2204, 65 L.Ed.2d 144 (1980), this Court discussed the historical purposes of the patent laws and in particular 35 U.S.C. § 101. * * *

* * *

In cases of statutory construction, we begin with the language of the statute. Unless otherwise defined, "words will be interpreted as taking their ordinary, contemporary, common meaning," *Perrin v. United States,* 444 U.S. 37, 42, 100 S.Ct. 311, 314, 62 L.Ed.2d 199 (1979), and, in dealing with the patent laws, we have more than once cautioned that "courts 'should not read into the patent laws limitations and conditions which the legislature has not expressed.'" *Diamond v. Chakrabarty, supra,* at 308, 100 S.Ct., at 2207 quoting *United States v.*

the Arrhenius equation for reaction time during the cure, which is

"In v = CZ + x

"where *v* is the total required cure time,

"repetitively comparing in the computer at said frequent intervals during the cure each said calculation of the total required cure time calculated with the Arrhenius equation and said elapsed time, and

"opening the press automatically when a said comparison indicates equivalence.

"2. The method of claim 1 including measuring the activation energy constant for the compound being molded in the press with a rheometer and automatically updating said data base within the computer in the event of changes in the compound being molded in said press as measured by said rheometer.

* * *

Dubilier Condenser Corp., 289 U.S. 178, 199, 53 S.Ct. 554, 561, 77 L.Ed. 1114 (1933).

* * *

Analyzing respondents' claims according to the above statements from our cases, we think that a physical and chemical process for molding precision synthetic rubber products falls within the § 101 categories of possibly patentable subject matter. That respondents' claims involve the transformation of an article, in this case raw, uncured synthetic rubber, into a different state or thing cannot be disputed. The respondents' claims describe in detail a step-by-step method for accomplishing such, beginning with the loading of a mold with raw, uncured rubber and ending with the eventual opening of the press at the conclusion of the cure. Industrial processes such as this are the types which have historically been eligible to receive the protection of our patent laws.

III

Our conclusion regarding respondents' claims is not altered by the fact that in several steps of the process a mathematical equation and a programmed digital computer are used. This Court has undoubtedly recognized limits to § 101 and every discovery is not embraced within the statutory terms. Excluded from such patent protection are laws of nature, natural phenomena, and abstract ideas. "An idea of itself is not patentable," *Rubber–Tip Pencil Co. v. Howard,* 20 Wall. 498, 507, 22 L.Ed. 410 (1874). "A principle, in the abstract, is a fundamental truth; an original cause; a motive; these cannot be patented, as no one can claim in either of them an exclusive right." * * *

* * *

* * * In *Benson,* we held unpatentable claims for an algorithm used to convert binary code decimal numbers to equivalent pure binary numbers. The sole practical application of the algorithm was in connection with the programming of a general purpose digital computer. We defined "algorithm" as a "procedure for solving a given type of mathematical problem," and we concluded that such an algorithm, or mathematical formula, is like a law of nature, which cannot be the subject of a patent.[9]

9. The term "algorithm" is subject to a variety of definitions. The petitioner defines the term to mean:

"'1. A fixed step-by-step procedure for accomplishing a given result; usually a simplified procedure for solving a complex problem, also a full statement of a finite number of steps. 2. A defined process or set of rules that leads [*sic*] and assures development of a desired output from a given input. A sequence of formulas and/or algebraic/logical steps to calculate or determine a given task; processing rules.'" Brief for Petitioner in *Diamond v. Bradley,* O.T.1980, No. 79–855, p. 6, n. 12, quoting C. Sippl & R. Sippl, Computer Dictionary and Handbook 23 (2d ed 1972).

This definition is significantly broader than the definition this Court employed in *Benson* and *Flook.* Our previous decisions regarding the patentability of "algorithms" are necessarily limited to the more narrow definition employed by the Court, and we do not pass judgment on whether processes falling outside the definition previously used by this Court, but within the defini-

Parker v. Flook, supra, presented a similar situation. The claims were drawn to a method for computing an "alarm limit." An "alarm limit" is simply a number and the Court concluded that the application sought to protect a formula for computing this number. Using this formula, the updated alarm limit could be calculated if several other variables were known. The application, however, did not purport to explain how these other variables were to be determined, nor did it purport "to contain any disclosure relating to the chemical processes at work, the monitoring of process variables, or the means of setting off an alarm or adjusting an alarm system. All that it provides is a formula for computing an updated alarm limit." 437 U.S., at 586, 98 S.Ct., at 2523.

In contrast, the respondents here do not seek to patent a mathematical formula. Instead, they seek patent protection for a process of curing synthetic rubber. Their process admittedly employs a well-known mathematical equation, but they do not seek to pre-empt the use of that equation. Rather, they seek only to foreclose from others the use of that equation in conjunction with all of the other steps in their claimed process. These include installing rubber in a press, closing the mold, constantly determining the temperature of the mold, constantly recalculating the appropriate cure time through the use of the formula and a digital computer, and automatically opening the press at the proper time. Obviously, one does not need a "computer" to cure natural or synthetic rubber, but if the computer use incorporated in the process patent significantly lessens the possibility of "overcuring" or "undercuring," the process as a whole does not thereby become unpatentable subject matter.

Our earlier opinions lend support to our present conclusion that a claim drawn to subject matter otherwise statutory does not become nonstatutory simply because it uses a mathematical formula, computer program, or digital computer. In *Gottschalk v. Benson,* we noted: "It is said that the decision precludes a patent for any program servicing a computer. We do not so hold." 409 U.S., at 71, 93 S.Ct., at 257. Similarly, in *Parker v. Flook,* we stated that "a process is not unpatentable simply because it contains a law of nature or a mathematical algorithm." 437 U.S., at 590, 98 S.Ct., at 2526. It is now commonplace that an *application* of a law of nature or mathematical formula to a known structure or process may well be deserving of patent protection. As Justice Stone explained four decades ago:

> "While a scientific truth, or the mathematical expression of it, is not a patentable invention, a novel and useful structure created with the aid of knowledge of scientific truth may be." *Mackay Radio & Telegraph Co. v. Radio of America,* 306 U.S. 86, 94, 59 S.Ct. 427, 431, 83 L.Ed. 506 (1939).[11]

tion offered by the petitioner, would be patentable subject matter.

11. We noted in *Funk Bros. Seed Co. v. Kalo Inoculant Co.,* 333 U.S. 127, 130, 68 S.Ct. 440, 441, 92 L.Ed. 588 (1948):

We think this statement in *Mackay* takes us a long way toward the correct answer in this case. Arrhenius' equation is not patentable in isolation, but when a process for curing rubber is devised which incorporates in it a more efficient solution of the equation, that process is at the very least not barred at the threshold by § 101.

In determining the eligibility of respondents' claimed process for patent protection under § 101, their claims must be considered as a whole. It is inappropriate to dissect the claims into old and new elements and then to ignore the presence of the old elements in the analysis. This is particularly true in a process claim because a new combination of steps in a process may be patentable even though all the constituents of the combination were well known and in common use before the combination was made. The "novelty" of any element or steps in a process, or even of the process itself, is of no relevance in determining whether the subject matter of a claim falls within the § 101 categories of possibly patentable subject matter.[12]

It has been urged that novelty is an appropriate consideration under § 101. Presumably, this argument results from the language in § 101 referring to any "new and useful" process, machine, etc. Section 101, however, is a general statement of the type of subject matter that is eligible for patent protection "subject to the conditions and requirements of this title." Specific conditions for patentability follow and § 102 covers in detail the conditions relating to novelty. The question therefore of whether a particular invention is novel is "wholly apart from whether the invention falls into a category of statutory subject matter." *In re Bergy,* 596 F.2d 952, 961 (Cust. & Pat.App., 1979) (emphasis deleted). See also *Nickola v. Peterson,* 580 F.2d 898 (CA6 1978). The legislative history of the 1952 Patent Act is in accord with this reasoning. * * *

* * *

> "He who discovers a hitherto unknown phenomenon of nature has no claim to a monopoly of it which the law recognizes. If there is to be invention from such a discovery, it must come from the application of the law of nature to a new and useful end."

Although we were dealing with a "product" claim in *Funk Bros.,* the same principle applies to a process claim. *Gottschalk v. Benson,* 409 U.S. 63, 68, 93 S.Ct. 253, 255, 34 L.Ed.2d 273 (1972).

12. It is argued that the procedure of dissecting a claim into old and new elements is mandated by our decision in *Flook* which noted that a mathematical algorithm must be assumed to be within the "prior art." It is from this language that the petitioner premises his argument that if everything other than the algorithm is determined to be old in the art, then the claim cannot recite statutory subject matter. The fallacy in this argument is that we did not hold in *Flook* that the mathematical algorithm could not be considered at all when making the § 101 determination. To accept the analysis proffered by the petitioner would, if carried to its extreme, make all inventions unpatentable because all inventions can be reduced to underlying principles of nature which, once known, make their implementation obvious. The analysis suggested by the petitioner would also undermine our earlier decisions regarding the criteria to consider in determining the eligibility of a process for patent protection. See, *e.g., Gottschalk v. Benson, supra;* and *Cochrane v. Deener,* 94 U.S. 780, 24 L.Ed. 139 (1877).

In this case, it may later be determined that the respondents' process is not deserving of patent protection because it fails to satisfy the statutory conditions of novelty under § 102 or nonobviousness under § 103. A rejection on either of these grounds does not affect the determination that respondents' claims recited subject matter which was eligible for patent protection under § 101.

IV

We have before us today only the question of whether respondents' claims fall within the § 101 categories of possibly patentable subject matter. We view respondents' claims as nothing more than a process for molding rubber products and not as an attempt to patent a mathematical formula. We recognize, of course, that when a claim recites a mathematical formula (or scientific principle or phenomenon of nature), an inquiry must be made into whether the claim is seeking patent protection for that formula in the abstract. A mathematical formula as such is not accorded the protection of our patent laws, *Gottschalk v. Benson,* 409 U.S. 63, 93 S.Ct. 253, 34 L.Ed.2d 273 (1972), and this principle cannot be circumvented by attempting to limit the use of the formula to a particular technological environment. *Parker v. Flook,* 437 U.S. 584, 98 S.Ct. 2522, 57 L.Ed.2d 451 (1978). Similarly, insignificant post-solution activity will not transform an unpatentable principle into a patentable process. *Ibid.* To hold otherwise would allow a competent draftsman to evade the recognized limitations on the type of subject matter eligible for patent protection. On the other hand, when a claim containing a mathematical formula implements or applies that formula in a structure or process which, when considered as a whole, is performing a function which the patent laws were designed to protect (*e.g.,* transforming or reducing an article to a different state or thing), then the claim satisfies the requirements of § 101. Because we do not view respondents' claims as an attempt to patent a mathematical formula, but rather to be drawn to an industrial process for the molding of rubber products, we affirm the judgment of the Court of Customs and Patent Appeals.

It is so ordered.

JUSTICE STEVENS, with whom JUSTICE BRENNAN, JUSTICE MARSHALL, and JUSTICE BLACKMUN join, dissenting.

The starting point in the proper adjudication of patent litigation is an understanding of what the inventor claims to have discovered. The Court's decision in this case rests on a misreading of the Diehr and Lutton patent application. Moreover, the Court has compounded its error by ignoring the critical distinction between the character of the subject matter that the inventor claims to be novel—the § 101 issue—and the question whether that subject matter is in fact novel—the § 102 issue.

I

[A portion of Justice Stevens' dissent presenting a historical review of the law relating to the patentability of computer programs is omitted here because it has already has been set forth above.]

II

As I stated at the outset, the starting point in the proper adjudication of patent litigation is an understanding of what the inventor claims to have discovered. Indeed, the outcome of such litigation is often determined by the judge's understanding of the patent application. This is such a case.

In the first sentence of its opinion, the Court states the question presented as "whether a process for curing synthetic rubber * * * is patentable subject matter." *Ante,* at 1051. Of course, that question was effectively answered many years ago when Charles Goodyear obtained his patent on the vulcanization process.[25] The patent application filed by Diehr and Lutton, however, teaches nothing about the chemistry of the synthetic rubber-curing process, nothing about the raw materials to be used in curing synthetic rubber, nothing about the equipment to be used in the process, and nothing about the significance or effect of any process variable such as temperature, curing time, particular compositions of material, or mold configurations. In short, Diehr and Lutton do not claim to have discovered anything new about the process for curing synthetic rubber.

As the Court reads the claims in the Diehr and Lutton patent application, the inventors' discovery is a method of constantly measuring the actual temperature inside a rubber molding press. As I read the claims, their discovery is an improved method of calculating the time that the mold should remain closed during the curing process. If the Court's reading of the claims were correct, I would agree that they disclose patentable subject matter. On the other hand, if the Court accepted my reading, I feel confident that the case would be decided differently.

There are three reasons why I cannot accept the Court's conclusion that Diehr and Lutton claim to have discovered a new method of constantly measuring the temperature inside a mold. First, there is not a word in the patent application that suggests that there is anything unusual about the temperature-reading devices used in this process—or indeed that any particular species of temperature-reading device should be used in it. Second, since devices for constantly measuring actual temperatures—on a back porch, for example—have been familiar articles for quite some time, I find it difficult to believe that a patent application filed in 1975 was premised on the notion that a "process of constantly measuring the actual temperature" had just been discovered. Finally, the Patent and Trademark Office Board of

25. In an opinion written over a century ago, the Court noted:

"A manufacturing process is clearly an art, within the meaning of the law. Goodyear's patent was for a process, namely, the process of vulcanizing india-rubber by subjecting it to a high degree of heat when mixed with sulphur and a mineral salt.

* * *

"The mixing of certain substances together, or the heating of a substance to a certain temperature, is a process." *Tilghman v. Proctor,* 102 U.S. 707, 722, 728, 26 L.Ed. 279 (1881).

* * *

Appeals expressly found that "the only difference between the conventional methods of operating a molding press and that claimed in [the] application rests in those steps of the claims which relate to the calculation incident to the solution of the mathematical problem or formula used to control the mold heater and the automatic opening of the press." This finding was not disturbed by the Court of Customs and Patent Appeals and is clearly correct.

A fair reading of the entire patent application, as well as the specific claims, makes it perfectly clear that what Diehr and Lutton claim to have discovered is a method of using a digital computer to determine the amount of time that a rubber molding press should remain closed during the synthetic rubber-curing process. There is no suggestion that there is anything novel in the instrumentation of the mold, in actuating a timer when the press is closed, or in automatically opening the press when the computed time expires. Nor does the application suggest that Diehr and Lutton have discovered anything about the temperatures in the mold or the amount of curing time that will produce the best cure. What they claim to have discovered, in essence, is a method of updating the original estimated curing time by repetitively recalculating that time pursuant to a well-known mathematical formula in response to variations in temperature within the mold. Their method of updating the curing time calculation is strikingly reminiscent of the method of updating alarm limits that Dale Flook sought to patent.

Parker v. Flook, 437 U.S. 584, 98 S.Ct. 2522, 57 L.Ed.2d 451 (1978), involved the use of a digital computer in connection with a catalytic conversion process. During the conversion process, variables such as temperature, pressure, and flow rates were constantly monitored and fed into the computer; in this case, temperature in the mold is the variable that is monitored and fed into the computer. In *Flook,* the digital computer repetitively recalculated the "alarm limit"—a number that might signal the need to terminate or modify the catalytic conversion process; in this case, the digital computer repetitively recalculates the correct curing time—a number that signals the time when the synthetic rubber molding press should open.

The essence of the claimed discovery in both cases was an algorithm that could be programmed on a digital computer. In *Flook,* the algorithm made use of multiple process variables; in this case, it makes use of only one. In *Flook,* the algorithm was expressed in a newly developed mathematical formula; in this case, the algorithm makes use of a well-known mathematical formula. Manifestly, neither of these differences can explain today's holding. What I believe does explain today's holding is a misunderstanding of the applicants' claimed invention and a failure to recognize the critical difference between the "discovery" requirement in § 101 and the "novelty" requirement in § 102.

III

The Court misapplies *Parker v. Flook* because, like the Court of Customs and Patent Appeals, it fails to understand or completely disregards the distinction between the subject matter of what the inventor *claims* to have discovered—the § 101 issue—and the question whether that claimed discovery is in fact novel—the § 102 issue. If there is not even a claim that anything constituting patentable subject matter has been discovered, there is no occasion to address the novelty issue. Or, as was true in *Flook,* if the only concept that the inventor claims to have discovered is not patentable subject matter, § 101 requires that the application be rejected without reaching any issue under § 102; for it is irrelevant that unpatentable subject matter—in that case a formula for updating alarm limits—may in fact be novel.

Proper analysis, therefore, must start with an understanding of what the inventor claims to have discovered—or phrased somewhat differently—what he considers his inventive concept to be. It seems clear to me that Diehr and Lutton claim to have developed a new method of programming a digital computer in order to calculate—promptly and repeatedly—the correct curing time in a familiar process. In the § 101 analysis, we must assume that the sequence of steps in this programming method is novel, unobvious, and useful. The threshold question of whether such a method is patentable subject matter remains.

If that method is regarded as an "algorithm" as that term was used in *Gottschalk v. Benson,* 409 U.S. 63, 93 S.Ct. 253, 34 L.Ed.2d 273 (1972), and in *Parker v. Flook,* 437 U.S. 584, 98 S.Ct. 2522, 57 L.Ed.2d 451 (1978), and if no other inventive concept is disclosed in the patent application, the question must be answered in the negative. In both *Benson* and *Flook,* the parties apparently agreed that the inventor's discovery was properly regarded as an algorithm; the holding that an algorithm was a "law of nature" that could not be patented therefore determined that those discoveries were not patentable processes within the meaning of § 101.

* * *

Even the Court does not suggest that the computer program developed by Diehr and Lutton is a patentable discovery. Accordingly, if we treat the program as though it were a familiar part of the prior art—as well-established precedent requires—it is absolutely clear that their application contains no claim of patentable invention. Their application was therefore properly rejected under § 101 by the Patent Office and the Board of Appeals.

IV

The broad question whether computer programs should be given patent protection involves policy considerations that this Court is not authorized to address. As the numerous briefs *amicus curiae* filed in *Gottschalk v. Benson, supra, Dann v. Johnston,* 425 U.S. 219, 96 S.Ct.

1393, 47 L.Ed.2d 692 (1976), *Parker v. Flook, supra,* and this case demonstrate, that question is not only difficult and important, but apparently also one that may be affected by institutional bias. In each of those cases, the spokesmen for the organized patent bar have uniformly favored patentability and industry representatives have taken positions properly motivated by their economic self-interest. Notwithstanding fervent argument that patent protection is essential for the growth of the software industry, commentators have noted that "this industry is growing by leaps and bounds without it." In addition, even some commentators who believe that legal protection for computer programs is desirable have expressed doubts that the present patent system can provide the needed protection.

Within the Federal Government, patterns of decision have also emerged. Gottschalk, Dann, Parker, and Diamond were not ordinary litigants—each was serving as Commissioner of Patents and Trademarks when he opposed the availability of patent protection for a program-related invention. No doubt each may have been motivated by a concern about the ability of the Patent Office to process effectively the flood of applications that would inevitably flow from a decision that computer programs are patentable. The consistent concern evidenced by the Commissioner of Patents and Trademarks and by the Board of Appeals of the Patent and Trademark Office has not been shared by the Court of Customs and Patent Appeals, which reversed the Board in *Benson, Johnston,* and *Flook,* and was in turn reversed by this Court in each of those cases.

Scholars have been critical of the work of both tribunals. Some of that criticism may stem from a conviction about the merits of the broad underlying policy question; such criticism may be put to one side. Other criticism, however, identifies two concerns to which federal judges have a duty to respond. First, the cases considering the patentability of program-related inventions do not establish rules that enable a conscientious patent lawyer to determine with a fair degree of accuracy which, if any, program-related inventions will be patentable. Second, the inclusion of the ambiguous concept of an "algorithm" within the "law of nature" category of unpatentable subject matter has given rise to the concern that almost any process might be so described and therefore held unpatentable.

In my judgment, today's decision will aggravate the first concern and will not adequately allay the second. I believe both concerns would be better addressed by (1) an unequivocal holding that no program-related invention is a patentable process under § 101 unless it makes a contribution to the art that is not dependent entirely on the utilization of a computer, and (2) an unequivocal explanation that the term "algorithm" as used in this case, as in *Benson* and *Flook,* is synonymous with the term "computer program." Because the invention claimed in the patent application at issue in this case makes no contribution to the art that is not entirely dependent upon the utilization of a computer in a familiar process, I would reverse the decision of the Court of Customs and Patent Appeals.

Notes and Questions

1. Compare the definitions of "algorithm" used by Stevens, at the end of his dissent, with that used by the government (majority opinion, footnote 9) and by the majority (text accompanying footnote 9). Query: Is this a holding or dictum? Compare the dictionary definition of this term in 1971 to that found in 1981 dictionaries.

2. If *Benson* holds that no invention can preempt all possible uses of an algorithm, then what is the "legal" meaning of the term algorithm after *Diehr?*

3. Compare *In re Christensen,* 478 F.2d 1392, 1396 (C.C.P.A.1973), where Judge Rich, in a concurring opinion, said with reference to *Benson:*

> Thus the reasoning of the Supreme Court's opinion has more bearing on the facts in this case than it had on the facts before it in *Benson.* The claims in this case do contain a mathematical formula; in *Benson* they did not. * * *
>
> * * *
>
> * * * "Algorithm" has been used in the sense of a "procedure for solving a given type of mathematical problem" and "formula" is used in the sense of a mathematical formula. The Supreme Court in *Benson* appears to have held that claims drafted in such terms are not patentable—for what reason remaining a mystery. Under the rules of the legal game, we are obliged to follow its lead as best we can.
>
> But for the *Benson* decision, I would reverse the rejection here because I see no reason why such a specific, useful, technological process as a process for determining subsurface porosity, concededly a contribution to the useful arts, cannot be defined in the language of mathematics which is widely used as a medium of communication in that field. I have no more doubt it is a "process" within the meaning of § 101 than I had about Benson's process; but on that point I seem to have been reversed.

4. Note that the majority in *Diehr* does not address the patentability of a program standing by itself. Compare the *Diehr* invention with that of Atkinson in the patent set forth towards the beginning of this chapter. Note that both involve the use of equipment in conjunction with a computer and a program. In *Diehr,* rubber is "cured" or transformed into something new. In the Atkinson patent, the "user" of a computer is able to navigate through commands with a "one button" mouse, rather than with the confusing "two-button" mouse whose use is taught by "Xerox Smalltalk," the prior art.

Apply the *Diehr* approach and the *Flook* approach to the Atkinson invention and determine if the Atkinson invention is patentable under both approaches. Are the two decisions consistent, as the majority in *Diehr* suggest? Or are they irreconcilable, as Stevens suggests in his lengthy dissent?

5. Does it matter if, in the Atkinson patent, the program is considered "prior art," as Stevens teaches in *Flook,* as opposed to considering § 101, § 102, and § 103 separately as "three doors" as Rich teaches in *Bergy?*

6. The majority in *Diamond v. Diehr* took the opposite view from Stevens' in *Flook* and approved the logic of *Bergy.* Since *Diehr* did not overrule *Flook,* the status of Justice Stevens's rule, which treats the unpatentable program as a "familiar part of the prior art," is somewhat uncertain.

Note on Practical Application of Benson, Flook, and Diehr

The Supreme Court only rarely addresses the patentability of computer program inventions. So it has been left to the Court of Customs and Patent Appeals and its successor, the Court of Appeals for the Federal Circuit, to create practical rules that can be applied by the examiners and district court judges in actual cases.

The four cases which follow—the first two handed down shortly following *Diehr* and the last two quite recently—set forth these practical rules. Based upon these decisions, the Patent and Trademark Office has prepared guidelines that are set forth following the second and fourth case in this series.

IN RE PARDO

United States Court of Customs and Patent Appeals, 1982.
684 F.2d 912.

Before MARKEY, CHIEF JUDGE, RICH, BALDWIN, MILLER, and NIES, ASSOCIATE JUDGES.

MILLER, JUDGE.

This is an ex parte *pro se* appeal from a decision of the Patent and Trademark Office ("PTO") Board of Appeals ("board") affirming the examiner's rejection of appellants' claims 26–61 under 35 U.S.C. § 101 as directed to nonstatutory subject matter and, pursuant to 37 CFR 1.196(b), entering a new rejection of the same claims for obviousness, 35 U.S.C. § 103. We reverse.

BACKGROUND

The Invention

Appellants characterize their invention as a method for controlling the internal operations of a computer. The invention converts a computer from a sequential processor (which executes program instructions in the order in which they are presented) to a processor which is not dependent on the order in which it receives program steps. This capability is important when the execution of certain program steps requires as a condition precedent the results of other program steps.

Appellants' specification describes the invention as involving an "algorithm" of a compiler program. Claims 26–43 are directed to a method of controlling the internal operations of a programmed computer, and claims 44–61 are directed to a computer controlled according to the method. Claims 30 and 48 are representative:

> 30. A process of operating a general purpose data processor of known type to enable the data processor to execute formulas in an object program comprising a plurality of formulas, such that the same results will be produced when using the same given data, regardless of the sequence in which said formulas are presented in said object program, comprising the steps of:
>
> (a) examining each of said formulas in a storage area of the data processor to determine which formulas can be designated as defined;
>
> (b) executing, in the sequence in which each formula is designated as defined, said formulas designated as defined;
>
> (c) repeating steps (a) and (b) for at least undefined formulas as many times as required until all said formulas have been designated as defined and have been executed;
>
> whereby to produce the same results upon execution of the formulas in the sequence recited in step (b) when using the same given data, regardless of the order in which said formulas were presented in the object program prior to said process.
>
> 48. A general purpose data processor of known type operating under the control of a stored program containing a set of instructions for enabling the data processor to execute formulas in an object program comprising a plurality of formulas, such that the same results will be produced when using the same given data, regardless of the sequence in which said formulas are presented in said object program, said data processor performing the following functions:
>
> (a) examining each of said formulas in a storage area of the data processor to determine which formulas can be designated as defined;
>
> (b) executing, in the sequence in which each formula is designated as defined, said formulas designated as defined;
>
> (c) repeating steps (a) and (b) for at least undefined formulas as many times as required until all said formulas have been designated as defined and have been executed;
>
> whereby to produce the same results upon execution of the formulas in the sequence recited in step (b) when using the same given data, regardless of the order in which said formulas were presented in the object program prior to said functions.

Prosecution History

The application was filed August 12, 1970. On July 28, 1972, the examiner indicated that all claims were allowable and that prosecution on the merits was closed. A notice of allowance, however, was not forthcoming, and subsequent to the decision in *Gottschalk v. Benson,* 409 U.S. 63, 93 S.Ct. 253, 34 L.Ed.2d 273, 175 USPQ 673 (1972), the PTO reopened prosecution and rejected the claims under 35 U.S.C. § 101.

The Board's Decision

The board affirmed the examiner's rejection, stating:

> The courts above us have consistently said that a claim directed in its entirety to an algorithm is nonstatutory. An algorithm is defined * * * as a procedure for solving a given type of mathematical problem.
>
> * * *

Thus, the board treated appellants' use of the word "algorithm" to describe their invention as an admission that their claims are drawn to nonstatutory subject matter.

The board then entered the following new rejection under 37 CFR 1.196(b):

> Claims 26 through 61 are rejected under 35 USC 103 as obvious. As we said before, the appellants' invention is directed to a method and apparatus for automatically rearranging random formulae for sequential execution by a computer. Suppose a user provides the following information:
>
> (1) values for a, b, c and d;
>
> (2) $A = X + Y$;
>
> (3) $X = a + b$; and
>
> (4) $Y = c + d$.
>
> Obviously, a computer cannot execute these operations in the order presented because step (2) cannot be performed until the results of steps (3) and (4) are obtained. What the appellants' algorithm does is rearrange the order of the formulae as presented by the user so that the computer can execute the operations. Thus, using our example, the appellants' algorithmic process would rearrange the formulae as follows:
>
> (1) values for a, b, c and d;
>
> (2) $X = a + b$;
>
> (3) $Y = c + d$; and
>
> (4) $A = X + Y$.
>
> These formulae, as arranged, can be executed by the computer in a logical, sequential fashion. In our opinion, this algorithmic process would have been obvious to the artisan facing the problem within the meaning of 35 USC 103.

OPINION

The issues before us are: (1) whether appellants' claims constitute statutory subject matter; and (2) whether the invention defined by the claims would have been obvious to a person of ordinary skill in the art on August 12, 1970, the date of appellants' constructive reduction to practice.

I. Statutory Subject Matter

A. No Admission

The method adopted by this court for analyzing mathematical algorithm-statutory subject matter cases in *In re Freeman,* 573 F.2d 1237, 197 U.S.P.Q. 464 (CCPA 1978), as modified by *In re Walter,* 618 F.2d 758, 205 U.S.P.Q. 397 (CCPA 1980), comprises a two part test: First, the claim is analyzed to determine whether a mathematical algorithm is directly or indirectly recited. Next, if a mathematical algorithm is found, the claim as a whole is further analyzed to determine whether the algorithm is "applied in any manner to physical elements or process steps," and, if it is, it "passes muster under § 101." 618 F.2d at 767, 205 U.S.P.Q. at 407. The second part of this test conforms to the opinion of the Supreme Court in *Diamond v. Diehr,* 450 U.S. 175, 101 S.Ct. 1048, 67 L.Ed.2d 155, 209 U.S.P.Q. 1 (1981). *In re Abele,* 684 F.2d 902 (CCPA 1982); *In re Taner,* 681 F.2d 787, at 790, 791 (CCPA 1982).

Appellants argue that their use of the word "algorithm" to describe their process is an insufficient basis to hold that their claims are drawn to nonstatutory subject matter. It has often been recognized that the word "algorithm" is subject to a number of definitions. The Supreme Court has defined it as a "procedure for solving a given type of mathematical problem." *Diamond v. Diehr, supra* 450 U.S. at 186, 101 S.Ct. at 1056, 209 U.S.P.Q. at 8. It is this type of algorithm that constitutes nonstatutory subject matter, and this court has consistently rejected attempts to enlarge the "mathematical algorithm" exception to the definition of patentable subject matter in section 101 to include nonmathematical algorithms. In *In re Freeman, supra* at 1246, 197 U.S.P.Q. at 471, the court said, "a refusal to recognize that *Benson* was concerned only with *mathematical* algorithms leads to the absurd view that the Court was reading the word 'process' out of the statute." * * *

Appellants filed their patent application containing the word "algorithm" more than two years before the decision in *Gottschalk v. Benson, supra,* where the court used the word in a limited sense to describe nonstatutory subject matter. There is no indication that "algorithm," as used by appellants, means "mathematical algorithm" as that term has been used by the Supreme Court. Therefore, appellants' use of the term to describe their invention is not an admission that they are claiming nonstatutory subject matter and is not dispositive of the issue before us.

B. Mathematical Algorithm

Applying the first part of the *Freeman* analysis to the appealed claims, we are unable to find any mathematical formula, calculation, or algorithm either directly or indirectly recited in the claimed steps of examining, compiling, storing, and executing. Indeed, the examiner acknowledged that "[t]he 'algorithm' of the present application is not 'mathematical' (although it deals with the proper sequence for performing mathematics), but it does establish the rules which are to be followed by a data processor and which appellants want to protect when so used." We perceive no essential distinction between appellants' claimed invention and the subject matter of *In re Chatfield, supra,* which comprised a timesharing method for operating a computer on several programs simultaneously. *Chatfield,* like this case, involved a method for controlling the internal operations of a computer to govern the manner in which programs are executed.

Nevertheless, despite the absence of an expressly-recited mathematical algorithm, the solicitor argues that appellants' claims *indirectly* amount to mathematical calculations, because the programs subjected to appellants' process are exemplified as mathematical formulae. * * *

* * *

Appellants' method claims are directed to executing programs in a computer. The method operates on *any* program and *any* formula which may be input, regardless of mathematical content. That a computer controlled according to the invention is capable of handling mathematics is irrelevant to the question of whether a mathematical algorithm is recited by the claims.

Section 101 encompasses a broad range of subject matter. "[A] claim drawn to subject matter otherwise statutory does not become nonstatutory simply because it uses a mathematical formula, computer program, or digital computer." *Diamond v. Diehr, supra* 450 U.S. at 187, 101 S.Ct. at 1056, 209 U.S.P.Q. at 8. Indeed, any process, machine, manufacture, or composition of matter constitutes statutory subject matter *unless* it falls within a judicially determined exception to section 101. The appealed claims do not fall within any such exception.

Accordingly, we hold that appellants' claims constitute statutory subject matter, and the section 101 rejection is *reversed.*

II. Obviousness

The obviousness rejection made by the board is only applicable to claims 26–27, 32–33, 40–41, 44–45, 50–51, and 58–59. The remainder of the claims do not require rearrangement of the process instructions, but achieve the stated objective of nonsequential operation in a different manner.

The board cited no references in support of the rejection, but relied on its own logic to hold that the invention would have been obvious. * * *

In the present case, the board, in entering the new rejection, exemplified a portion of one claimed method (*viz.,* rearrangement of the order of the formulae) and expressed the opinion that it would have been obvious to one of ordinary skill in the art in 1970. However, the skill of a person of ordinary skill in either computer programming or design in 1970 is not a proper subject for judicial notice today, no matter how simple a claimed invention may seem in hindsight. Appellants point out that computers were in general use as sequential processors for 18 years prior to their filing date, and yet the PTO has been unable to cite even one reference against their claims. * * *

* * *

In making the obviousness rejection, the board failed to follow the three-pronged analysis required by *Graham v. John Deere Co.,* 383 U.S. 1, 86 S.Ct. 684, 15 L.Ed.2d 545 (1966), whenever the obviousness of patent claims is in issue. The board did not determine the scope and content of the prior art or even indicate that there was any prior art; it did not determine the differences between the prior art and the claimed invention; and it did not ascertain the level of ordinary skill in the art at the time the invention was made.

Accordingly, we hold that the PTO has failed to establish that the claims would have been obvious to a person of ordinary skill in the art on August 12, 1970, and the section 103 rejection must also be *reversed.*

Reversed.

In re ABELE

United States Court of Customs and Patent Appeals, 1982.
684 F.2d 902.

Before MARKEY, CHIEF JUDGE, and RICH, BALDWIN, MILLER and NIES, JUDGES.

NIES, JUDGE.

This appeal is from the decision of the Patent and Trademark Office Board of Appeals (board) affirming the rejection of claims 5–7 and 33–47 [1] in their application serial No. 850,892, filed November 15, 1977, for "Tomographic Scanner." The claims stand rejected under 35 U.S.C. § 101 as being drawn to nonstatutory subject matter. We *affirm* the rejection of claims 5 and 7 and *reverse* with respect to all remaining claims on appeal.

THE INVENTION

Appellants' invention is in the field of image processing particularly as applied to computerized axial tomography or CAT scans. Specifically, appellants' invention is directed to an improvement in computed tomography whereby the exposure to X-ray is reduced while the reliability of the produced image is improved. * * *

* * *

THE REJECTION

The examiner rejected the claims on appeal under the authority of *Parker v. Flook,* 437 U.S. 584, 98 S.Ct. 2522, 57 L.Ed.2d 451 (1978). In the final rejection and in the examiner's answer before the board, the examiner construed *Flook* as mandating the following test:

1. Claims 2, 3, 8–9, 23 and 48 have been allowed. Claims 49–57 were withdrawn in accordance with 37 CFR 1.142(b).

> Taking each claim as a whole, it is assumed, for analysis purposes only, that any mathematical calculation in the claim is part of the prior art. If what is left is new and unobvious, then the claim, taken as a whole, protects more than a mathematical calculation and it is deemed statutory. But if the remainder of the claim is not novel nor unobvious, then the claim, taken as a whole, merely seeks to protect the mathematical calculation and, as such, does not comprise statutory subject matter.

Applying the above test, the examiner determined that, apart from the mathematical calculations, the remaining steps were well known or were "merely a necessary antecedent step to provide values for solving the mathematical equations," and, thus, were directed to nonstatutory subject matter, citing *In re Richman,* 563 F.2d 1026, 195 USPQ 340 (Cust. & Pat.App.1977).

THE BOARD'S DECISION

The board did not address the examiner's contentions, relying instead on *In re Freeman,* 573 F.2d 1237, 197 USPQ 464 (CCPA 1978), as modified by *In re Walter,* 618 F.2d 758, 205 USPQ 397 (Cust. & Pat.App.1980). Without resort to detailed claim language, the board affirmed the rejection under 35 U.S.C. § 101 as follows:

> When the claims are analyzed in [the manner dictated by *Walter*], it is manifest that the mathematical algorithm is not implemented in a manner to define structural relationships between physical elements in the apparatus claims or to refine or limit claim steps in the process claims. The claims do no more than present and solve a mathematical algorithm and are manifestly nonstatutory.

One member dissented with respect to rejection of claims 6 and 33–47 concluding that these claims are directed to "producing a product, an improved tomographic X-ray image," and are, therefore, directed to statutory subject matter citing *Diamond v. Diehr,* 450 U.S. 175, 101 S.Ct. 1048, 67 L.Ed.2d 155 (1981).

OPINION

I

A

We agree with the board that a two-part analysis is the proper vehicle for resolution of issues here presented under 35 U.S.C. § 101. However, we agree with appellants that the second step of the analysis is not as limited as the board held it to be.

B

In *Gottschalk v. Benson,* 409 U.S. 63, 93 S.Ct. 253, 34 L.Ed.2d 273 (1972), the Supreme Court concluded that claims directed to a particular "algorithm," conversion of binary coded decimal numbers to binary numbers, did not define patentable subject matter. In that case the Court defined the term "algorithm" as "[a] procedure for solving a given type of mathematical problem." *Id.* at 65, 93 S.Ct. at 254. The

Court's holding in *Benson* became the basis for the first part of the two-part analysis set forth by this court in *In re Freeman,* 573 F.2d 1237, 197 USPQ 464 (Cust. & Pat.App.1978).

In *Freeman,* 573 F.2d at 1245, 197 USPQ at 470, this court concluded:

> As a bare minimum, application of *Benson* in a particular case requires a careful analysis of the claims, to determine whether, as in *Benson,* they recite a "procedure for solving a given type of *mathematical* problem." [Citation omitted. Emphasis in original.]

Hence, the first part of the analysis requires:

> First, it must be determined whether the claim directly or indirectly recites an "algorithm" in the *Benson* sense of that term. * * * [*Id.* at 1245, 197 USPQ at 471.]

The second part of the *Freeman* analysis is derived from the further holding in *Benson,* 409 U.S. at 72, 93 S.Ct. at 257, that any patent issued in that case "would wholly pre-empt the mathematical formula and in practical effect would be a patent on the algorithm itself." Thus, it was concluded that the presence of an "algorithm" in a claim would not render a claimed invention nonstatutory unless the invention claimed *only* the "algorithm." Stating this conclusion in the language of *Benson,* this court declared:

> Second, the claim must be further analyzed to ascertain whether in its entirety it wholly preempts that algorithm. [*Freeman, Id.* at 1245, 197 USPQ at 471.]

This latter step in the *Freeman* analysis was not reached because of this court's conclusion that the claims did not recite an "algorithm." In *In re Toma,* 575 F.2d 872, 197 USPQ 852 (Cust. & Pat.App.1978), the same test was discussed but, again, the second part of the analysis was not reached. Subsequently, the Supreme Court handed down its decision in *Parker v. Flook,* 437 U.S. 584, 98 S.Ct. 2522, 57 L.Ed.2d 451 (1978), making clear that the second part of the above analysis was erroneous. The Court held that the claim need "not * * * cover every conceivable application of the formula" to be nonstatutory. *Id.* at 586, 98 S.Ct. at 2523.

In sum, the Court's decisions have made clear that a claim does not present patentable subject matter if it would wholly preempt an algorithm, *Benson,* supra, or if it would preempt the algorithm but for limiting its use to a particular technological environment, *Flook,* supra. However, these decisions leave undefined what does constitute statutory subject matter.

* * *

[I]n *In re Walter,* 618 F.2d 758, 205 USPQ 397 (Cust. & Pat.App. 1980), the second part of the two-step analysis[5] was defined as follows:

5. The first part of our analysis was not altered because the definition of an algorithm used by the court in *Flook* was identical to that used in *Benson, Flook,* 437 U.S. at 585 n.1, 98 S.Ct. at 2523 n.1, *quoting Benson,* 409 U.S. at 65, 93 S.Ct. 254.

> If it appears that the mathematical algorithm is implemented in a specific manner to define structural relationships between the physical elements of the claim (in apparatus claims) or to refine or limit claim steps (in process claims), *the claim being otherwise statutory,* the claim passes muster under § 101. If, however, the mathematical algorithm is merely presented and solved by the claimed invention, as was the case in *Benson* and *Flook,* and is not applied in any manner to physical elements or process steps, no amount of post-solution activity will render the claim statutory; nor is it saved by a preamble merely reciting the field of use of the mathematical algorithm. [*Id.* at 767, 205 USPQ at 407 (emphasis added).]

* * *

In *Walter,* the claims were directed to a process for correlating and cross-correlating signals. All of the claims steps were algorithm steps for performing the correlation or cross-correlation. There were no limitations in the claims, other than a field of use set forth in the preamble of the claims which stated that the algorithm was for use in connection with seismic surveying. The court concluded that the claims were directed to claiming only the algorithm, were not applied in any manner to any process steps, and were, therefore, directed to nonstatutory subject matter. *Id.* at 769, 205 USPQ at 409.

Appellants summarize the *Walter* test as setting forth two ends of a spectrum: what is now clearly nonstatutory, i.e., claims in which an algorithm is merely presented and solved by the claimed invention (preemption), and what is clearly statutory, i.e., claims in which an algorithm is implemented in a specific manner *to define structural relationships* between the physical elements of the claim (in an apparatus claim) or *to refine or limit claim steps* (in a process). Appellants urge that the statement of the test in *Walter* fails to provide a useful tool for analyzing claims in the "gray area" which falls between the two ends of that spectrum. We agree that the board's understanding and application of the *Walter* analysis justifies appellant's position. However, the *Walter* analysis quoted above does not limit patentable subject matter only to claims in which structural relationships or process steps are defined, limited or refined by the application of the algorithm.

Rather, *Walter* should be read as requiring no more than that the algorithm be "applied in any manner to physical elements or process steps," provided that its application is circumscribed by more than a field of use limitation or non-essential post-solution activity. Thus, if the claim would be "otherwise statutory," *id.,* albeit inoperative or less useful without the algorithm, the claim likewise presents statutory subject matter when the algorithm is included. This broad reading of *Walter,* we conclude, is in accord with the Supreme Court decisions.

* * *

Finally, the purpose of the two-part analysis supports the view taken here. The goal is to answer the question "What did applicants invent?" If the claimed invention is a mathematical algorithm, it is improper subject matter for patent protection, whereas if the claimed invention is an application of the algorithm, § 101 will not bar the grant of a patent.

* * *

II

In this case, each of the independent claims and, necessarily, each of the dependent claims, includes the limitation "calculating * * * the difference" either as a step in a process or as a means in an apparatus. Accordingly, all of the claims may be directed to nonstatutory subject matter as each presents a mathematical formula or a sequence of mathematical operations. * * * In any event, appellants concede that their claims "implement a mathematical algorithm."

III

A

We now turn to the second part of our analysis to determine whether what is claimed is a statutory process or apparatus or a nonstatutory algorithm.

We begin by contrasting the two broadest process claims, claims 5 and 6:

> 5. A method of displaying data in a field comprising the steps of
>
> calculating the difference between the local value of the data at a data point in the field and the average value of the data in a region of the field which surrounds said point for each point in said field, and
>
> displaying the value of said difference as a signed gray scale at a point in a picture which corresponds to said data point.
>
> 6. The method of claim 5 wherein said data is X-ray attenuation data produced in a two dimensional field by a computed tomography scanner.

We conclude that claim 5 is directed solely to the mathematical algorithm portion of appellants' invention and is, thus, not statutory subject matter under § 101. We reach the opposite conclusion with respect to claim 6.

The method of claim 6, unlike that of claim 5, requires "X-ray attenuation data." The specification indicates that such attenuation data is available only when an X-ray beam is produced by a CAT scanner, passed through an object, and detected upon its exit. Only after these steps have been completed is the algorithm performed, and the resultant modified data displayed in the required format.

Were we to view the claim absent the algorithm, the production, detection and display steps would still be present and would result in a conventional CAT-scan process. Accordingly, production and detection cannot be considered mere antecedent steps to obtain values for solving the algorithm as in *In re Richman,* cited by the examiner. Indeed, claim 6 presents data gathering steps not dictated by the algorithm but by other limitations which require certain antecedent steps. It is these antecedent steps that dictate what type of data must be obtained. * * * In any event, we view the production, detection, and display steps as manifestly statutory subject matter and are not swayed from this conclusion by the presence of an algorithm in the claimed method.

* * * In the instant case, claim 6 defines the variables and places the algorithm in a particular relationship to a series of steps in a particular type of process, permitting the algorithm to be applied as a further process step.

The algorithm, when properly viewed, is merely applied to the "attenuation data" to eliminate what would otherwise appear as artifacts upon display of the data in the manner claimed. The algorithm does not necessarily refine or limit the earlier steps of production and detection as would be required to achieve the status of patentable subject matter by the board's narrow reading of *Walter.* What appellants have done is to discover an application of an algorithm to process steps which are themselves part of an overall process which is statutory. Hence, claim 6 cannot be construed as a mere procedure for solving a given mathematical problem. As was the case in *Diehr* and *Johnson,* both supra, the algorithm is but a part of the overall claimed process.

We are faced simply with an improved CAT-scan process comparable to the improved process for curing synthetic rubber in *Diehr,* supra. The improvement in either case resides in the application of a mathematical formula within the context of a process which encompasses significantly more than the algorithm alone.

B

We do not reach the same conclusion with respect to claim 5. This claim presents no more than the calculation of a number and display of the result, albeit in a particular format.

The specification provides no greater meaning to "data in a field" than a matrix of numbers regardless of by what method generated. Thus, the algorithm is neither explicitly nor implicitly applied to any certain process. Moreover, that the result is displayed as a shade of gray rather than as simply a number provides no greater or better information, considering the broad range of applications encompassed by the claim. Indeed, this claim does not even attempt to "limit the use of the formula to a particular technological environment," *Diehr,* 450 U.S. at 191, 101 S.Ct. at 1058, as was done in *Flook,* supra. Hence, we view claim 5 as directed merely to a mathematical formula which is not proper subject matter under § 101.

* * *

Modified.

PATENTABLE SUBJECT MATTER MATHEMATICAL ALGORITHMS AND COMPUTER PROGRAMS

1106 Official Gazette of the United States Patent and Trademark Office 5 (September 5, 1989).

The following represents a recent legal analysis done by Associate Solicitor Lee E. Barrett, an attorney in the Office of the Solicitor of the Patent and Trademark Office, on the subject of the patentability of mathematical algorithms and computer programs. The analysis is published for the benefit of the public.

August 9, 1989 FRED E. McKELVEY
Solicitor

Table of Contents

DISCUSSION

I. Statutory Subject Matter—35 U.S.C. § 101

Inventions may be patented only if they fall within one of the four statutory classes of subject matter of 35 U.S.C. § 101: "process, machine, manufacture, or composition of matter." *See Kewanee Oil Co. v. Bicron Corp.,* 416 U.S. 470, 483, 181 USPQ 673, 679 (1974):

> [N]o patent is available for a discovery, however useful, novel, and nonobvious, unless it falls within one of the express categories of patentable subject matter of 35 U.S.C. § 101.

Subject matter that does not fall within one of the statutory classes of 35 U.S.C. § 101 is said to be "nonstatutory" or to be "unpatentable subject matter."

The broad language of § 101 is intended to dilineate a "general industrial boundary" of patentable invention. *In re Bergy,* 596 F.2d 952, 974 n. 11, 201 USPQ 352, 372 n. 11 (CCPA 1979), *vacated,* 444 U.S. 1028, *aff'd sub nom., Diamond v. Chakrabarty,* 447 U.S. 303, 206 USPQ 193 (1980). The first statutory class, process, is defined in 35 U.S.C. § 100(b) and refers to *acts,* while the last three classes, machine, manufacture and composition of matter, refer to physical *things;* therefore, the general field of patentable invention consists of new acts and new things. *Id.* The classes relevant to this discussion are "process" and "machine." A "process" is equivalent to a "method." *Bergy,* 596 F.2d at 965, 201 USPQ at 364. The term "machine" is used interchangeably with "apparatus." *In re Prater,* 415 F.2d 1393, 1395 n. 11, 162 USPQ 541, 543 n. 11 (CCPA 1969).

The question of whether a claimed invention satisfies the other conditions for patentability is "wholly apart from whether the invention falls into a category of statutory subject matter" (emphasis deleted). *Diamond v. Diehr,* 450 U.S. 175, 190, 209 USPQ 1, 9 (1981) (citing *Bergy,* 596 F.2d at 961, 201 USPQ at 361). As stated in *Parker v. Flook,* 437 U.S. 584, 593, 198 USPQ 193, 198–99 (1978):

> The obligation to determine what type of discovery is sought to be patented must precede the determination of whether that discovery is, in fact, new [i.e., novel under § 102] or obvious [§ 103].

* * *

II. Mathematical Algorithms

A. Mathematical algorithms per se are not a statutory "process" under § 101

A mathematical algorithm is defined as a "procedure for solving a given type of mathematical problem." *Gottschalk v. Benson,* 409 U.S. 63, 65, 175 USPQ 673, 674 (1972); *Flook,* 437 U.S. at 585 n. 1, 198 USPQ at 195 n. 1; *Diehr,* 450 U.S. at 186, 209 USPQ at 8. Mathematical algorithms are nonstatutory because they have been determined not to fall within the § 101 statutory class of a "process." *Benson.* "[A]n algorithm, or mathematical formula, is like a law of nature, which cannot be the subject of a patent." *Diehr,* 450 U.S. at 186, 209 USPQ at 8. The exception applies only to *mathematical* algorithms since any process is an "algorithm" in the sense that it is a step-by-step procedure to arrive at a given result. *In re Walter,* 618 F.2d 758, 764 n. 4, 205 USPQ 397, 405 n. 4. (CCPA 1980); *Pardo,* 684 F.2d at 915, 214 USPQ at 676.

Although mathematical algorithms *per se* are nonstatutory, as stated in *Diehr,* 450 U.S. at 187–88, 209 USPQ at 8–9:

> [A] claim drawn to subject matter otherwise statutory does not become nonstatutory simply because it uses a mathematical formula, computer program, or digital computer. * * * [I]n *Parker v. Flook* we stated that "a process is not unpatentable simply because it contains a law of nature or a mathematical algorithm." 437 U.S. at 590. It is now commonplace that an *application* of a law of nature or mathematical formula to a known structure or process may well be deserving of patent protection. As Justice Stone explained four decades ago:
>
> > "While a scientific truth, or the mathematical expression of it, is not a patentable invention, a novel and useful structure created with the aid of knowledge of scientific truth may be." *Mackay Radio & Telegraph Co. v. Radio Corp. of America,* 306 U.S. 86, 94 (1939). [Citations omitted.]

The Supreme Court thus recognizes that mathematical algorithms are "the basic tools of scientific and technological work," *Benson,* 409 U.S. at 67, 175 USPQ at 675, and should not be the subject of exclusive rights, whereas technological application of scientific principles and mathematical algorithms furthers the constitutional purpose of promoting "the Progress of * * * Useful arts." U.S. Const. art. I, § 8. It is also recognized that mathematical algorithms may be the most precise way to describe the invention.

Where claims involve mathematical algorithms, as stated in *In re Abele,* 684 F.2d 902, 907, 214 USPQ 682, 687 (CCPA 1982):

> The goal is to answer the question "What did applicants invent?" If the claimed invention is a mathematical algorithm, it is improper subject matter for patent protection, whereas if the claimed invention is an application of the algorithm, § 101 will not bar the grant of a patent.

The tests for determining whether claims containing mathematical algorithms are statutory have gradually evolved in the courts since the Supreme Court's decision in *Benson* in 1972.

B. Evolution of the two-part test for mathematical algorithm-statutory subject matter

The proper legal analysis of mathematical algorithm-statutory subject matter cases is the two-part test of *In re Freeman,* 573 F.2d 1237, 197 USPQ 464 (CCPA 1978), as modified by *Walter* and *Abele.* * * *

* * *

Under the second test of Abele, the claims are considered without the algorithm to determine whether what remains is "otherwise statutory," *not* to determine whether what remains is novel and nonobvious.

C. Application of the two-part test

1. Step 1—presence of a mathematical algorithm

a. Mathematical algorithm

A mathematical algorithm is a "procedure for solving a given type of mathematical problem." In this sense, a mathematical algorithm refers "to methods of calculation, mathematical formulas, and mathematical procedures generally." *Walter,* 618 F.2d at 764–65 n. 4, 205 USPQ at 405 n. 4. "The type of mathematical computation involved does not determine whether a procedure is statutory or nonstatutory." *In re Gelnovatch,* 595 F.2d 32, 41, 201 USPQ 136, 145 (CCPA 1979). A "claim for an improved method of calculation, even when tied to a specific end use, is unpatentable subject matter under § 101." *Flook,* 437 U.S. at 595 n. 18, 198 USPQ at 199 n. 18.

Mathematical algorithms may represent scientific principles, laws of nature, or ideas or mental processes for solving complex problems. *See Meyer,* 688 F.2d at 794–95, 215 USPQ at 197:

> Scientific principles, such as the relationship between mass and energy [$E = mc^2$], and laws of nature, such as the acceleration of gravity, namely $a = 32$ ft./sec.^{2}, can be represented in mathematical format. However, some mathematical algorithms and formulae do not represent scientific principles or laws of nature; they represent ideas or mental processes and are simply logical vehicles for communicating possible solutions to complex problems.

No distinction is made between mathematical algorithms invented by man, and mathematical algorithms representing discoveries of scientific principles and laws of nature which reveal a relationship that has always existed.

b. "Process" versus "apparatus" claims

Since mathematical algorithms have been determined not to fall within the § 101 statutory class of a "process," attempts have been made to circumvent the nonstatutory subject matter rejection by drafting mathematical algorithms as "machine" claims. The technique used is to draft the method steps in terms of "means for" language permitted by 35 U.S.C. § 112, sixth paragraph. While such a claim is technically a "machine" or "apparatus" claim, the courts have held that form of the claim does not control whether the subject matter is statutory.

* * *

* * * A claim is not presumed to be statutory simply because it is in apparatus form.

c. Form of the mathematical algorithm

The first step of the analysis is to determine whether the claim directly or indirectly recites a mathematical algorithm. A mathematical algorithm can appear in many forms. As stated in *Freeman,* 573 F.2d at 1246, 197 USPQ at 471:

> The manner in which a claim recites a mathematical algorithm may vary considerably. In some claims, a formula or equation may be expressed in traditional mathematical symbols so as to be immediately recognizable as a mathematical algorithm. * * *

Claims which include mathematical formulas or calculations expressed in mathematical symbols clearly include a mathematical algorithm. Mathematical algorithms in prose form may be expressed as literal translations of the mathematical algorithm (e.g., substituting the expression "division" or "taking the ratio" for a division sign) or may be expressed in words which indicate the mathematical algorithm.

It is not always possible to determine by inspection of the claim whether it indirectly recites a mathematical algorithm; in such instances the analysis "requires careful interpretation of each claim in the light of its supporting disclosure." *Johnson,* 589 F.2d at 1079, 200 USPQ at 208. * * *

2. Step 2—is the mathematical algorithm "applied in any manner to physical elements or process steps?"

The second test is to determine whether the mathematical algorithm is "applied in any manner to physical elements or process steps." The guideline for the analysis should be the CCPA's suggestion in *Abele* to view the claim without the mathematical algorithm to determine whether what remains is "otherwise statutory"; if it is, it does not become nonstatutory simply because it uses a mathematical algorithm. It is recognized that "[t]he line between a patentable 'process' and an unpatentable 'principle' is not always clear." *Flook,* 437 U.S. at 589, 198 USPQ at 197. There are no definitive "tests for determining whether a claim positively recites statutory subject matter." *Meyer,* 688 F.2d at 796 n. 4, 215 USPQ at 198 n. 4. Nevertheless, some useful guidelines may be synthesized out of the court decisions.

a. Post-solution activity

If the only limitation aside from the mathematical algorithm is insignificant or non-essential "post-solution activity," the claimed subject matter is nonstatutory. * * *

Insignificant post-solution activity by itself is insufficient to constitute a statutory process. In *Flook,* the final step of adjusting an alarm limit was not sufficient. * * *

The absence of post-solution activity or the fact that any post-solution activity may be trivial is only one factor to be considered. On one hand, as stated in *Walter,* 618 F.2d at 767–68, 205 USPQ at 407:

> if the end-product of a claimed invention is a *pure number,* as in *Benson* and *Flook,* the invention is nonstatutory regardless of any post-

solution activity which makes it available for use by a person or machine for other purposes.

On the other hand, as stated in *Abele,* 684 F.2d at 908 n. 9, 214 USPQ at 687 n. 9:

> "the fact that [the] equation is the final step is not determinative of the section 101 issue."

The particular order of the steps should not be determinative of the statutory subject matter inquiry.

b. Field of use limitations

A mathematical algorithm is not made statutory by "attempting to limit the use of the formula to a particular technological environment." *Diehr,* 450 U.S. at 191, 209 USPQ at 10. Thus, "field of use" or "end use" limitations in the claim preamble are insufficient to constitute a statutory process. This is consistent with the usual treatment of preambles as merely setting forth the environment. * * *

c. Data-gathering steps

If the only limitations in the claims in addition to the mathematical algorithm are data-gathering steps which "merely determine values for the variables used in the mathematical formulae used in making the calculations," such antecedent steps are insufficient to change a nonstatutory method of calculation into a statutory process. * * *

d. Transformation of something physical

In determining whether the claim recites a statutory process or a nonstatutory mathematical algorithm, it is useful to analyze whether there is transformation of something physical into a different form. One distinction is made between transformation of physical "signals" from one physical state to a different physical state, a statutory process in the electrical arts, and mere mathematical manipulation of "data" which, by itself, is not a statutory process. * * * It is manifest that the statutory nature of the subject matter does not depend on the labels "signals" or "data."

e. Structural limitations in process claims

Another issue is the effect of structural limitations in method claims. While structural limitations in method claims are not improper, they are usually not entitled to patentable weight unless they somehow affect or form an essential part of the process. * * *

III. COMPUTER PROGRAMS

A. "Computer programs" versus "computer processes"

A "process" or "algorithm" is a step-by-step procedure to arrive at a given result. In the patent area, a "computer process" or "computer algorithm" is a process, i.e., a series of steps, which is performed by a computer. A "[computer] program is a sequence of coded instructions for a digital computer." *Benson,* 409 U.S. at 65, 175 USPQ at 674. Computer programs are equivalently known as "software."

* * *

B. Statutory nature of computer processes

1. The Supreme Court has not ruled on the patentability of computer programs.

The Supreme Court has not ruled on whether computer processes are *per se* statutory or nonstatutory. The decisions in *Benson, Flook* and *Diehr* all dealt with claims viewed as mathematical algorithms. In *Benson* and *Diehr,* the claims contained mathematical algorithms implemented by a computer. In *Benson,* the Court held that the claims preempted the use of the mathematical algorithm, but did not hold that "any program servicing a computer" would be nonstatutory. In *Diehr,* the Court held that the claims otherwise defined a statutory process for curing rubber, and that the inclusion of a mathematical algorithm or computer program did not make claim nonstatutory. The claim in *Flook* did not involve a computer process.

* * *

2. The CCPA has held that computer processes are statutory unless they fall within a judicially determined exemption.

In *Pardo,* the most recent CCPA case on computer processes, the CCPA stated that, 684 F.2d at 916, 214 USPQ at 677:

> any process, machine, manufacture, or composition of matter constitutes statutory subject matter *unless* it falls within a judicially determined exception to section 101.

The major (and perhaps only) exception in the area of computer processes is the mathematical algorithm. Although not binding precedent on the Federal Circuit, the district court in *Paine, Webber, Jackson & Curtis, Inc. v. Merrill Lynch, Pierce, Fenner & Smith,* 564 F.Supp. 1358, 1367, 218 USPQ 212, 218 (D.Del.1983) stated:

> The CCPA [has] * * * held that a computer algorithm, as opposed to a mathematical algorithm, is patentable subject matter.

If a computer process claim does not contain a mathematical algorithm in the *Benson* sense, the second step of the *Freeman–Walter–Abele* test is not reached, and the claimed subject matter will usually be statutory.

The traditional approach by the CCPA to the PTO's rejection of computer processes as nonstatutory subject matter has been to apply the two-part test for mathematical algorithms and to find statutory subject matter if the claims do not recite a mathematical algorithm. * * *

If the computer process is found to contain a mathematical algorithm, it must then pass the second part of the *Freeman–Walter–Abele* test for statutory subject matter. *See, e.g., Sherwood; Maucorps; Gelnovatch.*

Arguably, other exceptions such as "methods of doing business" and "mental steps" may be raised if a claim is not a true computer process, but merely recites that an otherwise nonstatutory process is performed on a computer. * * *

* * *

IN RE GRAMS

United States Court of Appeals, Federal Circuit, 1989.
888 F.2d 835.

ARCHER, CIRCUIT JUDGE.

Applicants Ralph A. Grams and Dennis C. Lezotte (Grams) appeal from the decision of the Board of Patent Appeals and Interferences (Board), United States Patent and Trademark Office, Appeal No. 88–1391 (December 28, 1988), affirming the examiner's rejection of claims 1 and 3–16, which constitute all the claims remaining in Application S.N. 625,247, filed June 27, 1984. The claims were rejected under 35 U.S.C. § 101 as being directed to nonstatutory subject matter because they in essence claim either a mathematical algorithm or a method of doing business. We affirm.

BACKGROUND

The invention provides a method of testing a complex system to determine whether the system condition is normal or abnormal and, if it is abnormal, to determine the cause of the abnormality. As disclosed in the specification, the invention is applicable to any complex system, whether it be electrical, mechanical, chemical, biological, or combinations thereof. The system comprises a plurality of constituent subsystems or parts, some characteristic of which is represented by a set of correlated parameters susceptible of measurement and representative of the overall system. The disclosed invention involves considering the entire set of parameters, diagnosing the existence of an abnormality, and identifying which particular parameters of the set are responsible for the abnormality.

The claims limit the disclosed invention to the diagnosis of an individual. Claim 1, on which the other claims depend, reads:

> 1. A method of diagnosing an abnormal condition in an individual, the individual being characterized by a plurality of correlated parameters of a set of such parameters that is representative of the individual's condition, the parameters comprising data resulting from a plurality of clinical laboratory tests which measure the levels of chemical and biological constituents of the individaul [sic] and each parameter having a reference range of values, *the method comprising* [a] performing said plurality of clinical laboratory tests on the individual to measure the values of the set of parameters; [b] producing from the set of measured parameter values and the reference ranges of values a first quantity representative of the condition of the individual; [c] comparing the first quantity to a first predetermined value to determine

> whether the individual's condition is abnormal; [d] upon determining from said comparing that the individual's condition is abnormal, successively testing a plurality of different combinations of the constituents of the individual by eliminating parameters from the set to form subsets corresponding to said combinations, producing for each subset a second quantity, and comparing said second quantity with a second predetermined value to detect a non-significant deviation from a normal condition; and [e] identifying as a result of said testing a complementary subset of parameters corresponding to a combination of constituents responsible for the abnormal condition, said complementary subset comprising the parameters eliminated from the set so as to produce a subset having said non-significant deviation from a normal condition.

(Emphasis and bracketed letters added.) Thus, step [a] requires the performance of clinical laboratory tests on an individual to obtain data for the parameters (*e.g.*, sodium content). The remaining steps, [b]–[e], analyze that data to ascertain the existence and identity of an abnormality, and possible causes thereof. In that regard, steps [b]–[e] are in essence a mathematical algorithm, in that they represent "[a] procedure for solving a given type of mathematical problem." *Gottschalk v. Benson,* 409 U.S. 63, 65, 93 S.Ct. 253, 254, 34 L.Ed.2d 273 (1972).

Applicants do not dispute that claim 1 includes a mathematical algorithm. However, they contend that the mere recital of an algorithm does not automatically render a claim nonstatutory. They are correct in that regard, but the inclusion of a mathematical algorithm in a claim can render it nonstatutory if the claim in essence covers only the algorithm. The Board held that was the case here.

Issue

Whether the algorithm-containing claims at issue are drawn to statutory subject matter.

Opinion

Section 101 of Title 35 states:

> Whoever invents or discovers *any new and useful process,* machine, manufacture, or composition of matter, or *any* new and useful improvement thereof, may obtain a patent therefor, subject to the conditions and requirements of this title.

(Emphasis added.) Intuitively, one might conclude that the statute's "any * * * process" would include the diagnostic method claimed by applicants. Indeed, even without physical step [a] present in the claims, application of the algorithm in steps [b]–[e] seems to be a type of "process". The Supreme Court recognized as much in *Parker v. Flook,* 437 U.S. 584, 588–89, 98 S.Ct. 2522, 2524–25, 57 L.Ed.2d 451 (1978).

Flook makes clear, however, as did its forerunner, *Gottschalk v. Benson,* 409 U.S. 63, 93 S.Ct. 253, 34 L.Ed.2d 273 (1972), that even though the application of an algorithm to data is a "process" in the literal sense, it is not one that is contemplated by section 101, *i.e.*, it is "nonstatutory subject matter." Thus, mathematical algorithms join the list of non-patentable subject matter not within the scope of section 101, including methods of doing business, naturally occurring phenomenon, and laws of nature.

Construing section 101 as excluding mathematical algorithms seems somewhat at odds with the liberal view of that section expressed in a more recent Supreme Court opinion, *Diamond v. Chakrabarty,* 447 U.S. 303, 308–09, 314–16, 100 S.Ct. 2204, 2207–08, 2210–11, 65 L.Ed.2d 144 (1980). There, the Court decided that a living man-made micro-organism fell within the terms "manufacture" or "composition of matter" in section 101. In choosing such "expansive terms", stated the Court, "modified by the comprehensive 'any,' Congress plainly contemplated that the patent laws would be given wide scope." *Id.* The Court went so far as to note that Congress intended statutory subject matter to include " 'anything under the sun that is made by man.' " *Chakrabarty,* 447 U.S. at 309, 100 S.Ct. at 2207–08 (quoting S.Rep. No. 1979, 82d Cong., 2d Sess. 5 (1952); H.R.Rep. No. 1923, 82d Cong., 2d Sess. 6 (1952)), U.S.Code Cong. & Admin.News 1952, p. 2394.

Chakrabarty expressly rejects the argument that patentability in a new area, "micro-organisms[,] cannot qualify as patentable subject matter until Congress expressly authorizes such protection." *Id.* at 314–15, 100 S.Ct. at 2210–11. Although the Court distinguished *Parker v. Flook* in its opinion, *id.* at 315, 100 S.Ct. at 2210–11, the court's rejection of this argument seems to reflect a change from *Flook's* admonition that "we must proceed cautiously when we are asked to extend patent rights into areas wholly unforeseen by Congress." *Flook,* 437 U.S. at 596, 98 S.Ct. at 2528. *See also Gottschalk v. Benson,* 409 U.S. at 72, 93 S.Ct. at 257.

Another recent case, *Diamond v. Diehr,* 450 U.S. 175, 182, 101 S.Ct. 1048, 1054, 67 L.Ed.2d 155 (1981), repeats the "anything under the sun" statement of *Chakrabarty,* in the context of determining that the algorithm-containing claim at issue there was statutory subject matter under section 101. *Diehr* adds that in cases of statutory construction, which is involved here because the issue is whether applicants' claims fall within the statutory meaning of "process," "we begin with the language of the statute" and, unless otherwise defined, "words will be interpreted as taking their ordinary, contemporary, common meaning." *Id. Diehr* notes that the Court has "more than once cautioned that 'courts should not read into the patent laws limitations and conditions which a legislature has not expressed.' " *Id.* at 182, 101 S.Ct. at 1054 (quoting *Chakrabarty,* 447 U.S. at 308, 100 S.Ct. at 2207).

Notwithstanding those statements in *Diehr* and *Chakrabarty, Benson* remains the law. Indeed, *Benson* is cited in both *Diehr* and *Chakrabarty,* with no apparent attempt in either opinion to overrule or disapprove of it. Thus, "an algorithm, or mathematical formula * * * like a law of nature * * * cannot be the subject of a patent." *Diamond v. Diehr,* 450 U.S. at 186, 101 S.Ct. at 1056.

On the other hand, "the mere presence of a mathematical exercise, as a step or steps in a process involving nonmathematical steps, should not slam the door of the Patent and Trademark Office upon an applicant[.]" *In re Sarkar,* 588 F.2d 1330, 1333, 200 USPQ 132, 137 (CCPA 1978). Thus, if there are physical steps included in the claim in addition to the algorithm, the claim might be eligible for patent protection. As stated in *In re Walter,* 618 F.2d 758, 205 USPQ 397 (CCPA 1980):

> Once a mathematical algorithm has been found, the claim *as a whole* must be further analyzed. If it appears that the mathematical algorithm is implemented in a specific manner to define structural relationships between the physical elements of the claim (in apparatus claims) or to refine or limit claim steps (in process claims), the claim being otherwise statutory, the claim passes muster under § 101.

Id. at 767, 205 USPQ at 407 (emphasis in original; footnote omitted).

The *Walter* test, of deciding whether the algorithm "define[s] structural relationships" or "refine[s] or limit[s] claim steps" in an otherwise statutory claim, "was not intended to be the exclusive test for determining the presence of statutory subject matter." *In re Meyer,* 688 F.2d 789, 796, 215 USPQ 193, 198 (CCPA 1982). Thus, though satisfaction of the *Walter* test necessarily depicts statutory subject matter, failure to meet that test does not necessarily doom the claim. As stated in *In re Abele,* 684 F.2d 902, 907, 214 USPQ 682, 686 (CCPA 1982), "*Walter* should be read as requiring *no more than* that the algorithm be 'applied in any manner to physical elements or process steps[.]' " (Emphasis added.) * * *

* * *

Hence, the analysis requires careful interpretation of each claim in light of its supporting disclosure.

Though that analysis can be difficult, it is facilitated somewhat if, as here, the only physical step involves merely gathering data for the algorithm. * * *

* * *

Whether section 101 precludes patentability in every case where the physical step of obtaining data for the algorithm is the only other significant element in mathematical algorithm-containing claims is a question we need not answer. Analysis in that area depends on the claims as a whole and the circumstances of each case. Rather, we address only the claims and other circumstances involved here.

The sole physical process step in Grams' claim 1 is step [a], *i.e.,* performing clinical tests on individuals to obtain data. The specification does not bulge with disclosure on those tests. To the contrary, it focuses on the algorithm itself, although it briefly refers to, without describing, the clinical tests that provide data. Thus, it states: "The [computer] program was written to analyze the results of up to eighteen clinical laboratory tests produced by a standard chemical analyzer that measures the levels of the chemical biological components listed. * * * " The specification also states that "[t]he invention is applicable to any complex system, whether it be electrical, mechanical, chemical or biological, or combinations thereof." From the specification and the claim, it is clear to us that applicants are, in essence, claiming the mathematical algorithm, which they cannot do under *Gottschalk v. Benson.* The presence of a physical step in the claim to derive data for the algorithm will not render the claim statutory.

Applicants argue that *In re Abele,* 684 F.2d 902, 214 USPQ 682, warrants a reversal. We disagree.

Allowed claim 6 in *Abele* required operation of an algorithm on x-ray attenuation data, with a subsequent display. The data were available for the algorithm only after the production and detection steps, *i.e.,* after an x-ray beam was passed through an object using a CAT scanner, and detected upon exit. The court concluded that in the absence of the algorithm, "the production, detection, and display steps would still be present and would result in a conventional CAT-scan process." 684 F.2d at 908, 214 USPQ at 687. Thus, the production and detection steps were not viewed as mere antecedent steps to obtain values to solve the algorithm; instead "[w]e are faced simply with an improved CAT-scan[.]" 684 F.2d at 909, 214 USPQ at 688. "The improvement in either case resides in the application of a mathematical formula within the context of a process which encompasses significantly more than the algorithm alone." *Id.*

In *Abele,* therefore, the algorithm served to improve the CAT-scan process. As such, the algorithm satisfied the *Walter* guideline of "refining a process step in a process that is otherwise statutory," and hence, it presented statutory subject matter. In this case, because algorithm steps [b]–[e] do not operate to change any aspect of the physical process of step [a], the claim does not satisfy the *Walter* guideline. Though this by itself is not dispositive (see discussion of *Walter, supra*), patentability here is precluded by the fact that physical step [a] merely provides data for the algorithm.

* * *

Thus, claim 1 is unpatentable. Claims 3–15 were not argued separately from claim 1; hence they fall with our treatment of that claim. Claim 16, which requires that the method be performed with a programmed computer, is argued separately, but applicants have not persuaded us that performing the method of claim 1 with a computer requires a different result.

Because we affirm the Board's holding that the applicants' claims are unpatentable under section 101 as being drawn to a nonstatutory mathematical algorithm, we need not address the issue of whether they are also unpatentable as a method of doing business.

Affirmed.

IN RE IWAHASHI

United States Court of Appeals, Federal Circuit, 1989.
888 F.2d 1370.

RICH, CIRCUIT JUDGE.

This appeal is from the decision of the United States Patent and Trademark Office (PTO) Board of Patent Appeals and Interferences (Board), dated May 24, 1988, adhered to on reconsideration, affirming the examiner's final rejection of the single claim of applicants' patent application serial No. 454,022, filed December 28, 1982, entitled "Auto–Correlation Circuit for Use in Pattern Recognition." The sole ground of rejection is that the subject matter claimed is nonstatutory under 35 U.S.C. § 101 because it is merely a mathematical algorithm. We reverse.

The real party in interest, according to appellants' brief, is Sharp Kabishiki Kaisha (Sharp Corporation).

The opening sentence of the specification states: "This invention relates to an auto-correlation unit for use in pattern recognition to obtain auto-correlation coefficients as for stored signal samples." The embodiment more particularly discussed as a species of pattern recognition is voice recognition. The prior art calculation of auto-correlation coefficients is described as being based on a calculation formula involving a multiplication step. The specification states the disadvantage to be as follows:

> Those state-of-the-art units for calculation of the auto-correlation coefficients have the disadvantage of requiring expensive multipliers and also complicated circuitry. As a result the auto-correlation unit circuitry within the entire pattern recognition apparatus is proportionately large and auto-correlation calculation demands a greater amount of time during recognition.
>
> * * *
>
> The principal object of this invention is to provide an auto-correlation unit for pattern recognition which evaluates auto-correlation coefficients by means of a simple circuitry without the need for an expensive multiplier as well as eliminating the above discussed disadvantages.

Underlying the auto-correlation unit claimed, is a plethora of mathematical demonstration by which the applicants purport to show that the approximated value of the desired coefficient can be obtained *without multipliers* by obtaining the *square* of the sum of two of the factors in the equation and calculating the auto-correlation coefficient therefrom according to a stated formula. The specification concludes:

> As explained in the foregoing, this invention offers a highly cost effective auto-correlation unit for pattern recognition with simple circuitry without the need to use an expensive multiplier, but which

has comparatively high accuracy and can, moreover, calculate autocorrelation coefficients at high speed.

Fig. 1 of the application drawings is described as "a block diagram schematically showing an embodiment of this invention" and appears as follows:

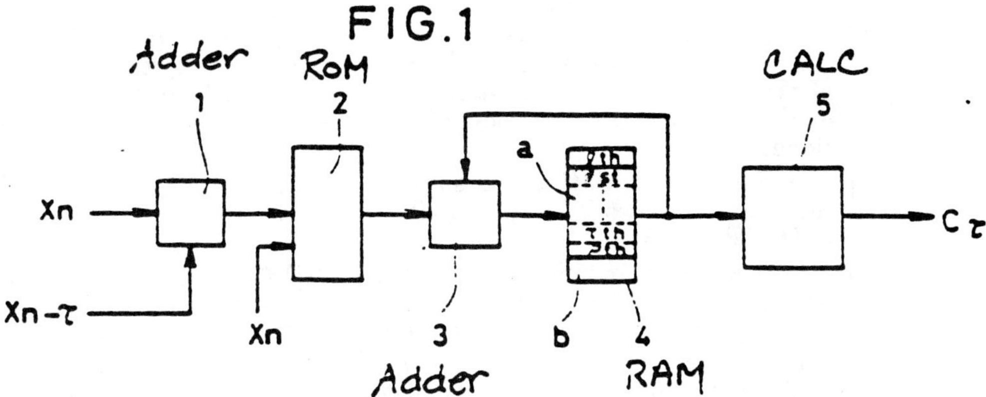

Fig. 2 is described as "a block diagram showing in more detail the embodiment of this invention" and appears as follows: * * *

We shall not attempt a description of the electronic circuitry shown by these drawings beyond explaining, for the better understanding of the claim, that the units designated "ROM" and "RAM" are, respectively, a read only memory and a random access memory, terms well understood by those skilled in the art. * * * In this case, the function of the ROM, 2 or 15, which is a permanent information storage device, is to deliver as output the *square* of a number fed to it as input. It is the electronic equivalent of a table in which one can look up the square of numbers over a desired range.

We next reproduce the claim on appeal and do so by presenting a copy of the claim as it has been presented in the Solicitor's brief, to which we have added the letters in brackets designating at [a] the preamble or introductory clause and at [b] through [h] the several means-plus-function and other elements of the combination of elements recited. Under the heading "Drawings" (the Solicitor's heading was "Fig. 1") we have copied verbatim the Solicitor's designations. Element [d], it will be noted, is not in means-plus-function form but specifies a "read only memory" or ROM, as the Solicitor says. Element [f] is an anomolous clause seemingly intended to indicate what data are stored in the ROM. It is not clear that a *means* for storing anything in the ROM is part of the disclosed "unit" since the application indicates that the squared values are "previously memorized" in the ROM. However that has nothing to do with the sole question before us which is whether the claim as a whole is, in the words of the Solicitor, "directed to nonstatutory subject matter," so we shall not comment further on element [f].

Claim	Drawings
[a] An auto-correlation unit for providing auto-correlation coefficients for use as feature parameters in pattern recognition for N pieces of sampled input values X_n (n = 0 to N − 1), said unit comprising:	
[b] means for extracting N pieces of sample input values X_n from a series of sample values in an input pattern expressed with an accuracy of optional multi-bits;	Not shown in Fig. 1; analog to digital converter 11 in Fig. 2.
[c] means for calculating the sum of the sample values X_n and $X_n - Z$ (t = O − P, P<N);	Adder 1.
[d] a read only memory associated with said means for calculating;	ROM 2.
[e] means for feeding to said read only memory the sum of the sampled input values as an address signal;	Signal path connecting adder 1 to ROM 2.
[f] means for storing in said read only memory the squared value of each sum, $(X_n + X_n - Z)^2$;	Internal structure of ROM 2 after being programmed to store squared values.
[g] means for fetching and outputting the squared values of each such sum of the sample input values from said read only memory when said memory is addressed by the sum of the sample input values; and	Read pulse (not shown) which is applied to ROM 2; in Fig. 2, signal f_1 or f_2, applied to ROM 15.
[h] means responsive to the output $(X_n + X_n - Z)^2$ of said read only memory for providing an auto-correlation coefficient for use as a feature parameter according to the following formula: $$\frac{\sum_{n=o}^{N-1} (X_n + X_n - Z)^2}{2 \cdot \sum_{n=o}^{N-1} X_n^2} - 1$$	Calculating circuit 5.

This is one more in the line of cases stemming from the Supreme Court decision in *Gottschalk v. Benson,* 409 U.S. 63, 93 S.Ct. 253, 34 L.Ed.2d 273 (1972), decided by our predecessor, the United States Court of Customs and Patent Appeals. * * *

Out of these cases came the *Freeman–Walter* test to determine whether a claim defines nonstatutory subject matter. It was stated in *Freeman* as follows:

> Determination of whether a claim preempts nonstatutory subject matter as a whole, in the light of *Benson,* requires a two-step analysis.

> First, it must be determined whether the claim directly or indirectly recites an "algorithm" in the *Benson* sense of that term, for a claim which fails even to recite an algorithm clearly cannot wholly preempt an algorithm. Second, the claim must be further analyzed to ascertain whether in its entirety it wholly preempts that algorithm.

573 F.2d at 1245, 197 USPQ at 471. The opinion next discusses the meaning of "algorithm" quoting from *Chatfield* footnote 5:

> Over-concentration on the word "algorithm" alone, for example, may mislead. The Supreme Court carefully supplied a definition of the particular algorithm before it [in *Benson*], i.e., "[a] procedure for solving a given type of *mathematical* problem." The broader definition of algorithm is "a step-by-step procedure for solving a problem or accomplishing some end." *Webster's New Collegiate Dictionary (1976).*
>
> * * * It would be unnecessarily detrimental to our patent system to deny inventors patent protection on the *sole* ground that their contribution could be broadly termed an "algorithm". [Emphasis of "sole" original, otherwise ours.]

In footnote 8 of the *Freeman* opinion the court further said:

> The preferred definition of "algorithm" in the computer art is: "A fixed step-by-step procedure for accomplishing a given result; usually a simplified procedure for solving a complex problem, also a full statement of a finite number of steps." C. Sippl & C. Sippl, Computer Dictionary and Handbook (1972).

Id. at 1246 n. 8, 197 USPQ at 471 n. 8. Appellants state that the apparatus claimed "may properly be characterized as a computer."

We note these discussions of the meaning of "algorithm" to take the mystery out of the term and we point out once again that every step-by-step process, be it electronic or chemical or mechanical, involves an algorithm in the broad sense of the term. Since § 101 expressly includes processes as a category of inventions which may be patented and § 100(b) further defines the word "process" as meaning "process, art or method, and includes a new use of a known process, machine, manufacture, composition of matter, or material," it follows that it is no ground for holding a claim is directed to nonstatutory subject matter to say it includes or is directed to an algorithm. This is why the proscription against patenting has been limited to *mathematical* algorithms and abstract *mathematical* formulae which, like the laws of nature, are not patentable subject matter.

The above-listed line of CCPA cases held some claims statutory and other claims nonstatutory, depending entirely on what they said. We have to do the same here. Appellants cautiously admit that their claim "at least indirectly, recites an algorithm in some manner," and thus meets the first part of the *Freeman–Walter* test, but argue strenuously and convincingly that it does not meet the second part of the test, relying, inter alia, on the following statement in *Walter* (footnote omitted):

> Once a mathematical algorithm has been found, the claim *as a whole* must be further analyzed. If it appears that the mathematical algorithm is implemented in a specific manner to define structural relationships between the physical elements of the claim (in apparatus claims) or to refine or limit claim steps (in process claims), the claim being otherwise statutory, the claim passes muster under § 101.

618 F.2d at 767, 205 USPQ at 407 (footnote omitted). Though the claim starts out by saying in clause [a] that it is a "unit", appellants prefer to characterize what they claim as apparatus with specific structural limitations. By the Solicitor's own analysis of the claim in the column labeled "Drawings", supra, we are constrained to agree. Appellants emphasize that they specify a ROM in clause [d] to which is fed an input from an adder specified in clause [c]. The Solicitor states that [c] and [d] are connected together by a signal path. Next are means in the form of disclosed electronic circuitry which take from the ROM its output in the form of squares of numbers supplied as ROM input and feed them to a calculating circuit [h]. The claim as a whole certainly defines apparatus in the form of a combination of interrelated means and we cannot discern any logical reason why it should not be deemed statutory subject matter as either a machine or a manufacture as specified in § 101. The fact that the apparatus operates according to an algorithm does not make it nonstatutory. We therefore hold that the claim is directed to statutory subject matter.

* * *

The decision of the board is *reversed.*

* * *

NOTICE INTERPRETING IN RE IWAHASHI (FED.CIR.1989)

1112 Official Gazette of the United States Patent and Trademark Office 16 (March 13, 1990).

The Patent and Trademark Office's (PTO's) policy on the patentability of claims reciting mathematical algorithms and computer programs, published at 1106 Off.Gaz.Pat.Office 5–12 (Sept. 5, 1989), is unaffected by *In re Iwahashi,* 888 F.2d 1370, 12 USPQ2d 1980 (Fed.Cir. 1989). The following comments are intended as the PTO's interpretation of *Iwahashi.*

Iwahashi reversed a rejection of appellants' apparatus claim 1 (the sole claim) under 35 U.S.C. § 101. The rejection maintained that claim 1 was directed to nonstatutory subject matter in the form of a mathematical algorithm. Appellants developed an approximation to the conventional equation for auto-correlation coefficients for use in pattern recognition which uses a term which is the square of the sum of two variables, instead of the product of the two variables. Appellants' claim to an autocorrelation unit is in "means-plus-function" format except for a recited "read only memory" ("ROM") for implementing the squaring term. PTO argued that the term "read only memory" as used in this claim is as broad as a means-plus-function recitation with the result that the claim is effectively entirely in means-plus-function format and indistinguishable for § 101 purposes from a method claim; it was argued that such a corresponding method claim would be nonstatutory. PTO also argued that appellants' apparatus claim is nonstatutory when directly analyzed according to the two-part *Freeman–Walter* test because (1) it recites a mathematical algorithm and (2) the algorithm does not "define" a structural relationship between physical elements and is not "applied" in any manner to physical elements.

The Federal Circuit determined that a read only memory is a "term[ ] well understood by those skilled in the art," 888 F.2d at 1372, 12 USPQ2d at 1909, and that the claimed read only memory element "is not in means-plus-function form," *id.* at 1373, 12 USPQ2d at 1909, but "is a specific piece of apparatus," *id.* at 1375, 12 USPQ2d at 1912. The Court states that appellants' apparatus claim does not meet the second part of the *Freeman–Walter* test, detailing the relationship between the ROM and the other means in the claim. Therefore, the Court concluded, *id.* at 1375, 12 USPQ2d at 1911:

> The claim as a whole certainly defines apparatus in the form of a combination of interrelated means and we cannot discern any logical reason why it should not be deemed statutory subject matter as either a machine or a manufacture as specified in § 101. The fact that the apparatus operates according to an algorithm does not make it nonstatutory. * * * We therefore hold that the claim is directed to statutory subject matter.

Because the Court determined a ROM to be a specific piece of apparatus for implementing a table look-up function, and not as broad as a means-plus-function recitation, appellants carried their burden of demonstrating that the claim is "truly drawn to specific apparatus distinct from other apparatus capable of performing the identical functions," *Walter,* 618 F.2d at 768, 205 USPQ at 408; as a matter of claim interpretation, the claim cannot be treated as equivalent to a method. The *Walter* test for whether an apparatus claim is equivalent to a method claim is the same as applying the *Freeman–Walter* test to an apparatus claim. *See In re Maucorps,* 609 F.2d 481, 486, 203 USPQ 812, 816 (CCPA 1979) (application of second part of two-part *Freeman* test to apparatus claim in "means for" format considers whether the "claimed invention as a whole comprises each and every means for carrying out a [mathematical algorithm]").

Once it is determined that the claim is truly drawn to specific apparatus, it necessarily follows that the apparatus is statutory subject matter under § 101. True apparatus does not invoke the mathematical algorithm exception because the mathematical algorithm remains free for use by anyone not employing the specific apparatus, i.e., there is no preemption, in whole or in part, of the mathematical algorithm itself. * * *

The Court's holding that the claim defines apparatus because of ROM is a specific piece of apparatus for implementing the mathematical algorithm is consistent with precedent and PTO policy as set forth at 1106 Off.Gaz.Pat.Office 5–12. Every case, however, must be determined on its facts and, to be consistent with previous decisions, *Iwahashi* does not "hold that the mere presence of apparatus language in a claim will, of itself, save that claim from rejection as nonstatutory," *id.* at 1247 n. 11, 197 USPQ at 472 n. 11. Under *Walter,* the inquiry with every apparatus claim should be whether the apparatus encompasses any and every means for performing the recited functions and, if this appears to be the case, the burden should be placed on the applicant to show that it does not.

The Court's dicta in footnote 1 (the sole footnote) suggests that § 112 ¶ 6 may require the PTO to construe means-plus-function limitation to the apparatus disclosed in the application and equivalents thereof. Under this suggestion, even a claim which is *entirely* in means-plus-function format could not be treated as indistinguishable from a corresponding method claim for § 101 purposes. Such a result would be directly contrary to precedent, including *Freeman, Walter, Abele* and *Meyer.* In the opinion of the PTO, means-plus-function limitations should be not treated differently for § 101 purposes than for § 102 and § 103 purposes for rejections over prior art. Indeed, during prosecution claims should be given their broadest reasonable interpretation. * * *

Feb. 15, 1990

JAMES E. DENNY
Acting Assistant Commissioner
for Patents

F. INFRINGEMENT BY EQUIVALENTS OF CLAIM ELEMENTS

The decisions studied so far make it clear that programmed computer and computer program inventions can be claimed either as methods or as apparatuses. Under 35 U.S.C.A. § 112, "An element in a claim for a combination may be expressed as a means or step for performing a specified function without the recital of structure, material, or acts in support thereof, and such claims shall be construed to cover the corresponding structure, material, or acts described in the specification and equivalents thereof." Accordingly, patent claims directed to apparatus frequently contain a series of "means for" steps. As an example, review "apparatus" claim 9 of the Atkinson patent and compare it to "method" claim 11. Since the "means for" language utilized in claim 9 is "construed to cover the corresponding structure ... described ... and equivalents thereof" under § 112, the question arises as to how widely a court should read a claim as covering substituted equivalents for the structure disclosed in the patent. The patent holder will argue for a broad interpretation of the claim; the alleged infringer will argue that what it has substituted in some way is not "equivalent" to the "structure ... described" in the claims.

The following two cases each address this question. *Pennwalt* holds that an equivalent structure must be found for each "means for" element of a claim, and it is improper to lump together several "means for" elements which collectively, but not individually, are equivalent to the infringing structural elements. Note that the practical effect of *Pennwalt* is to prevent a software implementation of an invention from infringing a hardware patent even though the "invention," broadly defined, appears to be present in both. As you read *Pennwalt,* think how the claims might have been drafted differently to cover both embodiments of the invention. The "doctrine of equivalents" discussed in this case provides a way in which courts can stretch any claim language to cover more infringers than the literal claim language might otherwise warrant.

The Texas Instruments case, which follows *Pennwalt,* sets limits on how far one may go in substituting "equivalents" for the structures disclosed in a patent. This case is also of interest because the "infringement" action was instituted by Texas Instruments before the International Trade Commission, an administrative agency, rather than before a Federal District Court. The standard of review adopted by the Court of Appeals for the Federal Circuit in this case is the weaker "substantial evidence" standard applicable to most court reviews of agency action, where considerable deference is given to agency findings of fact if supported by "substantial evidence" on the record taken as a whole. Had Texas Instruments prevailed, then their patent would thereafter have been enforced by the Customs Service in "In rem" proceedings without the need for Texas Instruments to be a party to the Customs examination and impoundment of the infringing goods.

While not discussed in this case, there also exists a "reverse doctrine of equivalents" that permits a court to find no infringement for reasons of fairness even when the claim language applies literally to an infringing apparatus or method.

PENNWALT CORP. v. DURAND–WAYLAND, INC.

United States Court of Appeals, Federal Circuit, 1987.
833 F.2d 931; *cert. denied,* 485 U.S. 961, 108 S.Ct. 1226, 99 L.Ed.2d 426 (1988), *cert. denied,* 485 U.S. 1009, 108 S.Ct. 1474, 99 L.Ed.2d 703 (1988).

BISSELL, CIRCUIT JUDGE.

This appeal and cross-appeal are from a judgment of the United States District Court for the Northern District of Georgia, 225 USPQ 558 (N.D.Ga.1984). The district court found that Durand–Wayland's accused devices do not infringe any claim, literally or under the doctrine of equivalents. Unable to view that finding as clearly erroneous under Fed.R.Civ.P. 52(a), we affirm the judgment of noninfringement and vacate, as moot, that part of the judgment concerning the validity of Pennwalt's patent.

Background

Pennwalt sued Durand–Wayland for infringing claims 1, 2, 10 and 18 (claims-at-issue) of its U.S. Patent No. 4,106,628 (the '628 patent) on an invention of Aaron J. Warkentin and George A. Mills, entitled "Sorter for Fruit and the Like." Following a nonjury trial on the issues of patent infringement and validity, the district court, on March 22, 1984, issued an opinion concluding that (1) the claims-at-issue were not anticipated by the prior art, (2) the '628 patent had not run afoul of the "on sale" bar of 35 U.S.C. § 102(b) (1982), and (3) the accused devices did not infringe any of the claims-at-issue, either literally or under the doctrine of equivalents. In an unpublished supplemental order of April 26, 1984, the district court concluded as a matter of law that the claims-at-issue would not have been obvious in light of the prior art.

Pennwalt appeals from the district court's holding of noninfringement, both literally and under the doctrine of equivalents, and its award of costs against Pennwalt. Durand–Wayland appeals from the district court's validity holdings and its denial of Durand–Wayland's request for recovery of its attorney fees.

Issue

Our disposition of this appeal requires resolution of the single question of whether the district court's finding of no infringement was clearly erroneous.

Opinion

The '628 patent claims a sorter. The principal object of the invention is to provide a rapid means for sorting items, such as fruit, by color, weight, or a combination of these two characteristics. The sorter recited in claims 1 and 2 conveys items along a track having an electronic-weighing device that produces an electrical signal proportional to the weight of the item, along with signal comparison means, clock means, position indicating means, and discharge means, each of which performs specified functions. The specification describes the details of a "hard-wired" network consisting of discrete electrical components which perform each step of the claims, e.g., by comparing the signals from the weighing device to reference signals and sending an appropriate signal at the proper time to discharge the item into the container corresponding to its weight. The combined sorter of claims 10 and 18 is a multifunctional apparatus whereby the item is conveyed across the weighing device and also carried past an optical scanner that produces an electrical signal proportional to the color of the item. The signals from the weighing device and color sensor are combined and an appropriate signal is sent at the proper time to discharge the item into the container corresponding to its color and weight.

Durand–Wayland manufactures and sells two different types of sorting machines. The first accused device, the "Microsizer," sorts by weight only and employs software labeled either Version 2 or Version

5. The second accused device employs software labeled Version 6 and sorts by both color and weight through the use of the "Microsizer" in conjunction with a color detection apparatus called a "Microsorter."

A more complete description of the claimed invention and of the accused devices is set forth in the district court's opinion. *Pennwalt,* 225 USPQ at 559–60. The claims-at-issue are set forth in the district court's opinion. *Id.* at 564–65.

I.

Literal Infringement

Pennwalt asserts on appeal that all limitations set forth in claims 1 and 2 and some limitations set forth in claims 10 and 18 can be read literally on the accused devices. Pennwalt contends that the district court erred in interpreting the claims by going beyond the means-plus-function language of a claim limitation and comparing the structure in the accused devices with the *structure* disclosed in the specification. Such comparison allegedly resulted in the court's reading nonexistent structural limitations into the claims. * * *

* * *

Thus, section 112, paragraph 6, rules out the possibility that any and every means which performs the function specified in the claim *literally* satisfies that limitation. While encompassing equivalents of those disclosed in the specification, the provision, nevertheless, acts as a restriction on the literal satisfaction of a claim limitation. If the required function is not performed *exactly* in the accused device, it must be borne in mind that section 112, paragraph 6, equivalency is not involved. Section 112, paragraph 6, plays no role in determining whether an equivalent function is performed by the accused device under the doctrine of equivalents.

Thus, it was not legal error (as Pennwalt asserts) for the district court to have made a comparison between Durand–Wayland's structure and the structure disclosed in the specification for performing a particular function. The statute means exactly what it says: To determine whether a claim limitation is met literally, where expressed as a means for performing a stated function, the court must compare the accused structure *with the disclosed structure,* and must find equivalent *structure* as well as *identity* of claimed *function* for that structure.

Where the issue is raised, it is part of the ultimate burden of proof of the patent owner to establish, with respect to a claim limitation in means-plus-function form, that the structure in the accused device which performs that function is the same as or an equivalent of the structure disclosed in the specification. In essence, Pennwalt erroneously argues that, if an accused structure performs the function required by the claim, it is per se structurally equivalent. That view entirely eliminates the section 112, paragraph 6, restriction and has been rejected in the above-cited precedent of this court.

We need not, and do not, determine whether the district court correctly found no equivalency in structure because the district court also found that the accused devices, in any event, did not perform the same functions specified in the claim. For example, the district court found that the accused devices had no position indicating means which tracked the location of the item being sorted. That finding negates the possibility of finding literal infringement.

II.

Infringement under the Doctrine of Equivalents

Under the doctrine of equivalents, infringement *may* be found (but not necessarily [1]) if an accused device performs substantially the same overall function or work, in substantially the same way, to obtain substantially the same overall result as the claimed invention. That formulation, however, does not mean one can ignore claim limitations. * * *

* * *

Pennwalt argues that the "accused machines simply do in a computer what the patent *illustrates* doing with hard-wired circuitry," and asserts that "this alone is insufficient to escape infringement," citing *Decca Ltd. v. United States,* 544 F.2d 1070, 1080–81, 210 Ct.Cl. 546, 563–64, 191 USPQ 439, 447 (1976). If Pennwalt was correct that the accused devices differ only in substituting a computer for hard-wired circuitry, it might have a stronger position for arguing that the accused devices infringe the claims. The claim limitations, however, require the performance of certain specified functions. Theoretically, a microprocessor could be programmed to perform those functions. However, the district court found that the microprocessor in the accused devices was not so programmed.

After a full trial, the district court made findings that certain functions of the claimed inventions were "missing" from the accused devices and those which were performed were "substantially different." *Pennwalt,* 225 USPQ at 572. The district court observed that "because the 'Microsizer' uses different elements and different operations (on the elements it does use) than the elements and operations disclosed in the patent-in-suit to achieve the desired results, infringement can only be found if the different elements and operations are the legal equivalents of those disclosed in the patent-in-suit." *Id.* It is clear from this that the district court correctly relied on an element-by-element comparison to conclude that there was no infringement under the doctrine of equivalents, because the accused devices did not perform substantially the same functions as the Pennwalt invention. * * *

* * *

1. The doctrine of equivalents is limited in that the doctrine will not extend (1) to cover an accused device in the prior art, and (2) to allow the patentee to recapture through equivalence certain coverage given up during prosecution.

Pennwalt argues that the district court erred as a matter of law in interpreting the claims which led to these findings. Pennwalt asserts that the district court looked to the specification and compared the accused devices with the preferred embodiment. As indicated, under the section 112, paragraph 6, analysis, such comparison was entirely correct, but it is readily apparent that the court did not so limit its infringement analysis. The court also looked for equivalent *functions.*

It is not the province of this court to determine *de novo* what is the preponderance of the evidence underlying the ultimate finding of no infringement or the subsidiary facts supporting that finding. Indeed, Fed.R.Civ.P. 52(a) prohibits our undertaking the role of the fact finder, which is the domain of the trial court. * * *

Here, if the district court was not clearly erroneous in finding that even a single function required by a claim or an equivalent function is not performed by the Durand–Wayland sorters, the court's finding of no infringement must be upheld.

Pennwalt asks us to reweigh the testimony, urging that the testimony of the court-appointed expert, Dr. Vacroux, is so strongly supportive of the contrary finding of infringement under the doctrine of equivalents that the district court's finding of no infringement cannot stand. Pennwalt, however, misconstrues the effect of Dr. Vacroux's testimony. Dr. Vacroux was a technical, not a legal, expert. He was not expected to, and did not, analyze infringement under a legal standard. He was not concerned, for example, with the scope of equivalents to which the claims were entitled in view of the prosecution history. In this light, the reports and testimony of Dr. Vacroux fully support the district court's finding of no infringement, rather than Pennwalt's position.

Pennwalt relies on the conclusory statement in Dr. Vacroux's initial written report in which he characterized the accused devices as "functionally equivalent" to the "invention." However, Dr. Vacroux also stated therein that "the new designs could be totally equivalent to those they replaced, *although the components and methods* used *differed significantly.*" (Emphasis added.) Further, when Dr. Vacroux was called to testify, and, in response to detailed questioning by the court, Dr. Vacroux testified that the accused devices performed "*some*" of the same type of operations but "in a different way" from the claimed invention. Specifically, Dr. Vacroux answered a question by the court as follows:

> Dr. Vacroux: They [the accused and claimed devices] are not equivalent, but functionally the internal operations I would say internally are functionally equivalent because they perform *some of the same type of operations.* They compare, they shift, they add so we do have the same type of functions internally *but done in a different way.* [Emphasis added.]

Dr. Vacroux's statement that the accused devices performed only "some of the same type of operations" supports the court's finding that some were not. It does not conflict with any of his other testimony or with his written report. Thus, on the issue of whether the accused devices performed *each* of the functional limitations of the claim or its equivalent and, thus, operated in substantially the same way, the district court followed its expert precisely. The court cannot be faulted for finding no infringement where the expert's testimony as to facts negates a finding of equivalency under the correct legal standard.

With respect to the scope of equivalent functions, the court correctly limited the claims, based upon review of the prosecution history, stating that "the claims of the patent should be read in light of the careful phraseology [of functions] chosen by the inventors" because "the machine disclosed in the patent-in-suit was carefully described so that it did not read on the prior art." *Pennwalt,* 225 USPQ at 570. As the court correctly noted, the invention was not a pioneer, but an improvement in a crowded art. The claims are "broad" with respect to what type of product can be sorted, i.e., "items" and, thus, sorters of all types of "items" fall within the relevant prior art. The claims are *narrow,* however, with respect to how the claimed sorter operates. Originally, the claims contained no position indicating means element with its associated functional limitations. The addition of that element was crucial to patentability. A device that does not satisfy this limitation at least equivalently does not function in substantially the same way as the claimed invention.

The trial court found that the accused devices do not have any position indicating means to determine *positions* of the items to be sorted. Specifically with respect to claims 10 and 18, the court correctly held that "the microprocessor stores weight and color data, not the positions of the items to be sorted." *Pennwalt,* 225 USPQ at 569. Since each of the claims-at-issue requires a position indicating means and the same analysis applies to each, we set forth only the relevant language of claim 10:

first position indicating means responsive to a signal from said clock means and said signal from said second comparison means for continuously indicating the position of an item to be sorted while the item is in transit between said optical detection means and said electronic weighing means,

second position indicating means responsive to the signal from said clock means, the signal from said first comparison means and said first position indicating means for generating a signal continuously indicative of the position of an item to be sorted after said item has been weighed.

The testimony of Dr. Alford, Durand–Wayland's expert, was that the accused machine had no component which satisfied either of the above limitations defining position indicating means, and Pennwalt has admitted that the accused machines do not sort by keeping track of the physical location of an item in transit, continuously or otherwise, as required by each of these limitations.

Pennwalt argues that there is a way to find out where an item is physically located on the track in the accused machine. Its witness, Dr. Moore, testified "*you could find* the location of a particular fruit as it moves from the scale to the drop by counting the distance from the stored value for that fruit back to the place the pointer is indicating at the start of the queue." (Emphasis added.) Dr. Alford, Durand–Wayland's expert, admitted this was *possible.* Thus, Pennwalt asserts that the accused devices have "position indicating means."

One need not explain the technology to understand the inadequacy of Dr. Moore's testimony. As Dr. Moore himself indicates, the accused machine simply *does not do* what he explains "could" be done. It is admitted that the physical tracking of fruit is not part of the way in which the Durand–Wayland sorter works, in contrast to the claimed sorter which requires some means for "continuously indicating the position of an item to be sorted." While a microprocessor theoretically could be programmed to perform that function, the evidence led the court to a finding that the Durand–Wayland machines performed a *substantially different* function from that which each of the claims requires.

With respect to the other limitations of claim 10, Pennwalt admits that the asserted "position indicating means" of Durand–Wayland does not meet the limitation that the means must be "responsive to * * * said signal from said second comparison means" because no comparison is made on the Durand–Wayland machine before the discharge point. However, Pennwalt contends that Durand–Wayland "has merely changed the position of an operable element, but the operation and results achieved are the same as those claimed." Pennwalt's analysis is flawed in significant respects.

First, the claim requires that the "position indicating means" must be responsive to certain specified signals. Thus, finding some combination of components in the accused device that might also be *labeled* a "position indicating means" is a meaningless exercise when such combination is not responsive to the specified signal.

* * *

Second, the district court correctly rejected Pennwalt's assertion that the memory component of the Durand–Wayland sorter which stores information as to weight and color of an item performed substantially the same functions as claimed for the position indicating means. The district court found that a memory function is not the same or substantially the same as the function of "continuously indicating" where an item is physically located in a sorter. On this point the record is indisputable that before the words "continuously indicating" were added as an additional limitation, the claim was unpatentable in view of *prior art* which, like the accused machines, stores the information with respect to sorting criteria in memories, but did not "continuously" track the location. *See, e.g.,* U.S. Patent No. 3,289,832 issued to Ramsey.

Thus, the facts here do not involve later-developed computer technology which should be deemed within the scope of the claims to avoid the pirating of an invention. On the contrary, the inventors could not obtain a patent with claims in which the functions were described more broadly. Having secured claims only by including very specific *functional* limitations, Pennwalt now seeks to avoid those very limitations under the doctrine of equivalents. This it cannot do. Simply put, the memory components of the Durand–Wayland sorter were not programmed to perform the same or an equivalent function of physically tracking the items to be sorted from the scanner to the scale or from the scale to its appropriate discharge point as required by the claims.[2]

Contrary to Pennwalt's arguments, the district court did not disregard the need to consider a range of equivalent *functions* under the doctrine of equivalents. Rather, upon evaluation of the evidence, the court concluded, as a fact, that no component in the Durand–Wayland devices performed a function within the permissible range of equivalents for the function of the first position indicating means. That function is required by all of the claims-at-issue. No means in the accused devices performs that function and thus there could be no literal infringement. No means with an equivalent function was substituted in the accused devices and thus there can be no infringement under the doctrine of equivalents. The district court's finding of no infringement is not clearly erroneous.

* * *

Conclusion

We affirm the judgment based on the finding of no infringement, the award of costs, and the denial of attorney fees to Durand–Wayland. There being no indication that Durand–Wayland's cross-appeal on validity extends beyond the litigated claims or the accused devices found to be noninfringing, we dismiss the cross-appeal as moot and vacate that part of the judgment concerning the validity of Pennwalt's patent.

Affirmed-in-part and Vacated-in-part.

Bennett, Senior Circuit Judge, dissenting in part, with whom Cowen, Senior Circuit Judge, and Edward S. Smith and Pauline Newman, Circuit Judges, join.

I agree with the majority that the district court's finding of no literal infringement of the '628 patent claims has not been shown to be clearly erroneous. However, I believe that the district court failed to consider the doctrine of equivalents issue in accord with the precedents of both this court and the Supreme Court. The in banc majority in this case, in affirming the district court, does not follow the precedents of

2. That a patent applicant narrows his claim to secure a patent does not always mean that prosecution history estoppel completely prohibits the patentee from recapturing some of what was originally claimed. The amount of coverage retained depends on the circumstances of each case.

this court. While the court sitting or hearing a case in banc can overrule its prior decisions, *see Capital Elec. Co. v. United States,* 729 F.2d 743, 746 (Fed.Cir.1984), it must do so openly and affirmatively, not sub silentio. The majority apparently, curiously, prefers not to acknowledge expressly the significant number of our prior decisions being overruled by its opinion. Therefore, I respectfully dissent from the majority's discussion of and conclusion on the issue of infringement under the doctrine of equivalents.

The majority opinion contravenes Supreme Court precedents, which do not leave the majority free to rewrite the doctrine of equivalents without regard for stare decisis principles. In so doing, the majority has made shortsighted policy choices. The majority has contrived an analytical framework for the doctrine of equivalents that is little more than a redundant literal infringement inquiry, which renders the doctrine of equivalents so unduly restrictive and inflexible as to end its usefulness as judicial doctrine. As this court is confronted in the future with different factual settings in the varied and increasingly complex technologies that comprise this court's patent cases, the court will be forced to admit (or ignore) the full extent of the ties with which it has bound itself today.

* * *

TEXAS INSTRUMENTS, INC. v. UNITED STATES INTERNATIONAL TRADE COMMISSION

United States Court of Appeals, Federal Circuit, 1986.
805 F.2d 1558.

PAULINE NEWMAN, CIRCUIT JUDGE.

In this action brought under section 337 of the Tariff Act of 1930 as amended, 19 U.S.C. § 1337, Texas Instruments, Inc. ("TI") appeals the final decision of the United States International Trade Commission. The Commission held that there was no statutory violation in that TI's U.S. Patent No. 3,819,921 ("'921 patent") was not infringed by certain imported calculators, and that there was no industry in the United States practicing an invention covered by any claim of the '921 patent. We affirm the decision of non-infringement, and thus do not reach the issue of whether there was injury to a domestic industry.

COMMISSION PROCEEDINGS

Texas Instruments alleged unfair methods of competition and unfair acts in the importation and sale of certain portable electronic calculators, based on the infringement of claims 1, 2, 6, 7, 30, 37, 41 and 53 of the '921 patent, and that the effect or tendency of the unfair methods and acts was to destroy or substantially injure an efficiently and economically operated industry in the United States. The Commission ordered an investigation. 49 Fed.Reg. 29,162 (1984). Twenty-one respondents were named. For details as to the parties and the proceedings, reference is made to the Commission's decision, familiarity with which is presumed. Three respondents settled with TI during the course of the proceedings, and respondents Nam Tai Electronics Co. Ltd., International Merchandising Associates Hong Kong, and Enterprex appeared at the hearing. Nam Tai subsequently settled with TI, taking worldwide licenses to all of TI's calculator patents including the '921 patent.

In the initial determination of April 18, 1985, the administrative law judge ("ALJ") considered first the defense of patent invalidity under 35 U.S.C. §§ 103 and 112, and held that the claims at issue had not been proven invalid, stating: "The presumption of validity afforded those claims under 35 U.S.C. § 282 remains unrebutted and in full effect." The Commission affirmed, and this aspect of the decision has not been appealed.

The ALJ held that TI had not sustained its burden of proving that any of the patent claims was infringed by any of the imported calculators, and that because "complainant does not produce calculators in accordance with the claims in issue of the '921 patent, no domestic industry exists." The Commission adopted these determinations. None of the respondents participated in this appeal. The Commission is the sole appellee, and appears to defend the merits of its decision.

A.

The '921 patent entitled "Miniature Electronic Calculator" was issued on June 25, 1974 to inventors Jack S. Kilby, Jerry D. Merryman and James H. Van Tassel, assignors to Texas Instruments. The '921 patent derives, through a series of continuation applications, from application Serial No. 671,777 filed September 29, 1967. It represents a pioneering invention, for which the inventors and TI have been recognized. The prototype calculator was accepted for the permanent collection of the Smithsonian's Museum of History and Technology. Patent claim 1 is representative:

1. A miniature, portable, battery operated electronic calculator comprising:

a. input means including a keyboard for entering digits of numbers and arithmetic commands into said calculator and generating signals corresponding to said digits and said commands, the keyboard including only one set of decimal number keys for entering plural digits of decimal numbers in sequence and including a plurality of command keys;

b. electronic means responsive to said signals for performing arithmetic calculations on the numbers entered into the calculator and for generating control signals, said electronic means comprising an integrated semiconductor circuit array located in substantially one plane, the area occupied by the integrated semiconductor array being no greater than that of the keyboard, said integrated semiconductor circuit array comprising:

i. memory means for storing digits of the numbers entered into the calculator,

ii. arithmetic means coupled to said memory means for adding, subtracting, multiplying and dividing said numbers and storing the resulting answers in the memory means, and

iii. means for selectively transferring numbers from the memory means through the arithmetic means and back to the memory means in a manner dependent upon the commands to effect the desired arithmetic operation;

c. means for providing a visual display coupled to said integrated semiconductor circuit array and responsive to said control signals for indicating said answer; and

d. the entire calculator including keyboard, electronic means, means for providing a visual display, and battery being contained within a "pocket sized" housing.

The specification contains a detailed description of the then preferred means of performing each step of the claims. In the seventeen years between the first filing of the patent application and filing of the complaint with the Commission, each such means has undergone technological advance. TI asserts that the means used in the accused calculators perform the functions that are specifically set forth in the '921 claims, and that by correct claim interpretation these claims are infringed because the means used in the accused calculators are substantially the same as, or equivalent to, the means illustrated in the specification.

The Commission adopted the ALJ's extensive findings and conclusions, wherein the ALJ construed the claims in light of the specification and found no claim infringed, either literally or in terms of the doctrine of equivalents.

TI argues that substantial evidence does not support the finding of non-infringement, in that the invention as embodied in the accused calculators is fundamentally the same as that of the '921 claims, that the '921 patent represents the giant step in the development of semiconductor technology and integrated circuitry on which is based the entire industry of hand-held calculators, and that the claims are not restricted to the preferred embodiments as they existed at the time the patent application was filed.

TI points to the established law that it is not necessary that the specification have described or that the inventors have foreseen each specific means now used to perform each of the functions of the claims. TI emphasizes that this basic patent on a pioneering invention is entitled to be interpreted broadly, and indeed this proposition is long-established, *see, e.g., Continental Paper Bag Co. v. Eastern Paper Bag Co.,* 210 U.S. 405, 415, 28 S.Ct. 748, 749–50, 52 L.Ed. 1122 (1908).

Analysis of patent infringement entails two inquiries: determination of the scope of the claims, as a matter of law; and the factual finding of whether properly construed claims encompass the accused structure. This analytical framework applies whether claims are asserted to be infringed literally or by application of the doctrine of equivalents.

Literal infringement requires that the accused device embody every element of the claim as properly interpreted. If the claim describes a combination of functions, and each function is performed by a means described in the specification or an equivalent of such means, then literal infringement holds. This prescription derives from 35 U.S.C. § 112 paragraph 6:

> An element in a claim for a combination may be expressed as a means or step for performing a specified function without the recital of structure, material, or acts in support thereof, and such claim shall be construed to cover the corresponding structure, material, or acts described in the specification and equivalents thereof.

The statute thus provides, and extensive judicial analysis has reinforced, that when the claimed invention is a novel combination of steps, all possible methods of carrying out each step of the combination are not required to be described in the specification. Correctly construed claims cover "equivalents of the described embodiments".

* * *

These principles are not unlimited in their application, but reflect the equitable concept that claims should be read in a way that avoids enabling an infringer to "practice a fraud on a patent." *Graver Tank & Manufacturing Co. v. Linde Air Products Co.,* 339 U.S. 605, 608, 70 S.Ct. 854, 856, 94 L.Ed. 1097, 85 USPQ 328, 330 (1950). It has long been recognized that the range of permissible equivalents depends upon the extent and nature of the invention, and may be more generously interpreted for a basic invention than for a less dramatic technological advance. The questions of claim interpretation raised in this case turn on the issue of the breadth of equivalents to which the claims are entitled. As in many aspects of patent law, the legal conclusions are intertwined with, and depend upon, the technological facts.

It is not required that those skilled in the art knew, at the time the patent application was filed, of the asserted equivalent means of performing the claimed functions; that equivalence is determined as of the time infringement takes place.

Devices that have been modified to such an extent that the modification may be separately patented may nonetheless infringe the claims of the basic patent. Similarly, the modification of an accused device does not negate infringement when that device has adopted the features of the claims or their equivalents.

TI argues that the Commission required too narrow a construction of the '921 patent claims, contrary to this body of precedent, so that the Commission in effect limited the claims to the means that were illustrated in the specification. * * *

* * *

* * * TI asserts that the accused devices perform all the steps of the claims, and that the detailed means by which these steps are carried out, where not described or predicted by the patentees, are the same as or equivalent to the means described in the specification.

The ALJ considered each step of the claims, and made extensive findings as to the structure and operation of the accused calculators in comparison with that described in the '921 specification. The ALJ's findings on the structure of the various devices are generally uncontroverted on this appeal, but his findings as to their operation, as well as his construction of the claims, are contested as is the conclusion of noninfringement.

In brief summary, either the ALJ found, or it was uncontested, that each of the accused calculators was a miniature, portable, battery operated device contained within a "pocket-sized" housing (preamble and clause d of claim 1); having a keyboard for entering digits of numbers and arithmetic commands into the calculator (clause a); an integrated semiconductor circuit located in substantially one plane and having memory, arithmetic, and transfer means (clause b and subclauses i, ii, and iii); and a visual display (clause c). The ALJ found that each of the functions of clauses a, b, and c was performed in the accused devices by a means that was not described in the '921 patent, and that each such means was not equivalent to the means shown in the specification. Although we conclude that substantial evidence did not support each such determination of non-equivalence as to each claim clause considered separately, we conclude that the accused devices do not infringe properly construed claims when the invention and the accused devices are viewed as a whole.

* * *

THE INVENTION AS A WHOLE

The '921 patent claims are all written in the form appropriate to a multi-step combination invention, wherein each step of a novel combination is described in terms of its function in the total combination. Each such function is presented in the "means" form contemplated by 35 U.S.C. § 112 paragraph 6, and each such means is illustrated in the specification in accordance with the statutory requirement under 35 U.S.C. § 112 paragraph 1 to set forth the best mode then known to the inventors.

TI correctly states and the ALJ so found, that every function described in the '921 patent claims is performed by the accused calculators. There was not substantial evidence to the contrary. The ALJ, finding that each of the means of performing these functions in the accused calculators embodied, to varying degrees, new or improved technology over that known or developed at the time the '921 patent application was filed, held that the means of each step was not equivalent to that shown in the specification, and thus found the claims not infringed. As a matter of law, subsequent improvements do not in themselves preclude a finding of infringement.

We conclude that the ALJ interpreted the claims too narrowly when he, in effect, limited each means to the embodiment shown in the specification. As stated in *D.M.I.:*

> The statute, § 112–6, was written precisely to avoid a holding that a means-plus-function limitation must be read as covering only the means disclosed in the specification.

755 F.2d at 1574, 225 USPQ at 238.

As an aid in determining the breadth of equivalents to be afforded means plus function clauses under section 112, the prosecution history, the other claims in the patent, expert testimony, and the language of the asserted claims may be considered in addition to the specification. The pioneer status of the invention also requires consideration.

* * *

While the scope of patent claims under section 112 paragraph 6, is a legal determination, it is not devoid of equitable considerations, particularly when determining the breadth of "means" claims on complex and rapidly-evolving technologies. * * *

* * *

However, this does not mean that there is no limit on changed means of performing a claimed function, such that literal infringement can never be avoided. There must be outer boundaries to the scope of these rules, as for most rules, when the factual situation strains their rote application and requires a fresh look at the rules in the new context in which they are presented. There is no abstract guide to determining when a modified device crosses the boundary with respect to the reasonable scope of patent claims. Indeed, the determination of infringement is not made in the abstract, but in the context of the claimed invention and the accused devices.

TI argues eloquently that consideration of the breadth of equivalents for its pioneering invention requires emphasis on the function of each step of the combination as claimed, and not on the specific means of performing each step that is set forth in the patent's disclosure. Before the Commission TI asserted that the '921 invention created a totally new market for electronic calculating devices, that there is nothing remotely similar in the prior art, and that "[t]his portable, miniature, battery operated calculator is a dramatic advance deserving pioneer status." Indeed, we agree.

TI asserts that the correct interpretation of the '921 claims does not limit the claims to the means described in the specification and to those equivalents that are operationally identical, but extends to include corresponding means that perform substantially the same function in substantially the same way to obtain the same result within the combination of the claims. We agree, and as we have stated, we conclude that when each changed means is considered separately, as part of the overall device as described by the inventors, substantial evidence may not support the finding that the resultant device is not an infringement of the '921 claims. However, this is not the situation before us.

Mindful of the admonition so often urged by us, it is the claimed invention as a whole that must be considered in determining whether there is infringement by the accused devices also considered as a whole. It is not appropriate in this case, where all of the claimed functions are performed in the accused devices by subsequently developed or improved means, to view each such change as if it were the only change from the disclosed embodiments of the invention. It is the entirety of the technology embodied in the accused devices that must be compared with the patent disclosure. Any other view distorts both the correct interpretation of the claims and their application to the accused devices.

* * *

* * * We agree with TI that a mere change in size due to improved miniaturization by technological advance does not in itself save the accused devices from infringement, and that the Commission erred to the extent that it construed the claims as limited to the 1967 state of the art of integrated semiconductor circuitry. Were the electronic means of clause b the only change, the record may not contain substantial evidence in support of the ALJ's finding of non-infringement. But viewing all of the modifications in the accused devices, we conclude that they reflect more than mere substitution of "an embellishment made possible by [improved] technology", as discussed in *Hughes Aircraft*, 717 F.2d at 1365, 219 USPQ at 483 (citing *Bendix,* 600 F.2d at 1382, 204 USPQ at 631).

To summarize the totality of changes: The input means in the '921 patent is a keyboard encoder that operates through conductive strips under the keys, whereas in the accused devices it is a scanning matrix encoder. The electronic means in the '921 patent is an integrated semiconductor array based on bipolar semiconductor technology; the accused devices use metal oxide semiconductors and embody significant advances in chip design and integrated circuitry. The display means in the '921 patent is a thermal printer, whereas the accused calculators use liquid crystal displays. Taken together, these accumulated differences distinguish the accused calculators from that contemplated in the '921 patent and transcend a fair range of equivalents of the '921 invention. Each individual difference, standing alone, could conceivably lead to a different result, by application of this court's precedent. It is to the invention as a whole to which this same precedent directs our analysis.

* * *

Equivalence of the subsequently-developed devices is not established by showing only accomplishment of the same result.

* * *

We conclude that the total of the technological changes beyond what the inventors disclosed transcends the equitable limits illustrated, for example, in *Graver Tank, D.M.I., Hughes Aircraft,* and *Atlas Powder,* and propels the accused devices beyond a just scope of the '921 claims. The record before us contains substantial evidence to support the ALJ's conclusion that TI did not sustain its burden of proving infringement by the accused calculators under 35 U.S.C. § 112 paragraph 6.

B.

TI presented the alternative argument that if the claims are not deemed literally infringed in terms of 35 U.S.C. § 112 paragraph 6, they should be held infringed in terms of the doctrine of equivalents.

When literal infringement under section 112 paragraph 6 is not present the doctrine of equivalents may nevertheless apply, and thereby secure to the patentee the fair scope of the patent. In this case, however, where the claimed functions are all performed in the accused devices, the considerations discussed in part A also apply to an infringement determination in terms of the doctrine of equivalents.

Whether the issue is equivalency of a means that is described in the specification to perform a function in a "means" clause of a combination claim (*i.e.,* literal infringement), or equivalency to the claimed invention as a whole (*i.e.,* infringement by the *doctrine* of equivalents), the test is the same three-part test of history: does the asserted equivalent perform substantially the same function in substantially the same way to accomplish substantially the same result. (In the case of "means" clauses, of course, the function is that stated in the claim.) * * *

In the case of literal infringement of a claim containing a "means" clause in terms of section 112 paragraph 6, the accused structure, composition, or process is compared with that described in the specification for performing the claimed function. In the case of infringement under the doctrine of equivalents, the accused structure, composition, or process is compared with the claimed invention as a whole.

* * *

The determination of equivalency by its nature is inimical to the basic precept of patent law that the claims are the measure of the grant. The doctrine of equivalents, ubiquitous since its origin in *Winans v. Denmead,* 56 U.S. (15 How.) 330, 14 L.Ed. 717 (1853), exists solely for the equitable purpose of "prevent[ing] an infringer from stealing the benefit of an invention." *Graver Tank,* 339 U.S. at 608, 70 S.Ct. at 856. To achieve this purpose, equivalency is judicially determined by reviewing the content of the patent, the prior art, and the accused device, and essentially redefining the scope of the claims. This constitutes a deviation from the need of the public to know the precise legal limits of patent protection without recourse to judicial ruling.

For the occasional pioneering invention, devoid of significant prior art—as in the case before us—whose boundaries probe the policy behind the law, there are no immutable rules. We caution that the incentive to innovation that flows from "inventing around" an adversely held patent must be preserved. To the extent that the doctrine of equivalents represents an exception to the requirement that the claims define the metes and bounds of the patent protection, we hearken to the wisdom of the Court in *Graver Tank,* that the purpose of the rule is "to temper unsparing logic" and thus to serve the greater interest of justice.

The decision of the Commission that the claims are not infringed is Affirmed.

Note

The opinion denying a rehearing, 846 F.2d 1369, indicates this decision is consistent with *Pennwalt,* 846 F.2d at 1372.

Exercise

U.S. Patent No. 4,216,528 (filed on August 3, 1972 and issued on August 5, 1980) discloses a set of computer programs designed to monitor signals generated by an industrial process (a rolling mill, an annealing furnace, or the like) and to generate control signals for the industrial process. Unlike the Apple patent, which contains a single flow chart, this patent contains 354 sheets of flow charts and a highly detailed written description. The patent is 1¾ inches thick.

Claim 1 of this patent reads as follows:

1. A computer-implemented logic director comprising: a digital computer system having signal inputs and signal outputs;

means within said computer system for maintaining a record of the status of system logical variables including at least some of said signal inputs and signal outputs;

a series of executable job definitions residing within said computer system each of which relates to a group of at least one logical variable and each of which defines a relationship that is to be maintained between the variables in the related group of variables;

linkages connecting at least some of said job definitions to at least one of the related logical variables; and

means responsive to a change in the status of a system logical variable for initiating execution of any job definitions which are linked to the variable;

whereby, in response to a change in the status of an input signal, selected job definitions are automatically executed in cascade to establish a new equilibrium set of output signals.

1. Consider whether a modern spreadsheet program infringes this claim.

a. Is there literal infringement?

b. If so, are there equitable reasons for applying the reverse doctrine of equivalents and finding no infringement?

c. If no literal infringement, is there infringement when the doctrine of equivalents is applied?

2. Consider whether this claim is infringed by a modern operating system that automatically calls upon one program to alter one document when the user causes another program to alter another document. For example, when the user alters numeric data in a spreadsheet, the operating system automatically triggers the execution of a word processing program to update a report that contains results taken from the spreadsheet.

a. Is there literal infringement?

b. If so, are there equitable reasons for applying the reverse doctrine of equivalents and finding no infringement?

c. If no literal infringement, is there infringement when the doctrine of equivalents is applied?

d. In the "preferred embodiment" of the invention as disclosed, the logic initiator monitors and controls an industrial process. Under 35 U.S.C.A. § 112, the "means for" claim elements apply to what is disclosed "and equivalents thereof." Claim 1 is not expressly limited to a process monitoring and control system. Does the use of "means for" language in claim 1 limit the scope of the claim to industrial process control systems? In other words, does the "means for" language prevent the claims from covering a spreadsheet or an operating system?

3. Consider the applicability of the two part analysis set forth in *Application of Freeman,* 573 F.2d 1237, 1245; 197 USPQ 464, 471 (C.C.P.A. 1978) to the above claim:

a. Does this claim directly or indirectly recite an "algorithm" in the *Benson* sense of that term?

b. Assuming it does, in its entirety does the claim wholly preempt the algorithm?

c. Does your answer to (b) change depending upon whether you limit the scope of the claim to industrial process control applications or expand its scope to cover spreadsheets and/or operating systems?

4. The trier of fact can be a district court judge, a jury, or a hearing officer from the ITC. Which of these forums is most likely to find infringement and why? In what ways would your arguments differ depending upon which is the trier of fact?

Chapter IV

MISAPPROPRIATION OF COMPUTER TECHNOLOGY

A. TRADE SECRETS

Trade secrecy was long the principal means of protecting computer technology and is still an important means of protection. During the 1960s and the early 1970s, when expensive mainframes and minicomputers dominated computer technology, there were a relatively small number of customers who could afford computers. Obviously, only the relatively few organizations that owned computers were in the market for software. The fact that there were a small number of transactions, each involving a relatively large amount of money, meant that it was practical for sellers of hardware and software to insist that buyers (or lessees) sign agreements to keep the hardware and software technology secret. The hardware and software companies also made their own employees sign trade secret agreements. Their legal advisors, conservative like most lawyers, liked the idea of relying on trade secret law, which was well-defined by numerous court precedents dating back to the nineteenth century. They were reluctant to rely on copyright or patent protection, because before the 1980s, there was great doubt about the availability and scope of copyright and patent protection for software and mixed software/hardware technology.

Three major changes occured in the 1980s. As demonstrated in the previous chapters, copyright and patent law developed into significant forms of protection for computer technology. The incredible growth of microcomputer ownership made it impossible to negotiate trade secret contracts with every purchaser of hardware and software. Microcomputer manufacturers discovered that hardware sales depended upon software availability and that software developers had to have unrestricted access to technical data about the microcomputers for which they were developing software. These three factors resulted in a major but not complete shift from trade secrecy to copyright and patents in the microcomputer industry. By 1990, the microcomputer industry was, in dollar volume, the majority of the computer industry.

Trade secrecy remains important in some areas of the computer industry. Mainframe manufacturers and custom software houses continue to use trade secrecy, as they have since the 1960s. Software developers nearly always keep "source code" secret when they sell "object code" to the general public or license "object code" to individual users. Developers often keep new products secret until they are released, to delay market entry by competitors. Because of the need to test new products and adapt software for them, developers do, however, distribute advance versions to trusted organizations, but require those organizations to sign trade secrecy agreements.

UNIFORM TRADE SECRETS ACT

§ 1. Definitions.

As used in this [Act], unless the context requires otherwise:

(1) "Improper means" includes theft, bribery, misrepresentation, breach or inducement of a breach of a duty to maintain secrecy, or espionage through electronic or other means;

(2) "Misappropriation" means:

(i) acquisition of a trade secret of another by a person who knows or has reason to know that the trade secret was acquired by improper means; or

(ii) disclosure or use of a trade secret of another without express or implied consent by a person who

(A) used improper means to acquire knowledge of the trade secret; or

(B) at the time of disclosure or use, knew or had reason to know that his knowledge of the trade secret was

(I) derived from or through a person who had utilized improper means to acquire it;

(II) acquired under circumstances giving rise to a duty to maintain its secrecy or limit its use; or

(III) derived from or through a person who owed a duty to the person seeking relief to maintain its secrecy or limit its use; or

(C) before a material change of his [or her] position, knew or had reason to know that it was a trade secret and that knowledge of it had been acquired by accident or mistake.

(3) "Person" means a natural person, corporation, business trust, estate, trust, partnership, association, joint venture, government, governmental subdivision or agency, or any other legal or commercial entity.

(4) "Trade secret" means information, including a formula, pattern, compilation, program, device, method, technique, or process, that:

(i) derives independent economic value, actual or potential, from not being generally known to, and not being readily ascertainable by proper means by, other persons who can obtain economic value from its disclosure or use, and

(ii) is the subject of efforts that are reasonable under the circumstances to maintain its secrecy.

§ 2. Injunctive Relief.

(a) Actual or threatened misappropriation may be enjoined. Upon application to the court, an injunction shall be terminated when the trade secret has ceased to exist, but the injunction may be continued for an additional reasonable period of time in order to eliminate commercial advantage that otherwise would be derived from the misappropriation.

(b) In exceptional circumstances, an injunction may condition future use upon payment of a reasonable royalty for no longer than the period of time for which use could have been prohibited. Exceptional circumstances include, but are not limited to, a material and prejudicial change of position prior to acquiring knowledge or reason to know of misappropriation that renders a prohibitive injunction inequitable.

(c) In appropriate circumstances, affirmative acts to protect a trade secret may be compelled by court order.

§ 3. Damages.

(a) Except to the extent that a material and prejudicial change of position prior to acquiring knowledge or reason to know of misappropriation renders a monetary recovery inequitable, a complainant is entitled to recover damages for misappropriation. Damages can include both the actual loss caused by misappropriation and the unjust enrichment caused by misappropriation that is not taken into account in computing actual loss. In lieu of damages measured by any other methods, the damages caused by misappropriation may be measured by imposition of liability for a reasonable royalty for a misappropriator's unauthorized disclosure or use of a trade secret.

(b) If willful and malicious misappropriation exists, the court may award exemplary damages in an amount not exceeding twice any award made under subsection (a).

§ 4. Attorney's Fees.

If (i) a claim of misappropriation is made in bad faith, (ii) a motion to terminate an injunction is made or resisted in bad faith, or (iii) willful and malicious misappropriation exists, the court may award reasonable attorney's fees to the prevailing party.

§ 5. Preservation of Secrecy.

In an action under this [Act], a court shall preserve the secrecy of an alleged trade secret by reasonable means, which may include granting protective orders in connection with discovery proceedings, holding in-camera hearings, sealing the records of the action, and ordering any person involved in the litigation not to disclose an alleged trade secret without prior court approval.

§ 6. Statute of Limitations.

An action for misappropriation must be brought within 3 years after the misappropriation is discovered or by the exercise of reasonable diligence should have been discovered. For the purposes of this section, a continuing misappropriation constitutes a single claim.

§ 7. Effect on Other Law.

(a) Except as provided in subsection (b), this [Act] displaces conflicting tort, restitutionary, and other law of this State providing civil remedies for misappropriation of a trade secret.

(b) This [Act] does not affect:

(1) contractual remedies, whether or not based upon misappropriation of a trade secret;

(2) other civil remedies that are not based upon misappropriation of a trade secret; or

(3) criminal remedies, whether or not based upon misappropriation of a trade secret.

§ 8. Uniformity of Application and Construction.

This [Act] shall be applied and construed to effectuate its general purpose to make uniform the law with respect to the subject of this [Act] among states enacting it.

§ 11. Time of Taking Effect.

This [Act] takes effect on ______, and does not apply to misappropriation occurring prior to the effective date. With respect to a continuing misappropriation that began prior to the effective date, the [Act] also does not apply to the continuing misappropriation that occurs after the effective date.

Note

For convenience, the whole Uniform Trade Secrets Act is reproduced here. However, the provisions on damages will not be discussed until the next chapter, which takes a comparative approach to copyright, patent, and trade secret damages in computer cases.

UNIVERSITY COMPUTING COMPANY v. LYKES–YOUNGSTOWN CORPORATION

United States Court of Appeals, Fifth Circuit, 1974.
Rehearing and Rehearing En Banc Denied, 1974.
504 F.2d 518.

TUTTLE, CIRCUIT JUDGE:

I. FACTS

This case involves three separate claims for damages arising out of a complicated series of transactions between four corporations and a number of their executive officers. The trial lasted three weeks and the record is correspondingly lengthy and complex. We begin by briefly summarizing the critical facts.

A. Joint Venture Agreement Between UCC and LYC

University Computing Company (UCC), a Texas corporation, and Lykes–Youngstown Corp. (LYC), a Delaware corporation, entered into a written agreement on July 1, 1969 to create jointly a new corporation, to be called Lykes–University Computing Company (Lykes/UCC), which was to offer computer services [1] in the southeastern United States. This enterprise was a new venture for LYC, which is a large diversified holding company active in insurance, shipping and other manufacturing enterprises. UCC was active in other parts of the country, particularly in the southwest, offering essentially the same services as Lykes/UCC was to offer. The joint venture was designed to open new markets for the sale of UCC's computer systems.[2]

* * *

B. Misappropriation of AIMES III By LYCSC

Among the computer systems Lykes/UCC was to market was a retail inventory control system owned by UCC called "AIMES III." (Automated Inventory Management Evaluation System). This system

1. Computer services entail both the sale of computer programs to customers who own their own computer equipment, and leasing of time on in-house computers. This latter type of service is referred to as functioning on a "service bureau basis" in the industry.

2. Computer systems are a series of computer programs designed to accomplish specific business tasks. Normally this entails programming the computer to generate specific reports to be used in making business decisions. The type of package sold by UCC included programs, programming instructions and computer language listings. In the industry the generic name for these materials is "software." For any given task any number of different systems can be used and vigorous competition exists between different computer systems firms selling retail merchandising systems. The technical information contained in a package sold by UCC would be valuable to a competitor and is regarded by UCC as a trade secret.

The costs of designing, developing, implementing and converting a business function such as accounts receivable accounting or retail merchandise inventory reporting, to an automated computer program are very large. Naturally programs which accomplish their functions efficiently and which contain unique procedures and methods are valuable in that they provide a competitive advantage for their owner.

was designed to maintain information on inventory in retail department stores.[5] UCC had previously sold the system to Leonard's Department Store in Fort Worth, Texas, subject to a restrictive use agreement which limited Leonard's to private and confidential use of the system. Leonard's paid $41,700 for the rights to restricted use of AIMES III. Lykes/UCC was to offer this system, as well as several others designed and owned by UCC, to customers in the southeast. The joint venture agreement provided for discount sales of these systems to Lykes/UCC at no more than 20% of UCC's development costs.

Following the incorporation of LYCSC (the newly created subsidiary of LYC), the new corporation proceeded to offer AIMES III to customers. Rather than purchase unrestricted rights to the system from UCC, LYCSC elected to steal the system from Leonard's. In December, 1969, LYCSC bribed an employee of Leonard's for $2500 to deliver a suitcase filled with computer tapes and other materials to an employee of LYCSC. In February, 1970, this same Leonard's employee was paid to fly to Atlanta from Dallas with additional tapes and documents once the materials originally obtained were found to be insufficient to run the system. With the new materials and the help of the Leonard's employee in installing the system in the LYCSC in-house computer, LYCSC was able to run the system in its entirety.[6]

After receiving these materials in December, LYCSC attempted to market the AIMES III system. This marketing effort continued until April of the following year. Salesmen for LYCSC made offers to department stores in Atlanta, New Orleans and Tampa, Florida. In addition the system was offered to another computer services firm in Atlanta. While none of these offers was accepted, in several cases detailed sales presentations were made by sales representatives of LYCSC. A brochure was printed by LYCSC to assist the sales effort.[7]

5. The system was designed to generate reports on volume of inventory, broken down by specific items, and assess the quantity of each item sold for specific reporting periods.

6. By running the programs, LYCSC compiled a complete set of Cobol listings for the system. These listings, using a type of computer language designed to correspond to common business English, showed the various data the system could generate.

7. The system was offered both as "AIMES III" and as "MIMIC" (Maximum Information Through Merchandising Inventory Control), a system represented as having been developed by LYCSC. Rich's Department Store in Atlanta was offered MIMIC for $45,000; Colony Shops in Tampa was offered AIMES III for $42,000; and Technical Resources, a computer consulting firm, was offered MIMIC for restricted use only for $30,000.

The brochure identified the MIMIC system as being a retail merchandising inventory control system owned by LYCSC. LYCSC also occasionally used UCC sales literature after removing the UCC logo from the corner of the printed publications.

A former sales representative of UCC, David Hudson, was hired by LYCSC to direct this sales campaign. Hudson had negotiated the original Leonard's sales agreement when he was with UCC. After joining LYCSC, he arranged the theft and accepted delivery of the AIMES III system. Hudson had been trained by UCC to teach selling techniques, and had even conducted a course for Lykes/UCC sales personnel on techniques to be used in selling AIMES III prior to the termination of the joint venture. At this sales seminar, the sales literature and other publications on the AIMES III system which LYCSC subsequently used in its marketing campaign were distributed.

C. Judgment in District Court

UCC brought this suit against LYC, LYCSC and Oliver Shinn claiming damages under seven Counts. * * * Count 3 charged a conspiracy among the three defendants to misappropriate UCC's trade secret, AIMES III. * * *

[The jury] returned verdicts * * * against all three defendants on Count 3. The jury awarded * * *; $220,000 against all three defendants for misappropriation of UCC's trade secret, AIMES III (Count 3) * * *.

Defendants bring this appeal attacking these verdicts on a number of different grounds. * * * We affirm the judgment of the court below on the jury verdict on * * * on Count 3 against defendants LYC, LYCSC and Oliver Shinn. * * *

* * *

III. Misappropriation of UCC's Trade Secret, AIMES III, By LYC, LYCSC, and Oliver Shinn

The defendants admit that LYCSC paid one Ron Clinton, an employee of Leonard's Department Store in Fort Worth, Texas, $2500 to induce him to steal Leonard's copy of the AIMES III system and deliver the tapes and documents comprising that system to an LYCSC employee. The defendants do not now claim that this conduct was lawful or even defensible.

The defendants do not challenge the finding of the jury that they acted in concert. If the jury finding of misappropriation of AIMES III is thus upheld, all three defendants properly share liability.

A. Legal Standards on Protection of Trade Secrets

A trade secret is protected against illegal appropriation and commercial use by a competitor. The development of this area of the law has been progressive, and most jurisdictions have developed similar standards. What Georgia law exists in this area seems to follow the Restatement, Torts § 757. * * *

Under the Restatement § 757 formulation, a trade secret is defined as:

> "Any formula, pattern, device or compilation of information which is used on one's business and which gives him an opportunity to obtain an advantage over competitors who do not know or use it."

In large measure the requirements simply are that "the parties view the process or device as a secret and that the secret be revealed in confidence. * * * " *Water Services, supra,* 410 F.2d at 172.

Liability attaches under the Restatement if one "who discloses or uses another's trade secrets without a privilege to do so. * * *

(a) * * * discovered the secret by improper means

or (b) his disclosure or use constitutes a breach of confidence reposed in him by the (owner of the secret) in disclosing the secret to him, or (c) he learned from a third person with notice of the facts that it was a secret and that the third person's disclosure of it was otherwise a breach of his duty to the (owner of the secret) * * * "

Unlike a patent which is totally protected for the period of time for which it is granted, the protection afforded a trade secret is limited—for it is protected only so long as competitors fail to duplicate it by legitimate, independent research.

While the defendants in this action have deprecated the value of AIMES III and made an effort at trial to challenge its uniqueness, they do not appeal the finding of the jury that AIMES III was a trade secret within the meaning of the § 757. Certainly it was undisputed that UCC viewed the system as a valuable and unique property, and used great caution in attempting to preserve its confidentiality. LYCSC itself described the system to one potential customer as " * * * the finest automated merchandising system available today," and proceeded to offer it to that customer for $45,000. Evidence was adduced at trial that AIMES III had unique capabilities and features which make it a valuable competitive product. The jury could properly find that the AIMES III computer system owned by UCC was a trade secret. The jury further could find that LYCSC's appropriation of the system was unlawful and a knowing violation of Leonard's restrictive use agreement with UCC. The requirements for liability under § 757 were satisfied in this case.

* * *

Notes

1. The Court, in *University Computing,* relies upon Restatement First of Torts. After the Restatement First of Torts, the American Law Institute decided to exclude trade secrets law from future Torts Restatements. However, trade secret law has been relatively stable, so courts still cite the trade secret sections of Restatement First. It is likely that the forthcoming Restatement Third of Unfair Competition will include trade secrets law. (There is no Restatement First or Second of Unfair Competition—the "Third" in the title indicates that the new Restatement will be in the same generation as the Restatement Third of Torts.)

2. *University Computing* presents the simplest trade secret situation—outright theft of trade secret material. A common, but more complex situation, involves an employee taking an employer's trade secret.

3. The next chapter includes the damages portion of the opinion in *University Computing.*

MINUTEMAN, INC. v. L.D. ALEXANDER

Supreme Court of Wisconsin, 1989.
147 Wis.2d 842, 434 N.W.2d 773.

DAY, JUSTICE.

This is a review of an unpublished opinion by the court of appeals which affirmed in part and reversed in part a decision by the circuit court for Dane county, Honorable P. Charles Jones, judge. 140 Wis.2d 868, 412 N.W.2d 902. The circuit court denied a motion for a temporary injunction against L.D. Alexander, George Cash, and Amity, Inc., (Defendants) on behalf of Minuteman, Inc. (Minuteman). Minuteman alleged the Defendants had misappropriated trade secrets and computer data. Minuteman sought the temporary injunction to prevent the Defendants from using these materials. The court of appeals reversed the circuit court's determination on one of the trade secrets and remanded the issue to the circuit court. On all other questions, the court of appeals affirmed the circuit court's conclusions. We affirm in part and reverse in part the court of appeals' decision and remand to the circuit court for further proceedings not inconsistent with this opinion.

The basic question to be answered in this review is: what is the proper test for determining what is a "trade secret?" The answer is to be found in sec. 134.90, Stats. * * *

Several other issues are raised: (A)(1) What remedy, if any, is available if a trade secret is improperly acquired, but not subsequently used, by a wrongful taker? We conclude that under section 134.90(2)(a), Stats., an improper acquisition is enough to constitute a misappropriation of a trade secret, and therefore, all remedies in sec. 134.90 are available. (2) What effect, if any, does the possibility of reverse engineering [1] the chemical formula of a trade secret have on remedies available under sec. 134.90? We hold the possibility of reverse engineering is not enough to prevent a temporary injunction from being issued, but rather should be considered when determining the length of the temporary injunction.

(B) What is the trade secret status of customer lists and lists of persons who have made inquiries as a result of a businesses' advertisements? We conclude these lists may be eligible for trade secret protection under sec. 134.90, Stats.

(C) Did the circuit court abuse its discretion by refusing to grant a temporary injunction against the use of allegedly misappropriated computer data in violation of sec. 943.70(2), Stats., of the criminal code? We conclude that because the circuit court articulated acceptable reasons as stated in *Werner v. A.L. Grootemaat & Sons, Inc.,* 80 Wis.2d 513, 519, 259 N.W.2d 310 (1977), for refusing to issue the temporary injunction, it did not abuse its discretion.

Minuteman and Amity, Inc., (Amity) are both engaged in the furniture stripping business. Both sell products to people in the furniture restoration business, usually small enterprises. Chemicals, tubs for dipping the furniture, and other related products are sold to customers mostly from catalogs. Their products are essentially the same and both companies consider the other a direct competitor.

1. "Reverse engineering" is "starting with a known product and working backward to find the method by which [the item] was developed." Note, 1985 Wis.Act 236, sec. 6.

This case arises out of events occurring during March and April of 1986. Some facts are in dispute. In March, 1986, Defendants L.D. Alexander (Alexander) and George Cash (Cash) were employed by Minuteman. Alexander was vice president and general manager. Cash was the vice president in charge of Research and Development. Both were employees at will and had not signed any form of non-competition or non-disclosure agreement with Minuteman.

In late March, Alexander and Cash met with Jerry Cook, president of Amity. It is unclear what was discussed, but Minuteman alleged that Alexander and Cash discussed the possibility of leaving Minuteman to join Amity.

On April 7, 1986, the president of Minuteman, Jim Gauthier (Gauthier), returned from a two week vacation. Upon his return to work he was allegedly met by Alexander and Cash who gave him their immediate resignations. Gauthier stated he did not take the two seriously and told them to take that day off.

On the morning of April 8, Alexander was observed removing boxes of materials from Minuteman's premises. Shortly thereafter, Minuteman allegedly discovered both Cash's and Alexander's work stations completely empty of normal business materials. Minuteman claimed it was unable to locate various business related items. They thought Cash and Alexander had taken the materials.

Several days later, Alexander and Cash began working for Amity. Immediately thereafter, Minuteman filed a complaint against the Defendants. Minuteman claimed numerous causes of action against the Defendants, four of which are the subject of this review. The first allegation claimed the Defendants had misappropriated the trade secret formula for Minuteman's Stripper '76 (formula). The second allegation claimed the Defendants had misappropriated a list of inquiries made in response to Minuteman's advertisements (Inquiry list). The third allegation claimed the Defendants had misappropriated a list of Minuteman's customers which included information about what and how much each customer had ordered (Customer list). The fourth allegation claimed the Defendants had misappropriated various computer data from Minuteman. None of the items involved were protected by trademarks or patents.

Minuteman requested relief in the form of monetary damages, a temporary restraining order, and a temporary injunction against the Defendants. Although Amity did not concede the allegations contained in the complaint, it did, however, stipulate to the temporary restraining order.

A three day hearing was later held on the matter which included conflicting testimony about what happened. There was testimony about Cash's and Alexander's behavior just before they left Minuteman. In early March 1986, Alexander had requested a printout of the entire Inquiry list. Alexander told Minuteman's computer operator he needed the list for promotional reasons. A complete printout of the list had never been prepared for anyone before, nor had there ever been a complete printed copy of the list routinely maintained in the office. There was also testimony that Minuteman took some security measures to protect the contents of the list from being known by those outside the company. The list was provided to Alexander because of his executive position within Minuteman. After Alexander left Minuteman, it is claimed the list was never found.

* * *

Minuteman asserted additional computer data assigned to Cash and Alexander by Minuteman were also discovered missing, including a recent printout of the Customer list.

A list of Amity's business solicitation mailings made by Cash and Alexander, on April 16 and 17, 1986, was also introduced into evidence. Minuteman argued this list was based on the Customer and Inquiry lists allegedly taken by Cash and Alexander. Minuteman's computer manager testified that the list was in the same sequence as Minuteman's Customer and Inquiry lists and that Minuteman's lists were the sources of Amity's list. Both Minuteman's and Amity's lists were basically in the same zip code order with some random additions in Amity's list. There were also similar mistakes in spelling and addressing on each list. Alexander stated he had written a list for his personal use while he was at Minuteman and used this personal list as the basis for the Amity mailings.

* * *

On the second and third allegations, the circuit court ruled Amity had used the Inquiry and Customer lists but the lists were not protected trade secrets because they failed to satisfy the six part test of the 4 *Restatement (First) of Torts,* sec. 757 (comment b) (1939), as required by *Corroon & Black,* 109 Wis.2d at 295, 325 N.W.2d 883. The circuit court also ruled that injunctive relief was inappropriate for Minuteman's fourth allegation of computer data misappropriation. Minuteman appealed to the court of appeals.

* * *

The court of appeals, however, affirmed the circuit court's ruling on the second and third allegations that the Customer and Inquiry lists were not trade secrets. The court of appeals also applied the six factor *Restatement* test and held the circuit court had correctly found the lists lacking the required elements. The court of appeals also affirmed the circuit court's decision to refuse to issue a temporary injunction for Minuteman's fourth allegation of computer data misappropriation. Minuteman then petitioned this court for review.

The first question is: what is the proper test for determining what is a trade secret? * * *

* * *

In 1986, the legislature passed the Wisconsin version of the Uniform Trade Secret Act (UTSA). Section 134.90, Stats., created a new definition of trade secret as well as establishing possible remedies available to those injured by trade secret misappropriation. * * *

* * *

The new definition of trade secret is found in sec. 134.90(1)(c), Stats., which states:

> Uniform trade secrets act. * * * (c) 'Trade secret' means information, including a formula, pattern, compilation, program, device, method, technique or process to which all of the following apply:
>
> 1. The information derives independent economic value, actual or potential, from not being generally known to, and not being readily ascertainable by proper means by, other persons who can obtain economic value from its disclosure or use.
>
> 2. The information is the subject of efforts to maintain its secrecy that are reasonable under the circumstances.

The Commissioners of the Uniform Laws Commission who drafted the UTSA, as well as our legislature, noted "[t]hat the definition of 'trade secret' contains a reasonable departure from the *Restatement of Torts* (first) definition which required that a trade secret be 'continuously used in one's business.'" 1985 Wis.Act. 236, sec. 6, note; *Uniform Trade Secrets Act,* sec. 1, comment, 14 U.L.A. 543 (1985).

We still find, however, the *Restatement's* definition helpful. The *Restatement* was the basic source of the UTSA's definition of trade secret. In addition, the UTSA's Comments state it "codifies the results of the better reasoned cases concerning the remedies for trade secret misappropriation." 1985 Wis.Act. 236, Prefatory Note; *Uniform Trade Secrets Act,* sec. 1, comment, 14 U.L.A. 543 (1985). We hold that although all six elements of the *Restatement*'s test are no longer required, the *Restatement* requirements still provide helpful guidance in deciding whether certain materials are trade secrets under our new definition.

* * *

When examining an alleged violation of sec. 134.90, Stats., three questions arise. First, whether the material complained about is a trade secret under sec. 134.90(1)(c), Stats. Second, whether a misappropriation has occurred in violation of sec. 134.90(2). And finally, if both of the above requirements are met, what type of relief is appropriate under sec. 134.90(3) or (4).

* * *

The circuit court's finding that "Cash obtained the formula without permission" constitutes an "improper means" as defined in sec. 134.-90(1)(a), Stats.[4] * * *

4. Section 134.90(1)(a), Stats., provides: Uniform trade secrets act. (1) Definitions. In this section: (a) "Improper means" includes espionage, theft, brib-

* * *

B. The Customer and Inquiry Lists:

Although the lists are distinct, both the circuit court and the court of appeals decided the second and third allegations in a similar fashion. Both courts interpreted sec. 134.90, Stats., as still embodying the trade secret definition in *Corroon* which required all six factors of the *Restatement* test be met before a trade secret could be found. As discussed above, the *Corroon* test no longer embodies the definition of trade secret. We, therefore, reverse the court of appeals' decision and remand for further determination using the statutory definition in sec. 134.90, Stats.

Some customer lists are afforded protection under the UTSA:

> This is not to say that every customer list would be denied trade secret status under the uniform act. We are well aware, for example, * * * that in certain sectors of the business community identical or nearly identical products and/or services are sold to a small, fixed group of purchasers. In such an intensely purchaser-oriented market, a supplier's customer list could well constitute a trade secret.

Steenhoven v. College Life Ins. Co. of Am., 460 N.E.2d 973, 974, n. 5 (Ind.Ct.App.1984).

In *Kozuch v. CRA–MAR Video Center, Inc.,* 478 N.E.2d 110 (Ind.Ct. App.1985), the customer list of a video rental club was found to constitute a trade secret under the Indiana version of the UTSA. An injunction was permitted to stop the use of the misappropriated trade secret. Others have noted the possibility of trade secret protection for Customer Lists under the UTSA. Decisions by other jurisdictions on questions involving the UTSA are to be given careful consideration by the courts in Wisconsin. Section 134.90(7), Stats.[5]

The court of appeals is reversed on this issue and the cause is remanded for an inquiry as to whether the lists are trade secrets as defined in sec. 134.90, Stats.

* * *

The decision of the court of appeals is affirmed in part and reversed in part and the cause is remanded for further proceedings not inconsistent with this opinion.

Notes

1. The trade secret here appears to have been a customer list maintained in a computer. Trade secret protection of computer-related informa-

ery, misrepresentation and breach or inducement of a breach of duty to maintain secrecy.

5. Section 134.90(7), Stats., provides:

Uniform trade secrets act. * * * (7) Uniformity of application and construction. This section shall be applied and construed to make uniform the law relating to misappropriation of trade secrets among states enacting substantially identical laws.

tion includes such "low technology" information as well as high technology information found in complex software source code.

2. The plaintiff appears to have overlooked a copyright claim. Federal copyright law protects customer lists as "compilations." Recall the protection successfully claimed by West Publishing Co. for compilations of cases.

3. Since there is no contract claim, it appears that the owner of the customer lists was remiss in not having negotiated non-disclosure contracts with its employees.

4. There is doubt in some states that trade secret law protects customer lists. It is important, therefore, for a business to protect such lists by having employees sign non-disclosure agreements. It is also important to include theories alternative to trade secret law in any lawsuit by the employer.

5. This case represents an archetypal trade secret situation—the employee who takes secret information to a new employer.

HEALTHCARE AFFILIATED SERVICES, INC. v. LIPPANY

United States District Court, Western District of Pennsylvania, 1988.
701 F.Supp. 1142.

BLOCH, DISTRICT JUDGE.

[Plaintiff, Healthcare Affiliated Services sued Defendant, Lippany, a former employee of Healthcare. Healthcare proved that Lippany was marketing as his own programs strikingly similar to those he had developed while a Healthcare employee.]

* * *

This Court has jurisdiction over the copyright claims at issue in this action pursuant to 28 U.S.C. § 1338, and may exercise jurisdiction over the state law claims pursuant to the doctrine pendent jurisdiction. *Carnegie Mellon University v. Cohill,* ___ U.S. ___, 108 S.Ct. 614, 98 L.Ed.2d 720 (1988).

In order to be entitled to a grant of a preliminary injunction, the moving party must show a likelihood of success on the merits of the litigation and irreparable harm. *Freixenet, S.A. v. Admiral Wine & Liquor Co.,* 731 F.2d 148, 151 (3d Cir.1984). In addition to these two requirements, the district court "should take into account, when they are relevant, * * * the possibility of harm to other interested persons from the grant or denial of the injunction, and * * * the public interest." *In re Arthur Treacher's Franchisee Litigation,* 689 F.2d 1137, 1143 (3d Cir.1982). Each of these elements will be addressed in turn.

I. LIKELIHOOD OF SUCCESS ON THE MERITS

Plaintiffs' complaint sets forth claims of copyright infringement and misappropriation of trade secrets and confidential information. In addition, plaintiffs seek recovery on the theories of fraudulent misrepresentation, breach of an employment contract, unfair competition, tortious interference with contractual and business relations, and diversion of corporate opportunities. The Court's factual findings on the issues presented in the context of the motion for a preliminary injunction will not be binding in the final outcome of this matter; the defendant has demanded a jury trial and the jury eventually will be making the final determination on the merits. Therefore, the Court finds it necessary to address only plaintiffs' claims regarding copyright infringement and misappropriation of trade secrets and confidential information. Plaintiffs have demonstrated substantial likelihood of success on the merits of their trade secrets and confidential information claims; this finding permits the Court to grant plaintiffs the relief they are seeking. * * *

A. Copyright claims

* * *

* * * In short, plaintiffs have not met their burden of demonstrating that the methodologies of their systems comprise the "structure, sequence and organization" of a computer program within the meaning of the copyright law and the *Whelan* decision. Accordingly, the Court concludes that plaintiffs have failed to establish a likelihood of success on the merits of their copyright claims.

B. Breach of employment agreement and disclosure of trade secrets

1. The Employment Agreement: Confidential Information

On June 1, 1987, defendant and HAS entered into an employment agreement; this employment agreement was executed in connection with defendant's promotion and an associated increase in salary. Under Pennsylvania law, the duty of an employee not to disclose the secrets of his employer may arise either from an express contract, as it does in the instant case, or may be implied from the confidential relationship existing between the master and servant. It is apparent that a confidential relationship existed between defendant and HAS. Where such a confidential relationship exists, injunctive relief will be granted to protect against the disclosure of information held secret by the employer, of which the employee gained knowledge as the result of his former employment situation.

The evidence presented during the hearing in this matter would strongly support the finding that the defendant has used the knowledge he acquired during his employment in the development of his five software programs, specifically his knowledge regarding existing software and software under development at HAS and customer needs and requirements. Defendant has admitted that he turned over detailed methodology to the programmers he employed to develop the software for his five programs; the evidence establishes that these methodologies were developed by plaintiffs' employees during their employment with plaintiffs.

Although defendant did demonstrate that plaintiffs had, on a limited number of occasions, given presentations concerning their hospital management systems in general, no evidence was presented that the methodologies of these systems ever were revealed to even a limited segment of the general public. Therefore, the methodologies constitute confidential information within the meaning of defendant's employment agreement.

The use of such confidential information would constitute a breach of the employment agreement. The evidence presented would support a finding that such a breach began prior to the termination of defendant's employment with plaintiffs and that it is of an ongoing nature; defendant derived the software systems he is marketing from plaintiffs' methodologies and has been utilizing plaintiffs' confidential information in his ongoing consulting arrangement with Altoona Hospital.

2. The Employment Agreement: Products Developed During Defendant's Employment

In addition to the provision concerning the preservation of confidential information, defendant's employment agreement states that all "products, processes, methodologies and services, including but not limited to systems and software developments and improvements * * * developed by [defendant] alone, or in conjunction with any other person or persons during his employment with HAS which in any way relate to the future business of HAS shall be the sole and exclusive property of HAS." Defendant does not dispute that he developed his five software programs during the period of time that he was employed by HAS, i.e., between 1984 and 1987. Defendant argues, however, that he performed the work associated with the programs' development at home, and not during the hours for which he was being paid by HAS.

While the evidence submitted on this point was not substantial, that which was introduced tends to contradict defendant's assertions that all of the development of the five programs was done on defendant's own time. This fact is not dispositive of the issue, in any case. It is abundantly clear that the five software programs which defendant has developed are products which defendant was assigned the task of developing as part of his normal job duties as a consultant with HAS. Defendant failed to develop the programs as assigned; rather, utilizing the methodologies, confidential information and trade secrets of plaintiffs (*see infra*), he developed five products which fulfilled the customer needs which plaintiffs' had foreseen and were attempting to serve. Defendant agreed that any software which he developed during his employment which "in any way relate[d] to the present or future business of HAS" belongs to HAS. Consequently, plaintiffs have made a substantial showing of likelihood of success on the merits of their claim that the five software programs developed by defendant in fact are the property of HAS, and that defendant has no right to the use of the same.

3. Trade Secrets

Under the law of Pennsylvania, in order to be entitled to injunctive relief against an employee for misappropriation of trade secrets, the employer bears the burden of demonstrating the following factors: (1) that there is a trade secret or secret process of manufacture; (2) that it is of value to the employer and important in the conduct of its business; (3) that by reason of discovery or ownership the employer has the right to use an enjoyment of the secret; and (4) that the secret was communicated to the employee while he was employed in a position of trust and confidence, under such circumstances as to make it inequitable and unjust for him to disclose it to others, or to make use of it himself, to the prejudice of his employer.

Section 757, comment B, of the Restatement of Torts, which has been adopted as the law of Pennsylvania, is determinative of the existence of a trade secret. Section 757, comment B, provides as follows:

> A trade secret may consist of any formula, pattern, device or compilation of information which is used in one's business and which gives him an opportunity to obtain an advantage over competition who do not know or use it. It may be a formula for a chemical compound, a process of manufacturing, treating or preserving materials, a pattern for a machine or other device, or a list of customers. * * * A trade secret is a process or device for continuous use in the operation of the business.

Trade secrets, in order to be entitled to protection, must be "particular secrets of the complaining employer and not general secrets of the trade in which he is engaged." *Capital Bakers v. Townsend,* 426 Pa. 188, 231 A.2d 292 (1967). Computer software programs are a proper subject of trade secret protection. *Computer Print Systems, Inc. v. Lewis,* 281 Pa.Super. 240, 422 A.2d 148 (1980).

In determining whether given information constitutes a trade secret, this Court is required to examine the following factors: the extent to which the information is known outside of the owner's business; the extent to which it is known by employees and others involved in the owner's business; the extent of measures taken by the owner to guard the secrecy of the information; the value of the information to the owner and to his competitors; the amount of effort or money expended by the owner in developing the information; and the ease or difficulty with which the information could be properly acquired or duplicated by others. *S.I. Handling Systems, Inc. v. Heisley,* 753 F.2d 1244, 1256 (3d Cir.1985).

As the foregoing factual findings establish, plaintiffs have presented substantial evidence going to each of the aforesaid six factors. Plaintiffs' methodologies have been developed by plaintiffs through the expenditure of considerable employee time and financial resources. These methodologies could be developed by others only via an equivalent expenditure of time and money. Plaintiffs have been careful to guard against the unauthorized disclosure of their methodologies to persons outside Blue Cross and HAS and have not revealed the methodologies to the general public. Access to the methodologies within plaintiffs' business structure has been on a limited, need-to-know basis. Maintenance of the confidentiality of the methodologies is essential to the future conduct of plaintiffs' hospital management consulting business. Therefore, the methodologies constitute trade secrets within the meaning of § 757.

Plaintiffs also must establish that the trade secret is of value to them and important in the conduct of their business. As stated above, and set forth in the factual findings, plaintiffs' status in the hospital management consulting field depends in large measure upon their continued exclusive use of their methodologies; therefore, this element is satisfied.

Plaintiffs likewise must establish that, by reason of discovery or ownership thereof, they have the right to use and enjoyment of the trade secret. The testimony establishes that plaintiffs' employees developed the methodologies during their employment with plaintiffs. Therefore, plaintiffs have the right to use the enjoyment of the same.

The final element which the plaintiffs must establish is that the trade secret was communicated to the employee while he was employed in a position of trust and confidence, under such circumstances as to make it inequitable and unjust for him to disclose it to others or to make use of it himself. Under the law of Pennsylvania, a confidential relationship between employer and employee is created where the employer turns over to the employee a pre-existing trade secret. "A pledge of secrecy is impliedly extracted from the employee, a pledge which he carries with him even beyond the ties of his employment relationship." *Wexler v. Greenberg,* 399 Pa. 569, 160 A.2d 430 (1960). During his employment with plaintiffs, defendant had access to the methodologies at issue herein for the express purpose of developing and enhancing the same. Defendant, rather than developing plaintiffs' programs, as he had been directed to do, used plaintiffs' existing methodologies to develop five software programs which he intended to put to his own personal use. It would be inequitable for defendant to utilize these trade secrets for his own benefit.

In summary, plaintiffs have sustained their burden of demonstrating a substantial likelihood of success on the merits of their trade secret claim and, accordingly, are entitled to injunctive relief.

* * *

III. Conclusion

In summary, the Court finds that plaintiffs have made a substantial showing that defendant has misappropriated plaintiffs' confidential information and trade secrets and has used the same to develop his five software programs which he has used to his own benefit. Defendant has the capability to continue to use these programs. Such continued use would result in serious irreparable injury to plaintiffs' competitive status in the hospital management consulting field.

An appropriate Order will be issued.

* * *

Notes

1. In *Healthcare,* the plaintiff did right what the plaintiff in *Minuteman* did wrong. Plaintiff in *Healthcare* had made its employees sign written agreements to protect confidential information, thus giving plaintiff a good contract claim. Plaintiff in *Healthcare* also added a copyright claim to its trade secret claim.

2. The key to victory in intellectual property disputes often is obtaining a preliminary injunction. An injunction puts the defendant "out of business" and so in a mood to settle. By bringing claims on multiple theories, plaintiff increased its chances of getting an injunction.

3. Although plaintiff failed to prove its copyright claim sufficiently to get a preliminary injunction, the claim was adequate to get plaintiff into Federal court and to bring in plaintiff's other claims under the doctrine of pendant jurisdiction. It is often procedurally advantageous to be in Federal court rather than state court.

B. TAKING OF NON-SECRET INFORMATION

1. PREEMPTION

Constitution of the United States, Art. I, sec. 8

The Congress shall have power * * *

(8) To promote the Progress of Science and useful Arts by securing for limited Times to Authors and Inventors the exclusive Right to their respective Writings and Discoveries. * * *

Generally, the taking of non-secret information by competitors is perfectly legal, provided that the information is not protected by copyright, patent, trade secret, or contract. There is a line of cases going back to *International News Service v. Associated Press,* 248 U.S. 215 (1918), however, that hold in some circumstances, such taking is illegal "misappropriation." (In that case International News Service was found liable for taking uncopyrighted information from Associated Press dispatches.) Even where the older precedents on "misappropriation" would give protection, the courts today regularly hold that such protection is unavailable, being "preempted" by Congress's exercise of its powers under the Patent and Copyright Clause of the Constitution.

COPYRIGHT ACT OF 1976
17 U.S.C.A. § 301

§ 301. Preemption with respect to other laws

(a) On and after January 1, 1978, all legal or equitable rights that are equivalent to any of the exclusive rights within the general scope of copyright as specified by section 106 in works of authorship that are fixed in a tangible medium of expression and come within the subject matter of copyright as specified by sections 102 and 103, whether created before or after that date and whether published or unpublished, are governed exclusively by this title. Thereafter, no person is entitled to any such right or equivalent right in any such work under the common law or statutes of any State.

(b) Nothing in this title annuls or limits any rights or remedies under the common law or statutes or any State with respect to—

(1) subject matter that does not come within the subject matter of copyright as specified by sections 102 and 103, including works of authorship not fixed in any tangible medium of expression; or

* * *

(3) activities violating legal or equitable rights that are not equivalent to any of the exclusive rights within the general scope of copyright as specified by section 106.

* * *

(d) Nothing in this title annuls or limits any rights or remedies under any other Federal statute.

(e) The scope of Federal preemption under this section is not affected by the adherence of the United States to the Berne Convention or the satisfaction of obligations of the United States thereunder.

* * *

SYNERCOM TECHNOLOGY, INC. v. UNIVERSITY COMPUTING COMPANY

United States District Court, Northern District of Texas, 1979.
474 F.Supp. 37.

PATRICK E. HIGGINBOTHAM, DISTRICT JUDGE.

BACKGROUND

This order concerns the only unresolved liability question in this lawsuit, the claim of unfair competition asserted by Synercom Technology, Inc. against University Computing Company (UCC) and Engineering Dynamics, Inc. (EDI). The claims of copyright infringement were decided by this court in a memorandum and order issued August 24, 1978 and reported at 462 F.Supp. 1003 (N.D.Tex.1978). The facts of this lawsuit were there set forth. No useful purpose would be served by reiteration of the facts except those directly relevant to the question of unfair competition.

First, this court found that, in developing new input formats, instruction manuals and related services to provide more simplified access to a computer program for structural analysis (STRAN), Synercom expended "approximately four man years at a cost in the range of $100,000." Moreover, by the time EDI entered the computerized structural analysis market with its SACS II program, Synercom had incurred costs approaching $500,000. Thus "without the cost of developing the input formats or of training customers in their usage, EDI was in position to simply pluck the fruits of Synercom's labors and risks, if SACS II was as good or better than STRAN."

This court found further that EDI's marketing strategy was to make its SACS II program compatible with the STRAN format so that STRAN users could switch to SACS II with minimum expense, and to capture the market aided in its pricing by lower cost. Additionally, the court found that in 1976, when the relationship between UCC and Synercom was deteriorating, UCC and EDI embarked upon a marketing effort that "if not aimed squarely at the old Synercom accounts included them in its sights." Finally, this court found that EDI and UCC willfully infringed Synercom's copyrights in its User's Manuals and that EDI's original counsel "conducted this litigation in a manner calculated to delay hearing on the merits and to increase the costs of litigation to Synercom as much as possible."

Analysis

The question for decision is whether EDI and UCC engaged in unfair competition by creating a structural analysis package designed specifically to be adaptable to an input methodology developed at great expense by Synercom and by directing its marketing program in significant part at Synercom's accounts.

The central legal doctrine upon which Synercom premises its claim of unfair competition is the doctrine of misappropriation. That doctrine was born into widespread acceptance in 1918 with the decision of the United States Supreme Court in *International News Service v. Associated Press,* 248 U.S. 215, 39 S.Ct. 68, 63 L.Ed. 211 (1918), a case decided under the pre-*Erie* federal common law. In that case the court enjoined I.N.S. from copying from A.P. bulletin boards uncopyrighted news gathered by A.P. correspondents and then selling the stories to I.N.S. member papers. The effect of the decision was not to grant A.P. a monopoly in the news stories gathered by its reporters, but to postpone reproduction and dissemination by I.N.S. until the immediate commercial value of the news was gone. The court emphasized the peculiarly short-lived value of news, and found that A.P. had a "quasi-property" right in freshly gathered news.

From this rather spectacular beginning there emerged a widely accepted action for the business tort of misappropriation, classified by several states under the general heading of unfair competition.[1] The

1. Strictly speaking, the tort of unfair competition requires the additional element of secondary meaning, or "passing off." As there is no claim that EDI or UCC passed off their product as that of Synercom, the analysis here will focus upon the doctrine of misappropriation.

courts of Texas have embraced the doctrine. In its typical formulation, the doctrine of misappropriation is said to require proof of three elements: "(i) the creation of plaintiff's product through extensive time, labor, skill and money, (ii) the defendant's use of that product in competition with the plaintiff, thereby gaining a special advantage in that competition (*i.e.,* a 'free ride') because defendant is burdened with little or none of the expense incurred by the plaintiff, and (iii) commercial damage to the plaintiff." Dannay, The Sears–Compco Doctrine Today: Trademarks and Unfair Competition, 67 Trademark Review 132 (1976).

Even casual analysis will reveal, however, that the doctrine's reach cannot be as broad as is indicated by this formulation of elements. Literally applied, for instance, the doctrine as set out would encompass the manufacture by a non-patentee of a product upon which a patent had expired. Obviously, then, the doctrine of misappropriation has limits, both inherent to the doctrine itself and externally imposed by the United States Constitution and the federal patent and copyright laws. The analysis here will proceed upon the assumption that the activity involved in this case is unlawful under the common law doctrine of misappropriation, whatever may be the inherent limits of that doctrine. The initial inquiry, then, will be whether the states, here the State of Texas, may legitimately punish the conduct engaged in by EDI and UCC, or whether Texas is foreclosed from regulating that conduct by federal law. More succinctly, the question, as it is so often in cases of this nature, is one of preemption.

The starting point for the effort to measure the permissible scope of state regulation of intellectual property is the analysis of the Supreme Court in two cases decided the same day, *Sears, Roebuck & Co. v. Stiffel Co.,* 376 U.S. 225, 84 S.Ct. 784, 11 L.Ed.2d 661 (1964) and *Compco Corp. v. Day–Brite Lighting, Inc.,* 376 U.S. 234, 84 S.Ct. 779, 11 L.Ed.2d 669 (1964). Both cases involved mechanical devices (a pole-lamp in *Sears* and a lighting fixture in *Compco*) created and patented (both cases involved design patents) by the plaintiff and copied by the defendant. In both cases the lower court had held the design patent invalid but had granted the plaintiffs relief under the state law of unfair competition. The Supreme Court reversed the lower court decisions, finding the state laws preempted under the Supremacy Clause of the Constitution, U.S. Const. Art. VI, the Patent–Copyright Clause, U.S. Const. Art. I, § 8, cl. 8, and the patent and copyright laws enacted by Congress. The court reasoned that one of the essential goals of the patent laws was to ensure that all inventions and discoveries were freely available to the public except those that were found to merit the temporary (17 years) reward of protection from competition by meeting the stringent requirements of patentability. Devices that did not meet those standards, the court reasoned, were intended by Congress to be freely available to the public, and state laws that effectively removed such devices from the public domain conflicted with the Congressional purpose and, consequently, were preempted.

The language of the decisions is broad,[2] giving a wide reading to the preemptive sweep of patent and copyright legislation:

> [W]hen an article is unprotected by a patent or a copyright, state law may not forbid others to copy that article. To forbid copying would interfere with the federal policy, found in article I, § 8, cl. 8, of the Constitution and in the implementing federal statutes, of allowing free access to copy whatever the federal patent and copyright laws leave in the public domain. 376 U.S. at 237, 84 S.Ct. at 782.

Despite the broad language of the decisions, it is important to note the precise factual context in which the cases arose. The devices in question were clearly the *type* of things to which the patent laws applied; these devices had simply been found not to meet the requirements of patentability. Thus if state law protection had been accorded to the plaintiffs in these cases, state law would have operated essentially as an extension of the patent system and, in fact, would have effectively subsumed the scheme of patent legislation by granting protection for a presumably unlimited period of time to devices that failed to meet the tests for federal patent protection. Thus the holdings of *Sears* and *Compco* are unremarkable; a contrary holding would have significantly eviscerated the purposes of federal patent legislation.[3]

Nonetheless, were these decisions the last word on the subject of preemption in the patent and copyright fields, this court would be constrained to hold state protection of the activity complained of here preempted, simply because of the broad language of *Sears* and *Compco.* But since those cases the Supreme Court has issued several decisions that have cut back on at least the language of *Sears* and *Compco* and have attempted to fashion some sort of workable interplay between state and federal law in the field of intellectual property. The result of these more recent decisions is that the precise dimensions of the preemptive sweep of federal law, and, consequently, the permissible reach of state law in this area has become a matter of difficulty and confusion that requires careful analysis of each case in the light of the relevant case law. The line between the permissible and the impermissible exercise of state power has become difficult to discern.

The first significant step back from the sweeping language of *Sears* and *Compco* was taken in *Goldstein v. California,* 412 U.S. 546, 93 S.Ct. 2303, 37 L.Ed.2d 163 (1973). Involved in that case was a California penal statute outlawing tape piracy. Goldstein and others who had been convicted under the statute challenged the power of California to

2. The breadth of language appears to have been intentional. Indeed, the cases could conceivably have been decided on the basis of a failure to adequately prove secondary meaning, without ever reaching the preemption issue.

3. It is also noteworthy that neither case involved "culpable" conduct on the part of the defendant in the sense that there was no breach of a confidential or contractual relationship and no theft of secrets.

punish tape piracy, arguing that state regulation of the activity was preempted by the federal copyright laws. The Supreme Court found, however, that the California law was not preempted and it upheld the convictions, reasoning that Congress, which until 1971 did not legislate with respect to copyright in musical recordings, had not determined that recordings were unworthy of any protection but had simply left the area "unattended." Hence the states were free to regulate with respect to musical recordings.

In a narrow sense, the *Goldstein* decision is as unremarkable as the *Sears* and *Compco* decisions. The case involved a penal statute regulating conduct that might be termed "culpable" in a sense that the conduct involved in *Sears* and *Compco* was not. Thus the statute in question was more an exercise of the state police power than were the laws found preempted in *Sears* and *Compco;* enforcement of the California law could not be said to conflict with the scheme of federal copyright regulation. In a sense, then, the *Goldstein* decision did not appear to work a significant departure from *Sears* and *Compco.*

On the other hand, the tone and language of the *Goldstein* decision altered at least the angle of approach to preemption problems. That is, whereas the court in *Sears* and *Compco* appeared to start with the presumption that intellectual property not specifically given protection by federal law was not a legitimate subject for state law protection, the court in *Goldstein* began with the premise that state regulation is permissible absent a Congressional intention to occupy the field. Still, the analysis in the three cases is along the same lines. In each case the court's central concern was whether the state law conflicted unacceptably with the goals of federal legislation.

That analysis was further elucidated by the Supreme Court in *Kewanee Oil Co. v. Bicron Corp.,* 416 U.S. 470, 94 S.Ct. 1879, 40 L.Ed.2d 315 (1974), a decision that represents the most significant departure from *Sears* and *Compco.* The plaintiff in *Kewanee* was a corporation that, after more than a decade of work, had succeeded in growing a valuable 17-inch crystal useful in the detection of ionizing radiation. Several employees, all of whom had signed trade secret agreements, joined the defendant Bicron Corporation, which then succeeded in growing a 17-inch crystal in only nine months. While the trial court permanently enjoined the defendant from making use of the crystal on the basis of Ohio trade secret law, the Sixth Circuit reversed that decision, finding state protection preempted under *Sears* and *Compco.* The Supreme Court, however, reinstated the trial court's decision, finding Ohio's trade secret law not preempted. Before considering the court's analysis, it is important to consider the facts of *Kewanee* and their relation to those in *Sears* and *Compco.*

First, *Kewanee* involved an invention clearly subject to the reach of the patent laws. No patent was applied for because the requirement of novelty could not be satisfied—the crystal had been in commercial use for more than one year prior to its development by the plaintiff. Yet the effect of the court's decision was to permanently prevent its use by the defendant unless the defendant could discover the process through its own independent efforts or through "working backwards" from the plaintiff's product. At least in a temporal sense, then, enforcement of the Ohio trade secrets law afforded the plaintiff greater protection against the defendant than a patent would have.[4] On the other hand, *Kewanee,* unlike *Sears* and *Compco,* involved an element of culpable conduct—the breach of trade secret agreements—so that the enforcement of the state law was in the nature of an exercise of the state's police power.

In reaching its decision, the court closely examined the effect of the trade secret law in order to determine if its enforcement would conflict with either of the dual purposes of the patent laws—namely, the policies of encouraging invention and of ensuring disclosure of invention. First, the court set out the standard for determining whether state law is preempted:

> The only limitation on the States is that in regulating the area of patents and copyrights they do not conflict with the operation of the laws in this area passed by Congress * * *.
>
> The question of whether the trade secret law of Ohio is void under the Supremacy Clause involves a consideration of whether that law "stands as an obstacle to the accomplishment of the full purposes and objectives of Congress." *Hines v. Davidowitz,* 312 U.S. 52, 67, 61 S.Ct. 399, 85 L.Ed. 581 (1941). 416 U.S. at 479, 94 S.Ct. at 1885.

Applying this test, the court found that enforcement of the Ohio trade secret law did not conflict with the purposes of the federal patent laws.

It is in the context of these decisions, then, that this court must determine whether the state law doctrine of misappropriation may properly be applied to the activities of UCC and EDI, or whether application of the doctrine would "stand as an obstacle to the accomplishment of the full purposes and objectives of Congress." That standard, of course, does not draw a clearly defined boundary around the preemptive scope of federal law. In a literal sense, any state regulation of writings and inventions conflicts in some way with the goals of the federal patent and copyright laws. The question, then, is how much state interference with federal goals can be tolerated. In that regard, the cases suggest several lines of inquiry.

First, and perhaps most important, is the concept of federalism. Preemption analysis involves by its very nature the problem of federalism, and a state law is far more likely to avoid preemption if it is an exercise of the traditional state power to provide for the health and welfare of its citizens. In both *Goldstein* and *Kewanee,* where state law was found not to be preempted, the activity in question was the type of

4. Of course, trade secret protection did not protect the plaintiff from competition by others who grew their own 17-inch crystal, even if that were accomplished by working backward from the plaintiff's product. In this sense the trade secret law afforded less protection from competition than a patent would have.

culpable conduct traditionally governed by state law. Thus in discussing trade secret laws in *Kewanee,* Justice Burger wrote as follows:

> [t]here is the inevitable cost to the basic decency of society when one firm steals from another. A most fundamental human right, that of privacy, is threatened when industrial espionage is condoned or is made profitable; the state interest in denying profit to such illegal ventures is unchallengeable. 416 U.S. at 487, 94 S.Ct. at 1889.

Thus the state interest in enforcing its law is far more compelling where theft of secrets or "industrial espionage" is involved.

A second line of inquiry suggested by the cases is whether there is a need for uniformity of legislation; that is, whether enforcement of state law would create a risk of conflicting legal standards governing a given type of conduct. This was a concern of the court in *Sears* and *Compco.*

In addition, it is important to determine whether Congress has expressed an intention to leave a matter free of protection, or whether it has simply left the matter "unattended." *Kewanee* may have stripped much of the force from this inquiry but it should be remembered that each of these inquiries is but an avenue of approach to the fundamental question of whether enforcement of a state law would interfere unacceptably with the purposes of federal legislation.

In this case there was no theft of trade secrets by EDI or UCC, no breach of contract, and no breach of a confidential relationship. In that sense application of the state misappropriation doctrine here would not be an exercise of the state police power, at least not to the extent of the state laws involved in *Goldstein* and *Kewanee.*

The input formats appropriated by the defendants here are not matters left "unattended" by Congress. They are writings within the meaning of the federal copyright laws, and this court found in its order of August 24, 1978 that the formats embody only an idea not an expression, and hence are not copyrightable. Thus the formats are the *type* of things covered by the copyright laws, but they simply do not qualify for protection under those laws; alternatively, if they do, the protection is very narrow. Nor would the format qualify for patent protection. These determinations, however, are not dispositive of the question of preemption in the light of *Kewanee.*

In addition, there is some risk that permitting states to limit the availability of the type of material involved here would result in substantial confusion as to whether use of such formats in a particular state was legal. This is hardly a compelling factor, though, as the *Kewanee* result produced the possibility of an equally nonuniform level of protection for trade secrets.

The overriding question is whether enforcement of the misappropriation doctrine here would conflict unacceptably with the goals of the federal patent and copyright laws. Enforcement of the state law would certainly not interfere with the federal policy of encouraging invention and creativity. On the contrary, that policy would be advanced by permitting the states to protect the input formats involved here. The more difficult question is whether application of the misappropriation doctrine here interferes unacceptably with the federal policy of full disclosure and free use of discoveries except where, in carefully limited circumstances, federal law grants temporary protection.

It is clear, first of all, that application of the misappropriation doctrine here would conflict with the federal policy of disclosure of and free access to discoveries. The result would be that no one could copy Synercom's input formats, and so Synercom would have a favored access to customers using its program, unless a competing package were devised with costs so much lower than Synercom's as to justify the expense of retraining users and of starting anew in the creation of stored data input. Thus the more precise question is whether this conflict with federal law would be so great as to require preemption of the state law.

It is this court's conclusion that the conflict with federal policy would be unacceptable, and that, consequently, the state law doctrine of misappropriation may not be applied to limit the use of Synercom's input format by EDI and UCC. To begin with, this court has found that the input format embodied is an idea and not an expression. None of the cases discussed has permitted a state to regulate the use of ideas. In fact, the court in *Goldstein* was careful to point out that "[n]o restraint has been placed on the use of an idea or concept." 412 U.S. at 571, 93 S.Ct. at 2317. Furthermore, the consequences of applying the misappropriation doctrine here would be significantly greater than the application of the state laws involved in *Goldstein* or *Kewanee.* The tape piracy statute in *Goldstein* did not prevent competition from recording "the same composition in precisely the same manner and with the same personnel as appeared on the original recording." *Id.* The trade secrets law enforced in *Kewanee* did not prevent others from growing a crystal identical to the plaintiff's by independent effort or by working backwards from the plaintiff's product. Application of the misappropriation doctrine here, however, would have a greater competitive impact, for Synercom's competitors would have to produce a package of substantially lower cost in order to attract any of Synercom's customers. Moreover, the focus of the misappropriation doctrine is much closer to the focus of the federal patent and copyright laws than either a tape piracy statute or a trade secret law, which are more concerned with ethical conduct than with the use of concepts and ideas. Thus the state interest here is not so great as it was in either *Kewanee* or *Goldstein,* where "industrial espionage" was involved. Finally, whereas the misappropriation doctrine typically extends protection for a limited period of time to matters with time value, as in *I.N.S.,* here permanent protection is sought under the statute.[7] Thus enforcement

7. Whether the doctrine of misappropriation even extends beyond the realm of matters with time value such as news or

of the doctrine here would work a more significant interference with federal policy than it would in the typical misappropriation case. In sum, assuming that the state law doctrine of misappropriation would prevent the defendants from copying Synercom's input format, the operation of the doctrine here is preempted.

Synercom advances two other theories in support of its claim of unfair competition. The first of these theories is that the defendants, in developing a structural analysis package patterned after that developed by Synercom, breached a duty of confidence owed to Synercom. The premise of the argument is that UCC learned of Synercom's STRAN program as a licensee of Synercom, and EDI learned of it through Bonner & Moore, Inc., another former licensee of Synercom.

An action for unfair competition based upon breach of confidence requires both a confidential relationship—usually by employment, contract, or agency—and confidential material. *Hyde v. Huffines,* 158 Tex. 566, 314 S.W.2d 763 (1958). While there may have been a confidential relationship here between Synercom and the defendants, the evidence indicates that the matter appropriated—including Synercom's program and input format—was *not* confidential. On the contrary, the input formats were published when the forms for their use were published. With respect to the program itself, the evidence at trial was insufficient to show that EDI's SACS II program was developed from confidential information about the STRAN program obtained by Bonner and Moore during its relationship with Synercom. Thus the breach of confidence theory must be rejected.

Synercom's final argument in support of its unfair competition claim is based on this court's finding that EDI and UCC engaged in willful, and hence criminal copyright infringement. Synercom argues from this premise that any illegal conduct in the course of business competition constitutes unfair competition. The problem with the argument is that it relates solely to the defendant's infringement of Synercom's copyright in its user manuals and not to the defendant's use of Synercom's input format. This court has already granted relief for the copyright infringement, and further relief for the same conduct under the theory of unfair competition would be unwarranted.

For the reasons discussed, each of Synercom's arguments in support of its unfair competition claim must be rejected. Thus Synercom's relief is limited to that awarded in this court's order of August 24, 1978.

VAULT CORPORATION v. QUAID SOFTWARE LIMITED

United States Court of Appeals, Fifth Circuit, 1988.
847 F.2d 255.

REAVLEY, CIRCUIT JUDGE:

* * *

broadcasts of sports events is a question that need not be decided here.

II

* * *

III. Vault's Federal Claims

* * *

IV. Vault's Louisiana Claims

Seeking preliminary and permanent injunctions and damages, Vault's original complaint alleged that Quaid breached its license agreement by decompiling or disassembling Vault's program in violation of the Louisiana Software License Enforcement Act (the "License Act"), La.Rev.Stat.Ann. § 51:1961 *et seq.* (West 1987), and that Quaid misappropriated Vault's program in violation of the Louisiana Uniform Trade Secrets Act, La.Rev.Stat.Ann. § 51:1431 *et seq.* (West 1987). On appeal, Vault abandons its misappropriation claim,[26] and, with respect to its breach of license claim, Vault only seeks an injunction to prevent Quaid from decompiling or disassembling PROLOK version 2.0.

Louisiana's License Act permits a software producer to impose a number of contractual terms upon software purchasers provided that the terms are set forth in a license agreement which comports with La.Rev.Stat.Ann. §§ 51:1963 & 1965, and that this license agreement accompanies the producer's software. Enforceable terms include the prohibition of: (1) any copying of the program for any purpose; (2) modifying and/or adapting the program in any way, including adaptation by reverse engineering, decompilation or disassembly. La.Rev. Stat.Ann. § 51:1964.[28] The terms "reverse engineering, decompiling or

26. While the district court held that the Louisiana Uniform Trade Secrets Act, La.Rev.Stat.Ann. § 51:1431 *et seq.*, was not preempted by the Copyright Act, the court held that the process of ascertaining information by "reverse engineering," used by Quaid to analyze the operation of Vault's program, did not constitute a violation of the Louisiana Trade Secrets Act. *Vault,* 655 F.Supp. at 761. This holding is not challenged on appeal.

28. Section 51:1964 reads, in full:

Terms of which shall be deemed to have been accepted under R.S. 51:1963, if included in an accompanying license agreement which conforms to the provisions of R.S. 51:1965, may include any or all of the following:

(1) Provisions for the retention by the licensor of title to the copy of the computer software.

(2) If title to the copy of computer software has been retained by the licensor, provisions for the prohibition of any copying of the copy of computer software for any purpose and/or limitations on the purposes for which copies of the computer software can be made and/or limitations on the number of copies of the computer software which can be made.

(3) If title to the copy of computer software has been retained by the licensor, provisions for the prohibition or limitation of rights to modify and/or adapt the copy of the computer software in any way, including without limitation prohibitions on translating, reverse engineering, decompiling, disassembling, and/or creating derivative works based on the computer software.

(4) If title to the copy of computer software has been retained by the licensor, provisions for prohibitions on further transfer, assignment, rental, sale, or other disposition of that copy or any other copies made from that copy of the computer software, provided that terms which prohibit the transfer of a copy of computer software in connection with the sale or transfer by operation of law of all or substantially all of the operating assets of a licensee's business shall to that extent only not be deemed to have been accepted under R.S. 51:1963.

disassembling" are defined as "any process by which computer software is converted from one form to another form which is more readily understandable to human beings, including without limitation any decoding or decrypting of any computer program which has been encoded or encrypted in any manner." La.Rev.Stat.Ann. § 51:1962(3).

Vault's license agreement, which accompanies PROLOK version 2.0 and comports with the requirements of La.Rev.Stat.Ann. §§ 51:1963 & 1965, provides that "[y]ou may not * * * copy, modify, translate, convert to another programming language, decompile or disassemble" [29] Vault's program. Vault asserts that these prohibitions are enforceable under Louisiana's License Act, and specifically seeks an injunction to prevent Quaid from decompiling or disassembling Vault's program.

The district court held that Vault's license agreement was "a contract of adhesion which could only be enforceable if the [Louisiana License Act] is a valid and enforceable statute." *Vault,* 655 F.Supp. at 761. The court noted numerous conflicts between Louisiana's License Act and the Copyright Act, including: (1) while the License Act authorizes a total prohibition on copying, the Copyright Act allows archival copies and copies made as an essential step in the utilization of a computer program, 17 U.S.C. § 117; (2) while the License Act authorizes a perpetual bar against copying, the Copyright Act grants protection against unauthorized copying only for the life of the author plus fifty years, 17 U.S.C. § 302(a); and (3) while the License Act places no restrictions on programs which may be protected, under the Copyright Act, only "original works of authorship" can be protected, 17 U.S.C. § 102. *Vault,* 655 F.Supp. at 762–63. The court concluded that, because Louisiana's License Act "touched upon the area" of federal copyright law, its provisions were preempted and Vault's license agreement was unenforceable. *Id.* at 763.

In *Sears, Roebuck & Co. v. Stiffel Co.,* 376 U.S. 225, 84 S.Ct. 784, 11 L.Ed.2d 661 (1964), the Supreme Court held that "[w]hen state law touches upon the area of [patent or copyright statutes], it is 'familiar doctrine' that the federal policy 'may not be set at naught, or its benefits denied' by the state law." *Id.* at 229, 84 S.Ct. at 787. Section 117 of the Copyright Act permits an owner of a computer program to make an adaptation of that program provided that the adaptation is either "created as an essential step in the utilization of the computer program in conjunction with a machine," § 117(1), or "is for archival purpose only," § 117(2). The provision in Louisiana's License Act, which permits a software producer to prohibit the adaptation of its licensed computer program by decompilation or disassembly, conflicts with the rights of computer program owners under § 117 and clearly "touches upon an area" of federal copyright law. For this reason, and the reasons set forth by the district court, we hold that at least this

(5) Provisions for the automatic termination without notice of the license agreement if any provisions of the license agreement are breached by the licensee.

29. *See supra* note 2.

provision of Louisiana's License Act is preempted by federal law, and thus that the restriction in Vault's license agreement against decompilation or disassembly is unenforceable.

V. CONCLUSION

We hold that: (1) Quaid did not infringe Vault's exclusive right to reproduce its program in copies under § 106(1); (2) Quaid's advertisement and sale of RAMKEY does not constitute contributory infringement; (3) RAMKEY does not constitute a derivative work of Vault's program under § 106(2); and (4) the provision in Vault's license agreement, which prohibits the decompilation or disassembly of its program, is unenforceable.

The judgment of the district court is Affirmed.

2. NON-PREEMPTION

MINUTEMAN, INC. v. L.D. ALEXANDER

Supreme Court of Wisconsin, 1989.
147 Wis.2d 842, 434 N.W.2d 773.

* * *

[The facts and trade secret issues of this case are printed earlier in this chapter.]

C. COMPUTER DATA:

Minuteman also challenges the decision of the court of appeals because Minuteman asserts both lower courts erred in their determinations on the fourth allegation of computer data misappropriation. Minuteman argues that the Defendants have violated sec. 943.70(2), Stats.,[6] with their alleged misappropriation of Minuteman's computer data. The circuit court found Minuteman's "evidence at the hearing fails to support the broad, conclusionary accusations" of the other alleged acts. The circuit court stated that even if the allegations could be supported by the evidence, damages represented an adequate remedy at law (relying on *Forest Laboratories, Inc. v. Formulations, Inc.*, 299 F.Supp. 202, 211 (E.D.Wis.1969)). Injunctive relief was therefore ruled inappropriate. The court of appeals affirmed the circuit court on this issue and we agree.

6. Section 943.70(2), Stats., provides:

Computer crimes. * * * (2) Offenses against computer data and programs (a) Whoever wilfully, knowingly and without authorization does any of the following may be penalized as provided in part (b):

1. Modifies data, computer programs or supporting documentation.

2. Destroys data, computer programs or supporting documentation.

3. Accesses data, computer programs or supporting documentation.

4. Takes possession of data, computer programs or supporting documentation.

5. Copies data, computer programs or supporting documentations.

6. Discloses restricted access codes or other restricted access information to unauthorized persons.

The denial of a temporary injunction is a matter of discretion of the circuit court. The sole issue on appeal is whether the circuit court abused its discretion. *Werner v. A.L. Grootemaat & Sons, Inc.*, 80 Wis.2d 513, 519, 259 N.W.2d 310 (1977). The circuit court found that Minuteman would not suffer irreparable harm and that damages represented an adequate remedy at law. In addition, the circuit court concluded that Minuteman had not established a reasonable probability of success on its fourth allegation. These are all satisfactory reasons for denying a temporary injunction. *Id.* 80 Wis.2d at 520, 259 N.W.2d 310. Minuteman has failed to show the circuit court abused its discretion. We, therefore, affirm the court of appeals on this issue.

The decision of the court of appeals is affirmed in part and reversed in part and the cause is remanded for further proceedings not inconsistent with this opinion.

STATE v. TANNER

Court of Appeal of Louisiana, Fifth Circuit, 1988.
534 So.2d 535.

KLIEBERT, JUDGE.

The defendant, Michael Tanner, was charged by bill of information with an offense against intellectual property (LSA–R.S. 14:73.2) and simple burglary (LSA–R.S. 14:62). A six-person jury found the defendant guilty on the former charge but was unable to reach a verdict on the latter charge. The defendant was sentenced to one year in parish prison, suspended, and was placed on one year's active probation subject to the conditions that he pay a $500.00 fine, court costs, and a monthly probation supervision fee of $25.00. The defendant appeals and assigns five errors, which we find to be meritless. Hence, defendant's conviction is affirmed and the sentence corrected to give credit for time served and, as corrected, affirmed.

Bill Groome owns Groome Enterprises, Inc., which operates a radio beeper rental business under the name First Page Beeper Service. In organizing the business Groome purchased a state-of-the-art communications business management system produced by D.B.C. Software for the beeper industry. The copyrighted system was based on a modified version of Cosmos/Revelations program and cost approximately $5,000.00. The serial number was 15156. The system tracked inventory, accounts, profits, and losses. In January of 1986 Groome hired Lane Geiger as a bookkeeper. Included in her responsibilities was the routine entry of business data into the data banks. Personnel from D.B.C. Software taught Geiger how to use the communications business management system.

Groome hired Michael Tanner in March of 1986 to act as sales manager of First Page Beeper Service. Approximately two months later Tanner began organizing his own beeper rental company, which was incorporated under the name Advanced Paging Services. Advanced Paging Services entered into a marketing agreement whereby it became an independent, non-exclusive sales and marketing contractor for Groome Enterprises, Inc.'s radio paging services. Several employees of First Page Beeper Service, including Geiger, began working for Advanced Paging Services in August of 1986. Geiger was to set up the computer billing program and act as bookkeeper.

On two occasions, in August and September of 1986, Tanner and Geiger used a key to enter First Page Beeper Services' offices after hours. Geiger made floppy disc copies of the Cosmos/Revelations program. Photocopies were made of the accompanying manuals. Relations between Tanner and Geiger became strained in November of 1986. Geiger approached Groome, informed him about the surreptitious copying of the program, and asked for her old job. Groome notified the police. A warrant search of Advanced Paging Services' offices uncovered the pirate copies of the software program and manuals. Tanner disclaimed any knowledge about the system or how it was obtained by Geiger.

* * *

Assignments of error numbers three and four address the sufficiency of the evidence in support of the verdict of guilty of violating LSA–R.S. 14:73.2. In *State v. Jacobs,* 504 So.2d 817, 820 (La.1987) the court stated:

> "[2] An appellate court in Louisiana, reviewing the sufficiency of the evidence to support a conviction, is controlled by the standard enunciated by the Supreme Court of the United States in *Jackson v. Virginia,* 443 U.S. 307 [99 S.Ct. 2781, 61 L.Ed.2d 560] (1979). Under that standard, the appellate court must determine that the evidence, viewed in the light most favorable to the prosecution, was sufficient to convince a rational trier of fact that all of the elements of the crime had been proved beyond a reasonable doubt.
>
> [3] When the conviction is based on both direct and circumstantial evidence, the reviewing court must resolve any conflict in the direct evidence by viewing that evidence in the light most favorable to the prosecution. When the direct evidence is thus viewed, the facts established by the direct evidence and the facts reasonably inferred from the circumstantial evidence must be sufficient for a rational juror to conclude beyond a reasonable doubt that defendant was guilty of every essential element of the crime. *State v. Sutton,* 436 So.2d 471 (La. 1983)." (Footnotes omitted)

To support a conviction of an offense against intellectual property the state must prove the defendant intentionally destroyed, inserted, modified, disclosed, used, copied, took or accessed, without consent, intellectual property. LSA–R.S. 14:73.2. Intellectual property is defined as data, computer programs, computer software, trade secrets, copyrighted materials, and confidential or proprietary information, in any form or medium, when such is stored in, produced by, or intended for use or storage with or in a computer, a computer system, or a computer network. LSA–R.S. 14:73.1.(9). All persons concerned in the commission of a crime, whether present or absent, and whether they directly commit the act constituting the offense, aid and abet in its commission, or directly or indirectly counsel or procure another to commit the crime are principals. LSA–R.S. 14:24.

The evidence offered by the state in support of the conviction was substantial. Copies of the programs, manuals and software bearing serial number 15156 were found in the offices of Advanced Paging Services. Neither Bill Groome nor his operations manager, Mary Condon, authorized anyone to copy the Cosmos/Revelations program. Lane Geiger admitted she copied the program at Tanner's request after he promised to pay her $1200.00 per month to work as bookkeeper for Advanced Paging Services. According to Geiger, she, Tanner, and Victor Bergeron entered First Page Beeper Service's offices in August of 1986 with a key supplied by Tanner. While Bergeron took pictures of paging systems for a training film being prepared by Tanner, Geiger made floppy disc copies of the Cosmos/Revelations program. Tanner "rummaged" around for information on accounts and proposals. Tanner and Geiger made a second entry in September of 1986 in order that additional copies could be made. Geiger downloaded the program onto the Advanced Paging Services' computer and, after printing out a master list of accounts, began deleting data entries in order that the files could be restarted at zero. It was during this period of time that Geiger approached Groome and informed him of the events at issue.

According to Tanner, Geiger offered to set up a computer billing system and act as bookkeeper for a salary of $1200.00 per month. Geiger was delegated the responsibility for the computer. Tanner disclaimed any knowledge about the program. He admitted he went to First Page Beeper Service's offices on two occasions with Geiger but claimed he did not know she was copying the Cosmos/Revelations system. He thought she was tying up loose ends with First Page Beeper Service. Tanner claimed that he found out about the Cosmos/Revelations program in September of 1986 and immediately called a computer consultant, Briant Manix, to erase the program. However, Manix testified that Tanner asked him to purge the data entries from the program, not the program itself. The program was still on the computer when the search warrant was executed in December of 1986.

Considered in the light most favorable to the prosecution, the evidence is sufficient to convince a rational trier of fact beyond a reasonable doubt that the defendant was a principal to an offense against intellectual property. The fact that the jury was unable to reach a verdict on the burglary charge has no bearing on our determination of the sufficiency of the evidence supporting the intellectual property conviction, for the infinite number of possible reasons for the jury's inability to reach a verdict reduces any attempt at rationalization to sheer speculation.

These assignments of error are meritless.

* * *

Accordingly, we affirm the conviction. * * *

Notes

1. One of the editors of this casebook conducted an extensive search in WESTLAW for cases *not* holding that Federal copyright law preempts the application of misappropriation theory to computer data or software. Only two cases appeared. The *Minuteman* case appears to treat the state computer crime statute as creating a tort of misappropriation of computer data, though it holds that the lower court was within its discretion in denying a preliminary injunction on the evidence presented. The *Tanner* case actually applies criminal sanctions for misappropriation of computer software.

2. Should the courts in these two cases have held that the misappropriation tort and crime respectively were preempted by Section 301 of the Copyright Act?

3. How should a computer crime/tort statute be drafted to avoid the preemption argument?

4. In *United States Golf Association v. St. Andrews Systems,* 749 F.2d 1028 (3d Cir.1984), defendant used plaintiff's golf handicapping formula as the basis for the programming of a commercially-marketed golf handicapping computer. The court dismissed a misappropriation claim because it found that the defendant was not in competition with the plaintiff, since the plaintiff did not exploit its golf handicapping formula commercially. Would there be a valid misappropriation claim if the plaintiff had in fact been selling its own pocket computers using the formula?

5. Defendant sells a stock index futures contract. Defendant openly advertises, "We have no connection with Dow Jones & Co., but we have programmed our computer with the Dow Jones stock market averaging formula as the basis for our futures contract." Does Dow Jones & Co. have a cause of action for misappropriation against defendant? See *Board of Trade v. Dow Jones & Co.* 98 Ill.2d 109, 74 Ill.Dec. 582, 456 N.E.2d 84 (1983) and *Standard & Poor's Corp. v. Commodity Exchange, Inc.,* 683 F.2d 704 (2d Cir.1982).

Chapter V

INTERNATIONAL INTELLECTUAL PROPERTY PROTECTION

A. TREATIES PROTECTING INTELLECTUAL PROPERTY

Almost all countries have intellectual property laws that grant legal protection for computer software and computer-related inventions. Economically-developed countries generally enforce these laws strictly; some less developed countries do not. Many influential people in less developed countries regard intellectual property legislation as a burden upon economic development, since the country has great needs for the import of intellectual property, but little opportunity for the export of export intellectual property. The lack of legal protection in these countries hurts the large multinational companies that are the main owners of intellectual property, because they lose profits when their technology is copied. These companies and their governments have retaliated by reducing investments and withholding favorable legal treatment.

The developed countries, and to an increasing extent the developing countries, are joined by treaties designed to secure minimum worldwide protection of intellectual property. These treaties cover areas important for computer technology: copyright, patent, trademark, and unfair competition.

Two treaties offer copyright protection: (1) The Berne Convention for the Protection of Literary and Artistic Works and (2) the Universal Copyright Convention (U.C.C.). Neither international convention offers worldwide protection of computer software, but both require that the domestic laws of each member country conform to minimum standards.

On October 31, 1988, the United States ratified the Berne Convention For The Protection of Literary and Artistic Works. In enacting the Berne Convention Implementation Act of 1988, Congress declared that the articles are "not self-executing under the Constitution and laws of the United States," and "[t]he obligations of the United States under the Berne Convention may be performed only pursuant to appropriate domestic law." Under the Convention, each member grants the same copyright protection to member nations as to its own nationals. Two clauses had prevented ratification of the Berne Convention by the United States, and resulted in the creation of the U.C.C.: (1) Moral Rights of creator, and (2) the no formalities requirement. The Moral Rights clause allows the author to object to "any distortion, mutilation or other alteration thereof, or any other action in relation to the said work which would be prejudicial to his honor or reputation." The moral rights even apply after transfer of the copyright. According to the Congressional proviso for ratification, moral rights have no effect under U.S. law. This right, however, has been found to exist under the Lanham Unfair Competition Act and the Copyright Act of 1976.

The "No Formalities" clause states that "the enjoyment and the exercise of these rights shall not be subject to any formality." This clause directly conflicts with the strict requirements for copyright notice, registration, and recordation under the Copyright Act of 1976. The 1988 Act eliminates the mandatory requirement for copyright notice of works published after March 1, 1989. As a strong incentive to encourage voluntary copyright notice however, the courts will not give any right to a claim of innocent infringement if there is not proper notice.

Under the 1988 Act, works of American origin must still meet the mandatory registration requirements. If the works are of foreign origin, the requirements are excused. The mandatory recordation requirements have been eliminated for all works, both American and foreign in origin. As an additional incentive to voluntarily comply with the copyright registration requirements, the 1988 Act doubles the amount of damages that may be recovered for registered works to between $500 and $20,000, up to a maximum of $100,000 if it is a willful infringement.

Each country must decide if computer software is excluded from copyright protection. All computer documentation, including flow charts, user manuals, source code and comments, and maintenance manuals are protected under the Berne Convention. There are no formalities that an author must follow before its software is protected under the Berne Convention. U.S. protection is for 50 years after the life of the author and is independent of protection extended by the country of origin. The author also has exclusive translation rights.

The U.C.C. requires each country to grant authors the same protection that it grants to its nationals. The United States, upon ratification of the U.C.C. in 1954, required that a work first published in the U.S. or any works authored by U.S. nationals or residents, even if published in a member state, must comply with domestic law. Under the U.C.C., the author must also comply with the country's formality for copyright protection. The U.C.C. also sets forth the formalities that must be followed: (1) there must be a "C" in a circle or the word copyright, (2) the name of the copyright owner, and (3) the year of first publication. Given the ratification of the Berne Convention, the importance of the U.C.C. has greatly declined.

The 1883 Paris Convention on Industrial Property is the basic international agreement on patents, trademarks and unfair competition. The convention establishes two rights for protection of industrial property. The right of uniform international treatment of patents: (1) each member country grants to an inventor from any other member country, the same protection as to its own nationals; and (2) the right of priority in which the applicant retains the date of the first application to establish priority and has a grace period of twelve months to apply for a subsequent patent in any other member country. The owner of a United States patent, or any other member country patent, must comply with patent laws of the member countries. This may become a problem when patenting software, given the varying treatment from none to qualified acceptance of software patents.

The second patent treaty is the Patent Cooperation Treaty (PCT) which was ratified by the United States in 1973. This treaty of thirty-nine member nations provides for a standardized patent application and centralized patent filing procedure. A patent applicant under this treaty is allowed time to decide whether to seek patent protection from the individual member nations without losing the priority date. Article 33 of Chapter II of the PCT provides for an international preliminary examination report on the patentability of an invention. The objective of this report is to:

> formulate a preliminary and non-binding opinion on the questions whether the claimed invention appear to be novel, to involve an inventive step (to be nonobvious), and to be industrially applicable. (Patent Cooperation Treaty, June 19, 1970, 28 U.S.Y. 7645, T.I.A.S. No. 8733)

Trade Secret Laws

Trade secret protection is generally not available outside the United States and the European Economic Community. If a country does have a trade secret law, it is most likely that trade secrets are protected by criminal laws rather than civil laws. Trade secret protection is also generally imposed by contract.

B. GENERAL AGREEMENT ON TARIFFS AND TRADE

The General Agreement on Tariffs and Trade (GATT) has served as a basis for world trade negotiations since 1947. The basic objective of GATT is to provide for uniformity in member country economic relations, and to allow member nations to enter into:

> reciprocal and mutually advantageous arrangements directed to the substantial reductions of tariffs and other barriers to trade and to the elimination of discriminatory treatment in international commerce.

The agreements formulated under GATT are not binding. Rather, GATT merely establishes policies to be followed by its members. The agreements under GATT apply only between governments, not between a government and a private party. The GATT trade agreements are not self-executing, and thus, do not have independent effect under United States law. According to the Protocol of Provisional Application, GATT does not have to be applied when it conflicts with existing legislation. Rather than possessing the status of binding domestic law, GATT has served as a forum for international trade negotiation. Even though the United States is a party to GATT, Congress has noted that GATT agreements do not completely determine United States foreign trade policies.

There are four basic principles that underlie GATT. Member countries should:

(1) try to reduce tariffs and eliminate quotas,

(2) adopt a most-favored-nation policy,

(3) not rescind tariff concessions, unless the other party is compensated, and

(4) settle trade conflict by negotiations.

These principles are not absolute and there are many exceptions. The problem with GATT stems from countries adopting non-tariff barriers in order to avoid these principles.

In late 1990, the chairman of the GATT negotiating Group on Trade Relations drafted the following proposals for GATT to adopt in protecting software by concepts similar to traditional copyright, trade secret, and the 1984 Chip Act provisions. Permitted antitrust limitations were also included. The proposals require agreement among GATT participants before the proposals become binding. Relevant portions follow.

C. PROPOSALS FOR SOFTWARE PROTECTION

DRAFT TEXTS ON TRADE–RELATED ASPECTS OF INTELLECTUAL PROPERTY RIGHTS, INCLUDING TRADE IN COUNTERFEIT GOODS

[GATT] Negotiating Group on Trade–Related Aspects of Intellectual Property Rights, including Trade in Counterfeit Goods, November 23, 1990.

The attached texts contain the results of the negotiations on trade-related aspects of intellectual property rights, including trade in counterfeit goods, as of 22 November 1990. They are put forward by the

Chairman on his own responsibility, but have been used by the Negotiating Group as the basis for negotiations. * * *

* * *

Part II: Standards Concerning the Availability, Scope and Use of Intellectual Property Rights

Section 1: Copyright and Related Rights

Article 9: Relation to Berne Convention

PARTIES shall comply with the substantive provisions [on economic rights] of the Berne Convention (1971). [However, PARTIES shall not have rights or obligations under this Agreement in respect of the rights conferred under Article *6bis* of that Convention or of the rights derived therefrom].

Article 10: Computer Programs and Compilations of Data

1. Computer programs, whether in source or object code, shall be protected as [literary] works under the Berne Convention (1971). [Such protection shall not extend to ideas, procedures, methods of operation or mathematical concepts.] [This shall not prevent PARTIES from requiring, as a condition of protection of computer programs, compliance with procedures and formalities consistent with the principles of Part IV of this Agreement or from making adjustments to the rights of reproduction and adaptation and to moral rights necessary to permit normal exploitation of a computer program, provided that this does not unreasonably prejudice the legitimate interests of the right holder.]

2. Compilations of data or other material, whether in machine-readable or other form, which by reason of the selection and arrangement of their contents constitute intellectual creations shall be protected as such. Such protection, which shall not extend to the data or material itself, shall be without prejudice to any copyright subsisting in the data or material itself.

Article 11: Rental Rights

In respect of at least computer programs and cinematographic works, a PARTY shall provide authors and their successors in title the right to authorise or prohibit the commercial rental to the public of originals or copies of their copyright works [, or alternatively the right to obtain an equitable remuneration corresponding to the economic value of such use] [, where circumstances arise by which the commercial rental of originals or copies of copyright works has led to [unauthorised] copying of such works which is materially impairing the exclusive right of reproduction conferred in that PARTY on authors and their successors in title].

Article 12: Term of Protection

Whenever the term of protection of a work, other than a photographic work, a work of applied art [or a computer program], is calculated on a basis other than the life of a natural person, such term shall be no less than 50 years from the end of the calendar year of authorised publication, or, failing such authorised publication within 50 years from the making of the work, 50 years from the end of the calendar year of making.

Article 13: Limitations and Exemptions

1. PARTIES shall confine limitations or exemptions to exclusive rights to certain special cases which do not conflict with a normal exploitation of the work and do not unreasonably prejudice the legitimate interests of the right holder.

[2. Translation and reproduction licences permitted under the Appendix to the Berne Convention (1971) shall not be granted where the legitimate local needs of a PARTY could be met by voluntary actions of right holders but for obstacles resulting from measures taken by the government of that PARTY.]

Article 14: Definition of Public

The term "public" shall not be defined in the domestic law of PARTIES in a manner that conflicts with a normal commercial exploitation of a work and unreasonably prejudices the legitimate interests of right holders.

Section 6: Layout–Designs (Topographies) of Integrated Circuits

Article 38: Relation to Washington Treaty

PARTIES agree to provide protection to the layout-designs (topographies) of integrated circuits (hereinafter referred to as "layout-designs") in accordance with the substantive provisions of the Treaty on Intellectual Property in Respect of Integrated Circuits as opened for signature on 26 May 1989 and, in addition, to comply with the following provisions.

Article 39: Scope of the Protection

Subject to the provisions of Article 40.1 below, PARTIES shall consider unlawful the following acts if performed without the authorisation of the holder of the right: importing, selling, or otherwise distributing for commercial purposes a protected layout-design, an integrated circuit in which a protected layout-design is incorporated [, or an article incorporating such an integrated circuit. Rights extend to an article incorporating an integrated circuit only insofar as it continues to contain an unlawfully reproduced layout-design.]

Article 40: Acts not Requiring the Authorisation of the Holder of the Right

1. Notwithstanding Article 39 above, no PARTY shall be obliged to consider unlawful the performance of any of the acts referred to in that paragraph in respect of an integrated circuit incorporating an unlawfully reproduced layout-design [or any article incorporating such an integrated circuit] where the person performing or ordering such acts did not know and had no reasonable ground to know, when acquiring

the integrated circuit [or article incorporating such an integrated circuit], that it incorporated an unlawfully reproduced layout-design. [PARTIES shall provide that, after the time that such person has received sufficient notice that the layout-design was unlawfully reproduced, he may perform any of the acts with respect to the stock on hand or ordered before such time, but shall be liable to pay to the holder of the right a sum equivalent to a reasonable royalty in a freely negotiated license in respect of the layout-design.]

2. The conditions set out in sub-paragraphs (a)–(*l*) and (*o*) of Article 34 above shall apply *mutatis mutandis* in the event of any non-voluntary licensing of a layout-design or of its use by or for the government without the authorisation of the right holder.

Article 41: Term of Protection

1. In PARTIES requiring registration as a condition of protection, the term of protection of layout-designs shall not end before the expiration of a period of 10 years counted from the date of filing an application for registration or from the first commercial exploitation wherever in the world it occurs.

2. In PARTIES not requiring registration as a condition for protection, layout-designs shall be protected for a term of no less than 10 years from the date of the first commercial exploitation wherever in the world it occurs.

3. Notwithstanding paragraphs 1 and 2 above, a PARTY may provide that protection shall lapse 15 years after the creation of the layout-design.

Section 7: Protection of Undisclosed Information

Article 42

1A. In the course of ensuring effective protection against unfair competition as provided in Article 10*bis* of the Paris Convention (1967), PARTIES shall protect undisclosed information in accordance with paragraphs 2 and 3 below and data submitted to governments or governmental agencies in accordance with paragraph 4 below.

2A. PARTIES shall provide in their domestic law the legal means for natural and legal persons to prevent information lawfully within their control from being disclosed to, acquired by, or used by others without their consent in a manner contrary to honest commercial practices [1] so long as such information:

— is secret in the sense that it is not, as a body or in the precise configuration and assembly of its components, generally known

1. For the purpose of this provision, "a manner contrary to honest commercial practices" shall [include] [mean] practices such as breach of contract, breach of confidence and inducement to breach, and includes the acquisition of undisclosed information by third parties who knew, or were grossly negligent in failing to know, that such practices were involved in the acquisition.

among or readily accessible to persons within the circles that normally deal with the kind of information in question;

— has commercial value because it is secret; and

— has been subject to reasonable steps under the circumstances, by the person lawfully in control of the information, to keep it secret.

3A. PARTIES shall not discourage or impede voluntary licensing of undisclosed information by imposing excessive or discriminatory conditions on such licenses or conditions which dilute the value of such information.

4A. PARTIES, when requiring, as a condition of approving the marketing of new pharmaceutical products or of a new agricultural chemical product, the submission of undisclosed test or other data, the origination of which involves a considerable effort, shall [protect such data against unfair commercial use. Unless the person submitting the information agrees, the data may not be relied upon for the approval of competing products for a reasonable time, generally no less than five years, commensurate with the efforts involved in the origination of the data, their nature, and the expenditure involved in their preparation. In addition, PARTIES shall] protect such data against disclosure, except where necessary to protect the public.

Section 8: Control of Abusive or Anti-competitive Practices in Contractual Licenses

Article 43

1. PARTIES agree that some licensing practices or conditions pertaining to intellectual property rights which restrain competition may have adverse effects on trade and may impede the transfer and dissemination of technology.

2B. PARTIES may specify in their national legislation licensing practices or conditions that may be deemed to constitute an abuse of intellectual property rights or to have an adverse effect on competition in the relevant market, and may adopt appropriate measures to prevent or control such practices.

COUNCIL OF THE EUROPEAN COMMUNITIES DIRECTIVE ON THE PROTECTION OF COMPUTER PROGRAMS

The Council of The European Communities,

Having regard to the Treaty establishing the European Economic Community and in particular Article 100a thereof.

Having regard to the proposal from the Commission.

In co-operation with the European Parliament.

Having regard to the Opinion of the Economic and Social Committee.

Whereas computer programs are at present not clearly protected in all Member States by existing legislation and such protection, where it exists, has different attributes;

Whereas the development of computer programs requires the investment of considerable human, technical and financial resources while computer programs can be copied at a fraction of the cost needed to develop them independently;

Whereas computer programs are playing an increasingly important role in a broad range of industries and computer program technology can accordingly be considered as being of fundamental importance for the Community's industrial development;

Whereas certain differences in the legal protection of computer programs offered by the laws of the Member States have direct and negative effects on the functioning of the common market as regards computer programs and such differences could well become greater as Member States introduce new legislation on this subject;

Whereas existing differences having such effects need to be removed and new ones prevented from arising while differences not adversely affecting the functioning of the common market to a substantial degree need not be removed or prevented from arising;

Whereas the Community's legal framework on the protection of computer programs can accordingly in the first instance be limited to establishing that Member States should accord protection to computer programs under copyright law as literary works and, further, to establishing who and what should be protected, the exclusive rights on which protected persons should be able to rely in order to authorize or prohibit certain acts and for how long the protection should apply;

Whereas, for the purpose of this Directive, the term "computer program" shall include programs in any form, including those which are incorporated into hardware; whereas this term also includes preparatory design work leading to the development of a computer program provided that the nature of the preparatory work is such that a computer program can result from it at a later stage;

Whereas, in respect of the criteria to be applied in determining whether or not a computer program is an original work, no tests as to the qualitative or aesthetic merits of the program should be applied;

Whereas the Community is fully committed to the promotion of international standardization;

Whereas the function of a computer program is to communicate and work together with other components of a computer system and with users and, for this purpose, a logical and, where appropriate, physical interconnection and interaction is required to permit all elements of software and hardware to work with other software and hardware and with users in all the ways in which they are intended to function;

Whereas the parts of the program which provide for such interconnection and interaction between elements of software and hardware are generally known as "interfaces";

Whereas this functional interconnection and interaction is generally known as "interoperability"; whereas such interoperability can be defined as the ability to exchange information and mutually to use the information which has been exchanged;

Whereas, for the avoidance of doubt, it has to be made clear that only the expression of a computer program is protected and that ideas and principles which underlie any element of a program, including those which underlie its interfaces, are not protected by copyright under this Directive;

Whereas, in accordance with this principle of copyright, to the extent that logic, algorithms and programming languages comprise ideas and principles, those ideas and principles are not protected under this Directive;

Whereas, in accordance with the legislation and jurisprudence of the Member States and the international copyright conventions, the expression of those ideas and principles is to be protected by copyright;

Whereas, for the purposes of this Directive, the term "rental" means the making available for use, for a limited period of time and for profit-making purposes, of a computer program or a copy thereof; whereas this term does not include public lending, which, accordingly, remains outside the scope of this Directive;

Whereas the exclusive rights of the author to prevent the unauthorized reproduction of his work have to be subject to a limited exception in the case of a computer program to allow the reproduction technically necessary for the use of that program by the lawful acquirer;

Whereas this means that the acts of loading and running necessary for the use of a copy of a program which has been lawfully acquired, and the act of correction of its errors, may not be prohibited by contract; whereas, in the absence of specific contractual provisions, including when a copy of the program has been sold, any other act necessary for the use of the copy of a program may be performed in accordance with its intended purpose by a lawful acquirer of that copy;

Whereas a person having a right to use a computer program should not be prevented from performing acts necessary to observe, study or test the functioning of the program, provided that these acts do not infringe the copyright in the program;

Whereas the unauthorized reproduction, translation, adaptation or transformation of the form of the code in which a copy of a computer program has been made available constitutes an infringement of the exclusive rights of the author;

Whereas, nevertheless, circumstances may exist when such a reproduction of the code and translation of its form within the meaning of

Article 4(a) and (b) are indispensable to obtain the necessary information to achieve the interoperability of an independently created program with other programs;

Whereas it has therefore to be considered that in these limited circumstances only, performance of the acts of reproduction and translation by or on behalf of a person having a right to use a copy of the program is legitimate and compatible with fair practice and must therefore be deemed not to require the authorization of the rightholder;

Whereas an objective of this exception is to make it possible to connect all components of a computer system, including those of different manufacturers, so that they can work together;

Whereas such an exception to the author's exclusive rights may not be used in a way which prejudices the legitimate interests of the rightholder or which conflicts with a normal exploitation of the program;

Whereas, in order to remain in accordance with the provisions of the Berne Convention for the Protection of Literary and Artistic Works, the term of protection should be the life of the author and fifty years from the first of January of the year following the year of his death or, in the case of an anonymous or pseudonymous work, 50 years from the first of January of the year following the year in which the work is first published;

Whereas protection of computer programs under copyright laws should be without prejudice to the application, in appropriate cases, of other forms of protection; whereas, however, any contractual provisions contrary to Article 6 or to the exceptions provided for in Article 5(2) and (3) should be null and void;

Whereas the provisions of this Directive are without prejudice to the application of the competition rules under Articles 85 and 86 of the Treaty if a dominant supplier refuses to make information available which is necessary for interoperability as defined in this Directive;

Whereas the provisions of this Directive should be without prejudice to specific requirements of Community law already enacted in respect of the publication of interfaces in the telecommunications sector or Council Decisions relating to standardization in the field of information technology and telecommunication;

Whereas this Directive does not affect derogations provided for under national legislation in accordance with the Berne Convention on points not covered by this Directive.

HAS ADOPTED THIS DIRECTIVE:

Article 1: Object of Protection

1. In accordance with the provisions of this Directive Member States shall protect computer programs, by copyright, as literary works within the meaning of the Berne Convention for the Protection of Literary and Artistic Works. For the purposes of this Directive the

term "computer programs" shall include their preparatory design material.

2. Protection in accordance with this Directive shall apply to the expression in any form of a computer program. Ideas and principles which underlie any element of a computer program, including those which underlie its interfaces, are not protected by copyright under this Directive.

3. A computer program shall be protected if it is original in the sense that it is the author's own intellectual creation. No other criteria shall be applied to determine its eligibility for protection.

Article 2: Authorship of programs

1. The author of a computer program shall be the natural person or group of natural persons who has created the computer program or, where the legislation of the Member State permits, the legal person designated as the rightholder by that legislation. Where collective works are recognized by the legislation of a Member State, the person considered by the legislation of the Member State to have created the work shall be deemed to be its author.

2. In respect of a computer program created by a group of natural persons jointly, the exclusive rights shall be owned jointly.

3. Where a computer program is created by an employee in the execution of his duties or following the instructions given by his employer, the employer exclusively shall be entitled to exercise all economic rights in the computer program so created, unless otherwise provided by contract.

Article 3: Beneficiaries of protection

Protection shall be granted to all natural or legal persons eligible under national copyright legislation as applied to literary works.

Article 4: Restricted Acts

Subject to the provisions of Articles 5 and 6, the exclusive rights of the rightholder within the meaning of Article 2, shall include the right to do or to authorize:

(a) the permanent or temporary reproduction of a computer program by any means and in any form, in part or in whole. Insofar as loading, displaying, running, transmission or storage of the computer program necessitate such reproduction, such acts shall be subject to authorization by the rightholder;

(b) the translation, adaptation, arrangement and any other alteration of a computer program and the reproduction of the results thereof, without prejudice to the rights of the person who alters the computer program;

(c) any form of distribution to the public, including the rental, of the original computer program or of copies thereof. The first sale in the Community of a copy of a program by the rightholder or with his consent shall exhaust the distribution right within the Community of that copy, with the exception of the right to control further rental of the program or a copy thereof.

Article 5: Exceptions to the restricted acts

1. In the absence of specific contractual provisions, the acts referred to in Article 4(a) and (b) shall not require authorization by the rightholder where they are necessary for the use of the computer program by the lawful acquirer in accordance with its intended purpose, including for error correction.

2. The making of a back-up copy by a person having a right to use the computer program may not be prevented by contract insofar as it is necessary for that use.

3. The person having a right to use a copy of a computer program shall be entitled, without the authorization of the rightholder, to observe, study or test the functioning of the program in order to determine the ideas and principles which underlie any element of the program, if he does so while performing any of the acts of loading, displaying, running, transmitting or storing the program which he is entitled to do.

Article 6: Decompilation

1. The authorization of the rightholder shall not be required where reproduction of the code and translation of its form within the meaning of Article 4(a) and 4(b) are indispensable to obtain the information necessary to achieve the interoperability of an independently created computer program with other programs, provided that the following conditions are met:

(a) these acts are performed by the licensee or by another person having a right to use a copy of a program, or on their behalf by a person authorized to do so;

(b) the information necessary to achieve interoperability has not previously been readily available to the persons referred to in subparagraph (a); and

(c) these acts are confined to the parts of the original program which are necessary to achieve interoperability.

2. The provisions of paragraph 1 shall not permit the information obtained through its application:

(a) to be used for goals other than to achieve the interoperability of the independently created computer program;

(b) to be given to others, except when necessary for the interoperability of the independently created computer program; or

(c) to be used for the development, production or marketing of a computer program substantially similar in its expression, or for any other act which infringes copyright.

3. In accordance with the provisions of the Berne Convention for the Protection of Literary and Artistic Works, the provisions of this Article may not be interpreted in such a way as to allow its application to be used in a manner which unreasonably prejudices the rightholder's legitimate interests or conflicts with a normal exploitation of the computer program.

Article 7: Special measures of protection

1. Without prejudice to the provisions of Articles 4, 5 and 6, Member States shall provide, in accordance with their national legislation, appropriate remedies against a person committing any of the acts listed in subparagraphs (a), (b) and (c) below:

(a) any act of putting into circulation a copy of a computer program knowing, or having reason to believe, that it is an infringing copy;

(b) the possession, for commercial purposes, of a copy of a computer program knowing, or having reason to believe, that it is an infringing copy;

(c) any act of putting into circulation, or the possession for commercial purposes of, any means the sole intended purpose of which is to facilitate the unauthorized removal or circumvention of any technical device which may have been applied to protect a computer program.

2. Any infringing copy of a computer program shall be liable to seizure in accordance with the legislation of the Member State concerned.

3. Member States may provide for the seizure of any means referred to in paragraph 1(c).

Article 8: Term of protection

1. Protection shall be granted for the life of the author and for fifty years after his death or after the death of the last surviving author; where the computer program is an anonymous or pseudonymous work, or where a legal person is designated as the author by national legislation in accordance with Article 2(1), the term of protection shall be fifty years from the time that the computer program is first lawfully made available to the public. The term of protection shall be deemed to begin on the first of January of the year following the above mentioned events.

2. Member States which already have a term of protection longer than that provided for in paragraph 1 are allowed to maintain their present term until such time as the term of protection for copyright works is harmonized by Community law in a more general way.

Article 9: Continued application of other legal provisions

1. The provisions of this Directive shall be without prejudice to any other legal provisions such as those concerning patent rights, trade

marks, unfair competition, trade secrets, protection of semi-conductor products or the law of contract. Any contractual provisions contrary to Article 6 or to the exceptions provided for in Article 5(2) and (3) shall be null and void.

2. The provisions of this Directive shall apply also to computer programs created before 1 January 1993 without prejudice to any acts concluded and rights acquired before that date.

Article 10: Final provisions

1. Member States shall bring into force the laws, regulations and administrative provisions necessary to comply with this Directive before 1 January 1993. When Member States adopt these measures, the latter shall contain a reference to this Directive or shall be accompanied by such reference on the occasion of their official publication. The methods of making such a reference shall be laid down by the Member States.

2. Member States shall communicate to the Commission the provisions of national law which they adopt in the field governed by this Directive.

Article 11

This Directive is addressed to the Member States.

Done at Brussels.

For the Council
The President

Note

In the early 1980s the European Commission became concerned about the lack of uniform software protection among the member states. The scope of copyright protection varied greatly among the member states. The Commission recognized that computer software was an integral part of the economic development of the Community. The Community market was distorted due to the different degrees of copyright protection. In addition, business firms in the Community were hesitant to develop software programs due to the amount of pirating in the industry and lack of uniform law. In order to encourage investment and development from businesses into the computer software industry, the Commission proposed the protection of computer programs.

Compare the Directive to United States copyright law for differences and similarities. Consider whether the Directive is more efficient or narrow than the U.S. copyright laws.

Notes and Questions

1. The U.S. copyright law protects the copyrighted work for 50 years after the death of the author. The EC proposed directive protects the work for 50 years after the creation of the work. Which term of protection is more efficient? More fair to the author?

2. The proposed directive in Article I, Section 3 does not extend to "ideas, principals, logic, algorithms or programming language underlying the program". Is this Section 3 similar to the idea/expression concept in U.S. copyright law?

3. Article I, Section 3 of the proposed directive discusses the protection of interfaces. How does this compare to the *Lotus* case?

4. The proposed directive differentiates between restricted acts and "secondary infringement". Does U.S. copyright law also make this distinction?

5. The EC's proposed directive equates computer programs with literary works which results in programs being subject to originality and creativity requirements. Does this unnecessarily limit the application of the directive?

6. Article 6 contains the word "interoperability," which is a political compromise. What will "interoperability" mean?

Chapter VI

COMPUTER CONTRACTS

A. APPLICABILITY OF THE UNIFORM COMMERCIAL CODE

UNIFORM COMMERCIAL CODE

§ 2–102. Scope; Certain Security and Other Transactions Excluded From This Article.

Unless the context otherwise requires, this Article applies to transactions in goods; it does not apply to any transaction which although in the form of an unconditional contract to sell or present sale is intended to operate only as a security transaction nor does this Article impair or repeal any statute regulating sales to consumers, farmers or other specified classes of buyers.

§ 2–105. Definitions: Transferability; "Goods"; "Future" Goods; "Lot"; "Commercial Unit".

(1) "Goods" means all things (including specially manufactured goods) which are movable at the time of identification to the contract for sale other than the money in which the price is to be paid, investment securities (Article 8) and things in action. "Goods" also includes the unborn young of animals and growing crops and other identified things attached to realty as described in the section on goods to be severed from realty (Section 2–107).

* * *

§ 2A–102. Scope.

This Article applies to any transaction, regardless of form, that creates a lease.

§ 2A–103. Definitions and Index of Definitions.

(1) In this Article unless the context otherwise requires:

* * *

(h) "Goods" means all things that are movable at the time of identification to the lease contract, or are fixtures (Section 2A–309), but the term does not include money, documents, instruments, accounts, chattel paper, general intangibles, or minerals or the like, including oil and gas, before extraction. The term also includes the unborn young of animals.

* * *

(j) "Lease" means a transfer of the right to possession and use of goods for a term in return for consideration, but a sale, including a sale on approval or a sale or return, or retention or creation of a security interest is not a lease. Unless the context clearly indicates otherwise, the term includes a sublease.

* * *

Notes and Questions

1. Article 2 of the UCC applies to the sale of goods; Article 2A applies to leases of goods. Both exclude services. A sale of an "off the shelf" computer program is a sale of goods, but a contract for a custom software program is a service. What happens when there is a contract to customize an "off the shelf" program?

2. Microsoft Word, WordPerfect, and Wordstar periodically appear in enhanced versions. Their makers usually allow the user to obtain the new version at a reduced cost. Is the new transaction a service upgrading the old version, or a separate sale of the new version?

3. Many businesses lease programs for mainframe computers. Does Article 2A apply to such leases?

NEILSON BUSINESS EQUIPMENT CENTER, INC. v. MONTELEONE

Supreme Court of Delaware, 1987.
524 A.2d 1172.

MOORE, JUSTICE.

Following a nonjury trial in the Superior Court, defendant Neilson Business Equipment Center, Inc. (Neilson), appeals a judgment awarding plaintiff, Dr. Italo V. Monteleone, P.A., damages of $34,983.42 for breaches of the warranties of merchantability and fitness arising from a lease contract for computer hardware, software and related services. The trial court found that the objects of the lease constituted "goods" under the Uniform Commercial Code and granted relief under the Code's implied warranties of merchantability and fitness. 6 *Del.C.* §§ 2–314(1) and 2–315.

Neilson's primary contentions are that the trial court erred (1) in classifying the computer software and related technical services as goods, and (2) in applying the Uniform Commercial Code's warranties to this transaction. Thus, we address for the first time the issue of computer software (programs) being treated as "goods" under the Code.

* * * We find that the classification of the contract as one involving "goods" is supported by substantial evidence. * * *

I.

Dr. Monteleone is a neurologist. In March, 1982, his office began investigating various computer information systems, since record keeping was entirely manual. The doctor gave Toni Reed, his bookkeeper and office manager, complete authority to acquire a suitable computer system. However, Ms. Reed had no prior experience in buying computer technology.

She initially considered four possible computer dealers, including Neilson. An advertisement in the local telephone directory listed Neilson as a dealer in microcomputers. Ultimately, Ms. Reed chose Neilson, in part because she had previously purchased an office photocopier from the defendant with satisfactory results.

After an initial meeting at Neilson's office, the company sent two representatives to study Dr. Monteleone's manual billing system. The parties ultimately signed a lease/purchase option agreement covering hardware equipment and software. As part of the agreement, Neilson agreed to customize the computer system to meet Dr. Monteleone's needs. The purchase price was $18,995, but Dr. Monteleone chose to lease the equipment in order to obtain favorable cash flow and tax benefits. The total of all lease payments amounted to $32,800.80. Dr. Monteleone retained an option to purchase the system at the end of the lease at fair market value, not exceeding 10% of the original purchase price. In addition to the lease, the parties executed a separate maintenance agreement valued at $2,182.00. To facilitate the transaction, Neilson sold the equipment and software to Tri–Continental Leasing Corporation, who in turn leased the items to Dr. Monteleone.

Although Neilson did not design the software, it renamed the program it had acquired elsewhere the "Neilson Medical Office Management System." However, Neilson did alter the program at various times in an attempt to make it meet the doctor's needs.

The computer was delivered in July, 1982, and problems immediately developed. For example, the system printed a separate bill for each treatment rather than one bill encompassing the doctor's services to a patient for a specific period; the bills and medical insurance forms were not compatible with Dr. Monteleone's records; patient information was not as detailed as required; and incorrect balances appeared in the accounts receivable register. Attempts to modify the system failed, and in August, 1982, Neilson hired a program consultant to solve the problems.

In February, 1983, Dr. Monteleone notified Neilson that the lease was terminated for cause. Thereafter, plaintiff stopped using the computer, although in March, 1983, Neilson's program consultant successfully effected some modifications. In June, 1983, Neilson took possession of the system pursuant to an agreement which allowed

Neilson to try and resell it. While in possession of the computer, Neilson modified the billing program and returned the system to Dr. Monteleone's office. The doctor never used the machine after its return, but continued timely lease payments under the contract.

The Superior Court ruled that the transaction involved goods and applied the warranty provisions of the Uniform Commercial Code. The trial court found that Neilson had breached the implied warranties of merchantability and fitness for a particular purpose, and awarded Dr. Monteleone damages totaling $34,983.42, with interest from March 11, 1983.

II.

This Court's standard and scope of review of the trial court's factual findings is governed by *Levitt v. Bouvier,* Del.Supr., 287 A.2d 671 (1972). Accordingly, those determinations will not be disturbed if they are supported by the record and are the product of an orderly and logical deductive process. *Id.* at 673.

The central issue before us is whether a contract for a computer system consisting of computer hardware, software and services constitutes "goods" under the Uniform Commercial Code. In our opinion, the parties agreed to a lease/purchase of a turnkey computer system which may properly be classified as a package constituting goods.

Article Two of the Uniform Commercial Code applies to "transactions in goods." 6 *Del.C.* § 2–102. The contract between Dr. Monteleone and Neilson is a mixed contract for both goods and services. When a mixed contract is presented, it is necessary for a court to review the factual circumstances surrounding the negotiation, formation and contemplated performance of the contract to determine whether the contract is predominantly or primarily a contract for the sale of goods. If so, the provisions of Article Two of the Uniform Commercial Code apply.

Neilson urges us to separate the contract into three distinct subparts—hardware, software and services. Defendant contends that only the hardware can be classified as "goods" under the Code, that there was nothing defective about the hardware, and thus plaintiff's claims for breaches of implied warranties fail. Neilson further argues that software is an intangible, and that intangibles do not constitute "goods" subject to the Code.

That argument is innovative, but unpersuasive. Neilson contracted to supply a turn-key computer system; that is, a system sold as a package which is ready to function immediately. The hardware and software elements are combined into a single unit—the computer system—prior to sale. The trial court's factual conclusion that the computer system is predominantly "goods" is supported by substantial evidence. Dr. Monteleone did not intend to contract separately for hardware and software. Rather, he bought a computer system to meet his information processing needs. Any consulting services rendered by

Neilson were ancillary to the contract, and cannot reasonably be treated as standing separately to escape the implied warranties of the Uniform Commercial Code.

Here, the parties cast their agreement in terms of a lease with an option granted Dr. Monteleone to purchase the computer system later. Although structured as a lease, it is clear that the parties intended to enter into the equivalent of a purchase and sale. Dr. Monteleone decided to lease because of favorable cash flow and tax benefits. Though structured as a lease, the substance of the transaction was a sale, and the trial court properly characterized it as such. *Earman Oil Co., Inc. v. Burroughs Corp.*, 625 F.2d 1291, 1293 n. 5 (5th Cir.1980).

Every contract of sale entered into by a merchant includes an implied warranty that the goods sold be "merchantable." The computer system, to be merchantable, must have been capable of passing without objection in the trade under the contract description, and be fit for the ordinary purposes for which it was intended. 6 *Del.C.* § 2–314(1) and (2). There is no dispute that the computer system failed in that regard. In general, the computer system did not meet Dr. Monteleone's expressed record and bookkeeping needs, even though Neilson's sales representatives informed Ms. Reed that the system would do so. The trial court correctly found that plaintiff had established all the elements necessary to prove a breach of the warranty of merchantability, namely: (1) that a merchant sold the goods; (2) that such goods were not "merchantable" at the time of sale; (3) that plaintiff was damaged; (4) that the damage was caused by the breach of the warranty of merchantability; and (5) that the seller had notice of the damage.

* * *

Here, Neilson knew that Dr. Monteleone, through his assistant, Ms. Reed, sought a computer system to meet specific information processing needs. Neilson admits that it was responsible for selecting the proper equipment, and also agreed to customize the software so that the computer system would be compatible with Dr. Monteleone's manual records. There could hardly be a clearer case where a buyer relies on the professional expertise of the seller than that presented here. Dr. Monteleone needed a system that would perform specific functions, and relied on Neilson's professional expertise and experience in the computer and information processing field to develop and deliver a satisfactory computer system. Neilson clearly had reason to know of Monteleone's reliance on the company's expertise and breached the warranty of fitness for a particular purpose. Its liability is established under the Uniform Commercial Code.

* * *

Accordingly, we affirm the Superior Court's finding that Neilson breached the Uniform Commercial Code warranties of merchantability and fitness * * *.

Notes and Questions

1. The court in *Monteleone* determined that the contract was a sale of goods, and that there had been a breach in the warranties of fitness for a particular purpose and merchantability. The computer software system, however, was to be customized for the needs of the lessee. Was this a contract for goods, or did the court extend protection to something that was really a service?

2. If a software program can be considered a good, therefore making the UCC applicable, what forms of warranties are available? What types of damages could a plaintiff seek?

B. WARRANTIES AND WARRANTY DISCLAIMERS

COMMUNICATIONS GROUPS, INC. a/k/a CGI v. WARNER COMMUNICATIONS INC.

Civil Court of the City of New York, New York County, Special Term, Part 1, 1988.
138 Misc.2d 80, 527 N.Y.S.2d 341.

LEONARD N. COHEN, JUDGE.

* * *

This action arises out of an alleged breach of a written agreement dated July 18, 1986 for the licensing, installation and servicing of a certain computer software package (the "Agreement"). Subsequently, the parties entered into two subcontracts for additional software and related hardware. As per the Agreement, defendant paid 50% of the amount due upon signing the Agreement. The remaining 50% was to be paid upon installation of the software. It is undisputed that defendant has not paid this remaining amount due under the Agreement.

The complaint, dated October 23, 1987, sets forth three causes of action for breach of contract to recover payment in the total amount of $16,650.00 still due and owing from defendant to plaintiff. Defendant does not dispute nonpayment, but defendant's Answer asserts four affirmative defenses and three counterclaims: the second affirmative defense/first counterclaim (first counterclaim) claims breach of an implied warranty of fitness of the computer software for defendant's specified known purposes; the third affirmative defense/second counterclaim (second counterclaim) claims breach of an express and/or implied warranty of merchantability of the software system and the good working order of its system and repair services; and the fourth affirmative defense/third counterclaim (third counterclaim) claims breach of contract in failing to provide support services to keep the system operational and in good working order.

As to the first and second counterclaims alleging implied warranties of merchantability and fitness for a specified known business purpose, the movant, CGI, contends that the Agreement provided for a software system or package which was neither for a tangible and movable product or goods nor a transaction for a sale or lease of either services or goods. Rather, CGI claims the Agreement was a license for computer software as an intangible service for limited use by defendant of "copyrightable information" and for the acquisition of the "abstract right" only "to listen" as with music on a record or disk. As a consequence, CGI argues that since implied warranties of fitness for a particular purpose or merchantability are remedies exclusively for contracts of the sale of goods and because the Agreement herein is not such a transaction of goods, the implied warranty counterclaims lack merit and cannot be maintained either under common law or under the Uniform Commercial Code (UCC).

Moreover, movant contends that even if the contract was for a sale of goods or a lease of goods, the contract, by its terms, provides for an express disclaimer of any implied warranties of fitness and merchantability. Therefore, movant urges that the first two counterclaims should be dismissed on this ground.

As for the third counterclaim, movant characterizes this claim as a breach of express warranties of the good working order and adequate support services of the computer software. Movant contends that such express warranties are lacking under the terms of the Agreement. Movant argues that any prior or subsequent oral promises or warranties which may have been made by movant cannot be considered part of the Agreement based on the parol evidence rules under common law and the UCC. Therefore, movant contends that the third counterclaim also lacks merit and fails to state a cause of action and should be dismissed.

The threshold issue presented is whether the software computer package or system provided for under the Agreement involved a transaction of "goods" as defined under UCC 2–105(1) to mean "all things (including specially manufactured goods) which are movable at the time of identification to the contract for sale * * *."

A review of the Agreement, the sole documentary and evidentiary matter submitted on these motion papers, shows that the computer software referred to therein is not defined. Nor have either of the parties in their motion papers articulated the precise form of the instant software. Software, however, is a widely used term and has several meanings.

Regardless of the software's specific form or use, it seems clear that computer software, generally, is considered by the courts to be a tangible, and movable item, not merely an intangible idea or thought and therefore qualifies as a "good" under Article 2 of the UCC. Moreover, UCC Sec. 1–102 provides that the Act shall be liberally construed and applied to promote its underlying purposes and policies.

Here, the Agreement clearly provides, in part, for the installation by CGI of its specially designed software equipment for defendant's particular telephone and computer system, needs and purposes. This equipment is expressly listed on schedules annexed and made a part of the Agreement. Said schedules clearly reflect installation by CGI of identifiable and movable equipment such as recording, accounting and traffic analysis and optimizations, modules, buffer, directories and an operational user guide and other items. A review of the counterclaim allegations shows that a software computer system and equipment were designed for defendant's special and unique known needs to store data relating to thousands of defendant's monthly telephone calls and to process and print this data on defendant's main computer frame so that defendant's operations would prove more time and labor efficient. Although the ideas and concepts of the CGI designed software system remained its intellectual and copyrightable property under the Agreement, the court finds in the context of the case law and the UCC that the contract terms clearly provided for a transaction of computer software equipment involving movable, tangible and identifiable products or goods and not solely intangible ideas and services and, in fact, such goods were installed by CGI for defendant's special purposes. Therefore, the first and second counterclaims are not dismissable on the ground of an exclusive contractual intangible services transaction as urged by movant.

The next issue raised by movant is that the contractual transaction failed to constitute either a sale or lease but merely was a license to use and service the software, therefore precluding defendant from relying on the common law or the UCC implied warranties of merchantability (UCC Sec. 2–314) and fitness for a particular known purpose (UCC 2–315).

The court finds that the Agreement clearly constituted a lease for the use of CGI's goods despite the terms expressed therein of a "license to use" CGI "proprietary" software for the payment of a one-time perpetual license fee in accordance with attached pricing schedules. The Agreement, although labelled a license agreement, is clearly analogous to a lease for chattels or goods. The movant has not addressed nor presented a distinction, factually or legally, between a license to use goods from an ordinary lease to use goods. Plaintiff's argument is based on an alleged contractual license to provide intangible services which, as hereinabove, the court rejects. Therefore, the court finds the Agreement clearly is a lease for the use of plaintiff's goods, despite the contractual label of a "license".

The law is clear that common law rights exist to state a cause of action or counterclaim for breach of implied warranties of merchantability and/or fitness for a particular known purpose involving the lease of chattels or goods without reliance on the UCC. * * *

Therefore, the defendant has sufficiently stated in its first and second counterclaims a common law breach of implied warranties under a contractual lease of goods. However, these counterclaims allege a purchase and sale of the software products. In this regard the contract specifically provided that the CGI software was to be its sole and exclusive property and upon termination of the agreement the defendant would return the software to CGI. Thus, CGI contends the transaction was not a sale within the meaning of UCC Sec. 2–106 (UCC 2–401) as no title passed from seller to buyer for a price and therefore defendant is precluded from asserting UCC's implied warranties.

However, New York courts have liberally construed the meaning of "transaction" under UCC 2–102, choosing to analyze the underlying facts of the agreement at issue in determining whether it sufficiently resembles a sale.

Courts in this jurisdiction have consistently applied Article 2 of the UCC to the leasing of chattels. Even if the lessor retains title to the goods, where the contract price of a lease is as large as the sales price of the same item, the transaction is analogous to a sale and will be covered by the UCC.

Therefore, the analysis used by the courts in this jurisdiction to determine whether or not a lease sufficiently resembles a sale so as to bring it within the scope of the UCC may be applicable to the Agreement herein. Although the Agreement specifically provides that plaintiff will retain title to the software, the Agreement appears to have no term and, in fact, is referred to as a "perpetual license." The economic effect of the Agreement is unclear from the sole submitted documentary evidence of the Agreement itself. Despite the Agreement spelling out the fee to be paid by defendant to plaintiff for use of the software, the court lacks information as to the actual value of the software.

Neither party has submitted an affidavit by a person with knowledge of the transaction at issue nor is the intent of the parties and surrounding circumstances of the whole transaction between the parties clear from the Agreement alone as to whether this transaction was a sale or only a lease of computer software goods. In the context of the case law as hereinabove, the contractual retention of title to the goods by CGI in and of itself is not determinative of whether this lease transaction resembled a sale for UCC applicability. There are factual triable issues raised in this regard and therefore dismissal of the implied warranty counterclaims for a sale for failure to sufficiently state a counterclaim or affirmative defense is not warranted. The court for purposes of this type of motion must accept the facts as alleged in the counterclaim as true. Here there is a sufficient showing to support legally cognizable counterclaims for the breach of implied warranties of fitness and merchantability for a sale of goods within the scope of the UCC.

Finally, as to the first and second counterclaims, the CGI contention that the Agreement contains an express and/or implied disclaimer of implied warranties lacks merit. The contractual provision relied on by CGI in this regard fails to alert or call to defendant's attention the exclusion of any warranty of merchantability or fitness for a particular known purpose but relates solely to CGI's maintenance, service and repair obligations for the software systems. Nor does this clause use the words "merchantability", "fitness", "disclaimer", "as is", "warranty" or "all faults".

The courts look to the relevant sections of the UCC, and even movant refers to the UCC, to test the validity of warranty disclaimers. The above words or other commonly understood language must be set forth in the contract, specifically and conspicuously, to call attention to the exclusion of warranties and make plain that there is no implied warranty in order to validate the exclusion of implied warranties. UCC Sec. 2–316 and Sec. 1–201(10). Therefore the plaintiff's motion to dismiss the first and second counterclaims is denied.

* * *

The court finds that the allegations in the third counterclaim sufficiently set forth a cognizable legal claim for breach of that portion of the Agreement as stated above which clearly imposed a duty on CGI to provide maintenance support services for the adequate functioning and operation of the system. It is noted that no affidavits or other evidence has been submitted relating to the specifications and criteria to be applied for the software operational performance. This appears to raise triable factual issues as to the merits of the alleged contractual breach. It is further noted that there is no explicit language in the Agreement that it is the complete and exclusive statement between the parties. Therefore, plaintiff's branch of the motion to dismiss the third counterclaim is denied.

Accordingly, the plaintiff's motion is denied in its entirety.

C. TORT AS AN ALTERNATIVE TO CONTRACT CLAIMS

1. MISREPRESENTATION

CLEMENTS AUTO COMPANY v. SERVICE BUREAU CORPORATION

United States Court of Appeals, Eighth Circuit, 1971.
444 F.2d 169.

HEANEY, CIRCUIT JUDGE.

The Service Bureau Corporation, a wholly-owned subsidiary of International Business Machines Corporation, appeals from a judgment awarding SM Supply Company $480,811 in damages, the basis of the award being actionable misrepresentations made by SBC to SM in connection with the sale of data processing services.

SBC asks this Court to set aside the judgment. It contends: (1) that the trial court erred in finding that SBC had made actionable misrepresentations, and (2) that the trial court's award of damages was improper.

* * *

SBC is engaged in the business of electronic data processing, offering to the public its services in eighty-four branch offices throughout the United States. It sells data processing services in the following areas: payroll, personnel records, accounts receivable, billing, sales accounting, marketing studies, cost accounting, inventory record, budgets and general accounting.

SM operates wholesale supply houses at Mankato and Rochester, Minnesota, and at Eau Claire, Wisconsin. It operated a similar supply house in LaCrosse, Wisconsin, through 1965. It deals in automotive parts and supplies, electrical construction materials, and electronic parts, supplies and equipment. Each outlet stocks more than sixty thousand items, ranging in value from a few cents per item to hundreds of dollars per item and in quantities of from one to several thousands each. SM's volume of business exceeded $6,900,000 each year from 1962 through 1966.

The first business relationships between the plaintiff and the defendant developed in 1961. In that year, SBC agreed to furnish data processing service to a Chevrolet dealership affiliated with SM. The services proved satisfactory and led SM's president to discuss SM's inventory problems with SBC. SBC indicated that it did not, at that time, have the computer capacity to provide the required data processing services. In the summer of 1962, however, SBC informed SM that, early in 1963, it would be acquiring an IBM 1401 computer which would have the capacity to produce data processing service for SM.

SBC made a study of SM's operations during the summer of 1962, with the view of providing data processing services to SM. SBC conferred with SM frequently during the study period and subsequent thereto. In February, 1963, SM signed two contracts dated December 20, 1962, under which SBC agreed to provide certain basic data processing services to SM. The two contracts were "accepted" by SBC in New York on April 4, 1963. Twelve additional contracts providing for additional services were signed by the parties during the succeeding four years. Processing of cards to be used in the system was initiated at the Mankato outlet in September, 1963; at the Rochester outlet in late 1963; and in the Wisconsin stores in the spring of 1964.

The nature of the data processing services provided during the four-year relationship between SBC and SM may be conveniently categorized into three basic stages. Initially, SBC automated SM's accounting and billing. At the same time, SBC used this input material to prepare certain monthly sales analysis reports and a weekly report of inventory movement. The inventory reports contained a six-week history of sales for all of SM's inventory. In August of 1964, the weekly inventory report was changed to a bi-weekly report which provided twelve weeks of history.

Second generation inventory reports began in January, 1965, and continued through December 4, 1965. These were bi-weekly reports which provided a twelve-week movement history, a record of inventory purchases, receipts and inter-branch transfers, and, for the first time, an on-hand balance of items for certain vendors selected by SM.

Finally, in December, 1965, SM signed a contract to obtain a third generation of inventory reports. These reports were to contain a detailed history for each item for the previous year, a movement history during specified months, an on-hand figure, and a computation of the number of weeks' supply of each item on hand. These reports were to be delivered beginning in January, 1966, but were not received until July, 1966, due to the discovery of an earlier programming error by SBC.

The services proved to be unsatisfactory to SM. It charges that the input method was slow and expensive, and that the reports were too error-prone and voluminous to be of use in purchasing inventory. SM finally terminated all contracts with SBC in January, 1967.

SM then brought the present lawsuit against SBC in September of 1967. It proceeded on the theories of rescission, breach of implied warranty, breach of contract, reformation and fraudulent misrepresentation. SBC counterclaimed for payments due.

The action was tried to the court without a jury. The court filed a detailed memorandum opinion and order on March 31, 1969. Clements Auto Company v. Service Bureau Corporation, 298 F.Supp. 115 (D.Minn.1969). The court denied recovery on all grounds other than misrepresentation, but found that SBC had made one central actionable misrepresentation to SM, i.e., that the proposed data processing system would, when fully implemented, be capable of providing SM sufficient information in a form such that when properly utilized, it would constitute an effective and efficient tool to be used in inventory control.

It further found that SBC had made several other specific actionable misrepresentations to SM:

(1) that the only way SM would ever get an inventory control system such as that in use at the Chevrolet dealership would be by automating the firm's accounting;

(2) that there were controls built into the system which were adequate to prevent any but a minimal number of errors;

(3) that Friden Flexowriters were a suitable input device to be used in the data processing system, that eight Flexowriters would be sufficient to do the job, that the Flexowriters could be operated by normal clerical personnel, and that the Flexowriters would produce a typed hard copy of the invoice which could be sent along with the customer's order; and

(4) that weekly sales management reports provided by the contract would allow management by exception.

It is conceded by the parties that the trial court properly relied on Hanson v. Ford Motor Company, 278 F.2d 586 (8th Cir.1960), in enumerating the essential elements of a fraud action in Minnesota:

"1. There must be a representation;

"2. That representation must be false;

"3. It must have to do with a past or present fact;

"4. That fact must be material;

"5. It must be susceptible of knowledge;

"6. The representer must know it to be false, or in the alternative, must assert it as of his own knowledge without knowing whether it is true or false;

"7. The representer must intend to have the other person induced to act, or justified in acting upon it;

"8. That person must be so induced to act or so justified in acting;

"9. That person's action must be in reliance upon the representation;

"10. That person must suffer damage;

"11. That damage must be attributable to the misrepresentation, that is, the statement must be the proximate cause of the injury."

Id. at 591.

It is important to emphasize that, in Minnesota, the element of scienter, or intent to deceive, or even recklessness, is not necessary to actionable fraud. * * *

* * *

While accepting the above as a correct statement of Minnesota law, SBC raises two arguments in opposition to the trial court's finding of liability for fraud. It first argues that the trial court erred in applying the Minnesota law of fraud to the present situation. The argument is rooted in what SBC considers to be a legal inconsistency in the trial court's findings. It is developed by SBC as follows:

(1) The trial court found certain aforementioned representations made to SM to be actionable under the Minnesota law of fraud.

(2) The trial court found that these same representations did not give rise to an express warranty because there was no valid agreement by the parties incorporating these representations into the contract, and that a disclaimer in the various contracts effectively negated all implied warranties.

(3) Under the relevant law, innocent misrepresentations and warranties, either express or implied, are substantially similar in nature.

(4) The passage of the Uniform Commercial Code by the legislature evinced an intent to have that body of law control all commercial transactions.

* * *

SBC candidly admits that this question has never been squarely faced by the Minnesota Supreme Court, but suggests that the governing policy of the U.C.C. compels its interpretation of the relationship between contract and tort law.

We cannot agree that this argument dictates a result other than that reached by the trial court. We start with the premise that the Erie Doctrine requires the application of Minnesota law. In the absence of explicit authority from the Minnesota Supreme Court, our obligation is "* * * to determine what the Supreme Court of Minnesota would declare the Minnesota law to be were this case before it." Village of Brooten v. Cudahy Packing Company, 291 F.2d 284, 288 (8th Cir.1961).

The first argument raised by SBC necessarily rests on two assumptions, both of which must be valid to sustain SBC's position:

(1) That the trial court's ruling as to the warranties was a correct assessment of Minnesota law.

(2) That the Minnesota Supreme Court would not permit the same representations to result in liability for fraud, but not for breach of warranty.

Assuming, arguendo, that the trial court correctly found the warranty disclaimer valid, we nevertheless believe that the Minnesota Supreme Court would find liability for fraud. SBC's conclusion that liability for innocent misrepresentation cannot exist without liability for breach of warranty compels two further conclusions:

(1) A contract provision which validly negates warranties is sufficient to negate liability for innocent misrepresentations.

(2) The Minnesota Supreme Court would be willing to distinguish between innocent and intentional misrepresentations. Both of these conclusions appear to be contrary to the main thrust of Minnesota law.

* * *

SBC relies to a great extent on our decision in First Acceptance Corp. v. Kennedy, 8 Cir., 194 F.2d 819 (1952), wherein we held that, under Iowa law, statements to the effect that an air conditioning system "would do the job" were statements of opinion rather than fact.

* * *

In finding that representations that the air conditioning system "would do the job" were predictions only, the Court relied heavily upon the fact that both parties knew that the storage system and the air conditioning system were completely new and experimental concepts. * * * As a practical matter, the Court noted that the ultimate design was a product of the knowledge of both parties and there was no proof whether the system failed because of inherent problems in the air conditioning design or because of problems with the new storage method.

In a less extraordinary situation, the Minnesota Supreme Court has indicated that the statement that "an ice machine, * * * when installed, could and would keep the buyer's ice box at a temperature low enough to prevent meat from spoiling" was a statement of an existing fact—the inherent capacity or power of the machine.

While the representation in question here would appear to fall somewhere between these two cases, we think that there was sufficient evidence from which the trial court could determine that the statement was one of fact rather than opinion and could reasonably have been relied upon as such. SBC was clearly an expert in the data processing area and was known to have extensive experience in the area of inventory control. There is nothing in the record to indicate that SM presented or thought it presented any special problems in regard to designing data processing services for inventory control. SM sought inventory control and was told by the expert in the field that the system designed would provide it.

Further, the fact that there were a number of specific representations made which were ancillary to and supportive of the main representation supports our view that, taken as a whole, the statements were factual rather than mere predictions. SBC was found to have made representations concerning the error-control features of the system it designed, the suitability and capabilities of the Friden Flexowriters, the input device it suggested and the usefulness of the weekly sales reports as a tool for management by exception. Each of these representations were statements of existing fact dealing with the inherent capabilities of the system designed by SBC. To a large extent, the accuracy of these more fundamental statements was essential to the validity of SBC's representation that its system would be a useful tool for inventory control.

* * *

Here, while the issue was controverted, there was sufficient expert evidence from which the trial court could find that these ancillary representations were not true. SBC argues that the difficulties occurred not because these representations were inherently inaccurate, but rather because they were based on false assumptions of volume made by SM. For example, it appears from the record that SBC's proposal was based on estimations of 45,000 parts and 6,000 customers per outlet when, in fact, substantially more parts and customers were involved. The record is also clear that these discrepancies caused some of the specific representations to be false and had some effect on the overall system. We agree with SBC that they cannot be held responsible for problems created by SM's lack of knowledge of its own operations. SBC's two-week study of SM's operation could not reasonably have given them this kind of detailed knowledge, nor could SM expect that it did.

Thus, the fact that eight Flexowriters were insufficient to keep up with the volume of input and that a hard copy of the invoices was not produced in time to be sent along with the customer's order cannot properly be attributed to SBC. More importantly, however, there was sufficient testimony in this record to support a finding that the SBC-designed system had inadequate error-control features, that the Flexowriters were not a suitable input device for SM's needs, and that it was difficult for normal clerical personnel to operate the Flexowriters. These errors of fact, as found by the trial court, are solely within SBC's field of expertise in data processing. Furthermore, there was testimony which directly linked these misrepresentations to the ultimate failure of the system to provide SM with satisfactory inventory control reports.

Finally, the trial court found that SM was told that the only way it would ever obtain an inventory control system such as that in use at the Chevrolet dealership would be by automating the firm's accounting. This is clearly a statement of fact. SBC does not contend otherwise. It is also conceded by SBC to be false. SBC responds by contending that the statement was not made and that it is so patently unbelievable that no reasonable reliance could be placed on it. However, there is evidence in the record which supports the trial court's finding to the contrary on both of these issues. There is also considerable evidence that the problems encountered by the system occurred, at least in part, because of the monumental effort involved in automating SM's accounting.

SBC next argues that there was no actual or justifiable reliance by SM on any representations made by SBC. We think this contention is without merit when applied to the initial relationship between SM and SBC.

We first note that we have previously discussed and disposed of SBC's contention that the merger and disclaimer provisions of the contracts negate reliance on the representations.

Secondly, we take notice of the inequality of knowledge as between the two parties. SBC was clearly the expert in the computer field and must be held responsible for superior knowledge in that field. The Minnesota Court has frequently looked to the relative knowledge of the parties in determining whether reliance on the representations was justified. * * *

* * *

Here, it is clear that, in entering into their initial agreements, SM relied upon the representations made by SBC regarding the usefulness and accuracy of the various reports. We agree with the trial court that SM had no basis for relying on representations such as that six weeks of inventory history would be sufficient. Such a statement was more peculiarly within SM's own business expertise. However, SBC's statements regarding the overall usefulness of its system, the presence of error-control features, the properties of the Flexowriters and the necessity of automating SM's accounting were all statements upon which SM, with its limited knowledge of computers and data processing systems, could reasonably rely, given the superior knowledge of SBC.

It is also clear that SM did rely on these statements in entering into the SBC contracts. SM wanted inventory control, and the record is clear that SM's management relied to some extent on the overall representations of SBC in deciding that SBC's proposal would provide it.

Nor can we agree with SBC's contention that the evidence concerning SM's investigation of the Flexowriters indicates as a matter of law that there was no reliance on SBC's representations. * * *

* * *

The evidence of the investigation may well have raised an issue of fact, but on the record before us, we cannot say that the trial court's determination was erroneous.

Lastly, SBC contends that even if SM was initially justified in their reliance on SBC's representations, SM discovered the falsity of the statements long before the relationship was terminated in January, 1967. The trial court found that while SM may have been aware of the problems with the system by the end of 1964, no duty to mitigate damages by terminating the contracts arose before September of 1966. It so held on the theory that SM was not aware of the exact cause of the problems and was so financially committed to the system that it was unreasonable for it to sever its contracts with SBC before that date.

Having carefully reviewed the applicable law and the lengthy record in this case, we conclude that the trial court erred in this finding.

The general rule in Minnesota is that "* * * a party defrauded cannot, after discovery of the fraud, increase his damages by continuing to expend money on the property retained and recover for such expenditures * * *." Perkins v. Meyerton, 190 Minn. 542, 251 N.W. 559, 560 (1934).

Following these principles, it is clear that a party to an executory contract, who prior to its performance discovers fraud, may not go forward with performance of the contract and subsequently sue for damages. The exception to the above principle is that where the defrauded party discovers the fraud after substantial performance or where it would be economically unreasonable to terminate the relationship, he may affirm or continue the contract and then bring suit for his entire damages.

In attempting to apply these legal principles, we must recognize two basic facts:

(1) The relationship involved here was based on a number of different contracts which were entered into over a period of approximately four years. Each of the basic contracts provided for continuing services and was terminable by either party upon thirty days' notice.

(2) The essential problems with the reports were apparent soon after they were provided to SM during 1963. While each of the three phases of the reports was progressively more sophisticated, the basic bulk and error-proneness of all the reports problems from the start.

Having considered the problem in light of the legal principles and factual relationship set out above, we conclude that as of April 30, 1965, SM was fully aware of the problems in the system and no longer had a basis for relying on the representations made by SBC.

* * *

At this point, we believe there is still support in the record for a finding that SM's actions resulted from SBC's representations. Even though the problems were visible, the system was new to SM and its employees. With some progress having been made in obtaining reliable input, and with the prospect of a longer history and more sophisticated report, SM may well have been justified in continuing the program.

However, when the second generation reports were received, beginning in January, 1965, SM clearly became aware of the debilitating nature of the problems in the system. The reports were still error-prone and difficult to use. Since the history was for a twelve-week period, we find that SM was justified in continuing with the system through March 31, 1965. At that point, reliance was no longer justified, and SM had the choice of terminating the contracts pursuant to the notice provisions or of assuming responsibility for further damages. Since the contract provided for thirty days' notice before cancellation, we find the cutoff date to be April 30, 1965.

At this point, we do not believe continued reliance can be justified by economic compulsion or by the fact that SM may not have fully realized the technical cause of the system's flaws. SM's contracts with SBC were for services and were terminable on a month's notice. While SM had paid substantial sums to SBC at this point, these payments had not resulted in any equity which might be lost by termination. Continuation of the contracts meant a continuation of the same monthly payments. On two occasions, the Minnesota Supreme Court has held that a party who discovers that he has been induced by fraud to enter into a 99–year lease shortly after the lease has begun to run cannot recover damages for the entire term of the contract. The court has so held on the basis that, in such a situation, the unperformed portion of the contract must be treated as a severable executory contract. Here, it is even more apparent that the doctrine of substantial performance is inapplicable. SM's efforts and expense did justify some attempt to salvage the SBC system. However, we have already taken that factor into account in our conclusion. As Judge Blackmun stated in Hanson v. Ford Motor Company, *supra,* 278 F.2d at 598, " * * * the representer is not a guarantor."

Nor can SM's continued reliance be justified by the fact that they were not necessarily aware of the technical cause of their problems. While this factor would have some initial importance in permitting SM an opportunity to correct the system's faults, we believe that by March 31, 1965, it had unsuccessfully explored sufficient corrective measures to be no longer justified in relying on SBC's original representations.

In arriving at this conclusion, we have also recognized that all of the representations complained of occurred prior to the signing of the initial contracts in December, 1962. SM makes no claim that its subsequent conduct was induced by continued fraudulent misrepresentations. As a matter of fact, the record clearly indicates that at least one of SBC's employees cautioned SM, in late 1964, against further expansion of the system.

We, therefore, conclude that SBC is liable in fraud for the representations it made to SM. However, we further find that this liability ended on April 30, 1965, and that SM may not recover for contracts entered after that date or for payments made after that date under existing contracts. We recognize that this finding imposes a burden on SBC, but we believe that it is one that would be imposed by the Minnesota Court. * * *

* * *

We now turn to the issue of

DAMAGES

The trial court awarded the following damages to SM:

(1) The sum paid by SM to SBC for data processing services from December, 1962, through January, 1967	$192,551.65
(2) The expenses incurred by SM in leasing the Flexowriters through January 31, 1967, plus the expense incurred in maintaining them, less their salvage value as of January 31, 1967 ($4,500)	$102,198.11
(3) The increased cost of clerical personnel to SM in the years 1963 through 1965	$ 24,135.43
(4) The increased cost of office supplies to SM in the years 1963 through 1966	$ 37,921.60
(5) A portion of the salaries paid by SM to its executives for the supervision of the data processing system in the years 1963 through 1966	$ 50,500.00
(6) Excess inventory purchased in 1966 and still on hand at the date of trial	$ 68,094.00
(7) Interest on Items (1) through (5)	$ 74,241.71
TOTAL	$549,642.50

Less, Benefits Received by SM:

Original Contracts	$15,000.00
(Unpaid)	$ 1,700.00
	$16,700.00
Second and Third Generation Reports	$18,698.98
(Unpaid)	$ 5,140.31
	$23,839.29
Interest on Counterclaim Award	$ 867.88
Year-end Inventory Contracts	$14,799.00
Executive Salaries	$12,625.00

TOTAL	$ 68,831.17
NET RECOVERY	$480,811.33

We have previously accepted SBC's contention that the representations it made to SM could not have been relied upon throughout the life of the contracts between the parties. We have fixed the outer limits of reliance as of March 31, 1965, and have indicated that SM should be given an additional thirty days thereafter to terminate its contracts with SBC.

It follows that SM's award must be reduced to reflect the fact that it is not entitled to recover for payments to SBC for services rendered after April 30, 1965, or for the increased cost of clerical personnel, supplies or executive salaries after that date. Furthermore, the award must be reduced to reflect any savings SM might have effected had it been able to cancel its lease agreement with the Transport Leasing Company as of March 31, 1965; any saving that it might have effected by cancelling its maintenance agreement as of the same date; and any increase in the salvage value of the Flexowriters in excess of $8,500 by virtue of being able to cancel at an earlier date. Finally, the award must be reduced to reflect the interest allowed on those payments or costs which we have disallowed.

Our computations indicate that these changes will reduce the award by approximately $153,000, depending on whether SM had a right to cancel its lease agreement with Transport Leasing on March 31, 1965, and a right to terminate its maintenance agreement with Friden on the same date. SBC contends, however, that the award should be reduced further. It urges (1) that because of contract provisions, the total award cannot exceed the total charges for services, and that no special or consequential damages can be awarded; (2) that no award can be made for interest prior to the decision; and (3) that no award is justified for the excess inventory purchased in 1966 and still on hand at the date of trial. We consider these contentions seriatim.

Contractual Limitation of Liability

The contracts between SBC and SM contained the following provision:

> "* * * SBC's liability with respect to this agreement is limited to the total charge for the services provided herein and no special or consequential damages may be recovered."

SBC argues that this provision validly limits the damages which can be awarded here. Such contract provisions appear to be valid under New York law. Farris Engineering Corp. v. Service Bureau Corp., 406 F.2d 519 (3rd Cir.1969). There is also authority for the proposition that contract provisions may operate to limit liability in suits brought for breach of contract under Minnesota law.

* * * We think the issue is properly posed as follows: Where a cause of action for fraud has been established, would Minnesota law

give effect to a contract provision limiting liability in awarding damages proven to result from the fraud? We believe that Minnesota law controls because in the final analysis the issue is controlled by the law of fraud.

In many ways, this question is substantially similar to SBC's earlier contention that a merger and warranty provision is effective to negate fraud. As it did there, SBC concedes that the contract provision is ineffective against intentional deceit, but argues it must be given effect where the fraud is based on "innocent misrepresentations." SBC again emphasizes the anomaly of obtaining different results in contract actions as opposed to fraud actions which do not include an element of bad faith.

However, we remain unconvinced that this difference in result would lead the Minnesota Court to give effect to the contract provision. In reaching this decision, we have relied to a large extent on our earlier analysis of the Minnesota law of fraud vis-a-vis Minnesota contract law. Minnesota's strong policy of providing an effective remedy in fraud would be substantially undermined were we to give effect to this severe restriction on the amount of liability. Having previously held that Minnesota would not give effect to a contract provision which would negate the fact of liability, we believe it inconsistent to hold that the court would then give effect to a provision limiting the amount of liability.

At least two of the Minnesota cases which have indicated that a particular contract limitation on damages or remedies is valid have done so only in the absence of allegations or proof of fraud. In the context of the Minnesota law of fraud, we believe it would be improper to read these cases as referring only to intentional fraudulent conduct.

* * *

INVENTORY

There are at least two reasons why no recovery can be permitted on a fraud theory for the "obsolete inventory":

(1) The inventory was purchased long after the date which we have fixed as being the date beyond which there could be reliance by SM on representations made to it by SBC.

(2) The record is bare of any testimony directly relating the purchases of the obsolete inventory to misrepresentations made to SM by SBC. The testimony relied upon by the trial court to establish the alleged loss was that of Charles C. Butler. He testified only that $363,000 of inventory purchased in 1966 remained on the shelves in 1969, and that this inventory had a value, as of the date of trial, of $181,000.

No recovery for the "obsolete inventory" can be permitted on a breach of warranty theory, because the trial court expressly found that no express or implied warranties had been made by SBC and no cross-appeal is taken by SM on this finding.

Recovery on a breach of contract theory for the "obsolete inventory" is, as the trial court suggests in its opinion, a possibility, but we feel there is too little evidence in this record to justify a remand to the trial court for a determination as to whether SM can recover under such a theory. The sampling technique used to compute the value of the obsolete inventory as of December 31, 1966, is subject to serious question, and SM failed to establish that the "obsolete inventory" was larger on December 31, 1966, than it had been in any of the earlier years. The latter point is particularly important in the light of SM's contention that it purchased the data processing services because its inventory was out of control.

The appellant's final contention is that evidence as to damages is so speculative and the evidence as to benefits received so negligible that the trial court erred in granting any award. We cannot agree. The Supreme Court and this Court have stated on a number of occasions that, once the fact of damages has been established, the courts are allowed considerable leeway in arriving at the amount of damages.

We do not believe, except as hereinbefore pointed out, that the trial court abused its discretion in awarding damages. Contrary to the defendant's contention, the position of SM did not improve during the years that it justifiably relied on SBC's representations. Its average inventories increased from $1,823,000 in 1962 to $2,106,000 in 1965. The rate of turnover of inventory fluctuated, but it was worse in 1965 than it had been in 1962. Inventories as a percent of sales also increased.

SM's sales did increase during the period of reliance, from $6,918,000 in 1962 to $7,750,000 in 1965, but this increase only led to increased losses.

SM's losses were higher during the three years of reliance than they were in the three preceding years. While it can be argued that the largest loss occurred in 1963 before the contracts became effective, it can also be argued that at least a portion of the $445,000 loss in 1967 was attributable to SBC's misrepresentations.

We acknowledge that there is evidence in this record from which the trial court could have found that SM caused or substantially contributed to its own losses by poor management, inferior clerical personnel, absence of a uniform pricing policy for its merchandise, absence of a uniform discount policy, and by contracting for second and third generation reports before it was ready to use them; but the trial court found to the contrary, and we are not prepared to say it made a mistake in so doing.

The judgment of the lower court is affirmed in part and reversed in part. We remand to the District Court for recomputation of damages in accordance with this opinion.[18]

The parties are to bear the costs of their own briefs and are to share the costs of the appendix equally. All other costs in this Court are to be borne by the Appellant.

2. ALTERNATIVES TO CONTRACT CLAIMS: FRAUD AND NEGLIGENCE

GLOVATORIUM, INC. v. NCR CORPORATION

United States Court of Appeals, Ninth Circuit, 1982.
684 F.2d 658.

ALARCON, CIRCUIT JUDGE:

Glovatorium filed this action against NCR Corporation (NCR) in state court alleging breach of contract, intentional and negligent misrepresentation, breach of warranty, and fraud for conversion of equipment. NCR removed the action to the federal district court on the basis of diversity of citizenship. After a jury trial, Glovatorium was awarded compensatory damages for intentional misrepresentation, breach of warranty, and breach of the implied covenant of good faith. Punitive damages were also awarded.

18. As an aid to the trial court on remand, we have attempted to estimate the amount of SM's award based on our opinion. In so doing, we followed the trial court's method of computing damages whenever it was consistent with our opinion. We also assumed that SM's total expenses in leasing and maintaining the Flexowriters were permanently fixed as of April 30, 1965. To the extent that this assumption is not accurate, the trial court should reduce the amount awarded for those items and for the corresponding interest.

ESTIMATED AWARD PURSUANT TO OUR OPINION

(1) The sum paid by SM to SBC for data processing services from December, 1962, through April, 1965		$ 89,000.00
(2) The expense incurred by SM in leasing the Flexowriters through April 30, 1965, plus the expense incurred in maintaining them, less their salvage value as of April 30, 1965 ($8,500.00)		$ 98,198.00
(3) The increased cost of clerical personnel to SM in the years 1963 through April 30, 1965		$ 19,922.00
(4) The increased cost of office supplies to SM in the years 1963 through April 30, 1965		$ 29,086.00
(5) A portion of the salaries paid by SM to its executives for the supervision of the data processing system in the years 1963 through 1966		$ 32,417.00
(6) Excess inventory purchased in 1966 and still on hand at the date of trial		$ .00
(7) Interest on Items (1) and (2)		$ 30,671.00
TOTAL		$299,294.00
Less, Benefits Received by SM:		
Original Contracts	$ 7,500.00	
Second and Third Generation Reports	$ .00*	
Year-end Inventory Contracts	$10,000.00	
Executive Salaries	$ 8,104.00	
Counterclaims for Amounts Unpaid after 4–30–65	$23,014.83	
Interest on Counterclaim Award	$ 2,930.00	
TOTAL		$ 51,548.83
NET RECOVERY		$247,745.17

* Assuming that no payments were made for these services prior to April 30, 1965.

NCR appeals from the judgment of the district court.

I. Sufficiency of the Evidence of Fraud by NCR

NCR contends that the evidence adduced at trial did not establish that it acted fraudulently in the sale of the SPIRIT/8200 computer system to Glovatorium. Under California law, fraud is established when a misrepresentation is knowingly made with the intent to induce reliance, and justifiable reliance results, causing plaintiff damage. Review of whether there is sufficient evidence to support the finding of fraud is, however, a procedural matter in which we must apply federal law. This court will not disturb a jury verdict unless the evidence is such "that no reasonable man would accept it as adequate to establish the existence of each fact essential to the liability." It is the function of the jury, not of this court, to weigh conflicting evidence and judge the credibility of witnesses. *Standard Oil Co. v. Perkins,* 347 F.2d 379, 383 (9th Cir.1965).

A.

Glovatorium sought to show fraud by NCR in that NCR sold the SPIRIT system with knowledge of its defects. Review of the record indicates that the evidence supports the claim that NCR had knowledge of the defects. First, Norman Cohen, a former district manager for NCR, testified that he notified the SPIRIT support group in Dayton, Ohio of problems with the system. He also stated that he advised "headquarters" about these problems. Second, NCR's own witness, Peter Ford, who was associated with the SPIRIT support group stated that as project leader for the SPIRIT development team, he "was responsible for the time and delivery of the system and *reporting progress to management at NCR.*" (emphasis added). It can reasonably be inferred that as project leader he knew of the problems and that as part of his report to NCR management about the progress of the system, he advised them of the problems with the system. Third, there was evidence that NCR "corporate" attempted to cover up defects in the system. For instance, one of the problems experienced with the system was that it was so slow that many clients found they could accomplish the same task faster if it were done manually rather than using the SPIRIT system. NCR, however, developed and distributed a demonstrator model for the system to be used as a sales tool that "was specifically designed to function very, very effectively, and very fast, much more so than the actual SPIRIT programs did." Thus, it is reasonable to infer knowledge of this defect on the part of NCR since the demonstrator was specifically designed to cover it up.

B.

Fraud on the part of NCR was also claimed with regard to the sales representations made to Glovatorium concerning the route accounting system.

Under California law, fraud is properly inferred from the immediate failure to perform a promise. *Kaylor v. Crown Zellerbach, Inc.,* 643

F.2d 1362, 1368 (9th Cir.1981). In the matter before us, it was represented to Glovatorium that the computer would perform route accounting functions and that it would be delivered with the system by September, 1975. The computer was delivered in September, 1975, but could not be used for any route accounting functions. The payroll function was not operating until late 1975 or early 1976, and once in operation, it never ran properly. The route accounting system (without the other systems) was not available until March, 1976. Only one of Glovatorium's five routes was ever put on the computer because of problems with the system. The accounts payable and general ledger systems were *never* installed because of problems. Under *Kaylor,* the immediate failure to perform in terms of the installation and the operation of the computer systems for which Glovatorium contracted is evidence from which fraud on the part of NCR is properly inferred.

Further evidence of fraud is shown by Warman's testimony that the 8200/SPIRIT system was never designed to perform a route accounting function. Yet, Glovatorium was sold the 8200/SPIRIT system to perform a route accounting function. Moreover, NCR had also determined that the SPIRIT system should not be modified. Yet, Glovatorium was sold a modified version of SPIRIT.[3]

C.

NCR contends that even if the above evidence shows fraud on the part of NCR employees, there is no evidence to establish fraud by NCR.

California law provides for corporate liability where "the advance knowledge, ratification, or act of oppression, fraud, or malice [is] * * * on the part of an officer, director, or managing agent of the corporation." Cal.Civil Code § 3294(b). The key inquiry in the determination of whether an employee is a managing agent is "the degree of discretion the employees possess in making decisions that will ultimately determine corporate policy." *Egan v. Mutual of Omaha Insurance Co.,* 24 Cal.3d 809, 822–23, 620 P.2d 141, 148, 169 Cal.Rptr. 691, 698 (1979), *cert. denied & appeal denied,* 445 U.S. 912, 100 S.Ct. 1271, 63 L.Ed.2d 597 (1980).

Warman testified that his conduct in connection with the Glovatorium sales transaction was, to his knowledge, "consistent * * * with NCR's *general policies and practices.*" (emphasis added). Indeed, the record demonstrates fraudulent acts by several NCR employees. First, Warman made the sale to Glovatorium of the computer system with the

3. NCR Corporate headquarters rejected the original contracts signed by Glovatorium which indicated a modification of SPIRIT. RT: 206–07. Thomas Warman, the NCR salesman, then prepared the contracts in such a way that the proposed modification was not apparent on the face of the contracts and they were approved. RT: 1010. Information concerning the anticipated volume of transactions, referred to as a configurator, was also sent with both sets of contracts. The configurator sent the first time was accurate. RT: 213–14. The configurator sent with the second set of contracts, however, was one in which the volume of transactions had been falsely reduced so that it had no relationship to the Glovatorium installation. RT: 216, 235–36.

knowledge that it was not designed to perform the functions for which it was sold. Second, the Oakland office manager for NCR and his assistant told one of their employees to switch the serial numbers on the drive from a loaner with the serial numbers on the Glovatorium drive. Glovatorium, however, had been told that the loaner was temporary.

There is also, as discussed above, evidence of fraudulent sales practices regarding the SPIRIT system at the direction of NCR headquarters. NCR seeks to distinguish such alleged fraud from the sales representations made to Glovatorium. The evidence of directions from headquarters is, however, probative of intent and, therefore establishes lack of good faith on the part of NCR and its sales personnel in the representations made concerning the route accounting systems. Even in criminal cases, probative evidence of willingness to participate in similar crimes is admissible.

The above evidence and the inferences that can reasonably be drawn from it are adequate to support the jury's conclusion that someone at NCR who was an officer or a director or who qualified as a managing agent participated in or ratified the fraudulent sale representations made to Glovatorium. This is particularly true in light of the fact that NCR offered no evidence to rebut such an inference. A reasonable person might accept the above evidence as adequate to establish NCR's liability; we will not disturb the jury verdict.

II. Requested Jury Instruction Defining Managing Agent

Appellant claims prejudicial error in the refusal of the trial court to give its requested instruction which would have defined the term "managing agent."

NCR requested that the judge instruct the jury that corporate liability existed, inter alia, if a managing agent "having power to bind the corporation" was involved in the fraud. No error existed in the trial judge's refusal to give the proffered instruction because the definition of a managing agent is not restricted to those who have power to bind the corporation. As discussed above, the California Supreme Court has held that focus in determining whether one is a managing agent is the degree of discretion the employee has to make decisions that will ultimately determine corporate policy. *Egan,* 24 Cal.3d at 822–23, 620 P.2d at 148, 169 Cal.Rptr. at 698. NCR's reliance on *Toole v. Richardson–Merrell, Inc.,* 251 Cal.App.2d 689, 711, 60 Cal.Rptr. 398, 414 (1967), as support for its requested instruction is misplaced. The court in *Toole* did not define a managing agent as one having power to bind the corporation; it referred only to "corporate officials having power to bind the corporation." *Id.* Moreover, even if the *Toole* court meant to define a managing agent as such, the more recent decision of the California Supreme Court in *Egan* is controlling.

The trial court's instruction on this point gave adequate guidance to the jury. The court, in effect, required that a person in the corporate hierarchy other than the salesman must have approved or aided the fraud, before punitive damages could be awarded. The relevant language given was: "you would have to find that an officer, director, or managing agent other than Mr. Warman, either over ratified or approved or confirmed these acts of fraud, oppression or the character of those acts, or that such a person personally participated in the acts of fraud, oppression or malice." No better or more complete instruction was proffered by NCR and, on the facts of this case, none was needed.

It is also clear from NCR's closing argument that it did not base its theory of defense on the grounds that any fraudulent acts that occurred were committed by employees who were not of the level of managing agents and that no one in authority at NCR knew about or ratified such acts. In speaking to the jury about intentional fraud, NCR stated that the issue "gets down to Mr. Warman, and it gets down to NCR." RT: 1520. NCR then discusses Warman's credibility, RT: 1521, and the fact that he had no incentive to make intentional misrepresentations. RT: 1523–25. With regard to NCR itself, Appellant claims that NCR acted in good faith and that "there was nothing nefarious, or underhanded, or fraudulent about the whole transaction." RT: 1533. NCR did not argue that if any fraud took place, there was insufficient evidence upon which to hold NCR liable under Cal.Civil Code § 3294. It is difficult to find prejudice due to an error based upon a theory that NCR did not argue to the jury.

Based on the foregoing, we conclude that any error committed by the trial judge was not prejudicial.

III. The Punitive Damage Award

NCR argues that the punitive damages awarded to Glovatorium by the jury were excessive and must be reversed. An award of punitive damages that is approved by the district court will not be disturbed by the appellate court "unless it appears that the jury was influenced by passion or prejudice." *Moore v. Greene,* 431 F.2d 584, 593–94 (9th Cir.1970). NCR contends that the award is unjustifiable punishment because it was based "upon a fraud judgment absent any malice, reprehensible or outrageous conduct, or evidence of wilful disregard of plaintiff's interest." They also point to the fact that the punitive damage award exceeded the compensatory damage award by 9.1 times. These claims fail to demonstrate that the jury was influenced by passion or prejudice.

As discussed in section I, *supra,* there is adequate evidence in the record to support the jury's finding of fraud on the part of NCR. There is no requirement under Cal.Civil Code § 3294 that malice, reprehensible or outrageous conduct or wilful disregard be shown in addition to the fraud. *Horn v. Guaranty Chevrolet Motors,* 270 Cal.App.2d 477, 484, 75 Cal.Rptr. 871, 875–76 (1969). Thus, only the fact that the punitive damages were 9.1 times the compensatory damages remains.

Without anything more, this is not an adequate basis for this court to find that the jury was impassioned or prejudiced.

IV. THE COMPENSATORY DAMAGE AWARD

NCR claims that the jury awarded over $32,000 in damages that were not proved at trial and that damages were improperly awarded for Glovatorium's lost profits.

We must determine whether the verdict is grossly excessive or monstrous absent a total lack of evidence on all or certain portions of the case and absent prejudice. *Barzelis v. Kulikowski,* 418 F.2d 869, 870 (9th Cir.1969).

A.

NCR focuses its argument that excessive damages were awarded on the fact that, during closing argument, Glovatorium requested $253,000 in damages, *see, e.g.,* Reply Brief for Appellant at 18, while the jury awarded over $32,000 more. This fact, however, is not an adequate basis upon which to disturb the jury verdict. The jury was entitled to disregard the amount asked for when there was other evidence from which the jurors could draw their own conclusions. *Luria Brothers & Co. v. Pielet Brothers Scrap Iron & Metal, Inc.,* 600 F.2d 103, 115 (9th Cir.1979). In the case before us, there was such evidence. For instance, the president of Glovatorium testified that lost profits could have been as high as $150,000. *See* RT: 565. To be conservative, however, he asked only for $24,000 in lost profits. *Id.* This evidence alone is enough to support the amount awarded by the jury.

B.

NCR contends that damages were improperly awarded on the basis of Glovatorium's lost profits. NCR, however, failed to raise any objection at trial to the instruction by the court that lost profits constituted a proper element of damages. NCR thereby waived its objection.

CONCLUSION

Based on the foregoing, the judgment entered by the district court is Affirmed.

Notes and Questions

1. If a particular contract is not considered a transaction in goods, so the UCC does not apply, the plaintiff may rely upon common law contract law, and, if the appropriate conditions are present, tort law. Are *Monteleone* and *Clements Auto Company* similar? Should *Monteleone* have been a tort case instead?

2. In *Glovatorium* the plaintiff acquired a defective software program from the defendant. The contract did not require the defendant to provide services. Was this a sale of a good? Why did the plaintiff sue in tort rather than under the UCC?

3. *Glovatorium* is a good example of a small-business plaintiff and a large, deep-pocket defendant. Although the actual damages were $253,000,

the defendant won $2,073,000 in punitive damages. This case shows the importance for the vendor to keep a record of all representations and actions of sales representatives. What could NCR's counsel have done during the contract negotiations to have reduced the possibility of such a large punitive damage award? See the unreported oral decision in Bigelow, Robert P., *Computer Contracts: Negotiating and Drafting Guide,* (Vol. 3) (April 1987) (8 CLSR 171).

DIVERSIFIED GRAPHICS, LTD. v. GROVES

United States Court of Appeals, Eighth Circuit, 1989.
868 F.2d 293, rehearing denied, 1989.

LAY, CHIEF JUDGE.

* * * Diversified Graphics, Ltd. was awarded money damages on a negligence claim and for breach of fiduciary duty. The suit was brought against Ray J. Groves, chairman of Ernst & Whinney, a partnership that engages in the practice of public accounting and related fields. Groves represents the class of partners; he now appeals. We affirm in part and reverse in part.

I. BACKGROUND

Diversified Graphics, Ltd. (D.G.) is a screen printer and apparel manufacturer. It hired Ernst & Whinney (E & W) to assist it in obtaining a computer system to fit its data processing needs. The parties dispute the extent to which E & W was involved in the selection and implementation stages of the new system.

E & W claims that it was retained for the limited purposes of evaluating D.G.'s needs, preparing a "Request for Proposal" to distribute to potential vendors of computer hardware and software, and to make a recommendation of a vendor. After it recommended Richter Management Services, Inc., E & W claims that it had no subsequent involvement in the project except to provide D.G. with a representative, William Byrne, who acted in a very limited advisory role. E & W contends that the subsequent difficulties in the implementation of the new computer system were due to unwise decisions made by D.G.'s management.

D.G. maintains that it had a longstanding relationship with E & W during which the former developed great trust and reliance upon the latter's services. Because D.G. lacked computer expertise, it decided to entrust E & W with the selection and implementation of an in-house computer data processing system. According to D.G., E & W had promised to locate a "turnkey" system which would be fully operational without need of extensive employee training. D.G. instead received a system that was difficult to operate and failed to adequately meet its needs.

D.G. filed this action asserting claims of negligence, breach of fiduciary duty, and breach of contract. At trial, the jury found in favor of D.G. on its negligence and breach of fiduciary duty claims and against D.G. on its breach of contract claim. On appeal, E & W argues that the district court improperly defined the conduct that gives rise to a breach of a fiduciary duty, applied an incorrect standard of care, and permitted a duplicative damage award. E & W also asserts that D.G. failed to make an adequate showing of the causation and damage portions of its case.

II. Discussion

A. *Duplicative Damages*

* * *

* * * Regardless of whether the harm was the result of negligence or breach of fiduciary duty or a combination of both, there is only a single injury and there may only be a single recovery. We therefore find that the district court erred in awarding D.G. the aggregate of the jury award.

B. *Negligence*

E & W argues that it should have been held to an ordinary, rather than a professional, standard of care. E & W further contends that the district court erred in denying its motion for a directed verdict on this claim because D.G. failed to offer expert testimony as to the appropriate standard and whether it had been breached in this case.

A breach of a professional standard is more exacting and difficult to prove than breach of ordinary care. Accordingly, it would appear that a finding that E & W breached the former standard would necessarily encompass a finding that it failed to exercise ordinary care. In any event, D.G. presented sufficient evidence to support the jury's finding of lack of professional care.

D.G.'s theory for recovery based on negligence encompasses the notion of a consultant-client relationship and therefore the existence of a professional standard of care: E & W failed to act reasonably in light of its superior knowledge and expertise in the area of computer systems. * * * D.G. claims that it retained E & W as a consultant during its purchase and implementation of an in-house data processing system. It is implicit in alleging the existence of an agreement that D.G. anticipated that E & W possessed superior knowledge in this area; D.G. contracted for the benefit of E & W's expertise. Based on D.G.'s allegations, E & W was properly held to a professional standard of care.

The degree of skill and care that may be required of a professional is a question of fact for the jury. On review, the evidence on the breach of the professional standard of care must be considered in the light most favorable to the plaintiff, according it all of the reasonable inferences and disregarding all of the defendant's evidence except as it supports the plaintiff's case. In the instant case, E & W argues that D.G. did not make a submissible case on negligence because D.G.'s expert, Norton Lee Hoffman, failed to both state the applicable professional standard and explain how E & W had violated that standard.

Upon review of Hoffman's testimony, we must agree with E & W that Hoffman could have stated the professional standard of care required of a computer systems consultant in a more straightforward manner. Much of his testimony recited only his personal opinion. Hoffman's testimony nonetheless contained significant discussion of the applicable professional standard of care and E & W's actions in relation to that standard. Furthermore, we find that there was substantial evidence elsewhere in the record regarding the applicable standards of a professional consultant.

The evidence contains E & W's Guidelines to Practice which incorporates the Management Advisory Services Practice Standards which were adopted by the American Institute of Certified Public Accountants, Inc. (AICPA Standards). The AICPA Standards require that "due professional care" is to be exercised in providing management advisory services. These standards in part generally provide:

> In performing management advisory services, a practitioner must act with integrity and objectivity and be independent in mental attitude.
>
> Engagements are to be performed by practitioners having competence in the analytical approach and process, and in the technical subject matter under consideration.
>
> Due professional care is to be exercised in the performance of a management advisory services engagement.
>
> Before accepting an engagement, a practitioner is to notify the client of any reservations he has regarding anticipated benefits.
>
> Before undertaking an engagement, a practitioner is to inform his client of all significant matters related to the engagement.
>
> Engagements are to be adequately planned, supervised, and controlled.
>
> Sufficient relevant data is to be obtained, documented, and evaluated in developing conclusions and recommendations.
>
> All significant matters relating to the results of the engagement are to be communicated to the client.

AICPA Standards Nos. 1–8. The expert witnesses of the plaintiff as well as those called by the defendant establish sufficient evidence from which the jury could find that the defendant did not meet the above-stated standards.

The record reflects that D.G. had determined that it required a "turnkey" computer system that would fully perform all of its data processing in-house. The term "turnkey" is intended to describe a self-sufficient system which the purchaser need only "turn the key" to commence operation. The record makes clear that the purchaser should not have to hire programmers and that current employees should not have to undergo extensive training to be able to operate the system. The evidence shows that to procure this type of customized and fully operational system, great care must be taken to carefully detail a business' needs and to properly develop specifications for the computer system. Potential vendors must be carefully scrutinized to discover all of the inadequacies of their data processing systems. Once a vender is chosen, proper implementation is imperative to ensure that the purchaser truly need only "turn the key" to commence full operation of the system. A fundamental part of implementation involves testing the system through parallel data processing operation. Finally, the existence of adequate documentation regarding the operation of the system is crucial once the system is up and running. As previously stated, employees will have had only minimal training and will depend heavily on the instructions for operation. Moreover, documentation is particularly important because this type of system is highly customized and standard instruction sources will have only limited value.

Thus, the record reflects sufficient information from which a jury could determine the applicable professional standard of care and upon which the jury could conclude that E & W's conduct fell short of adhering to that standard. The record also contains sufficient evidence to support the jury's finding that the inadequacies of the data processing system caused D.G. to incur considerable expense necessary for modifications, employee training, and additional staffing and consultation. We therefore find that D.G.'s claim for damages was properly submitted to the jury. * * *

Finally, E & W has asserted that D.G. failed to provide adequate proof of damages. We have reviewed the record and find that there is sufficient evidence contained therein to support the reasonableness and the amount of the jury's verdict. We therefore sustain the judgment awarded to D.G. for its negligence claim.

In light of our ruling that the judgment entry was duplicative and the fact that the jury's negligence award was higher than its award for breach of fiduciary duty, we find it unnecessary to address E & W's claim regarding the propriety of the submission of the claim for breach of fiduciary duty.

We therefore affirm the judgment entered by the district court insofar as it awards D.G. $82,500 for its negligence claim and vacate the judgment awarding D.G. $50,000 for its breach of fiduciary duty claim.

Affirmed in part and reversed in part.

Notes and Questions

1. Only a few cases have discussed whether or not computer specialists should be held to a "professional standard" like that applied to doctors or lawyers. Plaintiffs naturally prefer the professional standard, since it is easier to prove that a defendant failed to exercise professional skill than to prove that defendant was negligent, but courts have not accepted plaintiffs' argument.

2. Is *Diversified* a solid precedent supporting the application of a "professional standard" to computer specialists?

D. SOFTWARE SALES AND LICENSING

1. CHANNELS OF SOFTWARE DISTRIBUTION

The nature of the contractual arrangements governing software sales typically depends upon how it is sold. There are at least five fairly distinct methods for marketing software: (1) mass marketing through mail order houses and computer stores, (2) "shareware" distribution, (3) direct sales to major buyers, (4) custom-written software and (5) sales to United States government agencies. In terms of dollar sales, the largest category of software distribution is mass marketing. Mass marketing is incompatible with individually negotiated or even individually signed contracts between customers and software makers. The software makers, therefore, have sought substitutes for signed contracts. The expense of advertising and creating dealer networks has led to the development of the shareware industry, which distributes software free and relies mainly upon customer conscience for payment. Major buyers, such as large companies and universities, usually negotiate licenses with software companies for software used on mainframes and for software used in multiple copies on personal computers. Negotiated licenses are also the rule for custom-written software. The United States government has promulgated elaborate rules governing software acquisition by government agencies.

2. SALES AND LICENSING OF MASS-MARKETED SOFTWARE

Makers of personal computer software generally rely upon dealers to sell the software. Dealers, however, are unwilling or unable to make buyers sign individual contracts. Absent a contract, the relations of the maker, dealer, and buyer are governed by the Uniform Commercial Code and the Copyright Act. Software manufacturers view this legislation as overly favorable to buyers. They have sought to change their relations with buyers by contract and by lobbying for changes in legislation.

The most common contractual approach is the use of "shrink-wrap" licenses. The term "shrink-wrap" refers to the fact that when computer stores and mail-order houses sell software for personal computers, they usually sell it in packages covered with clear plastic wrap that has been "shrunk" to make it fit. The plastic covering protects the software and manuals from dust (potentially fatal to diskettes) and provides the buyer assurance that the merchandise is new. Almost all software companies include, inside the plastic shrink-wrap, a document stating that the software is only licensed, not sold to the customer and that the software is subject to a variety of restrictions. This document is called a "shrink-wrap" license.

UNIFORM COMMERCIAL CODE

§ 1–201. General Definitions.

Subject to additional definitions contained in the subsequent Articles of this Act which are applicable to specific Articles or Parts thereof, and unless the context otherwise requires, in this Act:

* * *

(19) "Good faith" means honesty in fact in the conduct or transaction concerned.

* * *

§ 2–103. Definitions and Index of Definitions.

(1) In this Article unless the context otherwise requires

* * *

(b) "Good faith" in the case of a merchant means honesty in fact and the observance of reasonable commercial standards of fair dealing in the trade.

* * *

§ 2–207. Additional Terms in Acceptance or Confirmation.

(1) A definite and seasonable expression of acceptance or a written confirmation which is sent within a reasonable time operates as an acceptance even though it states terms additional to or different from those offered or agreed upon, unless acceptance is expressly made conditional on assent to the additional or different terms.

(2) The additional terms are to be construed as proposals for addition to the contract. Between merchants such terms become part of the contract unless:

(a) the offer expressly limits acceptance to the terms of the offer;

(b) they materially alter it; or

(c) notification of objection to them has already been given or is given within a reasonable time after notice of them is received.

(3) Conduct by both parties which recognizes the existence of a contract is sufficient to establish a contract for sale although the writings of the parties do not otherwise establish a contract. In such case the terms of the particular contract consist of those terms on which the writings of the parties agree, together with any supplementary terms incorporated under any other provisions of this Act.

§ 2–209. Modification, Rescission and Waiver.

(1) An agreement modifying a contract within this Article needs no consideration to be binding.

* * *

§ 2–302. Unconscionable Contract or Clause.

(1) If the court as a matter of law finds the contract or any clause of the contract to have been unconscionable at the time it was made the court may refuse to enforce the contract, or it may enforce the remainder of the contract without the unconscionable clause, or it may so limit the application of any unconscionable clause as to avoid any unconscionable result.

(2) When it is claimed or appears to the court that the contract or any clause thereof may be unconscionable the parties shall be afforded a reasonable opportunity to present evidence as to its commercial setting, purpose and effect to aid the court in making the determination.

§ 2–403. Power to Transfer; Good Faith Purchase of Goods; "Entrusting".

(1) A purchaser of goods acquires all title which his transferor had or had power to transfer except that a purchaser of a limited interest acquires rights only to the extent of the interest purchased. A person with voidable title has power to transfer a good title to a good faith purchaser for value. When goods have been delivered under a transaction of purchase the purchaser has such power even though

(a) the transferor was deceived as to the identity of the purchaser, or

(b) the delivery was in exchange for a check which is later dishonored, or

(c) it was agreed that the transaction was to be a "cash sale", or

(d) the delivery was procured through fraud punishable as larcenous under the criminal law.

(2) Any entrusting of possession of goods to a merchant who deals in goods of that kind gives him power to transfer all rights of the entruster to a buyer in ordinary course of business.

(3) "Entrusting" includes any delivery and any acquiescence in retention of possession regardless of any condition expressed between the parties to the delivery or acquiescence and regardless of whether the procurement of the entrusting or the possessor's disposition of the goods have been such as to be larcenous under the criminal law.

* * *

Notes and Questions

1. It seems highly likely that most states would apply the Uniform Commerical Code to mass-marketed software, whether they considered the software purchaser to be a buyer under Article 2 or a lessee under Article 2A. This means that the buyer would have the advantage of the implied warranty of merchantability (Article 2–314) and of the right to receive consequentional damages (Article 2–715). Furthermore, since software makers typically advertise directly to buyers, it is quite likely that buyers

would have these rights against the makers as well as against the dealers. Express claims in the makers' software advertisements would probably create express warranties against the makers (Article 2–312). Software makers would like to limit the very broad rights the U.C.C. gives software buyers. Although legislation and court decisions often invalidate warranty disclaimers and limitations on liability in sales to consumers, they generally allow such disclaimers and limitations in sales to businesses.

2. The copyright law gives owners of copies of software a number of rights, including the right to make certain modifications and the right to resell the copy. Software makers may wish to limit these rights as well.

3. The problem that software vendors face is that it is impractical to force software stores to make buyers sign contracts. The vendors therefore include "shrink-wrap" license contracts with their products, hoping that buyers will somehow be bound by these contracts.

4. After rereading the Uniform Commercial Code sections above, decide if, in a typical software purchase, a shrink-wrap "contract" is enforceable.

5. Often the software maker will include an "owner registration card in the software package." Literature in the package encourages the buyer to fill out the card and mail it to the maker. The owner registration card typically contains the following language in fine print, "I accept the license terms enclosed with this software." The software maker may or may not offer some additional incentive to the buyer. It may say, "If you send in this card you will receive announcements of new versions of this software."

6. Reread the sections of the Uniform Commercial Code printed above. Is the buyer who sends in such a registration card bound to the terms of the shrink-wrap license?

7. In some cases the buyer needs a license contract as much as the seller does. For instance a buyer of a program with illustrations for use in desktop publishing ("clip-art") needs written permission to incorporate these illustrations in the buyer's publications. A software developer who buys components to be included in a software package also needs a license.

3. SHAREWARE

Small companies and amateur software developers cannot afford the costs of mass-marketing software. They cannot pay $10,000 a page for advertisements in computer magazines; they cannot create and supervise dealer networks. Shareware distribution offers an inexpensive alternative. The shareware concept is simple. Software is made available for free copying, usually by putting it on computer bulletin boards from which it may be transferred to other computers. (A computer bulletin board is a computer system connected to the telephone lines and open to calls from other computers.) Users are asked to send a small amount (typically around $25) if they like the program and use it regularly. Some shareware distributors disclaim copyright, relying only on customers' honor. Others claim copyright, both to provide additional incentive for shareware payments and to provide a basis for bargaining prices with large institutional users.

TELEREPLICA LICENCE AGREEMENT

TeleReplica is a set of copyrighted programs developed by Douglas Thomson. You may, without charge, use and distribute exact copies of TeleReplica subject to the following limitations:

— You may make and keep as many copies of the TeleReplica files as you wish.

— You may distribute copies of the TeleReplica files to others provided you distribute ALL the files listed below and provided NONE of these files is modified in any way.

— You may charge for such distribution, provided that you inform your prospective customers that the payment is only for the distribution, and that their payment is not registration of TeleReplica.

— You may provide TeleReplica along with another product or service, even if you charge for that product or service, provided that your prospective customers or clients are aware that they are NOT paying for TeleReplica, and provided that YOU have registered TeleReplica yourself.

— You may use TeleReplica for as long as you wish prior to registering. However, you must register your copy as soon as you believe the value you have gained from TeleReplica exceeds the registration fee. Support from users will permit improvements to TeleReplica to be made, and may also result in other products being made available on similar terms.

— TeleReplica is to be registered once for each simultaneous link. Hence a consultant using one modem to support multiple clients need only register once (the clients do not need to register at all unless they use TeleReplica for other purposes), and a company running a local area network with a single PC connected to a modem to provide access to multiple users need only register once. However, a company providing three computers/modems/telephone lines to permit three simultaneous remote logins via TeleReplica must register three times.

— Since TeleReplica has been made available free of charge for evaluation, you must agree not to hold Douglas Thomson liable for any damages resulting from the use of or inability to use this software. Douglas Thomson specifically disclaims all warranties, expressed or implied, including but not limited to implied warranties of merchantability and fitness for a particular purpose. In no event shall Douglas Thomson be liable for any loss of profit or any other commercial damage, including but not limited to special, incidental, consequential or other damages.

TeleReplica is not licensed to be used at all in places where this exclusion is not legal.

TELEREPLICA REGISTRATION FORM

Note: It is assumed you have already obtained and evaluated a copy of TeleReplica. This form is provided for registration only. No disk or documentation will be sent to you (the shareware version is the only version there is, and the documentation in the shareware release is all the documentation there is); your payment is for the benefit you have already received from TeleReplica. There is no incentive to register apart from your own honesty!

The following details are optional. If you provide them, then you will be notified of any further release of TeleReplica. As a registered user, you are entitled to use all future releases without additional registration fees. You should obtain any new release in whatever way you obtained your first copy.

Date: ______

Name: ______________________________
Title: ______________________________
Company: ______________________________
Address: ______________________________
____
City: ______________________________
State: ______________________________
Postcode/Zip: ______________________________
Country: ______________________________

Please complete the form below. Cheques drawn on Australian accounts should be made out for AU$25.00. Cheques drawn on US accounts should be made out for US$25.00 (the exchange rate will cover my bank charges for currency conversion). Cheques drawn in other currencies are also acceptable—simply use the current exchange rate to calculate the equivalent of US$25.00. Personal cheques are acceptable.

Quantity	Description	Cost per link	Total Cost
	registration of TeleReplica release 3.9	AU$25.00 or US$25.00 or equivalent	

Send to: Mr Douglas Thomson
c/–M.U.C.G.

Switchback Road
Churchill
Victoria 3842
AUSTRALIA

4. UNITED STATES GOVERNMENT SOFTWARE LICENSE TERMS

RIGHTS IN TECHNICAL DATA AND COMPUTER SOFTWARE

48 CFR 252.227–7013

As prescribed at 227.473–1(e) and 227.481–2(b)(2), insert the following clause:

RIGHTS IN TECHNICAL DATA AND COMPUTER SOFTWARE (OCT 1988)

(a) Definitions

(1) "Commercial computer software", as used in this clause, means computer software which is used regularly for other than Government purposes and is sold, licensed, or leased in significant quantities to the general public at established market or catalog prices.

(2) "Computer" as used in this clause, means a data processing device capable of accepting data, performing prescribed operations on the data, and supplying the results of these operations; for example, a device that operates on discrete data by performing arithmetic and logic processes on the data, or a device that operates on analog data by performing physical processes on the data.

(3) "Computer data base", as used in this clause, means a collection of data in a form capable of being processed and operated on by a computer.

(4) "Computer program", as used in this clause, means a series of instructions or statements in a form acceptable to a computer, designed to cause the computer to execute an operation or operations. Computer programs include operating systems, assemblers, compilers, interpreters, data management systems, utility programs, sort-merge programs, and ADPE maintenance/diagnostic programs, as well as applications programs such as payroll, inventory control, and engineering analysis programs. Computer programs may be either machine-dependent or machine-independent, and may be general-purpose in nature or be designed to satisfy the requirements of a particular user.

(5) "Computer software", as used in this clause, means computer programs and computer data bases.

(6) "Computer software documentation", as used in this clause, means technical data, including computer listings and printouts, in human-readable form which (i) documents the design or details of computer software, (ii) explains the capabilities of the software, or (iii) provides operating instructions for using the software to obtain desired results from a computer.

(7) "Data", as used in this clause, means recorded information, regardless of form or method of the recording.

(8) "Detailed design data", as used in this clause, means technical data that describes the physical configuration and performance characteristics of an item or component in sufficient detail to ensure that an item or component produced in accordance with the technical data will be essentially identical to the original item or component.

(9) "Detailed manufacturing or process data", as used in this clause, means technical data that describes the steps, sequences, and conditions of manufacturing, processing or assembly used by the manufacturer to produce an item or component or to perform a process.

(10) "Developed", as used in this clause, means that the item, component, or process exists and is workable. Thus, the item or component must have been constructed or the process practiced. Workability is generally established when the item, component or process has been analyzed or tested sufficiently to demonstrate to reasonable people skilled in the applicable art that there is a high probability that it will operate as intended. Whether, how much, and what type of analysis or testing is required to establish workability depends on the nature of the item, component, or process, and the state of the art. To be considered "developed", the item, component, or process need not be at the stage where it could be offered for sale or sold on the commercial market, nor must the item, component or process be actually reduced to practice within the meaning of Title 35 of the United States Code.

(11) "Developed Exclusively with Government Funds", as used in this clause, means, in connection with an item, component, or process, that the cost of development was paid for in whole by the Government or that the development was required for the performance of a Government contract or subcontract.

(12) "Developed Exclusively at Private Expense", as used in this clause, means, in connection with an item, component, or process, that no part of the cost of development was paid for by the Government and that the development was not required for the performance of a Government contract or subcontract. Independent research and development and bid and proposal costs, as defined in FAR 31.205–18 (whether or not included in a formal independent research and development program), are considered to be at private expense. All other indirect costs of development are considered Government funded when development was required for the performance of a Government contract or subcontract. They are considered funded at private expense when development was not required for the performance of a Government contract or subcontract.

(13) "Form, fit, and function data", as used in this clause, means technical data that describes the required overall physical, functional, and performance characteristics, (along with the qualification requirements, if applicable) of an item, component, or process to the extent

necessary to permit identification of physically and functionally interchangeable items.

(14) "Government purpose license rights" (GPLR), as used in this clause, means rights to use, duplicate, or disclose data (and in the SBIR Program, computer software), in whole or in part and in any manner, for Government purposes only, and to have or permit others to do so for Government purposes only. Government purposes include competitive procurement, but do not include the right to have or permit others to use technical data (and in the SBIR Program, computer software) for commercial purposes.

(15) "Limited rights", as used in this clause, means rights to use, duplicate, or disclose technical data, in whole or in part, by or for the Government, with the express limitation that such technical data shall not, without the written permission of the party asserting limited rights, be: released or disclosed outside the Government; used by the Government for manufacture, or in the case of computer sofware documentation, for preparing the same or similar computer software; or used by a party other than the Government, except that the Government may release or disclose technical data to persons outside the Government, or permit the use of technical data by such persons, if—

(i) Such release, disclosure, or use—

(A) Is necessary for emergency repair and overhaul; or

(B) Is a release or disclosure of technical data (other than detailed manufacturing or process data) to, or use of such data by, a foreign government that is in the interest of the Government and is required for evaluational or informational purposes;

(ii) Such release, disclosure, or use is made subject to a prohibition that the person to whom the data is released or disclosed may not further release, disclose, or use such data; and

(iii) the contractor or subcontractor asserting the restriction is notified of such release, disclosure, or use.

(16) "Required for the Performance of a Government Contract or Subcontract", as used in this clause, means, in connection with the development of an item, component, or process, that the development was specified in a Government contract or subcontract or that the development was accomplished during and was necessary for performance of a Government contract or subcontract.

(17) "Restricted rights", as used in this clause, means rights that apply only to computer software, and include, as a minimum, the right to—

(i) Use computer software with the computer for which or with which it was acquired, including use at any Government installation to which the computer may be transferred by the Government;

(ii) Use computer software with a backup computer if the computer for which or with which it was acquired is inoperative;

(iii) Copy computer programs for safekeeping (archives) or backup purposes; and

(iv) Modify computer software, or combine it with other software, subject to the provision that those portions of the derivative software incorporating restricted rights software are subject to the same restricted rights.

In addition, restricted rights include any other specific rights not inconsistent with the minimum rights in (a)(17)(i)–(iv) above that are listed or described in the contract or described in a license agreement made a part of the contract.

(18) "Technical data", as used in this clause, means recorded information, regardless of the form or method of the recording of a scientific or technical nature (including computer software documentation). The term does not include computer software or data incidental to contract administration, such as financial and/or management information.

(19) "Unlimited rights", as used in this clause, means rights to use, duplicate, release, or disclose, technical data or computer software in whole or in part, in any manner and for any purpose whatsoever, and to have or permit others to do so.

(20) "Unpublished", as used in this clause, means that technical data or computer software has not been released to the public or furnished to others without restriction on further use or disclosure. Delivery of other than unlimited rights technical data or computer software to or for the Government under the contract does not, in itself, constitute release to the public.

* * *

(c) Rights in Computer Software

(1) *Restricted Rights.* (i) The Government shall have restricted rights in computer software, listed or described in a license agreement made a part of this contract, which the parties have agreed will be furnished with restricted rights. Notwithstanding any contrary provision in any such license agreement, the Government shall have the rights included in the definition of "restricted rights" in paragraph (a)(17) above. Unless the computer software is marked by the Contractor with the following legend:

RESTRICTED RIGHTS LEGEND

Use, duplication or disclosure is subject to restrictions stated in Contract No. ______ with (Name of Contractor) and the related computer software documentation includes a prominent statement of the restrictions applicable to the computer software, the Government shall have unlimited rights in the software. The Contractor may not place any legend on computer software restricting the Government's rights in such software unless the restrictions are set forth in a license agreement made a part of this contract prior to the delivery date of the software. Failure of the Contractor to apply a restricted rights legend to the computer software shall relieve the Government of liability with respect to the unmarked software.

(ii) Notwithstanding subparagraph (c)(1)(i) above, commercial computer software and related documentation developed at private expense and not in the public domain may be marked with the following Legend:

RESTRICTED RIGHTS LEGEND

Use, duplication, or disclosure by the Government is subject to restrictions as set forth in subparagraph (c)(1)(ii) of the Rights in Technical Data and Computer Software clause at DFARS 252.227–7013.

____

(Name of Contractor and Address)

When acquired by the Government, commercial computer software and related documentation so legended shall be subject to the following:

(A) Title to and ownership of the software and documentation shall remain with the Contractor.

(B) User of the software and documentation shall be limited to the facility for which it is acquired.

(C) The Government shall not provide or otherwise make available the software or documentation, or any portion thereof, in any form, to any third party without the prior written approval of the Contractor. Third parties do not include prime contractors, subcontractors and agents of the Government who have the Government's permission to use the licensed software and documentation at the facility, and who have agreed to use the licensed software and documentation only in accordance with these restrictions. This provision does not limit the right of the Government to use software, documentation, or information therein, which the Government has or may obtain without restrictions.

(D) The Government shall have the right to use the computer software and documentation with the computer for which it is acquired at any other facility to which that computer may be transferred; to use the computer software and documentation with a backup computer when the primary computer is inoperative; to copy computer programs for safekeeping (archives) or backup purposes; and to modify the software and documentation or combine it with other software, *Provided,* that the unmodified portions shall remain subject to these restrictions.

(2) *Unlimited Rights.* The Government shall have unlimited rights in:

(i) Computer software resulting directly from performance of experimental, developmental or research work which was specified as an element of performance in this or any other Government contract or subcontract;

(ii) Computer software required to be originated or developed under a Government contract, or generated as a necessary part of performing a contract;

(iii) Computer data bases, prepared under a Government contract, consisting of information supplied by the Government, information in which the Government has unlimited rights, or information which is in the public domain;

(iv) Computer software prepared or required to be delivered under this or any other Government contract or subcontract and constituting corrections or changes to Government-furnished computer software; and

(v) Computer software which is otherwise publicly available, or has been, or is normally released, or disclosed by the Contractor or subcontractor without restriction on further release or disclosure.

(d) Technical Data and Computer Software Previously Provided Without Restriction

Contractor shall assert no restrictions on the Government's rights to use or disclose any data or computer software which the Contractor has previously delivered to the Government without restriction. The limited or restricted rights provided for by this clause shall not impair the right of the Government to use similar or identical data or computer software acquired from other sources.

(e) Copyrights

(1) In addition to the rights granted under the provisions of paragraphs (b) and (c) above, the Contractor hereby grants to the Government a nonexclusive, paid-up license throughout the world, of the scope set forth below, under any copyright owned by the Contractor, in any work of authorship prepared for or acquired by the Government under this contract, to reproduce the work in copies or phonorecords, to distribute copies or phonorecords to the public, to perform or display the work publicly, and to prepare derivative works thereof, and to have others do so for Government purposes. With respect to technical data and computer software in which the Government has unlimited rights, the license shall be of the same scope as the rights set forth in the definition of "unlimited rights" in (a)(19) above. With respect to technical data in which the Government has limited rights, the scope of the license is limited to the rights set forth in the definition of "limited rights". With respect to computer software which the parties have agreed will be furnished with restricted rights, the scope of the license is limited to such rights.

(2) Unless written approval of the Contracting Officer is obtained, the Contractor shall not include (in technical data or computer software prepared for or acquired by the Government under this contract) any works of authorship in which copyright is not owned by the Contractor without acquiring for the Government any rights necessary to perfect a copyright license of the scope specified herein.

(3) The Contractor shall be considered the "person for whom the work was prepared" for the purpose of determining authorship under 17 U.S.C. 201(b).

(4) Technical data delivered under this contract bearing a copyright notice shall also include the following statement:

This material may be reproduced by or for the U.S. Government pursuant to the copyright license under the clause at DFARS 252.227–7013 (date).

* * *

(g) Relation to Patents

Nothing contained in this clause shall imply a license to the Government under any patent or be construed as affecting the scope of any license or other right otherwise granted to the Government under any patent.

* * *

(1) Acquisition of Technical Data and Computer Software from Subcontractors

(1) The Contractor must satisfy its contractual obligation to the Government while ensuring that the rights afforded its subcontractors under 10 U.S.C. 2320 and 2321 are recognized and protected. In satisfying its obligation, the Contractor must accomplish the balancing of interests described at DFARS 227–472–1 in dealing with its subcontractors.

(2) Whenever any technical data or computer software is to be obtained from a subcontractor under this contract, the Contractor shall use this same clause in the subcontract, without alteration, and no other clause shall be used to enlarge or diminish the Government's or the Contractor's rights in the subcontractor data or computer software.

(3) Technical data required to be delivered by a subcontractor shall normally be delivered to the next higher-tier contractor. However, when there is a requirement in the prime contract for data which may be submitted with other than unlimited rights by a subcontractor, then said subcontractor may fulfill its requirement by submitting such data directly to the Government, rather than through the prime Contractor.

(4) The Contractor and higher-tier subcontractors will not use their power to award subcontracts as economic leverage to obtain rights in technical data or computer software from their subcontractors.

(5) The Contractor shall ensure that subcontractor rights are recognized and protected in the notification and listing process at paragraphs (j) and (k) below.

(6) In no event shall the Contractor use its obligation to recognize and protect subcontractor rights in technical data as an excuse for failing to satisfy its contractual obligation to the Government.

(j) Notice of Limitations on Government Rights

(1) The Offeror/Contractor shall notify the Contracting Officer of its or its potential subcontractor's use in the performance of the contract or subcontract of items, components, processes and computer software that—

(i) Have been developed exclusively at private expense;

(ii) Have been developed in part at private expense; or

(iii) Embody technology that has been developed exclusively with Government funds which the Offeror or Contractor or subcontractor desires exclusive rights to commercialize, with Government approval.

(2) Such notification is not required with respect to items, components, processes or computer software if no technical data is required to be delivered or if the required technical data is delivered with unlimited rights.

(3) Such notification shall be accompanied by the following representation;

REPRESENTATION OF PRIVATE DEVELOPMENT

The Offeror/Contractor/Subcontractor represents that, to the best of its knowledge and belief, the information contained in this notification is current, accurate, and complete.

Date ____________________

Name and Title ____________

Official __________________

This representation shall be dated and the signing official (identified by name and title) shall be duly authorized to bind the Contractor.

(4) Upon request by the Contracting Officer, the Offeror or Contractor shall provide sufficient information to enable the Contracting Officer to identify and evaluate the Contractor's or subcontractor's assertions made in (j)(1) above.

(k) Identification of Restrictions on Government Rights

Technical data and computer software shall not be tendered to the Government with other than unlimited rights, unless the technical data or computer software are identified in a list made part of this contract. This list is intended to facilitate review and acceptance of the technical data and computer software by the Government and does not change, waive, or otherwise modify the rights or obligations of the parties under the clause at DFARS 252.227–7037. As a minimum, this list must—

(1) Identify the items, components, processes, or computer software to which the restrictions on the Government apply;

(2) Identify or describe the technical data or computer software subject to other than unlimited rights; and

(3) Identify or describe, as appropriate, the category or categories of Government rights, the agreed-to time limitations, or any special restrictions on the use of disclosure of the technical data or computer software.

(l) Postaward Negotiation—Disputes

In the case of an item, component, or process that is developed in part with Government funds and in part at private expense, if, after exhausting all reasonable efforts, the parties fail to agree on the apportionment of the rights in technical data furnished under this contract by the date established in the contract for agreement, or within any extension established by the Contracting Officer, then the Contracting Officer may establish the respective data rights of the parties, subject to Contractor appeal as provided in the Disputes clause. In any event, the Contractor shall proceed with completion of the contract.

(End of clause)

* * *

5. DATA BASE ACCESS CONTRACTS

Major database access services, such as WESTLAW and DIALOG, require every user to sign a contract before they provide services. Most of the contract provisions are those that one might find in any service contract. The service company agrees to provide access to databases. The customer agrees to pay in accordance with a fee schedule. The contract limits liability for consequential damages. There is one set of provisions, however, that is unique to database contracts. These provisions define the rights of the customer to transfer parts of databases to the customer's own computer.

These provisions must strike a balance between customer needs and protection of the database access service's most valuable assets, the databases themselves. The contracts allow customers to copy citations and quotations from databases to print out for study or to include in articles, books, legal briefs, and other written works. The contracts forbid retention of substantial quantities of material, in order to prevent customers from creating competing database access systems. These provisions are particularly important to companies providing access to uncopyrightable database materials. It has long been clear that United States government publications, statutes, and court decisions cannot be protected by copyright. *Feist Publications v. Rural Telephone Service Co.* has expanded the area of clearly uncopyrightable materials to include many compilations of facts. Thus clauses limiting copying will be even more important in the future.

The demise of the "sweat of the brow" copyright doctrine is no great threat to companies that distribute information from a central computer system. Such companies can restrict access by granting passwords only to those who have signed contractual agreements restricting copying from the databases. Automatic monitoring programs can detect unusually copying activity. With access prices sometimes exceeding $1 a minute, most users would be bankrupt before they could copy a whole database. An emerging technology, the CD ROM, allows putting large databases on the same type of compact disks used for music recordings. Ideally, such CD ROM databases would be sold in stores and by mail, just as software, books, and records are now sold. But it is impossible to negotiate a contract with each buyer of mass marketed merchandise. Even if one could negotiate a contract, the buyer could sell the CD ROM to a bona fide purchaser who might take clear of the contractual restrictions. Thus uncopyrightable databases on CD ROM would be unprotected. There may be a need for change in the law to encourage CD ROM distribution of databases. See Ginsburg, "Creation and Commercial Value: Copyright Protection of Works of Information," 90 *Colum.L.Rev.* 1865 (1990).

6. NEGOTIATED CONTRACTS

Individually negotiated contracts may be for computer hardware or software. Hardware contracts have the features typically of other types of contracts for the purchase or lease of complex machinery. They are governed by Article 2 or 2A of the Uniform Commercial Code. Software contracts may involve either standardized or custom made software. The United States Government software license terms above, show the sort of contract a buyer might wish to negotiate.

Although off-the-shelf software supplies more and more of the needs of computer users, the custom software business is still flourishing. As personal computers become more complex and more powerful and are linked into networks, the need arises for highly skilled help in configuring standard network software and adapting it to hardware configurations and user needs. It may be much more effective to pay $50 to $100 an hour to outside consultants for these needs, than to keep a software specialist on the payroll full time. Since these contracts are generally negotiated on a "per-hour" basis, there is usually little litigation—dissatisfied customers generally just switch to another consultant. The one area where there has been substantial litigation is that of the rights to custom-written software. Do they belong to the customer, the consultant or both? The law with respect to ownership of consultant-developed software is unclear, so clear contract terms are essential.

Software licensees may invest considerable amounts of money in making new and better versions of licensed software. Unless the license contract is absolutely clear, the licensee and licensor may come into conflict over rights in the improvements. The next case shows that even the best of software companies may have this problem.

APPLE COMPUTER INC. v. MICROSOFT CORP.

United States District Court, Northern District of California, 1991.
759 F.Supp. 1444.

WALKER, J.

Apple Computer, Inc. ("Apple") filed this copyright infringement action on March 17, 1988, against Microsoft Corporation ("Microsoft") and Hewlett–Packard Company ("HP"), claiming that Microsoft's Windows computer operating system software and HP's New Wave computer application software infringed Apple's copyrights. The copyrights at issue protect the visual displays of Apple's Macintosh computer user interface.

I. THE VISUAL DISPLAYS OF THE MACINTOSH INTERFACE

In developing the Macintosh computer operating system software, Apple made one of the major commercial breakthroughs of the 1980's. The graphic user interface generated by the Macintosh system software consists of windows, icons, pull-down menus, and other images or visual displays projected on the computer screen. The Macintosh user interface [1] proved so intuitive that users were able to learn quickly how to manipulate the screen displays and mouse and thus accomplish what had theretofore been the daunting task of learning to operate a computer. This breakthrough vaulted Apple to the top of the personal computer industry.

The visual displays in a computer user interface owe their appearance to system software and application programs. System software is a computer program that controls the computer hardware and schedules the execution of its functions. Such software is keyed to the computer hardware which it runs and establishes the visual framework or environment for the images on the computer screen, as does a proscenium in a theatre. In order to put a computer to a specific task, however, the user also needs an application program—to further the stage analogy, the play. Application programs must be keyed to a particular system software and work within that system's framework or environment to carry out a specific application or task, e.g., word processing, accounting, and charting.

The obvious difference between a stage play and a computer interface is that in the latter, the user directs the action. The "user

1. This case deals only with the graphic elements or visual displays of the Macintosh user interface. The whole Macintosh user interface includes both its graphic elements or visual displays and the mouse technology which enables the user to point on these graphic elements and command some computer operation.

friendliness" of the Macintosh interface gave Apple a competitive edge over other personal computer manufacturers.

The commercial success of the Macintosh user interface and competition produced by Microsoft's analogous Windows Version 1.0 system software for IBM and IBM–compatible personal computers spawned a dispute between Apple and Microsoft over the rightful ownership of visual displays in this interface. The parties' dispute extended to ownership of visual displays in Microsoft Windows Version 1.0, and certain application programs; Microsoft Multiplan and Microsoft Excel, both spread-sheet programs; Microsoft Chart, a graphics program; Microsoft File, a database program; and Microsoft Word, a word processing program.[2] On November 22, 1985, Apple and Microsoft entered into an agreement ("1985 Agreement") to settle this dispute. The effect of that agreement upon the parties' rights was the first matter which the Honorable William W. Schwarzer, to whom this case was previously assigned, sought to determine.

The 1985 Agreement provided that: (1) Microsoft acknowledged that the visual displays in the Microsoft Windows Version 1.0 operating system and the disputed application programs were derivative works of the visual displays generated by Apple's Macintosh operating system and that of an earlier Apple effort, the Lisa; (2) Apple granted to Microsoft a non-exclusive, royalty-free, nontransferable license to use these derivative visual displays in present and future software programs and to license them to third parties for use in new software programs; (3) Microsoft agreed not to offer a new application program similar in function to Microsoft Excel prior to October 1, 1986; (4) Apple waived any copyright, patent, trade secret or other claim it may have as to Windows Version 1.0; (5) Microsoft granted to Apple a non-exclusive, royalty-free, nontransferable license to use any new visual displays created by Microsoft during the next five years as part of the Microsoft Windows retail software products; and (6) Microsoft agreed to revise Microsoft Word, which operates on the Macintosh operating system, by enhancing and improving that program by July 31, 1986.

Relying on this agreement, Microsoft apparently granted HP a license to use the Microsoft Windows system software in the development of what came to be known as HP's NewWave application program. Sewell Declaration with Appendix in Support of Apple's Summary Judgment Motion, Exh. 39. After learning of the HP NewWave application program and evidently fearing that Microsoft's licensing activities would soon diminish the Macintosh competitive advantage, Apple filed this lawsuit.

Apple's complaint alleged three claims: (1) copyright infringement of Apple's audiovisual works by HP's NewWave and Microsoft's Windows Version 2.03; (2) contributory infringement against Microsoft for

2. Microsoft developed Multiplan, Chart and File under an earlier agreement with Apple.

licensing Apple's visual displays to HP; and (3) unfair competition. Microsoft and HP asserted a variety of affirmative defenses, including two addressed in this order: Apple's allegedly fraudulent procurement of its copyrights and the asserted lack of originality of the Macintosh graphic user interface.

By orders dated March 20 and July 25, 1989,[3] Judge Schwarzer summarily adjudicated that: (1) the 1985 Agreement was not a complete defense to Apple's claim of copyright infringement; (2) the 1985 Agreement granted Microsoft a license to use in current and future software products the visual displays in Windows Version 1.0 and the five named Microsoft application programs; and (3) the visual displays in Windows 2.03 are in Windows 1.0 and the named application programs except for those relating to the use of overlapping main application windows and to certain changes in the appearance and manipulation of icons. Judge Schwarzer granted Microsoft partial summary judgment on Apple's infringement claim to the extent that Windows 2.03 and NewWave used visual displays that had appeared in Windows Version 1.0 and the five application programs named in the 1985 Agreement. 717 F.Supp. at 1435. Such visual displays were protected from Apple's infringement claims by virtue of the 1985 Agreement's licensing provisions. In reaching this conclusion, Judge Schwarzer rejected Apple's contention that the 1985 Agreement forbade Microsoft from developing in later system software an overall visual appearance more similar to that of the Macintosh than Windows Version 1.0. 717 F.Supp. at 1431. Judge Schwarzer determined that the 1985 Agreement licensed only those visual displays in Windows Version 1.0 and the five application programs named therein. 717 F.Supp. at 1435.

Judge Schwarzer's approach entailed analysis of the works' discrete "visual displays."[4] Pursuant to Judge Schwarzer's direction, Apple identified 189 Macintosh visual displays which it claimed appear in Windows Version 2.03 and NewWave.[5] Judge Schwarzer reorganized these visual displays into six categories and decided that with respect to Windows Version 2.03, all visual displays except the use of overlapping application windows and certain changes in the appearance and manipulation of icons were protected from Apple's infringement claims by virtue of the 1985 Agreement.[6] 717 F.Supp. at 1433–35.

By an order to which the parties stipulated during Judge Schwarzer's supervision of the litigation, this court limited the current phase

3. *Apple Computer, Inc. v. Microsoft Corp.*, 709 F.Supp. 925, 717 F.Supp. 1428 (N.D.Cal.1989).

4. The term "visual displays" comes from the 1985 Agreement. *See* Appendix to Microsoft's Memorandum in Support of Motion for Partial Summary Judgment, Exh. K.

5. Apple's document entitled "Similarities between Apple's Copyrighted Audiovisual Works and Microsoft's Windows 2.03 and Hewlett–Packard's NewWave" shall hereinafter be referred to as "Apple's List."

6. This holding did not affect the visual displays which Apple claimed are found only in NewWave. 717 F.Supp. at 1433 n. 8.

of litigation to issues regarding the validity and scope of Apple's copyrights in the works in suit and whether any of the ten remaining visual displays are licensed under the 1985 Agreement between Apple and Microsoft.

Presently before the court are: (1) Microsoft's motion for partial summary judgment, seeking a determination that seven of the ten remaining visual displays from Apple's List are licensed by the 1985 Agreement, and that none of the remaining ten features is protectible expression within the scope of any of Apple's copyrights; (2) HP's motion seeking partial summary adjudication that: (a) each of the 50 remaining items [7] on Apple's list of similarities applicable to NewWave is not original; (b) each of the remaining items does not constitute protectible expression under copyright law; or (c) the scope of protection for such items is so narrow that only virtually identical copying can constitute infringement; and (d) 11 of the remaining 50 items are licensed visual displays under the 1985 Agreement and are protected against Apple's claim of copyright infringement; and (3) Apple's motion for partial summary adjudication that Apple's audiovisual copyrights are valid and the Microsoft and HP affirmative defenses should be dismissed.

Implicit in Judge Schwarzer's approach to the case is a rejection of Apple's fundamental contention that the "total concept and feel" of the Macintosh graphic user interface is protectible expression. Rather, Judge Schwarzer's approach appears to have been to exclude licensed visual displays prior to applying the substantial similarity of idea and expression tests. The undersigned has considered a different approach to the litigation from that adopted by Judge Schwarzer, one that would not begin by an attempt to parse the visual displays of the Macintosh system software. However appealing such an approach might seem in the abstract, the 1985 Agreement appears to license individual visual displays rather than an overall "total concept and feel."[8] After lengthy consideration, the undersigned has concluded that Judge Schwarzer correctly began his analysis of the issues in the litigation with the 1985 Agreement. The court thus turns to the motions directed to the remaining issues involving the 1985 Agreement.

II. Microsoft's Motion for Partial Summary Judgment

In his July 25, 1989 order,[9] Judge Schwarzer found that particular changes in the appearance and use of icons, namely, the storage of icons anywhere on the screen rather than just at the bottom of the screen, the display of the icon's name below the icon, and changes in

7. Although HP correctly states that there are fifty visual displays on Apple's List which pertain only to NewWave, there are additional visual displays on Apple's List which refer to both NewWave and Windows 2.03.

8. An evaluation of whether the "total concept and feel" of the works is substantially similar should occur after unprotectible elements of expression have been identified and excluded from consideration. *See Data East USA, Inc. v. Epyx, Inc.*, 862 F.2d 204, 208 (9th Cir.1988).

9. *Apple Computer, Inc. v. Miscrosoft Corp.*, 717 F.Supp. 1428 (N.D.Cal.1989).

visual displays necessary to implement the overlapping windows system, were not licensed under the 1985 Agreement. 717 F.Supp. at 1433–1435. The remaining visual displays are:

A1 overlapping windows in front of a muted background;

A8 windows appearing partly on and off screen;

B1 top overlapping window displayed as the active window;

B2 window brought to top of stack when mouse clicked;

D1 gray outline of window dragged along with cursor when mouse pressed on window's title bar;

D2 window dragged to a new position when the mouse is released after dragging the window's outline;

D3 newly exposed areas on screen are redisplayed after the window is moved;

G4 icon may be moved to any part of screen by dragging along with cursor when user presses mouse on icon;

G5 display of icons on screen behind any open windows; and

G6 icon's title displayed beneath icon.

In support of its contention that seven of the remaining visual displays (A1, A8, B1, B2, D1, D2, D3) are licensed, Microsoft has submitted a videotape, Exhibit H, which shows that each of the seven visual displays appeared in the 1985 version of Microsoft Excel. Microsoft argues that any visual displays in Windows Version 1.0 and the five application programs developed by Microsoft (Word, Chart, File, Excel, and Multiplan) are licensed under the 1985 Agreement and, hence, are protected from Apple's claims of copyright infringement.

Apple contends that each of the Microsoft application programs developed for the Macintosh computer owes its distinctive Macintosh-like appearance to the Macintosh system software without which the application programs could not run. The visual displays which appear on the screen when an application program is running on a Macintosh computer are generated by the interaction between the Macintosh system software and the application program. Therefore, contends Apple, the only visual displays in the five named application programs which are licensed under the 1985 Agreement are those which are created by the code of the Microsoft application programs, not those generated by application calls to the Macintosh system software. The visual displays which are generated by the Macintosh system software include the window frames, moving animation, and the redisplay of those portions of the screen exposed by a window which has been moved. The visual displays which are generated by the Microsoft Excel application program are the contents of the windows. Capps Supp. Decl. ¶¶ 3, 4 and Exh. 1.

The issue of which visual displays are generated by the Microsoft application programs and which by the Macintosh system software was raised earlier before Judge Schwarzer, in a slightly different context.

In his March 20, 1989 Order, Judge Schwarzer declined to consider whether the visual displays in issue were generated by the Microsoft application programs or by the Macintosh system software. The point arose in connection with Microsoft's argument that the 1985 Agreement licensed to Microsoft application programs on the Macintosh system software then or in the future. 709 F.Supp. at 929. Judge Schwarzer concluded that Microsoft's contention would "defy common sense." *Id.*

Microsoft refers to the depositions of Albert Eisenstat, Apple's Senior Vice President, and John Sculley, Apple's President and CEO, in which these negotiators of the 1985 Agreement did not remember discussing the distinction between visual displays generated by the Microsoft application software code and those generated by the Macintosh system software code. Appendix to Microsoft's Reply to Apple's Response to Microsoft's Motion for Partial Summary Judgment. Furthermore, Microsoft contends that it would have been extremely difficult for the negotiators of the 1985 Agreement to determine which visual displays were attributable to which program codes because such information would require a detailed analysis of the images created by each software program.

Apple contends that: (1) the controversy which resulted in the 1985 license related entirely to Microsoft Windows Version 1.0; (2) Apple did not present any complaint formally or informally regarding any of the Microsoft application programs; and (3) Microsoft's Chairman Gates repeatedly explained that he sought confirmation of Microsoft's ownership of the visual displays in only those application programs that Microsoft created and owned. Apple's Response to Defendants' Motions for Partial Summary Judgment at 10.

Under California law, ambiguities in a written agreement are to be interpreted against the drafter, in this case, Microsoft.

Moreover, the Ninth Circuit has directed district courts to interpret copyright licenses narrowly, consistent with the federal copyright policy of providing incentives in the form of copyright protection to authors. *See S.O.S. Payday,* 886 F.2d at 1088 ("copyright licenses are assumed to prohibit any use not authorized"); *Cohen v. Paramount Pictures Corp.,* 845 F.2d 851, 854 (9th Cir.1988). In *S.O.S. v. Payday,* the court concluded that a software developer's grant of a "right of use" of several software programs to a company which provided financial services to clients did not confer the right to copy and prepare a modified version of the software programs without the licensor's permission. The court concluded that the licensee had only acquired the right to possess copies of the software programs for purposes of producing a product for its clients, and, therefore, had exceeded the scope of its license. Similarly, the *Cohen* court construed a license of a copyrighted work narrowly. *Cohen* involved a license to record and copy a motion picture and exhibit it "by means of television," which was construed not to include the distribution of videocassettes for home viewing, VCRs for home use not having been invented at the time the license was executed.

In light of these rules of construction and the 1985 Agreement's purpose to resolve the dispute over ownership of visual displays in Windows Version 1.0, the court concludes that the 1985 Agreement did not license the visual displays which are generated by calls from the Microsoft application programs to the Macintosh operating system. The mere fact that the Macintosh system software was designed so that the Macintosh interface could be used in conjunction with a variety of application programs written for the Macintosh computer,[10] should not open the door to a construction at odds with usual principles of contract law and the agreement's evident purpose. It would be astonishing if Apple had licensed those visual displays which had won for it great acclaim for aesthetic and intuitive appeal.

What Microsoft received in the 1985 Agreement was the right to continue to market its application programs written for the Macintosh and to use the visual displays generated by those application programs (not the visual displays generated by calls by the application programs to the Macintosh operating system) in present and future programs.

Although seven of the eleven remaining visual displays from Apple's List (A1, A8, B1, B2, D1, D2, and D3) do appear on the screen when the Microsoft Excel application program runs in conjunction with the Macintosh operating system, each of those seven visual displays owes its appearance to the Macintosh operating system. Capps Supp. Declaration. Therefore, those seven visual displays are not licensed under the 1985 Agreement. Microsoft's motion for summary adjudication that these displays are covered by virtue of being in the 1985 version of Microsoft Excel is, therefore, denied.

III. HP'S Motion for Partial Summary Judgment

As to the scope of the 1985 Agreement, HP contends that eleven of the fifty visual displays in Apple's List are covered by the 1985 Agreement and, therefore, are protected from Apple's claims of copyright infringement. These visual displays are: I3, I5, I10, I11, I12, F18, F19, G10, G19, G20, and G22.

A determination of the legal significance of undisputed historical facts, such as the visual displays in Windows Version 1.0 and NewWave, involves a mixed question of fact and law normally decided by the court and, therefore, appropriate for summary judgment. *See Cohen,* 845 F.2d at 853, 855 (reversal of summary judgment in favor of licensee).

As a preliminary matter, HP's motion for summary adjudication rests on the assumptions that the 1985 Agreement granted Microsoft the right to use and license to third parties visual displays in Windows

10. By permitting application programs to call upon the Macintosh system software to generate visual displays, the Apple software developers simplified the task of writing application programs for the Macintosh computer.

Version 1.0 and that HP is entitled to use those visual displays by virtue of a license from Microsoft to HP. The first assumption is plainly justified by Section 2A of the 1985 Agreement. Strangely, the second assumption is questionable. HP has not established the terms of the Microsoft–HP license. Absent such an agreement, HP has no right to rely on the 1985 Agreement between Microsoft and Apple as a defense to copyright infringement. Because the parties proceeded with two summary judgment motions without clarifying this issue and there are letters referring to a license between Microsoft and HP, the court can only assume that Microsoft did license the use of visual displays in Windows Version 1.0 to HP. The court is confident that the lawyers for these parties will be heard from if this is not the case and shall thus address the merits of HP's motion.

After reviewing the videotape exhibits submitted on this issue and comparing the appearance of these eleven visual displays in Apple's programs and in Microsoft Windows Version 1.0, the court drew the following conclusions.

Items I3, I5, I12, F18, F19, and G22 on Apple's List are all present in Windows Version 1.0 and hence are covered by the 1985 License.

Item I10 is licensed insofar as Windows Version 1.0 contains a "Select All" item in the Edit pull-down menu which allows the user to select all text in the window and display that text in reverse video. To the extent that the Windows Version 1.0 "Select All" item does not permit selection by reverse video of any icons, the "Select All" item is not licensed.

Item I11, a menu called "View" which presents the user with a number of menu items allowing the user to choose the folder's window display as icons or as a tabular list by name, type, or modification date, is licensed except insofar as Windows Version 1.0's "View" pull-down menu does not offer the user the option to display a folder's contents as icons in the window.

Item G19, selection of an icon by changing both the icon and its name into reverse video, is not licensed because in Windows Version 1.0 only disk drive icons and their names, which are not aligned directly below, can be selected by reverse video. The appearance of selecting only disk drive icons by reverse video in Windows Version 1.0 is significantly different from the selection of the variety of icons in the Macintosh and NewWave programs.

Items G10 and G20 do not appear to be licensed, but the association of different icon images with different types of objects and the use of a mouse to move icons around on a screen appear to be ideas. For purposes of the current motion, the court finds only that items G10 and G20 are not covered by the 1985 Agreement. The idea/expression distinction is properly raised in connection with the issue of substantial similarity, which is not presently before the court.

Therefore, the court concludes that items I3, I5, I12, F18, F19, and G22 on Apple's List are licensed to Microsoft pursuant to the 1985 Agreement and, assuming that Microsoft licensed the use of these visual displays to HP, are protected from Apple's claim of copyright infringement.

The following items on Apple's List are unlicensed and pertain to NewWave: A1, A8, B1, B2, D1–3, G1, G2, G4, G5, G6, G10–33, H1–6, I1, I2, I4, I6–11, J8–11 (55 items total).

* * *

7. SECURITY INTERESTS AND BANKRUPTCY—PROTECTING SOFTWARE SELLERS AND BUYERS

Inevitably some buyers and sellers of software will fail. Parties to software transactions must seek legal protection against the bankruptcy of their partners. Software sellers will seek protection in case buyers will not or cannot pay. Buyers will seek to continue software use even after sellers' bankruptcy.

* * *

BANKRUPTCY CODE
11 U.S.C.A. § 365

(n)(1) If the trustee rejects an executory contract under which the debtor is a licensor of a right to intellectual property, the licensee under such contract may elect—

(A) to treat such contract as terminated by such rejection if such rejection by the trustee amounts to such a breach as would entitle the licensee to treat such contract as terminated by virtue of its own terms, applicable nonbankruptcy law, or an agreement made by the licensee with another entity; or

(B) to retain its rights (including a right to enforce any exclusivity provision of such contract, but excluding any other right under applicable nonbankruptcy law to specific performance of such contract) under such contract and under any agreement supplementary to such contract, to such intellectual property (including any embodiment of such intellectual property to the extent protected by applicable nonbankruptcy law), as such rights existed immediately before the case commenced, for—

(i) the duration of such contract; and

(ii) any period for which such contract may be extended by the licensee as of right under applicable nonbankruptcy law.

(2) If the licensee elects to retain its rights, as described in paragraph (1) (B) of this subsection, under such contract—

(A) the trustee shall allow the licensee to exercise such rights;

(B) the licensee shall make all royalty payments due under such contract for the duration of such contract and for any period described in paragraph (1)(B) of this subsection for which the licensee extends such contract; and

(C) the licensee shall be deemed to waive—

(i) any right of setoff it may have with respect to such contract under this title or applicable nonbankruptcy law; and

(ii) any claim allowable under section 503(b) of this title arising from the performance of such contract.

(3) If the licensee elects to retain its rights, as described in paragraph (1)(B) of this subsection, then on the written request of the licensee the trustee shall—

(A) to the extent provided in such contract, or any agreement supplementary to such contract, provide to the licensee any intellectual property (including such embodiment) held by the trustee; and

(B) not interfere with the rights of the licensee as provided in such contract, or any agreement supplementary to such contract, to such intellectual property (including such embodiment) including any right to obtain such intellectual property (or such embodiment) from another entity.

(4) Unless and until the trustee rejects such contract, on the written request of the licensee the trustee shall—

(A) to the extent provided in such contract or any agreement supplementary to such contract—

(i) perform such contract; or

(ii) provide to the licensee such intellectual property (including any embodiment of such intellectual property to the extent protected by applicable nonbankruptcy law) held by the trustee; and

(B) not interfere with the rights of the licensee as provided in such contract, or any agreement supplementary to such contract, to such intellectual property (including such embodiment), including any right to obtain such intellectual property (or such embodiment) from another entity.

* * *

FLEMING v. CARROLL PUBLISHING COMPANY

District of Columbia Court of Appeals, 1990.
581 A.2d 1219.

STEADMAN, ASSOCIATE JUDGE:

This case presents several questions arising under Article 9 of the District of Columbia's version of the Uniform Commercial Code. A creditor that "leased" computer equipment and software to a user and later repossessed part of the property seeks to recover the balance due on the "lease." The issues include: (1) whether the controlling document was a "true lease" or a security agreement; (2) if a security agreement, whether the secured creditor's sale of part of the repossessed collateral without providing the requisite notice to the debtor bars the creditor from asserting rights either to a deficiency judgment or to collateral remaining in the debtor's possession; (3) if the creditor is not barred from asserting such rights, what the creditor's present rights are to the remaining collateral, which consists of computer software whose form has been significantly transformed; and (4) whether the creditor is, in any event, entitled to attorney's fees under the terms of the agreement between the parties. We uphold the trial court's rulings that the "lease" was a security agreement and that the creditor is barred from any deficiency judgment. We remand for further proceedings on the issues of the creditor's rights in the unrepossessed collateral and to attorney's fees.

I. The Facts

While unusually complicated in their detail, the facts relevant to disposition of this appeal may be summarized as follows. On December 29, 1980, Carroll Publishing Company ("Carroll") entered into an "Equipment Lease Agreement" (the "lease" or the "agreement") with three individual investors who had formed a partnership called Equity Leasing Joint Venture—80F ("Equity"). The lease covered certain computer hardware and software. These items were acquired through third-party vendors. Some of the software was "off-the-shelf" but at least two significant software packages were to be custom-written for Carroll by a third-party vendor. The lease term was for five years, with total payments of $87,328.25.[2]

A series of difficulties of various kinds developed, and on August 25, 1982, Carroll wrote to Equity's agent terminating the agreement, on the ground of nondelivery of certain items called for by the lease. Up to that point, Carroll had made sixteen regular lease payments totaling $26,198.46. On February 22, 1983, Equity filed the instant suit against Carroll, seeking recovery in the amount of $61,930.11 and attorney's fees. Carroll counterclaimed, alleging nondelivery of some of the leased items and seeking damages for fraud and for breach of contract.

While the case was pending, on September 29, 1983, Equity's agent went to Carroll's office armed with a court order and repossessed a number of pieces of hardware and one item of software, located in the drive of one of the repossessed machines. Subsequently, at least some

2. The lease did not provide for Carroll to purchase the equipment. In a subsequent Purchase Agreement of January 25, 1981, however, the parties agreed that "Buyer [Carroll] is hereby given the first right to purchase the Equipment at the estimated fair market value of 10% of the original value (see below) [.] Said purchase shall occur upon expiration of the lease." In addition, the Purchase Agreement provided that a "demand for purchase of the Equipment may be made by Equity or its successor or assigns at any time after the date hereof."

of the repossessed hardware was sold at a private sale, of which Carroll was given no form of notice.

Following a bench trial, the trial court denied Equity any relief. The court concluded first that the agreement was not a "true lease" but a security agreement governed by Article 9 of the District of Columbia's version of the Uniform Commercial Code. It concluded further that any claims for nondelivery were the sole responsibility of third-party vendors and not Equity; hence Equity was initially within its rights in proceeding under the agreement and under Article 9. However, it held, Equity's failure to give notice to Carroll of its proposed sale of repossessed collateral barred Equity from obtaining any deficiency judgment, and any rights in the software remaining in Carroll's possession had been lost because of the subsequent modification of the software. Hence, Equity took nothing by its complaint. Nonetheless, the court interpreted the agreement to permit Equity to recover reasonable attorney's fees and costs, which it awarded in the amount of $50,636.01.

II. Lease or Security Agreement

On appeal, Equity contends first that the trial court erred in concluding that the lease was not a "true lease" but a security agreement governed by Article 9 of the District of Columbia Uniform Commercial Code. D.C.Code §§ 28:9–101 to 28:9–507 (1989). District of Columbia Code § 28:1–201(37) (1989) provides, in pertinent part:

> "Security interest" means an interest in personal property or fixtures which secures payment or performance of an obligation. * * * Unless a lease or consignment is intended as security, reservation of title thereunder is not a "security interest". * * * Whether a lease is intended as security is to be determined by the facts of each case; however, (a) the inclusion of an option to purchase does not of itself make the lease one intended for security, and (b) an agreement that upon compliance with the terms of the lease the lessee shall become or has the option to become the owner of the property for no additional consideration or for a nominal consideration does make the lease one intended for security.

Thus, in determining whether a lease is a "true lease" or an Article 9 security agreement, the trial court must look to the intent of the parties, which depends on "the facts of each case." The trial court's determination as to the intent of the parties is essentially one of fact, *cf. Dodek v. Cf. 16 Corp.,* 537 A.2d 1086, 1093 (D.C.1988) ("the question of what the parties intended [by their contract] is clearly a question of fact" (internal quotation marks omitted)), and will not be upset unless it is "plainly wrong or without evidence to support it." D.C.Code § 17–305(a) (1989). Here, the trial court recognized that the intent of the parties is essential to a determination of whether a lease is a "true lease" or security agreement and the court detailed its reasons for finding that the parties intended the lease as a security agreement. In particular, the court noted that the lease allocated to Carroll several burdens typically associated with ownership of property, such as the obligation to pay license fees and taxes on the equipment, the obligation to keep the equipment in good repair and the assumption of "the entire risk of loss of and damage to Equipment from any and every cause whatsoever." In addition, the court noted that Equity's status was as financier, rather than manufacturer or seller, and that Equity had no storage facilities for the equipment. These are among the "factors" courts use in determining whether a lease is "intended for security." 2 J. White & R. Summers, Uniform Commercial Code § 23–3, at 251–52 (3d ed. 1988) (hereinafter, "White & Summers"). The court also noted that the total price Carroll was required to pay under the lease exceeded the purchase price of the equipment by $29,028.00 and that the customized system would be of little value to other potential lessees. "Under the totality of the evidence presented," the court found that the parties "intended to create a security agreement." We cannot say that this finding is "plainly wrong or without evidence to support it."

III. The Secured Creditor's Rights

A. *Deficiency Judgment*

Equity contends next that, even if the lease was a security agreement, the trial court erred in barring Equity from obtaining a deficiency judgment. * * *

* * *

* * * While a secured creditor ordinarily has the right to sue on the debt as well as proceed against the collateral, D.C.Code § 28:9–501(1), if he proceeds against the collateral, he is obligated to follow the applicable rule for its disposition. At least under the circumstances here, a failure to do so acts as a bar to any deficiency judgment, whatever rights the creditor may retain in the collateral itself. * * *

* * *

Although Equity lost its rights to a deficiency judgment, it does not follow that it has lost rights in the remaining collateral, and especially to the collateral not repossessed, *viz.*, the bulk of the "leased" software. We turn to this issue.

B. *Unrepossessed Collateral*

Even if barred from a deficiency judgment, Equity seeks in the alternative to assert rights against the unrepossessed balance of the software in Carroll's possession subject to the security agreement. We do not think that a bar to a deficiency judgment in itself constitutes any obstacle to the enforcement of a security interest in any collateral remaining in the debtor's possession. * * *

* * *

Chapter VII

INTELLECTUAL PROPERTY REMEDIES

A. DAMAGES

The issue of damages for intellectual property infringement is often as obscure as the basic issue of qualification for patent, copyright, or trade secret protection. While damages are available to the property owner, they are often difficult to determine or prove. The calculation of damages for patent, copyright, and trade secret violations have both similarities and differences.

Owners of all three types of intellectual property used to protect software—patents, copyrights, and trade secrets—are entitled to actual damages (also called compensatory damages). The Patent Act provides, "the court shall award the claimant damages adequate to compensate for the infringement, but in no event less than a reasonable royalty for the use made of the invention by the infringer * * *" (35 U.S.C.A. § 284). The Copyright Act provides, "The copyright owner is entitled to recover the actual damages suffered by him or her as a result of the infringement, and any profits of the infringer that are attributable to the infringement and are not taken into account in computing the actual damages." (17 U.S.C.A. § 504(b)). A further provision of the Copyright Act eases the burden of proof for copyright owners: "In establishing the infringer's profits, the copyright owner is required to present proof only of the infringer's gross revenue, and the infringer is required to prove his or her deductible expenses and the elements of profit attributable to factors other than the copyrighted work." (17 U.S.C.A. § 504(b)). Damages for trade secret infringement depend upon the statutory or common law of the jurisdiction involved.

Actual damages may be inadequate for a number of reasons. The plaintiff may have difficulty providing proof to answer the hypothetical question of how much more profit it would have made if the infringement had not occured. Legal expenses for plaintiffs in intellectual property cases are high. Since many violators of intellectual property escape detection, it is important to have severe sanctions against those who are caught. So it is not surprising that there are mechanisms to provide more than actual damages. In patent infringement cases, "the court may increase the damages up to three times the amount found or assessed." (35 U.S.C.A. § 284). A copyright owner may elect for statutory damages under a provision allowing the court to grant from $200 to $100,000 for a copyright violation without proof of actual damages. (17 U.S.C.A. § 504(c)). Courts may award punitive damages for wilful misappropriation of trade secrets.

UNIVERSITY COMPUTING CO. v. LYKES–YOUNGSTOWN CORP.

United States Court of Appeals, Fifth Circuit, 1974.
504 F.2d 518.

TUTTLE, CIRCUIT JUDGE:

[Defendants misappropriated plaintiff's inventory control software.]

* * *

C. Judgment in District Court.

UCC brought this suit against LYC, LYCSC and Oliver Shinn claiming damages under seven Counts. Counts 1 and 2 were combined at trial into a single count against LYC for breach of the joint venture agreement. Count 3 charged a conspiracy among the three defendants to misappropriate UCC's trade secret, AIMES III; Count 4 charged a conspiracy among the three defendants to convert unlawfully AIMES III; Count 5 charged a conspiracy among the three defendants to infringe UCC's common law copyright in AIMES III; Count 6 charged a conspiracy among the three defendants to violate Oliver Shinn's non-competition agreement with UCC; and finally Count 7 charged a conspiracy among the three defendants to induce a breach of the restrictive use agreement between Leonard's and UCC. Plaintiff conceded at trial Counts 3, 4, 5 and 7 all involved essentially the same damages for the misappropriation of the AIMES III system.

The district court granted a directed verdict for defendants on Counts 5 and 7. The remaining counts went to the jury, which returned verdicts against the plaintiff on Counts 4 and 6, against defendant LYC on Count 1 and against all three defendants on Count 3. The jury awarded $172,000 against LYC for its breach of the joint venture agreement (Counts 1 and 2); $220,000 against all three defendants for misappropriation of UCC's trade secret, AIMES III (Count 3); and finally the jury awarded $100,000 in attorneys' fees against LYC on Count 1.

Defendants bring this appeal attacking these verdicts on a number of different grounds. Plaintiff cross-appeals the directed verdict on Count 7, and the verdicts on Counts 4 and 6. We affirm the judgment of the court below on the jury verdict on Count 1 against defendant

LYC, and on Count 3 against defendants LYC, LYCSC and Oliver Shinn. We affirm judgment on the jury verdict on Counts 4 and 6 against plaintiff UCC and affirm the directed verdict against plaintiff UCC on Count 7. We reverse and remand for a new trial on the issue of attorneys' fees.

* * *

Once having determined that the jury finding that AIMES III was a trade secret wrongfully appropriated by the defendants was proper, the problem remains as to what is the appropriate measure of damages. It seems generally accepted that "the proper measure of damages in the case of a trade secret appropriation is to be determined by reference to the analogous line of cases involving patent infringement, just as patent infringement cases are used by analogy to determine the damages for copyright infringement." International Industries, Inc. v. Warren Petroleum Corp., 248 F.2d 696, 699 (3d Cir.1957). The case law is thus plentiful, but the standard for measuring damages which emerges is very flexible.

In some instances courts have attempted to measure the loss suffered by the plaintiff. While as a conceptual matter this seems to be a proper approach, in most cases the defendant has utilized the secret to his advantage with no obvious effect on the plaintiff save for the relative differences in their subsequent competitive positions. Largely as a result of this practical dilemma, normally the value of the secret to the plaintiff is an appropriate measure of damages only when the defendant has in some way destroyed the value of the secret. The most obvious way this is done is through publication, so that no secret remains. Where the plaintiff retains the use of the secret, as here, and where there has been no effective disclosure of the secret through publication the total value of the secret to the plaintiff is an inappropriate measure.

Further, unless some specific injury to the plaintiff can be established—such as lost sales—the loss to the plaintiff is not a particularly helpful approach in assessing damages.

The second approach is to measure the value of the secret to the defendant. This is usually the accepted approach where the secret has not been destroyed and where the plaintiff is unable to prove specific injury. In the case before us, then, the "appropriate measure of damages, by analogy to patent infringement, is not what plaintiff lost, but rather the benefits, profits, or advantages gained by the defendant in the use of the trade secret." International Industries, Inc. v. Warren Petroleum, *supra,* 248 F.2d at 699. The cases reveal, however, many variations in the way this benefit to the defendant can be measured.

Normally only the defendant's actual profits can be used as a measure of damages in cases where profits can be proved, and the defendant is normally not assessed damages on wholly speculative expectations of profits. Sheldon v. Metro–Goldwyn Pictures Corp., 309 U.S. 390, 60 S.Ct. 681, 84 L.Ed. 825 (1939). Had the defendants here been able to sell the AIMES III system at a profit, our task would be simplified. Because the defendants failed in their marketing efforts, no actual profits exist by which to value the worth to the defendants of what they misappropriated. However, the Supreme Court has held in a patent case that the lack of actual profits does not insulate the defendants from being obliged to pay for what they have wrongfully obtained in the mistaken belief their theft would benefit them. In re Cawood Patent, 94 U.S. 695, 24 L.Ed. 238 (1877).[29]

The rationale for this seems clearly to be that the risk of defendants' venture, using the misappropriated secret, should not be placed on the injured plaintiff, but rather the defendants must bear the risk of failure themselves. Accordingly the law looks to the time at which the misappropriation occurred to determine what the value of the misappropriated secret would be to a defendant who believes he can utilize it to his advantage, provided he does in fact put the idea to a commercial use.

This second technique frequently entails using what is called the "reasonable royalty" standard: while the parties to this action agree this is the appropriate standard, they are unable to agree on what the measure entails. Originally this measure was intended to deal with the situation where the misappropriated idea is used either to improve the defendant's manufacturing process, or is used as part of a larger manufactured product. In the early case of Egry Register Co. v. Standard Register Co., 23 F.2d 438 (6th Cir.1928), a patent infringement case, the defendant manufactured and sold cash registers which in part used a device developed by the plaintiff to roll paper through the machine. The trial court had awarded the plaintiff the total profits the defendant had made on all sales of the machines using this device. The Sixth Circuit Court of Appeals held this measure of damages was inequitable, because the device was only a part of the larger product sold by the defendant. Because no actual apportionment of profits based on what percentage of the success of the marketing of the machines was due to the plaintiff's device could be shown, the court held the proper measure of damages would be a reasonable royalty on defendant's sales, thereby creating an apportionment of profits based on an approximation of the actual value of the infringed device to the defendant.

* * *

The Court further held the proper standard would be a willing buyer-willing seller test: "* * * the primary inquiry * * * is what the parties would have agreed upon, if both were reasonably trying to reach agreement." *Egry Register, supra,* at 443.

The language of the *Egry* decision has been often quoted, but the type of measure used by the Court, based on actual sales, has taken many different forms. As the term is presently understood, the "rea-

29. Defendant's actual profits are now usually only one of a number of elements which can be considered in measuring damages for patent infringement. * * *

sonable royalty" measure of damages is taken to mean more than simply a percentage of actual profits. The measure now, very simply, means "[t]he actual value of what has been appropriated." Vitro Corporation of America v. Hall Chemical Co., 292 F.2d 678, 683 (6th Cir.1961). When this is not subject to exact measurement, a reasonable estimate of value is used. * * *

* * *

One other important variation on this "reasonable royalty" standard is the standard of comparison method, which also attempts to measure the value to the defendant of what he appropriated. * * *

* * *

Occasionally this has been taken to mean the difference in costs to the defendant of developing the trade secret on his own, using the actual development costs of the plaintiff as the complete measure of damages. Servo Corp. v. General Electric Co., 342 F.2d 993 (4th Cir.1965), cert. denied, 383 U.S. 934, 86 S.Ct. 1061, 15 L.Ed.2d 851 (1966). This measure of damages simply uses the plaintiff's actual costs, and in our view is frequently inadequate in that it fails to take into account the commercial context in which the misappropriation occurred.

In certain cases, where the trade secret was used by the defendant in a limited number of situations, where the plaintiff was not in direct competition with the defendant, where the development of the secret did not require substantial improvements in existing trade practices but rather merely refined the existing practices, and where the defendant's use of the plaintiff's trade secret has ceased, such a limited measure might be appropriate. In the type of case which we now consider, when the parties were potentially in direct competition and the course of conduct of the defendant extended over a period of time and included a number of different uses of the plaintiff's trade secret, and where the process of developing a computer system was very difficult and required substantial technical and theoretical advances, we believe a broader measure of damages is needed.

This broader measure should take into consideration development costs, but as only one of a number of different factors. We believe this type of measure is appropriate despite the fact that the inclusion of other factors means the final damages figure "need not be as precise as if the actual development costs for the trade secret were itself the measure of damages." Forest Laboratories, Inc. v. Pillsbury Co., 452 F.2d 621, 628 (7th Cir.1971).

Our review of the caselaw leads us to the conclusion that every case requires a flexible and imaginative approach to the problem of damages. We agree with the Court of Appeals for the Sixth Circuit that "each case is controlled by its own peculiar facts and circumstances," Enterprise Manufacturing Co. v. Shakespeare Co., 141 F.2d 916, 920 (6th Cir.1944), and accordingly we believe that the cases reveal that most courts adjust the measure of damages to accord with the commercial setting of the injury, the likely future consequences of the misappropriation, and the nature and extent of the use the defendant put the trade secret to after misappropriation. Naturally in some cases the damages will be subject to exact measurement, either because the parties had previously agreed on a licensing price as in Vitro Corp. v. Hall Chemical Co., supra, or because some industry standard provides a clear measure. Where the damages are uncertain, however, we do not feel that that uncertainty should preclude recovery; the plaintiff should be afforded every opportunity to prove damages once the misappropriation is shown.

Certain standards do emerge from the cases. The defendant must have actually put the trade secret to some commercial use. The law governing protection of trade secrets essentially is designed to regulate unfair business competition, and is not a substitute for criminal laws against theft or other civil remedies for conversion. If the defendant enjoyed actual profits, a type of restitutionary remedy can be afforded the plaintiff—either recovering the full total of defendant's profits or some apportioned amount designed to correspond to the actual contribution the plaintiff's trade secret made to the defendant's commercial success. Because the primary concern in most cases is to measure the value to the defendant of what he actually obtained from the plaintiff, the proper measure is to calculate what the parties would have agreed to as a fair price for licensing the defendant to put the trade secret to the use the defendant intended at the time the misappropriation took place.

In calculating what a fair licensing price would have been had the parties agreed, the trier of fact should consider such factors as the resulting and foreseeable changes in the parties' competitive posture; the prices past purchasers or licensees may have paid; the total value of the secret to the plaintiff, including the plaintiff's development costs and the importance of the secret to the plaintiff's business; the nature and extent of the use the defendant intended for the secret; and finally whatever other unique factors in the particular case which might have affected the parties' agreement, such as the ready availability of alternative processes. Hughes Tool Co. v. G.W. Murphy Industries, Inc., 491 F.2d 923, 931 (5th Cir.1973).

* * *

D. Challenges to Admission of Evidence on Value of AIMES III.

The defendants challenge the method by which UCC proved damages at trial. The only evidence introduced by either side on the question of damages for the AIMES III misappropriation was the expert testimony of one Stan Josephson, who estimated the value of a sale of unrestricted rights to AIMES III at $220,000. Defendants challenge both the expert qualifications of this witness and the legal sufficiency of his testimony. We deal with the first of these issues quickly.

The trial court has substantial discretion over the admission of evidence, Reuter v. Eastern Air Lines, 226 F.2d 443 (5th Cir.1955) and this includes the admission of expert testimony. In the absence of obvious error we will not disturb the ruling of the trial court. We find no error in permitting Josephson to testify as an expert. He was UCC Vice President of Technical Services. He testified he was responsible for developing software systems, pricing them for marketing, and then assisting as technical expert at sales presentations. He testified in pricing a software system he took into account such factors as development costs, the long-term potential for the system and UCC's sales objectives, as well as such extrinsic factors as the current market for such systems. We find Josephson was properly permitted to testify as to the value placed on the sale of unrestricted rights to the AIMES III system by UCC.

The second challenge to Josephson's testimony involves colloquy from the record during Josephson's cross-examination.

* * *

Defendants rightly point to the ambiguity created by Josephson's concession that what he was calculating was something other than what a willing buyer would agree to, which is the proper measure of damages.

In part our decision to sustain the jury verdict, which was heavily dependent on the Josephson testimony in view of the fact they assessed damages of $220,000, the precise estimate he had testified to, is based on our view that the jury was properly instructed in the law governing damages. The verdict of a jury properly instructed in the law clearly resolves ambiguities of this sort in testimony, and the jury had been fully instructed in the willing buyer-willing seller test.

But secondly we believe the ambiguity created by cross-examination was more apparent than real. Naturally, we read Mr. Josephson's testimony in its entirety and we do not find the above-quoted passage so inconsistent with his otherwise legally accurate description of how to calculate the value of unrestricted rights to AIMES III as to justify the jury verdict based on that testimony. Certainly estimating sales price as a function of costs is unexceptionable, and Josephson in our view had the expertise to opine that the proper way to calculate value is to multiply costs by a multiple of 2½.

What the disputed passage amounts to is Josephson's reluctance to claim that the figure he set as the proper sale price was necessarily that which a buyer would agree to. We can understand why he would demur from confidently asserting this is what the parties would agree to, for he had no prior transaction upon which to base his opinion. We believe it wasn't improper for UCC to prove its best estimate of the proper sales price, in part taking into consideration its policy of normally not offering its systems to potential competitors. While a certain amount of speculation is involved in this highly theoretical reconstruction of a sale which never took place, the aggrieved plaintiff must be permitted to present its best evidence on damages and not be foreclosed from seeking damages it deserves due to difficulty in measurement.

While we do not dispute the proper standard to be the "willing buyer-willing seller" test, we do not think a reconstruction of the agreement these two reasonable parties would arrive at can be taken too far. Nor do we feel that a witness as to value must cast his answers in the precise language that the Court uses in charging the jury. Both sides in such a hypothetical transaction have interests they wish to protect; such interests affect the price at which they are prepared to buy or sell—and in cases such as this one, the law is far more concerned with the rights and interests of the aggrieved plaintiff than in the interests of the defendants which they would have tried to protect had they dealt openly with the plaintiff from the beginning. As the Court in the *Egry Register* case acknowledged, the hypothetical agreement "must be modified by the commercial situation" *supra,* 23 F.2d at 443, and where the "willing seller" would have been unwilling to sell but for the theft of his secret, the Court reconstructing the agreement should consider the reasons the seller is unprepared to sell, and take into account such factors as the possible decline in the seller's future competitive posture.

This interest the holder of a trade secret has in retaining his rights to his secret is not a trivial one, and one which we do not intend to minimize. Courts should be reluctant to penalize an aggrieved plaintiff by too unrealistic and sterile a requirement of proving that the defendant *would* have agreed to the price the plaintiff thinks is fair. * * *

The proper method of fleshing out the dimensions of this hypothetical sale is by cross-examination and rebuttal testimony. The plaintiff fulfills its burden of proving damages by showing the misappropriation, the subsequent commercial use, and introduces evidence by which the jury can value the rights the defendant has obtained. This UCC did; the defendants introduced no evidence on the question of the value of unrestricted rights to AIMES III. The defendants chose to leave Josephson's testimony unchallenged as to how his estimate of value was arrived at, save for their belief his admission he couldn't guarantee a willing buyer would accept the $220,000 figure necessarily destroyed the value of all his testimony.

Because we read the record as presenting a valid issue of damages to the jury, with sufficient evidence by the plaintiff to permit the jury to value the system at $220,000, we cannot now decide that the $220,000 verdict was clearly excessive as defendants argue.

The defendants also attack the basis for Josephson's calculation of total development cost—claiming such factors as marketing expenses and the plaintiff's royalty agreement with the original developer of the system should not have been included as development costs. We believe these were questions for the jury; the defendants did not choose to cross-examine Josephson extensively on this point, nor did they present rebuttal evidence to dispute his inclusion of these amounts.

The jury was not obliged to accept Josephson's figures, but we hold they could reasonably do so.

The defendants next argue that permitting Josephson to testify as to the unaccepted offer UCC made to Honeywell for the sale of rights to unrestricted use of the AIMES III system was manifest error requiring reversal. It is clear that as a general rule, unaccepted offers are improper evidence by which to estimate value. Typically this problem will arise in condemnation proceedings where an expert witness estimates value by using sales of adjoining property, and occasionally uses unexercised options to purchase adjoining property. A second frequent problem occurs when the owner of the condemned property attempts to use past offers he has received to prove the value of the property.

* * *

Thus, while the rule is well entrenched in the caselaw, it is designed to serve specific purposes and we do not believe is meant to be enforced mechanically or without regard to the reasons for its existence. In the past where the offer was part of a continuing series of negotiations leading to ultimate agreement, it was held to be admissible. Where the offer was introduced for a purpose other than to prove value, it was held to be admissible. Where the offer was such a trivial part of the evidence offered as to be harmless, this Court has recognized the rule of Sharp v. United States is not to be automatically applied.

In sum, we find the admission of testimony concerning UCC's past offer to Honeywell of unrestricted rights to the AIMES III system of $220,000 to have been properly admitted. The past offer wasn't hearsay, for Josephson had personally been involved in the Honeywell transaction. Josephson was an expert and the rule against admitting proof of anonymous offers from unqualified third parties is clearly inapplicable to the facts of this case. Finally the figure of $220,000 was subject to full cross-examination. The defendants could explore with Josephson what factors he considered, what factors he ignored, how development costs were calculated, and finally how he arrived at the multiple of 2½ times development costs. We conclude they suffered no prejudice from the admission of evidence on the Honeywell offer.

There is a second, equally compelling, reason to uphold the admission of the evidence. The issue of the Honeywell offer was first raised on cross-examination of Josephson by the defendants. Josephson was asked whether UCC had ever offered unrestricted rights to anyone in the past, but was not asked what the offer actually was. We believe in the interests of elementary fairness the plaintiff had the right to then complete the account of the transaction which the defendants began. Had the jury only heard that an offer had been made to Honeywell, but did not learn of the amount, their likely reaction would be that UCC was concealing the facts of the Honeywell transaction because they had offered the AIMES III system for substantially less than $220,000. This untrue inference was properly rebutted.

* * *

* * * Similarly if the jury returns two inconsistent verdicts, the trial court may resubmit the issue to them for clarification.

* * *

V. Attorney's Fees.

Under Ga.Code Ann. § 20–1404, attorney's fees may be awarded "if the defendant has acted in bad faith, or has been stubbornly litigious, or has caused the plaintiff unnecessary trouble and expense * * *." The bad faith referred to has been consistently held by Georgia courts to refer to the conduct of the defendant in his dealings with the plaintiff out of which the suit arose, rather than the defendant's conduct in defending the suit.

The defendant LYC challenges the jury finding of bad faith in connection with Count 1. We find this to be without merit. There was sufficient evidence of secret meetings, confidential cost studies and the like, to permit the jury to find bad faith in LYC's dealings with UCC.

However, the Georgia courts have placed a gloss on the requirements of § 20–1404—adding to them the further requirement that in order for a plaintiff to be entitled to attorney's fees the jury must award the plaintiff substantially what he has requested in damages.

The plaintiff argues G.E.C. Corp. v. Levy, 126 Ga.App. 604, 191 S.E.2d 461 (1972) reverses this rule. We cannot agree with this reading of the case. In *Levy* the Georgia Court of Appeals specifically noted that "although the plaintiff did not recover all that he sought he did recover a substantial amount * * *." 126 Ga.App. at 608, 191 S.E.2d at 465. We believe this was in keeping with the rule announced in the cases cited above.

The plaintiff UCC did not recover substantially all that it sought in damages in Count 1. The amended complaint requested damages of three million dollars; the plaintiff put on proof of damages in excess of two million dollars at trial—yet recovered only $172,000. In our view this amount is so substantially less than the amount requested that the verdict for attorney's fees cannot stand, as it clearly amounts to a punitive measure which the Georgia cases expressly state § 20–1404 will not permit.

We cannot stop here, however, for we further find that the trial court erroneously charged the jury on assessing attorney's fees, and accordingly that issue must be retried.

The district court charged the jury:

> If you should render a verdict for the plaintiff on any of the four counts or more than one of the four counts, and if you should further determine—and this, again, is a matter entirely for you—that the plaintiff is entitled to attorney's fees on any of those counts, then you should go ahead and make a finding as to attorney's fees on each of those counts.

> In other words, don't split anything up; just go ahead and make a determination as to attorney's fees on each of these counts, and if you should return a verdict for the plaintiff on more than one count, I instruct you that the plaintiff would not be entitled to more than one award of attorney's fees, so that if you should return more than one award of attorney's fees, I will frame an appropriate judgment and will award to the plaintiff by said judgment only one of the awards indicated in your verdict.

We believe this instruction was erroneous. The jury was improperly denied the opportunity to apportion attorney's fees among the different counts and different defendants according to the proportion of total counsel time and effort which was devoted to each of the three substantive areas of the law suit, the joint venture breach, the AIMES III misappropriation and the violation of Shinn's non-competition agreement. The fact that the plaintiff's counsel refused to attempt to apportion his time in this manner, claiming the three were entwined, in no way concludes the matter. The jury heard the full case presented, and the jury would have known what percentage of the case was devoted to which substantive cause of action.

The jury should have been instructed to assess each count separately—evaluating each under the standards set out in § 20–1404 to determine whether attorney's fees should be awarded, and then determining whether to award fees for each area. While the trial court properly was concerned lest the plaintiff receive three times the fees it had proven, we do not believe the proper method of handling this potential problem is to take the matter from the jury entirely.

It is to be particularly noted that not all defendants were joined in all the counts. By charging the jury as the trial court did, the court may well have induced the jury to deliver one verdict of attorney's fees, against only one defendant, for possibly the entire amount which the jury felt the plaintiff's counsel should receive for the case—despite the fact that the jury found against the plaintiff on the non-competition agreement count, and we now hold found damages in an inadequate amount under the joint venture agreement count to support an award of attorney's fees.

We believe there was sufficient evidence in the record to sustain a jury finding of bad faith in the defendants' misappropriation of AIMES III, and thus we believe the issue of attorney's fees must be remanded for a new trial. Naturally because we do not disturb the original jury's findings as to liability and damages, only the AIMES III count can be the basis for attorney's fees, and the jury should be so instructed. The damages the jury assessed on the AIMES III count are, we believe, sufficient to support an award of attorney's fees. In evaluating what proportion of counsel's services are related to the AIMES III count, we believe it is proper to apportion counsel's efforts into the three substantive areas of the lawsuit, rather than by count. Thus the jury, if it wishes to award attorney's fees, should consider what proportion of counsel's time was devoted to the preparation of Counts 3, 4, 5 and 7, all of which relate to AIMES III, and it may properly award attorney's fees on Count 3 for the total time involved in preparing and trying the AIMES III claims.

The case is affirmed in part, reversed in part and remanded for further proceedings not inconsistent with this opinion.

Notes and Questions

1. The main elements in proving damages in a trade secret misappropriation case include: (1) a showing of the loss suffered by the plaintiff, (2) proof of the secret's value to the defendant, (3) calculation of the defendant's actual profits including what it should have paid as a reasonable royalty.

2. Note the importance of correct jury instructions to insure a valid jury verdict. Given the court's analysis of the jury instructions, would you have advised the plaintiff to propose alternative jury instructions?

3. Note the importance of Josephson's expert testimony concerning damages. If you were the plaintiff's counsel, would you have relied solely on Josephson's testimony or would you have presented additional evidence?

4. The Racketeer Influenced and Corrupt Organizations Act (RICO) provided for damages caused by racketeering activity. RICO provides treble damages for private plaintiffs who can meet the requirements of the act. Some thefts of trade secrets fall within the definition of racketeering activity.

B. INJUNCTION

Besides damages, another critically important remedy available to a patent, copyright, or trade secret owner is an injunction. Three types of injunctions are commonly sought: temporary restraining orders, preliminary, and permanent injunctions. Like damages, the courts often wrestle with the decision of whether certain injunctions should be granted. Some injunctive requests are relatively easy to grant, others are either difficult or inappropriate. Standards for granting injunctive relief are different in different states and in the various federal circuits. The discussion below gives typical rather than universal rules.

In cases involving a request for an injunction in a patent, copyright or trade secret infringement suit, plaintiff must show certain evidence before the court will grant the request. In a request for a temporary restraining order (TRO), the court must rely on the evidence presented by only one party—the party seeking the order. The other party to the dispute is either unaware of the suit or is not present at the time the order is sought. This places the alleged infringing party in a precarious situation should the order be inappropriate for the circumstances. A TRO, consequently, normally has a limited duration of 10 days. A TRO also generally requires posting a bond by the moving party. A preliminary injunction poses the same problems for the court as a TRO even though both parties to the dispute may present evidence. In granting a permanent injunction the court requires evidence of the possibility of future harm to the property owner. Where no evidence of future harm can be established, the request for the permanent injunction will be denied.

In patent cases where a TRO or preliminary injunction is sought, the court looks to two criteria: whether a patent in fact exists, and whether the alleged infringer appears to have infringed the patent. The patentee will be entitled to a permanent injunction if it can be shown that the risk of future harm exists.

In suits for copyright infringement the party seeking a TRO or a preliminary injunction must show: (1) it is the rightful owner of the copyright (with some exceptions, plaintiff must attach a copy of the copyright registration certificate to its complaint); (2) the possibility of irreparable harm should the injunction be denied; (3) that a strong possibility of success exists in winning the suit on the merits; and (4) that their copyright has been infringed. Where a party satisfies these four elements, a TRO or preliminary injunction would be appropriate.

A party seeking a TRO or preliminary injunction for trade secret infringement must first establish that the trade secret has been misappropriated. Then it must show: (1) it will suffer immediate irreparable injury from the infringing use, (2) it stands a strong likelihood of success in the dispute on the merits, and (3) that it would be harmed if relief were not granted.

Where a TRO or a preliminary injunction has been granted, the plaintiff may ask the court to impound the infringing property. Impoundment removes the articles from the market until the case has been resolved. In a permanent injunction, impoundment of the articles further deters infringers by causing severe financial loss.

JOHNSON CONTROLS, INC. v. PHOENIX CONTROL SYSTEMS, INC.

United States Court of Appeals, Ninth Circuit, 1989.
886 F.2d 1173.

Canby, Circuit Judge:

Phoenix Control Systems, Inc., appeals the district court's grant of a preliminary injunction against alleged copyright infringement and misappropriation of trade secrets. In addition to attacking the merits of the injunction, Phoenix Control argues that the district court erred in its use of a special master and in other evidentiary matters. We affirm.

Facts and Proceedings Below

Johnson Controls, Inc., is a Wisconsin corporation that designs and implements automated process control systems. Johnson developed a system of computer programs to control wastewater treatment plants. This product line is called the "JC–5000S." Derivatives of this program are used in several locations, and the program is customized for each location. Johnson registered its copyright in the JC–5000S.

Phoenix Control Systems, Inc., is a California corporation, formed by John Schratz in late 1983. It is a competitor of Johnson. Schratz and other individuals now working for Phoenix Control are former employees of Johnson. Johnson sued Phoenix Control for copyright infringement, misappropriation of trade secrets, unfair competition, trade libel, and interference with contractual relations. The district court granted Johnson's motion for a preliminary injunction, which prohibited Phoenix Controls from copying, distributing, preparing derivatives of, publishing, or representing that they have the ability to use Johnson's computer software referred to as the JC–5000S.

Standard of Review; Preliminary Injunctions

Our review of a preliminary injunction is limited. We will reverse the granting of a preliminary injunction only if the district court abused its discretion, or based its decision on an erroneous legal standard or clearly erroneous findings of fact. *Dumas v. Gommerman,* 865 F.2d 1093, 1095 (9th Cir.1989).

Johnson, the party requesting the preliminary injunction, had to show either a likelihood of success on the merits and the possibility of irreparable injury, or that serious questions going to the merits were raised and the balance of hardships tips sharply in its favor. *Dumas,* 865 F.2d at 1095; *Apple Computer Inc. v. Formula Int'l, Inc.,* 725 F.2d 521, 525 (9th Cir.1984). This test is viewed as a continuum. *Dumas,* 865 F.2d at 1095. The district court correctly noted that in a copyright infringement claim, a showing of a reasonable likelihood of success on the merits raises a presumption of irreparable harm. *Apple,* 725 F.2d at 525. As a result, Johnson need only show a reasonable likelihood of success on its copyright infringement claim to support the district court's grant of the preliminary injunction.[1]

* * *

Conclusion

Johnson demonstrated a reasonable likelihood of success on its copyright infringement claim. Nonliteral components of computer software may be protected by copyright where they constitute expression, rather than ideas. Access to Johnson's program was clear, and the record supports the finding of substantial similarity. The district court did not err in its application of law, nor were any of its factual findings clearly erroneous.

Affirmed.

1. Because we find that Johnson's copyright infringement claim supports the grant of the preliminary injunction, we need not reach the alternative ground of trade secret misappropriation.

C. SEIZURE AND DESTRUCTION

Some statutes allow the seizure of items that violate intellectual property rights. These remedies are, of course, particularly effective because they put a stop to the competitor's business and cause the competitor severe financial losses. The Copyright Act provides for impoundment, destruction, seizure, and forfeiture not only of the infringing copies, but also of the "means by which such copies * * * may be reproduced." (17 U.S.C.A. §§ 503, 509.) This provides a means for software copyright owners to put additional pressure on infringers by threatening the seizure of their computers. The 1984 Semiconductor Chip Act contained provisions for impounding and destruction not only of semiconductor chip products, but also of "products by means of which such [semiconductor chip products] may be reproduced." (17 U.S.C.A. § 911(e)(1)).

The trademark laws go even further, allowing *ex parte* seizure of products bearing counterfeit trade marks. (15 U.S.C.A. §§ 1118, 1124.)

D. INTERNATIONAL TRADE COMMISSION ACTION

As permitted under the General Agreement on Trade and Tariffs (GATT), the United States has enacted laws and regulations to restrict unfair import practices. The primary purpose of these laws is to protect U.S. industry from unfair foreign competition. (At times the U.S. has subjected foreign firms to more stringent requirements than U.S. firms, thus arguably violating its commitments under the GATT). The laws provide remedies when: (1) foreign firms "dump" goods—that is, they sell goods in the U.S. at prices lower than the price charged in the exporting country, (2) foreign governments subsidize the production and export of goods to the U.S., or (3) foreign firms import into the U.S. goods which infringe on U.S. intellectual property rights.

The International Trade Commission may act under Section 337 to prevent importation of goods which infringe U.S. intellectual property rights. Section 337, as modified in the Trade Agreements Act of 1979, has primarily been used to protect United States patents and other intellectual property rights against foreign infringements. Given the reliance of the computer industry on intellectual property laws and the large amount of imports, Section 337 is very important for the industry.

A United States party before the International Trade Commission may show a violation of Section 337 by proving an infringement of intellectual property rights. Before the 1988 Trade Act, the party also had to prove that the infringement harmed a domestic industry. The International Trade Commission may order injunctive relief, including permanent exclusion orders, temporary exclusion orders, and cease and desist orders. It cannot award damages. It can grant exclusion on a preliminary basis without a full trial and can issue a temporary exclusion order for 90 days, with the possibility of a 60–day extension. The power of the International Trade Commission to exclude infringing goods is particularly valuable in the technology field where the useful life of many new products is relatively brief.

Apple Computer has been very active in stopping imports which violate its patents and copyrights. *In re Certain Personal Computers* was decided before the 1988 amendments, so Apple had to prove injury as well as infringement. Major portions of this case appear in the copyright chapter of this book, so only the relevant remedy portion is printed below.

IN RE CERTAIN PERSONAL COMPUTERS AND COMPONENTS THEREOF

U.S. International Trade Commission, 1984.
224 U.S.P.Q. 270.

We concur in the finding of a violation of section 337 on the basis that (1) the patents and copyrights involved are valid, enforceable, and infringed; (2) there is an "industry, efficiently and economically operated, in the United States;" and (3) the importation of the subject articles has the tendency to substantially injure that industry. However, we have modified the ID in accordance with the standards adopted for review in our rules. We have found some conclusions of material fact clearly erroneous and some legal conclusions erroneous. Additionally, we have provided more complete reasoning in some instances where we have concurred in the finding of the ALJ.

* * *

Remedy

We have determined that a general exclusion order is the appropriate remedy in this case. The large number of sources of infringing imports actually established, and the apparent existence of even more, fully justify a general exclusion order. The only question is the form of the order. Our order, by its express terms, excludes from entry personal computers and components which directly infringe the involved patents and copyrights. Further, since the record shows that imports having motherboards substantially similar to the Apple motherboards contributorily infringe or induce infringement of the involved patents and copyrights, such imports are included in our exclusion order subject to the presentation of a license.

It is the intent of this order to remedy the violation we have found to exist without disrupting lawful trade in personal computers and components thereof. To avoid evasion of our order, it excludes from entry ROMless computers and components which can be shown to be associated with imports of infringing ROMs or which are intended to receive infringing ROMs in the United States. Any beneficiary or any person adversely affected by this order may petition this Commission for a modification or clarification to ensure that its intent is achieved.

The Commission may also modify or clarify the order on its own motion.[158]

* * *

BONDING

We find that the bond should be set at 200 percent of the entered value of the products involved.

The bond provided for by 19 U.S.C. § 1337(g)(3) is a reexportation bond requiring the reexportation of the articles covered by this exclusion order which are entered during the Presidential review period provided for by 19 U.S.C. § 1337(g)(2). Entry of such articles during this period is only conditionally lawful, the condition being that the President disapprove the Commission's determination, thus rendering the determination and order of no force or effect. If this condition is not satisfied, the bond requires that the articles be reexported, and if they are not, the penalty amount of the bond may be assessed. The Commission is charged with prescribing the penalty amount of this reexportation bond. The Commission's rules provide that the Commission take into consideration, among other things, "the amount which would offset any competitive advantage resulting from the alleged unfair methods of competition and unfair acts enjoyed by persons benefiting from the importation of the articles in question."

Both Apple and the Commission investigative attorney submit that a bond in the amount of 200 percent of entered value is such an amount. This was computed on the basis of the average retail sales price of the bulk of the involved imported personal computers. We find this amount to be appropriate.

Notes and Questions

1. What other remedies could Apple have requested? Is the exclusion remedy the best?

2. The Omnibus Trade Reform Bill (OTRB) requires that the United States Trade Representatives (USTRs) negotiate with foreign countries who have inadequate intellectual property laws. The USTRs may now identify and initiate cases against "priority" countries with trading practices that

158. On February 2, 1984, and March 7, 1984, the Commission received letters from the U.S. Customs Service (Customs) regarding the inherent difficulties in enforcing an exclusion order in this investigation in view of Customs' limited resources. The letters stated that, at the time of importation, Customs "must attempt to identify * * * whether the printed circuitry of a computer of component is in violation of an Apple patent * * *" Customs further stated that this might entail an examination of every computer and component importation regardless of make, model, and type. Further "difficulties" were noted, but Customs stated that they would endeavor to enforce the order to the best of their ability. (February 2, 1984, letter from the Director, Office of Trade Operations to the Chairman and letter dated March 7, 1984, from the Assistant Commissioner, Office of Commercial Operations to the Chairman). As discussed above, we have concluded that an exclusion order is the only way to remedy the violation found to exist. Commissioner Haggart notes that Apple states that it will provide Customs with technical support necessary to enforce such an order. Complainant's Brief on Remedy, Bonding, and the Public Interest 5–9.

infringe on U.S. intellectual property rights. USTRs can also initiate proceedings against the countries that deny "adequate and effective" intellectual property laws to U.S. industries or countries that deny "fair and equitable" market access for U.S. products that are patented or copyrighted. The time period for negotiations with foreign countries was limited to six months. If a country violates this section, USTRs can impose sanctions to suspend, withdraw, or prevent the application of trade agreement concessions. Duties and other import restrictions can also be imposed.

E. FEDERAL CRIMINAL REMEDIES

1. CRIMINAL COPYRIGHT VIOLATION

UNITED STATES v. GOSS

United States Court of Appeals, Eleventh Circuit, 1986.
803 F.2d 638.

EDMONDSON, CIRCUIT JUDGE:

Appellant Tom Goss was convicted for infringing copyright by distributing copies of audiovisual works of the video games Karate Champ and Kung Fu Master. An owner of a legally made copy, however, is entitled to sell or otherwise dispose of that particular copy without the copyright owner's authorization. 17 U.S.C. Sec. 109(a). In this case, the copies in which the audiovisual works were fixed were memory chips, also known as ROMs. The government totally failed to prove that the ROMs which Goss sold were illegally made or unowned by Goss, apparently because it did not realize that the ROMs were the copies. Instead, the government attempted to show that the circuit boards which Goss sold were "counterfeit."

At oral argument, the government forthrightly conceded that at trial it did not address the ROM issue at all. More specifically, the government conceded that at trial it never contended that the pertinent ROMs, themselves, were from illegitimate manufacturers. Because there was insufficient evidence against Goss, we hold that his motion for judgment of acquittal should have been granted and reverse with directions to enter a judgment of acquittal.

The first count of Goss's indictment charged him with criminally infringing

> the copyrights of audiovisual works * * * for the purposes of commercial advantage and private financial gain [by] *distribut[ing more than seven* but less than sixty-five] unlawfully manufactured and unauthorized *copies* of the *audiovisual works* "Karate Champ" and "Kung Fu Master". * * * (emphasis added).

Although the indictment included a second count, that count was dismissed on the government's motion.

At trial, the government attempted to prove Goss's guilt by showing that Irem Corp. ("Irem") and Data East, Corp. ("Deco"), two Japanese corporations, developed the Kung Fu Master and Karate Champ video games, respectively. These corporations transferred a portion of their rights as copyright holders in these games to Data East, U.S.A., an American company. Among the rights so transferred was the exclusive right to distribute these games in North America.

The government's evidence showed that Goss sold to an undercover F.B.I. agent four circuit boards for the Kung Fu Master game and five entire Karate Champ games in upright cabinet form. Moreover, a government witness, who is employed as vice-president of Data East, U.S.A., testified that Goss was not authorized to distribute these.

The government presented evidence that the five upright Karate Champ games sold by Goss displayed the same visual images and sounds as did an authorized, factory-made Karate Champ game. Likewise, when attached to a power supply and other hardware, the four Kung Fu Master circuit boards sold by Goss produced the same sights and sounds as did an authorized Kung Fu Master game.

During the trial, the government attempted to prove that the circuit boards sold by Goss, including the five in the upright complete games, were "counterfeit." To show this, the government demonstrated that Goss's boards lacked the manufacturer's label and custom chip which were affixed to authorized boards.

The government also played tape recordings of conversations in which Goss agreed to sell the games. In the first conversation, the undercover F.B.I. agent referred obliquely to a "problem." Goss responded by saying "ya can't be too brave or conspicuous with it. Ya gotta use a little common sense." Shortly thereafter, Goss also stated that the legal expenses of "pull[ing] a game off" are so great that "[t]here's nobody left that's got the money to pursue it." In this tape-recorded conversation, Mr. Goss also said that:

> The one thing they're after is the people that's bringin' the boards in the country. That's the ones they, they've never, I don't reckon they've ever got after an operator. * * * And if they do come in, all you gotta say is, you know, I bought this thing and so, off of so and so's truck or I bought it at an auction or somethin'. And the worst you're gonna lose, you're gonna lose the game.

After the government rested its case, Goss moved for a judgment of acquittal pursuant to Fed.R.Crim.P. 29, on the grounds that the government did not present sufficient evidence to sustain a conviction. At the close of all evidence, Goss renewed this motion. Both times, the judge denied it. The jury returned a verdict of guilty as charged.

Goss raises numerous arguments on appeal. One of Goss's contentions is that the district court erred by denying his motion for acquittal, because the government presented insufficient evidence that the copies which he sold were illegally made or that he did not own them.[1] Since

1. In his brief, Goss couches this argument in terms of the "first sale" doctrine which evolved under the former Copyright Act.

we agree with this contention, we do not address Goss's other arguments.

We apply a rigorous standard of review. A criminal conviction can be reversed by an appellate court for insufficiency of evidence only if a reasonable jury could not have found that the evidence established guilt beyond a reasonable doubt. When determining whether the evidence was insufficient, an appellate court must view the evidence and the inferences which can be drawn therefrom in the light most favorable to the government.

To determine whether the government presented sufficient evidence that Goss illegally distributed copies of audiovisual works, it is necessary to identify precisely the audiovisual works and the copies in which they were fixed. The Act defines an "audiovisual work" as a work:

> that consist[s] of a series of related images which are intrinsically intended to be shown by the use of machines or devises such as projectors, viewers, or electronic equipment, together with accompanying sounds, if any, regardless of the nature of the material objects, such as films or tapes, in which the works are embodied.

17 U.S.C. Sec. 101. Thus, the visual images and sounds of the video games, Kung Fu Master and Karate Champ, constitute "audiovisual works". Such video game audiovisual works can be copyrighted.

Under section 101 of the Act, "copies" are defined as:

> material objects, other than phonorecords, in which a work is fixed by any method now known, or later developed, and from which the work can be perceived, reproduced, or otherwise communicated, either directly or with the aid of a machine or device. * * *

17 U.S.C. Sec. 101. A video game has a number of physical components: e.g., a power supply, display screen, outer cabinet with graphics, controls (such as the "joy stick" and firing buttons), a circuit board, and memory chips attached to the circuit board. The material object or "copy" in which the audiovisual work is fixed must be one or more of these components.

At trial, the government attempted to show that the circuit boards were "counterfeit," which suggests that it believed that the entire circuit boards—including the hardware and attached memory chips—constituted the copies. The government appeared confused at oral argument regarding what were the copies. When asked to identify the copies which Goss sold, the government responded that the audiovisual works were the copies. This answer misconceives the statutory definition of "copies": "work" and "copy" are not synonymous terms; rather, a copy is the material object in which a work is fixed.

Goss presented uncontradicted testimony by two experts that the copies in which the audiovisual works were fixed were memory chips. Such memory devices can be either ROMs (read only memory), PROMs (programmable read only memory) or E–ROMs (erasable read only memory), and are sometimes referred to generically as ROMs.

Mr. Leskey, one of Goss's expert witnesses, testified that the memory which is programmed into the ROMs in a video game includes

> [a]ll of the memory in the unit, that is, all of the video or visuals, the foreground objects, the background imagery, the sound patterns, the controls for the sound patterns, the entire system controls * * * as to how the game operates, the logic of the game, how you win or lose. * * *

This testimony was uncontested.

Moreover, Goss presented uncontradicted expert testimony that the ROM chips in this case were placed in sockets on the circuit boards, and could be removed from the circuit boards. By replacing one set of ROM chips with another, these experts testified, it is possible for the same circuit board to produce many different games.

Also, Goss presented uncontroverted expert testimony that the circuit board is simply hardware which responds to instructions from the software (i.e., the program stored in the memory chips). One of Goss's experts testified that the circuit board is a mechanism similar to a video cassette player, whereas the set of ROMs is a copy similar to a video cassette tape. Another of Goss's expert's analogized the ROM chips to slides and the circuit board to a projector.

All of the evidence adduced at trial showed that the ROMs were the copies. A jury could not reasonably have found otherwise.[4] To prove that Goss illegally distributed copies, therefore, the government was required to show that Goss illegally distributed ROM chips.

Criminal infringement of copyright has three elements: (1) infringement of a copyright (2) done wilfully (3) for purposes of commercial advantage or private financial gain. 17 U.S.C. Sec. 506(a). Thus, one of the elements which the government must prove is "infringement." A person infringes copyright if he or she violates one of the exclusive rights of a copyright owner. 17 U.S.C. Sec. 501(a).

Goss was indicted and convicted for violating the exclusive right of a copyright holder to distribute copies. This exclusive right is set forth in Sec. 106 of the Act, which provides in pertinent part that:

> Subject to sections 107 through 118, the owner of copyright under this title has the exclusive rights to do and to authorize any of the following: * * *

4. We note the factual narrowness of our ruling. The technology of video games, like other computer technologies, is diverse and constantly changing. No single rule of law can be developed regarding what constitutes a "copy" in a video game. Instead, the question of what component or components of a video game constitutes the "copy" in which the audiovisual work is fixed is a determination of material fact which must be made by the trier of fact in each copyright case. We simply hold that, in light of extensive, uncontradicted expert testimony presented at trial, a reasonable jury could only conclude that the copies in this case were the ROMs.

> (3) to distribute copies or phonorecords of the copyrighted work to the public by sale or other transfer of ownership, or by rental, lease, or lending. * * *

This exclusive distribution right, however, is limited by section 109(a) of the Act, which provides that:

> Notwithstanding the provisions of section 106(3), *the owner of a particular copy* * * * *lawfully made* under this title, or any person authorized by such owner, is entitled, without the authority of the copyright owner, to sell or otherwise dispose of the possession of that copy. * * *

17 U.S.C. section 109(a) (emphasis added).

The effect of section 109(a) is that, if Goss owned a legally made copy (i.e., a legally made set of ROMs), he was entitled to sell or otherwise to distribute such ROMs. Selling such legally obtained ROMs would not infringe the copyright owner's exclusive distribution right, regardless of whether the ROMs were attached to a "counterfeit" board.

Our analysis would not be complete, however, without considering which party bears the burden of proof under section 109(a). Legislative history indicates that section 109(a) is a defense in civil copyright cases. After criticizing a district court opinion in a civil case which placed on the plaintiff the burden of proving that a copy had been unlawfully made or acquired, the House Committee on the Judiciary stated that "in an action to determine whether a defendant is entitled to the privilege established by Sec. 109(a) * * *, the burden of proving whether a particular copy was lawfully made or acquired should rest on the defendant." H.R.Rep. No. 94–1476, 94th Cong., 2d Sess. 80–81, *reprinted in* 1976 U.S. CODE CONG. & AD. NEWS 5659, 5694–95. Whether the Committee intended this comment to apply to criminal infringement actions is unclear.

Case law exists regarding the burden of proving in a criminal case that a copy is legally made and acquired. This case law, however, uses the terminology of the "first sale" doctrine.

The first sale doctrine developed under section 27 of the former Copyright Act, which provided in pertinent part that "nothing in this title shall be deemed to forbid, prevent, or restrict the transfer of any copy of a copyrighted work the possession of which has been lawfully obtained." Interpreting former section 27, courts held that a copyright owner's exclusive vending right extended only to the first sale of a copy. If a legally made copy had been the subject of a first sale, then further distribution of that copy did not infringe the copyright owner's exclusive vending right.

Courts applying the former Copyright Act consistently held that in a criminal case the government has the burden of proving the absence of a first sale.

The Eleventh Circuit has applied the "first sale" doctrine in a criminal case under the present Copyright Act. *United States v. Drum,*

733 F.2d 1503 (11th Cir.1984), *cert. denied sub nom., Cooper v. United States,* 469 U.S. 1061, 105 S.Ct. 543, 83 L.Ed.2d 431 (1984). In *Drum,* a criminal RICO case involving substantive copyright offenses under the 1976 Copyright Act, the Eleventh Circuit treated the "first sale" issue as a *defense.* The *Drum* Court indicated that, once the defense had been raised, the government had an obligation to rebut it. The Court reasoned as follows:

> McKinney attacks the sufficiency of the evidence to negate the "first sale" defense which he raised at trial. * * * The government may prove the absence of a first sale by direct evidence of the source of the pirated recordings or by circumstantial evidence that the recording was never authorized [i.e., illegally made]. * * * The evidence [presented at trial was] entirely adequate to rebut the first sale defense. *Id.* at 1507.

We are bound by *Drum,* even though it does not explicitly mention section 109(a). *Drum* was decided under the present Act and, like our case, involved the burden of proof with respect to whether a copy was legally made or acquired. Therefore, we hold that in a criminal copyright case involving unauthorized distribution of copies, section 109(a) is a defense. If a defendant presents any evidence that the copies were legally made and that he or she owned them, this is sufficient to create a jury issue with respect to the section 109(a) defense. When the defendant makes such a showing, the burden shifts to the government to demonstrate beyond a reasonable doubt that the pertinent copies were either not legally made or not owned by the defendant.

Goss's two expert witnesses compared the ROMs on an authorized, factory-built Kung Fu Master circuit board with the ROMs on a Kung Fu Master circuit board sold by Goss. According to these experts, the ROMs on both boards were the same size. One of the experts noted that the ROMs were the same shape, and that, indeed, some of the ROMs had identical serial numbers. Both experts testified that a visual inspection revealed no distinguishing physical characteristics between the ROMs on the two boards, and that it was impossible to determine by visual inspection where or by whom the ROMs had been programmed. Of course, the government's evidence indicated that the entire boards, including the ROMs, produced identical audiovisual works.

One of Goss's experts testified that it "might" be possible to use a method, which costs approximately ten thousand dollars, to examine the ROMs "address by address." If the test indicated a difference between the ROMs, he testified, "you might be able to tell something," but if it showed no differences between the ROMs, "you still wouldn't know."

In addition, the evidence at trial showed that there are numerous possible sources of legally made Kung Fu Master ROMs which could have been inserted into the boards Goss sold. Such sources include used and broken Kung Fu Master games, as well as thousands of boards sold abroad separately from the game cabinets.

Also, Goss presented uncontroverted evidence that he owned the ROMs in the Kung Fu Master boards which he sold to the F.B.I. agent. This evidence consisted of proof that he bought the boards, including the ROMs, from a firm in Kentucky. We hold that Goss made a sufficient showing to raise a section 109(a) defense with respect to the ROMs in the four Kung Fu Master boards he sold.[7]

Once Goss raised a section 109(a) defense with respect to the ROMs in the four Kung Fu Master boards, the burden shifted to the government to prove beyond a reasonable doubt that these Kung Fu Master copies were either illegally made or not owned by Goss. The government failed to meet this burden. *Indeed, the government concedes that it never focused on or addressed the ROMs at all.*

The government presented no evidence whatsoever that Goss did not own the ROMs he sold. Nor did the government present any direct evidence that the ROMs were illegally manufactured. Goss's highly ambiguous comments, which suggest that he thought he was doing something wrong, arguably constitute no evidence that the ROMs, in particular, were illegally manufactured. If these comments do constitute evidence, they are *at most* highly tenuous circumstantial evidence that the ROMs were illegally made.

The government's effort to prove that other components of the circuit boards were made without permission was misdirected. The ROMs were the copies, not the other components of the circuit board to which they were attached. Proof that these other elements were made without authorization does not show that the copies—the ROMs—were illegally manufactured. The government's evidence is analogous to proof, in a prosecution for illegal distribution of phonorecords, that defendant sold a record player which had been made without authorization. Manufacture and distribution of a record player without authorization does not infringe copyright in the phonorecord.[8]

In short, the government did not try to prove anything specifically with regard to the ROMs. If the government nonetheless happened to

7. Goss presented no expert testimony comparing the ROMs in the five Karate Champ games he sold with the ROMs in an authorized Karate Champ game. Also, these ROMs were apparently physically distinguishable, inasmuch as the Karate Champ ROMs sold by Goss lacked the "Deco" copyright notice attached to the ROMs on the authorized Karate Champ board. We do not decide whether Goss presented any evidence which raised a section 109(a) defense with respect to the ROMs in the five Karate Champ boards.

8. The evidence regarding the absence of the custom chip from the boards sold by Goss is also irrelevant. The testimony at trial established that the custom chip on each authorized board was a complicated relay device, which functioned as a "lock" by making it difficult to manufacture a board without permission. Proof that Goss sold boards without custom chips is irrelevant to whether the ROMs, in particular, were illegally manufactured. Indeed, such evidence is analogous to proof that defendant sold a record player without a lock on it. A copyright holder of a phonorecord has no rights with respect to the record player, and sale of a record player without a lock does not infringe copyright.

present evidence bearing on the ROMs, then such evidence was highly tenuous circumstantial evidence. No jury could have reasonably found that the government proved beyond a reasonable doubt that ROMs in the four Kung Fu Master boards which Goss sold were illegally made or not owned by Goss. Therefore, the government's proof with respect to these Kung Fu Master ROMs was insufficient.

We note that the burden imposed on the government is not an impossible one. Even where the distributed copies are physically indistinguishable from the authorized copies, the government can rebut a section 109(a) defense by direct evidence that the copies were illegally made (e.g., clear admissions by defendant, or testimony by a third party who saw the copies being made without authorization) or circumstantial evidence to this effect (e.g., facts indicating that defendant or an upstream supplier purchased reproducing equipment which would enable them to make the copies without authorization). Of course, where the copies are physically indistinguishable, the government is also free to show that the defendant did not own the copies.

The government argues that it did not need to prove anything with respect to the ROMs, because a copyrighted audiovisual work of a video game can be infringed separately from the program which produces it. Of course, the government is correct that the audiovisual work and the program of a video game are both copyrightable works, which can be infringed separately. *See Stern Electronics, supra,* 669 F.2d at 855. But the fact that the copyrighted audiovisual work *can be* separately infringed does not relieve the government of its burden of proving that it *was in fact* infringed.

A critical factor in this case is the limited nature of the exact crime charged: Goss was indicted and convicted for infringing the copyright holder's exclusive right to distribute *copies.* [9] Therefore, the government was required to focus on the *material objects* in which the audiovisual works were fixed and to show that these were distributed illegally. This the government has failed to do.

Goss was indicted for the felony of distributing more than seven but less than sixty-five copies of audiovisual works without authorization within a 180–day period. *See* 18 U.S.C. Sec. 2319(b)(2)(B); *cf.* 18 U.S.C. Sec. 1. To distribute seven or fewer copies can be a misdemeanor. 18 U.S.C. Sec. 2319(b)(3); *cf.* 18 U.S.C. Sec. 1. The government did not request a charge regarding the lesser included misdemeanor offense; and, indeed, the judge instructed the jury that it must find that Goss distributed more than seven copies in order to find him guilty. The jury returned a verdict of guilty as charged.

9. The government could have sought an indictment for violating one or more of the copyright holder's other four exclusive rights: i.e., to reproduce the work in copies, to prepare derivative works, to perform the work publicly, and to display the work publicly. *See* 17 U.S.C. Sec. 106. It did not. Even if it had, the government could not have prevailed by simply asserting that the audiovisual work can be separately infringed. It would have been required to show that infringement in fact occurred.

The government attempted to prove that Goss distributed nine copies without authorization: four Kung Fu Master copies and five Karate Champ copies. As the foregoing analysis demonstrates, Goss presented evidence sufficient to raise a section 109(a) defense with respect to the four Kung Fu Master copies; and the government failed to rebut it. Thus, with respect to the four Kung Fu Master copies, the government's evidence was insufficient.

Even assuming, arguendo, that the government's evidence was adequate with respect to the five Karate Champ copies, the government still failed to present sufficient evidence to sustain Goss's felony conviction. At most, the government proved illegal distribution of five copies. The fact that distribution of five copies can be enough for a misdemeanor conviction is immaterial, because Goss was neither charged for nor convicted of such a misdemeanor.

We infrequently reverse on insufficiency of evidence grounds. The government totally failed, however, once the burden shifted to it, to rebut Goss's section 109(a) defense with respect to the ROMs in the four Kung Fu Master boards. Therefore, we are constrained to conclude that the evidence was insufficient to support Goss's conviction. The crime was not proved.

Accordingly, the conviction is reversed with instructions to enter a judgment of acquittal.

Notes and Questions

1. The Copyright Act allows the owner of a legitimate copy of a copyright work to sell that copy. (17 U.S.C.A. § 109.) The "first sale doctrine" is a judicially-created rule that once an owner has sold even one copy of a copyrighted work, the burden of proof is on the government in a criminal copyright case to show that the defendant's copy is an illegal one. If, however, the government can show that the copyright owner has never sold a copy of the copyrighted work, this evidence is sufficient, unless rebutted, to show that defendant's copy is unauthorized.

2. If it were feasible to lease—instead of sell—computer chips, boards, and software, would the lessors be in a better position to fight infringers than are software vendors?

2. TRADE SECRET VIOLATION AS A FEDERAL CRIME

UNITED STATES v. ROBERT J. RIGGS, also known as Robert Johnson, also known as Prophet, and Craig Neidorf, also known as Knight Lightning, Defendants.

United States District Court, Northern District of Illinois, 1990.
739 F.Supp. 414.

BUA, DISTRICT JUDGE.

Over the course of the past decade, advances in technology and growing respect and acceptance for the powers of computers have created a true explosion in the computer industry. Quite naturally, the growth of computer availability and application has spawned a host of new legal issues. This case requires the court to wrestle with some of these novel legal issues which are a product of the marriage between law and computers.

The indictment charges that defendants Robert J. Riggs and Craig Neidorf, through the use of computers, violated the federal wire fraud statute, 18 U.S.C. § 1343, and the federal statute prohibiting interstate transportation of stolen property, 18 U.S.C. § 2314. Neidorf argues that the wire fraud statute and the statute prohibiting interstate transportation of stolen property do not apply to the conduct with which he is charged. Therefore, he has moved to dismiss the charges against him, as set forth in Counts II–IV of the indictment, which are based on those statutes.[1] Neidorf has also filed various other pretrial motions. For the reasons stated herein, Neidorf's motions are denied.

I. The Indictment

A. Factual Allegations

In about September 1988, Neidorf and Riggs devised and began implementing a scheme to defraud Bell South Telephone Company ("Bell South"), which provides telephone services to a nine-state region including Alabama, Georgia, Mississippi, Tennessee, Kentucky, Louisiana, North Carolina, South Carolina, and Florida. The objective of the fraud scheme was to steal Bell South's computer text file[2] which contained information regarding its enhanced 911 (E911) system for handling emergency calls to policy, fire, ambulance, and other emergency services in municipalities. The text file which Riggs and Neidorf planned to steal specifically details the procedures for installation, operation, and maintenance of E911 services in the region in which Bell South operates. Bell South considered this file to contain valuable proprietary information and, therefore, closely guarded the information from being disclosed outside of Bell South and its subsidiaries. Riggs and Neidorf wanted to obtain the E911 text file so it could be printed in a computer newsletter known as "PHRACK" which Neidorf edited and published.

In about December 1988, Riggs began the execution of the fraud scheme by using his home computer in Decatur, Georgia, to gain

1. The current indictment also contains three counts—V, VI, and VII—which set forth charges against Neidorf for violations of § 1030(a)(6)(A) of the Computer Fraud and Abuse Act of 1986, 18 U.S.C. § 1030(a)(6)(A). Although Neidorf also moves to dismiss those counts, the government has indicated that it is in the process of drafting a superseding indictment which may not contain any charges under the Computer Fraud and Abuse Act of 1986. Therefore, the court will reserve its ruling on Neidorf's motion to dismiss Counts V, VI, and VII until the superseding indictment is filed. The court will also reserve its ruling on Neidorf's motion for a bill of particulars, which by its terms pertains only to Counts V, VI, and VII.

2. A "computer text file" is a collection of stored data which, when retrieved from a disk or other computer storing device, presents typed English characters on a computer monitor, a printer, or other medium compatible with the computer storing the data.

unlawful access to Bell South's computer system located at its corporate headquarters in Atlanta, Georgia. After gaining access to Bell South's system, Riggs "downloaded" [3] the text file, which described in detail the operation of the E911 system in Bell South's operating region. Riggs then disguised and concealed his unauthorized access to the Bell South system by using account codes of persons with legitimate access to the E911 text file.

Pursuant to the scheme he had devised with Neidorf, Riggs then transferred the stolen computer text file to Neidorf by way of an interstate computer data network. Riggs stored the stolen text file on a computer bulletin board system [4] located in Lockport, Illinois, so as to make the file available to Neidorf. The Lockport bulletin board system was used by computer "hackers" [5] as a location for exchanging and developing software tools and other information which could be used for unauthorized intrusion into computer systems. Neidorf, a twenty-year-old student at the University of Missouri in Columbia, Missouri, used a computer located at his school to access the Lockport computer bulletin board and thereby receive the Bell South E911 text file from Riggs. At the request of Riggs, Neidorf then edited and retyped the E911 text file in order to conceal the fact that it had been stolen from Bell South. Neidorf then "uploaded" his revised version of the stolen file back onto the Lockport bulletin board system for Riggs' review. To complete the scheme, in February 1989, Neidorf published his edited edition of Bell South's E911 text file in his PHRACK newsletter.

B. Charges

The current indictment asserts seven counts. Count I charges that Riggs committed wire fraud in violation of 18 U.S.C. § 1343 by transferring the E911 text file from his home computer in Decatur, Georgia to the computer bulletin board system in Lockport, Illinois. Count II charges both Riggs and Neidorf with violating § 1343 by causing the edited E911 file to be transferred from a computer operated by Neidorf in Columbia, Missouri, to the computer bulletin board system in Lockport, Illinois. Counts III and IV assert that by transferring the E911 text file via an interstate computer network, Riggs and Neidorf violated the National Stolen Property Act, 18 U.S.C. § 2314, which prohibits interstate transfer of stolen property. Finally, Counts V–VII charge Riggs and Neidorf with violating § 1030(a)(6)(A) of the Computer Fraud and Abuse Act of 1986, 18 U.S.C. § 1030(a)(6)(A), which prohibits

3. "Downloading" is the process of transferring files, programs, or other computer-stored information from a remote computer to one's own computer. "Uploading" is the reverse process, *i.e.*, transferring computer-stored data from one's own computer to a remote computer. *Id.*

4. A computer bulletin board system is a computer program that simulates an actual bulletin board by allowing computer users who access a particular computer to post messages, read existing messages, and delete messages. The messages exchanged may contain a wide variety of information, including stolen credit card numbers, confidential business information, and information about local community events.

5. For a discussion of the definition of "hackers," see Part II, Subpart C, *infra*.

knowingly, and with intent to defraud, trafficking in information through which a computer may be accessed without authorization.

II. Discussion

A. Motion to Dismiss Count II

Neidorf claims that Count II of the indictment is defective because it fails to allege a scheme to defraud, one of the necessary elements for a wire fraud claim under 18 U.S.C. § 1343. *See Lombardo v. United States,* 865 F.2d 155, 157 (7th Cir.) (holding that the two elements of a wire fraud claim under § 1343 are a scheme to defraud and the use of wire communications in furtherance of the scheme), *cert. denied,* ___ U.S. ___, 109 S.Ct. 3186, 105 L.Ed.2d 695 (1989). All Count II charges, says Neidorf, is that he received and then transferred a computer text file, not that he participated in any scheme to defraud.

Unsurprisingly, Neidorf's reading of the indictment is self-servingly narrow. The indictment plainly and clearly charges that Neidorf and Riggs concocted a fraud scheme, the object of which was to steal the E911 text file from Bell South and to distribute it to others via the PHRACK newsletter. The indictment also clearly alleges that both Riggs and Neidorf took action in furtherance of the fraud scheme. Riggs allegedly used fraudulent means to access Bell South's computer system and then disguised his unauthorized entry. Neidorf allegedly furthered the scheme by redacting from the E911 text file references to Bell South and other information which would reveal the source of the E911 file, transmitting the redacted file back to the Lockport bulletin board for Riggs review, and publishing the redacted text file in the PHRACK newsletter for others' use. Moreover, both Neidorf and Riggs allegedly used coded language, code names, and other deceptive means to avoid the detection of their fraud by law enforcement officials. These allegations sufficiently set forth the existence of a scheme to defraud, as well as Neidorf's participation in the scheme. * * *

Neidorf also argues that Count II is deficient because it fails to allege that he had a fiduciary relationship with Bell South. To support this position, Neidorf relies on cases such as *United States v. Richter,* 610 F.Supp. 480 (N.D.Ill.1985), and *United States v. Dorfman,* 532 F.Supp. 1118 (N.D.Ill.1981). In each of those cases, as well as other similar cases cited by Neidorf, the court held that where a wire fraud charge is based on the deprivation of an intangible right, such as the right to honest and fair government or the right to the loyal service of an employee, the government must allege the existence of a fiduciary relationship between the defendant and the alleged victim to state a charge under § 1343.

In the instant case, however, the wire fraud charge is not based on the deprivation of an intangible right. The government charges Riggs and Neidorf with scheming to defraud Bell South out of *property*—the confidential information contained in the E911 text file. The indictment specifically alleges that the object of defendants' scheme was the

E911 text file, which Bell South considered to be valuable, proprietary, information. The law is clear that such valuable, confidential information is "property," the deprivation of which can form the basis of a wire fraud charge under § 1343. Therefore, Neidorf's argument misconstrues the wire fraud charge against him. Cases such as *Richter* and *Dorfman* are wholly inapposite.

As further support for his argument that fiduciary relationship between himself and Bell South must be alleged to state a wire fraud charge against him, Neidorf analogizes his role in the alleged scheme to that of an "innocent tippee" in the securities context, such as the defendants in *Dirks v. Securities Exchange Commission,* 463 U.S. 646, 103 S.Ct. 3255, 77 L.Ed.2d 911 (1983), and *Chiarella v. United States,* 445 U.S. 222, 100 S.Ct. 1108, 63 L.Ed.2d 348 (1980). This analogy, however, is fallacious. Those cases involved individuals who come upon information *lawfully;* the question in each of those cases was whether, once possessing that information, the individual had a duty to disclose it. In the instant case, in contrast, Neidorf is alleged to have planned and participated in the scheme to defraud Bell South. Although Riggs allegedly was the one who actually stole the E911 text file from Bell South's computer system, the government alleges that Neidorf was completely aware of Riggs' activities and agreed to help Riggs conceal the theft to make the fraud complete. Therefore, in no way can Neidorf be construed as being in a similar situation to the innocent tippees in *Dirks* and *Chiarella.* As a result, the court rejects his argument that Count II is defective for failing to allege a fiduciary duty between himself and Bell South. Neidorf's motion to dismiss Count II is accordingly denied.

B. Motion to Dismiss Counts III and IV

Counts III and IV charge Riggs and Neidorf with violating 18 U.S.C. § 2314, which provides, in relevant part:

> Whoever transports, transmits, or transfers in interstate or foreign commerce any goods, wares, merchandise, securities or money, of the value of $5000 or more, knowing the same to have been stolen, converted or taken by fraud * * * [s]hall be fined not more than $10,000 or imprisoned not more than ten years, or both.

The government concedes that charging Neidorf under § 2314 plots a course on uncharted waters. No court has ever held that the electronic transfer of confidential, proprietary business information from one computer to another across state lines constitutes a violation of § 2314. However, no court has addressed the issue. Surprisingly, despite the prevalence of computer-related crime, this is a case of first impression. The government argues that reading § 2314 as covering Neidorf's conduct in this case is a natural adaptation of the statute to modern society. Conversely, Neidorf contends that his conduct does not fall within the purview of § 2314 and that the government is seeking an unreasonable expansion of the statute. He urges the court to dismiss the charge on two grounds.

Neidorf's first argument is that the government cannot sustain a § 2314 charge in this case because the only thing which he allegedly caused to be transferred across state lines was "electronic impulses." Neidorf maintains that under the plain language of the statute, this conduct does not come within the scope of § 2314 since electronic impulses do not constitute "goods, wares, or merchandise."

The court is unpersuaded by Neidorf's disingenuous argument that he merely transferred electronic impulses across state lines. Several courts have upheld § 2314 charges based on the wire transfer of fraudulently obtained money, rejecting the arguments of the defendants in those cases that only electronic impulses, not actual money, crossed state lines. For example, in *United States v. Gilboe,* 684 F.2d 235 (2d Cir.1982), *cert. denied,* 459 U.S. 1201, 103 S.Ct. 1185, 75 L.Ed.2d 432 (1983), the court held, in affirming a § 2314 conviction based on the wire transfer of funds:

> The question whether [§ 2314] covers electronic transfers of funds appears to be one of first impression, but we do not regard it as a difficult one. Electronic signals in this context are the means by which funds are transported. The beginning of the transaction is money in one account and the ending is money in another. The manner in which the funds were moved does not affect the ability to obtain tangible paper dollars or a bank check from the receiving account. If anything, the means of transfer here were essential to the fraudulent scheme.

Id. at 238. Other circuits have followed the reasoning in *Gilboe.* In all of these cases, the courts held that money was transferred across state lines within the meaning of § 2314 because funds were actually accessible in one account prior to the transfer, and those funds were actually accessible in an out-of-state account after the transfer. The courts refused to accept the superficial characterization of the transfers as the mere transmittal of electronic impulses.

Similarly, in the instant case, Neidorf's conduct is not properly characterized as the mere transmission of electronic impulses. Through the use of his computer, Neidorf allegedly transferred proprietary business information—Bell South's E911 text file. Like the money in the case dealing with wire transfers of funds, the information in the E911 text file was accessible at Neidorf's computer terminal in Missouri before he transferred it, and the information was also accessible at the Lockport, Illinois computer bulletin board after Neidorf transferred it. Therefore, under *Gilboe, Kroh, Wright,* and *Goldberg,* the mere fact that the information actually crossed state lines via computer-generated electronic impulses does not defeat a charge under § 2314.

The question this case presents, then, is not whether electronic impulses are "goods, wares, or merchandise" within the meaning of § 2314, but whether the proprietary information contained in Bell South's E911 text file constitutes a "good, ware, or merchandise" within the purview of the statute. This court answers that question affirmatively. It is well-settled that when proprietary business information is affixed to some tangible medium, such as a piece of paper, it constitutes "goods, wares, or merchandise" within the meaning of § 2314.

Therefore, in the instant case, if the information in Bell South's E911 text file had been affixed to a floppy disk, or printed out on a computer printer, then Neidorf's transfer of that information across state lines would clearly constitute the transfer of "goods, wares, or merchandise" within the meaning of § 2314. This court sees no reason to hold differently simply because Neidorf stored the information inside computers instead of printing it out on paper. In either case, the information is in a transferrable, accessible, even salable form.

Neidorf argues in his brief that a § 2314 charge cannot survive when the "thing" actually transferred never takes tangible form. A few courts have apparently adopted this position. For example, in *United States v. Smith,* 686 F.2d 234 (5th Cir.1982), the court held that a copyright does not fit within the definition of "goods, wares, or merchandise" under § 2314. The court ruled that in order to come within that definition, "[t]he 'thing' or 'item' must have some sort of tangible existence; it must be in the nature of 'personal property or chattels.'" *Id.* at 241. Similarly, in *Bottone, supra,* where the court held that copies of documents describing a manufacturing process for a patented drug constitute "goods, wares, or merchandise" under § 2314, the court opined:

> To be sure, where no tangible objects were ever taken or transported, a court would be hard pressed to conclude that "goods" had been stolen and transported within the meaning of § 2314; the statute would presumably not extend to the case where a carefully guarded secret was memorized, carried away in the recesses of a thievish mind and placed in writing only after a [state] boundary had been crossed.

365 F.2d at 393.

Nevertheless, this court is not entirely convinced that tangibility is an absolute requirement of "goods, wares, or merchandise" under § 2314. Congress enacted § 2314 to extend the National Motor Vehicle Theft Act to cover all stolen property over a certain value ($5000) which is knowingly transported across state lines. In line with this broad congressional intent, courts have liberally construed the term "goods, wares, or merchandise" as "a general and comprehensive designation of such personal property and chattels as are ordinarily the subject of commerce." Reading a tangibility requirement into the definition of "goods, wares, or merchandise" might unduly restrict the scope of § 2314, especially in this modern technological age. For instance, suppose the existence of a valuable gas, used as an anesthetic, which is colorless, odorless, and tasteless—totally imperceptible to the human senses. If this gas is stored in a tank in Indiana, and a trucker hooks up to the tank, releases the valuable gas into a storage tank on his truck, and then takes the gas to Illinois to sell it for a profit, is there no violation of § 2314 simply because the gas is not technically tangible?

This court is reluctant to believe that any court would construe § 2314 so narrowly.

In any event, this court need not decide that issue to resolve this case, for even if tangibility is a requirement of "goods, wares or merchandise" under § 2314, in this court's opinion the computer-stored business information in this case satisfies that requirement. Although not printed out on paper, a more conventional form of tangibility, the information in Bell South's E911 text file was allegedly stored on computer. Thus, by simply pressing a few buttons, Neidorf could recall that information from computer storage and view it on his computer terminal. The information was also accessible to others in the same fashion if they simply pressed the right buttons on their computer. This ability to access the information in viewable form from a reliable storage place differentiates this case from the mere memorization of a formula and makes this case more similar to cases like *Greenwald, Bottone, Seagraves,* and *Lester,* where proprietary information was also stored, but in a more traditional manner—on paper. The accessibility of the information in readable form from a particular storage place also makes the information tangible, transferable, salable and, in this court's opinion, brings it within the definition of "goods, wares, or merchandise" under § 2314.

In order to sustain a charge against Neidorf under § 2314, however, the government cannot simply allege that Neidorf transferred "goods, wares, or merchandise" across state boundaries; the government must also allege that Neidorf executed the transfer knowing the goods were "stolen, converted or taken by fraud." This requirement forms the basis for Neidorf's second challenge to Counts III and IV. Relying on *Dowling v. United States,* 473 U.S. 207, 105 S.Ct. 3127, 87 L.Ed.2d 152 (1985), Neidorf maintains that the § 2314 charges should be dismissed because the "things" he allegedly transferred are not the type of property which is capable of being "stolen, converted or taken by fraud."

In *Dowling,* the government charged the defendant with violating § 2314 by shipping "bootleg" and "pirated" [10] phonorecords across state lines. *Id.* at 212, 105 S.Ct. at 3130–31. The government argued that the shipments came within § 2314 because the phonorecords embodied performances of copyrighted musical compositions which the defendant had no right to distribute. *Id.* at 214–15, 105 S.Ct. at 3131–32. The Court framed the issue in the case as follows:

> Dowling does not contest that he caused the shipment of goods in interstate commerce, or that the shipments had sufficient value to meet the monetary requirement. He argues, instead, that the goods shipped were not "stolen, converted or taken by fraud."

10. A "bootleg" phonorecord is an unauthorized copy of a commercially unreleased performance. A "pirated" phonorecord is an unauthorized copy of a performance already commercially released. *Dowling,* 473 U.S. at 209–10 n. 2, 105 S.Ct. at 3129 n. 2.

* * *

> We must determine, therefore, whether phonorecords that include the performance of copyrighted musical compositions for the use of which no authorization has been sought or royalties paid are consequently "stolen, converted or taken by fraud" for purposes of § 2314.

Id. at 214–16, 105 S.Ct. at 3131–32. The Court ruled that while the holder of a copyright possesses certain property rights which are protectible and enforceable under copyright law, he does not own the type of possessory interest in an item of property which may be "stolen, converted or taken by fraud." *Id.* at 216–18, 105 S.Ct. at 3132–34. Thus, the Court held that § 2314 does not apply to interstate shipments of "bootleg" and "pirated" phonorecords whose unauthorized distribution infringes on valid copyrights. *Id.* at 228–29, 105 S.Ct. at 3138–39.

Neidorf also cites *United States v. Smith,* 686 F.2d 234 (5th Cir. 1982), to support his argument. Like *Dowling, Smith* held that copyright infringement is not the equivalent of theft or conversion under § 2314. *Id.* at 241. The instant case, however, is distinguishable from *Dowling* and *Smith.* This case involves the transfer of confidential, proprietary business information, not copyrights. As *Dowling* and *Smith* recognized, the copyright holder owns only a bundle of intangible rights which can be infringed, but not stolen or converted. The owner of confidential, proprietary business information, in contrast, possesses something which has clearly been recognized as an item of *property. Carpenter,* 108 S.Ct. at 320; *Keane,* 852 F.2d at 205. As such, it is certainly capable of being misappropriated, which, according to the indictment, is exactly what happened to the information in Bell South's E911 text file.

In his final gasp, Neidorf points out that in *Dowling,* the Court based its ruling partly on the fact that Congress passed the Copyright Act to deal exclusively with copyright infringements. The Court reasoned that applying § 2314 to the infringement of copyrights would result in an unnecessary and unwarranted intrusion into an area already governed by the Copyright Act. 473 U.S. at 221–26, 105 S.Ct. at 3135–38. Neidorf makes a similar argument in this case. He notes that Congress has enacted a statute—the Computer Fraud and Abuse Act ("CFAA"), 18 U.S.C. § 1030—which is specifically designed to address computer-related crimes, such as unauthorized computer access. Neidorf claims that the enactment of the CFAA precludes a finding that § 2314 reaches his alleged conduct in this case.

The problem with Neidorf's argument, however, is that he does not cite, and this court is unable to find, anything in the legislative history of the CFAA which suggests that the statute was intended to be the exclusive law governing computer-related crimes, or that its enactment precludes the application of other criminal statutes to computer-related conduct. Therefore, the court rejects Neidorf's claim that applying § 2314 to the instant case would undermine the Congressional intent behind the CFAA. Similarly, the court rejects Neidorf's bald assertion that the legislative history behind § 2314 supports his argument. Nothing in the legislative history of § 2314 prevents the court from finding that the information in Bell South's E911 text file was "stolen, converted or taken by fraud" as that term is used in § 2314. Accordingly, Neidorf's motion to dismiss Counts III and IV is denied.

C. Motion to Strike Surplusage and Prejudicial Material

Pursuant to Rule 7(d) of the Federal Rules of Criminal Procedure, Neidorf moves to strike certain words and phrases from the indictment which he claims are unnecessary and prejudicial. He first argues that the terms "hackers" and "computer hackers" should be stricken because those terms are likely to cause confusion and prejudice. He contends that the government uses those terms in the indictment to lure the jury into predetermining his character and motives.

The court, however, is not convinced that the government's use of the term "hacker" in this case is unduly prejudicial. The government has specifically defined "hackers" in the indictment as "individuals involved with the unauthorized access of computer systems by various means." This definition is consistent with *Webster's II New Riverside University Dictionary* (1984), which defines hacker as follows: "*Slang.* One who gains unauthorized, usu[ally] non-fraudulent access to another's computer system." *Id.* at 557. The term "hackers" has also been understood to encompass both those who obtain unauthorized access to computer systems and those who simply enjoy using computers and experimenting with their capabilities as "innocent" hobbyists. *See* Staff of the Subcomm. on Transportation, Aviation & Materials of the House Comm. on Science & Technology, 98th Cong., 2d Sess., Report on Computer & Communications Security & Privacy 17 (Comm. Print 1984) (citing the testimony of Donn B. Parker, Senior Management Systems Consultant, SRI International, Computer Research Institute, wherein he stated, "Computer hackers are hobbyists with intense interest in exploring the capabilities of computers and communications and causing these systems to perform to their limits. * * * Hackers exhibit a spectrum of behavior from benign to malicious."); *see also* C. Stoll, *The Cuckoo's Egg,* at 10 (1989) ("The word hacker has two very different meanings. The people I knew who called themselves hackers were software wizards who * * * knew all the nooks and crannies of the operating system. * * * But in common usage, a hacker is someone who breaks into computers"). However, as pointed out in *The Cuckoo's Egg,* and as is evident from a review of the modern articles using the term, the definition set forth in the indictment is the one most commonly employed.

The court finds that the use of the term "hackers" in the indictment does not unduly prejudice Neidorf; it is simply a succinct method of describing the alleged activities of the persons with whom Neidorf was associated during the time period charged in the indictment. The term is both relevant and material, and, contrary to Neidorf's claim that it will cause confusion, the term is likely to be somewhat helpful to the jury in understanding the charges in this case. Thus, the court refuses to strike the term "hackers" from the indictment. *See United States v. Chaverra–Cardona,* 667 F.Supp. 609, 611 (N.D.Ill.1987) (information relevant to the charges and helpful to the jury's understanding of those charges should not be stricken from an indictment).

Neidorf also claims that references to the "Legion of Doom," a computer hacker group, should be deleted from the indictment. Neidorf, however, allegedly had close ties to the Legion of Doom and disseminated the E911 text file to some of its members. Therefore, references to the Legion of Doom are highly relevant to the charges in this case. Neidorf claims the name "Legion of Doom" "invites images of cult worshippers, satanism, terrorism or black magic," but this is a gross exaggeration of the potential effect of the term. The indictment clearly sets forth the purposes and activities of the group, none of which include the slightest reference to any type of satanism or the like. Thus, there is no reason to strike references to the "Legion of Doom."

Neidorf further contends that the court should strike the following portions of the indictment: (1) the second sentence of paragraph 8, which reads:

> The Lockport [computer bulletin board system] was also used by computer hackers as a location for exchanging and developing software tools for computer intrusion, and for receiving and distributing hacker tutorials and other information.

(2) the underlined words in paragraph 21, which reads:

> It was further part of the scheme that the defendants RIGGS and NEIDORF would publish information to other computer <u>hackers which could be used to gain unauthorized access to emergency 911 computer systems in the United States and thereby disrupt or halt 911 service in portions of the United States.</u>

and (3) the underlined parts of paragraph 3, which reads in part:

> The E911 Practice was a <u>highly</u> proprietary <u>and closely held</u> computerized text file belonging to the Bell South Telephone Company and stored on the company's AIMSX computer in Atlanta, Georgia. The E911 Practice described the computerized control and maintenance of the E911 system and <u>carried warning notices that it was not to be disclosed outside Bell South or any of its subsidiaries except under written agreement.</u>

Each of these allegations, however, are directly relevant to Neidorf's knowledge of the proprietary, confidential nature of the information in Bell South's E911 file and to Neidorf's motive and ability to aid in the misappropriation of that information. Therefore, those allegations are pertinent to the elements of the offenses charged and are not properly stricken. Neidorf's motion to strike is accordingly denied.

D. Motion for a Santiago Hearing

In order to offer the statements of a defendant's alleged co-conspirators into evidence against the defendant pursuant to Fed.R.Evid. 801(d)(2)(E), the government must make a preliminary showing, by a preponderance of the evidence, that: (1) a conspiracy existed; (2) the defendant and the declarant were members of the conspiracy when the statements were made; and (3) the statements were made during the course of and in furtherance of the conspiracy. *Bourjaily v. United States,* 483 U.S. 171, 107 S.Ct. 2775, 97 L.Ed.2d 144 (1989); *United States v. Santiago,* 582 F.2d 1128, 1135 (7th Cir.1978). Neidorf has moved for an order requiring the government to file a statement setting forth its evidence in support of each of the above factors. The government, however, filed a *Santiago* proffer subsequent to Neidorf's motion. Therefore, Neidorf's motion for a *Santiago* proffer is denied as moot. Moreover, after reviewing the government's case as detailed in its proffer, the court finds that the government has set forth sufficient evidence to support a preliminary finding of the admissibility of the statements of Neidorf's alleged coconspirators. Therefore, this court will conditionally admit those statements, offered pursuant to Rule 801(d)(2)(E), subject to proof by a preponderance of the evidence at trial that the *Santiago* factors are satisfied.

* * *

Conclusion

For the foregoing reasons, Neidorf's pretrial motions are denied, except for his motion to dismiss Counts V–VII and his motion for a bill of particulars, which are held in abeyance pending the filing of the superseding indictment.

It is so ordered.

Notes

1. The defense next moved to dismiss on the theory that the prosecution infringed upon First Amendment rights. The court denied this motion. 743 F.Supp. 556 (N.D.Ill.1990).

2. Excellent work by defendant Neidorf's lawyer and expert witness produced evidence that the information Neidorf was accused of stealing was, in fact, already available in published sources. At this point, the government dropped the prosecution against him. See Dorothy E. Denning, "The United States vs. Craig Neidorf: a Debate on Electronic Publishing, Constitutional Rights and Hacking, *Communications of the ACM,* vol. 34, no. 3, p. 24 (1991).

3. The other defendants entered guilty pleas and received substantial prison sentences. Michael Alexander, "Jail Time Sounds Sharp Note on Tampering," *Computerworld,* Nov. 26, 1990, p. 1.

UNITED STATES v. BROWN

United States Court of Appeals, Tenth Circuit, 1991.
925 F.2d 1301.

HOLLOWAY, CHIEF JUDGE.

The United States appeals from a dismissal by the district court of an indictment charging the defendant, John M. Brown, with three counts of violations of the National Stolen Property Act, 18 U.S.C. §§ 2314 and 2315.[1] The indictment was dismissed on the ground that the allegedly stolen property, a computer program in source code form, did not come within the ambit of 18 U.S.C. §§ 2314 and 2315 as goods, wares or merchandise. We affirm.

I

At the hearing on the motion to dismiss the indictment, government counsel stated that defendant Brown worked as a computer programmer for The Software Link, Inc. (hereinafter TSL), a computer software company located in Georgia (II R. 31). One asset of TSL was a computer program known as PC–MOS/386.[2] Later in New Mexico, Brown was the subject of an FBI investigation which culminated in the issuance and execution of a search warrant for his apartment. During the search of Brown's residence, the FBI discovered five three-ring notebooks and a hard disk which contained portions of the source code for the PC–MOS/386 program. II R. at 47.

A grand jury returned a three count indictment on November 16, 1989, charging Brown in one count with violating 18 U.S.C. § 2314 and in two counts with violating 18 U.S.C. § 2315.[5] At a pretrial motion

1. Section 2314 applies, in part, to whoever "transports, transmits, or transfers in interstate or foreign commerce any goods, wares, merchandise, securities or money, of the value of $5,000 or more, knowing the same to have been stolen, converted or taken by fraud." 18 U.S.C. § 2314.

Section 2315 applies, in part, to whoever "receives, possesses, conceals, stores, barters, sells, or disposes of any goods, wares, or merchandise, securities, or money of the value of $5,000 or more * * * which have crossed a State or United States boundary after being stolen, unlawfully converted, or taken, knowing the same to have been stolen, unlawfully converted, or taken." 18 U.S.C. § 2315.

2. PC–MOS/386 allows certain International Business Machines (IBM) compatible computers to perform complex activities such as multi-tasking and sharing of data among multiple users. II R. at 45–46.

5. Count I stated that Brown "did knowingly cause to be transported in interstate commerce from Norcross, in the State of Georgia, to Albuquerque, New Mexico, computer programs, software and manuals, to wit: a computer program with source code PC–MOS/386 an exclusive product of The Software Link, Inc., (TSL), such items having a value of $5,000.00 or more, and the Defendant, JOHN M. BROWN, then knew that the computer program and software manuals had been stolen, converted and taken by fraud."

Count II charged that Brown "knowingly possessed, concealed, stored, sold and disposed of computer programs, software and manuals, to wit: a computer program with source code PC–MOS/386 an exclusive product of The Software Link, Inc., (TSL), such items having a value of $5,000.00 or more and which had crossed a state or United States boundary after being stolen, and JOHN M. BROWN then knew the computer programs, software and manuals to have been stolen."

Count III was identical to Count II in all aspects other than the date of the offense

hearing, the district judge granted a motion to dismiss made by the defendant. The judge based his decision primarily on *Dowling v. United States,* 473 U.S. 207, 216, 226, 105 S.Ct. 3127, 3132, 3137, 87 L.Ed.2d 152 (1985), which held that § 2314 does not apply to crimes which involve mere copyright infringement and emphasized the fact that cases under § 2314 have always involved "physical 'goods, wares [or] merchandise' " that have themselves been "stolen, converted or taken by fraud."

* * *

In the pretrial stage of the proceedings, Brown filed a motion to dismiss. The motion alleged that upon his termination from TSL, the company shipped his materials from Georgia to his home in New Mexico; that these included his backup tapes, owned by him; that when packaged, the source code, PC–MOS/386, was on the tapes; that material from the government provided to defendant indicates the source code is copyright material belonging to TSL. The motion concluded that the source code was "intellectual property" and that the infringement the government alleges implicates complex copyright interests, and that this intellectual property cannot constitute goods, wares or merchandise under the National Stolen Property Act. For reasons that might appear at a full hearing, defendant asked that his motion to dismiss be granted.

* * *

We turn now to the charges of the indictment and to the evidentiary hearing on the motion to dismiss, including statements by counsel and testimony of witnesses, which developed essentially undisputed facts.

The indictment was stated in three counts. Count I alleged that Brown violated 18 U.S.C. § 2314, in February 1989 by transporting interstate, from Georgia to New Mexico, "computer programs, software and manuals, to wit: a computer program with source code PC–MOS/386 an exclusive product of The Software Link, Inc., (TSL), such items having a value of $5,000.00 or more." I R.Doc. 1 at 1. Count II alleged that Brown violated 18 U.S.C. § 2315 on July 28, 1989 because he "knowingly possessed, concealed, stored, sold and disposed of computer programs, software and manuals, to wit: a computer program with source code PC–MOS/386 * * * which had crossed a state or United States boundary after being stolen." *Id.* at 1–2. Count III was virtually identical to Count II, except that the date was August 2, 1989 and the "sold and disposed of" language was deleted. *Id.* at 2.

The primary focus of the hearing on the motion to dismiss was on the applicability of *Dowling* to the case. Brown argued that *Dowling* applied because the government was not "complaining that Mr. Brown took a physical object from this company in Georgia and transported it

and the deletion of the "sold and disposed of" language.

in interstate commerce" but instead that he took a source code and transported it. II R. at 24.

The government attempted to distinguish this case from *Dowling,* arguing that

> [t]he major distinction in this case * * * [is that the] source code took 15 years to develop by TSL. It is not something that Mr. Brown could have gone to TSL, talked to the engineers, talked to the computers, even if he is extremely literate and perhaps brilliant in the area of computer programming, left that area, not taken anything physically that was not his, come to New Mexico and recreated it.

Id. at 27.

Brown claimed that the government could at most show that a copy of the program was made at TSL and was then transported in interstate commerce. *Id.* at 33. The court questioned this characterization of the government case since the indictment did not state that only a "copy" was involved. *Id.* In an attempt to clarify the government's position, the court asked the prosecutor to describe what its proof would show as to "how the program got to New Mexico" or, specifically, what Brown did "physically to acquire the program in Georgia." *Id.*

The government reply was that "TSL has it in their computers. He acquired that, and he could either have done it on a floppy disk or a tape or a hard disk and brought that with him to New Mexico." *Id.* at 35. The district judge asked: "Will the government prove that it was not [sic] the company's hard disk that was brought, physically?" The prosecuting attorney stated that she did "not believe the government can prove that TSL owned hard disk A and he stole hard disk A. I don't believe we can prove that." *Id.* at 36. The court then stated that since the government could not prove that, "we have to assume that a copy was made." *Id.* The prosecutor responded "[t]hat's correct," but argued that it made no difference because "he still knows that it is not something that he has a right to take." *Id.*

The government again attempted to distinguish *Dowling* by emphasizing that *Dowling* involved recordings made "off of something that's open to the public", while in the instant case the source code was "removed from things that the victim thought they had protected * * *." *Id.* at 37. The court questioned as to "whether or not [something is] property depends on the method in which it's captured?" *Id.*[10]

10. A pertinent excerpt from the transcript follows:

"THE COURT: So whether or not it's property depends on the method in which it's captured? For example, this program that somebody devised, it's something intellectual.

MS. BURNETT: An idea.

THE COURT: An idea. Are you telling me that it depends on how you transfer that idea, or how or where you get—where you pick up that idea—I mean, where you steal that from?

MS. BURNETT: Well—

THE COURT: But is that what *Dowling* says?

MS. BURNETT: I think that what *Dowling* says is there is a difference between an intellectual property, which is this idea floating around and it's kind of intangible, and if you shrink it down and put it on

The court then directed both counsel to establish "a factual predicate * * * to show * * * what happened physically, and what physical objects were acted upon to bring the program to New Mexico." *Id.* at 39.

The government's first witness was Mr. Klossner, a special agent and local information systems administrator for the FBI in Albuquerque, who was present at the execution of the search warrant at Brown's apartment. *Id.* at 42. He stated that Mr. Roark, co-chairman of TSL and co-developer of PC–MOS/386, identified the source code from Brown's hard disk and bound paper printouts as being part of PC–MOS/386. *Id.* at 46. The judge attempted to determine the origin of this seized material by asking if the witness had "any information whatsoever insofar as the material that is contained in the five three-ring binders, that this was original material belonging to Software Link?" *Id.* at 51. Klossner replied that "it doesn't make sense to talk about original material." *Id.* Klossner further stated that he did not understand that Roark was indicating that the hard disk found in Brown's apartment, the physical object itself, was the property of TSL. *Id.* at 57. Klossner understood that Roark was saying that "the source code, the electronic signals on the hard disk, were the property of TSL, and the material, the source code as printed out in the binder were the property of TSL." *Id.* at 58.

The next government witness was FBI agent Gariay. He testified briefly about a tape recording, a transcript of which was offered into evidence. The recording was of a telephone conversation between Brown and Ben Brady. Brady was a cooperating witness for the government, who was to receive copies of the stolen source code.[11] Gariay testified that to his knowledge, Brown was discussing his appropriation of the source code itself. *Id.* at 65. When asked if these printouts could have been generated by Brown's own computer in Albuquerque, the witness stated that he had "no idea." *Id.* at 65.

The final witness was a defense witness, Peter Ives, who is an attorney specializing in intellectual property and computer law. Ives testified that "[t]he source code itself, under the copyright law, exists separate and apart from the tangible embodiment of that work." *Id.* at 68. Ives continued that "[t]he source code itself * * * is essentially an

paper. If it's on paper and what's on paper or some media is stolen, then that is 2314.

THE COURT: That's not what happened here.

MS. BURNETT: Well, it was put onto a disk. And there's no difference between a disk and a piece of paper. It was taken directly—this idea had been shrunk down and made into a program. Now it is in the banks of the computer of TSL. And it is there to be used for the benefit of TSL, and it lives there. And Mr. Brown then physically takes a copy of that out and—"

II R. at 37–38.

11. A pertinent portion of the conversation follows:

Brown: I've got five, three ring binders that's full of printouts.

Brady: Right that include PC MOS 3.0.

Brown: 3.1.

Brady: 3.1?

Brown: Yes.

Brady: When did you get that?

Brown: When I was out there.

Addendum to Appellant's Brief at 2.

intangible which then, for purposes of distribution and the like, would be put into some sort of tangible form as was discussed, disks, et cetera." *Id.* at 70. Ives concluded by agreeing with defense counsel's suggestion that the source code on a floppy disk was analogous to a song on a phono record. *Id.* at 72.

At this point the trial judge made his ruling "based upon the rationale in *Dowling.*" *Id.* at 72. The court found that the source code contained in the printouts in the binders, and which was contained in the hard disk, "is not the type of property which is contemplated * * * within the language of the statute, goods, wares or merchandise." *Id.* at 73. Furthermore, the court noted that it took "into consideration that which *Dowling* discusses, and that is[,] that a criminal statute must be construed strictly." *Id.* at 73. A brief written order followed this ruling, giving no further reasons, but stating that the indictment was "dismissed in its entirety." I R.Doc. 21.

IV

In *Dowling,* the defendant was convicted under § 2314 of the National Stolen Property Act following his distribution of "bootleg" phonograph recordings of Elvis Presley vocalizations, the copyrights for which were owned by other persons.[12] The Court reasoned that crimes involving copyright violations could be dealt with through a variety of means, chiefly civil, and that it was not Congress' intention that the National Stolen Property Act function as a criminalization of copyright infringement. *Id.* at 216–18, 105 S.Ct. at 3132–34. The Court noted that the courts have never required that the items stolen and transported remain in entirely unaltered form. The Court emphasized, however, that:

> *[T]hese cases and others prosecuted under § 2314 have always involved physical "goods, wares, [or] merchandise" that have themselves been "stolen, converted or taken by fraud."* This basic element comports with the common-sense meaning of the statutory language: by requiring that the "goods, wares, [or] merchandise" be "the same" as those "stolen, converted or taken by fraud," the provision seems clearly to contemplate a physical identity between the items unlawfully obtained and those eventually transported, and hence some prior physical taking of the subject goods.

473 U.S. at 216, 105 S.Ct. at 3132 (emphasis added). This essential ingredient of the statute—the involvement of physical "goods, wares, [or] merchandise" that were themselves "stolen, converted or taken by fraud"—was missing in *Dowling* and is likewise missing here.

The government argues that the case before us is distinguishable from *Dowling* primarily because the recordings in *Dowling* were taken off of the radio. Members of the public are allowed to listen to these recordings when broadcast and to make a copy for their own personal

12. "A 'bootleg' phonorecord is one which contains an unauthorized copy of a commercially unreleased performance." *Dowling,* 473 U.S. at 209 n. 2, 105 S.Ct. at 3129 n. 2.

use, but not to make numerous copies and sell them commercially, as Dowling did. *See Sony Corp. v. Universal City Studios, Inc.,* 464 U.S. 417, 104 S.Ct. 774, 78 L.Ed.2d 574 (1984). *Dowling* involves a bare copyright violation, since Dowling merely used recordings which he possessed legally, in a manner which went beyond what was permissible. In the instant case, however, the government says that an actual taking occurred because the "source code" which was found in Brown's apartment was never released to anyone outside TSL. The program, therefore, had to have been originally physically taken from TSL through illicit means.

As noted, *Dowling* holds that § 2314 applies only to physical "goods, wares or merchandise." Purely intellectual property is not within this category. It can be represented physically, such as through writing on a page, but the underlying, intellectual property itself, remains intangible. It is true that the intellectual property involved in the instant case was more nearly "stolen, converted or taken by fraud" in the sense that it was at no time freely presented to the public as had been the recordings in *Dowling.* In fact, the government says here that Brown himself, although a programmer at TSL, did not have authorized access to the PC–MOS/386 source code file. II R. at 58. This point, however, is not dispositive of the critical issue under *Dowling.* Here we agree that the property, PC–MOS/386, does not meet the requirement of §§ 2314 and 2315 respecting "goods, wares, or merchandise." We hold that the computer program itself is an intangible intellectual property, and as such, it alone cannot constitute goods, wares, merchandise, securities or moneys which have been stolen, converted or taken within the meaning of §§ 2314 or 2315.

The recent case of *United States v. Riggs,* 739 F.Supp. 414 (N.D.Ill. 1990), was cited by the government as supplemental authority for the proposition that source codes can be described as goods, wares, or merchandise. Mr. Riggs was convicted under 18 U.S.C. § 2314 for the theft of an electronic text file owned by Bell South. A text file is very similar to a source code file in most respects. Riggs stole the text file by accessing the Bell South computer and transferring the text file over phone lines to his own computer. No physical item was taken from Bell South.

The district court reasoned that "if the information in Bell South's E911 text file had been affixed to a floppy disk, or printed out on a computer printer, then [defendant's] transfer of that information across state lines would clearly constitute the transfer of 'goods, wares, or merchandise' within the meaning of § 2314." *Id.* The district court found "no reason to hold differently simply because [defendant] stored the information inside computers instead of printing it out on paper. In either case, the information is in a transferrable, accessible, even salable form." The court further reasoned that "reading a tangibility requirement into the definition of 'goods, wares, or merchandise' might unduly restrict the scope of § 2314, especially in this modern technological age." The court found that "[t]he accessability of the information in readable form from a particular storage place also makes the information tangible, transferable, salable and, in [the district] court's opinion, brings it within the definition of 'goods, wares, or merchandise' under § 2314." *Id.* at 422.

We disagree. We feel that the *Riggs* interpretation of the statute is in error in light of the Supreme Court's focus on "physical 'goods, wares [or] merchandise' that have themselves been 'stolen, converted or taken by fraud,' " 473 U.S. at 216, 105 S.Ct. at 3132. The element of physical "goods, wares, or merchandise" in §§ 2314 and 2315 is critical. The limitation which this places on the reach of the National Stolen Property Act is imposed by the statute itself, and must be observed. *See Dowling* at 218, 226, 105 S.Ct. at 3133, 3137.

"Federal crimes, of course, 'are solely creatures of statute * * *,' " *Dowling,* 473 U.S. at 213, 105 S.Ct. at 3131 (citations omitted). The language of the statutes involved here does not support the government's broad-ranging interpretation of §§ 2314 and 2315, and even if this were less apparent, the ambiguity concerning the ambit of the criminal statutes should be resolved in favor of lenity. *See Rewis v. United States,* 401 U.S. 808, 812, 91 S.Ct. 1056, 1059, 28 L.Ed.2d 493 (1971). Since the government could not establish that the defendant had transported, transmitted or transferred in interstate commerce (§ 2314), or received, possessed, concealed, stored, bartered, sold or disposed of (§ 2315) any physical "goods, wares or merchandise * * *," the indictment was properly dismissed.

Affirmed.

F. STATE CRIMINAL REMEDIES FOR TRADE SECRET VIOLATION

SCHALK v. STATE

Court of Appeals of Texas, Dallas, 1988.
767 S.W.2d 441.

McClung, Justice.

This is an appeal from a jury trial for the theft of trade secrets. Appellant was found guilty and assessed punishment at two years confinement and a fine of $5,000, probated for two years.

Specifically, appellant was indicted under Texas Penal Code section 31.05 for knowingly making a copy of five separately identified computer programs that were the trade secrets of his employer.

Appellant contends that: 1) the evidence is insufficient to establish that the five computer programs listed in the indictment were, in fact, trade secrets; 2) the evidence is insufficient to prove that appellant knowingly committed the offense charged. * * * Having found no error, we affirm the judgment of the trial court.

Facts

The complainant, appellant's former employer, is a major corporation with world-wide facilities and engaged primarily in the electronics industry in various capacities. This case involves a computer programming area sometimes referred to as speech synthesis, or voice recognition. It can be described in an oversimplified manner as a computer software program that causes a device to respond in a specified manner to commands issued orally or by voice. The complainant is generally understood to be a pioneer in this field and an industry leader in the research and development of this type of programming for various applications.

The complainant kept and maintained a facility on their premises in Dallas designated as the "speech research laboratory" where this type of programing, research and development was conducted. Appellant had been employed by the complainant for approximately twelve years as an engineer in the speech laboratory. The laboratory was kept physically separated from other facilities within the confines of the overall premises. Access to the laboratory was limited to only certain authorized personnel, estimated to be something less than one hundred out of the several thousand that were admitted daily through the gates of the fences around the perimeter. The exterior gates were monitored by security guards around the clock. Speech laboratory employees were required to wear a certain type identity badge to gain access to the laboratory. Appellant, as an employee in this speech laboratory, was provided with the appropriate identity badge and was one of the limited group of employees granted access to the laboratory.

While so employed, appellant was under the direct supervision and authority of the Branch Manager of the Speech Research Laboratory. This branch manager was also known as the Chief Speech Scientist. Over the years of appellant's employment, his relationship with the department head became somewhat informal; however, the branch manager was appellant's immediate superior, and appellant always received all job assignments from the Chief Speech Scientist and was responsible directly to him. Appellant's immediate superior had been associated with the complainant company for many years prior to appellant's employment and, as Chief Speech Scientist, had originally written many of the programs utilized in the research conducted in the speech laboratory. Part of appellant's primary job assignment was to modify or convert certain portions of those original programs so as to accomplish a specific result, such as producing sounds from a speaker rather than a visual output displayed on a video screen, on receipt of an oral command. The final product, while perhaps producing a different result, was primarily made up of the basic original program that had been previously developed and carefully preserved as confidential by the complainant company.

These programs were stored in a memory bank of a computer system in the speech laboratory. Appellant was allowed access to these programs through a code or password specifically assigned to him. The password or code assigned to an employee in the laboratory was personal to that employee and was assigned only if their job duties required access to the information and any of those confidential programs stored in the memory bank. Essentially, access was permitted on a "need to know basis" as it related to their duties. Only by the proper use of his assigned password or code could appellant withdraw information from a memory bank and into a computer terminal. Appellant could also call data from the memory bank into a computer terminal located off of the complainant's premises via telephone modem, with the right kind of computer equipment and the use of his personal password. On certain occasions, persons from outside the company were assigned a guest/user password or code so as to allow access to the computer within the laboratory. This decision and assignment, however, was made by persons within the company other than appellant, and appellant was not consulted or involved in such a decision.

As was customary with all laboratory employees, appellant had a "directory" designated as his and identified as such. Appellant's work product was saved or stored under this directory in the memory bank of the computer in the speech laboratory. Appellant also could, and did, store other data, programs and information in this same directory, some of which was personal to him. The speech laboratory computer equipment had the capability of receiving from, sending to, or copying to another medium, such as magnetic tape, any information stored in the memory when the appropriate instructions or commands were entered. Whenever a computer memory was accessed, the date, time, and identification of the user and the terminal was automatically logged into the memory. Appellant was experienced and very sophisticated in the use of this equipment and was a top level employee in the laboratory, working at a computer terminal regularly on a full time basis.

Appellant resigned his position with the complainant company to take a position as a vice-president with another company that also engaged in voice recognition and speech synthesis research and development. Although this new company was much smaller in overall size and scope and said to be utilizing a different method or system, the new employer was in fact a direct competitor of the complainant in the area of voice control technology. Appellant's background, knowledge, and experience in this field was a major factor in making the new job available to him.

Over a period of a few years, several other speech laboratory personnel had left the complainant's employment to take positions with this same new employer, primarily because their specialized knowledge in this field gave them unique qualifications that competitive companies would seek out. One such employee had occasion to see some information stored in the memory of the computer he was using on his new job that he believed he recognized and he thought belonged to his former employer, the complainant. Feeling something was amiss, this employee contacted complainant's company security to report what he had seen. (This informant acknowledged that he felt that he had been wrongfully terminated previously by the complainant and that he hoped that bringing this information to the complainant's attention would help get his old job back.) A series of meetings between security personnel and the informant took place and during these meetings, additional information was delivered. The informant was also recruited to act as a "mole" to search his employer's premises and equipment for further information or like material. The mole took several photos of various offices and their contents and made copies of some documents he thought belonged to the complainant and contained sensitive material. One of the photographs taken in appellant's office revealed a shelf containing one or more magnetic tapes of the type used to store computer data. Although the contents of the tapes were unknown at that time, at least one of them bore a label with the names of certain programs which the mole recognized from his former employment and job assignments with the complainant.

The information from the informant was passed along through the complainant's corporate structure, and an internal investigation within the speech laboratory took place. From the automatic entries made when the computer memory was accessed, the complainant determined that only a few hours before appellant left complainant's employ, a copy of the entire directory assigned to appellant was made onto a magnetic tape by someone using the personal access code assigned to the appellant. Imbedded within that directory and the information copied onto that tape from that directory were programs identified by the complainant to be trade secrets. Among these were the five programs that were ultimately made the subject of this indictment.

* * *

Appellant does not dispute the fact that he did copy the directory that had a plethora of data recorded on it, or that the programs on the indictment were included, or that he took the tape with him when he left complainant's employ.

TRADE SECRET

Section 31.05(b)(2) of the Texas Penal Code, entitled "Theft of Trade Secrets," provides:

> A person commits an offense if, without the owner's effective consent, he knowingly makes a copy of an article representing a trade secret.

Section 31.05 defines a trade secret in subsection (a):

> "Trade secret" means the whole or any part of any scientific or technical information, design, process, procedure, formula or improvement that has value and that the owner has taken measures to prevent from becoming available to persons other than those selected by the owner to have access for limited purposes.

To be a "trade secret" within the clear meaning of this section, the information, design, process, procedure, formula or improvement must not only be a secret, but must also be generally unavailable to the public and it must give one who uses it an advantage over competitors that do not know of or use the trade secret. A fair reading of this section suggests that to qualify as a "trade secret", the article in question must meet a three prong test:

1) Be all or part of scientific or technical information,

2) Be of value to the owner,

3) Be protected by measures taken by the owner from access, except those selected by the owner for limited purposes.

Appellant does not contest the first two prongs of the test, that is, the fact that the programs are a "part of any scientific or technical information * * * that has value. * * *" Rather, he asserts in his first point of error that the evidence is insufficient to support the third prong: He contends that the complainant failed to designate the computer programs as trade secrets or prevent access to the computer where this information was stored; therefore, the complainant did not take measures to prevent access to them. Appellant argues that the programs in question were not trade secrets at the time he made the copy, or, if they had been, they had lost their status as trade secrets because the complainant had not protected them. Clearly, if an article that is a trade secret becomes known to the community, it loses its status as a trade secret. *Furr's Inc. v. United Specialty Advertising Co.*, 338 S.W.2d 762, 765 (Tex.Civ.App.—El Paso 1960, writ ref'd n.r.e.). However, a limited disclosure to others pledged to secrecy will not destroy the trade secret's status as such. *Metallurgical Indus. Inc. v. Fourtek, Inc.*, 790 F.2d 1195, 1200 (5th Cir.1986). There is no question but that appellant was one of the limited persons that had been granted limited access to this information since his job function required him to work with this data on a regular basis. We must determine, therefore, if the data was ever a trade secret and, if so, whether it had lost its status as such for some reason at the time it was copied by appellant.

Appellant points out that several persons had been granted guest/user codes, including a summer intern who was allowed to utilize the laboratory equipment to write his college thesis. That intern testified, however, that he felt the information and codes entrusted to him were a secret and were not to be disclosed. Appellant argues that access could be gained through use of a telephone modem, but recognizes that it took the right kind of computer and user password to do so. Appellant claims that his superior, the Chief Speech Scientist and Branch Manager of the Speech Research Laboratory, had made a ten minute presentation at a seminar where he discussed the "concepts" involved concerning the series of programs listed on the indictment. Although concepts were briefly discussed, the algorithms used in the creations of the programs were not mentioned or disclosed. Appellant further maintains that certain data base programs were released to the National Bureau of Standards to aid them in establishing an industry standard. These programs were unrelated to those in the indictment. Appellant further argues that data was released to a university engaged in similar research. This release was only under a nondisclosure agreement. Appellant insists that the internal procedures manual provided to all employees set out the manner that trade secrets were to be identified and handled and these programs were not so identified. Significantly, the basic programs from which the items in question were derived were, in fact, listed in the Trade Secret Register kept by the complainant. While appellant points out certain areas that he feels show complainant's weaknesses in the security of the information, he presents no evidence to suggest that any of the series of programs in the indictment had ever been released to anyone outside the speech laboratory. The complainant vigorously and steadfastly denied that any of these programs and the algorithms had ever been published or given out to anyone and that none of complainant's speech recognition, speech synthesis, speaker verification, or voice verification software had ever been released nor had anyone ever been authorized to do so. Finally, appellant admitted that he had personally told fellow employees that such programs had not been given out.

It is an axiom in our jurisprudence that when interpreting a statute, we should start with the statute itself. A statute must generally be construed according to the fair import of its terms, and with a view to effect its objects and to promote justice. We must assume that the Legislature meant the section to be read as it was written and we cannot create an offense by enlarging on, or inserting or deleting words, nor should we do so by giving false meaning to its words. *State ex rel. Vance v. Hatten,* 600 S.W.2d 828, 830 (Tex.Crim.App.1980).

Turning to the statute, the pertinent portion reads "*that the owner has taken measures to prevent from becoming available to persons other than those selected by the owner.* * * * " This statute does not deal with the degree or extent to which an owner must go to protect a secret but simply specifies that for it to be an offense to copy information without the owners' permission, the owner must have taken some measures to protect the information from unauthorized disclosure. Although appellant's attack is directed more toward the type, degree, or extent of the measures taken to protect the data than it is toward the question of whether the " * * * owner has taken measures * * * " we, nevertheless, will treat this point as one of factual insufficiency and address the record under that standard.

The relevant question is whether, after viewing the evidence in the light most favorable to the prosecution, a rational trier of fact could find the essential elements of the offense beyond a reasonable doubt. *Jackson v. Virginia,* 443 U.S. 307 at 319, 99 S.Ct. 2781 at 2789, 61 L.Ed.2d 560 (1979). This standard is applicable to both direct and circumstantial evidence cases. *Taylor v. State,* 684 S.W.2d 682, 684 (Tex.Crim.App.1984).

This voluminous record is replete with evidence detailing the strict security measures taken by the complainant to prevent any and all information emanating from the speech laboratory from falling into the hands of unauthorized persons. All employees, including appellant, signed nondisclosure agreements when hired. This was a necessary condition of the employment of the appellant. Various applications of identification badges were provided to all employees and these badges had to be displayed at all times and places while on or about the premises. Different levels of security were applied to different areas and the badges carried features to delineate whether a particular employee was cleared to enter a particular area. The full time security guards, regular employees, receptionist, and so forth, were required to remain alert for anyone they might observe without a proper identification badge for a particular section or area. Visitors were subjected to sign-in procedures and were provided escorts and special identification badges. The entry gates were manned by security guards. Security guards were stationed in selected locations, and closed circuit television monitors were used throughout the building. Entry to the speech laboratory was limited to only a very small segment of the total employee population, and was contained in a separate wing or building and isolated with security doors from other areas. Within this area, all print-outs or hard copies of any data were kept put away. Night time security checks were made for data left out on desks. In the event any documents were seen by security personnel during routine off-hour inspections, they were put away and the incident made the subject of a report. Appellant was assigned a password or access code which allowed limited access to some information stored in the computer memory but other data stored in restricted directories was not available. Any access at all required certain code clearance or password information to be given before the computer would respond. A highly confidential Trade Secret Register was kept and maintained as a permanent record in the legal department which contained reference to the "speech processing" programs being utilized in the laboratory. Employees in the laboratory were given an admonition that they were to protect any software programs being used, developed, or being researched by the laboratory. In addition, an "exit" interview was conducted with any employee whose job involved sensitive proprietary and confidential information by a member of the Legal Department staff for the specific purpose of re-emphasizing their non-disclosure responsibility upon termination.

We conclude that these facts are sufficient for this jury, as a rational trier of fact, to find beyond a reasonable doubt that these elaborate security precautions were taken by the owner/complainant to protect its information, that such information was secret and intended by the owner to remain so. Having determined that the evidence is sufficient to meet the test of "measures taken by the owner to protect", we hold the programs listed in the indictment were trade secrets as defined in Texas Penal Code section 31.05(a). Appellant's point of error number one is overruled.

Knowledge

In his second point of error, appellant maintains that the evidence is insufficient to prove that he "knowingly" made copies of trade secrets. Appellant having admitted that he made the copy, and our having previously held the items to be trade secrets, we then come to the question of whether appellant "knew" the items were trade secrets when he made the copy, thus that he acted knowingly as set out in Texas Penal Code section 31.05(b)(2). The necessary culpable mental state is described in Texas Penal Code section 6.03(b) thusly:

> A person acts knowingly, or with knowledge, with respect to the nature of his conduct or to circumstances surrounding his conduct when he is aware of the nature of his conduct or that the circumstances exist. A person acts knowingly, or with knowledge, with respect to a result of his conduct when he is aware that his conduct is reasonably certain to cause the result.

TEX.PENAL CODE ANN. (Vernon 1974).

Evidence in regard to a culpable mental state must be viewed in the light most favorable to the verdict. *See Humason v. State,* 728 S.W.2d 363 (Tex.Crim.App.1987). Absent a confession, proof that appellant acted knowingly must be based on circumstantial evidence. *Dillon v. State,* 574 S.W.2d 92, 94 (Tex.Crim.App.1978). Being mindful of the above and the standard of review of factual insufficiency claims as set out above, we again turn to the record.

Because appellant had been a full time, high level employee in the speech laboratory for twelve years, he had been subjected to the elaborate security precautions implemented by his employer every day. The controlled physical access to the plant through the use of guards, employee identification badges, visitor escorts and special sign-in procedures, confidential materials kept locked up or destroyed when no longer needed, closed circuit television monitoring, and the necessity of the regular use of secret identity codes on the computer all served as a constant reminder of the restricted environment in which appellant worked. Appellant signed a nondisclosure agreement when he was hired. He discussed the need for secrecy and the nature of the confidential aspects of their work with his immediate superior and fellow employees on a regular basis during his employment. Periodic staff meetings were held where the nature and progress of their work was discussed and the subject of much of the discussions was the secret and confidential aspects of work appellant and his fellow employees were doing. The value of work and how it did or would affect the complainant's competitive position in the general market place was a significant factor discussed in the regular staff meetings.

Appellant, during his testimony at trial, stated that it would have taken hours to have gone through the numerous programs and data in his directory to selectively pick out items for copying, so in the interest of time, he intentionally entered the commands that would copy all files in the directory, knowing that all files would be copied. He further stated that he had worked on the files that were in his directory and was familiar with them and what they were, but that he did not consider them to be trade secrets; that they were not so marked or designated in the computer and that they were readily accessible to him.

Significantly, appellant not only copied his own entire directory, but also copied one other directory called the "speech utility" directory. He did so very close to his last day on the job, and used his secret identity code to gain access to all of this data for copying. In his exit interview, which took place as one of the last official events on the job, he signed a document titled Trade Secret Listing for Termination of Employment where he acknowledged that his nondisclosure responsibility and the confidentiality of his work was discussed. Appellant testified he felt he had a right to copy and take anything he was interested in because he never had any intention of using this information. The issue of whether the data and information in question was wrongfully used is not before us. There was also testimony that during the time appellant was in the employ of the new company, he was heard to make reference to items belonging to the complainant as the "stolen data base" and the "stolen files," on a periodic basis.

We hold this evidence is sufficient to support the finding by the jury that appellant knowingly made copies of protected programs that were of value to his employer. Appellant's second point of error is overruled.

* * *

AFFIRMED.

Chapter VIII

TAXING INTELLECTUAL PROPERTY

A. LOCAL PROPERTY TAXES ON SOFTWARE

State taxation of hardware is reasonably well settled, with all states taxing hardware. The tax treatment of software, however, is in a state of flux. Many jurisdictions impose an annual net worth tax or personal property tax on various types of personal property. Generally, the annual property tax or net worth tax is imposed on tangible personal property, but not imposed on intangible personal property. The battleground is whether software is tangible or intangible. The following 1986 *Strayer* case is an example of this tangible/intangible software dispute.

MATTER OF PROTEST OF STRAYER

Supreme Court of Kansas, 1986.
716 P.2d 588, 239 Kan. 136.

LOCKETT, JUSTICE:

Taxpayer appeals the decision of the Graham County District Court upholding a ruling of the Kansas Board of Tax Appeals which determined that computer software was taxable as tangible personal property.

The appellant, Thomas D. Strayer, is a certified public accountant. In November of 1981, Strayer purchased a computer from Computax Systems, Inc. Additionally, Strayer executed a licensing agreement with Computax at a cost of $7,010. The agreement provided for the use of certain computer software programs. Annual renewal of the license agreement cost one-half of the initial fee. The agreement required Computax to update the software as needed during each year and to provide other services. The bulk of the annual fee paid for the use of an income tax preparation software program.

Under the agreement, the software program and later updates are shipped by Computax on eight-inch floppy disks. Since the disks wear out through usage and are subject to damage, Strayer may make as many copies of these disks as he needs before returning the originals to Computax.

In 1982, Strayer listed the computer for personal property tax assessment, but did not list the software programs. The Graham County Assessor asked to see invoices regarding the purchase, noted the initial fee charged for the software and insisted that the software was subject to personal property tax assessment. Personal property taxes were assessed, using the initial licensing fee paid as the market value. Strayer paid that portion of the 1982 taxes attributable to the software under protest and filed an application for refund of those taxes with the Board of Tax Appeals.

The Board of Tax Appeals determined that computer software was tangible personal property, subject to personal property taxation, and that since title to the software remained with Computax, Computax was liable for the personal property taxes. Computax's license agreement with the program utilizer requires him to reimburse the company for the tax assessed, and to challenge any taxation.

A statement of background is necessary for a general understanding of the technical aspects of the case. A functioning computer is a combination of hardware and computer programs, sometimes called "software." The electronic data processing industry is made up of a number of companies which offer numerous types of products and/or services to users of electronic data processing equipment. The data processing equipment is often referred to as computer hardware. Computer programs are the instructions which make the data processing equipment perform tasks and include "operational programs," which orchestrate the basic functions of the computer, and "application programs," which provide the particularized instructions adapted for specialized programs.

Computer software was traditionally viewed as an integral part of the computer hardware unit until 1969, when IBM announced that it would price its hardware separately from its software and services. Due to the uncertain nature of the software and the inexperience and lack of skill of both taxpayers and state assessment agencies in classifying software, local taxing authorities and taxpayers have been in conflict since that date over whether software constitutes tangible personal property or intangible intellectual property. Annot., 82 A.L.R.3d 606 § 2.

Following the IBM announcement, the Internal Revenue Service promulgated Rev.Proc. 69–21 § 3, 1969–2 C.B. 303, which provided guidelines for IRS agents in the tax treatment of computer software. Rev.Proc. 69–21 stated:

> "The costs of developing software (whether or not the particular software is patented or copyrighted) in many respects so closely resemble the kind of research and experimental expenditures that fall within the purview of Section 174 of the Internal Revenue Code of 1954 as to

warrant accounting treatment similar to that accorded such costs under that section."

Section 174 provides that a taxpayer may elect to treat development costs as current expenses or as a capital expenditure. Rev.Proc. 69–21 § 4, however, pointedly identifies all software as intangible. Note, The Revolt Against the Property Tax on Software: An Unnecessary Conflict Growing Out of Unbundling, 9 Suffolk U.L.Rev. 118, 131 (1975).

The taxpayer here, relying on the case law from our sister states, contends that computer software is intangible personal property and not subject to the Kansas personal property tax placed upon tangible personal property. The County contends that, under Kansas statutes, computer software is not classified as intangible property and is, therefore, taxable as tangible personal property.

Almost all states which have considered the nature of computer software have found that the software is intangible personal property. This is generally based on the idea that the information contained on the software is the product being sold, that this information can be transmitted in many forms, including over the telephone, and that the information often becomes outdated and must be replaced. Only one state has found that software is tangible personal property, but the appellate court noted it could not determine from the record how to apportion the purchase price between operational and application functions of the software.

One of the first cases discussing this issue was *District of Columbia v. Universal Computer Assoc., Inc.,* 465 F.2d 615 (D.C.Cir.1972). The District of Columbia Tax Court had held that certain computer software represented intangible values and was not subject to personal property tax. The software consisted of two sets of punched cards, one set containing the standard program developed by IBM to run the computer and one set containing a special tax program. The material of the punched cards themselves was of insignificant value. It was for the intangible value of the information stored on the cards that Universal was charged. How the information was created, who had title, and how the information was put on the computer—all supported the court's conclusion.

In *Commerce Union Bank v. Tidwell,* 538 S.W.2d 405 (Tenn.1976), the State argued that the purchase of consumer software was analogous to the purchase or lease of a motion picture film. The court distinguished the computer software from motion picture films, noting that the latter constituted an end product without which the labor, skills and thought processes which went into its creation would prove meaningless. Absent the film, the taxpayer had nothing. The computer tapes and cards, however, were not a finished product. It was the information they contained which constituted the valuable resource.

In *First National Bank v. Dep't of Revenue,* 85 Ill.2d 84, 51 Ill.Dec. 667, 421 N.E.2d 175 (1981), the Illinois court said that the test to determine whether property is tangible is whether the tape is the substance of the transaction or merely incidental to a service. The Illinois bank purchased the software as a means of programming its computer so that it could perform functions the bank needed to have performed. The tapes were certainly not the only medium through which the information could be transferred. In this way, the tapes differ from a movie film, a phonograph record or a book, whereby the media used are the only practicable ways of preserving those articles. Thus, while those articles and the tapes are similar in that they physically represent the transfer of ideas or artistic processes, a more significant distinction is that those articles are inseparable from the ideas or processes, whereas computer programs are separable from the tapes. Bryant & Mather, *Property Taxation of Computer Software,* 18 N.Y.L.F. 59, 67 (1972). It was not the tapes but the information which was the substance of the transaction.

Missouri reached a similar conclusion in *James v. Tres Computer Service, Inc.,* 642 S.W.2d 347 (Mo.1982). It concluded that the tapes used for the programs were not the ultimate object of the sale and that it was not necessary that the information purchased be put on tape for it to be transmitted to the user. It said that the presence of the data on the tapes is merely an incidental physical commingling of the tangible tapes and the intangible information which is actually the subject of the transaction. It concluded that if the tapes serve only to convey the computer data and then are discarded, the value of the professional services is not considered taxable as tangible personal property.

In *Maccabees v. Treasury Dep't,* 122 Mich.App. 660, 332 N.W.2d 561 (1983), the court noted, in holding that the software was intangible personal property, that any tangible personal property attendant to software is inconsequential because software can be entered into a computer via telephone lines; communications media, such as punched cards and tapes, are transitory and are destroyed or reused after the software is entered into a computer; the software program exists as imperceivable binary pulses; and the tangible communications media has little or no value apart from the program. It said the focus of the transaction is on the personalized service of the software vendors, an intangibles transaction.

Alabama held that computer software was intangible personal property in *State v. Central Computer Services, Inc.,* 349 So.2d 1156 (Ala.Civ.App.1977). The court concluded that it was the knowledge, the information contained on the tapes, which was the main characteristic of the software, and such information was intangible property.

Maryland is the only state to find that computer software is tangible personal property. In *Greyhound Computer v. St. Dep't,* 271 Md. 674, 320 A.2d 52 (1974), 82 A.L.R.3d 597, the court considered whether computer software—programs, educational services, and systems engineering services—which had been "bundled" in the cost of computers purchased by Greyhound and another company from IBM and leased to others was tangible personal property.

The State's major contention in that case was that even if software were severable from the hardware and even if a separate price could be established for it, these items still constituted tangible personal property since the value of an article consisted, in large part, of the cost and skill used in producing it and not primarily of the cost of the material from which it was made. The court could not determine from the record what portion of the purchase price was attributable to such of the software that was "systems software" or what portion was attributable to "applications software."

California has taken a different approach to the problem. The state legislature has amended the state's tax code so that software is divided into two types—systems software and application software. Cal.Rev. & Tax Code §§ 995, 995.2 (West 1986 Supp.). Only the basic operational programs are taxed on the theory that taxation of application programs would be detrimental to research and an expansion of business activity within the state.

The power to levy taxes is inherent in the power to govern, but the exercise of that power is dependent upon the existence of legislation designating the kinds of property to be taxed and nothing is taxable unless clearly within the taxing statute. Tax statutes are penal, and thus must be strictly construed in favor of the taxpayer. The liberal construction rule for statutes is subject to the principle that all rules of statutory construction are merely for the purpose of ascertaining the intention of the legislature as expressed in the statute. A liberal construction of a statute does not permit the courts to read into a statute something that does not come within the wording used in the statute. But, statutes must be construed with reason, considering the practicalities of the subject matter addressed.

Using the rules of statutory construction, can we determine from the Kansas statutes whether the legislature intended computer software programs to be taxed as personal property or fall within the definition of intangible property?

K.S.A. 79–101 provides for the taxation of all property in the state. K.S.A.1985 Supp. 79–201 describes what property is exempt from taxation. Generally, the legislature has the authority to provide that property other than that named in the Kansas Constitution may be exempt from taxation, but this exemption must have a public purpose and be designed to promote the public welfare. *Topeka Cemetery Ass'n v. Schnellbacher,* 218 Kan. 39, 542 P.2d 278 (1975). Computer software is not included in this listing and therefore must be either: (1) tangible personal property subject to the personal property tax; (2) intangible property; or (3) a mixture of personal property and intangible property, depending upon the character or function of the particular software program.

K.S.A. 79–102 defines personal property to include every "tangible" thing other than real property which is the subject of ownership. The legislature has not defined "tangible." K.S.A. 79–301, 79–303, 79–304 and 79–306 discuss the listing of "tangible" personal property for the purposes of taxation.

"Tangible" is not defined in the statutory sections dealing with personal property taxes. It is defined in K.S.A.1985 Supp. 79–3602(f), the sales tax section, as "corporeal personal property." Corporeal is not defined in the statutes. Black's Law Dictionary 310 (5th ed. 1979), defines corporeal as:

> "A term descriptive of such things as have an objective, material existence; perceptible by the senses of sight and touch; possessing a real body."

Under the intangibles tax law, K.S.A.1985 Supp. 12–1,101, intangibles are defined as "money, notes and other evidence of debt." K.S.A. 12–1,102(a) defines money to include gold and silver coin, United States treasury notes, and other forms of currency. Notes and other evidence of debt are defined in 12–1, 102(b) to include stock certificates, notes, bonds, debentures, claims secured by deed, liquidated claims and demands for money, accounts receivable, and all written instruments, contracts or other writings evidencing, calling for, or fixing or showing a fixed obligation. There are other forms of intangible property, such as good will, franchises, patents, copyrights and trademarks which are not listed within the statutes.

K.S.A. 84–9–106 of the Uniform Commercial Code defines "general intangibles" as "any personal property (including things in action) other than goods, accounts, chattel paper, documents, instruments and money." The Kansas Comment 1983 under 84–9–106 defines two key types of "intangibles." The term "general intangibles" continues as a catch-all to pick up collateral which does not fit any other Article 9 category. It includes, for example, a tax refund, *computer software,* patent rights, trademarks, goodwill, a vendor's interest in an installment land contract, certain partnership interests in commercial real estate, and other offbeat intangible collateral. "When the secured party is not sure how to categorize collateral, he should assume that it qualifies as a general intangible, and file accordingly." K.S.A. 84–9–106, Kansas Comment 1983.

For the most part, software has come into existence since the tax statutes in this state were written. The fact that the legislature has designated that certain property be taxed under the intangibles tax does not mean that there are no other types of intangible property or that all other types of property must thus be tangible. Whether computer software should be treated as tangible personal property subject to the personal property tax or as intangible personal property not subject to the tax must be determined with reason, considering the practicalities of the subject matter addressed.

Using the guidelines for statutory construction, we determine that under the tax statutes, software programs which constitute the operational programs, without which a computer cannot operate, have a value that is to be considered an essential portion of the computer hardware and are therefore taxable as tangible personal property in conjunction with the hardware. Application programs, those which are particularized instructions adopted for special programs, are intangible property not subject to the personal property tax for tangible property.

It is held that the tax program obtained by the taxpayer under the licensing agreement was composed of particularized instruction for the computation of taxes, and thus was an application software program. Application programs are intangible property and not subject to the personal property tax on tangible property.

Since we have determined that the tax program is an application software program, *i.e.,* intangible property, we need not discuss other issues raised by the taxpayer.

The decision of the district court is reversed.

B. LOCAL SALES OR USE TAXES ON COMPUTER SERVICES

The first item to consider is the difference between a state sales tax and a use tax. A sales tax is imposed on a retail sale of tangible personal property. The retailer is responsible for collecting the tax, which is passed on to the consumers, and remitting the tax to the state in exchange for the privilege of doing business within the state. States, by statute or regulation, may exempt certain transactions from sales tax. The more common exceptions are sales of services and sales for resale, which are taxed on the sale to the ultimate consumer.

A use tax is levied on the consumer who has "used, stored or consumed tangible personal property in the state." This occurs most often in situations where the customer orders merchandise and has it shipped from an out-of-state retailer. If the out-of-state retailer does not do business within the consumer's state, the out-of-state retailer may not be responsible for collecting and remitting a tax on the sale to the customer's state. The states recognize this could provide an unfair advantage to an out-of-state retailer and, therefore, impose a compensating use tax on the consumer. As with property taxation of software, the imposition of a sales or use tax on computer software turns on whether software is deemed to be tangible personal property.

Comptroller of the Treasury v. Equitable Trust Company is an early case examining this tangible/intangible debate.

COMPTROLLER OF THE TREASURY v. EQUITABLE TRUST COMPANY

Court of Appeals of Maryland. 1983.
296 Md. 459, 464 A.2d 248.

RODOWSKY, JUDGE.

This is a sales tax case. It involves computer programs in the business data processing field. At issue is how the computer program license transactions presented here are to be conceptualized under the statute which reaches sales of "any tangible personal property." Md. Code (1957, 1980 Repl.Vol.), Art. 81, § 324(f). Did the taxpayer, a computer user, acquire from the proprietors of canned, transactional computer programs

1. intangible personal property, namely, the right to use the programs, with copies of the programs transferred by the medium of magnetic tapes; or

2. intangible personal property, namely, "knowledge" or "information," which was transferred to the taxpayer by the temporary medium of magnetic tape; or

3. tangible personal property, namely, magnetic tapes which had been enhanced in value by the copies of the programs coded thereon?

Alternatives 1 and 2 result in no tax. An *amicus,* Data Processing Management Association, has raised the first alternative. The taxpayer, Equitable Trust Company (Equitable), emphasizes the second analysis. The Comptroller urges the third position, which we adopt.

As of September 16, 1974, Equitable entered into a written contract, delineated "License Agreement," with Auxton Computer Enterprises, Incorporated (AUXCO). AUXCO granted Equitable a nontransferable and nonexclusive right to use a program, the "AUXCO Project Management System," at a one-time price of $20,000. There was no termination date. Equitable covenanted not to publish or disclose to any third person any information concerning the program and not to copy the program tapes or documentation except for internal use. Paragraph 10 of the agreement in part provided that "[l]egal title to the System shall remain with AUXCO, and [Equitable] agrees that AUXCO may repossess the System" upon breach by Equitable of its obligations. This program was acquired for use by Equitable's systems and programming people in tracking project performance.

By a "License Agreement" of December 13, 1974 with PACE Applied Technology, Inc. (PACE), Equitable acquired the right to use two PACE programs in perpetuity. One was the "KOMAND Data Acquisition System" for the price of $10,800. The other was the "KOMAND Resource Billing System" for a price of $4,365. The agreement placed restrictions on Equitable's disclosing PACE's proprietary information. The PACE programs were described in testimony as an accounting system which would allow Equitable to know exactly how much its computer and peripheral equipment were used for running specific applications, such as the main deposit program or the time deposit program.

During an audit in 1975, the Comptroller assessed sales tax against Equitable based upon the prices paid pursuant to the foregoing agreements. That assessment was affirmed by a hearing officer in the Sales Tax Division whose decision was affirmed by the Maryland Tax Court. On appeal to the Baltimore City Court (now the Circuit Court for Baltimore City), the assessment was abated. That court concluded as a matter of law that the dominant purpose or essence of the transactions was the programs and that computer programs are intangible. The Comptroller appealed to the Court of Special Appeals. We issued the writ of certiorari on our own motion prior to consideration of the matter by the intermediate appellate court.

1

Before the legal contentions can be considered, some fundamentals should be stated. A computer is a machine. It does not think. It is designed to execute predetermined instructions. Ultimately a "program" is a set of such instructions. An "applicational program," as we shall use the term, is a set of instructions that will cause the machine to perform a specific task. An example from the banking field would be a program which listed certain information with respect to each installment loan account for which any payment was delinquent. Unless otherwise specified, "program" as used in this opinion will mean an applicational program.

* * *

The programs involved here are stipulated to be existing, prepackaged programs of general application, called "canned" programs. The stipulation further states:

> The programs assessed were not developed exclusively for use by Equitable but were developed to be sold to many different purchasers. None of the assessment for computer software relates to programs specially designed and developed exclusively for Equitable [, i.e., a custom program].

The advantage to a computer user of a canned program is that the user need not start from the beginning in developing the particular program. Reinventing the wheel is avoided. However, because the developer or proprietor is marketing a program for use by many different organizations of the same general type, and possibly for use on machines of various manufacture, there will ordinarily be a need for a particular user to make some adaptations in a canned program to meet the specifics of that user's situation. Equitable made some adaptations, but they are not described in evidence.

Each program received by Equitable was delivered to it on magnetic tape. This means that the proprietor of the program made a copy of it, directly or indirectly, from a master which was in some physical form. The physical form of the program copies, as delivered, was a coded series of magnetic impulses. Each code was readable by Equitable's computer and seems to have been in machine instructions. Equitable loaded the program copy tape into computer memory and started the process of adaptation. At that point, Equitable had no further need for the particular copy delivered from the standpoint of instructing its computer. That copy, however, was retained by Equitable.

In order for a program to instruct computer execution, the magnetic tape copy of the program is loaded into memory. "In loading a program, nothing is taken from the storage media and nothing is added to the memory; rather, the user's computer reads the storage media and *rearranges its memory* to create a corresponding pattern of magnetic impulses." Note, *Software and Sales Taxes: The Illusory Intangible,* 63 B.U.L.Rev. 181, 189 (1983) (the B.U. Note) (Emphasis in original. Footnote omitted.). *See also* Note, *Software Taxation: A Critical Reevaluation of the Notion of Intangibility,* 1980 B.Y.U.L.Rev. 859, 871–72. The process of making changes to a program also takes place while the program is in memory. Equitable did not store the reproductions of the subject programs, or any adaptations thereof, in memory when they were not in use. They were stored peripherally. On any day when adaptations were made to a program, Equitable represents that it produced at least two tapes of the program, as changed. One was for storage on the computer premises, and the other was for storage off premises.

2

The Comptroller's position is that Equitable acquired tapes containing program copies. Magnetic tapes are tangible personal property. Acquisition of such tapes under the license agreements is a sale, because Art. 81, § 324(d) provides that "sale" means "any transaction whereby title or possession, or both, of tangible personal property is or is to be transferred by any means whatsoever for a consideration including rental, lease, or license to use. * * *"

* * *

3

The starting point for our legal inquiry is the effect of the license agreements. There is no evidence that the subject programs are patented, or are part of any patent, even if we assume that programs can be patented. Nor is there any evidence of copyright. Indeed the "license agreements" involved here were made years prior to the Software and Copyright Amendment of 1980, Pub.L. 96–517, 94 Stat. 3015, 3028 (codified at 17 U.S.C. §§ 101, 117). One purpose of the license agreements is to protect, by reliance on the law of trade secrets, the economic interest of the proprietors in the expression of the programs and in any ideas embodied therein. The proprietors do not want some pirates to be the ones making money from the proprietors' having developed the programs. Furnishing Equitable with a complete copy of each program on tape destroyed, as to Equitable, any secrecy in program expression. With a program copy on tape, Equitable was in a position to make further copies and to distribute them commercially, unless Equitable were contractually restricted.

Space Aero viewed breach of contract to be one basis for the law of trade secrets, in addition to abuse of confidence or impropriety in the means of procurement. 238 Md. at 113, 208 A.2d at 84. Here Equitable was willing to pay for copies of the programs on magnetic tape which the proprietors were willing fully to disclose to Equitable, if Equitable contractually restricted its use. Consequently, the licenses involved here do not grant intangible rights from the proprietors to Equitable. The licenses simply erect contractual limitations on the use which Equitable might otherwise make of the statutorily unprotected program copies it acquired by proper means.

But while neither "license agreement" purports to transfer absolute legal title to anything, not even to the specific magnetic tapes used to deliver the program copies, Equitable has the right to use the specific tapes. This is a sale of the tapes under Art. 81, § 324(d).

4

Equitable's principal argument is that this Court should conceptually sever the program copy contained on the magnetic tape from the tangible tape itself. The argument is that the transaction should be viewed as operating on two levels, one the transfer of intangible knowledge or information and the other the delivery of a tangible tape. To have a scalpel for this legal surgery, it would be necessary for us to adopt as part of Maryland sales tax law a principle that the buyer's predominant purpose for a transaction controls the classification of the acquisition as either tangible or intangible.

Quotron Systems v. Comptroller, 287 Md. 178, 411 A.2d 439 (1980) recognized a predominant purpose test as one of several factors in determining use tax applicability to the type of transaction presented there. That taxpayer undertook concurrently to render two types of interrelated performances. One was to maintain and continuously to update a computerized data bank of economic information, such as the selling prices of securities, which its customers could randomly access through remote terminals. The other was to install Quotron-owned hardware, including the remote terminals, on customers' premises for their use in requesting and receiving electronic transmissions of the economic data. We held that the first analytical step was to characterize the performances as a single, overall function, either rental of equipment or the provision of services. *Id.* at 186, 411 A.2d at 443. The dominant purpose was to obtain services and not to rent hardware. Based on that factor, on the taxpayer's retention of control over the hardware, and on the fact that Quotron's hardware could not be obtained without subscribing to the service, we concluded that the transaction was the provision of services. *Id.* at 188, 411 A.2d at 444.

This approach is quite similar to that which we have used to determine whether a contract of sale is one for goods or for services under Art. 2 of the Uniform Commercial Code, where the performance involves both. See *Anthony Pools v. Sheehan,* 295 Md. 285, 455 A.2d 434 (1983); *Burton v. Artery Company,* 279 Md. 94, 367 A.2d 935 (1977). *Quotron* did not say that the dominant purpose of obtaining data made the subject of the contract intangible because information is intangible.

The rule of *Quotron* has been implicitly applied in the case at bar on an aspect which is not disputed by Equitable. In addition to providing program copies on tape, each proprietor agreed to furnish certain installation services. AUXCO also contracted to furnish a limited amount of training within the fixed contract price. Equitable does not argue, however, that these services predominate. Any intellectual effort rendered in the past in developing the programs is now embodied in the products for sale, the copies of the programs. That effort is reflected in the price for the copies just as engineering costs of a model of a television receiver are part of the selling price of a particular unit of that model.

We have no doubt that the dominant purpose of the subject transactions was to obtain a copy of the programs. But there are problems in adopting a dominant purpose test in order conceptually to sever information or data from the physical medium employed to deliver a copy of the information, and next to declare that the information predominates, so as thereby to classify the transaction as a sale of intangible property. One factor used in determining the dominant purpose is the admittedly insignificant value of a blank magnetic tape when compared to the price paid for a program copy on tape. But § 324(i) defines "price" to mean

> the aggregate value in money * * * promised to be paid or delivered by a purchaser to a vendor in the consummation and complete performance of a retail sale without any deduction therefrom on account of the cost of the property sold, cost of materials used, labor or service cost, or any other expense whatsoever.

While Equitable points out that the question of price is not reached unless it is first determined that property sold is tangible, the legislative policy embraced in the definition of price runs contrary to the conceptual severing of the insignificant blank tape from the valuable program copy superimposed thereon as magnetic impulses.

A second concern is the precedent established for apparently comparable transactions. If the dominant purpose is to obtain knowledge, information or data which thereby results in severing the dominant purpose object from the physical medium of transfer, the analogy to books, motion picture films, video display discs, phonorecords and music tapes immediately comes to mind. In sales of the latter, the purchaser's dominant purpose ordinarily is to obtain the knowledge, information or data thereby conveyed. While the book is in human readable form, the other media are machine readable. A purchase of any of these information conveying media is within the imposition of the sales tax as tangible personal property. Such transactions escape taxation only if there is an applicable statutory exclusion or exemption. These analogies, however, have been argued to other courts which have held that tape copies of programs are intangible. We turn now to a consideration of the rationale of those opinions.

5

* * *

We can take judicial notice, based on modern human experience, that the technology exists for producing a copy of a movie film on disc, of a phonograph record on tape, and of a book on microfiche. We have previously discussed how the program copy is not separated from the tape, when it is used in the computer. See B.U.Note, *supra,* at 188–89. To remove the program copy from the magnetic tape requires that it be over-written, or obliterated in a magnetic field, in the way in which one dictating on tape makes corrections or wipes the tape clean.

* * *

Here the parties have stipulated that the programs are "canned," by which they mean a program other than one originally developed exclusively for the buyer. While the record shows that adaptations were made to the programs acquired by Equitable, Equitable does not contend that services rendered to Equitable by the proprietors were of sufficient magnitude to classify either subject transaction as a purchase of services under the rule of *Quotron, supra.*

6

The tangible-intangible debate with respect to computer software can arise in contexts other than that of state and local sales, use and property taxes. The problem arises under the federal income tax as to eligibility for investment credit and accelerated depreciation. When the hardware manufacturers' segment of the industry unbundled their installation contracts and began separately to state prices for software, it was necessary for the Internal Revenue Service to adopt a position. Basically, bundled software is treated as part of the hardware, while unbundled software is treated as an intangible. *See* Rev.Proc. 69–21, 1969–2 C.B. 303; Rev.Rul. 71–177, 1971–1 C.B. 5; Bigelow, *The Computer And The Tax Collector,* 30 Emory L.J. 357, 362, 365 (1981).

Software, as embodied in tapes and documentation, has been held to be subject to the writ of replevin, over the objection that improved programs developed for the defendant's existing hardware were simply "a body of intangibles, that is, concepts or ideas. * * *" *F & M Schaefer Corp. v. Electronic Data Systems Corp.,* 430 F.Supp. 988, 992 (S.D.N.Y.1977), *aff'd mem.,* 614 F.2d 1286 (2d Cir.1979). *Cf. Institutional Management Corp. v. Translation Systems, Inc.,* 456 F.Supp. 661 (D.Md.1978) (documentation of program replevied, without discussion of tangibility issue).

The severability argument is not a new one in sales tax cases. It has been rejected in a line of cases where those who rent motion picture films from producers have argued that the intellectual property or the right to use the copy transmitted for commercial exhibition should be severed from the tangible copy of the film.

* * *

The movie film cases have been applied to reject the severability argument in the leasing of video tapes for television broadcasting. *See Turner Communications Corp. v. Chilivis,* 239 Ga. 91, 236 S.E.2d 251 (1977). A transfer of film negatives and master recordings used for making audio-visual aids for the training of medical personnel was held subject to sales tax, despite the purchaser's argument that its primary interest was not in the physical objects but in the right to exploit the intellectual products they embodied. *Simplicity Pattern Company, Inc. v. State Board of Equalization,* 27 Cal.3d 900, 167 Cal.Rptr. 366, 615 P.2d 555 (1980). That result, however, was aided by the fact that a statute, enacted too late to apply to the transaction, limited the tax on master sound tapes and records to the amounts paid for tangible elements exclusive of copyrightable, artistic or intangible elements.

* * *

7

From the standpoint of Maryland law, we conclude that the program copy acquisitions by Equitable are subject to sales tax for the following reasons.

We have indicated in parts (1) and (5) of this opinion both certain misconceptions in the technological underpinnings of the decisions holding taped copies to be intangible and our concerns with the apparent departures in reasoning from that usually applied in sales tax cases. Secondly, there is a substantial question whether the decision that set the course for the line of program cases, *Universal Computer, supra,* is consistent with existing Maryland law. That decision rested largely on *Washington Times–Herald* which held the acquisition of cartoon mats to be the purchase of personal services. Md.Code, Art. 81, § 326(dd) exempts, *inter alia,* the sale of mats under circumstances therein set forth. The exemption was added by Chapter 530 of the Acts of 1973. At a minimum, enactment of the exemption indicates a legislative recognition that the sales tax statute could be applied to purchases of mats. Similarly, § 326(k) exempts rentals of motion picture films to persons whose gross receipts are subject to amusement tax. The indication is that, absent the exemption, neither the artistic content nor the right to exhibit the film copy would be severed from the tangible medium and thereby placed beyond the reach of the sales tax act.

Additionally, this Court's discussion of computer software in the context of a bundled installation in the *Greyhound* case leads to the classification of the subject programs as tangible. After noting the

Maryland Tax Court's conclusion that software (programs, educational services and systems engineering services) was not severable from the hardware, we said (271 Md. at 677–78, 320 A.2d at 54–55):

> What is troublesome about [the tax court] approach is the fact that[,] while a substantial portion of the software is of a tangible nature, *i.e.,* punched cards, magnetic tapes, instructions covering operation or applications, [for property tax purposes] the remainder consists of personal services to be rendered after purchase. * * *

This passage reflects awareness of both operational and applicational programs, but makes no distinction between them as to their tangible nature, either in human readable documentation form or in machine readable tape or card form.

* * *

* * * A tape containing a copy of a canned program does not lose its tangible character, because its content is a reproduction of the product of intellectual effort, just as the phonorecord does not become intangible, because it is a reproduction of the product of artistic effort. The price paid for a copy of a canned program reflects the cost of developing the program which the proprietor hopes to recover, with profit, by spreading the cost among its customers. Simply because the canned program on tape is much more expensive than the typical phonorecord, the program tape is not any less tangible.

The phonorecord analogy is directly addressed by Equitable. It says that in the case of the recording "*the intangible information has no value without the tangible record.* * * * " (Emphasis in original.) The same is true of the program copies Equitable acquired in the transactions being taxed. The millions of magnetic impulses which in their precise order have meaning were conveyed to the computer, in the transactions as carried out, by tapes. A meaningful sequence of magnetic impulses cannot float in space. Equitable's argument has merit, if the direct input by keyboard, without documentation, alternative (a service transaction) or the electronic transmission, without documentation, alternative (no tangible carrier) is the form of transaction under consideration. But, because a taxable transaction might have been structured in a nontaxable form, it does not thereby become nontaxable.

It is said each tape is used only once. But a dress pattern purchased at retail and used to make only one dress (or, even if never used) is taxable.

Equitable points to the provisions of the contract under which a delivery copy of a program, if lost or destroyed, will be replaced by the proprietor at minimal or no additional cost. On the other hand, the purchaser of a phonorecord which is lost or destroyed would have to replace it by paying the current price for another copy. This economic fact simply reflects that the proprietors of canned programs are better able to obtain thousands of dollars for a program copy by eliminating the customer's risk of accidental loss. It would be over-reaching to attempt to charge a second retail price when a replacement copy is reproduceable at minor cost.

Finally, Equitable argues that a purchased program "can be and was in fact *severed and exists apart* from the tangible transfer medium. * * * " (Emphasis in original.) As shown above, the copy delivered to Equitable does not become severed in any physical sense from the tape when the tape is used to structure computer memory.

We do not discern any legally significant difference for sales tax purposes between the canned computer program on magnetic tape and music on a phonograph record. As stated in the *National Commission on New Technological Uses of Copyrighted Works, Final Report* at 10 (1978): "Both recorded music and computer programs are sets of information in a form which, when passed over a magnetized head, cause minute currents to flow in such a way that desired physical work is accomplished." In the case of the phonograph record, the sales tax statute in Maryland has never been viewed as conceptually severing the copy of the performance from the tangible carrier. We conclude that the statute does not sever copies of computer programs from the tangible carriers employed in the subject sales.

Judgment of the Circuit Court for Baltimore City reversed. Case remanded to that Court for the entry of a judgment affirming the order of the Maryland Tax Court as to the assessments on computer programs. Costs to be paid by Equitable Trust Company.

FIRST NATIONAL BANK OF SPRINGFIELD v. DEPARTMENT OF REVENUE

Supreme Court of Illinois, 1981.
85 Ill.2d 84, 51 Ill.Dec. 667, 421 N.E.2d 175.

CLARK, JUSTICE:

After an audit was conducted by defendant, the Department of Revenue, a deficiency tax assessment was asserted against the plaintiff, the First National Bank of Springfield. Liability for the deficiencies was alleged to be due under the Use Tax Act (Ill.Rev.Stat.1977, ch. 120, pars. 439.1 to 439.22), the Retailers' Occupation Tax Act (Ill.Rev.Stat. 1977, ch. 120, pars. 440 to 453), and the Municipal Retailers' Occupation Tax Act (Ill.Rev.Stat.1977, ch. 24, par. 8–11–1). The plaintiff protested the assessment and, after a hearing, the Department issued a final deficiency assessment in the amount of $12,131.10, including penalty and interest. The final assessment constituted a final administrative decision. The plaintiff filed a complaint for review of the Department's final assessment in the circuit court of Sangamon County. Subsequently, the parties agreed to reduce the final assessment by the amount of taxes attributable to the sales by plaintiff of repossessed machinery. As a result, the only remaining dispute concerned the taxability under the Use Tax Act of five computer software programs purchased by plaintiff for use in Illinois. The circuit court decided, as a matter law, that the plaintiff's purchase of computer software programs from out-of-state, nonresident suppliers were purchases of intangible personal property and therefore not subject to the use tax. The court set aside the Department's final assessment and entered judgment for the plaintiff. The Department moved for a direct appeal to this court under Rule 302(b) (73 Ill.2d R. 302(b)). We allowed the Department's motion. We affirm.

In the computer industry, computer hardware is the tangible part of the machinery itself. Software denotes the information loaded into the machine and the directions given to the machine (usually through the media of punch cards, discs or magnetic tapes) as to what it is to do and upon what command. Software also may include counseling and expert engineering assistance furnished by the seller of software, as well as flow charts and instruction manuals. (See *Honeywell, Inc. v. Lithonia Lighting, Inc.* (N.D.Ga.1970), 317 F.Supp. 406, 408.) The record in this case indicates that only magnetic tapes were delivered to the bank. There is no mention of any other materials accompanying the tapes.

There are two basic types of software programs. An operational program controls the hardware and actually makes the machine operate. It is fundamental and necessary to the functioning of the hardware. An applicational program is designed to perform specific functions once the programming information is fed into the computer.

In the instant case, the programs involved were applicational. Larry Thomson, an assistant vice president and manager of data processing at the plaintiff bank, testified that the bank purchased five applicational programs from five different sources. The programs purchased were a customer information file from the National City Bank of Cleveland which would enable the bank to compile information from all of the bank's accounting ledgers and make it available at one source. Another program computed installment-loan payments, while a third program computed commercial-loan payments. A fourth program, a programmer's information and index program, is, according to Thomson, "commonly known as a librarian system whereby [the bank] could take other programs, such as the National City program, place it on that library and use that as a method of keeping track of the program, making changes to it." The last program, an audit program, contained a set of instructions used to accumulate requested information from all other programs. Thomson also testified that the programs were delivered on magnetic tapes. The programs were then taken off the magnetic tapes and put into a library, where necessary modifications were made to the programs to accommodate the bank's particular needs. After the information was removed from the tapes and stored elsewhere, the tapes could either be used again or discarded. Thomson stated further that those instructions could have been conveyed to the bank through discs, punch cards or over the telephone.

Section 3 of the Use Tax Act provides:

> "A tax is imposed upon the privilege of using in this State tangible personal property * * * purchased at retail from a retailer." (Ill.Rev. Stat.1977, ch. 120, par. 439.3.)

Thus, the issue in this case is whether computer software is tangible personal property and is therefore taxable under the Use Tax Act.

The plaintiff contends that the magnetic tapes in question here constituted intangible personal property, because they were, in essence, merely a means of conveying programming instructions. The plaintiff argues that software primarily represents intangible services and not tangible goods. The Department, on the contrary, contends that the physical qualities of the tapes predominate over the information contained on them. The Department compares the tapes to films, phonograph records and books. All three examples, the Department argues, represent the physical manifestation of intangible ideas and artistic achievement, yet all three are taxable as tangible personal property.

Taxing statutes are to be strictly construed, and their language is not to be extended or enlarged by implication beyond its clear import, but in cases of doubt such laws are construed most strongly against the government and in favor of the taxpayer.

In our opinion, computer software, such as the instant magnetic tapes, is more properly characterized as intangible, than tangible, personal property. The Use Tax Act does not define the word "tangible," but this court abided by the following definition in *Farrand Coal Co. v. Halpin* (1957), 10 Ill.2d 507, 511, 140 N.E.2d 698:

> "An examination of the statute in question and the objectives intended to be accomplished thereby clearly indicates that the General Assembly when using the word tangible in referring to personal property had in mind the ordinary and popularly understood meaning of such term as indicated in Webster's first definition thereof, which is 'Capable of being touched; also, perceptible to the touch; tactile; palpable.' Webster's New International Dictionary, Second Edition, Unabridged, 1946."

Yet the foregoing definition does not altogether resolve this issue.

In *Time, Inc. v. Hulman* (1964), 31 Ill.2d 344, 201 N.E.2d 374, this court decided that magazines are tangible personal property and that the proceeds from their sale would be subject to the retailers' occupation tax were it not for an exclusion afforded to newspapers and other materials "such as" newsprint. (31 Ill.2d 344, 351–52, 201 N.E.2d 374.) In discussing whether magazines are tangible personal property, it was said:

> "The sale of a magazine is essentially not different from the sale of a loaf of bread, or an automobile. While it is true that the utility or value of plaintiffs' magazines is in their content and not the paper and ink with which they are printed, the taxability of the transaction is not determined by weighing the value of the intangible properties of the item of sale, such as form, organization and design, against the value of its tangible properties, such as weight, size and texture. *The test is,*

where tangible personal property is transferred, as the parties agree occurs in the transactions here involved, *whether the transfer is the substance of the transaction or merely incidental to a service.* In selling magazines by subscriptions, plaintiffs act as retailers of tangible personal property and as such are liable for retailers' occupation tax, if not otherwise exempt." (Emphasis added.) 31 Ill.2d 344, 350, 201 N.E.2d 374.

In *Commerce Union Bank v. Tidwell* (Tenn.1976), 538 S.W.2d 405, the Supreme Court of Tennessee held that computer software in the form of magnetic tapes or punch cards is intangible personal property and therefore not subject to that State's sales and use tax. The court reasoned that only information was being created and sold, "and the magnetic tapes which contain this information are only a method of transmitting these intellectual creations from the originator to the user. It is merely incidental that these intangibles are transmitted by way of a tangible reel of tape that is not even retained by the user." 538 S.W.2d 405, 407.

* * *

This court has previously held that where a service of skill was rendered in the manufacture of a special milling machine for the particular and exclusive use of a purchaser, the sale of the product was not taxable where it was merely incidental to the service.

The instant case is of a similar vein. The plaintiff bank purchased, in substance, the means of programming its computer so that it could perform functions the bank needed to have performed. The bank did not desire to spend the money or time to formulate the programs through its own data-processing staff. Therefore it purchased instruction programs from other sources. It simply happened that, for the sake of convenience and easy handling, the programs were recorded on magnetic tapes. The tapes were certainly not the only medium through which the information could be transferred. In this way, the tapes differ from a movie film, a phonograph record or a book, whereby the media used are the only practicable ways of preserving those articles. Thus, while those articles and the tapes are similar in that they physically represent the transfer of ideas or artistic processes, a more significant distinction is that those articles are inseparable from the ideas or processes, whereas computer programs are separable from the tapes. Not only may software information be conveyed any number of ways, but it may even be copied off of the tapes and stored, using another medium. In short, it is not the tapes which are the substance of the transaction, it is the information. We, therefore, hold that the sale of computer software in the instant transaction is, in substance, the transfer of intangible personal property and, as such, is not taxable under the Illinois Use Tax Act.

Accordingly, for the reasons stated, the judgment of the circuit court is affirmed.

Judgment affirmed.

SIMON, J., took no part in the consideration or decision of this case.

Notes and Questions

1. By the early 1990s, canned software programs were sales and use taxable in virtually all states. Custom programs, on the other hand, were taxable in less than half the states. Software was subject to property tax in about one-third of the states. Until all states have specific legislation or judicial precedent classifying software, disputes will continue, since software falls on the borderlines between goods and services and between tangible and intangible property.

2. Tax managers, attorneys and others must deal daily with the lack of consistency permeating the area. A tax manager, in filing a sales, use, or property tax declaration must take a position on the taxability of software. State to state differences in tax systems provide important planning opportunities. Companies can place data processing or computer intensive facilities in favorable tax jurisdictions.

C. FEDERAL INCOME TAX

1. KEY ISSUES

Federal tax treatment of computer resources revolves around two major concepts: (1) the definition and special treatment of research and development expenditures (§ 174), and (2) the depreciation of computer resources (§§ 167–168). Most businesses prefer to deduct the cost of all research and development in order to reduce their taxable income. Alternatively, taxpayers may amortize the research and development expenditures over the life of the computer product. The Internal Revenue Service (I.R.S.), quite naturally, wants taxpayers to amortize the research and development expenditures over the life of the computer products. Under amortization principals, taxpayers are allowed to depreciate the item over the life of the product with yearly depreciation deduction based on various formulas. The battle lines are thus drawn: taxpayers want to classify as many expenses as research and development expenditures and thus immediately deduct these expenses. IRS, on the other hand, wants to keep the definition of research and development expenditures as narrow as possible, and thus have as many expenses as possible amortized and depreciated over the life of the computer product.

Congress has added an additional level of complexity by allowing a few research and development expenses to be used as a credit by the taxpayer. In simple terms, a tax credit is a dollar-for-dollar reduction from the taxpayer's taxes, and thus most preferred by taxpayers. Although very complex accounting principles are involved, basically, most taxpayers first prefer tax credits, then deductions, and finally amortization and depreciation of the costs of acquiring computer resources.

The second major federal tax issue in computer industry is the rules for depreciating computer products once amortization is determined to be appropriate. This includes electing a cost recovery method for the amortization process.

2. RESEARCH AND EXPERIMENTAL EXPENDITURES

Section 174(a) of the Internal Revenue Code (the "Code") permits deductions for research or experimental expenditures paid or incurred by a taxpayer during the taxable year in connection with a trade or business. The § 174(a) deduction is available in certain circumstances for costs of developing computer software. Software development costs are not explicitly covered in Reg. § 1.174–2(a)(1). Pursuant to Rev. Proc. 69–21, however, a deduction is allowed for software development in accordance with "rules similar to those applicable under Section 174." The definition of "research and experimental expenditures," in Reg. § 1.174–2(a)(1) covers research and "development costs in the experimental or laboratory sense." Generally included are all costs incident to the development of an experimental or pilot model, a plant process, a product, a formula, an invention, or similar property. Not included are those expenditures for the ordinary testing or inspection of materials or products for quality control or those for efficiency surveys, management studies, consumer surveys, advertising, or promotions. The term does include the costs of obtaining a patent, including attorneys' fees. The provisions of § 174 apply to costs paid or incurred directly by the taxpayer for research or experimentation carried out on behalf of the taxpayer by another person or organization.

3. NORMAL EXPENSES AND DEDUCTIONS

Revenue Procedure 69–21 dictates that the costs of software developed internally by the taxpayer are to be deducted as current expenses. Costs of purchased software are to be capitalized and amortized over a five year period, or a shorter period if the taxpayer can demonstrate that the life of the software is less than five years.

4. WAYS OF TREATING R & D EXPENDITURES

Section 174 provides two methods for treating research or experimental expenditures paid or incurred by the taxpayer in connection with its trade or business; (1) Under § 174(a) the expenditures may be treated as expenses not chargeable to capital account and deducted in the year in which they are paid or incurred; or (2) they may be deferred and amortized under § 174(b). Research or experimental expenditures which are neither treated as expenses nor deferred and amortized under § 174 must be charged to capital account. Once an alternative is selected, the same accounting method must be used for all future software development costs. Generally, most businesses find it more advantageous to write these costs off currently. There may be situations, however, with a start-up situation or a company in a loss position, in which it may be better to capitalize and amortize these costs.

5. TREATMENT OF HARDWARE AND SOFTWARE FOR DEPRECIATION PURPOSES

The taxpayer may choose one of two basic methods to depreciate its expenses: MACRS or ADS.

a. MACRS

The Tax Reform Act of 1986, under § 168, created a Modified Accelerated Cost Recovery System (MACRS), which continued to classify computer equipment as five-year property. Under the modified ACRS, the 200% declining balance method is used, switching to the straight-line method in the later years. The new rules are effective for computer equipment placed in service after December 31, 1986.

b. ADS

Taxpayers may elect to compute depreciation deductions by using the Alternative Depreciation System (ADS) under I.R.C. § 168(g). This system utilized the straight-line method as well as the new ACRS recovery period with regard to computers. This results in slower depreciation deductions. The benefit of using ADS is to reduce the taxpayer's tax preferences and possible alternative minimum tax, since ADS is not an accelerated method of depreciation. The election to use ADS is irrevocable. ADS must be used to compute depreciation allowances for computer equipment used predominately outside the United States, leased or otherwise used by a tax-exempt entity, financed with the proceeds for tax-exempt bonds or imported from foreign countries that maintain discriminatory acts. ADS must also be used to compute depreciation deductions for mixed-use property. Mixed-used property includes a computer used for both business and personal purposes that is used 50% or less in the taxpayer's trade or business.

The choice of which depreciation system to use represents an advanced taxation course onto itself. In addition, advising clients on computer resource acquisition can be very complex given the pressure at the state level to classify as much of the acquisition as software and thus generally avoid state taxation of the software given the software is classed as intangible personal property, as compared to the general desirability at the federal level to classify as much of the acquisition as hardware to normally obtain more favorable depreciation treatment.

6. INCREMENTAL RESEARCH CREDIT

Section 41 is a credit for research activities as previously discussed, a tax credit is the most desirable element for a taxpayer. Under § 41, a taxpayer obtains a credit for 20% of the excess of qualified research expenditures of a taxable year over the average amount of the taxpayer's yearly qualified research expenditures in the preceding three taxable years. Computer software development expenses are divided into two distinct categories: (1) expenses to develop computer software, the primary purpose of which is sale, licensing or leasing to the public, and (2) expenses to develop computer software, the primary purpose of which is for the taxpayer's internal use. The TRA '86 substantially amended the definition of qualified research expenditures for taxable years after 1985. Section 41(d)(4)(E) incremental research credit applies to research expenditures that are: (1) research and development expenses in the experimental or laboratory sense (under § 174); (2) undertaken for the purpose of discovering information that is technological in nature and intended to be useful in the development of a new or improved business component of the taxpayer; and (3) substantial elements of a process of experimentation for certain functional purposes.

The following items are not eligible for the credit, being specifically excluded by § 174 and § 41:

(1) Research done outside the United States.

(2) Research in the social sciences, arts, or humanities.

(3) Ordinary testing or inspection of materials or products for quality control.

(4) Market and consumer research.

(5) Advertising or promotion expenses.

(6) Management studies and efficiency surveys.

(7) Acquisition or improvement of land or of certain depreciable or depletable property used in research.

(8) Acquisition of another person's patent, model, production, or process. Activities of obtaining a patent, including making and protecting a patent application (and attorneys' fees incurred), however, qualify for the credit.

(9) Research conducted after commercial production.

(10) Research for the adaptation of existing business components.

The cost of developing computer software, i.e. new or significantly improved programs or routines for computers, is eligible for the incremental research credit. The I.R.S. equates the costs of developing computer software to similar costs incurred in product development for purposes of § 174 deduction. The various limitations and exclusions built into the credit also apply to software. For example, the costs of adapting or modifying previously developed programs are not eligible for the credit. "Computer software" includes all programs or routines used to cause a computer to perform a desired task or set of tasks, and the documentation required to describe and maintain these programs.

In addition to the above tests, computer software that is developed for internal use is not deemed to be qualified research for purposes of the tax credit except to the extent that it meets the tests set forth in Regulations. In promulgating Regulations, the I.R.S. was instructed to include the following three part specific rule for internal use software in addition to the general requirements for qualified research:

(1) The software must be innovative, i.e., it results in a cost reduction or speed improvement that is substantial and economically significant.

(2) Software development must entail significant economic risk, i.e., substantial resources are committed by the taxpayer and substantial uncertainty exists that such resources can be recovered in a reasonable period.

(3) The software cannot be commercially available, i.e., it cannot be purchased, leased, or licensed for the intended purpose without modifications that satisfy the first two requirements.

Qualified research expenses include in-house research expenses and contract expenses paid or incurred by the taxpayer "in carrying on any trade or business of the taxpayer." "Contract research expenditures" means 65% of any amount paid or incurred by the taxpayer with respect to any person (other than an employee of the taxpayer) for qualified research. This would, therefore, apply to the research and development limited partnerships.

As seen from the above brief overview of the federal tax treatment of hardware and software, the issues are extremely complex, and critically important to each taxpayer, so they must be addressed early in the acquisition process.

Chapter IX

PRIVACY

Before the computer age, the greatest protection of individual privacy was the inefficiency of the data collection and distribution system. In the nineteenth century, a person could start a new life on the Western frontier. The quality of record-keeping and communications was such that there was little chance of being haunted by true or false reports about past. Record-keeping and distribution systems improved gradually over the first half of the twentieth century. Then, in the 1960s, the introduction of computer data banks caused a sudden, dramatic improvement in the keeping and distribution of records about individuals. Absent change in the law, this technological development would have meant a dramatic decrease in privacy and a drastic increase in the risk of harm from false information. This development also could have meant a shift in power in society, favoring those who had information over those who lacked it.

Congress enacted a variety of legislation in response to the problems posed by improvements in the collection and distribution of information about individuals. State legislatures and the courts have also contributed to the development of the law in this area. This Part of the casebook deals with the particular ways in which this new area of the law affects computer storage of information. Computer data banks threaten to make it impossible for individuals ever to escape minor mistakes and misdeeds, by recording and distributing information about them with computerized efficiency. The law of computer privacy, the subject of Chapter IX, attempts to curb this threat by restricting the gathering and distribution of true information about individuals. The efficiency of the computer is more dangerous when the information it stores is false. Chapter X deals with legal remedies designed to ensure that the information stored and distributed is true. Information is power. Chapter XI covers legislation aimed at forcing those with information in computers to share it with those who need the information. Financial information moving from computer to computer is the lifeblood of our economy. Chapter XII deals with the laws regulating the transfers of such information.

A. RESTRICTING DATA BASE GATHERING, ACCESSIBILITY, AND USE

Here are some questions to keep in mind in reading the following materials. What types of information should society suppress? Is the fear that the user of the information might interpret it incorrectly or that the user might interpret it correctly? What leads legislators to conclude that it is "fair" to use certain information and "unfair" to use other types of information? How should society suppress information—by restricting gathering, restricting distribution in general, restricting potential recipients, or restricting use? Who should have the right and who the duty to enforce the restrictions?

MERRIKEN v. CRESSMAN

United States District Court, Eastern District of Pennsylvania, 1973.
364 F.Supp. 913.

JOHN MORGAN DAVIS, DISTRICT JUDGE.

I. FINDINGS OF FACT

1. Plaintiff, Michael Merriken, is an eighth grade student at Stewart Junior High School, Marshall and Forrest Avenues, Norristown, Pa. Plaintiff, Sylvia Merriken, is the mother of Michael Merriken, is a resident of Montgomery County, and pays real estate and other taxes to the county.

2. Defendants are the Montgomery County Commissioners, the members of the Norristown Area School Board, the Superintendent of Schools of the Norristown Area School Board, and the Principal of Stewart Junior High School.

3. Defendants, acting in concert with each other and with Fred Streit Associates, intend to introduce a program entitled Critical Period of Intervention (CPI) into the Norristown Area School District to be administered to eighth grade students including Plaintiff, Michael Merriken.

4. Defendants intend to expend public tax monies to implement the CPI Program.

5. The stated purpose of the CPI Program is as a drug prevention approach as contrasted with drug rehabilitation efforts. It is designed to aid the local school district in identifying potential abusers, prepare the necessary interventions, identify resources to train and aid the district personnel to remediate the problems and, finally, to evaluate the results.

6. When suit was first instituted, Defendants did not intend to obtain the affirmative consent of parents to the participation of their

children in the CPI Program. Rather, Defendants proposed a "book of the month club" approach in which a parent's silence would be construed as acquiescence. It was only after suit was started that Defendants offered to change that format so that affirmative written parental consent to participation in the CPI Program would be required.

7. However, the revised letter to parents makes no provision whatsoever for allowing parents to see the test instrument itself.

8. As originally proposed, the CPI Program contained no provision for student consent. After commencement of litigation, Defendants did modify the test instrument to allow students to return a blank questionnaire. However, no affirmative written consent from the students is contemplated nor is any data made available to students in advance to assist them in their decision.

9. In addition to a letter, Defendants propose to send to parents a question and answer sheet explaining the CPI Program. (Plffs' Exh. 5) By the admission of its author, Mr. Streit, that document is a "selling device", "an attempt to convince the parent to allow the child to participate". The whole purpose in composing that document "was to convince parents that they ought to allow their children to participate". Mr. Streit acknowledged that "there is nothing in this document * * * that is critical of or negative about the CPI Program".

10. Two child psychiatrists testified without contradiction as to several negative, and indeed dangerous aspects of the CPI Program, none of which are mentioned or referred to in any of the materials to be made available to parents. These dangers include the risk that the CPI Program will operate as a self fulfilling prophecy in which a child labelled as a potential drug abuser will by virtue of the label decide to be that which people already think he or she is anyway. In fact, the CPI Program manual itself, not available to parents, acknowledges this risk. Another danger mentioned is that of scapegoating in which a child might be marked out by his peers for unpleasant treatment either because of refusal to take the CPI test or because of the results of the test. That this is not a mere hypothetical risk was illustrated by an incident involving Plaintiff, Michael Merriken, in which fellow students accused him of being a drug user because his mother does not want him to participate in the CPI Program. Drs. Gordon and Hanford also described the severe loyalty conflict that might result by asking children the types of personal questions about their relationship with parents and siblings which are included in the CPI questionnaire. A final example has to do with the qualifications of the personnel who will administer the so-called interventions once the results of the CPI questionnaire have been evaluated. As both psychiatrists pointed out, the types of psychotherapy that are suggested as interventions in the CPI Program are quite sophisticated and require the skills of trained psychotherapists, psychiatrists, psychologists, etc. who have undergone many years of training. However, the CPI Program contemplates that these sophisticated psychotherapy techniques will be administered by

school personnel, including teachers without any particular qualifications who have undergone only a short crash course.

11. According to the Program, CPI is a "drug prevention approach as contrasted with drug rehabilitation efforts * * * It is designed to aid the local school district in identifying potential abusers, prepare the necessary interventions, identify resources to train and aid the district personnel to remediate the problems and, finally, to evaluate the results". However, the Program nowhere defines the term "potential [drug] abuser". All that the Program does state is that it will identify patterns similar to marijuana, LSD, barbiturate or amphetamine user. There is no reference to such drugs as cigarettes, alcohol, opium, heroin or cocaine. Moreover, there is no statement as to what constitutes abuse. The study on which CPI is based, however, does contain "an arbitrary set of decisions * * * to define the degrees of use, known or experimental, moderate or heavy".

12. Identification of a potential drug abuser, emotionally handicapped student, or student with deviant behavior or student with specific problems is accomplished by requiring students such as Plaintiff and also their teachers to complete test questionnaires. (Plffs' Exhs. 1 and 2) The questionnaires ask such personal and private questions as the family religion, the race or skin color of the student (Defendants have since stipulated to dropping this question), the family composition, including the reason for the absence of one or both parents, and whether one or both parents "hugged and kissed me good night when I was small", "tell me how much they love me", "enjoyed talking about current events with me", and "make me feel unloved". In addition both students and teachers are asked to identify other students in the class who make unusual or odd remarks, get into fights or quarrels with other students, make unusual or inappropriate responses during normal school activities, or have to be coaxed or forced to work with other pupils. Students are at no time given any guidance as to what should be considered an odd or unusual remark or what is to be considered an inappropriate response. For example, there is no warning that political differences or unusual and imaginative insights should not be looked upon as odd remarks or inappropriate responses.

13. Although the CPI Program constantly refers to confidentiality, no specifics are given in the Program itself as to how confidentiality is to be maintained after evaluation. Mr. Streit did testify on this subject but that testimony is far different from what appears in the printed CPI materials. The Program, by its own terms, contemplates the development of a "massive data bank" and also dissemination of data relating to specific students to various school personnel, including superintendents, principals, guidance counsellors, athletic coaches, social workers, PTA officers, and school board members. (Plffs' Exh. 6) In fact, at a meeting of the Norristown School Board on Monday, October 23, 1972, parents were advised that teams of faculty members had already been selected to receive data back from the CPI Program in

order to implement the intervention stage of the Program in the various schools in Norristown.

14. Even if those who are to be working with the CPI Program were to try and be as confidential as possible, in accordance with Mr. Streit's testimony, there is absolutely no assurance that the materials which have been gathered would be free from access by outside authorities in the community who have subpoena power. Thus, there is no assurance that should an enterprising district attorney convene a special grand jury to investigate the drug problem in Montgomery County, the records of the CPI Program would remain inviolate from subpoenas and that he could not determine the identity of children who have been labeled by the CPI Program as potential drug abusers.

15. The second step of the CPI Program is "intervention" or "remediation". The stated purpose of this phase is "to change the cognitive and affective domains of potential drug abusers and other forms of deviant behavior". Intervention may take several forms, some of which are compulsory for the student and which seriously limit and infringe upon individual liberty. * * *

* * *

16. Intervention is also another major threat to the confidentiality of the CPI Program. For example, one form of intervention is Referral Intervention. Under this program, "responsible school personnel make referral interventions when remediation needed by a particular student far exceeds available school resources. This referral intervention utilizes community resources such as clinics, hospitals, rehabilitation centers, etc. to help the seriously disturbed or serious drug-user student." Another form of intervention is Adult Role Model in which "teachers [are] * * * asked to select two children from the list of identified emotionally handicapped children. They would be given background information on each child. * * *"

17. The CPI Program results will not be made available to parents unless they affirmatively request them.

II. Discussion

The CPI Program as presented above is considered by its advocates, the Defendants, as a voluntary program in which affirmative parental consent is now given before participation by the student; and a student may return a blank questionnaire when the test is administered without apparent recrimination. It is contended that the Program is constitutional and is within discretionary power of the School Board.

The Plaintiffs assert that the Program is not voluntary because individuals' constitutional rights are waived without knowing, intelligent and aware consent. Before the Court reaches the question of the voluntariness of this Program, we will examine the alleged violations of the Constitution and state why individual constitutional rights are involved in this litigation.

The Plaintiffs claim that the CPI Program will interfere with and impede the Plaintiffs' rights of freedom of religion, freedom of speech, freedom of assembly, privilege against self-incrimination and right to privacy guaranteed by the First, Fourth, Fifth, Ninth and Fourteenth Amendments to the Constitution of the United States.

The main thrust of the Plaintiffs' argument that the CPI Program is an involuntary invasion of constitutionally protected rights, is the violation of the right to privacy. They base their argument mainly on *Griswold v. Connecticut,* 381 U.S. 479, 85 S.Ct. 1678, 14 L.Ed.2d 510 (1965), in which the Supreme Court ruled that inherent in the first nine Amendments to the Constitution is a right to privacy which is binding on the States as well. In a more recent case, the Supreme Court re-emphasized its position on the right of privacy in *Roe v. Wade,* 410 U.S. 113, 93 S.Ct. 705, 35 L.Ed.2d 147 (1973), and restated some of the general factual situations to which this right would apply.

* * *

This Court will look closely at the factual situation as it relates to family relationships and child rearing. The CPI Program questionnaire asks whether the student's family is "very close, somewhat close, not too close, or not close at all." (Plffs' Exh. 1—Question 7) In addition, the student is asked to answer questions of such intimate things of his parents as to whether they "hugged and kissed him goodnight when he was small" (Question 53); whether they told him how "much they loved him or her" (Question 54); whether the parents "seemed to know what the student's needs or wants are" (Question 116); and whether the student "feels that he is loved by his parents" (Question 112).

The above questions are samples which represent the highly personal nature of the entire questionnaire. These questions go directly to an individual's family relationship and his rearing. There probably is no more private a relationship, excepting marriage, which the Constitution safeguards than that between parent and child. This Court can look upon any invasion of that relationship as a direct violation of one's Constitutional right to privacy.

The fact that the students are juveniles does not in any way invalidate their right to assert their Constitutional right to privacy.

* * *

This Court would add that the right to privacy is on an equal or possibly more elevated pedestal than some other individual Constitutional rights and should be treated with as much deference as free speech. The United States Court of Appeals for the Third Circuit held in *Stull v. The School Board of Western Beaver Junior–Senior High School,* 459 F.2d 339 (1972), in reversing the District Court, that high school dress codes governing the length of hair in the absence of any evidence of disruption or of a health hazard or of an affect on academic accomplishment was violative of due process. * * *

* * *

As this Court ascertains from the above authority that children who are students are entitled to exercise their Constitutional rights, the question then arises whether parents, as guardians of the children, can waive their children's Constitutional rights. In the case at Bar, the children are never given the opportunity to consent to invasion of their privacy; only the opportunity to refuse to consent by returning a blank questionnaire. Whether this procedure is Constitutional is questionable, but the Court does not have to face that issue because the facts presented show that the parents could not have been properly informed about the CPI Program and as a result could not have given informed consent for their children to take the CPI test.

Before dwelling on the question of "informed consent", it should be noted that the case before the Court is a civil case. The Supreme Court has indicated that in civil cases as well as criminal cases the Court should indulge in every reasonable presumption against waiver of procedural due process and an individual's Constitutional rights. * * *

* * *

The facts as stated show that the letters to the parents were "selling devices" aimed at gaining consent without giving negative information that would make the parents completely aware of "the relevant circumstances and likely consequences" of the Program. Mr. Streit, the man who conceived the CPI Program, admitted that the letter to the parents gave only one side of the test picture. There were no statements to the parents concerning the self-fulfilling prophecy, scapegoating of those children who opted not to participate or the ultimate use of the data as it would effect their children and law authorities who might find it necessary to use that information to learn more about the drug situation in the local community.

The Law does not abound with cases or expert treatises on the problem of personality testing and confidentiality, and the problems of informed consent. However, in a recent Federal Bar Journal article by Charles W. Sheerer and Ronald A. Roston, on "Some Legal and Psychological Concerns About Personality Testing in the Public Schools", 3 Fed.Bar Journal 111 (1971), there is some insight into the problem of scientific testing and the American parent. * * *

* * *

This Court feels that however good may be the intent and motive of the Defendant, the presentation of the CPI Program to the student and the students' parents is far from candid, and any attempt at informed consent does not reach the level that this Court would consider adequate as in the "consent ideally obtained by a physician prior to the performance of surgery". The parents are not aware of the consequences and there is no substitute for candor and honesty in fact, particularly by the school board who, as the ultimate decision maker as far as the education of our children is concerned, should give our citizenry a more forthright approach. The attempt to make the letter requesting consent similar to a promotional inducement to buy, lacks the necessary substance to give a parent the opportunity to give knowing, intelligent and aware consent.

The actual testing of the students and the results gained are suspect. All that the Program does state is that it will identify patterns similar to marijuana, LSD, barbiturate or amphetamine users. There is no reference to the use of drugs and there are no statements as to what constitutes abuse. The study nowhere defines what is a potential drug abuser and is vague in the relationship of its background analysis to the intended results.

There is a statement concerning the confidentiality of the test during its administration and during the immediate evaluation period that is comprehensive and well explained, but the credibility of the confidentiality of this Program breaks down when the potential drug abusers are reported to the school superintendent. The school will then attempt remediation by the use of teachers, guidance counselors and others, who have had little training in the area of psychological therapy in either individual or group therapy sessions. The ultimate use of this information, although possibly gained with a great deal of scientific success, is the most serious problem that faces the Court. How many children would be labeled as potential drug abusers who in actuality are not, and would be subjected to the problem of group therapy sessions conducted by inexperienced individuals?

Strict confidentiality is not maintained after evaluation and there are many opportunities for a child to suffer insurmountable harm from a labeling such as "drug abuser" at an age when the cruelty of other children is at an extreme. The seriousness of this problem is illustrated by the fact that if one child is so harmed and would be temporarily or permanently damaged by the label of "drug abuser" is this Program worth the effort to identify other actual "drug abusers".

When a program talks about labeling someone as a particular type and such a label could remain with him for the remainder of his life, the margin of error must be almost nil. The preliminary statistics and other evidence indicate there will be errors in identification. The Court recognizes that the Supreme Court has spoken and many Law Review authorities have spoken about a balancing test. What this means is that the Court balances the invasion of privacy against the public need for a program to learn and possibly prevent drug abuse in a society which has become highly aware of the dangers and effects of drug abuse. If the Court finds the public need so great and the invasion minimal, then it could sanction the Program in favor of public need. * * *

* * *

The Court, in balancing the right of an individual to privacy and the right of the Government to invade that privacy for the sake of public interest, strikes the balance in favor of the individual in the circumstances shown in this case. In short, the reasons for this are that the test itself and the surrounding results of that test are not sufficiently presented to both the child and the parents, as well as the Court, as to its authenticity and credibility in fighting the drug problem in this country. There is too much of a chance that the wrong people for the wrong reasons will be singled out and counselled in the wrong manner.

The Plaintiff also contends that other Constitutional rights will be violated if the Defendants are allowed to proceed with the CPI Program. There is no other Constitutional right that this Program would violate besides privacy. The protection against self-incrimination violation may be moot because of the new Pennsylvania Law which attempts to prevent the use of information, obtained confidentially from students, from being used against them in legal proceedings without consent. (24 P.S. § 13–1319)

The evidence presents no violation of the Constitutional right of the student to speak or assemble. The Court recognizes, however, that young people at the junior high school level are ostracized for unpopular views by their peers but no school authority is preventing the students from speaking or assembling. Although there may be a chilling effect or a step in the direction toward the prevention of free speech and assembly, this Court feels that there is no violation of Constitutional rights in this particular fact situation.

The Defendant maintains that the Legislature has vested the school board with discretionary power to act, that is, to test its students, and the burden placed on the Plaintiffs to show that this power is being abused is extremely heavy. However, as the facts presented in this case, vis-a-vis, a violation of one's Constitutional rights, so overwhelmingly carries the burden there is no question that the school board has overstepped its discretionary authority.

The CPI Program attempts to determine relative to today's problem of drug use and abuse what steps can be taken to prevent students from becoming drug abusers; and if such a program as presented here could be used to identify those who are potential drug abusers. Unfortunately, this Program does not meet the necessary Constitutional and procedural requirements. Setting precedents as to invasion of Constitutional rights without informed consent must be examined very closely and only employed when the balance weighs so heavily in favor of the public need. As the Program now stands the individual loses more than society can gain in its fight against drugs. The Court will enjoin this Program as it fails to meet Constitutional standards.

III. Conclusions of Law

1. This action is brought to redress the deprivation by Defendants, under color of state law, of the rights, privileges and immunities secured to Plaintiffs by Article I, Section 9, Clause 3 and the First, Fourth, Fifth, Ninth and Fourteenth Amendments of the United States

Constitution. The Court has jurisdiction of the action pursuant to 28 U.S.C. § 1343; 28 U.S.C. § 1331.

2. The CPI Program will violate the Plaintiffs' right to privacy inherent in the penumbras of the Bill of Rights of the United States Constitution.

3. Under the CPI Program, Defendants would unlawfully and without authority attempt to exercise the exclusive privileges of parents, extending into areas beyond matters of conduct and discipline, in excess of their power and contrary to law.

4. The CPI Program will be administered without the knowing, intelligent, voluntary and aware consent of parents or students.

5. Defendants, their agents, servants and employers and all persons acting in concert with them are permanently enjoined and restrained from implementing or in any other way proceeding with the CPI Program and from expending any further county or school district revenues on the CPI Program.

FAIR CREDIT REPORTING ACT
15 U.S.C. §§ 1681ff

§ 601. Short Title

This title may be cited as the Fair Credit Reporting Act.

§ 602. Findings and Purpose [15 U.S.C. § 1681]

(a) The Congress makes the following findings:

(1) The banking system is dependent upon fair and accurate credit reporting. Inaccurate credit reports directly impair the efficiency of the banking system, and unfair credit reporting methods undermine the public confidence which is essential to the continued functioning of the banking system.

(2) An elaborate mechanism has been developed for investigating and evaluating the credit worthiness, credit standing, credit capacity, character, and general reputation of consumers.

(3) Consumer reporting agencies have assumed a vital role in assembling and evaluating consumer credit and other information on consumers.

(4) There is a need to insure that consumer reporting agencies exercise their grave responsibilities with fairness, impartiality, and a respect for the consumer's right to privacy.

(b) It is the purpose of this title to require that consumer reporting agencies adopt reasonable procedures for meeting the needs of commerce for consumer credit, personnel, insurance, and other information in a manner which is fair and equitable to the consumer, with regard to the confidentiality, accuracy, relevancy, and proper utilization of such information in accordance with the requirements of this title.

§ 603. Definitions and Rules of Construction [15 U.S.C. § 1681a]

(a) Definitions and rules of construction set forth in this section are applicable for the purposes of this title.

(b) The term "person" means any individual, partnership, corporation, trust, estate, cooperative, association, government or governmental subdivision or agency, or other entity.

(c) The term "consumer" means an individual.

(d) The term "consumer report" means any written, oral, or other communication of any information by a consumer reporting agency bearing on a consumer's credit worthiness, credit standing, credit capacity, character, general reputation, personal characteristics, or mode of living which is used or expected to be used or collected in whole or in part for the purpose of serving as a factor in establishing the consumer's eligibility for (1) credit or insurance to be used primarily for personal, family, or household purposes, or (2) employment purposes, or (3) other purposes authorized under section 604. The term does not include (A) any report containing information solely as to transactions or experiences between the consumer and the person making the report; (B) any authorization or approval of a specific extension of credit directly or indirectly by the issuer of a credit card or similar device; or (C) any report in which a person who has been requested by a third party to make a specific extension of credit directly or indirectly to a consumer conveys his decision with respect to such request, if the third party advises the consumer of the name and address of the person to whom the request was made and such person makes the disclosures to the consumer required under section 615.

(e) The term "investigative consumer report" means a consumer report or portion thereof in which information on a consumer's character, general reputation, personal characteristics, or mode of living is obtained through personal interviews with neighbors, friends, or associates of the consumer reported on or with others with whom he is acquainted or who may have knowledge concerning any such items of information. However, such information shall not include specific factual information on a consumer's credit record obtained directly from a creditor of the consumer or from a consumer reporting agency when such information was obtained directly from a creditor of the consumer or from the consumer.

(f) The term "consumer reporting agency" means any person which, for monetary fees, dues, or on a cooperative nonprofit basis, regularly engages in whole or in part in the practice of assembling or evaluating consumer credit information or other information on consumers for the purpose of furnishing consumer reports to third parties, and which uses any means or facility of interstate commerce for the purpose of preparing or furnishing consumer reports.

(g) The term "file", when used in connection with information on any consumer, means all of the information on that consumer recorded and retained by a consumer reporting agency regardless of how the information is stored.

(h) The term "employment purposes" when used in connection with a consumer report means a report used for the purpose of evaluating a consumer for employment, promotion, reassignment or retention as an employee.

(i) The term "medical information" means information or records obtained, with the consent of the individual to whom it relates, from licensed physicians or medical practitioners, hospitals, clinics, or other medical or medically related facilities.

§ 604. Permissible Purposes of Reports [15 U.S.C. § 1681b]

A consumer reporting agency may furnish a consumer report under the following circumstances and no other:

(1) In response to the order of a court having jurisdiction to issue such an order, or a subpoena issued in connection with proceedings before a Federal grand jury.

(2) In accordance with the written instructions of the consumer to whom it relates.

(3) To a person which it has reason to believe—

(A) intends to use the information in connection with a credit transaction involving the consumer on whom the information is to be furnished and involving the extension of credit to, or review or collection of an account of, the consumer; or

(B) intends to use the information for employment purposes; or

(C) intends to use the information in connection with the underwriting of insurance involving the consumer; or

(D) intends to use the information in connection with a determination of the consumer's eligibility for a license or other benefit granted by a governmental instrumentality required by law to consider an applicant's financial responsibility or status; or

(E) otherwise has a legitimate business need for the information in connection with a business transaction involving the consumer.

§ 605. Obsolete Information [15 U.S.C. § 1681c]

(a) Except as authorized under subsection (b) of this section, no consumer reporting agency may make any consumer report containing any of the following items of information:

(1) Cases under Title 11 or under the Bankruptcy Act that, from the date of entry of the order for relief or the date of adjudication, as the case may be, antedate the report by more than 10 years.

(2) Suits and judgments which, from date of entry, antedate the report by more than seven years or until the governing statute of limitations has expired, whichever is the longer period.

(3) Paid tax liens which, from date of payment, antedate the report by more than seven years.

(4) Accounts placed for collection or charged to profit and loss which antedate the report by more than seven years.

(5) Records of arrest, indictment, or conviction of crime which, from date of disposition, release, or parole, antedate the report by more than seven years.

(6) Any other adverse item of information which antedates the report by more than seven years.

(b) The provisions of subsection (a) of this section are not applicable in the case of any consumer credit report to be used in connection with—

(1) a credit transaction involving, or which may reasonably be expected to involve, a principal amount of $50,000 or more;

(2) the underwriting of life insurance involving, or which may reasonably be expected to involve, a face amount of $50,000 or more; or

(3) the employment of any individual at an annual salary which equals, or which may reasonably be expected to equal $20,000, or more.

§ 606. Disclosure of Investigative Consumer Reports [15 U.S.C. § 1681d]

(a) A person may not procure or cause to be prepared an investigative consumer report on any consumer unless—

(1) it is clearly and accurately disclosed to the consumer that an investigative consumer report including information as to his character, general reputation, personal characteristics, and mode of living, whichever are applicable, may be made, and such disclosure (A) is made in a writing mailed, or otherwise delivered, to the consumer, not later than three days after the date on which the report was first requested, and (B) includes a statement informing the consumer of his right to request the additional disclosures provided for under subsection (b) of this section; or

(2) the report is to be used for employment purposes for which the consumer has not specifically applied.

(b) Any person who procures or causes to be prepared an investigative consumer report on any consumer shall, upon written request made by the consumer within a reasonable period of time after the receipt by him of the disclosure required by subsection (a)(1) of this section, shall [1] make a complete and accurate disclosure of the nature and scope of the investigation requested. This disclosure shall be made

1. So in original. Probably should be omitted.

in a writing mailed, or otherwise delivered, to the consumer not later than five days after the date on which the request for such disclosure was received from the consumer or such report was first requested, whichever is the later.

(c) No person may be held liable for any violation of subsection (a) or (b) of this section if he shows by a preponderance of the evidence that at the time of the violation he maintained reasonable procedures to assure compliance with subsection (a) or (b) of this section.

§ 607. Compliance Procedures [15 U.S.C. § 1681e]

(a) Every consumer reporting agency shall maintain reasonable procedures designed to avoid violations of section 1681c of this title and to limit the furnishing of consumer reports to the purposes listed under section 1681b of this title. These procedures shall require that prospective users of the information identify themselves, certify the purposes for which the information is sought, and certify that the information will be used for no other purpose. Every consumer reporting agency shall make a reasonable effort to verify the identity of a new prospective user and the uses certified by such prospective user prior to furnishing such user a consumer report. No consumer reporting agency may furnish a consumer report to any person if it has reasonable grounds for believing that the consumer report will not be used for a purpose listed in section 604.

(b) Whenever a consumer reporting agency prepares a consumer report it shall follow reasonable procedures to assure maximum possible accuracy of the information concerning the individual about whom the report relates.

§ 608. Disclosures to Governmental Agencies [15 U.S.C. § 1681f]

Notwithstanding the provisions of section 604, a consumer reporting agency may furnish identifying information respecting any consumer, limited to his name, address, former addresses, places of employment, or former places of employment, to a governmental agency.

BANKRUPTCY CODE
11 U.S.C.A. § 525

§ 525. Protection against discriminatory treatment

(a) Except as provided in the Perishable Agricultural Commodities Act, 1930 (7 U.S.C. 499a–499s), the Packers and Stockyards Act, 1921 (7 U.S.C. 181–229), and section 1 of the Act entitled "An Act making appropriations for the Department of Agriculture for the fiscal year ending June 30, 1944, and for other purposes," approved July 12, 1943 (57 Stat. 422; 7 U.S.C. 204), a governmental unit may not deny, revoke, suspend, or refuse to renew a license, permit, charter, franchise, or other similar grant to, condition such a grant to, discriminate with respect to such a grant against, deny employment to, terminate the employment of, or discriminate with respect to employment against, a person that is or has been a debtor under this title or a bankrupt or a debtor under the Bankruptcy Act, or another person with whom such bankrupt or debtor has been associated, solely because such bankrupt or debtor is or has been a debtor under this title or a bankrupt or debtor under the Bankruptcy Act, has been insolvent before the commencement of the case under this title, or during the case but before the debtor is granted or denied a discharge, or has not paid a debt that is dischargeable in the case under this title or that was discharged under the Bankruptcy Act.

(b) No private employer may terminate the employment of, or discriminate with respect to employment against, an individual who is or has been a debtor under this title, a debtor or bankrupt under the Bankruptcy Act, or an individual associated with such debtor or bankrupt, solely because such debtor or bankrupt—

(1) is or has been a debtor under this title or a debtor or bankrupt under the Bankruptcy Act;

(2) has been insolvent before the commencement of a case under this title or during the case but before the grant or denial of a discharge; or

(3) has not paid a debt that is dischargeable in a case under this title or that was discharged under the Bankruptcy Act.

Notes and Questions

1. Note that, as the provision above from the Bankruptcy Code shows, even where it is legal for data banks to collect and distribute information, it may be illegal to use it.

2. In the late 1980s there was a revolution in data base storage technology. Previously, only large mainframe computers could store giant data bases. New technology now allows data bases to be stored on inexpensive compact diskettes (like those used for music recording) or on videodisc. One disk can store information on millions of people. With the aid of an inexpensive adapter and appropriate software, an ordinary personal computer can retrieve information stored on these disks.

In April 1990, Lotus Development Corporation announced that, in cooperation with Equifax, a major national supplier of credit reports, it would distribute a new product called "Marketplace: Households," with personal and marketing information on 120 million people stored on compact disks. Purchasers of the product would be able to retrieve information using a personal computer equipped with a compact disk adapter. In January 1991, Lotus announced that it was canceling its plans due to privacy concerns. Lawrence M. Fisher, "New Data Base Ended By Lotus and Equifax," New York Times, Jan. 24, 1991, p. C3.

Computer experts had evaluated "Households" as completely feasible from a technical point of view. Perhaps another company will dare to go ahead with a similar product. Is existing privacy law sufficient to deal with this new technology? Should Congress enact new legislation before it is too late?

B. AGGREGATION

According to the Hegelian dialectic, when quantitative change becomes great enough, it at some point turns into qualitative change. Computers are extremely good at collecting large quantities of information and finding patterns in that information. This ability may be a threat to privacy, in that the patterns found will reveal information about individuals that they would rather keep secret.

WHALEN v. ROE, 1977

429 U.S. 589, 97 S.Ct. 869, 51 L.Ed.2d 64.

MR. JUSTICE STEVENS delivered the opinion of the Court.

The constitutional question presented is whether the State of New York may record, in a centralized computer file, the names and addresses of all persons who have obtained, pursuant to a doctor's prescription, certain drugs for which there is both a lawful and an unlawful market.

The District Court enjoined enforcement of the portions of the New York State Controlled Substances Act of 1972 which require such recording on the ground that they violate appellees' constitutionally protected rights of privacy. We noted probable jurisdiction of the appeal by the Commissioner of Health, 424 U.S. 907, 96 S.Ct. 1100, 47 L.Ed.2d 310, and now reverse.

Many drugs have both legitimate and illegitimate uses. In response to a concern that such drugs were being diverted into unlawful channels, in 1970 the New York Legislature created a special commission to evaluate the State's drug-control laws. The commission found the existing laws deficient in several respects. There was no effective way to prevent the use of stolen or revised prescriptions, to prevent unscrupulous pharmacists from repeatedly refilling prescriptions, to prevent users from obtaining prescriptions from more than one doctor, or to prevent doctors from over-prescribing, either by authorizing an excessive amount in one prescription or by giving one patient multiple prescriptions. In drafting new legislation to correct such defects, the commission consulted with enforcement officials in California and Illinois where central reporting systems were being used effectively.

The new New York statute classified potentially harmful drugs in five schedules. Drugs, such as heroin, which are highly abused and have no recognized medical use, are in Schedule I; they cannot be prescribed. Schedules II through V include drugs which have a progressively lower potential for abuse but also have a recognized medical use. Our concern is limited to Schedule II which includes the most dangerous of the legitimate drugs.

With an exception for emergencies, the Act requires that all prescriptions for Schedule II drugs be prepared by the physician in triplicate on an official form. The completed form identifies the prescribing physician; the dispensing pharmacy; the drug and dosage; and the name, address, and age of the patient. One copy of the form is retained by the physician, the second by the pharmacist, and the third is forwarded to the New York State Department of Health in Albany. A prescription made on an official form may not exceed a 30–day supply, and may not be refilled.

The District Court found that about 100,000 Schedule II prescription forms are delivered to a receiving room at the Department of Health in Albany each month. They are sorted, coded, and logged and then taken to another room where the data on the forms is recorded on magnetic tapes for processing by a computer. Thereafter, the forms are returned to the receiving room to be retained in a vault for a five-year period and then destroyed as required by the statute. The receiving room is surrounded by a locked wire fence and protected by an alarm system. The computer tapes containing the prescription data are kept in a locked cabinet. When the tapes are used, the computer is run "off-line," which means that no terminal outside of the computer room can read or record any information. Public disclosure of the identity of patients is expressly prohibited by the statute and by a Department of Health regulation. Willful violation of these prohibitions is a crime punishable by up to one year in prison and a $2,000 fine. At the time of trial there were 17 Department of Health employees with access to the files; in addition, there were 24 investigators with authority to investigate cases of overdispensing which might be identified by the computer. Twenty months after the effective date of the Act, the computerized data had only been used in two investigations involving alleged overuse by specific patients.

A few days before the Act became effective, this litigation was commenced by a group of patients regularly receiving prescriptions for Schedule II drugs, by doctors who prescribe such drugs, and by two associations of physicians. After various preliminary proceedings, a three-judge District Court conducted a one-day trial. Appellees offered evidence tending to prove that persons in need of treatment with Schedule II drugs will from time to time decline such treatment because of their fear that the misuse of the computerized data will cause them to be stigmatized as "drug addicts."

The District Court held that "the doctor-patient relationship intrudes on one of the zones of privacy accorded constitutional protection" and that the patient-identification provisions of the Act invaded this zone with "a needlessly broad sweep," and enjoined enforcement of the provisions of the Act which deal with the reporting of patients' names and addresses.

I

The District Court found that the State had been unable to demonstrate the necessity for the patient-identification requirement on the basis of its experience during the first 20 months of administration of the new statute. There was a time when that alone would have provided a basis for invalidating the statute. *Lochner v. New York,* 198 U.S. 45, 25 S.Ct. 539, 49 L.Ed. 937, involved legislation making it a crime for a baker to permit his employees to work more than 60 hours in a week. In an opinion no longer regarded as authoritative, the Court held the statute unconstitutional as "an unreasonable, unnecessary and arbitrary interference with the right of the individual to his personal liberty * * *." *Id.,* at 56, 25 S.Ct., at 543.

The holding in *Lochner* has been implicitly rejected many times. State legislation which has some effect on individual liberty or privacy may not be held unconstitutional simply because a court finds it unnecessary, in whole or in part. For we have frequently recognized that individual States have broad latitude in experimenting with possible solutions to problems of vital local concern.

The New York statute challenged in this case represents a considered attempt to deal with such a problem. It is manifestly the product of an orderly and rational legislative decision. It was recommended by a specially appointed commission which held extensive hearings on the proposed legislation, and drew on experience with similar programs in other States. There surely was nothing unreasonable in the assumption that the patient-identification requirement might aid in the enforcement of laws designed to minimize the misuse of dangerous drugs. For the requirement could reasonably be expected to have a deterrent effect on potential violators as well as to aid in the detection or investigation of specific instances of apparent abuse. At the very least, it would seem clear that the State's vital interest in controlling the distribution of dangerous drugs would support a decision to experiment with new techniques for control. For if an experiment fails—if in this case experience teaches that the patient-identification requirement results in the foolish expenditure of funds to acquire a mountain of useless information—the legislative process remains available to terminate the unwise experiment. It follows that the legislature's enactment of the patient-identification requirement was a reasonable exercise of New York's broad police powers. The District Court's finding that the necessity for the requirement had not been proved is not, therefore, a sufficient reason for holding the statutory requirement unconstitutional.

II

Appellees contend that the statute invades a constitutionally protected "zone of privacy." The cases sometimes characterized as protecting "privacy" have in fact involved at least two different kinds of interests. One is the individual interest in avoiding disclosure of personal matters, and another is the interest in independence in making certain kinds of important decisions. Appellees argue that both of these interests are impaired by this statute. The mere existence in readily available form of the information about patients' use of

Schedule II drugs creates a genuine concern that the information will become publicly known and that it will adversely affect their reputations. This concern makes some patients reluctant to use, and some doctors reluctant to prescribe, such drugs even when their use is medically indicated. It follows, they argue, that the making of decisions about matters vital to the care of their health is inevitably affected by the statute. Thus, the statute threatens to impair both their interest in the nondisclosure of private information and also their interest in making important decisions independently.

We are persuaded, however, that the New York program does not, on its face, pose a sufficiently grievous threat to either interest to establish a constitutional violation.

Public disclosure of patient information can come about in three ways. Health Department employees may violate the statute by failing, either deliberately or negligently, to maintain proper security. A patient or a doctor may be accused of a violation and the stored data may be offered in evidence in a judicial proceeding. Or, thirdly, a doctor, a pharmacist, or the patient may voluntarily reveal information on a prescription form.

The third possibility existed under the prior law and is entirely unrelated to the existence of the computerized data bank. Neither of the other two possibilities provides a proper ground for attacking the statute as invalid on its face. There is no support in the record, or in the experience of the two States that New York has emulated, for an assumption that the security provisions of the statute will be administered improperly. And the remote possibility that judicial supervision of the evidentiary use of particular items of stored information will provide inadequate protection against unwarranted disclosures is surely not a sufficient reason for invalidating the entire patient-identification program.

Even without public disclosure, it is, of course, true that private information must be disclosed to the authorized employees of the New York Department of Health. Such disclosures, however, are not significantly different from those that were required under the prior law. Nor are they meaningfully distinguishable from a host of other unpleasant invasions of privacy that are associated with many facets of health care. Unquestionably, some individuals' concern for their own privacy may lead them to avoid or to postpone needed medical attention. Nevertheless, disclosures of private medical information to doctors, to hospital personnel, to insurance companies, and to public health agencies are often an essential part of modern medical practice even when the disclosure may reflect unfavorably on the character of the patient. Requiring such disclosures to representatives of the State having responsibility for the health of the community, does not automatically amount to an impermissible invasion of privacy.

Appellees also argue, however, that even if unwarranted disclosures do not actually occur, the knowledge that the information is readily available in a computerized file creates a genuine concern that causes some persons to decline needed medication. The record supports the conclusion that some use of Schedule II drugs has been discouraged by that concern; it also is clear, however, that about 100,000 prescriptions for such drugs were being filled each month prior to the entry of the District Court's injunction. Clearly, therefore, the statute did not deprive the public of access to the drugs.

Nor can it be said that any individual has been deprived of the right to decide independently, with the advice of his physician, to acquire and to use needed medication. Although the State no doubt could prohibit entirely the use of particular Schedule II drugs, it has not done so. This case is therefore unlike those in which the Court held that a total prohibition of certain conduct was an impermissible deprivation of liberty. Nor does the State require access to these drugs to be conditioned on the consent of any state official or other third party. Within dosage limits which appellees do not challenge, the decision to prescribe, or to use, is left entirely to the physician and the patient.

We hold that neither the immediate nor the threatened impact of the patient-identification requirements in the New York State Controlled Substances Act of 1972 on either the reputation or the independence of patients for whom Schedule II drugs are medically indicated is sufficient to constitute an invasion of any right or liberty protected by the Fourteenth Amendment.

III

The appellee doctors argue separately that the statute impairs their right to practice medicine free of unwarranted state interference. If the doctors' claim has any reference to the impact of the 1972 statute on their own procedures, it is clearly frivolous. For even the prior statute required the doctor to prepare a written prescription identifying the name and address of the patient and the dosage of the prescribed drug. To the extent that their claim has reference to the possibility that the patients' concern about disclosure may induce them to refuse needed medication, the doctors' claim is derivative from, and therefore no stronger than, the patients'. Our rejection of their claim therefore disposes of the doctors' as well.

IV

A final word about issues we have not decided. We are not unaware of the threat to privacy implicit in the accumulation of vast amounts of personal information in computerized data banks or other massive government files. The collection of taxes, the distribution of welfare and social security benefits, the supervision of public health, the direction of our Armed Forces, and the enforcement of the criminal laws all require the orderly preservation of great quantities of information, much of which is personal in character and potentially embarrassing or harmful if disclosed. The right to collect and use such data for public purposes is typically accompanied by a concomitant statutory or regulatory duty to avoid unwarranted disclosures. Recognizing that in some circumstances that duty arguably has its roots in the Constitution, nevertheless New York's statutory scheme, and its implementing administrative procedures, evidence a proper concern with, and protection of, the individual's interest in privacy. We therefore need not, and do not, decide any question which might be presented by the unwarranted disclosure of accumulated private data—whether intentional or unintentional—or by a system that did not contain comparable security provisions. We simply hold that this record does not establish an invasion of any right or liberty protected by the Fourteenth Amendment.

Reversed.

MR. JUSTICE BRENNAN, concurring.

I write only to express my understanding of the opinion of the Court, which I join.

* * *

What is more troubling about this scheme, however, is the central computer storage of the data thus collected. Obviously, as the State argues, collection and storage of data by the State that is in itself legitimate is not rendered unconstitutional simply because new technology makes the State's operations more efficient. However, as the example of the Fourth Amendment shows the Constitution puts limits not only on the type of information the State may gather, but also on the means it may use to gather it. The central storage and easy accessibility of computerized data vastly increase the potential for abuse of that information, and I am not prepared to say that future developments will not demonstrate the necessity of some curb on such technology.

In this case, as the Court's opinion makes clear, the State's carefully designed program includes numerous safeguards intended to forestall the danger of indiscriminate disclosure. Given this serious and, so far as the record shows, successful effort to prevent abuse and limit access to the personal information at issue, I cannot say that the statute's provisions for computer storage, on their face, amount to a deprivation of constitutionally protected privacy interests, any more than the more traditional reporting provisions.

UNITED STATES DEPARTMENT OF JUSTICE v. REPORTERS COMMITTEE FOR FREEDOM OF THE PRESS, 1989

489 U.S. 749, 109 S.Ct. 1468, 103 L.Ed.2d 774.

JUSTICE STEVENS delivered the opinion of the Court.

The Federal Bureau of Investigation (FBI) has accumulated and maintains criminal identification records, sometimes referred to as "rap sheets," on over 24 million persons. The question presented by this case is whether the disclosure of the contents of such a file to a third party "could reasonably be expected to constitute an unwarranted invasion of personal privacy" within the meaning of the Freedom of Information Act (FOIA), 5 U.S.C. § 552(b)(7)(C) (1982 ed., Supp. IV).

I

In 1924 Congress appropriated funds to enable the Department of Justice (Department) to establish a program to collect and preserve fingerprints and other criminal identification records. 43 Stat. 217. That statute authorized the Department to exchange such information with "officials of States, cities and other institutions." *Ibid.* Six years later Congress created the FBI's identification division, and gave it responsibility for "acquiring, collecting, classifying, and preserving criminal identification and other crime records and the exchanging of said criminal identification records with the duly authorized officials of governmental agencies, of States, cities, and penal institutions." Ch. 455, 46 Stat. 554 (codified at 5 U.S.C. § 340 (1934)); see 28 U.S.C. § 534(a)(4) (providing for exchange of rap-sheet information among "authorized officials of the Federal Government, the States, cities, and penal and other institutions"). Rap sheets compiled pursuant to such authority contain certain descriptive information, such as date of birth and physical characteristics, as well as a history of arrests, charges, convictions, and incarcerations of the subject. Normally a rap sheet is preserved until its subject attains age 80. Because of the volume of rap sheets, they are sometimes incorrect or incomplete and sometimes contain information about other persons with similar names.

The local, state, and federal law enforcement agencies throughout the Nation that exchange rap-sheet data with the FBI do so on a voluntary basis. The principal use of the information is to assist in the detection and prosecution of offenders; it is also used by courts and corrections officials in connection with sentencing and parole decisions. As a matter of executive policy, the Department has generally treated rap sheets as confidential and, with certain exceptions, has restricted their use to governmental purposes. Consistent with the Department's basic policy of treating these records as confidential, Congress in 1957 amended the basic statute to provide that the FBI's exchange of rap-sheet information with any other agency is subject to cancellation "if dissemination is made outside the receiving departments or related agencies." 71 Stat. 61; see 28 U.S.C. § 534(b).

As a matter of Department policy, the FBI has made two exceptions to its general practice of prohibiting unofficial access to rap sheets. First, it allows the subject of a rap sheet to obtain a copy, see 28 CFR §§ 16.30–16.34 (1988); and second, it occasionally allows rap sheets to be used in the preparation of press releases and publicity designed to assist in the apprehension of wanted persons or fugitives. See § 20.33(a)(4).

In addition, on three separate occasions Congress has expressly authorized the release of rap sheets for other limited purposes. In 1972 it provided for such release to officials of federally chartered or insured banking institutions and "if authorized by state statute and approved by the Attorney General, to officials of State and local governments for purposes of employment and licensing. * * *" 86 Stat. 1115. In 1975, in an amendment to the Securities Act, Congress permitted the Attorney General to release rap sheets to self-regulatory organizations in the securities industry. See 15 U.S.C. § 78q(f)(2) (1982 ed., Supp IV). And finally, in 1986 Congress authorized release of criminal-history information to licensees or applicants before the Nuclear Regulatory Commission. See 42 U.S.C. § 2169(a). These three targeted enactments—all adopted after the FOIA was passed in 1966—are consistent with the view that Congress understood and did not disapprove the FBI's general policy of treating rap sheets as nonpublic documents.

Although much rap-sheet information is a matter of public record, the availability and dissemination of the actual rap sheet to the public is limited. Arrests, indictments, convictions, and sentences are public events that are usually documented in court records. In addition, if a person's entire criminal history transpired in a single jurisdiction, all of the contents of his or her rap sheet may be available upon request in that jurisdiction. That possibility, however, is present in only three States. All of the other 47 States place substantial restrictions on the availability of criminal-history summaries even though individual events in those summaries are matters of public record. Moreover, even in Florida, Wisconsin, and Oklahoma, the publicly available summaries may not include information about out-of-state arrests or convictions.

II

The statute known as the FOIA is actually a part of the Administrative Procedure Act (APA). Section 3 of the APA as enacted in 1946 gave agencies broad discretion concerning the publication of governmental records. In 1966, Congress amended that section to implement " 'a general philosophy of full agency disclosure.' " The amendment required agencies to publish their rules of procedure in the Federal Register, 5 U.S.C. § 552(a)(1)(C), and to make available for public inspection and copying their opinions, statements of policy, interpretations, and staff manuals and instructions that are not published in the Federal Register, § 552(a)(2). In addition, § 522(a)(3) requires every agency "upon any request for records which * * * reasonably describes such records" to make such records "promptly available to any person." If an agency improperly withholds any documents, the district court has jurisdiction to order their production. Unlike the review of other agency action that must be upheld if supported by substantial evidence and not arbitrary or capricious, the FOIA expressly places the burden "on the agency to sustain its action" and directs the district courts to "determine the matter de novo."

Congress exempted nine categories of documents from the FOIA's broad disclosure requirements. Three of those exemptions are arguably relevant to this case. Exemption 3 applies to documents that are specifically exempted from disclosure by another statute. § 552(b)(3). Exemption 6 protects "personnel and medical files and similar files the disclosure of which would constitute a clearly unwarranted invasion of personal privacy." § 552(b)(6).[7] Exemption 7(C) excludes records or information compiled for law enforcement purposes, "but only to the extent that the production of such [materials] * * * could reasonably be expected to constitute an unwarranted invasion of personal privacy." § 552(b)(7)(C).

Exemption 7(C)'s privacy language is broader than the comparable language in Exemption 6 in two respects. First, whereas Exemption 6 requires that the invasion of privacy be "clearly unwarranted," the adverb "clearly" is omitted from Exemption 7(C). This omission is the product of a 1974 amendment adopted in response to concerns expressed by the President. Second, whereas Exemption 6 refers to disclosures that "would constitute" an invasion of privacy, Exemption 7(C) encompasses any disclosure that "could reasonably be expected to constitute" such an invasion. This difference is also the product of a specific amendment. Thus, the standard for evaluating a threatened invasion of privacy interests resulting from the disclosure of records compiled for law-enforcement purposes is somewhat broader than the standard applicable to personnel, medical, and similar files.

III

This case arises out of requests made by a CBS news correspondent and the Reporters Committee for Freedom of the Press (respondents) for information concerning the criminal records of four members of the Medico family. The Pennsylvania Crime Commission had identified the family's company, Medico Industries, as a legitimate business dominated by organized crime figures. Moreover, the company allegedly had obtained a number of defense contracts as a result of an improper arrangement with a corrupt Congressman.

The FOIA requests sought disclosure of any arrests, indictments, acquittals, convictions, and sentences of any of the four Medicos. Although the FBI originally denied the requests, it provided the requested data concerning three of the Medicos after their deaths. In their complaint in the District Court, respondents sought the rap sheet for the fourth, Charles Medico (Medico), insofar as it contained "matters of public record." App. 33.

7. Congress employed similar language earlier in the statute to authorize an agency to delete identifying details that might otherwise offend an individual's privacy:

"To the extent required to prevent a clearly unwarranted invasion of personal privacy, an agency may delete identifying details when it makes available or publishes an opinion, statement of policy, interpretation, or staff manual or instruction." § 552(a)(2).

The parties filed cross-motions for summary judgment. In their briefs, respondents urged that any information regarding "a record of bribery, embezzlement or other financial crime" would potentially be a matter of special public interest. *Id.,* at 97. In answer to that argument, the Department advised respondents and the District Court that it had no record of any financial crimes concerning Medico, but the Department continued to refuse to confirm or deny whether it had any information concerning nonfinancial crimes. Thus, the issue was narrowed to Medico's nonfinancial-crime history insofar as it is a matter of public record.

The District Court granted the Department's motion for summary judgment, relying on three separate grounds. First, it concluded that 28 U.S.C. § 534, the statute that authorizes the exchange of rap-sheet information with other official agencies, also prohibits the release of such information to members of the public, and therefore that Exemption 3 was applicable. Second, it decided that files containing rap sheets were included within the category of "personnel and medical files and similar files the disclosure of which would constitute an unwarranted invasion of privacy," and therefore that Exemption 6 was applicable. The term "similar files" applied because rap-sheet information "is personal to the individual named therein." App. to Pet. for Cert. 56a. After balancing Medico's privacy interest against the public interest in disclosure, the District Court concluded that the invasion of privacy was "clearly unwarranted." [11] Finally, the court held that the rap sheet was also protected by Exemption 7(C) but it ordered the Department to file a statement containing the requested data *in camera,* to give it an opportunity to reconsider the issue if, after reviewing that statement, such action seemed appropriate. After the Department made that filing, the District Court advised the parties that it would not reconsider the matter but it did seal the *in camera* submission and make it part of the record on appeal.

The Court of Appeals reversed. 259 U.S.App.D.C. 426, 816 F.2d 730 (1987). It held that an individual's privacy interest in criminal-history information that is a matter of public record was minimal at best. Noting the absence of any statutory standards by which to judge the public interest in disclosure, the Court of Appeals concluded that it should be bound by the state and local determinations that such information should be made available to the general public. Accordingly, it held that Exemptions 6 and 7(C) were inapplicable. It also agreed with respondent that Exemption 3 did not apply because 28 U.S.C.

11. "It seems highly unlikely that information about offenses which may have occurred 30 or 40 years ago, as in the case of William Medico, would have any relevance or public interest. The same can be said for information relating to the arrest or conviction of persons for minor criminal offenses or offenses which are completely unrelated to anything now under consideration by the plaintiffs. That information is personal to the third party (Charles Medico), and it if exists, its release would constitute 'a clearly unwarranted invasion of personal privacy.' The Court concludes therefore that those documents and that information are exempt from disclosure pursuant to 5 U.S.C. § 552(b)(6) and (7)(C)." *Id.,* at 57a.

§ 534 did not qualify as a statute "specifically" exempting rap sheets from disclosure.

In response to rehearing petitions advising the court that, contrary to its original understanding, most States had adopted policies of refusing to provide members of the public with criminal-history summaries, the Court of Appeals modified its holding. 265 U.S.App.D.C. 365, 831 F.2d 1124 (1987). With regard to the public interest side of the balance, the court now recognized that it could not rely upon state policies of disclosure. However, it adhered to its view that federal judges are not in a position to make "idiosyncratic" evaluations of the public interest in particular disclosures, see 259 U.S.App.D.C., at 437, 816 F.2d, at 741; instead, it directed district courts to consider "the general disclosure policies of the statute." 265 U.S.App.D.C., at 367, 831 F.2d, at 1126. With regard to the privacy interest in nondisclosure of rap sheets, the court told the District Court "only to make a factual determination in these kinds of cases: Has a legitimate privacy interest of the subject in his rap sheets faded because they appear on the public record?" *Id.,* at 368, 831 F.2d, at 1127. In accordance with its initial opinion, it remanded the case to the District Court to determine whether the withheld information is publicly available at its source, and if so, whether the Department might satisfy its statutory obligation by referring respondents to the enforcement agency or agencies that had provided the original information.

Although he had concurred in the Court of Appeals' original disposition, Judge Starr dissented, expressing disagreement with the majority on three points. First, he rejected the argument that there is no privacy interest in "cumulative, indexed, computerized" data simply because the underlying information is on record at local courthouses or police stations:

> "As I see it, computerized data banks of the sort involved here present issues considerably more difficult than, and certainly very different from, a case involving the source records themselves. This conclusion is buttressed by what I now know to be the host of state laws requiring that cumulative, indexed criminal history information be kept confidential, as well as by general Congressional indications of concern about the privacy implications of computerized data banks. *See* H.R.Rep. No. 1416, 93d Cong., 2d Sess. 3, 6–9 (1974), *reprinted in Legislative History of the Privacy Act of 1974, Source Book on Privacy,* 296, 299–302 (1974)." *Id.,* at 369, 831 F.2d, at 1128.

Second, Judge Starr concluded that the statute required the District Court to make a separate evaluation of the public interest in disclosure depending upon the kind of use that would be made of the information and the identity of the subject:

> "Although there may be no public interest in disclosure of the FBI rap sheet of one's otherwise inconspicuously anonymous next-door neighbor, there may be a significant public interest—one that overcomes the substantial privacy interest at stake—in the rap sheet of a public figure or an official holding high governmental office. For guidance in

fleshing out that analysis, it seems sensible to me to draw upon the substantial body of defamation law dealing with 'public personages.' " *Id.,* at 370, 831 F.2d, at 1129.

Finally, he questioned the feasibility of requiring the Department to determine the availability of the requested material at its source, and expressed concern that the majority's approach departed from the original purpose of the FOIA and threatened to convert the Federal Government into a clearinghouse for personal information that had been collected about millions of persons under a variety of different situations:

> "We are now informed that many federal agencies collect items of information on individuals that are ostensibly matters of public record. For example, Veterans Administration and Social Security records include birth certificates, marriage licenses, and divorce decrees (which may recite findings of fault); the Department of Housing and Urban Development maintains data on millions of home mortgages that are presumably 'public records' at county clerks' offices. * * * Under the majority's approach, in the absence of state confidentiality laws, there would appear to be a virtual per se rule requiring all such information to be released. The federal government is thereby transformed in one fell swoop into *the* clearinghouse for highly personal information, releasing records on any person, to any requester, for any purpose. This Congress did not intend." *Id.,* at 371, 831 F.2d, at 1130 (emphasis in original).

The Court of Appeals denied rehearing en banc, with four judges dissenting. Because of the potential effect of the Court of Appeals' opinion on values of personal privacy, we granted certiorari. 485 U.S. ——, 108 S.Ct. 1467, 99 L.Ed.2d 697 (1988). We now reverse.

IV

Exemption 7(C) requires us to balance the privacy interest in maintaining, as the Government puts it, the "practical obscurity" of the rap sheets, against the public interest in their release.

The preliminary question is whether Medico's interest in the non-disclosure of any rap sheet the FBI might have on him is the sort of "personal privacy" interest that Congress intended Exemption 7(C) to protect.[13] As we have pointed out before, "[t]he cases sometimes characterized as protecting 'privacy' have in fact involved at least two different kinds of interests. One is the individual interest in avoiding disclosure of personal matters, and another is the interest in independence in making certain kinds of important decisions." *Whalen v. Roe,*

13. The question of the statutory meaning of privacy under FOIA is, of course, not the same as the question whether a tort action might lie for invasion of privacy or the question whether an individual's interest in privacy is protected by the Constitution. See, *e.g., Cox Broadcasting Corp. v. Cohn,* 420 U.S. 469, 95 S.Ct. 1029, 43 L.Ed.2d 328 (1975) (Constitution forbids State from penalizing publication of name of deceased rape victim obtained from public records); *Paul v. Davis,* 424 U.S. 693, 712–714, 96 S.Ct. 1155, 1165–1167, 47 L.Ed.2d 405 (1976) (no constitutional privacy right affected by publication of name of arrested but untried shoplifter).

429 U.S. 589, 598–600, 97 S.Ct. 869, 875–877, 51 L.Ed.2d 64 (1977) (footnotes omitted). Here, the former interest, "in avoiding disclosure of personal matters," is implicated. Because events summarized in a rap sheet have been previously disclosed to the public, respondents contend that Medico's privacy interest in avoiding disclosure of a federal compilation of these events approaches zero. We reject respondents' cramped notion of personal privacy.

To begin with, both the common law and the literal understandings of privacy encompass the individual's control of information concerning his or her person. In an organized society, there are few facts that are not at one time or another divulged to another. Thus the extent of the protection accorded a privacy right at common law rested in part on the degree of dissemination of the allegedly private fact and the extent to which the passage of time rendered it private.[15] According to Webster's initial definition, information may be classified as "private" if it is "intended for or restricted to the use of a particular person or group or class of persons: not freely available to the public." Recognition of this attribute of a privacy interest supports the distinction, in terms of personal privacy, between scattered disclosure of the bits of information contained in a rap sheet and revelation of the rap sheet as a whole. The very fact that federal funds have been spent to prepare, index, and maintain these criminal-history files demonstrates that the individual items of information in the summaries would not otherwise be "freely available" either to the officials who have access to the underlying files or to the general public. Indeed, if the summaries were "freely available," there would be no reason to invoke the FOIA to obtain access to the information they contain. Granted, in many contexts the fact that information is not freely available is no reason to exempt that information from a statute generally requiring its dissemination. But the issue here is whether the compilation of otherwise hard-to-obtain information alters the privacy interest implicated by disclosure of that information. Plainly there is a vast difference between the public records that might be found after a diligent search of courthouse files, county archives, and local police stations throughout the country and a computerized summary located in a single clearinghouse of information.

This conclusion is supported by the web of federal statutory and regulatory provisions that limit the disclosure of rap-sheet information. That is, Congress has authorized rap-sheet dissemination to banks, local licensing officials, the securities industry, the nuclear-power industry, and other law-enforcement agencies. See *supra,* at 1470–1471. Fur-

15. See Warren & Brandeis, The Right to Privacy, 4 Harv.L.Rev. 193, 198 (1890–1891) ("The common law secures to each individual the right of determining, ordinarily, to what extent his thoughts, sentiments, and emotions shall be communicated to others. * * * [E]ven if he has chosen to give them expression, he generally retains the power to fix the limits of the publicity which shall be given them"). The common law recognized that one did not necessarily forfeit a privacy interest in matters made part of the public record, albeit the privacy interest was diminished and another who obtained the facts from the public record might be privileged to publish it.

ther, the FBI has permitted such disclosure to the subject of the rap sheet and, more generally, to assist in the apprehension of wanted persons or fugitives. See *supra,* at 1471. Finally, the FBI's exchange of rap-sheet information "is subject to cancellation if dissemination is made outside the receiving departments or related agencies." 28 U.S.C. § 534(b). This careful and limited pattern of authorized rap-sheet disclosure fits the dictionary definition of privacy as involving a restriction of information "to the use of a particular person or group or class of persons." Moreover, although perhaps not specific enough to constitute a statutory Exemption under the FOIA Exemption 3, 5 U.S.C. § 552(b)(3),[17] these statutes and regulations, taken as a whole, evidence a congressional intent to protect the privacy of rap-sheet subjects, and a concomitant recognition of the power of compilations to affect personal privacy that outstrips the combined power of the bits of information contained within.

Other portions of the FOIA itself bolster the conclusion that disclosure of records regarding private citizens, identifiable by name, is not what the framers of the FOIA had in mind. Specifically, the FOIA provides that "[t]o the extent required to prevent a clearly unwarranted invasion of personal privacy, an agency may delete identifying details when it makes available or publishes an opinion, statement of policy, interpretation, or staff manual or instruction." 5 U.S.C. § 552(a)(2). Additionally, the FOIA assures that "[a]ny reasonably segregable portion of a record shall be provided to any person requesting such record after deletion of the portions which are exempt under [§ (b)]." 5 U.S.C. § 552(b) (1982 ed., Supp. IV). These provisions, for deletion of identifying references and disclosure of segregable portions of records with exempt information deleted, reflect a congressional understanding that disclosure of records containing personal details about private citizens can infringe significant privacy interests.

Also supporting our conclusion that a strong privacy interest inheres in the non-disclosure of compiled computerized information is the Privacy Act, codified at 5 U.S.C. § 552a (1982 ed. and Supp. IV). The Privacy Act was passed in 1974 largely out of concern over "the impact of computer data banks on individual privacy." H.R.Rep. No. 93–1416, p. 7 (1974). The Privacy Act provides generally that "[n]o agency shall disclose any record which is contained in a system of records * * * except pursuant to a written request by, or with the prior written consent of, the individual to whom the record pertains." 5 U.S.C. § 552a(b) (1982 ed., Supp. IV). Although the Privacy Act contains a variety of exceptions to this rule, including an Exemption for information required to be disclosed under the FOIA, see 5 U.S.C. § 552a(b)(2), Congress' basic policy concern regarding the implications of computerized data banks for personal privacy is certainly relevant in

17. The Court of Appeals reversed the District Court's holding in favor of petitioners on the Exemption 3 issue, and petitioners do not renew their Exemption 3 argument before this Court. See Pet. for Cert. 6, n. 1.

our consideration of the privacy interest affected by dissemination of rap sheets from the FBI computer.

Given this level of federal concern over centralized databases, the fact that most States deny the general public access to their criminal-history summaries should not be surprising. As we have pointed out, see *supra,* at 1471 and n. 2, in 47 States non-conviction data from criminal-history summaries are not available at all, and even conviction data are "generally unavailable to the public." See n. 2, *supra.* State policies, of course, do not determine the meaning of a federal statute, but they provide evidence that the law-enforcement profession generally assumes—as has the Department of Justice—that individual subjects have a significant privacy interest in their criminal histories. It is reasonable to presume that Congress legislated with an understanding of this professional point of view.

In addition to the common-law and dictionary understanding, the basic difference between scattered bits of criminal history and a federal compilation, federal statutory provisions, and state policies, our cases have also recognized the privacy interest inherent in the nondisclosure of certain information even where the information may have been at one time public. Most apposite for present purposes is our decision in *Department of the Air Force v. Rose,* 425 U.S. 352, 96 S.Ct. 1592, 48 L.Ed.2d 11 (1976). New York University law students sought Air Force Honor and Ethics Code case summaries for a Law Review project on military discipline. The Academy had already publicly posted these summaries on 40 squadron bulletin boards, usually with identifying names redacted (names were posted for cadets who were found guilty and who left the Academy), and with instructions that cadets should read the summaries only if necessary. Although the opinion dealt with Exemption 6's exception for "personnel and medical files and similar files the disclosure of which would constitute a clearly unwarranted invasion of personal privacy," and our opinion today deals with Exemption 7(C), much of our discussion in *Rose* is applicable here. We explained that the FOIA permits release of a segregable portion of a record with other portions deleted, and that *in camera* inspection was proper to determine whether parts of a record could be released while keeping other parts secret. See *id.,* at 373–377, 96 S.Ct., at 1604–1607; 5 U.S.C. §§ 552(b) and (a)(4)(B) (1982 ed. and Supp. IV). We emphasized the FOIA's segregability and *in camera* provisions in order to explain that the case summaries, *with identifying names redacted,* were generally disclosable. * * *

* * *

* * * First: We praised the Academy's tradition of protecting personal privacy through redaction of names from the case summaries. But even with names redacted, subjects of such summaries can often be identified through other, disclosed information. So, second: *Even though the summaries, with only names redacted, had once been public,* we recognized the potential invasion of privacy through later recogni-

tion of identifying details, and approved the Court of Appeals' rule permitting the District Court to delete "other identifying information" in order to safeguard this privacy interest. If a cadet has a privacy interest in past discipline that was once public but may have been "wholly forgotten," the ordinary citizen surely has a similar interest in the aspects of his or her criminal history that may have been wholly forgotten.

We have also recognized the privacy interest in keeping personal facts away from the public eye. In *Whalen v. Roe,* 429 U.S. 589, 97 S.Ct. 869, 51 L.Ed.2d 64 (1977), we held that "the State of New York may record, in a centralized computer file, the names and addresses of all persons who have obtained, pursuant to a doctor's prescription, certain drugs for which there is both a lawful and an unlawful market." *Id.,* at 591, 97 S.Ct., at 872. In holding only that the Federal Constitution does not *prohibit* such a compilation, we recognized that such a centralized computer file posed a "threat to privacy".

* * *

In sum, the fact that "an event is not wholly 'private' does not mean that an individual has no interest in limiting disclosure or dissemination of the information." Rehnquist, Is an Expanded Right of Privacy Consistent with Fair and Effective Law Enforcement?, Nelson Timothy Stephens Lectures, University of Kansas Law School, pt. 1, p. 13 (Sept. 26–27, 1974). The privacy interest in a rap sheet is substantial. The substantial character of that interest is affected by the fact that in today's society the computer can accumulate and store information that would otherwise have surely been forgotten long before a person attains the age of 80, when the FBI's rap sheets are discarded.

V

Exemption 7(C), by its terms, permits an agency to withhold a document only when revelation "could reasonably be expected to constitute an *unwarranted* invasion of personal privacy." We must next address what factors might *warrant* an invasion of the interest described in Part IV, *supra.*

Our previous decisions establish that whether an invasion of privacy is *warranted* cannot turn on the purposes for which the request for information is made. Except for cases in which the objection to disclosure is based on a claim of privilege and the person requesting disclosure is the party protected by the privilege, the identity of the requesting party has no bearing on the merits of his or her FOIA request. Thus, although the subject of a presentence report can waive a privilege that might defeat a third party's access to that report, *United States Department of Justice v. Julian,* 486 U.S. —, —, 108 S.Ct. 1606, —, 100 L.Ed.2d 1 (1988), and although the FBI's policy of granting the subject of a rap sheet access to his own criminal history is consistent with its policy of denying access to all other members of the general public, see *supra,* at 1471, the rights of the two press respondents in this case are no different from those that might be asserted by any other third party, such as a neighbor or prospective employer. As we have repeatedly stated, Congress "clearly intended" the FOIA "to give any member of the public as much right to disclosure as one with a special interest [in a particular document]." *NLRB v. Sears, Roebuck & Co.,* 421 U.S. 132, 149, 95 S.Ct. 1504, 1515, 44 L.Ed.2d 29 (1975). As Professor Davis explained: "The Act's sole concern is with what must be made public or not made public." [19]

Thus whether disclosure of a private document under Exemption 7(C) is warranted must turn on the nature of the requested document and its relationship to "the basic purpose of the Freedom of Information Act 'to open agency action to the light of public scrutiny.'" *Department of the Air Force v. Rose,* 425 U.S., at 372, 96 S.Ct., at 1604, rather than on the particular purpose for which the document is being requested. In our leading case on the FOIA, we declared that the Act was designed to create a broad right of access to "official information." *EPA v. Mink,* 410 U.S. 73, 80, 93 S.Ct. 827, 832, 35 L.Ed.2d 119 (1973). In his dissent in that case, Justice Douglas characterized the philosophy of the statute by quoting this comment by Henry Steele Commager:

> " 'The generation that made the nation thought secrecy in government one of the instruments of Old World tyranny and committed itself to the principle that a democracy cannot function unless the people are permitted to know *what their government is up to.*' " *Id.,* at 105, 93 S.Ct., at 845 (quoting from The New York Review of Books, Oct. 5, 1972, p. 7) (emphasis added).

This basic policy of " 'full agency disclosure unless information is exempted under clearly delineated statutory language,' " *Department of the Air Force v. Rose,* 425 U.S., at 360–361, 96 S.Ct., at 1599 (quoting S.Rep. No. 813, 89th Cong., 1st Sess., 3 (1965)), indeed focuses on the citizens' right to be informed about "what their government is up to." Official information that sheds light on an agency's performance of its statutory duties falls squarely within that statutory purpose. That purpose, however, is not fostered by disclosure of information about private citizens that is accumulated in various governmental files but that reveals little or nothing about an agency's own conduct. In this case—and presumably in the typical case in which one private citizen is seeking information about another—the requester does not intend to discover anything about the conduct of the agency that has possession of the requested records. Indeed, response to this request would not shed any light on the conduct of any Government agency or official.

The point is illustrated by our decision in *Rose, supra.* As discussed earlier, we held that the FOIA required the United States Air Force to honor a request for *in camera* submission of disciplinary-hearing summaries maintained in the Academy's Honors and Ethics

19. Davis, The Information Act: A Preliminary Analysis, 34 U.Chi.L.Rev. 761, 765 (1966–1967), quoted in JUSTICE SCALIA's dissenting opinion in *United States Department of Justice v. Julian,* 486 U.S. ___, ___, 108 S.Ct. 1606, ___, 100 L.Ed.2d 1 (1988).

Code reading files. The summaries obviously contained information that would explain how the disciplinary procedures actually functioned and therefore were an appropriate subject of a FOIA request. All parties, however, agreed that the files should be redacted by deleting information that would identify the particular cadets to whom the summaries related. The deletions were unquestionably appropriate because the names of the particular cadets were irrelevant to the inquiry into the way the Air Force Academy administered its Honor Code; leaving the identifying material in the summaries would therefore have been a "clearly unwarranted" invasion of individual privacy. If, instead of seeking information about the Academy's own conduct, the requests had asked for specific files to obtain information about the persons to whom those files related, the public interest that supported the decision in *Rose* would have been inapplicable. In fact, we explicitly recognized that "the basic purpose of the [FOIA is] to open agency action to the light of public scrutiny." *Id.*, at 372, 96 S.Ct., at 1604.

Respondents argue that there is a two-fold public interest in learning about Medico's past arrests or convictions: He allegedly had improper dealings with a corrupt Congressman and he is an officer of a corporation with defense contracts. But if Medico has, in fact, been arrested or convicted of certain crimes, that information would neither aggravate nor mitigate his allegedly improper relationship with the Congressman; more specifically, it would tell us nothing directly about the character of the *Congressman's* behavior. Nor would it tell us anything about the conduct of the *Department of Defense* (DOD) in awarding one or more contracts to the Medico Company. Arguably a FOIA request to the DOD for records relating to those contracts, or for documents describing the agency's procedures, if any, for determining whether officers of a prospective contractor have criminal records, would constitute an appropriate request for "official information." Conceivably Medico's rap sheet would provide details to include in a news story, but, in itself, this is not the kind of public interest for which Congress enacted the FOIA. In other words, although there is undoubtedly some public interest in anyone's criminal history, especially if the history is in some way related to the subject's dealing with a public official or agency, the FOIA's central purpose is to ensure that the *Government's* activities be opened to the sharp eye of public scrutiny, not that information about *private citizens* that happens to be in the warehouse of the Government be so disclosed. Thus, it should come as no surprise that in none of our cases construing the FOIA have we found it appropriate to order a Government agency to honor a FOIA request for information about a particular private citizen.[21]

21. In fact, in at least three cases we have specifically *rejected* requests for information about private citizens. See *CIA v. Sims,* 471 U.S. 159, 105 S.Ct. 1881, 85 L.Ed.2d 173 (1985); *FBI v. Abramson,* 456 U.S. 615, 102 S.Ct. 2054, 72 L.Ed.2d 376 (1982); *United States Department of State v. Washington Post Co.,* 456 U.S. 595, 102 S.Ct. 1957, 72 L.Ed.2d 358 (1982).

What we have said should make clear that the public interest in the release of any rap sheet on Medico that may exist is not the type of interest protected by the FOIA. Medico may or may not be one of the 24 million persons for whom the FBI has a rap sheet. If respondents are entitled to have the FBI tell them what it knows about Medico's criminal history, any other member of the public is entitled to the same disclosure—whether for writing a news story, for deciding whether or not to employ Medico, to rent a house to him, to extend credit to him, or simply to confirm or deny a suspicion. There is, unquestionably, *some* public interest in providing interested citizens with answers to their questions about Medico. But that interest falls outside the ambit of the public interest that the FOIA was enacted to serve.

Finally, we note that Congress has provided that the standard fees for production of documents under the FOIA shall be waived or reduced "if disclosure of the information is in the public interest because it is likely to contribute significantly to public understanding of the operations or activities of the government and is not primarily in the commercial interest of the requester." 5 U.S.C. § 552(a)(4)(A)(iii) (1982 ed., Supp. IV). Although such a provision obviously implies that there will be requests that do not meet such a "public interest" standard, we think it relevant to today's inquiry regarding the public interest in release of rap sheets on private citizens that Congress once again expressed the core purpose of the FOIA as "contribut[ing] significantly to public understanding *of the operations or activities of the government.*"

VI

Both the general requirement that a court "shall determine the matter de novo" and the specific reference to an "unwarranted" invasion of privacy in Exemption 7(C) indicate that a court must balance the public interest in disclosure against the interest Congress intended the Exemption to protect. Although both sides agree that such a balance must be undertaken, *how* such a balance should be done is in dispute. The Court of Appeals majority expressed concern about assigning federal judges the task of striking a proper case-by-case, or ad hoc, balance between individual privacy interests and the public interest in the disclosure of criminal-history information without providing those judges standards to assist in performing that task. Our cases provide support for the proposition that categorical decisions may be appropriate and individual circumstances disregarded when a case fits into a genus in which the balance characteristically tips in one direction. * * *

* * *

Finally: The privacy interest in maintaining the practical obscurity of rap-sheet information will always be high. When the subject of such a rap sheet is a private citizen and when the information is in the Government's control as a compilation, rather than as a record of "what the Government is up to," the privacy interest protected by

Exemption 7(C) is in fact at its apex while the FOIA-based public interest in disclosure is at its nadir. See Parts IV and V, *supra.* Such a disparity on the scales of justice holds for a class of cases without regard to individual circumstances; the standard virtues of bright-line rules are thus present, and the difficulties attendant to ad hoc adjudication may be avoided. Accordingly, we hold as a categorical matter that a third party's request for law-enforcement records or information about a private citizen can reasonably be expected to invade that citizen's privacy, and that when the request seeks no "official information" about a Government agency, but merely records that the Government happens to be storing, the invasion of privacy is "unwarranted." The judgment of the Court of Appeals is reversed.

* * *

Notes and Questions

1. Do you agree with the Supreme Court's holding? Should a convicted criminal have a right to keep his or her past record from being reported? What about the public's right to know about criminal activity?

2. Many governmental agencies, due to recent technological advances, have computers that "link" to the computer systems of other governmental agencies. This makes criminal records easier to locate and compile.

3. Conceivably an independent private company could collect public court records from around the country and compile its own "rap sheets." Would this be an invasion of privacy?

4. As with many constitutional issues, courts generally end up applying some type of balancing test when deciding privacy cases. Given the constant growth of governmental data bases, future privacy disputes, with appropriate balancing tests can be expected.

Chapter X

RIGHT TO ACCURACY OF INFORMATION

A. RIGHTS OF PERSONS ABOUT WHOM DATA IS KEPT

1. FALSE OR INCOMPLETE INFORMATION

THOMPSON v. SAN ANTONIO RETAIL MERCHANTS ASS'N

United States Court of Appeals, Fifth Circuit, 1982.
682 F.2d 509.

Before RUBIN, JOHNSON and GARWOOD, CIRCUIT JUDGES.

PER CURIAM:

This case involves the liability of the San Antonio Retail Merchants Association (SARMA) for an inaccurate credit report. Gulf Oil Corporation (Gulf) and Montgomery Ward (Ward's) denied credit to William Douglas Thompson, III, on the basis of erroneous credit information furnished by SARMA. The district court, after a nonjury trial, entered judgment for Thompson in the sum of $10,000 actual damages and $4,485 attorneys' fees. SARMA appeals.

I. BACKGROUND

SARMA provides a computerized credit reporting service to local business subscribers. This service depends heavily upon credit history information fed into SARMA's files by subscribers. A key mechanism used by SARMA to update its files is a computerized "automatic capturing" feature. A subscriber must feed certain identifying information from its own computer terminal into SARMA's central computer in order to gain access to the credit history of a particular consumer. When presented with this identifying information, SARMA's computer searches its records and displays on the subscriber's terminal the credit history file that most nearly matches the consumer. The decision whether to accept a given file as being that of a particular consumer is left completely to the terminal operator. When a subscriber does accept a given file as pertaining to a particular consumer, however, the computer automatically captures into the file any information input from the subscriber's terminal that the central file did not already have.

The disadvantage of an automatic capturing feature is that it may accept erroneous information fed in by subscribers, unless special auditing procedures are built into the system. In the instant case, SARMA failed to check the accuracy of a social security number obtained by its automatic capturing feature. The social security number is the single most important identifying factor for credit-reference purposes. As a result, the computer erroneously began to report the bad credit history of "William Daniel Thompson, Jr.," to subscribers inquiring about "William Douglas Thompson, III."

In November 1974, William Daniel Thompson, Jr., opened a credit account with Gordon's Jewelers (Gordon's) in San Antonio, listing his social security number as 457–68–5778, his address as 132 Baxter, his occupation as truck loader, and his marital status as single. He subsequently ran up a delinquent account of $77.25 at Gordon's that was ultimately charged off as a bad debt. When Gordon's voluntarily reported the bad debt, SARMA placed the information and a derogatory credit rating into file number 5867114, without any identifying social security number.

In early 1978, the plaintiff, William Douglas Thompson, III, applied for credit with Gulf and with Ward's in San Antonio. He listed his social security as 407–86–4065, his address as 6929 Timbercreek, his occupation as grounds keeper, and his wife as Deborah C. On February 9, 1978, Gulf's terminal operator mistakenly accepted file number 5867114 as that of the plaintiff. SARMA's computer thereupon automatically captured various information about William Douglas Thompson, III, including his social security number, into file number 5867114. At that point, the original file, which was on William Daniel Thompson, Jr., became a potpourri of information on both the plaintiff and the original William Daniel Thompson, Jr. The name on the file remained that of William Daniel Thompson, Jr. The social security number became that of the plaintiff, the current address and employer became that of the plaintiff, a former address and employer became that of William Daniel Thompson, Jr., and the wife's name became that of the plaintiff's wife.

Shortly thereafter, Ward's terminal operator ran a credit check on the plaintiff, was given the garbled data, and accepted file number 5867114 as that of the plaintiff. As a result of the adverse information regarding the Gordon's account, Ward's denied the plaintiff credit. The plaintiff applied for credit at Ward's in May 1979 and was again rejected.

On February 21, 1978, Gulf requested a "revision" of file number 5867114, a procedure which entails a rechecking of information in a file with respect to a particular creditor or creditors. Following its usual procedures, SARMA would call Gordon's to verify in detail the information in the file. Although this was probably done, whoever contacted Gordon's apparently failed to check the social security number of Gordon's delinquent customer and take corrective action when it was received. Instead, the adverse information remained in the file under the plaintiff's social security number after Gulf's revision request, and Gulf denied the plaintiff credit.

The adverse information remained in the plaintiff's file during 1978 and the first five and a half months of 1979. During all of this time the plaintiff thought he had been denied credit from Ward's and Gulf because of a 1976 Texas felony conviction for burglary. He had received a five-year probationary sentence, but subsequently gained fulltime employment and straightened out his life. In June of 1979, plaintiff's wife learned from her credit union in processing an application for a loan that her husband's adverse credit rating resulted from a bad debt at Gordon's. The plaintiff knew he had never had an account at Gordon's so he and his wife went directly to their place of business. After waiting some two hours he was informed that there had indeed been a mistake, their credit record was for William Daniel Thompson, Jr.

The plaintiff and his wife went to SARMA with this information in an attempt to purge the erroneous credit information. They spoke with an individual and showed birth registration and drivers license information revealing his name to be William Douglas Thompson III. The entire process required some three hours. Nevertheless SARMA thereafter mailed appellee a letter addressed to William Daniel Thompson III. Appellee's wife again returned to SARMA. Following this SARMA once again addressed appellee in another letter as William Daniel Thompson III. Appellee again returned to SARMA—yet again SARMA wrote still another letter with the same incorrect name. Further, though SARMA's policy was to send corrections made on a file to any subscribers who had made inquiry about it within the last six months, SARMA failed to notify Ward's of the corrections. The plaintiff filed an action in state court on October 4, 1979. It was not until October 16, 1979, that SARMA informed Ward's of the erroneous credit information. On November 5, 1979, the action was removed to the federal district court. After a bench trial, the district court found that denials of credit to the appellee by Gulf and Ward's were caused by SARMA's failure to follow reasonable procedures to assure the maximum possible accuracy of its files. The district court awarded plaintiff actual damages in the sum of $10,000 plus attorneys' fees in the sum of $4485.

II. The Liability Issue

Under 15 U.S.C. § 1681o of the Fair Credit Reporting Act (Act), a "consumer reporting agency" is liable to "any consumer" for negligent failure to comply with "any requirement imposed" by the Act. In the instant case, the district court determined that SARMA was liable under section 1681o for negligent failure to comply with section 1681e(b) of the Act, which provides:

> When a consumer reporting agency *prepares* a consumer report, it shall follow *reasonable procedures* to assure *maximum possible accuracy* of information concerning the individual about whom the report relates.

15 U.S.C. § 1681e(b) (emphasis added).

Section 1681e(b) does not impose strict liability for any inaccurate credit report, but only a duty of reasonable care in preparation of the report. That duty extends to updating procedures, because "preparation" of a consumer report should be viewed as a continuing process and the obligation to insure accuracy arises with every addition of information. *Lowry v. Credit Bureau, Inc. of Georgia,* 444 F.Supp. 541, 544 (N.D.Ga.1978). The standard of conduct by which the trier of fact must judge the adequacy of agency procedures is what a reasonably prudent person would do under the circumstances.

Applying the reasonable-person standard, the district court found two acts of negligence in SARMA's updating procedures. First, SARMA failed to exercise reasonable care in programming its computer to automatically capture information into a file without requiring any minimum number of "points of correspondence" between the consumer and the file or having an adequate auditing procedure to foster accuracy. Second, SARMA failed to employ reasonable procedures designed to learn the disparity in social security numbers for the two Thompsons when it revised file number 5867114 at Gulf's request. This Court can reverse the district court on these findings of fact only if there is a definite and firm conviction that the judgment of the district court is clearly erroneous.

With respect to the first act of negligence, George Zepeda, SARMA's manager, testified that SARMA's computer had no minimum number of points of correspondence to be satisfied before an inquiring subscriber could accept credit information. Moreover, SARMA had no way of knowing if the information supplied by the subscriber was correct. Although SARMA did conduct spot audits to verify social security numbers, it did not audit all subscribers. With respect to the second act of negligence, SARMA's verification process failed to uncover the erroneous social security number even though Gulf made a specific request for a "revision" to check the adverse credit history ascribed to the plaintiff. SARMA's manager, Mr. Zepeda, testified that what should have been done upon the request for a revision, was to pick up the phone and check with Gordon's and learn, among other things, the social security number for William Daniel Thompson, Jr. It was the manager's further testimony that the social security number is the single most important information in a consumer's credit file. In light of this evidence, this Court cannot conclude that the district court was clearly erroneous in finding negligent violation of section 1681e(b).

III. Award of Damages

The district court's award of $10,000 in actual damages was based on humiliation and mental distress to the plaintiff. Even when there are no out-of-pocket expenses, humiliation and mental distress do constitute recoverable elements of damage under the Act. In the instant case, the amount of damages is a question of fact which may be reversed by this Court only if the district court's findings are clearly erroneous.

SARMA asserts that Thompson failed to prove any actual damages, or at best proved only minimal damages for humiliation and mental distress. There was evidence, however, that Thompson suffered humiliation and embarassment from being denied credit on three occasions. Thompson testified that the denial of credit hurt him deeply because of his mistaken belief that it resulted from his felony conviction:

> I was trying to build myself back up, trying to set myself up, get back on my feet again. I was working sixty hours a week and sometimes seventy. I went back to school. I was going to school at night three nights a week, four nights a week, three hours a night, and [denial of credit] really hurt. It made me disgusted with myself.
>
> * * * [I needed credit to] be able to obtain things that everybody else is able to obtain, to be able to buy clothes or set myself up where I can show my ability to be trusted.
>
> We didn't even have a bed. It was pretty bad. We were hurting. Everything we had to do, we had to save up and pay cash for strictly. It was just impossible to do it any other way.

Further, the inaccurate information remained in SARMA's files for almost one and one-half years after the inaccurate information was inserted. Even after the error was discovered, Thompson spent months pressing SARMA to correct its mistakes and fully succeeded only after bringing a lawsuit against SARMA. This Court is of the opinion that the trial judge was entitled to conclude that the humiliation and mental distress were not minimal but substantial.

SARMA contends that the instant damage award is excessive when compared to similar cases such as *Millstone,* 528 F.2d at 834–35 and *Bryant,* 487 F.Supp. at 1239–40. In *Millstone,* an insurance company cancelled an automobile insurance policy after a consumer credit report alleged the insured was a political activist disliked by his neighbors. The insurer first cancelled the insured's policy and then reinstated it when an agent discovered the insured was in fact a highly respected assistant managing editor of the *St. Louis Post Dispatch.* Even though the incorrect report involved a mere $68.00 insurance policy, the district court awarded $2500 in actual damages for Millstone's mental anguish over the report. In *Bryant,* an inaccurate credit report was issued on a consumer in connection with a mortgage application for a house purchase. The credit report resulted in denial of the mortgage. The consumer called the inaccuracy to the attention of the credit reporting agency, yet the same inaccurate information was issued in connection with a later mortgage application. A jury determination of $8,000 in actual damages was sustained in that instance. *Bryant,* 487 F.Supp. at 1242–43. The damage award in the instant case is not so out of line with *Bryant* and *Millstone* as to be clearly erroneous. The case *sub judice* was a trial before the court without a jury. The trial judge was in a position to weigh the credibility of testimony on humiliation and mental distress and, therefore, should be given considerable latitude; it cannot be said that his determination was clearly erroneous.

SARMA finally asserts that Thompson was required to mitigate his damages by first exhausting alternative remedies. SARMA cites section 1681i of the Act which sets forth a procedure for consumers to challenge the completeness or accuracy of any disputed information in this file. The Act, however, does not require that a consumer pursue the remedies provided in section 1681i before bringing suit under section 1681o for violation of section 1681e. If a consumer can prove a violation of section 1681e, he can sue directly on that basis without first exhausting alternative remedies. *McPhee v. Chilton Corp.,* 468 F.Supp. 494, 498 n. 7 (D.Conn.1978). Thompson was not required to mitigate his damages by formally disputing the accuracy of information contained in his file.

IV. Award of Attorneys' Fees

Section 1681o also allows an award of attorneys' fees. The district court may determine the amount of attorneys' fees on the basis of the guidelines set forth in *Johnson v. Georgia Highway Express, Inc.,* 488 F.2d 714 (5th Cir.1974). The district court explicitly applied the *Johnson* criteria and awarded $4485 in attorneys' fees based on 41.5 hours of work at $90 per hour and other special fees. The determination of a reasonable attorneys' fee is a matter within the discretion of the trial judge and should not be set aside absent clear abuse of discretion. This Court cannot say that the district court clearly abused its discretion.

The judgment of the district court is Affirmed.

ROGAN v. CITY OF LOS ANGELES

United States District Court, Central District of California, 1987.
668 F.Supp. 1384.

Kelleher, Senior District Judge.

I. Introduction

This is an action under 42 U.S.C. section 1983 for money damages, declaratory relief, litigation costs and attorneys' fees against: (a) the City of Los Angeles ("the Defendant City"); and (b) two police officers employed by the city, Defendant Crotsley and Defendant Slack (referred to hereinafter collectively as "the Defendant Officers"). The action arises out of the alleged deprivation of Plaintiff Terry Dean Rogan's constitutional rights resulting from his mistaken arrests for robbery and murder.

Pending before the Court are the parties' cross motions for summary judgment on the issue of liability. The material evidentiary facts are uncontroverted.

II. Analysis

A. *42 U.S.C. 1983 Action Against the City of Los Angeles*

In order to state a civil rights claim against a municipality under 42 U.S.C. section 1983, a plaintiff must show that: (1) he has suffered a deprivation of a constitutionally protected interest; and (2) said deprivation was caused by an official policy, custom or usage of the municipality. Each element will be discussed below.

1. *Deprivation of a Constitutionally Protected Interest*

a. *Relevant Facts*

During 1981, Bernard McKandes ("McKandes"), an escapee from an Alabama state prison, started using Plaintiff's name after he obtained Plaintiff's birth certificate. McKandes obtained the birth certificate at Saginaw, Michigan, Plaintiff's birthplace and place of residence.[2]

After obtaining Plaintiff's birth certificate, McKandes proceeded to California. McKandes there used Plaintiff's birth certificate to obtain a California driver's license and various other identification documents in Plaintiff's name.

Sometime during 1982, McKandes was arrested by the Los Angeles Police Department ("LAPD") on suspicion of murder. McKandes was using the false identification in Plaintiff's name at the time of his arrest. The LAPD released McKandes for reasons presently unknown.

Approximately three months later, but still during 1982, McKandes left Los Angeles and stopped using the identification in Plaintiff's name.

On or about April 20, 1982, Defendant Crotsley caused an arrest warrant to issue in the name of Terry Dean Rogan, charging him with two robbery-murders which occurred in Los Angeles that month. Said warrant listed Plaintiff's name and an alias, but did not contain McKandes' known physical characteristics (e.g., scars, tattoos, height, weight, etc.).

On approximately May 10, 1982, Defendant Slack caused the warrant information to be placed into the national computer arrest war-

2. McKandes obtained a copy of Plaintiff's birth certificate from one Derrick Smith ("Smith"). Said birth certificate was in good condition. Plaintiff testified that he tore up and threw away his copy of his birth certificate because it was mutilated. Plaintiff further testified that he has known Smith since he was young, and that Smith went to school with his brothers and sisters. Defendants strongly emphasize this evidence, but fail to explain it's significance, if any. Defendants apparently infer that Plaintiff was improperly involved in the transfer of his birth certificate from Smith to McKandes.

* * *

rant notification system known as the National Crime Information Center ("NCIC"). Entry of said information into the NCIC system ensured that any police officer in the United States having access to the system would be made aware that a robbery-murder warrant in the name of Terry Dean Rogan was outstanding in California. Like the warrant upon which it was based, said information set forth Plaintiff's name and an alias, but did not contain McKandes' known physical characteristics.

On or about June 7, 1982, Defendant Crotsley requested that an official police bulletin be completed and forwarded to certain police departments through official channels. Said bulletin contained, *inter alia:* (a) Plaintiff's name; (b) three aliases, one of which contained McKandes' correct surname; (c) McKandes' photograph; (d) McKandes' fingerprint; (e) McKandes' height; (f) McKandes' weight; and (g) notice that the suspect had the tattoo "Connie" on the right side of his chest. The bulletin also stated that the suspect should be considered armed and extremely dangerous. The bulletin's widest area of distribution was achieved by or about March 21, 1983, at which time it was sent to: (a) Chicago, Illinois; (b) Mobile, Alabama; and (c) Detroit, Michigan. None of Plaintiff's arrests at issue herein were made by police departments which relied upon the bulletin or had it in their possession.

During July, 1982, Defendant Slack reentered the pertinent NCIC record without modification or amendment.

On or about October 31, 1982, Plaintiff came into contact with officers of the Carrollton Township Police Department in Saginaw County, Michigan, during the course of a trespassing dispute. Plaintiff was arrested on a charge of resisting arrest. The police officers made an inquiry of the NCIC system. The resulting computer report reflected the existence of the California robbery-murder warrant in Plaintiff's name.

On or about November 1, 1982, the Carrollton police contacted LAPD about the California arrest warrant. The Carrollton police established four days later through fingerprint comparison and Plaintiff's lack of certain scars and tattoos that were visible on the body of the wanted suspect, McKandes, that Plaintiff was not the man wanted by the LAPD. Plaintiff then pleaded (either guilty or *nolo contendre,* the record does not reveal which) to the charge of resisting arrest and was sentenced to "time served" of five days, and released. Upon Plaintiff's initial arrest, the NCIC record regarding the California warrant was automatically removed from the NCIC system.

Later during November, 1982, Defendant Crotsley caused the arrest warrant information in Plaintiff's name to be reentered into the NCIC system without modifying same to reflect either the suspect's (i.e., McKandes') known unique physical characteristics (i.e., scars, tattoos) or the duplicate name-misidentification problem. As reflected by the relevant NCIC data entry form, an NCIC computer record contains a miscellaneous field that allows for the entry of up to 121 characters of information regarding identifying physical characteristics or possible mistaken identity-duplicate name situations.

During February or March, 1983, Plaintiff was a passenger in an automobile which was stopped by Bay County sheriff's deputies outside of Saginaw, Michigan, for failure to use a turn signal. The officers ran a computer check on Plaintiff after he showed the officers his identification. The California robbery-murder warrant was reported back to the officers in response to their computer check. As a result, Plaintiff was ordered out of the car at gunpoint, searched, handcuffed, and transported to the jail in Bay City, Michigan. Plaintiff was there handcuffed to metal bars while the sheriff's deputies made telephone calls to the Saginaw police and the LAPD in order to determine Plaintiff's status. Plaintiff was released after being held in jail for approximately two hours.

During early 1983, Plaintiff was stopped for a traffic offense by Saginaw police officers and was again detained until the California robbery-murder warrant problem could be clarified. Plaintiff testified that he did not recall the details of this encounter.

Plaintiff then sought the assistance of the local Federal Bureau of Investigation ("FBI") office in Saginaw. An FBI agent confirmed the existence of a murder warrant in Plaintiff's name in the NCIC system, but informed Plaintiff that only the originating state agency (i.e., the LAPD) could delete, amend, or correct the computer warrant entry.

During July, 1983, Plaintiff traveled from Michigan to Hugo, Oklahoma to visit relatives and to look for employment there and in Kolleen, Texas. On or about July 18, 1983, while driving through Denton County, Texas, Plaintiff was stopped by the police for speeding. The officer's inquiry to the NCIC system again revealed the existence of the outstanding robbery-murder warrant in Plaintiff's name. As a result, Plaintiff was arrested at gunpoint, handcuffed and taken to the nearest jail facility, where he was held for investigation of his true identity. Plaintiff was released after being held in custody for approximately three hours when the relevant fingerprints were transmitted to Texas.

Also on or about July 18, 1983, Defendant Crotsley again reactivated the NCIC file in Plaintiff's name without modification.

On or about January 14, 1984, Plaintiff was stopped while driving his car in Saginaw, Michigan, by a county deputy for not having his headlights on. The resulting inquiry into the NCIC system again revealed the existence of the California robbery-murder warrant. Two or three more police cars arrived, including officers armed with shotguns. Plaintiff was apprehended at gunpoint, searched, handcuffed, and taken to the county jail. Plaintiff was then released after officers there on duty vouched for his true identity.

During January, 1984, a reporter for the Saginaw News informed Defendant Crotsley that McKandes, who was by then again incarcerated in an Alabama prison, was the person actually wanted for the robbery-murders in Los Angeles. An FBI agent verified that the fingerprints of the suspect wanted in Los Angeles were those of McKandes.

On January 23, 1984, Defendant Crotsley forwarded the suspect's fingerprints to the Alabama Department of Corrections, and removed the NCIC record in Plaintiff's name.

McKandes was later convicted of the California robbery and murder charges.

During the period of their investigation, the Defendant Officers tried to check the NCIC system at least once per month, and more often if possible, to make sure that the warrant information was still in the system.

b. Application of the Law to the Relevant Facts

The leading case in this area of the law is *Baker v. McCollan,* 443 U.S. 137, 99 S.Ct. 2689, 61 L.Ed.2d 433 (1979). In *Baker* the plaintiff's brother procured a duplicate of the plaintiff's driver's license. *Baker,* 443 U.S. at 140, 99 S.Ct. at 2693. The plaintiff's brother, masquerading as the plaintiff, was arrested on narcotics charges and signed various documents in the plaintiff's name during the booking and bail procedures. *Baker,* 443 U.S. at 140–141, 99 S.Ct. at 2693. The plaintiff's brother then absconded and an arrest warrant was issued in the plaintiff's name. *Baker,* 443 U.S. at 141, 99 S.Ct. at 2693. The plaintiff was subsequently arrested pursuant to said warrant. *Id.* The plaintiff was held in custody for a three day period over a New Year's weekend before the police recognized their error and released him. *Id.* The Supreme Court rejected the plaintiff's Fourth and Fourteenth Amendment claims, holding:

> *Absent an attack on the validity of the warrant under which he was arrested,* respondent's complaint is simply that despite his protests of mistaken identity, he was detained in * * * jail from December 30 * * * until January 2, when the validity of his protests was ascertained. Whatever claims this situation might give rise to under state tort law, we think it gives rise to no claim under the United States Constitution.

Baker, 443 U.S. at 143–144, 99 S.Ct. at 2694 (Emphasis added.).

* * *

Several post-*Baker* decisions have found that a mistaken arrest can deprive a person of his Fourth and Fourteenth Amendment rights when: (a) the arrest warrant is constitutionally infirm; or (b) the arrest warrant is valid but (i) the detention resulting from the arrest becomes too lengthy in light of the plaintiff's repeated protests of innocence or (ii) the plaintiff is subjected to repeated arrests despite the fact that after the warrant's issuance the police receive notice of information exonerating the plaintiff.

Plaintiff contends that (1) the NCIC record and the arrest warrant upon which it was based violated the particular description requirement of the Fourth Amendment; and (2) the maintenance and reentry of the warrant information in the NCIC system without modification after his November, 1982, Michigan arrest deprived him of his rights under the Fourth and Fourteenth Amendments. Plaintiff's contentions are correct.

* * *

* * * The Court is guided by the reasoning set forth in *United States v. Mackey,* 387 F.Supp. 1121 (D.Nev.1975).

Mackey involved a motion to suppress the admission into evidence of a shotgun that was seized during a search incident to the defendant's arrest. *Mackey,* 387 F.Supp. at 1121–22. The defendant was arrested in Nevada pursuant to an NCIC notice that he was wanted in Monterey, California for a probation violation. *Id.* However, the warrant for the defendant's arrest for a probation violation had been satisfied approximately five months prior to said arrest. *Id.* The Court noted that under the heading "Steps to Assure Accuracy of Stored Information", the relevant NCIC policy statement provides:

> A. The FBI/NCIC and state control terminal agencies will make continuous checks on records being entered in the system to assure system standards and criteria are being met.
>
> B. Control terminal agencies shall adopt a careful and permanent program of data verification including:
>
> 1. Systemic audits conducted to insure that files have been regularly and accurately updated.
>
> 2. *Where errors or points of incompleteness are detected the control terminal shall take immediate action to correct or complete the NCIC record as well as its own state records.*

Mackey, 387 F.Supp. at 1123 (Emphasis added.) (Quoting "National Crime Information Center (NCIC) Computerized Criminal History Program Background, Concept and Policy," approved June 11, 1974, at 12.); *see also:* 28 C.F.R. 20.35(b), (e), (h) (1986) (Policies proposed by the Board become binding when adopted by the Director of the FBI.); *Cf.* 28 C.F.R. 20.37 (1986) ("It shall be the responsibility of each criminal justice agency contributing data to [the] * * * system to assure that information on individuals is kept complete, accurate and current. * * * "); *see also:* 28 C.F.R. 20.30, 20.31(a) (1986) (Section 20.37 governs the NCIC system.). The Court observed that:

> Because of the inaccurate listing in the NCIC computer, defendant was a "marked man" for the five months prior to his arrest. * * * At any time, as demonstrated by this situation, a routine check by the police could well result in defendant's arrest, booking, search and detention. Further, there is no evidence to suggest that defendant would not continue to be subject to such humiliation until Monterey police officials cleared the computer of the warrant. * * * Moreover, this

> could happen anywhere in the United States where law enforcement officers had access to NCIC information. Defendant was subject to being deprived of his liberty at any time and without any legal basis.

The Court went on to hold:

> The Court finds that a computer inaccuracy of this nature and duration, even if unintended, amounted to a capricious disregard for the rights of the defendant as a citizen of the United States. The evidence compels a finding that the government's action was equivalent to an arbitrary arrest, and that an arrest on this basis deprived defendant of his liberty without due process of law.

Mackey, 387 F.Supp. at 1125. The Court granted the defendant's motion to suppress. *Id.*

The decision in *Mackey* reflects the fact that information produced by the NCIC system is used as the functional equivalent and extension of arrest warrants. *See: Mackey,* 387 F.Supp. at 1122. Most importantly, the reasoning in *Mackey* persuasively supports the proposition that such information must be judged, at minimum, by the same standards as those applicable to arrest warrants. To rule otherwise in this highly computerized age would largely obviate the protection afforded by the Fourth Amendment's particularity requirement.

In the present case, like *Mackey,* probable cause for all but Plaintiff's initial arrest (as opposed to the reason for the traffic stops) was based solely on the NCIC information. Moreover, as previously noted, each NCIC computer record provides a 121 character field for additional information regarding, *inter alia,* the suspect's description and misidentification-duplicate name problems. Significantly, Defendants have neither contended nor produced evidence indicating that it was not possible, or even merely impractical, to insert information regarding McKandes' tattoos and scars and Plaintiff's misidentification in said field because, for example, it contained more important information. The relevant data entry form reflects that at any given time at least 71 spaces were available for additional information even assuming, *arguendo,* the information already set forth in said field was of overriding importance. As noted above, the pertinent NCIC policy statement expressly requires that the inputing agency "take immediate action to correct or complete the NCIC record" when "errors or points of incompleteness are detected." *Mackey,* 387 F.Supp. at 1123; *Cf.* 28 C.F.R. 20.37 (1986). * * *

* * * By analogy, Plaintiff herein has the burden of proving that a given incarceration was caused, prolonged, or otherwise adversely effected by the local authorities' reliance upon the NCIC record. It is clear that Plaintiff's last four (4) arrests and detentions after traffic stops satisfy this requirement. However, Plaintiffs first incarceration was the result of a trespassing dispute and the related charge of resisting arrest. Plaintiff pleaded (either guilty or *nolo contendre,* the record does not reflect which) to the charge of resisting arrest and was sentenced to "time served." The Court recognizes that Plaintiff *may*

have: (i) been initially held in custody, rather than released on bail on the charge of resisting arrest, because of the NCIC record; and (ii) found it advisable, having already spent five (5) days in jail, to plead to the charge of resisting arrest with the understanding that the district attorney would recommend that he be sentenced to time served. However, Plaintiff has neither contended that he was innocent of the charge of resisting arrest nor offered any evidence tending to support any of the possibilities delineated above. Moreover, Plaintiff's sentence of "time served" establishes that his period of incarceration was not prolonged because of the NCIC record. Thus, the Court holds that: (a) Plaintiff's initial arrest was not caused by the NCIC record; (b) the duration of his resulting incarceration was not prolonged by same; and (c) Plaintiff was neither subjected to an illegal seizure in violation of the Fourth Amendment nor deprived of his liberty without due process of law in violation of the Fourteenth Amendment.

In sum, the Court holds that Plaintiff was unconstitutionally deprived of his liberty during his last four arrests and detentions. The Court bases said holding upon two independently sufficient but mutually supportive grounds. First, the Court has determined that the NCIC record and the arrest warrant upon which it was based violated the particular description requirement of the Fourth Amendment. *See: Powe,* 664 F.2d at 649. Secondly, the Court finds that the maintenance and multiple reentry of the NCIC record without amendment after Plaintiff's initial misidentification as the suspect caused him to be arrested and detained without due process of law. The Court further holds that Plaintiff's first incarceration for resisting arrest was not caused, prolonged, or adversely effected by either the robbery-murder warrant or the NCIC record created pursuant thereto. *See: Powe,* 664 F.2d 648. Plaintiff therefore has carried his burden of proof on the first prong of the *Monell* municipal liability test only as to his last four incarcerations.

2. *Causation of the Deviation by Official Policy, Custom or Usage*

a. *The Law*

It is well settled that inadequate training or supervision can constitute an actionable policy or custom under the second prong of the *Monell* municipal liability test. *Bergquist v. County of Cochise,* 806 F.2d 1364, 1370 (9th Cir.1986). However, mere negligence does not give rise to section 1983 liability. *Daniels v. Williams,* 474 U.S. 327, 106 S.Ct. 662, 666–67, 88 L.Ed. 662 (1986); *Bergquist,* 806 F.2d at 1370. Conversely, a "policy" of *gross* negligence in training or supervision gives rise to section 1983 liability. Thus, a city may be held liable either for the grossly negligent failure to implement a training program for its officers or for implementing a program grossly inadequate to prevent the type of harm suffered. *Id.* Such gross negligence must manifest deliberate indifference to the resulting violations of the citizen's constitutional rights. *Languirand,* 717 F.2d at 227; *Herrera,* 653 F.2d at 1224; *Owens,* 601 F.2d at 1246.

The requisite policy, custom or usage may not be proved through reference to a single unconstitutional incident unless "proof of the incident includes proof that it was caused by an existing unconstitutional * * * policy." *City of Oklahoma v. Tuttle,* 471 U.S. 808, 105 S.Ct. 2427, 2436, 85 L.Ed.2d 791 (1985); *Bergquist,* 806 F.2d at 1370 n. 1. In contrast, it is sufficient to show a pattern of similar incidents in which citizens were injured or endangered by intentional or negligent police misconduct or that serious incompetence or misbehavior was general or widespread throughout the police force. *Languirand,* 717 F.2d at 228.

b. Relevant Facts

Information in the NCIC system can be withdrawn, added to, corrected, or amended by the law enforcement agency that originally inserted same. However, neither Defendant Slack nor Defendant Crotsley received any training in the procedures for or the necessity of amending information that had been entered into the NCIC system when additional or more accurate information becomes available. The Defendant Officers did not discuss the possibility of adding information to the NCIC record in response to Plaintiff's original misidentification as the suspect.

Defendant Slack has placed information into the NCIC system at least several hundred times during his career as a police officer. Defendant Slack never amended an NCIC file record when more complete or accurate information became available. Moreover, Defendant Slack did not know for sure if it was possible to do so.

Similarly, Defendant Crotsley never considered whether it was possible to insert information into the NCIC system that would alert the officers using the system about the misidentification-dual name problem. Defendant Crotsley was not aware of any LAPD policy addressing dual name-misidentification situations. Defendant Crotsley's policy in such situations was to give the innocent person a computer printout of the warrant and his business card as evidence of the person's innocence *only if* the person came to Los Angeles and picked the items up personally. Defendant Crotsley testified that he had followed this procedure on four prior occasions, and that "quite a few other police officers" followed the same procedure. During the seventeen years Defendant Crotsley was a police officer it was not the custom for investigators to obtain their superior's approval prior to inserting information into the system. Defendant Crotsley received no instructions or supervision from his superiors regarding the information to be inserted into the NCIC system in this case. However, Defendant Crotsely's superiors were aware of his reactivation of the NCIC entry after Plaintiff's initial misidentification.

LAPD's NCIC operators and supervisors do not make any independent decisions regarding the information inserted into the system, but instead follow the investigators' instructions.

There is one and only one reasonable and permissible factual inference possible given this uncontroverted evidence. *See:* n. 2, *supra.* Said inference is that the Defendant City (i) failed to adopt any policy, (ii) to train, and (iii) to supervise the Defendant Officers regarding: (a) the Fourth Amendment requirement that both the arrest warrant and the initial NCIC record describe the suspect with particularity; and (b) the procedures for and the necessity of amending the NCIC record when additional or more accurate descriptive information became available.

c. *Application of the Law to the Facts*

(i) The Defendant Officers' Failure to Adequately Describe the Suspect in the Warrant and the NCIC Record Created Pursuant Thereto

* * *

* * * The Defendant Officers tried to check the NCIC system at least once per month to make sure that the entry was still in the system. Moreover, the Defendant Officers reactivated the erroneous and incomplete NCIC record three times (i.e., once before Plaintiff's initial misidentification and twice afterward). Defendant Crotsley was aware of at least four prior occasions where such problems arose. Similarly, Defendant Crotsley testified that "quite a few other police officers" had dealt with the same problem in the same way in which he did. The only reasonable and permissible inference given the uncontroverted facts set forth in Section II.A.2.b. above (*See,* n. 2, *supra.*) is that the insufficiently descriptive warrant and NCIC record were: (i) systemic in nature; and (ii) the result of the Defendant City's grossly negligent and indifferent failure to adequately train and/or supervise the Defendant Officers, or to even adopt and make known appropriate policy.

(ii) The Defendants' Maintenance and Reentry of the Inadequately Descriptive NCIC Record After Receiving Notice of Plaintiff's Initial Misidentification as the Suspect

* * * Moreover, as previously noted, the relevant NCIC policy statement requires that state agencies "*adopt a careful and permanent program of data verification* including * * * tak[ing] immediate action to correct or complete the NCIC record as well as its own state records" when "errors or points of incompleteness are detected." *See: Mackey,* 387 F.Supp. at 1123; *Cf.* 28 C.F.R. 20.37 (1986). The purpose of this requirement is obviously to protect innocent persons. *See: Mackey,* 387 F.Supp. at 1123 ("In a national system * * * individual users are responsible for the accuracy, validity, and completeness of their record entries * * * and more stringent controls with respect to system discipline are required." Quoting "National Crime Information History Center (NCIC) Computerized History Program Background, Concept and Policy," approved June 11, 1974, at 3.). Thus, the Defendant City's failure to adopt such a program was negligent *per se.*

Most importantly, the breach of an official policy constitutes reckless disregard for the safety of those for whose protection it is adopted when omission of the required precautions involves a high degree of probability that serious harm will result. Restatement (Second) of Torts, section 500 comment e (1965); W. Keeton, D. Dobbs, R. Keeton & D. Owen, *Prosser and Keeton on the Law of Torts,* section 34, at 214 (5th Ed.1984); *see, e.g., Lewis v. Zell,* 279 Ala. 33, 181 So.2d 101 (1965). Such is the case here. Plaintiff was subjected to the pain and humiliation of being arrested, handcuffed, searched, booked, and incarcerated. Moreover, as Chief Judge Bazelon recognized, an arrest record creates a continuing disability:

> Information denominated a record of arrests, if it becomes known, may subject an individual to serious difficulties. Even if no direct economic loss is involved, the injury to an individual's reputation may be substantial. Economic losses themselves may be both direct and serious. Opportunities for schooling, employment, or professional licenses may be restricted or nonexistent as a consequence of the mere fact of an arrest, even if followed by acquittal or complete exoneration of the charges involved. An arrest record may be used by the police in determining whether subsequently to arrest the individual concerned, or whether to exercise their discretion to bring formal charges against an individual already arrested. Arrest records have been used in deciding whether to allow a defendant to present his story without impeachment by prior convictions, and as a basis for denying release prior to trial or an appeal; or then may be considered by a judge in determining the sentence to be given a convicted offender.

Menard v. Mitchell, 430 F.2d 486, 490, 491 (D.C.Cir.1970). Most compellingly, Plaintiff's life was endangered each time he was apprehended at gunpoint by police officers who believed that he was an armed and dangerous murder suspect. Said danger of serious harm was both highly probable and forseeable. Such reckless conduct, if not less, constitutes "gross negligence." Thus, the Defendant City's above-defined failure to train or supervise its police officers satisfies the gross negligence test.

(iii) Summary

The Court finds that the Defendant City's failure to (i) adopt any policy, (ii) train, and (iii) supervise its police officers regarding: (a) the Fourth Amendment requirement that the arrest warrant and the NCIC record created pursuant thereto describe the suspect with particularity; and (b) the procedures for and the necessity of amending the NCIC record when additional or more accurate descriptive information became available were both grossly negligent and systemic in nature.

3. Conclusion

For the reasons stated, the Court holds that there is no material question of fact and that Plaintiff is entitled to judgment against the City of Los Angeles on the 42 U.S.C. section 1983 liability issue as a matter of law. *See:* Fed.R.Civ.P. 56(c). The Court, however, believes it is appropriate to emphasize the limited scope of said holding.

The Court recognizes that: (i) the Defendant Officers were diligently seeking to apprehend a dangerous murder suspect; (ii) the suspect, McKandes, had used Plaintiff's name; and (iii) said officers had probable cause to place Plaintiff's name on the arrest warrant and the NCIC record created pursuant thereto (*See: Powe,* 664 F.2d at 647.). However, Defendants mistakenly contend that the officers were faced with the choice of either proceeding as they did or not acting at all. Defendants fail to recognize the third option which would allow the officers to discharge their duties to apprehend McKandes and to respect Plaintiff's constitutional rights. This option was to: (1) insert the additional descriptive information concerning McKandes (re: scars, tattoos, etc.) into the arrest warrant and NCIC record; and (2) amend same to reflect the misidentification-duplicate name problem after Plaintiff's initial misidentification.

B. 42 U.S.C. 1983 Action Against the Defendant Officers

The initial inquiry in a section 1983 action against an individual defendant must focus on whether: (a) the conduct complained of was committed under color of state law; and (b) this conduct deprived the plaintiff of rights secured by the Constitution or laws of the United States. *Parratt v. Taylor,* 451 U.S. 527, 535, 101 S.Ct. 1908, 1913, 68 L.Ed.2d 420 (1981); *McKay,* 730 F.2d at 1367. If the claim arises out of the defendant's performance of his discretionary functions, the Court must then determine whether he is entitled to the defense of qualified immunity.

* * *

b. Conclusion

For the reasons stated, the Court holds that there is no material question of fact and that the Defendant Officers are entitled to judgment against Plaintiff as a matter of law on: (a) the issue of qualified immunity; and therefore (b) Plaintiff's 42 U.S.C. section 1983 claim for damages. *See:* Fed.R.Civ.P. 56(c).

III. ORDER

Pursuant to the foregoing recital of undisputed facts, it is hereby ORDERED, ADJUDGED AND DECREED that:

1. There is no material question of fact and that Plaintiff is entitled to judgment against the City of Los Angeles on the 42 U.S.C. section 1983 liability issue as a matter of law.

2. There is no material question of fact and that the Defendant Officers are entitled to judgment against Plaintiff as a matter of law on: (a) the issue of qualified immunity; and therefore (b) Plaintiff's 42 U.S.C. section 1983 claim.

The Clerk shall send, by United States mail, a copy of this Memorandum of Decision and Order to counsel for the parties.

Notes and Questions

1. The Constitution guarantees protection of certain individual rights. One of the most carefully guarded rights is the right to personal liberty and to be free from false arrests. Would the courts have decided differently if the plaintiff had not suffered the deprivation of a constitutionally protected liberty?

2. As seen in *Rogan,* when dealing with personal data, training personnel in the proper use of complex computerized data bases is essential.

LOWRY v. CREDIT BUREAU, INC. OF GEORGIA

United States District Court, Northern District of Georgia, 1978.
444 F.Supp. 541.

HAROLD L. MURPHY, DISTRICT JUDGE.

ORDER

This is an action for damages predicated upon defendant's alleged violation of the Fair Credit Reporting Act, 15 U.S.C. § 1681 et seq. Plaintiffs contend defendant violated 15 U.S.C. § 1681e(b) in failing to follow reasonable procedures so as to insure maximum possible accuracy of information about the plaintiffs. Plaintiffs contend defendant violated 15 U.S.C. § 1681i in failing to undertake the reinvestigation required after the accuracy of a file is disputed. Plaintiffs contend defendant libelled them in reporting to Decatur Federal Savings and Loan Association that James F. Lowry had once been adjudicated bankrupt.

In reviewing the facts on a summary judgment motion, those facts are to be viewed in a manner most favorable to the party opposing the motion. *United States v. Hangar One, Inc.,* 563 F.2d 1155 (5th Cir. 1977). The facts of this case are that on August 1, 1976, plaintiffs formalized an application with Decatur Federal Savings and Loan Association ("Decatur Federal") for permanent financing of a home plaintiffs had recently constructed. On the loan application, Mr. Lowry listed his name as "James F. Lowry" and his former address as Solana Beach, California.

The loan application was sent to the South Regional Loan Office of Decatur Federal. At this office, Decatur Federal maintains a computer terminal which provides direct access to information stored in the computers of the defendant Credit Bureau on various consumers. This terminal affords Decatur Federal the opportunity to obtain credit information directly and without intervention by Credit Bureau personnel.

In seeking a consumer's credit history, the party desiring the information supplies the computer with as much relevant data as possible about the party as to whom they are inquiring. The computer will then provide the names of parties for whom it has credit histories and with whom there is a programmed minimum of correspondence between the identifying information of the party for whom information is sought and the parties for whom the computer has stored credit information. The computer will not provide the names of any party for whom it has credit information unless there are at least fifty "points" of correspondence between the subject of the inquiry's data and the relevant credit records. The operator chooses the credit histories he or she wishes to review from the computer proffered list of names and the number of "points" of correspondence.

The inquiry by the Decatur Federal operator resulted in the offering of a "James Frank Lowry" of San Francisco, California whose file showed 50 "points" of correspondence. The operator made the independent decision to have the computer supply its information on "James Frank Lowry" despite the fact that only the minimum of correspondence had been indicated. The computer disclosed that "James Frank Lowry" of San Francisco, California had been adjudicated bankrupt in 1967.

The facts that the applicant for the insurance, and the plaintiff in this litigation, was named James Francis, and not James Frank Lowry and had listed his prior address as Solano Beach, not San Francisco, California were not enough to dispel the notion that James Francis Lowry was a bankrupt not worthy of credit. Plaintiffs were informed that a problem existed with regard to the issuance of credit to them. Plaintiffs were informed a resolution of the difficulty must come from the Credit Bureau.

On August 19, 1976, Mr. Lowry visited defendant's office in Atlanta, Georgia. During the course of an inquiry which carried through the following day, Mr. Lowry was told by an employee of defendant Credit Bureau that there was indeed a bankruptcy on his record. On Monday, August 23, 1976, an inquiry was begun with the processing of a "request for investigation". The focus of the investigation was plaintiff's contention that he had never filed for bankruptcy nor had he lived at the address indicated for him in San Francisco.

During Credit Bureau's investigation, new reports were sought on "James F. Lowry" from the Credit Bureau's computer banks by Decatur Federal. The reports included the previously noted disclosure of a bankruptcy by a James Frank Lowry. On September 10, 1976, Decatur Federal issued a "decline letter" indicating a denial of plaintiff's loan application.

On September 13, 1976, Mr. Lowry notified Credit Bureau of the denial of his loan application and demanded a correction of his credit report. On October 8, 1976, defendant Credit Bureau notified Decatur Federal that a correction was being made in Mr. Lowry's report. The letter of October 8th suggested Decatur Federal might wish to reconsider Mr. Lowry's application on the basis of the correction. The corrected report included no allegations of bankruptcy.

Plaintiffs were not notified of the correction of the record nor were they informed of the outcome of the investigation they had requested. On December 9, 1976 plaintiffs' attorney was notified that plaintiffs would probably receive their loan if they were to reapply. Plaintiffs were offered a loan commitment on December 13, 1976 with slightly higher closing costs than those apparent on the loan application. The loan was closed on February 7, 1977.

1. Plaintiffs contend they have been the victim of a violation of defendant Credit Bureau's duty to insure the maximum possible accuracy of information. The Fair Credit Reporting Act provides in relevant part:

> Whenever a consumer reporting agency prepares a consumer report it shall follow reasonable procedures to assure maximum possible accuracy of the information concerning the individual about whom the report relates. 15 U.S.C. § 1681e(b).

This section imposes an obligation to insure maximum accuracy only in the preparation of a report. The crux of plaintiffs' complaint is the potential for confusion of reports inherent in defendant's computer system. Plaintiffs note the potential for confusion was realized in their case and resulted in at least the delay in the grant of a loan.

Plaintiffs' concern is not accuracy in the preparation of credit reports; plaintiffs' concern is the confusion of those reports. Confusion of reports did result, but that does not provide a basis for a federal claim. This district has previously recognized that "in order to pursue a cause of action predicated upon willful or negligent violation of 15 U.S.C. § 1681e(b), the report sought to be attacked must be inaccurate". *Middlebrooks v. Retail Credit Co.,* 416 F.Supp. 1013, 1015 (N.D.Ga. 1976); *Peller v. Retail Credit Co.,* No. 17900 (N.D.Ga. December 6, 1973).

The only inaccuracy in the questioned credit reports arises from the presence of plaintiff James Francis Lowry's social security number in the James Frank Lowry file. As noted by both sides, the plaintiff's social security number appeared with the bankrupt James Frank Lowry's file because the computer was programmed to add the information when Decatur Federal's operator accepted the file of James Frank Lowry the first time. The automatic addition of this information may constitute a violation of the 15 U.S.C. § 1681e(b) obligation to provide the maximum possible accuracy in the preparation of a credit report. Preparation may be viewed as a continuing process and the obligation to insure accuracy arises with every addition of information. Plaintiffs may have difficulty demonstrating the existence of damages sustained as a result of this breach [as required under 15 U.S.C. § 1681*o* (1)] but at this stage it cannot be said such proof would be impossible.

2. Plaintiffs contend there has been a breach of defendant Credit Bureau's duty to investigate the accuracy of information "in his file". 15 U.S.C. § 1681i(a). Preliminarily, it must be noted that the circumstances of this case indicate the necessity of reading the language "in his file" to include more than just the computer report which a two

month investigation discloses to be the only report relevant to the subject of the inquiry. As encountered in this instance, if a party has credit difficulties because of confusion of two similar computer reports, the subject's "file" must be viewed as the totality of the conflicting information which is causing the credit uncertainty. Under this view, and the language of 15 U.S.C. § 1681i(a), a consumer reporting agency is obligated to reinvestigate the accuracy of information as it relates to the subject of the inquiry. The agency's obligations are not terminated by the fact that the information is accurate about someone else if that information is presented in a manner such as to create inaccurate impressions as to the credit history of a particular individual. To permit the activity encountered here to go uncovered would be contrary to the broadly remedial aims disclosed in 15 U.S.C. § 1681.

The Fair Credit Reporting Act creates an obligation to investigate "within a reasonable period". There is no doubt an investigation was undertaken and changes were made. The only issue here is whether 49 days constitutes a "reasonable period" to determine if one party is the bankrupt referred to in a particular credit report. This element of the complaint is not proper for disposition on summary judgment.

3. Plaintiffs allege they were defamed by the order to attribution of a bankruptcy to them. Defendant responds to this contention by noting that the notation of a bankruptcy was clearly attributed to a James F. Lowry who is not the plaintiff.

The review of libel allegations must begin with a widely cited rule of Georgia law: "[t]he defamatory words must refer to some ascertained or ascertainable person, and that person must be the plaintiff." *Ledger–Enquirer Company v. Brown,* 214 Ga. 422, 423, 105 S.E.2d 229, 230 (1958); *Constitution Publishing Co. v. Leathers,* 48 Ga.App. 429, 431, 172 S.E. 923 (1934). The unquestioned fact is that the defendant's attribution of bankruptcy concerned a James F. Lowry who is not the plaintiff in this case. Defendant Credit Bureau has simply reported the truth of a bankruptcy by an individual with a name similar to that of the plaintiff, and that fact alone is not enough to support the specter of libel.

Georgia courts have noted that language susceptible to but one, non-defamatory meaning is for the court's interpretation. *Ledger–Enquirer,* supra, 214 Ga. at 424, 105 S.E.2d 229; *Constitution Publishing Co. v. Andrews,* 50 Ga.App. 116, 117, 177 S.E. 258 (1934). Georgia courts have previously held that a libel does not arise as to a third person when true information is stated as to another party. *Minday v. Constitution Publishing Co.,* 52 Ga.App. 51, 182 S.E. 53 (1935); *Atlanta Journal Co. v. Farmer,* 48 Ga.App. 273, 172 S.E. 647 (1934). Plaintiff has not demonstrated the requisite elements under Georgia law.

Jurisdiction is invoked on this count as pendant to federal claims. The tenuous nature of the federal claims would warrant a denial of the court's discretion to permit the defamation action even if the requisite elements were present.

4. Pending before the court is defendant's motion for award of expenses. The motion concerns expenses incurred in securing a disclosure of information. The disclosure was made after a motion to compel but was not the result of a court order.

Rule 37(a)(4), Federal Rules of Civil Procedure, permits the award of expenses to a party "[i]f the motion is granted". The motion was not granted in this case. Therefore the Federal Rules do not authorize such an award in this case. See, *Johnson v. Martin,* 137 Ga.App. 312, 223 S.E.2d 465 (1976). Additionally, there was some justification for plaintiffs' hesitance to disclose the requested information.

5. Accordingly, the motion for summary judgment is DENIED as to claims premised upon 15 U.S.C. § 1681e(b) and 1681i(a). The motion for summary judgment is GRANTED as to the state law claims of defamation. The motion for award of expenses is DENIED.

Notes and Questions

1. Despite the ever-increasing sophistication of computer software in matching and "filling in the blanks" among different data records, extreme care should be taken in designing any computer system which "automatically" matches different data records, and then supplements one record based on the information contained in the other record.

2. How does this case compare to the *Rogan* case? Did the court reach a similar conclusion?

2. RIGHT TO CHECK FOR ACCURACY AND HAVE MISTAKES CORRECTED

TRUTH IN LENDING ACT
15 U.S.C.A. § 1601ff

CHAPTER 4. CREDIT BILLING

§ 161. Correction of Billing Errors [15 U.S.C. § 1666]

(a) If a creditor, within sixty days after having transmitted to an obligor a statement of the obligor's account in connection with an extension of consumer credit, receives at the address disclosed under section 127(b)(10) a written notice (other than notice on a payment stub or other payment medium supplied by the creditor if the creditor so stipulates with the disclosure required under section 127(a)(7)) from the obligor in which the obligor—

(1) sets forth or otherwise enables the creditor to identify the name and account number (if any) of the obligor,

(2) indicates the obligor's belief that the statement contains a billing error and the amount of such billing error, and

(3) sets forth the reasons for the obligor's belief (to the extent applicable) that the statement contains a billing error,

the creditor shall, unless the obligor has, after giving such written notice and before the expiration of the time limits herein specified, agreed that the statement was correct—

(A) not later than thirty days after the receipt of the notice, send a written acknowledgment thereof to the obligor, unless the action required in subparagraph (B) is taken within such thirty-day period, and

(B) not later than two complete billing cycles of the creditor (in no event later than ninety days) after the receipt of the notice and prior to taking any action to collect the amount, or any part thereof, indicated by the obligor under paragraph (2) either—

(i) make appropriate corrections in the account of the obligor, including the crediting of any finance charges on amounts erroneously billed, and transmit to the obligor a notification of such corrections and the creditor's explanation of any change in the amount indicated by the obligor under paragraph (2) and, if any such change is made and the obligor so requests, copies of documentary evidence of the obligor's indebtedness; or

(ii) send a written explanation or clarification to the obligor, after having conducted an investigation, setting forth to the extent applicable the reasons why the creditor believes the account of the obligor was correctly shown in the statement and, upon request of the obligor, provide copies of documentary evidence of the obligor's indebtedness. In the case of a billing error where the obligor alleges that the creditor's billing statement reflects goods not delivered to the obligor or his designee in accordance with the agreement made at the time of the transaction, a creditor may not construe such amount to be correctly shown unless he determines that such goods were actually delivered, mailed, or otherwise sent to the obligor and provides the obligor with a statement of such determination.

After complying with the provisions of this subsection with respect to an alleged billing error, a creditor has no further responsibility under this section if the obligor continues to make substantially the same allegation with respect to such error.

(b) For the purpose of this section, a "billing error" consists of any of the following:

(1) A reflection on a statement of an extension of credit which was not made to the obligor or, if made, was not in the amount reflected on such statement.

(2) A reflection on a statement of an extension of credit for which the obligor requests additional clarification including documentary evidence thereof.

(3) A reflection on a statement of goods or services not accepted by the obligor or his designee or not delivered to the obligor or his designee in accordance with the agreement made at the time of a transaction.

(4) The creditor's failure to reflect properly on a statement a payment made by the obligor or a credit issued to the obligor.

(5) A computation error or similar error of an accounting nature of the creditor on a statement.

(6) Failure to transmit the statement required under section 127(b) of this Act to the last address of the obligor which has been disclosed to the creditor, unless that address was furnished less than twenty days before the end of the billing cycle for which the statement is required.

(7) Any other error described in regulations of the Board.

(c) For the purposes of this section, "action to collect the amount, or any part thereof, indicated by an obligor under paragraph (2)" does not include the sending of statements of account, which may include finance charges on amounts in dispute, to the obligor following written notice from the obligor as specified under subsection (a), if—

(1) the obligor's account is not restricted or closed because of the failure of the obligor to pay the amount indicated under paragraph (2) of subsection (a), and

(2) the creditor indicates the payment of such amount is not required pending the creditor's compliance with this section. Nothing in this section shall be construed to prohibit any action by a creditor to collect any amount which has not been indicated by the obligor to contain a billing error.

(d) Pursuant to regulations of the Board, a creditor operating an open end consumer credit plan may not, prior to the sending of the written explanation or clarification required under paragraph (B)(ii), restrict or close an account with respect to which the obligor has indicated pursuant to subsection (a) that he believes such account to contain a billing error solely because of the obligor's failure to pay the amount indicated to be in error. Nothing in this subsection shall be deemed to prohibit a creditor from applying against the credit limit on the obligor's account the amount indicated to be in error.

(e) Any creditor who fails to comply with the requirements of this section or section 162 forfeits any right to collect from the obligor the amount indicated by the obligor under paragraph (2) of subsection (a) of this section, and any finance charges thereon, except that the amount required to be forfeited under this subsection may not exceed $50.

§ 162. Regulation of Credit Reports [15 U.S.C. § 1666a]

(a) After receiving a notice from an obligor as provided in section 161(a), a creditor or his agent may not directly or indirectly threaten to report to any person adversely on the obligor's credit rating or credit standing because of the obligor's failure to pay the amount indicated by the obligor under section 161(a)(2), and such amount may not be reported as delinquent to any third party until the creditor has met the requirements of section 161 and has allowed the obligor the same number of days (not less than ten) thereafter to make payment as is provided under the credit agreement with the obligor for the payment of undisputed amounts.

(b) If a creditor receives a further written notice from an obligor that an amount is still in dispute within the time allowed for payment under subsection (a) of this section, a creditor may not report to any third party that the amount of the obligor is delinquent because the obligor has failed to pay an amount which he has indicated under section 161(a)(2), unless the creditor also reports that the amount is in dispute and, at the same time, notifies the obligor of the name and address of each party to whom the creditor is reporting information concerning the delinquency.

(c) A creditor shall report any subsequent resolution of any delinquencies reported pursuant to subsection (b) to the parties to whom such delinquencies were initially reported.

FAIR CREDIT REPORTING ACT
15 U.S.C.A. § 1681ff

§ 609. Disclosures to Consumers [15 U.S.C. § 1681g]

(a) Every consumer reporting agency shall, upon request and proper identification of any consumer, clearly and accurately disclose to the consumer:

(1) The nature and substance of all information (except medical information) in its files on the consumer at the time of the request.

(2) The sources of the information; except that the sources of information acquired solely for use in preparing an investigative consumer report and actually used for no other purpose need not be disclosed: *Provided,* That in the event an action is brought under this subchapter, such sources shall be available to the plaintiff under appropriate discovery procedures in the court in which the action is brought.

(3) The recipients of any consumer report on the consumer which it has furnished—

(A) for employment purposes within the two-year period preceding the request, and

(B) for any other purpose within the six-month period preceding the request.

(b) The requirements of subsection (a) of this section respecting the disclosure of sources of information and the recipients of consumer reports do not apply to information received or consumer reports furnished prior to the effective date of this subchapter except to the extent that the matter involved is contained in the files of the consumer reporting agency on that date.

§ 610. Conditions of Disclosure to Consumers [15 U.S.C. § 1681h]

(a) A consumer reporting agency shall make the disclosures required under section 609 during normal business hours and on reasonable notice.

(b) The disclosures required under section 609 shall be made to the consumer—

(1) in person if he appears in person and furnishes proper identification; or

(2) by telephone if he has made a written request, with proper identification, for telephone disclosure and the toll charge, if any, for the telephone call is prepaid by or charged directly to the consumer.

(c) Any consumer reporting agency shall provide trained personnel to explain to the consumer any information furnished to him pursuant to section 609.

(d) The consumer shall be permitted to be accompanied by one other person of his choosing, who shall furnish reasonable identification. A consumer reporting agency may require the consumer to furnish a written statement granting permission to the consumer reporting agency to discuss the consumer's file in such person's presence.

(e) Except as provided in sections 616 and 617, no consumer may bring any action or proceeding in the nature of defamation, invasion of privacy, or negligence with respect to the reporting of information against any consumer reporting agency, any user of information, or any person who furnishes information to a consumer reporting agency, based on information disclosed pursuant to section 609, 610, or 615, except as to false information furnished with malice or willful intent to injure such consumer.

§ 611. Procedure in Case of Disputed Accuracy [15 U.S.C. § 1681i]

(a) If the completeness or accuracy of any item of information contained in his file is disputed by a consumer, and such dispute is directly conveyed to the consumer reporting agency by the consumer, the consumer reporting agency shall within a reasonable period of time reinvestigate and record the current status of that information unless it has reasonable grounds to believe that the dispute by the consumer is frivolous or irrelevant. If after such reinvestigation such information is found to be inaccurate or can no longer be verified, the consumer reporting agency shall promptly delete such information. The presence of contradictory information in the consumer's file does not in and of itself constitute reasonable grounds for believing the dispute is frivolous or irrelevant.

(b) If the reinvestigation does not resolve the dispute, the consumer may file a brief statement setting forth the nature of the dispute. The consumer reporting agency may limit such statements to not more than one hundred words if it provides the consumer with assistance in writing a clear summary of the dispute.

(c) Whenever a statement of a dispute is filed, unless there is reasonable grounds to believe that it is frivolous or irrelevant, the consumer reporting agency shall, in any subsequent consumer report containing the information in question, clearly note that it is disputed by the consumer and provide either the consumer's statement or a clear and accurate codification or summary thereof.

(d) Following any deletion of information which is found to be inaccurate or whose accuracy can no longer be verified or any notation as to disputed information, the consumer reporting agency shall, at the request of the consumer, furnish notification that the item has been deleted or the statement, codification or summary pursuant to subsection (b) or (c) of this section to any person specifically designated by the consumer who has within two years prior thereto received a consumer report for employment purposes, or within six months prior thereto received a consumer report for any other purpose, which contained the deleted or disputed information. The consumer reporting agency shall clearly and conspicuously disclose to the consumer his rights to make such a request. Such disclosure shall be made at or prior to the time the information is deleted or the consumer's statement regarding the disputed information is received.

§ 612. Charges for Certain Disclosures [15 U.S.C. § 1681j]

A consumer reporting agency shall make all disclosures pursuant to section 609 and furnish all consumer reports pursuant to section 611(d) without charge to the consumer if, within thirty days after receipt by such consumer of a notification pursuant to section 615 of this title or notification from a debt collection agency affiliated with such consumer reporting agency stating that the consumer's credit rating may be or has been adversely affected, the consumer makes a request under section 609 or 611(d). Otherwise, the consumer reporting agency may impose a reasonable charge on the consumer for making disclosure to such consumer pursuant to section 609, the charge for which shall be indicated to the consumer prior to making disclosure; and for furnishing notifications, statements, summaries, or codifications to person designated by the consumer pursuant to section 611(d), the charge for which shall be indicated to the consumer prior to furnishing such information and shall not exceed the charge that the consumer reporting agency would impose on each designated recipient for a consumer report except that no charge may be made for notifying such persons of the deletion of information which is found to be inaccurate or which can no longer be verified.

§ 613. Public Record Information for Employment Purposes [15 U.S.C. § 1681k]

A consumer reporting agency which furnishes a consumer report for employment purposes and which for that purpose compiles and reports items of information on consumers which are matters of public record and are likely to have an adverse effect upon a consumer's ability to obtain employment shall—

(1) at the time such public record information is reported to the user of such consumer report, notify the consumer of the fact that public record information is being reported by the consumer reporting agency, together with the name and address of the person to whom such information is being reported; or

(2) maintain strict procedures designed to insure that whenever public record information which is likely to have an adverse effect on a consumer's ability to obtain employment is reported it is complete and up to date. For purposes of this paragraph, items of public record relating to arrests, indictments, convictions, suits, tax liens, and outstanding judgments shall be considered up to date if the current public record status of the item at the time of the report is reported.

§ 614. Restrictions on Investigative Consumer Reports [15 U.S.C. § 1681*l*]

Whenever a consumer reporting agency prepares an investigative consumer report, no adverse information in the consumer report (other than information which is a matter of public record) may be included in a subsequent consumer report unless such adverse information has been verified in the process of making such subsequent consumer report, or the adverse information was received within the three-month period preceding the date the subsequent report is furnished.

§ 615. Requirements on Users of Consumer Reports [15 U.S.C. § 1681m]

(a) Whenever credit or insurance for personal, family, or household purposes, or employment involving a consumer is denied or the charge for such credit or insurance is increased either wholly or partly because of information contained in a consumer report from a consumer reporting agency, the user of the consumer report shall so advise the consumer against whom such adverse action has been taken and supply the name and address of the consumer reporting agency making the report.

(b) Whenever credit for personal, family, or household purposes involving a consumer is denied or the charge for such credit is increased either wholly or partly because of information obtained from a person other than a consumer reporting agency bearing upon the consumer's credit worthiness, credit standing, credit capacity, character, general reputation, personal characteristics, or mode of living, the user of such information shall, within a reasonable period of time, upon the consumer's written request for the reasons for such adverse action received within sixty days after learning of such adverse action, disclose the nature of the information to the consumer. The user of such information shall clearly and accurately disclose to the consumer his right to make such written request at the time such adverse action is communicated to the consumer.

(c) No person shall be held liable for any violation of this section if he shows by a preponderance of the evidence that at the time of the alleged violation he maintained reasonable procedures to assure compliance with the provisions of subsections (a) and (b) of this section.

B. COMPUTERIZED RECORDS AS EVIDENCE

UNITED STATES v. BONALLO

United States Court of Appeals, Ninth Circuit, 1988.
858 F.2d 1427.

REINHARDT, CIRCUIT JUDGE:

Defendant/appellant Daniel Bonallo appeals his conviction on 12 counts of bank fraud under 18 U.S.C. § 1344 (1984). The appeal requires us to determine whether a scheme to defraud a bank under that statute requires that the misrepresentation actually precede the bank's transfer of money or property to the perpetrator. We also consider the sufficiency of the indictment as well as the sufficiency of the evidence. Bonallo also contests the admissibility of certain evidence. We affirm his conviction on 11 of the 12 counts.

[Bonallo was convicted of bank fraud. On appeal he contends that the trial court erred in admitting computerized records.]

IV. ADMISSIBILITY OF EXHIBITS "1" AND "3"

Government Exhibit "1" is a list of persons whose bank card numbers were used to obtain funds from ATMs [Automatic Teller Machines] of the Bank, and who reported to the Bank that they did not use a card for such transactions. The exhibit lists the person's name, account, type of card used, date and time of the transaction, and the amount of money obtained. The information in the exhibit was obtained from customer affidavits and from American Data's computer records.

Government Exhibit "3" is a list reflecting the date and time of the 12 transactions at issue, and also the pertinent times when Bonallo arrived at and left the American Data building after hours. The information in the exhibit comes from American Data computer logs.

The court admitted the exhibits over the objection of counsel. Bonallo challenges the evidence under Fed.R.Evid. 803(6), the business records exception.

We review evidentiary questions such as this for an abuse of discretion. *United States v. Catabran,* 836 F.2d 453, 456 (9th Cir.1988). Computer records are properly admissible as business records under

803(6). *Id.* at 456. Fed.R.Evid. 803(6) allows for the admission of business records when they are: "(1) made or based on information transmitted by a person with knowledge at or near the time of the transaction; (2) made in the ordinary course of business; and (3) trustworthy, with neither the source of information nor method or circumstances of preparation indicating a lack of trustworthiness." *Id.* at 457 (citing *United States v. Miller,* 771 F.2d 1219, 1237 (9th Cir. 1985)).

Bonallo argues that the computer data which served as the basis for Exhibits "1" and "3" was not sufficiently trustworthy under 803(6). He contends that proof of untrustworthiness lies in the fact that the government is claiming, as its central theory of the case, that he altered the computer records. Also, Bonallo points out, government witnesses testified that it was in fact possible to alter the transaction records, as well as the access logs of the American Data building. Bonallo does not dispute the admissibility of the exhibits on any ground other than that the computer data on which they were based was untrustworthy.

Bonallo's contention that proof of untrustworthiness may be found in the government's theory that the computer data was altered is entirely without merit. Had the government attempted to introduce into evidence what it contended to be ordinary records, made in the normal course of business, in their original form, then proof that the records had been altered would indeed tend to show that they were unreliable. Here, however, the government introduced what it contended to be *altered records* precisely to show that they were in fact altered. Thus, the government's theory that Bonallo altered the records is wholly consistent with its characterization of the records and the purpose for which it introduced them. Under these circumstances, the fact that the records reflected the alterations in no way tends to prove that they are untrustworthy.

Bonallo also argues that the records are untrustworthy because it is possible that someone else at American Data altered them in an effort to frame him. However, Bonallo does not provide any evidence to support that theory. The fact that it is possible to alter data contained in a computer is plainly insufficient to establish untrustworthiness. The mere possibility that the logs may have been altered goes only to the weight of the evidence not its admissibility. *See Catabran,* 836 F.2d at 458. We therefore conclude that the district court did not abuse its discretion in admitting these exhibits.

V. Admissibility of Exhibit "20"

Government Exhibit "20" is a computer printout in computer language and is referred to as the "fraud program". It was found by Kanable, Bonallo's replacement at American Data, in the Tandem computer program listings "owned" by Bonallo—i.e., in Bonallo's program library. The "fraud program" could alter ATM transaction records to make it appear that a cash withdrawal from an ATM was made by one cardholder when it was in fact made by another. Bonallo argues that the exhibit was irrelevant to the prosecution because the program was run by Kanable once he modified the computer programs and files, Kanable ran the program not on actual files but on "test" files, and the government failed to establish that Kanable's program was the same program Bonallo used to alter the records.

We find these arguments unpersuasive. Because the discovery of the program in Bonallo's program library likely had a "tendency to make the existence of [a] fact that is of consequence to the determination of the action more probable * * * than it would be without the evidence," Fed.R.Evid. 401, the district court did not abuse its discretion when admitting it. Again, Bonallo's criticisms of the evidence go to its weight rather than its admissibility.

For the above reasons, we affirm Bonallo's conviction on 11 counts of bank fraud in violation of 18 U.S.C. § 1344(a)(1).

* * *

Notes and Questions

1. The Court, while considering the admissibility of the computer records in *Bonallo,* seems to focus on the fact that computer records are exceptionally reliable. Is this a consistent analysis considering the previous cases of *Rogan* and *Lowery?*

2. What advice would you give American Data Personnel for the next time they discover a "fraud program"?

3. To insure a successful computer crime prosecution, the initial investigators must be well-trained on technical and legal aspects of computer crime.

C. COMPUTER CRIME—PUNISHING INTERFERENCE WITH COMPUTER SYSTEMS

Corporations and governmental agencies have become increasingly dependent upon their computer systems. A computer system shutdown could seriously disrupt business. Therefore most organizations have "locks" on their systems to prevent tampering. Employees often know enough to evade the security "locks." Clever outsiders sometimes succeed in "unlocking" the system. A careless or malicious person can cause immense damage with a few computer commands. For instance, a single command (which the authors will not reveal) is enough to destroy all the data on the hard disk of a personal computer. Most states have passed laws on computer tampering. The following case is one of the first cases to apply such a law.

PEOPLE v. VERSAGGI

City Court of Rochester, Monroe County, Criminal Branch, N.Y., 1987.
136 Misc.2d 361, 518 N.Y.S.2d 553.

JOSEPH D. VALENTINO, JUDGE.

FACTS

The SL-100 is the computer which runs Eastman Kodak Company's telephone system. In Rochester, New York, Kodak has two such computers—one located at Kodak Office on State Street, which operates the Kodak Office telephones, and one located at the Kodak Park complex which operates the Kodak Park telephones. In the early morning hours of November 10, 1986, several telephone access lines to the Kodak Park complex in Rochester "shut down". It took computer technicians approximately two hours to restore the lines by issuing commands on the computer. Just over a week later, on November 19, 1986, all phone lines at the Kodak Office in Rochester were disconnected. This time the system repaired itself by way of a program in the computer system.

In November 1986, defendant Robert Versaggi was employed by Kodak as a computer technician responsible for maintaining and effecting repairs on the Call Defender system, the Timeplex system, and the multiplexer to Colorado. He was not responsible for the SL-100 systems.

As part of his job, the defendant often was required to work from his home, for which he was provided with Kodak-owned computer equipment. He was one of a handful of technicians who had been provided with an accelerator—a security device which allowed him to "access" certain Kodak computer systems which were also equipped with accelerators, including the Tellabs local area network. Kodak also provided him with a telephone line held by New York Telephone, phone number 948-5385, for the purpose of connecting with the Kodak computers from his home. Kodak was billed directly for calls made on this line. As the defendant resided in Batavia, calls made to Rochester would appear as itemized long distance calls.

Just prior to the November 10th and November 19th incidents, the telecommunications supervisor, Joseph Doyle, instructed one of his technicians David Nentarz to set up a script file to monitor the Tellabs data channel. The Tellabs computer system serves as a data communications network router. In certain situations, a user calling from outside of Kodak would first access the Tellabs System, from which point access to other systems was possible. Technicians used Tellabs as a diagnostic route when diagnosing problems with other systems from home. Tellabs is equipped with a security device known as an accelerator. This device prevents external access to Tellabs except by those users who also have accelerators. In November, Kodak employees who had been provided with accelerators included David Nentarz, Larry

Comstock, Mike Russell and defendant Robert Versaggi. These people had access to Tellabs from their homes.

The script file set up by David Nentarz monitored the first dial-in channel, corresponding to telephone number 722–6916. This program was hooked up to the Tellabs supervisory mode, or monitor port, and constantly checked for a connection with the Tellabs network. Once a user accessed another system via Tellabs, the monitor observed everything that appeared on that person's screen, much like a hidden camera in a bank which watches customers once they come in the door. The user would not be able to detect that he was being monitored. Further, the program contained a capture function which was activated as soon as a connection with Tellabs was made. Like the film in a hidden camera, this capture program ("capture") recorded on disc everything that came across the screen after the connection was in place. Capture created on floppy disc a permanent record of the user's activity while he was connected to Tellabs through the 722–6916 channel, eliminating the need for someone to stand vigil over the screen while the script file was running.

Kodak initially investigated the matter to determine why the lines went down, and who, if anyone, had caused them to malfunction. Evidence before the investigators included printouts from the SL–100 log which documented all activity on the SL–100 systems for the time periods in question; printouts from the monitor port of the Tellabs local area network which documented all activity on Tellabs through line 722–6916 for the time periods in question; and two New York Telephone bills for the telephone line provided to defendant Robert Versaggi by Kodak for the dates in question. Based on this evidence, Kodak investigators determined that on each occasion, defendant Versaggi had accessed the Kodak SL–100 systems and entered commands which caused the systems to shut down phone lines.

Defendant was charged with two counts of computer tampering in the second degree, Penal Law 156.20, a class A misdemeanor, which provides: "A person is guilty of computer tampering in the second degree when he uses or causes to be used a computer or computer service and having no right to do so he intentionally alters in any manner or destroys computer data or a computer program of another person." The People charge that by accessing the SL–100's on two occasions and entering certain commands which caused the system to shut down phone lines, defendant altered the computer software program in violation of the statute. At a bench trial which lasted two days, the People elicited testimony from five witnesses, including two Kodak computer technicians and the supervisor of telecommunications at Eastman Kodak, defendant's immediate boss. Much of what was heard consisted of expert testimony relating to computer operations at Kodak and the analysis of computer printouts received in evidence. Defendant did not testify; nor did he raise any defense provided by statute. (See Penal Law 156.50). After trial, the defendant moved to dismiss on the ground of insufficient evidence. He further argued that the actions of which he is accused do not constitute an alteration under the statute.

LAW

This case involves perhaps the first prosecution under New York's new computer crime statute, Penal Law Article 156, which went into effect on November 1, 1986, just days before the incidents charged herein. As of yet, the statute has not been construed by any court, and the reported decisions involving prosecutions under similar statutes in other states offer little substantive guidance. (See e.g., *People v. Brown,* 726 P.2d 638 [Colo.1986]; *State ex rel. Hall v. Wolf,* 710 S.W.2d 302 [Mo.1986]).

1. Sufficiency of the Evidence

The People's case rests solely on circumstantial evidence. The defendant was not caught in the act at his computer terminal (see e.g., *Regina v. Christensen,* 7 CLSR 406 [Canada 1979]). Instead, the events of November 10, and November 19, were traced to him through two sets of computer printouts and two telephone bills. Where a conviction rests on circumstantial evidence, "the hypothesis of guilt should flow naturally from the facts proved, and be consistent with them, and * * * the facts proved must exclude to a moral certainty every reasonable hypothesis of innocence". (*People v. Morris,* 36 N.Y.2d 877, 878, 372 N.Y.S.2d 210, 334 N.E.2d 10 [1975], citing *People v. Lagana,* 36 N.Y.2d 71, 365 N.Y.S.2d 147, 324 N.E.2d 534 [1975].)

The testimony shows that on both occasions, someone, without any right or authority to do so, manually issued commands on the computer software causing the phone lines to disconnect. This was not disputed at trial. The real issue for the finder of fact is whether the evidence proved beyond a reasonable doubt that defendant was the perpetrator. After a careful review of the evidence, this court is convinced beyond a reasonable doubt that it was defendant who issued the commands.

Trial testimony included evidence that other methods of access to the SL–100 systems were available besides through Tellabs 6916. From this, the court was urged to draw the inference that any number of people might have been responsible for issuing commands, and that their access would have remained undetected by the Tellabs monitor port. The court must reject this theory. The commands issued to the SL–100 and captured on the Tellabs monitor are in each case identical to the commands appearing on the SL–100 log printouts. The logs revealed that no other commands were issued to the SL–100's causing them to fail. Furthermore, the relevant time periods correspond almost exactly on the two sets of printouts. From this evidence, the court finds that on each occasion the SL–100 telephone system was accessed and reprogrammed through Tellabs channel 6916, and that this activity is recorded in the capture file printouts in evidence.

If the proof had stopped there, the court would find the evidence insufficient to convict, for there would be no conclusive evidence that it was defendant rather than another technician with an accelerator who had accessed Tellabs. Certainly, some of the evidence would have pointed towards Robert Versaggi, such as testimony that only he and David Nentarz had access to the Defender control screen on November 10, and proof that the "Versaggi" PROFS account had been accessed on November 19. But these items of evidence would not lead the court to conclude beyond a reasonable doubt that defendant was the perpetrator.

The People did offer further evidence, however: the New York Telephone bills for defendant Versaggi's Kodak-provided telephone line, phone number 948–5385. The November 10th bill reveals that a phone call was made to Tellabs channel 722–6916 at 12:10 a.m. which lasted for thirty-four minutes. This call corresponds to the capture file printout which shows that after initially accessing the Defender system, the user accessed the Kodak Park SL–100 at 12:11:53 and remained in that system at least until 12:33. The November 19th bill reveals that three phone calls were made to Tellabs channel 722–6916. The first call, made at 12:40 a.m. for three minutes, corresponds to the first Tellabs connection at 12:40:33. The second phone call, made at 12:50 for four minutes, though not actually reflected on the printout, corresponds to the time period during which the user was in Tellabs but not in a host system. This call's absence from the printout is consistent with the order of events reflected on the capture file. The third phone call, made at 1:33 a.m. for five minutes, corresponds to the SL–100 log-in time of 1:34.

After careful consideration of this evidence, I am convinced that on each occasion the illicit SL–100 commands were issued over defendant's Kodak-provided telephone line from computer equipment in his home, and that defendant was the perpetrator.

Concerning the defendant's intent, it should be noted that specific warnings appeared on the user's screen and the illegal commands were entered even after these warnings appeared. Keeping in mind that the capture file could not pick up log-on times until a host system was accessed, and that the several clocks involved were not synchronized, I find that the relevant times correspond so closely as to rule out all other reasonable explanations for the origin of the commands.

Circumstantial evidence is treated with special care "not because of any inherent weakness in this form of evidence, but to ensure that the [fact finder] has not relied upon equivocal evidence to draw unwarranted inferences or to make unsupported assumptions". (*People v. Way,* 59 N.Y.2d 361, 365, 465 N.Y.S.2d 853, 452 N.E.2d 1181 [1983]). The evidence here is by no means equivocal. This court finds that the evidence proves unequivocally and beyond a reasonable doubt that on November 10 and November 19, defendant intentionally issued commands to the SL–100 systems, causing phone lines to disconnect.

2. *"Alteration" Under the Statute*

The defendant argues that the actions for which he is charged did not constitute "alterations" under the statute. The statute (Penal Law 156.20) provides:

> A person is guilty of computer tampering in the second degree when he uses or causes to be used a computer or computer service and having no right to do so he intentionally alters in any manner or destroys computer data or a computer program of another person.

The statute also defines "computer program":

> "Computer program" is property and means an ordered set of data representing coded instructions or statements that, when executed by computer, cause the computer to process data or direct the computer to perform one or more computer operations or both and may be in any form, including magnetic storage media, punched cards, or stored internally in the memory of the computer.

(Penal Law 156.00[2]).

The defendant has suggested that the criminal activity which took place constituted interrupting the operation of the computer system, as opposed to altering a computer program. In some states, interrupting the operation of a computer system is classified as a crime. (See, e.g., Cal.Penal Code, § 502[c]; Conn.Gen.Stat.Ann. § 53a–251[d]). This classification is absent, however, from New York's computer crime statute. The New York State Legislature has instead chosen to focus on the activity itself rather than the result of that activity. 33 Buffalo L.Rev. 777, 785 [1984]. Therefore, the court must look to the statute and the alleged activity to determine whether that activity is within the purview of the statute.

The software involved here was part of the SL–100 package that came from the manufacturer. Defendant contends that issuing the commands constituted merely a "use" of the program as opposed to an alteration. Clearly, the program was written so that such commands could be entered to achieve shutting down the hardware, if necessary. Defendant did not rewrite the program. In fact, Joseph Doyle testified that any generic changes in the software would have to be made by the manufacturer. He also testified that normally, the software is executing a set of instructions which directs the hardware to provide dial tone, place calls, receive digits and other functions necessary to the operation of the telephone system. To effect changes in the hardware, it must be taken off its normal course of action and instructed to do other things. Here, the defendant changed the usual instructions to the hardware, so that instead of operating the telephone system in its normal fashion, it turned itself off.

This court finds that by issuing commands to the software which changed the instructions to the hardware, taking it off its normal course of action and shutting down the phone lines, defendant "altered" a computer program within the meaning of Penal Law 156.20. To embrace defendant's contention would be to require proof, not merely that the commands were issued changing the instructions, but that the software in fact had been rewritten. Such a hypertechnical statutory interpretation would certainly defy the statute's plain language as well as its very purpose to deter this kind of activity by employees entrusted with special computer privileges.

Defendant also urges that any alteration under the statute must be permanent. In the November 10 incident, a technician spent almost two hours issuing "counter-commands" on the software in order to restore the system to normal. In the November 19 incident, the system fixed itself by means of a function written into the program. But simply because a program can be fixed does not mean that it has not been altered. The statute makes it criminal to intentionally "alter in any manner *or destroy*" a program. An altered program which cannot be fixed most likely is destroyed. Destruction suggests permanency. As the statute distinguishes between the two forms of tampering—alteration and destruction—it must be assumed that the Legislature intended these to involve different sets of circumstances. Not only would it be inconsistent to hold that an alteration must be permanent to be punishable under the statute, but it would render the words "or destroy" a redundancy.

Finally, defendant points out that the alteration did not result in physical damage or financial damage. These are not elements of computer tampering in the second degree. As previously noted, this is not a result-oriented statute. The only time a computer tampering prosecution must focus on results is when the alteration or destruction exceeds $1,000. When this occurs, the crime is raised to computer tampering in the first degree, a class E felony. (See PL 156.25[4]). This monetary sum merely parallels the distinction between misdemeanor and felony crimes defined by the value of the property involved. As the defendant has not been charged with a felony, there is no need to consider physical or financial damage.

Defendant's motions to dismiss are denied. Based on the foregoing, this court finds the defendant guilty on two counts of computer tampering in the second degree.

MAHRU v. SUPERIOR COURT

Court of Appeal, Second District, Division 2, 1987, As Modified May 22, 1987, Review Denied July 23, 1987.
191 Cal.App.3d 545, 237 Cal.Rptr. 298.

THE COURT:

Petitioner is charged with one count of violating Penal Code section 502, subdivision (c). In this petition for a writ of prohibition (Pen.Code, § 999a) he contends that under a proper interpretation of section 502, the evidence adduced at the preliminary examination does not create a reasonable suspicion he committed the offense.

At the preliminary examination, the evidence tended to establish the following facts. Petitioner (Mahru), an experienced computer programmer, was an employee, director, and 15% shareholder of BHI, a data-processing firm. In 1983 BHI contracted to provide on-site computerized data processing services for the Downey Schools Federal Credit Union. The credit union purchased a computer and software and resold them on credit to BHI, retaining a security interest. The computer equipment was located at the credit union, in space the credit union leased to BHI. It was operated by BHI employees, not credit union employees. In a daily routine, BHI employees started the computer and ran a share draft tape containing data received overnight. Then credit union tellers could use their terminals to enter deposits and withdrawals. BHI employees attended the computer all day and, at the end of the day, made backup tapes to be stored in the credit union's fireproof vault and ran closing routines before shutting the computer down. When the equipment needed servicing, BHI had it repaired.

The data processing service agreement between BHI and the credit union provided for termination by mutual consent or upon 182 days' written notice. Upon termination, BHI was required under the contract to deliver a magnetic tape containing all current credit union records.

On February 9, 1985, the credit union told BHI orally that it was terminating the contract because BHI's system was inadequate, and that it was replacing BHI with a different firm, ECOM. (Two days later, it signed a contract with ECOM.)

At that meeting, the credit union said it expected to complete the conversion to ECOM data processing by April 1. It asked BHI to continue doing the credit union's data processing until then and to cooperate with ECOM during the conversion. BHI responded that it had been losing money on its operations at the credit union and would propose a price for continued services during the conversion. The credit union had already paid, under the contract, for BHI's regular services through the end of February. The respective attorneys for BHI and the credit union thereafter attempted to negotiate an agreement covering the conversion period.

By Wednesday, February 20, negotiations had broken down. Hegardt, the head of BHI, instructed codefendant Walker (BHI's chief computer operator) not to bring the tellers on line after running the share draft tape. Mahru, who was a programming expert (Hegardt was not), gave Walker a written instruction to make specified changes in the names of two files in the computer program. One effect of these changes was to make doubly certain that credit union employees, none of whom were computer experts, would be unable to run the credit union's programs without assistance from either BHI personnel or another expert computer software technician. Another effect was to make it more difficult for a non-BHI expert to run these programs.

The computer could also be run using backup tapes kept in the credit union's vault. These tapes contained complete and current credit union accounting data. They also would automatically change the file names back to their original form. Walker told a credit union vice-president this, but she did not know enough about computers to be able to use the information.

The file name changes were not entirely concealed; Walker left Mahru's written instruction taped to the computer display screen.

No BHI employees returned to the credit union the next day, Thursday, February 21. Consequently, the credit union was unable to resume automated operations. The record does not show whether credit union employees attempted to run the computer system themselves. At the credit union's request, ECOM sent a programmer and an operator to get the system running. By Monday, February 25, ECOM had the computer running, but it took one more day to restore access to the programs used by the credit union, apparently because of the file name changes ordered by Mahru. The cost of ECOM's services to restore computer operations is not of record. From February 21 to February 26 the credit union did its bookkeeping by hand, as it normally had during briefer periods when the computer was inoperative.

Eventually BHI filed a petition in bankruptcy, and the credit union took possession of the computer pursuant to its security interest.

Hegardt, called by the defense, testified the purpose for changing the file names was to prevent amateurs at the credit union, who might attempt to run the computer without any expert assistance, from putting the system into operation, lest they accidentally destroy or otherwise harm part of the credit union's computerized financial records.

Mahru was charged with violating Penal Code section 502, subdivision (c), which reads, in full: "Any person who maliciously accesses, alters, deletes, damages, destroys or disrupts the operation of any computer system, computer network, computer program, or data is guilty of a public offense." "Maliciously" imports "a wish to vex, annoy, or injure another person, or an intent to do a wrongful act." (Pen.Code, § 7, subd. (4).)

From the evidence, the magistrate had reasonable cause to suspect petitioner accessed, altered, and disrupted the operation of, the computer system and programs. Despite the defense's evidence to the contrary, the facts also support a suspicion that petitioner desired to vex and annoy the credit union, and to injure it by putting it to additional expense, in retaliation for its termination of BHI's contract.

The question presented, though, is whether the court should blindly match the literal words of sections 502 and 7 to the facts of the case. We think not. The documentary evidence established that BHI, not the credit union, owned the computer hardware and software, and the credit union had only a security interest in it. (See Cal.U.Com.Code, §§ 1201, subd. (37); 2401, subds. (1)–(3); 9202.) There was no evidence to the contrary. Section 502, subdivision (c) cannot be properly construed to make it a public offense for an employee, with his employer's approval, to operate the employer's computer in the course of the employer's business in a way that inconveniences or annoys or inflicts expense on another person.

The urge to spite others is one of the more miserable concomitants of human intelligence. Compared to human behavior as a whole, relatively few forms of spiteful conduct are actionable in tort, contract, or crime. More often they are merely upsetting and reprehensible. The legislature could not have meant, by enacting section 502, to bring the Penal Code into the computer age by making annoying or spiteful acts criminal offenses whenever a computer is used to accomplish them. Individuals and organizations use computers for typing and other routine tasks in the conduct of their affairs, and sometimes in the course of these affairs they do vexing, annoying, and injurious things. Such acts cannot all be criminal.

Here, the credit union had informed BHI that it was terminating the contract. The parties devote substantial attention to analyzing the niceties of the contract dispute between BHI and the credit union; they seem to believe it important to establish whether BHI breached the contract by walking off the job. We cannot see what difference it makes who breached first and whether BHI was justified, as a matter of contract law, in abruptly ceasing its performance. Surely whether petitioner's conduct is to be judged criminal cannot turn on whether it constituted a breach of contract by BHI.

Petitioner relies in part on a legislative declaration of findings and purpose accompanying a 1984 amendment to section 502. This declaration speaks of an "increase in the incidence of misuse and intrusions by unauthorized individuals" and the need for "sanctions against unauthorized intrusions into computer systems." This declaration, he says, shows a legislative intent to deter and punish only browsers and hackers—outsiders who break into a computer system to obtain or alter the information contained there. But we cannot be confident that this brief declaration of purpose was intended to summarize every act covered by the statute. Hence we have not relied on the legislative declaration in construing subdivision (c) to exclude the acts shown here.

Finally, and in light of the foregoing discussion, petitioner should not be required to wait for an appeal to obtain judicial resolution of his legal contention. The expense and humiliation of trial and possible conviction and sentencing should not be inflicted on him in this case.

This is a proper case for issuance of a peremptory writ in the first instance. (Code Civ.Proc., § 1088; *Palma v. U.S. Industrial Fasteners, Inc.* (1984) 36 Cal.3d 171, 177–180, 203 Cal.Rptr. 626, 681 P.2d 893.) All parties were informed this court was considering issuing a peremptory writ in the first instance. The matter having been fully briefed, issuance of an alternative writ would add nothing to the exposition of the issues.

Let a peremptory writ of prohibition issue, directing respondent to vacate its order of February 18, 1987, denying petitioner's motion to set aside the information, and to enter a new and different order granting the motion.

Notes and Questions

1. What evidence would Versaggi have needed to prove he was not at his home computer terminal during the time periods when the computer "wrongs" occurred?

2. The court in *Mahru* stated that the "urge to spite others is one of the more miserable concomitants of human intelligence." Given the Credit Union in *Mahru* was the keeper of its depositors' money and needed to rely on computer hardware and software, should Mahru's actions (and his employer's) be a violation of federal and state criminal laws?

3. Research your state to determine if a similar statute to the one in *Versaggi* exists. Is the statute significantly similar? Have there been any cases applying the statute? If there has not been any cases applying the statute, what do you think the probable outcome of *Versaggi* would be in your jurisdiction. If there is not a similar statute to the New York statute, propose one.

UNITED STATES v. MORRIS

United States Court of Appeals, Second Circuit, 1991.
928 F.2d 504.

JON O. NEWMAN, CIRCUIT JUDGE:

This appeal presents two narrow issues of statutory construction concerning a provision Congress recently adopted to strengthen protection against computer crimes. Section 2(d) of the Computer Fraud and Abuse Act of 1986, 18 U.S.C. § 1030(a)(5)(A) (1988), punishes anyone who intentionally accesses without authorization a category of computers known as "[f]ederal interest computers" and damages or prevents authorized use of information in such computers, causing loss of $1,000 or more. The issues raised are (1) whether the Government must prove not only that the defendant intended to access a federal interest computer, but also that the defendant intended to prevent authorized use of the computer's information and thereby cause loss; and (2) what satisfies the statutory requirement of "access without authorization." These questions are raised on an appeal by Robert Tappan Morris from the May 16, 1990, judgment of the District Court for the Northern District of New York (Howard G. Munson, Judge) convicting him, after a jury trial, of violating 18 U.S.C. § 1030(a)(5)(A). Morris released into INTERNET, a national computer network, a computer program known as a "worm"[1] that spread and multiplied, eventually causing computers

1. In the colorful argot of computers, a "worm" is a program that travels from one computer to another but does not attach itself to the operating system of the com-

at various educational institutions and military sites to "crash" or cease functioning.

We conclude that section 1030(a)(5)(A) does not require the Government to demonstrate that the defendant intentionally prevented authorized use and thereby caused loss. We also find that there was sufficient evidence for the jury to conclude that Morris acted "without authorization" within the meaning of section 1030(a)(5)(A). We therefore affirm.

FACTS

In the fall of 1988, Morris was a first-year graduate student in Cornell University's computer science Ph.D. program. Through undergraduate work at Harvard and in various jobs he had acquired significant computer experience and expertise. When Morris entered Cornell, he was given an account on the computer at the Computer Science Division. This account gave him explicit authorization to use computers at Cornell. Morris engaged in various discussions with fellow graduate students about the security of computer networks and his ability to penetrate it.

In October 1988, Morris began work on a computer program, later known as the INTERNET "worm" or "virus." The goal of this program was to demonstrate the inadequacies of current security measures on computer networks by exploiting the security defects that Morris had discovered. The tactic he selected was release of a worm into network computers. Morris designed the program to spread across a national network of computers after being inserted at one computer location connected to the network. Morris released the worm into INTERNET, which is a group of national networks that connect university, governmental, and military computers around the country. The network permits communication and transfer of information between computers on the network. Morris sought to program the INTERNET worm to spread widely without drawing attention to itself. The worm was supposed to occupy little computer operation time, and thus not interfere with normal use of the computers. Morris programmed the worm to make it difficult to detect and read, so that other programmers would not be able to "kill" the worm easily. Morris also wanted to ensure that the worm did not copy itself onto a computer that already had a copy. Multiple copies of the worm on a computer would make the worm easier to detect and would bog down the system and ultimately cause the computer to crash. Therefore, Morris designed the worm to "ask" each computer whether it already had a copy of the worm. If it responded "no," then the worm would copy onto the computer; if it responded "yes," the worm would not duplicate. However, Morris was concerned that other programmers could kill the worm by program-

puter it "infects." It differs from a "virus," which is also a migrating program, but one that attaches itself to the operating system of any computer it enters and can infect any other computer that uses files from the infected computer.

ming their own computers to falsely respond "yes" to the question. To circumvent this protection, Morris programmed the worm to duplicate itself every seventh time it received a "yes" response. As it turned out, Morris underestimated the number of times a computer would be asked the question, and his one-out-of-seven ratio resulted in far more copying than he had anticipated. The worm was also designed so that it would be killed when a computer was shut down, an event that typically occurs once every week or two. This would have prevented the worm from accumulating on one computer, had Morris correctly estimated the likely rate of reinfection.

Morris identified four ways in which the worm could break into computers on the network:

(1) through a "hole" or "bug" (an error) in SEND MAIL, a computer program that transfers and receives electronic mail on a computer;

(2) through a bug in the "finger demon" program, a program that permits a person to obtain limited information about the users of another computer;

(3) through the "trusted hosts" feature, which permits a user with certain privileges on one computer to have equivalent privileges on another computer without using a password; and

(4) through a program of password guessing, whereby various combinations of letters are tried out in rapid sequence in the hope that one will be an authorized user's password, which is entered to permit whatever level of activity that user is authorized to perform.

On November 2, 1988, Morris released the worm from a computer at the Massachusetts Institute of Technology. MIT was selected to disguise the fact that the worm came from Morris at Cornell. Morris soon discovered that the worm was replicating and reinfecting machines at a much faster rate than he had anticipated. Ultimately, many machines at locations around the country either crashed or became "catatonic." When Morris realized what was happening, he contacted a friend at Harvard to discuss a solution. Eventually, they sent an anonymous message from Harvard over the network, instructing programmers how to kill the worm and prevent reinfection. However, because the network route was clogged, this message did not get through until it was too late. Computers were affected at numerous installations, including leading universities, military sites, and medical research facilities. The estimated cost of dealing with the worm at each installation ranged from $200 to more than $53,000. Morris was found guilty, following a jury trial, of violating 18 U.S.C. § 1030(a)(5)(A). He was sentenced to three years of probation, 400 hours of community service, a fine of $10,050, and the costs of his supervision.

Discussion

I. The Intent Requirement in Section 1030(a)(5)(A)

Section 1030(a)(5)(A), covers anyone who

(5) *intentionally* accesses a Federal interest computer without authorization, and by means of one or more instances of such conduct alters, damages, or destroys information in any such Federal interest computer, or prevents authorized use of any such computer or information, *and thereby*

(A) causes loss to one or more others of a value aggregating $1,000 or more during any one year period; * * * [emphasis added].

The District Court concluded that the intent requirement applied only to the accessing and not to the resulting damage. Judge Munson found recourse to legislative history unnecessary because he considered the statute clear and unambiguous. However, the Court observed that the legislative history supported its reading of section 1030(a)(5)(A).

Morris argues that the Government had to prove not only that he intended the unauthorized access of a federal interest computer, but also that he intended to prevent others from using it, and thus cause a loss. The adverb "intentionally," he contends, modifies both verb phrases of the section. The Government urges that since punctuation sets the "accesses" phrase off from the subsequent "damages" phrase, the provision unambiguously shows that "intentionally" modifies only "accesses." * * * In the present case, we do not believe the comma after "authorization" renders the text so clear as to preclude review of the legislative history.

* * *

Despite some isolated language in the legislative history that arguably suggests a scienter component for the "damages" phrase of section 1030(a)(5)(A), the wording, structure, and purpose of the subsection, examined in comparison with its departure from the format of its predecessor provision persuade us that the "intentionally" standard applies only to the "accesses" phrase of section 1030(a)(5)(A), and not to its "damages" phrase. II. The unauthorized access requirement in section 1030(a)(5)(A) [2] Section 1030(a)(5)(A) penalizes the conduct of an individual who "intentionally accesses a Federal interest computer without authorization." Morris contends that his conduct constituted, at most, "exceeding authorized access" rather than the "unauthorized access" that the subsection punishes. Morris argues that there was insufficient evidence to convict him of "unauthorized access," and that even if the evidence sufficed, he was entitled to have the jury instructed on his "theory of defense."

We assess the sufficiency of the evidence under the traditional standard. Morris was authorized to use computers at Cornell, Harvard, and Berkeley, all of which were on INTERNET. As a result, Morris was authorized to communicate with other computers on the network to send electronic mail (SEND MAIL), and to find out certain information about the users of other computers (finger demon). The question is whether Morris's transmission of his worm constituted exceeding authorized access or accessing without authorization.

The Senate Report stated that section 1030(a)(5)(A), like the new section 1030(a)(3), would "be aimed at 'outsiders,' i.e., those lacking authorization to access any Federal interest computer." Senate Report at 10, U.S.Code Cong. & Admin.News at 2488. But the Report also stated, in concluding its discussion on the scope of section 1030(a)(3), that it applies "where the offender is completely outside the Government, ... or where the offender's act of trespass is interdepartmental in nature." Id. at 8, U.S.Code Cong. & Admin.News at 2486 (emphasis added).

Morris relies on the first quoted portion to argue that his actions can be characterized only as exceeding authorized access, since he had authorized access to a federal interest computer. However, the second quoted portion reveals that Congress was not drawing a bright line between those who have some access to any federal interest computer and those who have none. Congress contemplated that individuals with access to some federal interest computers would be subject to liability under the computer fraud provisions for gaining unauthorized access to other federal interest computers. See, e.g., id. (stating that a Labor Department employee who uses Labor's computers to access without authorization an FBI computer can be criminally prosecuted). The evidence permitted the jury to conclude that Morris's use of the SEND MAIL and finger demon features constituted access without authorization. While a case might arise where the use of SEND MAIL or finger demon falls within a nebulous area in which the line between accessing without authorization and exceeding authorized access may not be clear, Morris's conduct here falls well within the area of unauthorized access. Morris did not use either of those features in any way related to their intended function. He did not send or read mail nor discover information about other users; instead he found holes in both programs that permitted him a special and unauthorized access route into other computers.

Moreover, the jury verdict need not be upheld solely on Morris's use of SEND MAIL and finger demon. As the District Court noted, in denying Morris' motion for acquittal,—

> Although the evidence may have shown that defendant's initial insertion of the worm simply exceeded his authorized access, the evidence also demonstrated that the worm was designed to spread to other computers at which he had no account and no authority, express or implied, to unleash the worm program. Moreover, there was also evidence that the worm was designed to gain access to computers at which he had no account by guessing their passwords. Accordingly, the evidence did support the jury's conclusion that defendant accessed without authority as opposed to merely exceeding the scope of his authority.

In light of the reasonable conclusions that the jury could draw from Morris's use of SEND MAIL and finger demon, and from his use of the trusted hosts feature and password guessing, his challenge to the sufficiency of the evidence fails. Morris endeavors to bolster his sufficiency argument by contending that his conduct was not punishable under subsection (a)(5) but was punishable under subsection (a)(3). That concession belies the validity of his claim that he only exceeded authorization rather than made unauthorized access. Neither subsection (a)(3) nor (a)(5) punishes conduct that exceeds authorization. Both punish a person who "accesses" "without authorization" certain computers. Subsection (a)(3) covers the computers of a department or agency of the United States; subsection (a)(5) more broadly covers any federal interest computers, defined to include, among other computers, those used exclusively by the United States, 18 U.S.C.s 1030(e)(2)(A), and adds the element of causing damage or loss of use of a value of $1,000 or more. If Morris violated subsection (a)(3), as he concedes, then his conduct in inserting the worm into the INTERNET must have constituted "unauthorized access" under subsection (a)(5) to the computers of the federal departments the worm reached, for example, those of NASA and military bases.

To extricate himself from the consequence of conceding that he made "unauthorized access" within the meaning of subsection (a)(3), Morris subtly shifts his argument and contends that he is not within the reach of subsection (a)(5) at all. He argues that subsection (a)(5) covers only those who, unlike himself, lack access to any federal interest computer. It is true that a primary concern of Congress in drafting subsection (a)(5) was to reach those unauthorized to access any federal interest computer. The Senate Report stated, "[T]his subsection [(a)(5)] will be aimed at 'outsiders,' i.e., those lacking authorization to access any Federal interest computer." Senate Report at 10, U.S.Code Cong. & Admin.News at 2488. But the fact that the subsection is "aimed" at such "outsiders" does not mean that its coverage is limited to them. Congress understandably thought that the group most likely to damage federal interest computers would be those who lack authorization to use any of them. But it surely did not mean to insulate from liability the person authorized to use computers at the State Department who causes damage to computers at the Defense Department. Congress created the misdemeanor offense of subsection (a)(3) to punish intentional trespasses into computers for which one lacks authorized access; it added the felony offense of subsection (a)(5) to punish such a trespasser who also causes damage or loss in excess of $1,000, not only to computers of the United States but to any computer within the definition of federal interest computers. With both provisions, Congress was punishing those, like Morris, who, with access to some computers that enable them to communicate on a network linking other computers, gain access to other computers to which they lack authorization and either trespass, in violation of subsection (a)(3), or cause damage or loss of $1,000 or more, in violation of subsection (a)(5).

Morris also contends that the District Court should have instructed the jury on his theory that he was only exceeding authorized access. The District Court decided that it was unnecessary to provide the jury with a definition of "authorization." We agree. Since the word is of common usage, without any technical or ambiguous meaning, the Court was not obliged to instruct the jury on its meaning. See, e.g., *United States v. Chenault,* 844 F.2d 1124, 1131 (5th Cir.1988) ("A trial court need not define specific statutory terms unless they are outside the common understanding of a juror or are so technical or specific as to require a definition.").

An instruction on "exceeding authorized access" would have risked misleading the jury into thinking that Morris could not be convicted if some of his conduct could be viewed as falling within this description. Yet, even if that phrase might have applied to some of his conduct, he could nonetheless be found liable for doing what the statute prohibited, gaining access where he was unauthorized and causing loss.

Additionally, the District Court properly refused to charge the jury with Morris's proposed jury instruction on access without authorization. That instruction stated, "To establish the element of lack of authorization, the government must prove beyond a reasonable doubt that Mr. Morris was an 'outsider,' that is, that he was not authorized to access any Federal interest computer in any manner." As the analysis of the legislative history reveals, Congress did not intend an individual's authorized access to one federal interest computer to protect him from prosecution, no matter what other federal interest computers he accesses.

Conclusion

For the foregoing reasons, the judgment of the District Court is affirmed.

D. PREVENTING RADIO FREQUENCY INTERFERENCE

One of the authors of this casebook bought one of the first home computers, a "Sol–20" in the late 1970s. The computer was in a handsome case with beautiful walnut wood sides. When the computer was operating, it generated high frequency radio waves, which passed unhindered through the wood to interfere with television reception throughout the house. As home computers spread, apartment dwellers found their television reception ruined by radio waves from nearby apartments. The Federal Communications Commission soon moved to protect the television viewers of the United States. It initiated requirements limiting radio wave emissions for computers. Today all computers and most computer peripheral devices must meet either the stiff standards for inclusion in Class B (for home computers) or the more lenient standards for Class A (for office computers). The cost of testing and dealing with Federal Communications Commission paperwork, unfortunately, made it more difficult for small companies to enter the computer and computer peripheral marketplace. Excerpts from the Federal Communications Commission regulations follow.

RADIO FREQUENCY DEVICES
47 C.F.R., Ch. 1

Subpart A—General

§ 15.1 Scope of this part

(a) This part sets out the regulations under which an intentional, unintentional, or incidental radiator may be operated without an individual license. It also contains the technical specifications, administrative requirements and other conditions relating to the marketing of Part 15 devices.

(b) The operation of an intentional or unintentional radiator that is not in accordance with the regulations in this part must be licensed pursuant to the provisions of section 301 of the Communications Act of 1934, as amended, unless otherwise exempted from the licensing requirements elsewhere in this chapter.

(c) Unless specifically exempted, the operation or marketing of an intentional or unintentional radiator that is not in compliance with the administrative and technical provisions in this part, including prior Commission authorization or verification, as appropriate, is prohibited under section 302 of the Communications Act of 1934, as amended, and Subpart I of Part 2 of this chapter. The equipment authorization and verification procedures are detailed in Subpart J of Part 2 of this chapter.

* * *

(h) *Class A digital device.* A digital device that is marketed for use in a commercial, industrial or business environment, exclusive of a device which is marketed for use by the general public or is intended to be used in the home.

(i) *Class B digital device.* A digital device that is marketed for use in a residential environment notwithstanding use in commercial, business and industrial environments. Examples of such devices include, but are not limited to, personal computers, calculators, and similar electronic devices that are marketed for use by the general public.

Note: The responsible party may also qualify a device intended to be marketed in a commercial, business or industrial environment as a Class B device, and in fact is encouraged to do so, provided the device complies with the technical specifications for a Class B digital device. In the event that a particular type of device has been found to repeatedly cause harmful interference to radio communications, the Commission may classify such a digital device as a Class B digital device, regardless of its intended use.

* * *

(k) *Digital device.* (Previously defined as a computing device). An unintentional radiator (device or system) that generates and uses timing signals or pulses at a rate in excess of 9,000 pulses (cycles) per second and uses digital techniques; inclusive of telephone equipment that uses digital techniques or any device or system that generates and uses radio frequency energy for the purpose of performing data processing functions, such as electronic computations, operations, transformations, recording, filing, sorting, storage, retrieval, or transfer. A radio frequency device that is specifically subject to an emanation requirement in any other FCC Rule part or an intentional radiator subject to Subpart C of this part that contains a digital device is not subject to the standards for digital devices, provided the digital device is used only to enable operation of the radio frequency device and the digital device does not control additional functions or capabilities.

Note: Computer terminals and peripherals that are intended to be connected to a computer are digital devices.

(*l*) *Field disturbance sensor.* A device that establishes a radio frequency field in its vicinity and detects changes in that field resulting from the movement of persons or objects within its range.

(m) *Harmful interference.* Any emission, radiation or induction that endangers the functioning of a radio navigation service or of other safety services or seriously degrades, obstructs or repeatedly interrupts a radiocommunications service operating in accordance with this chapter.

(n) *Incidental radiator.* A device that generates radio frequency energy during the course of its operation although the device is not intentionally designed to generate or emit radio frequency energy. Examples of incidental radiators are dc motors, mechanical light switches, etc.

* * *

(r) *Peripheral device.* An input/output unit of a system that feeds data into and/or receives data from the central processing unit of a digital device. Peripherals to a digital device include any device that is connected external to the digital device, any device internal to the digital device that connects the digital device to an external device by wire or cable, and any circuit board or card designed for interchangeable mounting, internally or externally, that increases the operating or processing speed of a digital device, e.g., "turbo cards" and "enhancement boards". Examples of peripheral devices include terminals, printers, external floppy disk drives and other data storage devices, video monitors, keyboards, control cards, interface boards, external memory expansion cards and other input/output devices that may or may not contain digital circuitry. However, an internal device that contains the central processing unit of a digital device is not a peripheral even though such a device may connect to an external keyboard or other components.

(s) *Personal computer.* An electronic computer that is marketed for use in the home, notwithstanding business applications. Such computers are considered Class B digital devices. Computers which use a standard TV receiver as a display device or meet all of the following conditions are considered examples of personal computers:

(1) Marketed through a retail outlet or direct mail order catalog.

(2) Notices of sale or advertisements are distributed or directed to the general public or hobbyist users rather than restricted to commercial users.

(3) Operates on a battery or 120 volt electrical supply.

If the responsible party can demonstrate that because of price or performance the computer is not suitable for residential or hobbyist use, it may request that the computer be considered to fall outside of the scope of this definition for personal computers.

* * *

(u) *Radio frequency (RF) energy.* Electromagnetic energy at any frequency in the radio spectrum between 9 kHz and 3,000,000 MHz.

* * *

(z) *Unintentional radiator.* A device that intentionally generates radio frequency energy for use within the device, or that sends radio frequency signals by conduction to associated equipment via connecting wiring, but which is not intended to emit RF energy by radiation or induction.

* * *

§ 15.15 General technical requirements

(a) An intentional or unintentional radiator shall be constructed in accordance with good engineering design and manufacturing practice. Emanations from the device shall be suppressed as much as practicable, but in no case shall the emanations exceed the levels specified in these rules.

(b) An intentional or unintentional radiator must be constructed such that the adjustments of any control that is readily accessible by or intended to be accessible to the user will not cause operation of the device in violation of the regulations.

(c) Parties responsible for equipment compliance should note that the limits specified in this part will not prevent harmful interference under all circumstances. Since the operators of Part 15 devices are required to cease operation should harmful interference occur to authorized users of the radio frequency spectrum, the parties responsible for equipment compliance are encouraged to employ the minimum field strength necessary for communications, to provide greater attenuation of unwanted emissions than required by these regulations, and to advise the user as to how to resolve harmful interference problems (for example, see § 15.105(b)).

* * *

§ 15.19 Labelling requirements

(a) In addition to the requirements in Part 2 of this chapter, a device subject to certification, notification, or verification shall be labelled as follows:

* * *

(3) All other devices shall bear the following statement in a conspicuous location on the device:

> This device complies with Part 15 of the FCC Rules. Operation is subject to the following two conditions: (1) This device may not cause harmful interference, and (2) this device must accept any interference received, including interference that may cause undesired operation.

(b) Where a device is constructed in two or more sections connected by wires and marketed together, the statement specified in this section is required to be affixed only to the main control unit.

(c) When the device is so small or for such use that it is not practicable to place the statement specified in this section on it, the information required by these paragraphs shall be placed in a prominent location in the instruction manual or pamphlet supplied to the user or, alternatively, shall be placed on the container in which the device is marketed. However, the FCC identifier or the unique identifier, as appropriate, must be displayed on the device.

§ 15.21 Information to user

The users manual or instruction manual for an intentional or unintentional radiator shall caution the user that changes or modifications not expressly approved by the party responsible for compliance could void the user's authority to operate the equipment.

* * *

§ 15.27 Special accessories

(a) Equipment marketed to a consumer must be capable of complying with the necessary regulations in the configuration in which the equipment is marketed. Where special accessories, such as shielded cables and/or special connectors, are required to enable an unintentional or intentional radiator to comply with the emission limits in this part, the equipment must be marketed with, i.e., shipped and sold with, those special accessories. However, in lieu of shipping or packaging the special accessories with the unintentional or intentional radiator, the responsible party may employ other methods of ensuring that the special accessories are provided to the consumer, without additional charge, at the time of purchase. Information detailing any alternative method used to supply the special accessories shall be included in the application for a grant of equipment authorization or retained in the verification records, as appropriate. The party responsible for the equipment, as detailed in § 2.909 of this chapter, shall ensure that these special accessories are provided with the equipment. The instruction manual for such devices shall include appropriate instructions on the first page of the text concerned with the installation of the device that these special accessories must be used with the device. It is the responsibility of the user to use the needed special accessories supplied with the equipment.

(b) If a device requiring special accessories is installed by or under the supervision of the party marketing the device, it is the responsibility of that party to install the equipment using the special accessories. For equipment requiring professional installation, it is not necessary for the responsible party to market the special accessories with the equipment. However, the need to use the special accessories must be detailed in the instruction manual, and it is the responsibility of the installer to provide and to install the required accessories.

(c) Accessory items that can be readily obtained from multiple retail outlets are not considered to be special accessories and are not required to be marketed with the equipment. The manual included with the equipment must specify what additional components or accessories are required to be used in order to ensure compliance with this part, and it is the responsibility of the user to provide and use those components and accessories.

(d) The resulting system, including any accessories or components marketed with the equipment, must comply with the regulations.

§ 15.29 Inspection by the Commission

(a) Any equipment or device subject to the provisions of this part, together with any certificate, notice of registration or any technical data required to be kept on file by the operator, supplier or party responsible for compliance of the device shall be made available for inspection by a Commission representative upon reasonable request.

(b) The owner or operator of a radio frequency device subject to this part shall promptly furnish to the Commission or its representative such information as may be requested concerning the operation of the radio frequency device.

(c) The party responsible for the compliance of any device subject to this part shall promptly furnish to the Commission or its representatives such information as may be requested concerning the operation of the device, including a copy of any measurements made for obtaining an equipment authorization or demonstrating compliance with the regulations.

(d) The Commission, from time to time, may request the party responsible for compliance, including an importer, to submit to the FCC Laboratory in Columbia, Maryland, various equipment to determine that the equipment continues to comply with the applicable standards. Shipping costs to the Commission's Laboratory and return shall be borne by the responsible party. Testing by the Commission will be performed using the measurement procedure(s) that was in effect at the time the equipment was authorized or verified.

§ 15.31 Measurement standards

(a) The following measurement procedures are used by the Commission to determine compliance with the technical requirements. Copies of these procedures are available from the National Technical Information Service (NTIS), 5285 Port Royal Road, Springfield, VA 22161 or from the Commission's current duplicating contractor whose name and address are available from the Commission's Consumer Assistance Office.

* * *

(4) FCC/OET MP–4: FCC Procedure for Measuring RF Emissions from Computing Devices.

* * *

(b) All parties making compliance measurements on equipment subject to the requirements of this part are urged to use these measurement procedures. Any party using other procedures should ensure that such other procedures can be relied on to produce measurement results compatible with the FCC measurement procedures. The description of the measurement procedure used in testing the equipment for compliance and a list of the test equipment actually employed shall be made part of an application for certification or included with the data required to be retained by the party responsible for devices subject to notification or verification.

* * *

Subpart B—Unintentional Radiators

§ 15.101 Equipment authorization of unintentional radiators

(a) Except as otherwise exempted in §§ 15.23, 15.103, and 15.113, unintentional radiators shall be authorized by the Commission or verified prior to the initiation of marketing, as follows:

Type of device	Equipment authorization required [1]
TV broadcast receiver	Verification.
FM broadcast receiver	Do.
CB receiver	Certification.
Superregenerative receiver	Do.
Scanning receiver	Do.
All other receivers subject to Part 15	Notification.
TV interface device	Certification.
Cable system terminal device	Notification.
Stand-alone cable input selector switch	Verification.
Class B personal computers & peripherals	Certification.
Other Class B digital devices & peripherals	Verification.
Class A digital devices & peripherals	Do.
External switching power supplies	Do.
All other devices	Do.

[1] See additional provisions in this section and in § 15.103 of this part.

* * *

(c) Personal computer mother boards (the circuit board performing the central processing) that are marketed assembled with an enclosure and a power supply must be certificated with that enclosure and power supply.

(d) Peripheral devices, as defined in § 15.3(r), shall be certified or verified, as appropriate, prior to marketing. However, if a peripheral always will be marketed with a specific personal computer, it is not necessary to obtain a separate grant of certification for that peripheral, provided the specific combination of personal computer and peripheral has received a grant of certification.

(e) Subassemblies to digital devices are not subject to the technical standards in this part unless they are marketed as part of a system in which case the resulting system must comply with the applicable regulations. Subassemblies include: Those devices that are enclosed solely within the enclosure housing the digital device and are not included in the definition of peripherals in § 15.3(r), such as internal disc drives and memory expansion units; digital devices marketed to another manufacturer to be incorporated into a final product; circuit boards containing the central processing unit that are marketed without an enclosure or power supply; and, switching power supplies that are separately marketed and are solely for use internal to a digital device.

(f) The procedures for obtaining a grant of certification or notification and for verification are contained in Subpart J of Part 2 of this chapter.

* * *

Chapter XI

ACCESS TO INFORMATION IN COMPUTERIZED FORM

A. ACCESS TO GOVERNMENT DATA BANKS

Freedom of Information Act

The Freedom of Information Act (5 U.S.C. § 552) was enacted in 1976 to force federal agencies to reveal their records, procedures, and statements of policy to requesting members of the public. The Act provides that each agency must publish a description of the place and method by which the public may obtain such information. The required publication is in the *Federal Register.* Exceptions are allowed in cases where the information request would:

1. Constitute a "clearly" unwarranted invasion of personal "privacy"
2. Jeopardize national defense matters
3. Impinge upon internal personnel rules
4. Release confidential financial information or trade secrets, personnel and medical files, geological information, and inter-office or intra-office agency memoranda
5. Reveal investigatory records which can be obtained only by a valid subpoena

Persons who are refused the right to inspect legitimate federal records may sue to enjoin the agency from withholding the information and recover costs and attorney's fees.

B. ACCESS TO COMPUTERIZED DATA IN LITIGATION

UNITED STATES v. LIEBERT, III.

United States Court of Appeals, Third Circuit, 519 F.2d 542, 1975.
Cert. denied 423 U.S. 985, 96 S.Ct. 392, 46 L.Ed.2d 301 (1975).

ROSENN, CIRCUIT JUDGE:

Despite more than a decade of experience with expanded pretrial discovery in criminal cases, the extent to which it should be permitted continues to be "a complex and controversial issue." [1] Whether pretrial discovery may be used to secure extrinsic evidence to impeach the reliability of computer printouts which are the fundament of the prosecution's case presents an issue of first impression.

Defendant, Peter P. Liebert, III, was charged in a three-count information on December 21, 1973, with willfully and knowingly having failed to file his income tax returns for the years 1967 through 1969, in violation of section 7203 of the Internal Revenue Code of 1954 (Code). Liebert was arraigned and pleaded not guilty to the charges. His attorneys have claimed he filed a tax return for each of the three years in question.

I. DISCOVERY MOTIONS

In a failure-to-file prosecution, the Government relies heavily upon a report compiled by the personnel of the appropriate service center that their computers have no record of the receipt of a taxpayer's return for the particular year. In preparation for challenging the reliability and accuracy of the computer report, Liebert filed on January 14, 1974, a motion seeking an order permitting his computer expert access to the Mid–Atlantic Service Center for the purpose of analyzing and testing the Internal Revenue Service's (IRS) data processing systems. After extended proceedings, the district court granted the motion.

On February 28, 1974, Liebert filed a second discovery motion seeking production of all records indicating the number of notices issued by the IRS for the years 1967 through 1973 to taxpayers advising that no tax return had been received.[2] On October 22, 1974, again after extended proceedings, the district court ordered the Government to furnish Liebert a "mutually agreeable portion of the lists" of the people whom the Government suspected as being probable nonfilers for

1. *See Advisory Committee's Note to Proposed Amendments to Rules of Criminal Procedure,* 34 F.R.D. 411, 423 (1964).

2. Liebert learned of the existence of such records when an Assistant United States Attorney introduced one page of the list into evidence in another failure-to-file

the years 1970 and 1971.[3] 383 F.Supp. 1060 (E.D.Pa.1974).

When the Government refused to produce the lists, the district court on November 26, 1974, dismissed the charges against Liebert. The Government appeals, arguing that the lists are not subject to disclosure under the Code. The Government also contends that even if the lists are not privileged under the Code, the information Liebert desires through the use of the lists may be obtained from alternative sources without invading the privacy of the persons listed. We find merit in the Government's latter contention, vacate the judgment of the district court, and remand.

An understanding of the nature of the lists in dispute is essential for the proper resolution of the problem confronting us. The lists are prepared in conjunction with the IRS Individual Master File Delinquency Check Program, which identifies individuals who filed in the previous year but apparently have not filed for the current year, and individuals who have not filed for either the current or the previous years.

About six months after the due date of the return in question, an inquiry is initiated by analyzing the individual master file for taxpayers who have filed in the prior year but apparently not for the current year. Also, certain other documents, such as Social Security Administration wage records and W–2 forms, are compared with the master file to identify possible nonfilers. After the potentially delinquent taxpayers have been identified, wage information for the current year, adjusted gross income from the last return filed, and other criteria are used to determine whether the taxpayer probably was required to file.

Within the limitations of available resources, certain of these apparent nonfilers are selected for contact. As soon as the first notices are sent to the apparently delinquent taxpayers, the service center prepares a listing identifying each nonfiling taxpayer. These listings are the lists in issue in this case. If the taxpayer does not respond satisfactorily to the notice, a taxpayer delinquency investigation is issued and forwarded to the local IRS office where an attempt is made to communicate with the taxpayer either by phone, letter, or in person to resolve the apparent delinquency.

Thus, although the lists are commonly referred to as the lists of nonfilers, that appellation is misleading in two aspects. First, the lists contain names of persons who, in fact, have filed. For example, the return may have been in process at the time the lists were prepared, the taxpayer may have moved and filed in a different service center, or

case. *See United States v. Greenlee,* No. 74–2106, 517 F.2d 899 (3d Cir., 1975).

3. The lists were not available for 1967 through 1969, the years for which Liebert had been charged with failure to file tax returns. The district court ordered the production of the 1970 and 1971 lists after determining that the system producing these lists had been upgraded since the preparation of the 1967 through 1969 lists. The court reasoned that if errors existed in the later lists, they in all probability would demonstrate the presence of an equal or greater number of errors in the earlier lists. The Government has not challenged this conclusion on appeal.

the taxpayer may have married and filed jointly under a different name. Second, the lists contain names of persons who did not file, but were under no duty to do so. Such people may have not earned enough adjusted gross income to be required to file, or indeed may have died during the year.

II. GOVERNMENT'S STATUTORY CONTENTIONS

The Government contends that the production of the lists is barred by section 6103(a) of the Code, which permits the public inspection of returns "only upon order of the President and under rules and regulations prescribed by the Secretary * * *."

Although recognizing that the nonfiling lists are not tax returns, as are 1040 forms, the Government argues that the lists are compiled from previous years' returns, and from documents normally attached to the current year's returns, such as W–2 forms, and therefore are encompassed within the administrative definition of "return" promulgated under authority of subsection (a).

Congress, in enacting section 6103(a), sought to protect the confidentiality of the information necessary for the determination of tax liability found in returns filed under compulsion of law. *Tax Analysts and Advocates v. IRS,* 505 F.2d 350, 354, n. 1 (D.C.Cir.1974); *Association of Am. Railroads v. United States,* 371 F.Supp. 114, 116 (D.D.C.1974) (three-judge court). This policy of confidentiality encourages the full disclosure of income by taxpayers who are assured that their neighbors or competitors "will not be apprised of the intimate details of [their] financial [lives]." *Association of Am. Railroads v. United States, supra,* 371 F.Supp. at 116.

Section 6103(a), however, is limited by section 6103(f) of the Code which mandates that the IRS furnish to an inquirer information as to whether a person has, or has not, filed an income tax return. Information about an individual's financial status necessarily revealed by disclosing whether or not an individual has filed his return cannot be confidential under subsection (a) because the fact of filing or nonfiling is public information under subsection (f). For example, the amount of an individual's adjusted gross income is confidential under subsection (a), but the information that an individual either has an adjusted gross income requiring a filing or lacks such income but desires a tax refund cannot be confidential because such information necessarily is revealed by the filing of a return.

The nonfiling list reveals two types of information about an individual taxpayer. First, the list reveals that as a result of an investigation, albeit preliminary and incomplete, the IRS has determined that the individual did not file a return notwithstanding his duty to file. This type of information is not covered by subsection (a). Second, the list contains limited information about an individual's financial status. Such information reveals at most that an individual either had filed in the previous year or had an adjusted gross income requiring a filing in the current year. This information is exactly the type of information necessarily revealed by the fact of filing, which is public knowledge under subsection (f).

We therefore conclude that neither section 6103(a) nor any reasonable construction thereof bars the production of the nonfiling lists pursuant to judicial order. Since the production of the lists is not barred by the statute, production may not be barred by the regulations promulgated under authority of the statute.

The Government also contends that disclosure of the lists is forbidden by section 7213(a)(1) of the Code which provides that it shall be unlawful for any federal employee "to permit any income return or copy thereof or any book containing any abstract or particulars thereof to be seen or examined by any person except as provided by law," and 18 U.S.C. § 1905 (1970) which is a more general anti-disclosure statute containing a similar prohibition. Under both statutes, the prohibition against the release of confidential information contains the proviso "except as provided by law." Such phrase permits the disclosure of confidential information pursuant to a lawfully issued judicial order. * * *

III. Rule 16(b)

Absent any statutory prohibition against the production of nonfiling lists, the authority of the district court to order the production of such lists is governed by Federal Rule of Criminal Procedure 16(b) which provides that "the court may order the attorney for the government to permit the defendant to inspect and copy * * * documents * * * within the possession * * * of the government, upon a showing of materiality to the preparation of his defense and that the request is reasonable." The use of the permissive term "may" calls for an exercise of discretion and indicates the absence of a hard and fast rule when discovery should be ordered. *United States v. McCarthy,* 292 F.Supp. 937, 941–42 (S.D.N.Y.1968). Thus, a district court's ruling on a discovery motion will be disturbed only for an abuse of discretion.

The nonfiling lists undoubtedly are material to the preparation of Liebert's defense. A defendant in a criminal trial enjoys the sixth amendment right of being confronted with the witnesses testifying against him and of having compulsory process for obtaining witnesses to testify in his favor. * * *

* * *

Included within the constitutional right of confrontation is the ability through cross-examination to challenge the credibility and reliability of the witnesses testifying against a defendant. A major "witness" confronting Liebert will be computer printouts indicating that the IRS has no record of having received his returns. The introduction of a computer printout is admissible in a criminal trial provided that the party offering the computer information lays a foundation sufficient to warrant a finding that such information is trustworthy and the opposing party is given the same opportunity to inquire into the accuracy of the computer and its input procedures as he has to inquire into the accuracy of written business records. *United States v. De Georgia,* 420 F.2d 889 (9th Cir.1969).

A party seeking to impeach the reliability of computer evidence should have sufficient opportunity to ascertain by pretrial discovery whether both the machine and those who supply it with data input and information have performed their tasks accurately. The nonfiling lists plainly are outputs of the computer system identifying individuals not filing returns. If an individual who in fact has filed is listed as a nonfiler due to computer error, such error casts doubt on the accuracy and reliability of the records identifying Liebert as a nonfiler. The lists, therefore, may be useful to Liebert in his efforts to impeach the reliability of the computer procedures indicating that he has not filed his returns.

Rule 16(b), however, does not allow discovery merely upon a showing that the requested documents are material to the defendant's preparation for trial; the reasonableness of the discovery request must also be demonstrated. The determination by the district court of the reasonableness of a request requires balancing the interest favoring and opposing discovery. Whether the scales are tipped for or against discovery depends upon where lies the most compelling need.

The interest favoring the discovery request in the instant case is, as just discussed, the usefulness of the nonfiling lists to the preparation of Liebert's defense. Opposing the request are weighty interests—the right of privacy of the individuals named on the lists, and the need to avoid the problems in managing the presentation of evidence developed from the lists.

As aptly described by Mr. Justice Brandeis almost a half century ago, and equally true today, "the right to be let alone [is] the most comprehensive of rights and the right most valued by civilized men." *Olmstead v. United States,* 277 U.S. 438, 478, 48 S.Ct. 564, 572, 72 L.Ed. 944 (1928) (Brandeis, J., dissenting). The district court characterized this right as "elusive," primarily because it believed the information in the lists could be obtained under section 6103(f) by addressing to the IRS numerous inquiries as to whether particular individuals had filed their returns. 383 F.Supp. at 1064. This characterization, however, disregards the existence of three different facets of individual privacy which may be violated by production of the nonfiling lists, only one of which is infringed to the same degree by subsection (f).

First, the failure of an individual to file a return is revealed by production of the lists. Although an individual may desire to keep such information confidential, the fact of nonfiling is public information under subsection (f).

Second, the production of such lists necessarily would lead to communications from Liebert. His specific purpose in seeking the list is to communicate with individuals named in the lists in a zealous effort to find inaccuracies. This he proposes to do in the face of "[t]he ancient concept that 'a man's home is his castle' into which 'not even the king may enter' has lost none of its vitality * * *." *Rowan v. United States Post Office Dep't,* 397 U.S. 728, 737, 90 S.Ct. 1484, 1490, 25 L.Ed.2d 736 (1970). While courts in some instances have ordered production of lists which might lead to contacts between the parties obtaining, and those named, in the lists, such production has been limited to instances where it advanced an important public interest and where the person contacted probably would not be offended. Where the contact is likely to prove offensive, the courts vigilantly have safeguarded the privacy of the individual.

An intrusive communication by a stranger about a failure to file a tax return well may prove disturbing to an individual. Moreover, such contact could prove disturbing apart from tax considerations by reviving dormant unpleasant memories.

Of course, inquiries may be made of individuals about their nonfiling as a result of subsection (f), but the probability of such inquiry is significantly less than through the production of the nonfiling lists. Only 450,000 of the estimated 6,000,000 probable nonfilers are contained in the nonfiling lists, thereby increasing the exposure to contact of the individuals named by a factor of twelve. Moreover, as Liebert recognizes, the identification of all nonfilers under subsection (f) is impractical, requiring culling of names from a phone book or street directory, transmitting the list to the appropriate internal revenue office, and tabulating the answers. As contrasted with this impractical procedure, the easy availability of the names in the nonfiling lists increases the likelihood of contact with such persons.

Third, and most important, the individuals on the nonfiling lists are not just individuals who the IRS believes have not filed, but are individuals who the IRS believes have not filed in violation of their legal obligation. Nothing in subsection (f) authorizes the release of information indicating that the IRS preliminarily suspects an individual of being in violation of the law. Although the great majority of persons on the lists in fact have filed a return or have legitimate reasons for not doing so, being a suspect under investigation by a government agency is a circumstance which every person except the bizarre would prefer to hold in confidence. The courts have respected this preference.

The other interest opposing discovery is the difficulty in managing at trial the information developed from the lists. Liebert hopes to be able to find persons listed as nonfilers but who in fact have filed, and introduce such evidence to the jury either by calling such persons as witnesses or by cross-examination of the IRS computer experts. The Government then may assume the burden of rebutting the accuracy of such evidence by attempting to prove that the persons cited by Liebert did not in fact file their returns or were listed as nonfilers for reasons other than computer error. The trial thus is likely to deteriorate into a series of minitrials centered upon the reasons individuals, not defendants in the case, were listed as nonfilers. The chief issue, Liebert's alleged willful failure to file his returns, may be obscured.

Balancing the need for disclosing all relevant information in a criminal proceeding against the need for protecting the privacy of individuals having no connection with it, and the further need for avoiding the potential misuse of such information is a difficult and delicate task. It may well be, as Liebert contends, that absent alternative sources of information and difficulty in managing such information at trial, "[t]he generalized assertion of privilege [based on confidentiality] must yield to the demonstrated, specific need for evidence in a pending criminal trial." *United States v. Nixon,* 418 U.S. 683, 713, 94 S.Ct. 3090, 3110, 41 L.Ed.2d 1039 (1974). We note that the foregoing cases required disclosure from witnesses, not extrinsic evidence from unrelated parties. Moreover, such cases do not control here because they involve discovery from the only available source of information. Further the information sought was either admissible in the case in chief or in a form manageable during cross-examination.

Even when the evidence sought in pretrial discovery is material for the defense of a criminal prosecution, we believe the mantle of the privacy of a person having no connection with the case should not be lifted, at least in the present context, if there are reasonable alternative means of securing the information. The principle has particular application when the intrusion on privacy runs a risk of being extraordinarily burdensome to the parties and also may tend to obscure the real issue in the case.

The Government, both voluntarily and as a result of the district court's order directing that Liebert's experts have access to the Mid–Atlantic Service Center for the purpose of testing and analyzing the computer facilities, represented to the district court that it would make available to Liebert: (a) all the relevant IRS handbooks documenting the procedures, machine operations, and other relevant information pertaining to its electronic data processing system; (b) statistical analyses relating to the Service's ability to discover and report accurately failures to file returns; (c) an expert familiar with all aspects of the nonfiling lists; (d) an expert familiar with all aspects of the processing of work through the Mid–Atlantic Service Center; and (e) an expert who has made studies on the reliability of the Service's data processing systems.[19] The experts may be deposed by Liebert on any subject not concerning confidential data obtained from tax returns filed by taxpayers. Moreover, the Government has offered to allow Liebert's computer experts to run any test on its computer system not unreasonably interrupting the Service Center operations. Finally, the Government has offered to conduct tests demonstrating the retrieval of a number of actual tax returns of taxpayers whose authorizations are obtained.

19. We assume that the information supplied by the Government will include the number of persons listed as nonfilers due to computer error in 1970 and 1971.

Such alternatives should provide Liebert with the information necessary to cross-examine the computer testimony confronting him by analyzing the reliability of the computer system in theory and checking the accuracy of the system in fact. Moreover, the alternatives should provide information focusing directly on the credibility of the computer testimony and more likely should develop the facts than the digression sought by Liebert. They should provide evidence adducible at trial in a more manageable manner without the risk of invading the privacy of, or inconveniencing, taxpayers wholly unconnected with the case. The order of the district court directing the production of the nonfiling lists was unreasonable in light of the alternatives offered by the Government.

The judgment of the district court will be vacated and the case remanded with directions to reinstate the information. Upon proper motion by the defendant, the district court should order the Government to produce the materials and experts indicated in this opinion. Each party will bear its own costs.

Notes and Questions

1. Could Liebert have obtained the IRS non-filers list through a FOIA request to the IRS?

2. Since the non-filers list is part of the IRS ongoing enforcement action against those who have not filed returns, the real reason the IRS refused to disclose the non-filers list may have been its sensitive nature.

NATIONAL UNION ELECTRIC CORPORATION v. MATSUSHITA ELECTRIC INDUSTRIAL CO., LTD. In re JAPANESE ELECTRONIC PRODUCTS ANTITRUST LITIGATION

United States District Court, Eastern District of Pennsylvania, 1980.
494 F.Supp. 1257.

EDWARD R. BECKER, DISTRICT JUDGE.

This Memorandum Opinion addresses a motion styled "Request of Certain Defendants for the Production by National Union Electric Corporation (NUE) of Certain Computer Materials." [1] More specifically, defendants request NUE to cause its computer experts to perform the work necessary to create a computer readable tape containing certain data previously supplied by NUE to defendants in printed form in answers to interrogatories.

The relevant interrogatories requested:

— NUE's annual and monthly sales, in dollars and units, for monochrome and color television receivers, by model (Interrogatories 1 and 2)

1. The motion arises in the course of a massive antitrust case in which NUE is one of the plaintiffs. The anatomy of the litigation is detailed elsewhere, and need not be repeated here. *See* Opinion 494 F.Supp. 1190 at 1193–1194 (April 14, 1980). Both motion and response (which comes in the form of NUE's motion for a protective order) are supported by affidavits and memoranda. We have held two hearings on the matter.

— NUE's annual and monthly production, in dollars and units, for monochrome and color television receivers, by model (Interrogatories 3 and 4)

— Model numbers for television receivers produced or sold by NUE, including various characteristics of the sets (e.g. the number of square inches on the viewing screen of the picture tube) (Interrogatory No. 5).

In answer to the interrogatories, NUE furnished certain TV sales and production data, and certain model by model price data in the form of a computer generated paper printout. The printout can, of course, be read by defense counsel. However, it cannot be read by defense counsel's computer. Because defense counsel contend that they cannot effectively analyze the data until the data can be read by their computer, they have brought the present motion.[2]

Defendants' counsel concede that they could themselves replicate what they seek from NUE if they were to undertake the expensive and time consuming process of having clerical personnel manually create a data base identical to NUE's by reading each piece of data in NUE's computer paper printout and key-punching it into a computer readable device.[3] They estimate that this process would take two months and cost many thousands of dollars. On the other hand, defendants submit that it would be a comparatively simple matter for NUE's computer people to rerun the program which caused the computer to assemble and to print this data in paper reports, substituting a new instruction to extract and print the same data onto a computer-readable form like magnetic tape. Defendants are willing to pay the cost of this operation.[4]

2. If the tape is provided, the exact data which defendants now have on paper would be provided on tape. Once the data is in defendants' computer, they propose to analyze the data according to computer programs which their experts will write to accomplish the types of analysis requested by defense counsel. Their proposal is congruent with the Manual for Complex Litigation which, in recommending that courts encourage cooperation between parties in discovering computer information, adds:

"The court, in its discretion, may prescribe that discovery take place in any one of a number of other ways. For example, it may be that the information has not been recorded in the computer in a form in which it will be of maximum utility to the examining party. Accordingly, it may be appropriate for the court to facilitate, or even encourage, the examining party to develop his own programs for the analysis or reorganization of the machine-readable data so as to convert the information into a form that is more germane to the examiner's defense or prosecution of the action." Manual for Complex Litigation § 2.715.

3. Defendants describe this process as involving the manual typing of over 1,000 pages of data containing literally hundreds of thousands of numbers (e.g., number of models sold for each month for each year for each screen size, etc.) followed by the manual verification that each number was typed correctly.

4. In connection with this procedure, defendants also request "record format information." The term "record format information" refers to the arrangement of the data in the computer-readable form provided. Without knowledge of the format and record length of the data contained on the tape, the defendants' computer system cannot be instructed to read the information because it does not know where to start or stop. The computer has no way to distinguish one record from another without being given record format instructions.

There is a subtle play on words involved in this motion. Lawyers and judges often talk of "production" in terms of Rule 34 of the Federal Rules of Civil Procedure as involving the delivery to the opposing party of some existing document or tangible object. In connection with the present motion, however, the word "produce" is used in the sense of "manufacture"; i.e. NUE is being asked to manufacture or produce something which did not exist theretofore. NUE maintains that the discovery rules do not cognize such a request and that, in any event, what defendants request is protected by the work product privilege, F.R.Civ.P. 26(b)(3), because it reflects mental impressions, analysis, conclusions or thoughts of NUE's counsel or their representatives. NUE thus resists the motion.[6]

NUE's work product objection stems ultimately from the fact that the data at issue was compiled under counsel's direction from raw data which has been available for defendants' inspection and copying in this litigation. NUE asserts that the process for establishing the computer base for the data at issue involved detailed "decision analysis", i.e. the sentient selection by counsel from voluminous raw material of a limited amount of data for inclusion in that base, and that the fruits of that process are therefore protected under the work product rubric. Acknowledging that the work product privilege is but a qualified evidentiary privilege, *see United States v. Nobles,* 422 U.S. 225, 95 S.Ct. 2160, 45 L.Ed.2d 141 (1975), NUE adds that the defendants do not have substantial need for the computer tape, within the meaning of F.R.Civ.P. 26(b)(3), because they could create the tape themselves by the method described above. Given the colossal cost of this litigation, NUE suggests that the time and cost necessary to produce the tape is modest and that it does not constitute undue hardship within the meaning of the rule.

When this matter first came on for hearing, we denied the motion for discovery, in part because we misunderstood it, and in part because it was couched in different form than it now is. We were under the impression at that time that the defendants were seeking data stored by the plaintiffs somewhere within their computer software, which differed from the material on the paper printout, and further that the data was arrayed in a particular way so that disclosure might have revealed something about NUE's trial strategy. So viewed, the information sought would have been similar to plaintiff's trial support system which was protected from discovery under the work product notion in *In re: IBM Peripherals EDP Devices Antitrust Litigation,* 5 Computer Law Service Rep. 878 (N.D.Cal.1975). *See also Montrose Chemical Corp. of California v. Train,* 491 F.2d 63 (D.C.Cir.1974). An affidavit filed by NUE's computer expert explains that NUE, through its counsel, did in fact create a litigation support system on the basis of selection by counsel of a number of documents out of many for inclu-

6. There is no dispute that the data sought is properly discoverable. Indeed, we ordered the plaintiffs to produce the information in Answers to Interrogatories, pursuant to a Rule 37 Motion.

sion in a computer data base. However, the defendants do not in fact seek a computer disc, or a computer tape extracted from that disc, which contains information selected for use in such a litigation support system. Rather, defendants' request is limited to exactly the same data (in the same arrangement) which NUE furnished defendants in paper computer printout reports. We are thus faced with a different question from that which we originally perceived.

It is true, as NUE complains, that no computer tape in the form requested by the defendants exists, and that the relief requested by defendants would require "the creation (e.g. manufacture) of a physical object not now in existence". The principal question before us, however, is whether that which defendants seek production (or manufacture) of is work product within the meaning of the Federal Rules. We conclude that it is not.

Ordinarily, in addressing the question whether given material is work product, we would turn to precedent, including the seminal case of *Hickman v. Taylor,* 329 U.S. 495, 67 S.Ct. 385, 91 L.Ed. 451 (1947). We have canvassed the cases, but find nothing helpful. We are, therefore, constrained to analyze the facts before us in terms of the language of Rule 26. We have done so, but have failed to discover any "mental impressions, conclusions, opinions, or legal theories" therein. Neither do we find any "trial strategy". Rather, we find that all the defendants seek is precisely the same data as is contained in the computer printouts which were furnished in discovery. To the extent that an issue exists as to selection and arrangement of that data, it appears that it is the defendants who decided what data NUE was to gather and how it should be arranged by virtue of the framing of their interrogatories. Moreover, to the extent that any "decision analysis" by NUE was involved, the paper computer printout has already revealed whatever data, activity, or other "decisional analysis" considerations were present.

As defendants note, the only difference between what defendants already have and what they request is that a computer cannot read what NUE has previously produced. That is a mechanical, not a qualitative, difference. It must be remembered that the actual data being sought is model-by-model production, sales, and price data, which is *not* claimed to have been the product of any attorney input. And, finally, it must be noted that it is clear from the affidavits which have been filed that NUE does not have to produce its entire data base or computerized trial support system in order to adequately respond to defendants' request.[8] Rather, as defendants' affidavits demonstrate, in order to produce the computer-printed information in a tape form, all that is necessary is for NUE's computer specialist to re-run the instructions used to extract and print the computer reports on paper with a new instruction to print the results on computer-readable form like

8. Thus, there is no concern that defendants will have access to proprietary information that might be on NUE's disc which stores the accumulated data.

magnetic tape rather than in paper copy form. To repeat, what is sought is not work product within the meaning of Rule 26.

In view of the foregoing analysis we must confront the only remaining question, i.e. whether there is anything in the federal discovery rules which relieves NUE from the obligation to perform the labor necessary to produce the requested tape. Notwithstanding NUE's protestations, both common sense and a growing body of precedent support defendants' request. While we can find no case in which the court has ordered the programming of a computer to manufacture a computer tape not theretofore in physical existence, a number of cases have ordered the production, in the Rule 34 sense, of computer materials.

In *Quadrini v. Sikorsky Aircraft Division, United Aircraft Corporation,* 74 F.R.D. 594 (D.Conn.1977) Judge Newman granted defendant's motion to compel plaintiff to produce, *inter alia,* data processing cards, which are a type of computer-readable materials. In *Pearl Brewing Co. v. Jos. Schlitz Brewing Co.,* 415 F.Supp. 1122, 1134–41 (S.D.Tex.1976), Judge Bue allowed defendants under Rule 26(b)(4)(B) to inspect and copy "the entire system documentation"—i.e., the underlying computer program which performed certain analysis—prepared by certain experts for plaintiff's computer-generated model. In *Adams v. Dan River Mills, Inc.,* 54 F.R.D. 220, 222 (W.D.Va.1972), the court ordered production of computer-readable data material, saying:

> "Because of the accuracy and inexpensiveness of producing the requested documents in the case at bar, this court sees no reason why the defendant should not be required to produce the computer cards or tapes * * * to the plaintiff."

And, in *United States v. Davey,* 543 F.2d 996 (2d Cir.1976), an Internal Revenue summons proceeding, the Court of Appeals ordered the respondent to produce magnetic tapes in its possession, which contained financial data, even though the same information had already been proffered to the Internal Revenue Service in printout form. The district court in *Davey* had ordered production of the computer tapes, commenting that their production would make unnecessary "a great deal of manual examination of many thousands of printout pages." 404 F.Supp. 1283, 1284 (S.D.N.Y.1975), *rev'd on other grounds, Davey, supra.* The Second Circuit affirmed on this point. It noted that "inspection of the requested tapes * * * would * * * insure greater accuracy and a substantial saving in auditing time," and held that the taxpayer could not "give the IRS requested information in an inconvenient form with a view to immunizing itself from demands for other records containing the same relevant information in a more convenient form." 543 F.2d at 1000.

As some of the decisions have observed, the 1970 amendments to Rule 34 of the Federal Rules of Civil Procedure made it clear that computerized records are subject to requests for production. Those amendments added to the list in Rule 34(a)(1) of matters subject to production the language "and other data compilations from which information can be obtained, translated, if necessary, by the respondent through detection devices into reasonably usable form." The 1970 Advisory Committee Notes explained:

> The inclusive description of "documents" is revised to accord with changing technology. It makes clear that Rule 34 applies to electronic data compilations from which information can be obtained only with the use of detection devices, and that when the data can as a practical matter be made usable by the discovering party only through respondent's devices, respondent may be required to use his devices to translate the data into usable form. In many instances, this means that respondent will have to supply a print-out of computer data.

48 F.R.D. 487, 527 (1970). The Rule thus provides that data be produced in a "reasonably usable form." The Advisory Committee contemplated that this usable form would often consist of a printout of the data stored electronically, but did not preclude production of the information in an electronic medium. *See* 8 C. Wright & A. Miller, Federal Practice and Procedure § 2218 (1970). The Manual for Complex Litigation, on the other hand, views the production of computer data records in machine-readable form as primary in complex cases, with the production of printouts as a secondary alternative:

> In the computer context, the basic types of machine records commonly utilized include: (1) punched cards; (2) paper and magnetic tapes; and (3) a variety of other machine oriented components which record and store data. In the absence of special considerations such as privilege, work product immunity, or the presence of industrial or trade secrets in the machine, readable computerized data (including computerized analyses) in any of the above-mentioned forms should be freely discoverable. If the discovering party has data processing equipment that is compatible with that of the owners of the computer records, *delivery of the machine-readable version of the information, or a copy thereof,* will often be sufficient. When the discovering party's equipment is not compatible, or he has no computer equipment, delivery of a print-out of the machine-readable records may provide a reasonable alternative mode of discovery.

Manual for Complex Litigation § 2.715 (emphasis added). While a printout might be "reasonably usable" within the meaning of Rule 34, the production of a party's data in a form which is directly readable by the adverse party's computers is the preferred alternative, according to the editors of the Manual for Complex Litigation.

Although there may be some difference between requiring the production of existing tapes and requiring a party to so program the computer as to produce data in computer-readable as opposed to printout form, we find it to be a distinction without a difference, at least in the circumstances of this case. As we have noted, the defendants have expressed their willingness to pay the costs of whatever operations are necessary to manufacture a computer-readable tape. As a result, the problem of allocating the burden of discovery expense, which might be significant in otherwise similar situations, *see* Horning, *supra,* at 675–87, is nonexistent here. Apart from the possible expense, the manufacture of a machine-readable copy of a computer disc is in principle no different from the manufacture of a photocopy of a written document, a common enough method of responding to a request for document production.

It may well be that Judge Charles E. Clark and the framers of the Federal Rules of Civil Procedure could not foresee the computer age. However, we know we now live in an era when much of the data which our society desires to retain is stored in computer discs. This process will escalate in years to come; we suspect that by the year 2000 virtually all data will be stored in some form of computer memory. To interpret the Federal Rules which, after all, are to be construed to "secure the just, speedy, and *inexpensive* determination of every action," F.R.Civ.P. 1, (emphasis added), in a manner which would preclude the production of material such as is requested here, would eventually defeat their purpose.

Defendants' request will be granted.

An appropriate order follows.

Notes

1. Different agencies may have specific filing requirements for requests. Information concerning the requirements can be found in the Code of Federal Regulations.

2. A FOIA request that has been denied may be appealed within the agency. If the appeal is administratively denied, judicial appeal of the FOIA request may be pursued.

ADAMS v. DAN RIVER MILLS, INC.

United States District Court, Western District of Virginia, 1972.
54 F.R.D. 220.

DALTON, DISTRICT JUDGE.

On August 30, 1971, the plaintiffs, by counsel, filed a request for the production of documents pursuant to Rule 34 of the Federal Rules of Civil Procedure, 28 U.S.C.A., asking the defendant, Dan River Mills, Inc., to allow inspection and copying of certain documents. Specifically, the plaintiffs sought the defendant's current computerized master payroll file and all computer print-outs for W–2 forms of the defendant's employees as far back as they were retained. The defendant did not comply with the request and on November 29, 1971, the plaintiffs filed a motion asking this court to enter an order pursuant to Rule 37 of the Federal Rules of Civil Procedure, 28 U.S.C.A., compelling the production of these documents. Counsel for both parties have filed memoranda in support of their respective positions on this issue.

The plaintiffs take the position that the information sought is vital and relevant to their case which involves alleged racially discriminatory employment practices by the defendant. The defendant in contesting the plaintiffs' motion contends that the request is beyond the scope of allowable discovery because it is too broad, that much of the information sought is repetitive and irrelevant, and that the information is privileged since it involves labor costs which the defendant contends are trade secrets.

The plaintiffs state [that] they need the current computer cards or tapes and the W–2 print-outs in order to prepare accurate, up-to-date statistics which will be relevant in determining whether or not discriminatory practices have occurred. Furthermore, the plaintiffs contend that the use of this computerized data is the most inexpensive and reliable method which can be used since making the necessary studies with human labor is not only extremely time-consuming and expensive, but also is more susceptible to error. On the other hand, the defendant states that the plaintiffs have computer print-outs on which this information appears and therefore the production of these documents would be repetitive. The defendant further contends that under the rules of discovery documents do not have to be produced in any specific form.

Examination of the notes of the Advisory Committee on Rules pertaining to Rule 34 of the Federal Rules of Civil Procedure reveals that the Committee was aware of the effect which technology in the field of electronic data processing might have in discovery. The notes of the Committee state in part:

> The inclusive description of "documents" is revised to accord with changing technology. It makes clear that Rule 34 applies to electronic data compilations from which information can be obtained only with the use of detection devices, and that when the data can as a practical matter be made usable by the discovering party only through respondent's devices, respondent may be required to use his devices to translate the data to usable form. In many instances, this means that respondent will have to supply a print-out of computer data. The burden thus placed on respondent will vary from case to case, and the courts have ample power under Rule 26(c) to protect respondent against undue burden or expense, either by restricting discovery or requiring that the discovering party pay costs.
>
> Fed.Rules Civ.Proc. Rule 34, 28 U.S.C.A.

While it appears to this court that the above language only directly covers the situation where the respondent can be required to prepare the information in a usable form, such as a print-out, it does not appear to preclude the production of computer in-put information such as computer cards or tapes. Likewise, this court is aware of no reason why documents of this nature should not be subject to discovery.

Because of the accuracy and inexpensiveness of producing the requested documents in the case at bar, this court sees no reason why the defendant should not be required to produce the computer cards or tapes and the W–2 print-outs to the plaintiffs.

After due consideration of the memoranda presented by both parties, this court feels that the information sought should not be denied on the ground that it constitutes a privileged trade secret. While labor costs may well be "secret" information in the competitive textile industry, this court fails to see how the defendant can be damaged by requiring production of the documents sought. However, if the defendant desires, this court will entertain its motion to put the documents under a protective order pursuant to the provisions of Rule 26(c) of the Federal Rules of Civil Procedure.

For the reasons herein given, it is hereby ordered and adjudged that the defendant produce the current master payroll file and the requested W–2 print-outs in the appropriate computerized form.

It is further ordered and adjudged that the plaintiffs shall pay the cost of preparing these documents and that all other costs related to this motion shall be borne by the respective parties.

Questions

Would plaintiff have been wiser to have requested and offered to pay the appropriate costs to the defendant to sort the payroll data into specified categories before producing the payroll file to the plaintiff?

MANUAL FOR COMPLEX LITIGATION SECOND, ¶ 21.446

21.446 Discovery of Computerized Data

The potential benefits that may be derived from computerized data—as well as the problems such data may create—are substantial both in the discovery process and at the trial. At the outset of the litigation the court should inquire into the existence of computerized data and processes for its retrieval. Under Fed.R.Civ.P. 34 discovery may be obtained of "data compilations from which information can be obtained, translated, if necessary, by the respondent through detection devices into reasonably usable form." Accordingly, a party may be required not only to furnish pre-existing hard copies of computerized data but also to provide new print-outs of pertinent items or of data bases. Sometimes a party should be required to provide this information in machine-readable form, so that the data may be stored by the discovering parties for later analysis on their own computers without the time, expense, and potential for errors that would result if data from a print-out were re-entered manually.

Parties sometimes request production in a form that can be created only at substantial expense for additional programming; if so, payment of such costs by the requesting party should be made a condition to production. Although trade secrets, privileged information, and trial preparation materials may require protection, and indeed the methodology of a company's computer system may itself be a valuable asset that should not be handed over to others without good reason, protective orders under Rule 26(c) may be entered by the court to prevent abuse or misuse.

Materials not previously computerized are often encoded by counsel in anticipation of or during complex litigation. Frequently the objective will be to produce studies and tabulations for introduction in evidence or for use by experts. In such situations, discovery should usually be allowed in essentially the same manner as for pre-existing computerized materials, subject, however, to appropriate protection of "work product" materials. If production is required, provision ordinarily should be made for those who benefit from the computerization process to share the expense. As discussed in § 21.444, in appropriate cases counsel may be able to agree upon a system for establishing a common computerized depository.

The discovery program should also include inquiry into those facts that will affect the use of computerized data at trial either as direct evidence or as information relied upon by experts. In part, the same kinds of questions must be considered as with non-computerized records because the Federal Rules of Evidence have been written to accommodate both types of evidence. However, special inquiry must also usually be made into matters affecting the accuracy of the data output. Notwithstanding the capacity of computers to make tabulations and calculations involving enormous quantities of information—and to do so more quickly and reliably than if done manually—several sources of potential errors of great magnitude exist. The more common include incorrect or incomplete entry of data, mistakes in output instructions, programming errors, damage and contamination of storage media, power outages, and equipment malfunction.

The proponent of computerized evidence has the burden of laying a proper foundation by establishing its accuracy. Exploring matters relating to the reliability of such data for the first time at trial, however, may waste time and either be unfair to the parties against whom they are offered or result in elimination of evidence that (had problems been identified and corrected earlier) would have been beneficial in expediting trial and understanding the issues. Therefore, well in advance of trial, appropriate discovery should be undertaken concerning the reliability of computerized evidence that may be used later. This will usually include inquiry into the accuracy of the underlying source materials, the procedures for storage and processing, and some testing of the reliability of the results obtained. If it is impracticable to identify and correct all errors, counsel should nevertheless attempt to ascertain and stipulate the statistical probability of the range of error.

Notes and Questions

Would a computerized litigation system developed by one party in a complex litigation, be discoverable by the other party? See *In re IBM Peripheral EDP Devices Antitrust Litigation,* 5 *Computer L.Serv.* 878 (N.D.Calif.1975).

C. DUTY TO USE DATA BANKS

Suppose a business or government agency fails to use available computer technology to locate critical information. If avoidable harm occurs, should there be liability?

HERMES v. PFIZER, INC.

United States Court of Appeals, Fifth Circuit, 1988.
848 F.2d 66.

Before BROWN, KING, and HIGGINBOTHAM, CIRCUIT JUDGES.

PER CURIAM:

In this Mississippi diversity suit a jury returned a verdict of $800,000 against defendant Pfizer, Inc. as compensation for plaintiff Laura Hermes' personal injury resulting from the use of the prescription drug Sinequan, a Pfizer product. We reject Pfizer's arguments that the evidence of the drug's potential side effect was insufficient to trigger a duty to warn and that there was insufficient evidence that the drug was a cause of injury, and we affirm.

I

A gynecologist prescribed Sinequan, a tricyclic antidepressant, for Laura Hermes, a 50–year old post-hysterectomy patient. Several days after taking the medication, Hermes developed "extrapyramidal" symptoms or a "hunting jaw."[2] Hermes sought treatment by an oral surgeon who referred her to a neurologist. The condition appears to be permanent.

Hermes filed this suit against Pfizer alleging strict liability and negligence. Hermes offered the testimony of Dr. Dewey Metts, the oral surgeon, Dr. Joe Jackson, the treating neurologist, Dr. Michael Bourgeois, the prescribing gynecologist, Dr. James O'Donnell, an expert in adverse drug reactions and licensed pharmacist, and, as an adverse witness, Salvatore Giorgiani a Pfizer employee responsible for maintaining adverse drug reactions reports. Pfizer presented the testimony of Dr. James Matheny, an expert in pharmacology. Dr. Armin Haerer, a neurologist who examined Hermes under court order, also testified at trial.

II

Pfizer argues that the court erred in denying its motions for directed verdict, judgment n.o.v., and new trial because the evidence on the issues of duty to warn and causation was insufficient to support a jury verdict. On review of a motion for directed verdict or judgment n.o.v., we apply the test announced in *Boeing Co. v. Shipman,* whether,

2. "Hunting jaw" is characterized by joint pain, lack of control of the jaw and tongue muscles, slurred speech, drooling, and difficulty chewing.

in a light most favorable to the party opposing the motion, reasonable people could not arrive at a contrary verdict. In reviewing a motion for new trial, we ask whether the verdict is against the great weight of the evidence.

A

A key issue in this appeal is whether Pfizer had a duty to warn Hermes of the possible side effect she experienced, whether it knew or should have known that the taking of Sinequan could cause permanent hunting jaw. Whether there is a duty to warn turns on the manufacturer's actual knowledge and its "constructive knowledge as measured by scientific literature and other available means of communication." A manufacturer has a duty to keep abreast of research, adverse reaction reports, and other scientific literature pertaining to its product.

Pfizer argues that there was insufficient evidence of any knowledge of the possible side effect. It argues that not one expert testified that there had been any report of symptoms such as those experienced by Hermes. It cites to *Johnston v. Upjohn Co.*, in which the court held that "if such a reaction had never occurred before, defendant could not know about it or in the exercise of the required degree of care could not have found out about it, and absent knowledge of such reaction, there could be no duty to warn."

Pfizer argues that in any event there is no evidence that it breached any duty to warn, pointing to its instructions insert and reference in *Physician's Desk Reference,* which noted the possibility of *temporary* extrapyramidal symptoms. Pfizer contends that it had no duty to warn of *permanent* symptoms because it "knew" of none.

Hermes argues, on the other hand, that Pfizer knew or should have known of the side effect. Her expert, O'Donnell, unequivocally stated that Sinequan could cause temporary and permanent hunting jaw. The jury also had before it an FDA computer printout of adverse drug reaction reports concerning Sinequan, evidence that reports of extrapyramidal symptoms were recorded as early as 1970.

We are persuaded that this evidence was enough for the jury to have concluded that Pfizer had sufficient knowledge to trigger a duty to warn. The court did not err in denying Pfizer's motion on this ground.

* * *

Questions

1. Assume that a hospital is contemplating acquiring a sophisticated computer system to assist in detection of illness. What factors, as an attorney, would you consider in the formulation of your advice to your client, the hospital, about whether or not to acquire the system?

2. Should a computer company which provides a service be required to do so in such a way as to maximize (or nearly maximize) the benefits of the system? Should it matter if health and/or safety are involved?

For example, should a computer company which provides computerized analysis of blood be required to:

a. keep its programs current with the latest blood tests?

b. develop sophisticated blood tests on its own in order to provide maximum service?

AKINS v. DISTRICT OF COLUMBIA

Court of Appeals, District of Columbia, 1987.
526 A.2d 933.

STEADMAN, ASSOCIATE JUDGE:

Appellant contests dismissal of his suit pursuant to Super.Ct.Civ.R. 12(b)(6), for failure to state a claim under which relief can be granted. Upon review of the pleadings and the relevant case law, we affirm.

I

Appellant initiated this lawsuit after having been gravely wounded during an armed robbery on May 11, 1982. The perpetrator, Clifford Henry Williams, was out on $3000 bond for two previous armed robberies at the time. The arraignment judges who had twice released Williams in the preceding three-month period had done so on the basis of information which failed to include the record of the disposition of Williams' prior juvenile offenses. The Pretrial Services Agency (PSA) report did note, however, that Williams had a number of prior juvenile arrests. The disposition information was not included in the PSA report because the computer, installed and maintained by defendant IBM, failed to operate and the defendant PSA employees failed to manually retrieve the information. Nonetheless, the PSA report recommended that a hearing be conducted pursuant to D.C.Code § 23–1322(a) (1981) to determine whether Williams would pose a threat to community safety.

II

Appellant alleges the following facts to demonstrate appellees' liability for negligence: (1) The PSA computer, installed and maintained by IBM, failed to operate on two important occasions; (2) each time, the PSA discovered that their computer was not working, and they could not obtain a full record of Williams' arrest and conviction record; (3) rather than searching for the information by hand, both times the PSA informed the arraignment court that the computer did not work and they could not provide all of the requested information; therefore; (4) the arraignment judge released Williams, once on his own recognizance and then on a $3000 bond, because he was unaware of the full scope of Williams' previous record. After a hearing, the motions court granted all defendants' motions to dismiss under Rule 12(b)(6). The court based its decision on a number of grounds. We will address only those necessary to resolve this litigation, construing the complaint in the light most favorable to plaintiff, taking his allegations as true. *McBryde v. Amoco Oil Co.*, 404 A.2d 200, 202 (D.C.1979).

A.

Appellees District of Columbia, PSA, and PSA employees. This court has recognized that the District of Columbia and its law enforcement officials "generally may not be held liable for failure to protect individuals from harm caused by criminal conduct." *Morgan v. District of Columbia,* 468 A.2d 1306, 1310 (D.C.1983) (en banc). *Morgan,* like most cases on this subject, deals with a situation where the police have failed to protect an individual from a specific criminal threat. *Id.,* and cases cited therein. We have employed this doctrine, however, to suits which allege negligence by building inspectors in inspection and enforcement of fire safety standards, *Platt v. District of Columbia,* 467 A.2d 149 (D.C.1983); and to suits involving the fire department's alleged breach of duty of care in its ability to respond to a fire, *Chandler v. District of Columbia,* 404 A.2d 964 (D.C.1979). In short, our case law has prohibited suits against the District of Columbia and its employees in situations where the alleged breach of duty involves a duty to the general public to ensure its safety.

The PSA is an agency charged with providing to the courts information regarding prior criminal records. They do so in order to assist the judiciary in determining how to balance public safety concerns against an accused's right to liberty. This duty, like the duty of a building inspector, a firefighter or a police officer, "is a public duty, for neglect of which the officer is amenable to the public, and punishable by indictment only." *South v. Maryland,* 59 U.S. (18 How.) 396, 403, 15 L.Ed. 433 (1855).

We have allowed an exception to this rule only where a specific undertaking to protect a particular individual has occurred, and that individual has justifiably relied upon such an undertaking. *Morgan, supra,* 468 A.2d at 1314–15. Nowhere in the record has appellant alleged any specific undertaking toward appellant by PSA, much less a justifiable reliance thereon. We conclude, then, that appellant's suit against the District and the PSA employees is barred by this "public duty doctrine".

B.

Appellee IBM. For this court to conclude that IBM might be held liable to appellant for its assumptively negligent maintenance of the PSA computers, we would have to conclude that IBM's negligence could be characterized as a legal proximate cause of the injury to appellant. When a criminal act intervenes between a defendant's negligence and the injury to the plaintiff, we have required that the injury be highly foreseeable before finding the negligent party liable, due to the "extraordinary nature of criminal conduct." *Lacy v. District of Columbia,* 424 A.2d 317, 322 (D.C.1980). In *Lacy* we approved an instruction which required that the defendants have "actual knowledge that the assaults on [appellant] would occur or [have] good reason to anticipate the assaults. * * * " *Id.* Standing alone, Williams' criminal assault of appellant might possibly be considered a remotely foreseeable result of computer failure at the PSA, but when combined with the intervening inaction of the PSA, and the discretionary decision of the arraignment judge, there is no way to interpret appellant's allegations as showing that appellee IBM had actual knowledge of, or good reason to anticipate, Williams' assault.

Affirmed.

Notes and Questions

Assume that the District of Columbia relied on PSA and IBM for properly functioning computer resources. In addition, assume that PSA knew that the computers were providing the District of Columbia with erroneous information due to internal computer malfunctions. Given these two assumptions, would Akins have prevailed against PSA? Suppose that PSA did not know, but should have known that erroneous information was being generated by the computer, then would Akins have prevailed against PSA?

Chapter XII

REGULATING THE TRANSFER OF INFORMATION

A. ELECTRONIC FUNDS TRANSFER

Electronic funds transfer is the generic term for a whole spectrum of transactions involving an exchange of value between financial institutions and among consumers by way of electronic impulses. These transactions include: cash withdrawals, deposits, credit card authorization, check verification, billing operations, point-of-sale payments, clearing house services, balance inquiries, shifting of funds from one account to another, direct payroll deposits, and preauthorized periodic payments. The simplest way to view electronics funds transfer is that electronic blips and bleeps are being substituted for paper in our current, paper-based, payments system.

The exchange of financial information by means other than paper is not really new. At the time of the passage of the Federal Reserve Act, the transfer of financial data was accomplished by telegraph, using a Morse code system. By the late 1930s, the Federal Reserve converted to teletype machines, and then, in the 1960s, computers were introduced into the Federal Reserve Communications System.

The types of electronics funds transfer services which are potentially available to both individual and business customers can be classified into two broad categories: (1) *information services* which involve the access to or transmission of data related to financial transactions and (2) *funds transfer* which involve the actual movement of funds in or out of a deposit account. Information services include credit authorization for credit card purchases, check verification (that permits a nondepository institution to verify the existence of funds), and check guarantee, whereby a consumer has a check payment guaranteed. Also included are "file look-up" functions which permit a consumer or financial institution to access account files for information. Funds transfer services are divided into four functions: deposit, debit, debit with overdraft privilege, and credit functions. Within the debit function, there are four subareas: (1) debit for cash withdrawal, (2) debit for bill or loan payment, (3) debit for purchase, and (4) debit for interaccount transfer. Credit functions are classified into the areas of credit purchase and cash advance against an existing line of credit.

While electronic funds transfer (EFT) systems promise to provide more convenience and service, many consumers are concerned with protective safeguards. Because our present payments system is paper-based, the source of consumer rights for paper payments is the Uniform Commercial Code (UCC). Consumer protection in the computer world came into existence as one of the titles of the Consumer Credit Protection Act of the Financial Institutions Regulatory and Interest Rate Control Act of 1978, known as the Electronic Funds Transfer Act (15 U.S.C.A. §§ 1693–1963). Regulation E (12 CFR § 205.s) is the rule implementing the Act.

Value exchanges are governed by a combination of Federal and state law. The Expedited Funds Availability Act of 1987 authorized the Board of Governors of the Federal Reserve System to regulate the check collection process. Regulations issued and planned by the Federal Reserve System preempt state law on check collection. The main sources of state law governing non-cash value exchanges are Articles 3, 4, and 4A of the Uniform Commercial Code. The Commissioners on Uniform State Laws and the American Law Institute have proposed revised versions of these Articles that would accommodate electronic funds transfer and Federal preemption of check collection. Article 3 of the UCC is entitled "Negotiable Instruments" and deals with such instruments as checks, drafts, and promissory notes. Article 4 deals with the check collection process and is entitled "Bank Deposits and Collections." The new Article 4A, "Funds Transfers" deals in detail with problems of electronic funds transfers. Many of the details of electronics funds transfers are governed by contracts negotiated among banks.

ELECTRONIC FUNDS TRANSFER ACT
15 U.S.C. § 1693

§ 901. Short Title

This Act may be cited as the "Electronic Fund Transfer Act."

§ 902. Findings and Purpose [15 U.S.C. § 1693]

(a) The Congress finds that the use of electronic systems to transfer funds provides the potential for substantial benefits to consumers. However, due to the unique characteristics of such systems, the application of existing consumer protection legislation is unclear, leaving the rights and liabilities of consumers, financial institutions, and intermediaries in electronic fund transfers undefined.

(b) It is the purpose of this title to provide a basic framework establishing the rights, liabilities, and responsibilities of participants in electronic fund transfer systems. The primary objective of this title, however, is the provision of individual consumer rights.

§ 903. Definitions [15 U.S.C. § 1693a]

As used in this title—

(1) the term "accepted card or other means of access" means a card, code, or other means of access to a consumer's account for the purpose of initiating electronic fund transfers when the person to whom such card or other means of access was issued has requested and received or has signed or has used, or authorized another to use, such card or other means of access for the purpose of transferring money between accounts or obtaining money, property, labor, or services;

(2) the term "account" means a demand deposit, savings deposit, or other asset account (other than an occasional or incidental credit balance in an open end credit plan as defined in section 103(i) of this Act), as described in regulations of the Board, established primarily for personal, family, or household purposes, but such term does not include an account held by a financial institution pursuant to a bona fide trust agreement;

(3) the term "Board" means the Board of Governors of the Federal Reserve System;

(4) the term "business day" means any day on which the offices of the consumer's financial institution involved in an electronic fund transfer are open to the public for carrying on substantially all of its business functions;

(5) the term "consumer" means a natural person;

(6) the term "electronic fund transfer" means any transfer of funds, other than a transaction originated by check, draft, or similar paper instrument, which is initiated through an electronic terminal, telephonic instrument, or computer or magnetic tape so as to order, instruct, or authorize a financial institution to debit or credit an account. Such term includes, but is not limited to, point-of-sale transfers, automated teller machine transactions, direct deposits or withdrawals of funds, and transfers initiated by telephone. Such term does not include—

(A) any check guarantee or authorization service which does not directly result in a debit or credit to a consumer's account;

(B) any transfer of funds, other than those processed by automated clearinghouse, made by a financial institution on behalf of a consumer by means of a service that transfers funds held at either Federal Reserve banks or other depository institutions and which is not designed primarily to transfer funds on behalf of a consumer;

(C) any transaction the primary purpose of which is the purchase or sale of securities or commodities through a broker-dealer registered with or regulated by the Securities and Exchange Commission;

(D) any automatic transfer from a savings account to a demand deposit account pursuant to an agreement between a consumer and a financial institution for the purpose of covering an overdraft or maintaining an agreed upon minimum balance in the consumer's demand deposit account; or

(E) any transfer of funds which is initiated by a telephone conversation between a consumer and an officer or employee of a financial institution which is not pursuant to a prearranged plan and under which periodic or recurring transfers are not contemplated;

as determined under regulations of the Board;

(7) the term "electronic terminal" means an electronic device, other than a telephone operated by a consumer, through which a consumer may initiate an electronic fund transfer. Such term includes, but is not limited to, point-of-sale terminals, automated teller machines, and cash dispensing machines;

(8) the term "financial institution" means a State or National bank, a State or Federal savings and loan association, a mutual savings bank, a State or Federal credit union, or any other person who, directly or indirectly, holds an account belonging to a consumer;

(9) the term "preauthorized electronic fund transfer" means an electronic fund transfer authorized in advance to recur at substantially regular intervals;

(10) the term "State" means any State, territory, or possession of the United States, the District of Columbia, the Commonwealth of Puerto Rico, or any political subdivision of any of the foregoing; and

(11) the term "unauthorized electronic fund transfer" means an electronic fund transfer from a consumer's account initiated by a person other than the consumer without actual authority to initiate such transfer and from which the consumer receives no benefit, but the term does not include any electronic fund transfer (A) initiated by a person other than the consumer who was furnished with the card, code, or other means of access to such consumer's account by such consumer, unless the consumer has notified the financial institution involved that transfers by such other person are no longer authorized, (B) initiated with fraudulent intent by the consumer or any person acting in concert with the consumer, or (C) which constitutes an error committed by a financial institution.

§ 904. Regulations [15 U.S.C. § 1693b]

(a) The Board shall prescribe regulations to carry out the purposes of this title. In prescribing such regulations, the Board shall:

(1) consult with the other agencies referred to in section 917 and take into account, and allow for, the continuing evolution of electronic banking services and the technology utilized in such services,

(2) prepare an analysis of economic impact which considers the costs and benefits to financial institutions, consumers, and other users of electronic fund transfers, including the extent to which additional documentation, reports, records, or other paper work would be required, and the effects upon competition in the provision of electronic banking services among large and small financial institutions and the availability of such services to different classes of consumers, particularly low income consumers,

(3) to the extent practicable, the Board shall demonstrate that the consumer protections of the proposed regulations outweigh the compliance costs imposed upon consumers and financial institutions, and

(4) any proposed regulations and accompanying analyses shall be sent promptly to Congress by the Board.

(b) The Board shall issue model clauses for optional use by financial institutions to facilitate compliance with the disclosure requirements of section 905 and to aid consumers in understanding the rights and responsibilities of participants in electronic fund transfers by utilizing readily understandable language. Such model clauses shall be adopted after notice duly given in the Federal Register and opportunity for public comment in accordance with section 553 of Title 5. With respect to the disclosures required by section 905(a)(3) and (4), the Board shall take account of variations in the services and charges under different electronic fund transfer systems and, as appropriate, shall issue alternative model clauses for disclosure of these differing account terms.

(c) Regulations prescribed hereunder may contain such classifications, differentiations, or other provisions, and may provide for such adjustments and exceptions for any class of electronic fund transfers, as in the judgment of the Board are necessary or proper to effectuate the purposes of this title, to prevent circumvention or evasion thereof, or to facilitate compliance therewith. The Board shall by regulation modify the requirements imposed by this title on small financial institutions if the Board determines that such modifications are necessary to alleviate any undue compliance burden on small financial institutions and such modifications are consistent with the purpose and objective of this title.

(d) In the event that electronic fund transfer services are made available to consumers by a person other than a financial institution holding a consumer's account, the Board shall by regulation assure that the disclosures, protections, responsibilities, and remedies created by this title are made applicable to such persons and services.

§ 905. Terms and Conditions of Transfers [15 U.S.C. § 1693c]

(a) The terms and conditions of electronic fund transfers involving a consumer's account shall be disclosed at the time the consumer contracts for an electronic fund transfer service, in accordance with regulations of the Board. Such disclosures shall be in readily understandable language and shall include, to the extent applicable—

(1) the consumer's liability for unauthorized electronic fund transfers and, at the financial institution's option, notice of the advisability of prompt reporting of any loss, theft, or unauthorized use of a card, code, or other means of access;

(2) the telephone number and address of the person or office to be notified in the event the consumer believes that an unauthorized electronic fund transfer has been or may be effected;

(3) the type and nature of electronic fund transfers which the consumer may initiate, including any limitations on the frequency or dollar amount of such transfers, except that the details of such limitations need not be disclosed if their confidentiality is necessary to maintain the security of an electronic fund transfer system, as determined by the Board;

(4) any charges for electronic fund transfers or for the right to make such transfers;

(5) the consumer's right to stop payment of a preauthorized electronic fund transfer and the procedure to initiate such a stop payment order;

(6) the consumer's right to receive documentation of electronic fund transfers under section 906;

(7) a summary, in a form prescribed by regulations of the Board, of the error resolution provisions of section 908 and the consumer's rights thereunder. The financial institution shall thereafter transmit such summary at least once per calendar year;

(8) the financial institution's liability to the consumer under section 910; and

(9) under what circumstances the financial institution will in the ordinary course of business disclose information concerning the consumer's account to third persons.

(b) A financial institution shall notify a consumer in writing at least twenty-one days prior to the effective date of any change in any term or condition of the consumer's account required to be disclosed under subsection (a) of this section if such change would result in greater cost or liability for such consumer or decreased access to the consumer's account. A financial institution may, however, implement a change in the terms or conditions of an account without prior notice when such change is immediately necessary to maintain or restore the security of an electronic fund transfer system or a consumer's account. Subject to subsection (a)(3) of this section, the Board shall require subsequent notification if such a change is made permanent.

(c) For any account of a consumer made accessible to electronic fund transfers prior to the effective date of this title, the information required to be disclosed to the consumer under subsection (a) of this section shall be disclosed not later than the earlier of—

(1) the first periodic statement required by section 906(c) after the effective date of this title; or

(2) thirty days after the effective date of this title.

§ 906. Documentation of Transfers; Periodic Statements [15 U.S.C. § 1693d]

(a) For each electronic fund transfer initiated by a consumer from an electronic terminal, the financial institution holding such consumer's account shall, directly or indirectly, at the time the transfer is initiated, make available to the consumer written documentation of such transfer. The documentation shall clearly set forth to the extent applicable—

(1) the amount involved and date the transfer is initiated;

(2) the type of transfer;

(3) the identity of the consumer's account with the financial institution from which or to which funds are transferred;

(4) the identity of any third party to whom or from whom funds are transferred; and

(5) the location or identification of the electronic terminal involved.

(b) For a consumer's account which is scheduled to be credited by a preauthorized electronic fund transfer from the same payor at least once in each successive sixty-day period, except where the payor provides positive notice of the transfer to the consumer, the financial institution shall elect to provide promptly either positive notice to the consumer when the credit is made as scheduled, or negative notice to the consumer when the credit is not made as scheduled, in accordance with regulations of the Board. The means of notice elected shall be disclosed to the consumer in accordance with section 905.

(c) A financial institution shall provide each consumer with a periodic statement for each account of such consumer that may be accessed by means of an electronic fund transfer. Except as provided in subsections (d) and (e) of this section, such statement shall be provided at least monthly for each monthly or shorter cycle in which an electronic fund transfer affecting the account has occurred, or every three months, whichever is more frequent. The statement, which may include information regarding transactions other than electronic fund transfers, shall clearly set forth—

(1) with regard to each electronic fund transfer during the period, the information described in subsection (a) of this section, which may be provided on an accompanying document;

(2) the amount of any fee or charge assessed by the financial institution during the period for electronic fund transfers or for account maintenance;

(3) the balances in the consumer's account at the beginning of the period and at the close of the period; and

(4) the address and telephone number to be used by the financial institution for the purpose of receiving any statement inquiry or notice of account error from the consumer. Such address and telephone number shall be preceded by the caption "Direct Inquiries To:" or other similar language indicating that the address and number are to be used for such inquiries or notices.

(d) In the case of a consumer's passbook account which may not be accessed by electronic fund transfers other than preauthorized electronic fund transfers crediting the account, a financial institution may, in lieu of complying with the requirements of subsection (c) of this section, upon presentation of the passbook provide the consumer in writing with the amount and date of each such transfer involving the account since the passbook was last presented.

(e) In the case of a consumer's account, other than a passbook account, which may not be accessed by electronic fund transfers other than preauthorized electronic fund transfers crediting the account, the financial institution may provide a periodic statement on a quarterly basis which otherwise complies with the requirements of subsection (c) of this section.

(f) In any action involving a consumer, any documentation required by this section to be given to the consumer which indicates that an electronic fund transfer was made to another person shall be admissible as evidence of such transfer and shall constitute prima facie proof that such transfer was made.

§ 907. Preauthorized Transfers [15 U.S.C. § 1693e]

(a) A preauthorized electronic fund transfer from a consumer's account may be authorized by the consumer only in writing, and a copy of such authorization shall be provided to the consumer when made. A consumer may stop payment of a preauthorized electronic fund transfer by notifying the financial institution orally or in writing at any time up to three business days preceding the scheduled date of such transfer. The financial institution may require written confirmation to be provided to it within fourteen days of an oral notification if, when the oral notification is made, the consumer is advised of such requirement and the address to which such confirmation should be sent.

(b) In the case of preauthorized transfers from a consumer's account to the same person which may vary in amount, the financial institution or designated payee shall, prior to each transfer, provide reasonable advance notice to the consumer, in accordance with regulations of the Board, of the amount to be transferred and the scheduled date of the transfer.

§ 908. Error Resolution [15 U.S.C. § 1693f]

(a) If a financial institution, within sixty days after having transmitted to a consumer documentation pursuant to section 906(a), (c), or (d) or notification pursuant to section 906(b), receives oral or written notice in which the consumer—

(1) sets forth or otherwise enables the financial institution to identify the name and account number of the consumer;

(2) indicates the consumer's belief that the documentation, or, in the case of notification pursuant to section 906(b), the consumer's account, contains an error and the amount of such error; and

(3) sets forth the reasons for the consumer's belief (where applicable) that an error has occurred,

the financial institution shall investigate the alleged error, determine whether an error has occurred, and report or mail the results of such investigation and determination to the consumer within ten business days. The financial institution may require written confirmation to be provided to it within ten business days of an oral notification of error if, when the oral notification is made, the consumer is advised of such requirement and the address to which such confirmation should be sent. A financial institution which requires written confirmation in accordance with the previous sentence need not provisionally recredit a consumer's account in accordance with subsection (c) of this section, nor shall the financial institution be liable under subsection (e) of this section if the written confirmation is not received within the ten-day period referred to in the previous sentence.

(b) If the financial institution determines that an error did occur, it shall promptly, but in no event more than one business day after such determination, correct the error, subject to section 909, including the crediting of interest where applicable.

(c) If a financial institution receives notice of an error in the manner and within the time period specified in subsection (a) of this section, it may, in lieu of the requirements of subsections (a) and (b) of this section, within ten business days after receiving such notice provisionally recredit the consumer's account for the amount alleged to be in error, subject to section 909, including interest where applicable, pending the conclusion of its investigation and its determination of whether an error has occurred. Such investigation shall be concluded not later than forty-five days after receipt of notice of the error. During the pendency of the investigation, the consumer shall have full use of the funds provisionally recredited.

(d) If the financial institution determines after its investigation pursuant to subsection (a) or (c) of this section that an error did not occur, it shall deliver or mail to the consumer an explanation of its findings within 3 business days after the conclusion of its investigation, and upon request of the consumer promptly deliver or mail to the consumer reproductions of all documents which the financial institution relied on to conclude that such error did not occur. The financial institution shall include notice of the right to request reproductions with the explanation of its findings.

(e) If in any action under section 915, the court finds that—

(1) the financial institution did not provisionally recredit a consumer's account within the ten-day period specified in subsection (c) of this section, and the financial institution (A) did not make a good faith investigation of the alleged error, or (B) did not have a reasonable basis for believing that the consumer's account was not in error; or

(2) the financial institution knowingly and willfully concluded that the consumer's account was not in error when such conclusion could not reasonably have been drawn from the evidence available to the financial institution at the time of its investigation,

then the consumer shall be entitled to treble damages determined under section 915(a)(1).

(f) For the purpose of this section, an error consists of—

(1) an unauthorized electronic fund transfer;

(2) an incorrect electronic fund transfer from or to the consumer's account;

(3) the omission from a periodic statement of an electronic fund transfer affecting the consumer's account which should have been included;

(4) a computational error by the financial institution;

(5) the consumer's receipt of an incorrect amount of money from an electronic terminal;

(6) a consumer's request for additional information or clarification concerning an electronic fund transfer or any documentation required by this title; or

(7) any other error described in regulations of the Board.

§ 909. Consumer Liability for Unauthorized Transfers [15 U.S.C. § 1693g]

(a) A consumer shall be liable for any unauthorized electronic fund transfer involving the account of such consumer only if the card or other means of access utilized for such transfer was an accepted card or other means of access and if the issuer of such card, code, or other means of access has provided a means whereby the user of such card, code, or other means of access can be identified as the person authorized to use it, such as by signature, photograph, or fingerprint or by electronic or mechanical confirmation. In no event, however, shall a consumer's liability for an unauthorized transfer exceed the lesser of—

(1) $50; or

(2) the amount of money or value of property or services obtained in such unauthorized electronic fund transfer prior to the time the financial institution is notified of, or otherwise becomes aware of, circumstances which lead to the reasonable belief that an unauthorized electronic fund transfer involving the consumer's account has been or may be effected. Notice under this paragraph is sufficient when such steps have been taken as may be reasonably required in the ordinary course of business to provide the financial institution with the pertinent information, whether or not any particular officer, employee, or agent of the financial institution does in fact receive such information.

Notwithstanding the foregoing, reimbursement need not be made to the consumer for losses the financial institution establishes would not have occurred but for the failure of the consumer to report within sixty days of transmittal of the statement (or in extenuating circumstances such as extended travel or hospitalization, within a reasonable time under the circumstances) any unauthorized electronic fund transfer or account error which appears on the periodic statement provided to the consumer under section 906. In addition, reimbursement need not be made to the consumer for losses which the financial institution establishes would not have occurred but for the failure of the consumer to report any loss or theft of a card or other means of access within two business days after the consumer learns of the loss or theft (or in extenuating circumstances such as extended travel or hospitalization, within a longer period which is reasonable under the circumstances), but the consumer's liability under this subsection in any such case may not exceed a total of $500, or the amount of unauthorized electronic fund transfers which occur following the close of two business days (or such longer period) after the consumer learns of the loss or theft but prior to notice to the financial institution under this subsection, whichever is less.

(b) In any action which involves a consumer's liability for an unauthorized electronic fund transfer, the burden of proof is upon the financial institution to show that the electronic fund transfer was authorized or, if the electronic fund transfer was unauthorized, then the burden of proof is upon the financial institution to establish that the conditions of liability set forth in subsection (a) of this section have been met, and, if the transfer was initiated after the effective date of section 905, that the disclosures required to be made to the consumer under section 905(a)(1) and (2) were in fact made in accordance with such section.

(c) In the event of a transaction which involves both an unauthorized electronic fund transfer and an extension of credit as defined in section 103(e) of this Act pursuant to an agreement between the consumer and the financial institution to extend such credit to the consumer in the event the consumer's account is overdrawn, the limitation on the consumer's liability for such transaction shall be determined solely in accordance with this section.

(d) Nothing in this section imposes liability upon a consumer for an unauthorized electronic fund transfer in excess of his liability for such a transfer under other applicable law or under any agreement with the consumer's financial institution.

(e) Except as provided in this section, a consumer incurs no liability from an unauthorized electronic fund transfer.

§ 910. Liability of Financial Institutions [15 U.S.C. § 1693h]

(a) Subject to subsections (b) and (c) of this section, a financial institution shall be liable to a consumer for all damages proximately caused by—

(1) the financial institution's failure to make an electronic fund transfer, in accordance with the terms and conditions of an account, in the correct amount or in a timely manner when properly instructed to do so by the consumer, except where—

(A) the consumer's account has insufficient funds;

(B) the funds are subject to legal process or other encumbrance restricting such transfer;

(C) such transfer would exceed an established credit limit;

(D) an electronic terminal has insufficient cash to complete the transaction; or

(E) as otherwise provided in regulations of the Board;

(2) the financial institution's failure to make an electronic fund transfer due to insufficient funds when the financial institution failed to credit, in accordance with the terms and conditions of an account, a deposit of funds to the consumer's account which would have provided sufficient funds to make the transfer, and

(3) the financial institution's failure to stop payment of a preauthorized transfer from a consumer's account when instructed to do so in accordance with the terms and conditions of the account.

(b) A financial institution shall not be liable under subsection (a)(1) or (2) of this section if the financial institution shows by a preponderance of the evidence that its action or failure to act resulted from—

(1) an act of God or other circumstance beyond its control, that it exercised reasonable care to prevent such an occurrence, and that it exercised such diligence as the circumstances required; or

(2) a technical malfunction which was known to the consumer at the time he attempted to initiate an electronic fund transfer or, in the case of a preauthorized transfer, at the time such transfer should have occurred.

(c) In the case of a failure described in subsection (a) of this section which was not intentional and which resulted from a bona fide error, notwithstanding the maintenance of procedures reasonably adapted to avoid any such error, the financial institution shall be liable for actual damages proved.

§ 911. Issuance of Cards or Other Means of Access [15 U.S.C. § 1693i]

(a) No person may issue to a consumer any card, code, or other means of access to such consumer's account for the purpose of initiating an electronic fund transfer other than—

(1) in response to a request or application therefor; or

(2) as a renewal of, or in substitution for, an accepted card, code, or other means of access, whether issued by the initial issuer or a successor.

(b) Notwithstanding the provisions of subsection (a) of this section, a person may distribute to a consumer on an unsolicited basis a card, code, or other means of access for use in initiating an electronic fund transfer from such consumer's account, if—

(1) such card, code, or other means of access is not validated;

(2) such distribution is accompanied by a complete disclosure, in accordance with section 905, of the consumer's rights and liabilities which will apply if such card, code, or other means of access is validated;

(3) such distribution is accompanied by a clear explanation, in accordance with regulations of the Board, that such card, code, or other means of access is not validated and how the consumer may dispose of such code, card, or other means of access if validation is not desired; and

(4) such card, code, or other means of access is validated only in response to a request or application from the consumer, upon verification of the consumer's identity.

(c) For the purpose of subsection (b) of this section, a card, code, or other means of access is validated when it may be used to initiate an electronic fund transfer.

§ 912. Suspension of Obligations [15 U.S.C. § 1693j]

If a system malfunction prevents the effectuation of an electronic fund transfer initiated by a consumer to another person, and such other person has agreed to accept payment by such means, the consumer's obligation to the other person shall be suspended until the malfunction is corrected and the electronic fund transfer may be completed, unless such other person has subsequently, by written request, demanded payment by means other than an electronic fund transfer.

§ 913. Compulsory Use of Electronic Fund Transfers [15 U.S.C. § 1693k]

No person may—

(1) condition the extension of credit to a consumer on such consumer's repayment by means of preauthorized electronic fund transfers; or

(2) require a consumer to establish an account for receipt of electronic fund transfers with a particular financial institution as a condition of employment or receipt of a government benefit.

§ 914. Waiver of Rights [15 U.S.C. § 1693*l*]

No writing or other agreement between a consumer and any other person may contain any provision which constitutes a waiver of any right conferred or cause of action created by this title. Nothing in this section prohibits, however, any writing or other agreement which grants to a consumer a more extensive right or remedy or greater protection than contained in this title or a waiver given in settlement of a dispute or action.

§ 915. Civil Liability [15 U.S.C. § 1693m]

(a) Except as otherwise provided by this section and section 910, any person who fails to comply with any provision of this title with respect to any consumer, except for an error resolved in accordance with section 908, if liable to such consumer in an amount equal to the sum of—

(1) any actual damage sustained by such consumer as a result of such failure;

(2)(A) in the case of an individual action, an amount not less than $100 nor greater than $1,000; or

(B) in the case of a class action, such amount as the court may allow, except that (i) as to each member of the class no minimum recovery shall be applicable, and (ii) the total recovery under this subparagraph in any class action or series of class actions arising out of the same failure to comply by the same person shall not be more than the lesser of $500,000 or 1 per centum of the net worth of the defendant; and

(3) in the case of any successful action to enforce the foregoing liability, the costs of the action, together with a reasonable attorney's fee as determined by the court.

(b) In determining the amount of liability in any action under subsection (a) of this section, the court shall consider, among other relevant factors—

(1) in any individual action under subsection (a)(2)(A) of this section, the frequency and persistence of noncompliance, the nature of such noncompliance, and the extent to which the noncompliance was intentional; or

(2) in any class action under subsection (a)(2)(B) of this section, the frequency and persistence of noncompliance, the nature of such noncompliance, the resources of the defendant, the number of persons

adversely affected, and the extent to which the noncompliance was intentional.

(c) Except as provided in section 910, a person may not be held liable in any action brought under this section for a violation of this title if the person shows by a preponderance of evidence that the violation was not intentional and resulted from a bona fide error notwithstanding the maintenance of procedures reasonably adapted to avoid any such error.

(d) No provision of this section or section 916 imposing any liability shall apply to—

(1) any act done or omitted in good faith in conformity with any rule, regulation, or interpretation thereof by the Board or in conformity with any interpretation or approval by an official or employee of the Federal Reserve System duly authorized by the Board to issue such interpretations or approvals under such procedures as the Board may prescribe therefor; or

(2) any failure to make disclosure in proper form if a financial institution utilized an appropriate model clause issued by the Board,

notwithstanding that after such act, omission, or failure has occurred, such rule, regulation, approval, or model clause is amended, rescinded, or determined by judicial or other authority to be invalid for any reason.

(e) A person has no liability under this section for any failure to comply with any requirement under this title if, prior to the institution of an action under this section, the person notifies the consumer concerned of the failure, complies with the requirements of this title, and makes an appropriate adjustment to the consumer's account and pays actual damages or, where applicable, damages in accordance with section 910.

(f) On a finding by the court that an unsuccessful action under this section was brought in bad faith or for purposes of harassment, the court shall award to the defendant attorney's fees reasonable in relation to the work expended and costs.

(g) Without regard to the amount in controversy, any action under this section may be brought in any United States district court, or in any other court of competent jurisdiction, within one year from the date of the occurrence of the violation.

§ 916. Criminal Liability [15 U.S.C. § 1693n]

(a) Whoever knowingly and willfully—

(1) gives false or inaccurate information or fails to provide information which he is required to disclose by this title or any regulation issued thereunder; or

(2) otherwise fails to comply with any provision of this title;

shall be fined not more than $5,000 or imprisoned not more than one year, or both.

(b) Whoever—

(1) knowingly, in a transaction affecting interstate or foreign commerce, uses or attempts or conspires to use any counterfeit, fictitious, altered, forged, lost, stolen, or fraudulently obtained debit instrument to obtain money, goods, services, or anything else of value which within any one-year period has a value aggregating $1,000 or more; or

(2) with unlawful or fraudulent intent, transports or attempts or conspires to transport in interstate or foreign commerce a counterfeit, fictitious, altered, forged, lost, stolen, or fraudulently obtained debit instrument knowing the same to be counterfeit, fictitious, altered, forged, lost, stolen, or fraudulently obtained; or

(3) with unlawful or fraudulent intent, uses any instrumentality of interstate or foreign commerce to sell or transport a counterfeit, fictitious, altered, forged, lost, stolen, or fraudulently obtained debit instrument knowing the same to be counterfeit, fictitious, altered, forged, lost, stolen, or fraudulently obtained; or

(4) knowingly receives, conceals, uses, or transports money, goods, services, or anything else of value (except tickets for interstate or foreign transportation) which (A) within any one-year period has a value aggregating $1,000 or more, (B) has moved in or is part of, or which constitutes interstate or foreign commerce, and (C) has been obtained with a counterfeit, fictitious, altered, forged, lost, stolen, or fraudulently obtained debit instrument; or

(5) knowingly receives, conceals, uses, sells, or transports in interstate or foreign commerce one or more tickets for interstate or foreign transportation, which (A) within any one-year period have a value aggregating $500 or more, and (B) have been purchased or obtained with one or more counterfeit, fictitious, altered, forged, lost, stolen, or fraudulently obtained debit instrument; or

(6) in a transaction affecting interstate or foreign commerce, furnishes money, property, services, or anything else of value, which within any one-year period has a value aggregating $1,000 or more, through the use of any counterfeit, fictitious, altered, forged, lost, stolen, or fraudulently obtained debit instrument knowing the same to be counterfeit, fictitious, altered, forged, lost, stolen, or fraudulently obtained—

shall be fined not more than $10,000 or imprisoned not more than ten years, or both.

(c) As used in this section, the term "debit instrument" means a card, code, or other device, other than a check, draft, or similar paper instrument, by the use of which a person may initiate an electronic fund transfer.

§ 917. Administrative Enforcement [15 U.S.C. § 1693*o*]

(a) *Enforcing agencies.* Compliance with the requirements imposed under this subchapter shall be enforced under—

(1) section 8 of the Federal Deposit Insurance Act, in the case of—

(A) national banks, by the Comptroller of the Currency;

(B) member banks of the Federal Reserve System (other than national banks), by the Board;

(C) banks insured by the Federal Deposit Insurance Corporation (other than members of the Federal Reserve System), by the Board of Directors of the Federal Deposit Insurance Corporation;

(2) section 8 of the Federal Deposit Insurance Act [12 U.S.C.A. § 1818], by the Director of the Office of Thrift Supervision, in the case of a savings association the deposits of which are insured by the Federal Deposit Insurance Corporation;

(3) the Federal Credit Union Act, by the Administrator of the National Credit Union Administration with respect to any Federal credit union;

(4) the Federal Aviation Act of 1958, by the Civil Aeronautics Board, with respect to any air carrier or foreign air carrier subject to that Act; and

(5) the Securities Exchange Act of 1934, by the Securities and Exchange Commission, with respect to any broker or dealer subject to that Act.

(b) For the purpose of the exercise by any agency referred to in subsection (a) of this section of its powers under any Act referred to in that subsection, a violation of any requirement imposed under this title shall be deemed to be a violation of a requirement imposed under that Act. In addition to its powers under any provision of law specifically referred to in subsection (a) of this section, each of the agencies referred to in that subsection may exercise, for the purpose of enforcing compliance with any requirement imposed under this title, any other authority conferred on it by law.

(c) Except to the extent that enforcement of the requirements imposed under this title is specifically committed to some other Government agency under subsection (a) of this section, the Federal Trade Commission shall enforce such requirements. For the purpose of the exercise by the Federal Trade Commission of its functions and powers under the Federal Trade Commission Act, a violation of any requirement imposed under this title shall be deemed a violation of a requirement imposed under that Act. All of the functions and powers of the Federal Trade Commission under the Federal Trade Commission Act are available to the Commission to enforce compliance by any person subject to the jurisdiction of the Commission with the requirements imposed under this title, irrespective of whether that person is engaged in commerce or meets any other jurisdictional tests in the Federal Trade Commission Act.

§ 918. Reports to Congress [15 U.S.C. § 1693p]

(a) Not later than twelve months after the effective date of this subchapter and at one-year intervals thereafter, the Board shall make reports to the Congress concerning the administration of its functions under this title, including such recommendations as the Board deems necessary and appropriate. In addition, each report of the Board shall include its assessment of the extent to which compliance with this title is being achieved, and a summary of the enforcement actions taken under section 917. In such report, the Board shall particularly address the effects of this title on the costs and benefits to financial institutions and consumers, on competition, on the introduction of new technology, on the operations of financial institutions, and on the adequacy of consumer protection.

(b) In the exercise of its functions under this title, the Board may obtain upon request the views of any other Federal agency which, in the judgment of the Board, exercises regulatory or supervisory functions with respect to any class of persons subject to this title.

§ 919. Relation to State Laws [15 U.S.C. § 1693q]

This title does not annul, alter, or affect the laws of any State relating to electronic fund transfers, except to the extent that those laws are inconsistent with the provisions of this title, and then only to the extent of the inconsistency. A State law is not inconsistent with this title if the protection such law affords any consumer is greater than the protection afforded by this title. The Board shall, upon its own motion or upon the request of any financial institution, State, or other interested party, submitted in accordance with procedures prescribed in regulations of the Board, determine whether a State requirement is inconsistent or affords greater protection. If the Board determines that a State requirement is inconsistent, financial institutions shall incur no liability under the law of that State for a good faith failure to comply with that law, notwithstanding that such determination is subsequently amended, rescinded, or determined by judicial or other authority to be invalid for any reason. This title does not extend the applicability of any such law to any class of persons or transactions to which it would not otherwise apply.

§ 920. Exemption for State Regulation [15 U.S.C. § 1693r]

The Board shall by regulation exempt from the requirements of this title any class of electronic fund transfers within any State if the Board determines that under the law of that State that class of electronic fund transfers is subject to requirements substantially similar to those imposed by this title, and that there is adequate provision for enforcement.

UCC ART. 4A

PREFATORY NOTE

The National Conference of Commissioners on Uniform State laws and The American Law Institute have approved a new Article 4A to the Uniform Commercial Code. Comments that follow each of the sections of the statute are intended as official comments. They explain in detail the purpose and meaning of the various sections and the policy considerations on which they are based.

Description of transaction covered by Article 4A.

There are a number of mechanisms for making payments through the banking system. Most of these mechanisms are covered in whole or part by state or federal statutes. In terms of number of transactions, payments made by check or credit card are the most common payment methods. Payment by check is covered by Articles 3 and 4 of the UCC and some aspects of payment by credit card are covered by federal law. In recent years electronic funds transfers have been increasingly common in consumer transactions. For example, in some cases a retail customer can pay for purchases by use of an access or debit card inserted in a terminal at the retail store that allows the bank account of the customer to be instantly debited. Some aspects of these point-of-sale transactions and other consumer payments that are effected electronically are covered by a federal statute, the Electronic Fund Transfer Act (EFTA). If any part of a funds transfer is covered by EFTA, the entire funds transfer is excluded from Article 4A.

Another type of payment, commonly referred to as a wholesale wire transfer, is the primary focus of Article 4A. Payments that are covered by Article 4A are overwhelmingly between business or financial institutions. The dollar volume of payments made by wire transfer far exceeds the dollar volume of payments made by other means. The volume of payments by wire transfer over the two principal wire payment systems—the Federal Reserve wire transfer network (Fedwire) and the New York Clearing House Interbank Payments Systems (CHIPS)—exceeds one trillion dollars per day. Most payments carried out by use of automated clearing houses are consumer payments covered by EFTA and therefore not covered by Article 4A. There is, however, a significant volume of nonconsumer ACH payments that closely resemble wholesale wire transfers. These payments are also covered by Article 4A.

There is some resemblance between payments made by wire transfer and payments made by other means such as paper-based checks and credit cards or electronically-based consumer payments, but there are also many differences. Article 4A excludes from its coverage these other payment mechanisms. Article 4A follows a policy of treating the transaction that it covers—a "funds transfer"—as a unique method of payment that is governed by unique principles of law that address the operational and policy issues presented by this kind of payment.

The funds transfer that is covered by Article 4A is not a complex transaction and can be illustrated by the following example which is used throughout the Prefatory Note as a basis for discussion. X, a debtor, wants to pay an obligation owed to Y. Instead of delivering to Y a negotiable instrument such as a check or some other writing such as a credit card slip that enables Y to obtain payment from a bank, X transmits an instruction to X's bank to credit a sum of money to the bank account of Y. In most cases X's bank and Y's bank are different banks. X's bank may carry out X's instruction by instructing Y's bank to credit Y's account in the amount that X requested. The instruction that X issues to its bank is a "payment order." X is the "sender" of the payment order and X's bank is the "receiving bank" with respect to X's order. Y is the "beneficiary" of X's order. When X's bank issues an instruction to Y's bank to carry out X's payment order, X's bank "executes" X's order. The instruction of X's bank to Y's bank is also a payment order. With respect to that order, X's bank is the sender, Y's bank is the receiving bank, and Y is the beneficiary. The entire series of transactions by which X pays Y is known as the "funds transfer." With respect to the funds transfer, X is the "originator," X's bank is the "originator's bank," Y is the "beneficiary" and Y's bank is the "beneficiary's bank." In more complex transactions there are one or more additional banks known as "intermediary banks" between X's bank and Y's bank. In the funds transfer the instruction contained in the payment order of X to its bank is carried out by a series of payment orders by each bank in the transmission chain to the next bank in the chain until Y's bank receives a payment order to make the credit to Y's account. In most cases, the payment order of each bank to the next bank in the chain is transmitted electronically, and often the payment order of X to its bank is also transmitted electronically, but the means of transmission does not have any legal significance. A payment order may be transmitted by any means, and in some cases the payment order is transmitted by a slow means such as first class mail. To reflect this fact, the broader term "funds transfer" rather than the narrower term "wire transfer" is used in Article 4A to describe the overall payment transaction.

Funds transfers are divided into two categories determined by whether the instruction to pay is given by the person making payment or the person receiving payment. If the instruction is given by the person making the payment, the transfer is commonly referred to as a "credit transfer." If the instruction is given by the person receiving payment, the transfer is commonly referred to as a "debit transfer." Article 4A governs credit transfers and excludes debit transfers.

Why is Article 4A needed?

There is no comprehensive body of law that defines the rights and obligations that arise from wire transfers. Some aspects of wire transfers are governed by rules of the principal transfer systems. Transfers made by Fedwire are governed by Federal Reserve Regulation J and transfers over CHIPS are governed by the CHIPS rules. Transfers made by means of automated clearing houses are governed by uniform rules adopted by various associations of banks in various parts of the nation or by Federal Reserve rules or operating circulars. But the various funds transfer system rules apply to only limited aspects of wire transfer transactions. The resolution of the many issues that are not covered by funds transfer system rules depends on contracts of the parties, to the extent that they exist, or principles of law applicable to other payment mechanisms that might be applied by analogy. The result is a great deal of uncertainty. There is no consensus about the juridical nature of a wire transfer and consequently of the rights and obligations that are created. Article 4A is intended to provide the comprehensive body of law that we do not have today.

Characteristics of a funds transfer.

There are a number of characteristics of funds transfers covered by Article 4A that have influenced the drafting of the statute. The typical funds transfer involves a large amount of money. Multimillion dollar transactions are commonplace. The originator of the transfer and the beneficiary are typically sophisticated business or financial organizations. High speed is another predominant characteristic. Most funds transfers are completed on the same day, even in complex transactions in which there are several intermediary banks in the transmission chain. A funds transfer is a highly efficient substitute for payments made by the delivery of paper instruments. Another characteristic is extremely low cost. A transfer that involves many millions of dollars can be made for a price of a few dollars. Price does not normally vary very much or at all with the amount of the transfer. This system of pricing may not be feasible if the bank is exposed to very large liabilities in connection with the transaction. The pricing system assumes that the price reflects primarily the cost of the mechanical operation performed by the bank, but in fact, a bank may have more or less potential liability with respect to a funds transfer depending upon the amount of the transfer. Risk of loss to banks carrying out a funds transfer may arise from a variety of causes. In some funds transfers, there may be extensions of very large amounts of credit for short periods of time by the banks that carry out a funds transfer. If a payment order is issued to the beneficiary's bank, it is normal for the bank to release funds to the beneficiary immediately. Sometimes, payment to the beneficiary's bank by the bank that issued the order to the beneficiary's bank is delayed until the end of the day. If that payment is not received because of the insolvency of the bank that is obliged to pay, the beneficiary's bank may suffer a loss. There is also risk of loss if a bank fails to execute the payment order of a customer, or if the order is executed late. There also may be an error in the payment order issued by a bank that is executing the payment order of its customer. For example, the error might relate to the amount to be paid or to the identity of the person to be paid. Because the dollar amounts involved in funds transfers are so large, the risk of loss if something goes wrong in a transaction may also be very large. A major policy issue in the drafting of Article 4A is that of determining how risk of loss is to be allocated given the price structure in the industry.

Concept of acceptance and effect of acceptance by the beneficiary's bank.

Rights and obligations under Article 4A arise as the result of "acceptance" of a payment order by the bank to which the order is addressed. Section 4A–209. The effect of acceptance varies depending upon whether the payment order is issued to the beneficiary's bank or to a bank other than the beneficiary's bank. Acceptance by the beneficiary's bank is particularly important because it defines when the beneficiary's bank becomes obligated to the beneficiary to pay the amount of the payment order. Although Article 4A follows convention in using the term "funds transfer" to identify the payment from X to Y that is described above, no money or property right of X is actually transferred to Y. X pays Y by causing Y's bank to become indebted to Y in the amount of the payment. This debt arises when Y's bank accepts the payment order that X's bank issued to Y's bank to execute X's order. If the funds transfer was carried out by use of one or more intermediary banks between X's bank and Y's bank, Y's bank becomes indebted to Y when Y's bank accepts the payment order issued to it by an intermediary bank. The funds transfer is completed when this debt is incurred. Acceptance, the event that determines when the debt of Y's bank to Y arises, occurs (i) when Y's bank pays Y or notifies Y of receipt of the payment order, or (ii) when Y's bank receives payment from the bank that issued a payment order to Y's bank.

The only obligation of the beneficiary's bank that results from acceptance of a payment order is to pay the amount of the order to the beneficiary. No obligation is owed to either the sender of the payment order accepted by the beneficiary's bank or to the originator of the funds transfer. The obligation created by acceptance by the beneficiary's bank is for the benefit of the beneficiary. The purpose of the sender's payment order is to effect payment by the originator to the beneficiary and that purpose is achieved when the beneficiary's bank accepts the payment order. Section 4A–405 states rules for determining when the obligation of the beneficiary's bank to the beneficiary has been paid.

Acceptance by a bank other than the beneficiary's bank.

In the funds transfer described above, what is the obligation of X's bank when it receives X's payment order? Funds transfers by a bank on behalf of its customer are made pursuant to an agreement or arrangement that may or may not be reduced to a formal document signed by the parties. It is probably true that in most cases there is either no express agreement or the agreement addresses only some aspects of the transaction. Substantial risk is involved in funds transfers and a bank may not be willing to give this service to all customers, and may not be willing to offer it to any customer unless certain safeguards against loss such as security procedures are in effect. Funds transfers often involve the giving of credit by the receiving bank to the customer, and that also may involve an agreement. These considerations are reflected in Article 4A by the principle that, in the absence of a contrary agreement, a receiving bank does not incur liability with respect to a payment order until it accepts it. If X and X's bank in the hypothetical case had an agreement that obliged the bank to act on X's payment orders and the bank failed to comply with the agreement, the bank can be held liable for breach of the agreement. But apart from any obligation arising by agreement, the bank does not incur any liability with respect to X's payment order until the bank accepts the order. X's payment order is treated by Article 4A as a request by X to the bank to take action that will cause X's payment order to be carried out. That request can be accepted by X's bank by "executing" X's payment order. Execution occurs when X's bank sends a payment order to Y's bank intended by X's bank to carry out the payment order of X. X's bank could also execute X's payment order by issuing a payment order to an intermediary bank instructing the intermediary bank to instruct Y's bank to make the credit to Y's account. In that case execution and acceptance of X's order occur when the payment order of X's bank is sent to the intermediary bank. When X's bank executes X's payment order the bank is entitled to receive payment from X and may debit an authorized account of X. If X's bank does not execute X's order and the amount of the order is covered by a withdrawable credit balance in X's authorized account, the bank must pay X interest on the money represented by X's order unless X is given prompt notice of rejection of the order. Section 4A–210(b).

Bank error in funds transfers.

If a bank, other than the beneficiary's bank, accepts a payment order, the obligations and liabilities are owed to the originator of the funds transfer. Assume in the example stated above, that X's bank executes X's payment order by issuing a payment order to an intermediary bank that executes the order of X's bank by issuing a payment order to Y's bank. The obligations of X's bank with respect to execution are owed to X. The obligations of the intermediary bank with respect to execution are also owed to X. Section 4A–302 states standards with respect to the time and manner of execution of payment orders. Section 4A–305 states the measure of damages for improper execution. It also states that a receiving bank is liable for damages if it fails to execute a payment order that it was obliged by express agreement to execute. In each case consequential damages are not recoverable unless an express agreement of the receiving bank provides for them. The policy basis for this limitation is discussed in Comment 2 to Section 4A–305.

Error in the consummation of a funds transfer is not uncommon. There may be a discrepancy in the amount that the originator orders to be paid to the beneficiary and the amount that the beneficiary's bank is ordered to pay. For example, if the originator's payment order instructs payment of $100,000 and the payment order of the originator's bank instructs payment of $1,000,000, the originator's bank is entitled to receive only $100,000 from the originator and has the burden of recovering the additional $900,000 paid to the beneficiary by mistake. In some cases the originator's bank or an intermediary bank instructs payment to a beneficiary other than the beneficiary stated in the originator's payment order. If the wrong beneficiary is paid the bank that issued the erroneous payment order is not entitled to receive payment of the payment order that it executed and has the burden of recovering the mistaken payment. The originator is not obliged to pay its payment order. Section 4A–303 and Section 4A–207 state rules for determining the rights and obligations of the various parties to the funds transfer in these cases and in other typical cases in which error is made.

Pursuant to Section 4A–402(c) the originator is excused from the obligation to pay the originator's bank if the funds transfer is not completed, i.e. payment by the originator to the beneficiary is not made. Payment by the originator to the beneficiary occurs when the beneficiary's bank accepts a payment order for the benefit of the beneficiary of the originator's payment order. Section 4A–406. If for any reason that acceptance does not occur, the originator is not required to pay the payment order that it issued or, if it already paid, is entitled to refund of the payment with interest. This "money-back guarantee" is an important protection of the originator of a funds transfer. The same rule applies to any other sender in the funds transfer. Each sender's obligation to pay is excused if the beneficiary's bank does not accept a payment order for the benefit of the beneficiary of that sender's order. There is an important exception to this rule. It is common practice for the originator of a funds transfer to designate the intermediary bank or banks through which the funds transfer is to be routed. The originator's bank is required by Section 4A–302 to follow the instruction of the originator with respect to intermediary banks. If the originator's bank sends a payment order to the intermediary bank designated in the originator's order and the intermediary bank causes the funds transfer to miscarry by failing to execute the payment order or by instructing payment to the wrong beneficiary, the originator's bank is not required to pay its payment order and if it has already paid it is entitled to recover payment from the intermediary bank. This remedy is normally adequate, but if the originator's bank already paid its order and the intermediary bank has suspended payments or is not permitted by law to refund payment, the originator's bank will suffer a loss. Since the originator required the originator's bank to use the failed intermediary bank, Section 4A–402(e) provides that in this case the originator is obliged to pay its payment order and has a claim against the intermediary bank for the amount of the order. The same principle applies to any other sender that designates a subsequent intermediary bank.

Unauthorized payment orders.

An important issue addressed in Section 4A–202 and Section 4A–203 is how the risk of loss from unauthorized payment orders is to be allocated. In a large percentage of cases, the payment order of the originator of the funds transfer is transmitted electronically to the originator's bank. In these cases it may not be possible for the bank to know whether the electronic message has been authorized by its customer. To ensure that no unauthorized person is transmitting messages to the bank, the normal practice is to establish security procedures that usually involve the use of codes or identifying numbers or words. If the bank accepts a payment order that purports to be that of its customer after verifying its authenticity by complying with a security procedure agreed to by the customer and the bank, the customer is bound to pay the order even if it was not authorized. But there is an important limitation on this rule. The bank is entitled to payment in the case of an unauthorized order only if the court finds that the security procedure was a commercially reasonable method of providing security against unauthorized payment orders. The customer can also avoid liability if it can prove that the unauthorized order was not initiated by an employee or other agent of the customer having access to confidential security information or by a person who obtained that information from a source controlled by the customer. The policy issues are discussed in the comments following Section 4A–203. If the bank accepts an unauthorized payment order without verifying it in compliance with a security procedure, the loss falls on the bank.

Security procedures are also important in cases of error in the transmission of payment orders. There may be an error by the sender in the amount of the order, or a sender may transmit a payment order and then erroneously transmit a duplicate of the order. Normally, the sender is bound by the payment order even if it is issued by mistake. But in some cases an error of this kind can be detected by a security procedure. Although the receiving bank is not obliged to provide a security procedure for the detection of error, if such a procedure is agreed to by the bank Section 4A–205 provides that if the error is not detected because the receiving bank does not comply with the procedure, any resulting loss is borne by the bank failing to comply with the security procedure.

Insolvency losses.

Some payment orders do not involve the granting of credit to the sender by the receiving bank. In those cases, the receiving bank accepts the sender's order at the same time the bank receives payment of the order. This is true of a transfer of funds by Fedwire or of cases in which the receiving bank can debit a funded account of the sender. But in some cases the granting of credit is the norm. This is true of a payment order over CHIPS. In a CHIPS transaction the receiving bank usually will accept the order before receiving payment from the sending bank. Payment is delayed until the end of the day when settlement is made through the Federal Reserve System. If the receiving bank is an intermediary bank, it will accept by issuing a payment order to another bank and the intermediary bank is obliged to pay that payment order. If the receiving bank is the beneficiary's bank, the bank usually will accept by releasing funds to the beneficiary before the bank has received payment. If a sending bank suspends payments before settling its liabilities at the end of the day, the financial stability of banks that are net creditors of the insolvent bank may also be put into jeopardy, because the dollar volume of funds transfers between the banks may be extremely large. With respect to two banks that are dealing with each other in a series of transactions in which each bank is sometimes a receiving bank and sometimes a sender, the risk of insolvency can be managed if amounts payable as a sender and amounts receivable as a receiving bank are roughly equal. But if these amounts are significantly out of balance, a net creditor bank may have a very significant credit risk during the day before settlement occurs. The Federal Reserve System and the banking community are greatly concerned with this risk, and various measures have been instituted to reduce this credit exposure. Article 4A also addresses this problem. A receiving bank can always avoid this risk by delaying acceptance of a payment order until after the bank has received payment. For example, if the beneficiary's bank credits the beneficiary's account it can avoid acceptance by not notifying the beneficiary of the receipt of the order or by notifying the beneficiary that the credit may not be withdrawn until the beneficiary's bank receives payment. But if the beneficiary's bank releases funds to the beneficiary before receiving settlement, the result in a funds transfer other than a transfer by means of an automated clearing house or similar provisional settlement system is that the beneficiary's bank may not recover the funds if it fails to receive settlement. This rule encourages the banking system to impose credit limitations on banks that issue payment orders. These limitations are already in effect. CHIPS has also proposed a loss-sharing plan to be adopted for implementation in the second half of 1990 under which CHIPS participants will be required to provide funds necessary to complete settlement of the obligations of one or more participants that are unable to meet settlement obligations. Under this plan, it will be a virtual certainty that there will be settlement on CHIPS in the event of failure by a single bank. Section 4A–403(b) and (c) are also addressed to reducing risks of insolvency. Under these provisions the amount owed by a failed bank with respect to payment orders it issued is the net amount owing after setting off amounts owed to the failed bank with respect to payment orders it received. This rule allows credit exposure to be managed by limitations on the net debit position of a bank.

PORT CITY STATE BANK v. AMERICAN NATIONAL BANK

United States Court of Appeals, Tenth Circuit, 1973.

486 F.2d 196.

HILL, CIRCUIT JUDGE.

This appeal is from a judgment entered against appellant Port City State Bank in its suit to collect upon two checks forwarded to appellee and not returned as insufficient before the appropriate midnight deadline. Following a trial without a jury, the United States District Court for the Western District of Oklahoma ruled that the failure to notify of dishonor prior to the deadline was excused in this case by Regulation J of the Federal Reserve Regulations, 12 C.F.R. 210.14, and 12A O.S.A. 4–108(2).

This court has jurisdiction by virtue of the diversity of citizenship of the parties and the allegation in the complaint of liability greatly exceeding the jurisdictional amount.

The record discloses that appellant was the holder of two checks drawn upon the J.H. McClung Coin Shop account with American National. Both items were forwarded through collecting channels for payment. The first check arrived at American National on Friday, November 28, 1969. That check contained two conflicting amounts: in figures $72,000.00 and in words seventy-two dollars and no/100 dollars. It was processed manually and stamped insufficient funds on Saturday, November 29; however, it was not returned immediately but was placed in Monday's business to determine if any deposits were forthcoming on Monday which would balance the account. Notice of dishonor was given to the last endorser of the check, the Federal Reserve Bank at Oklahoma City, on Wednesday, December 3, and the check was returned to the Federal Reserve on December 4.

The second check, in the amount of $120,377.20, arrived at American National on Tuesday, December 2, 1969. The first notice of its dishonor was by telephone to the Federal Reserve on Friday, December 5; it was returned to the Federal Reserve the same day.

It was stipulated by the parties that the "midnight deadline" for these items as established by Regulation J, 12 C.F.R. 210.12, and 12A O.S.A. 4–104(1)(h) was midnight December 1 for the first check and midnight December 3 for the second check. Additionally, it was stipulated that neither check was dishonored before the applicable deadline.

These facts establish a prima facie case for the application of 12 C.F.R. 210.12 and 12A O.S.A. 4–302(a), both concerning the necessity of fulfilling the midnight deadline, and thus it became the obligation of appellee at the trial to prove an excuse from these provisions under 12 C.F.R. 210.14 and 12A O.S.A. 4–108(2). The latter regulations in essence prevent the operation of the midnight deadline in cases when the delay by the payor bank is caused by the interruption of communication facilities, suspension of payments by another bank, war, emergency condition or other circumstances beyond the control of the bank provided it exercises such diligence as the circumstances require.

In furtherance of its contention, American National presented evidence that prior to December 1, 1969, it had performed its bookkeeping functions by machine posting, a so-called manual system. During 1969, however, a decision was made to implement a computer bookkeeping operation, and a rental agreement was entered into with a large computer company. That lease provided that all repairs and maintenance were the obligation of the computer firm, and American National was not authorized to undertake any such tasks. After the installation of the computer, American National paralleled its manual system with computer operations for approximately two weeks. Finally the decision was made to change over to computer processing beginning on December 1. A last manual posting was made on Saturday, November 29, and the manual bookkeeping equipment was removed from the bank during that weekend.

At approximately 10:00 a.m. on December 1, the first day for use of computer operations, the American National computer developed a "memory error" which rendered it unusable. Though the computer manufacturer indicated repairs would not take "too long", they lasted until late Monday night and the testing procedure extended into the early hours of Tuesday, December 2.

In reliance upon the belief that the computer would be repaired without prolonged delay, American National took no extraordinary steps to process Monday's business during the business day. However, when it became apparent that evening that the computer was not going to be ready immediately, American National decided to utilize an identical computer in a bank which was a trip of some 2½ hours away, in accord with a backup agreement they had made with the other banking institution. Thus at about 11:30 p.m. personnel from American National and the computer company began processing Monday's business on the backup computer and continued processing through the night. This work had proceeded to the point of capturing the items on discs when, because the backup computer was required by its owner and because they were informed their own computer was operational, the American National personnel returned to their bank to complete the work on their own machine. After returning to American National, the work was processed to the point of completing the printing of the trial balances when another memory error developed which again rendered the computer unusable. No further use could be made of the appellee's computer until a new memory module was installed on Thursday, December 4.

Because of the second failure, American National was forced to utilize the backup computer both Wednesday and Thursday during times it was not required by its owner. Monday's business was completed and work was begun on Tuesday's items the evening of Tuesday, December 2. Tuesday's items were not completed until either Wednesday, the third, or Thursday, the fourth. When the second check arrived in Tuesday's business, it was held to determine if a later deposit had balanced the account. Through the use of the backup computer and then its own computer during the next weekend, American National was fully "caught up" by Monday, December 8.

Based upon this evidence, the trial court held that the computer malfunction suffered by American National was the cause of its failure to meet its required midnight deadline on the checks, and that such malfunction constituted both an emergency condition and a circumstance beyond the control of the bank as outlined in 12 C.F.R. 210.14 and 12A O.S.A. 4–108(2). The court further held that the reaction to the situation by American National fulfilled the requirements of diligence imposed by those regulations, and therefore the court entered judgment for American National on both checks.

Appellant has urged several grounds for the reversal of this judgment, none of which we find merits that action. Though § 4–108(2) of the Uniform Commercial Code is in effect in the vast majority of states, we find no reported cases interpreting or defining this particular provision of the Code. And, of course, our obligation in this appeal is to apply this statute as would the Supreme Court of the State of Oklahoma. Primarily we are faced with reviewing a factual determination by the trial court, and its findings will be affirmed unless clearly erroneous.

Appellant's first contention is that the computer malfunction experienced by appellee was not the cause of the failure to notify on either check and thus could not excuse that lack of action. Though the trial court did not expressly rule upon this causation issue, it impliedly held that the delay in notification was a result of the computer breakdown in both instances, we believe that holding is not clearly erroneous.

As to the first check, it is true that it was processed and stamped insufficient on Saturday, however it was held for Monday's business to allow any deposits made on Monday to balance the account before notice was required. This procedure is reasonable, and only the subsequent computer breakdown prevented timely notice upon the check. In the case of the second check, appellant contends that problems involved in balancing the "proof batches" caused the delay, not the unavailability of the computer. Such a contention ignores the problems encountered by the bank on Tuesday as a result of the delay in processing Monday's business. Tuesday's work was delayed first by the necessity of driving 2½ hours each day before work could commence, and second by the necessity that Monday's business be completed first. Without doubt, both of these delays resulted from the computer problems at American National.

Further appellant contends that a computer failure, as a matter of law, is not an event which can impose the application of 12A O.S.A. 4–108(2). In our opinion, such a determination is a mixed question of fact and law; however, neither treatment justifies the reversal of the trial court's determination in this case. Factually, it was in no way erroneous to conclude that the malfunction created an emergency condition in the bank and was also a condition beyond the control of the bank. Appellant's argument that in law this malfunction is not included within the prescribed contingencies of § 4–108(2) is without foundation. The statute is clear and unambiguous on its face, and we need not resort to interpretive aids as urged by appellant. Our judgment coincides with that of the trial court that a computer failure such as in this case qualifies for the application of the statute. Additionally, this court has previously indicated that the views of a district judge who is a resident of the state where the controversy arose in a case involving interpretation of laws of that state carries extraordinary persuasive weight on appeal.

Port City next alleges that the trial court erred in its determination that American National exercised "such diligence" as the circumstances required. Basically, appellant asserts three alternative procedures that American National could have employed, and asserts that if any of these alternatives would have resulted in meeting the deadline, then appellee did not exercise diligence under the circumstances. As the trial court correctly concluded, the statute does not require perfection on the part of appellee, and American National's performance should not be judged on the basis of 20–20 hindsight.

It must first be noted that appellee quickly notified the computer firm of the breakdown, and that company began an immediate repair effort. Further, there was evidence to indicate that such computer breakdowns are generally repaired very quickly. Thus it would appear that appellee was justified in its initial delay in adopting emergency procedures based on its belief such measures would prove unnecessary. Additionally, we must agree with the trial court that appellee's duty under these circumstances was much broader than one requiring merely that it meet its midnight deadline. It was further obligated to keep the bank open and to serve its customers. To abandon the orderly day by day process of bookkeeping to adopt radical emergency measures would have likely prolonged the delay in returning the bank to normal operations.

As to appellant's assertion that appellee should have returned to manual posting, it was shown that the equipment for this procedure was no longer in the bank. Further, no clear evidence was presented to indicate such a procedure would have allowed appellee to fulfill its deadlines if the procedure had been implemented. Any decision to return to manual posting would have to have been made very soon after the discovery of the initial failure. At that time, because of their own experience with computers and the industry history, and also because the manufacturer did not foresee the serious nature of the repairs, American National was justified in believing its computer would be back in service soon. Their delay in commencing emergency operations was reasonable, and these facts prevented a return to manual posting in time to fulfill the deadlines.

As to the possibility of utilizing another backup computer at the regional headquarters of the computer leasing firm, we must agree with the trial court that there was no evidence that this alternative would have proved any more successful than the method actually employed by appellee.

In regard to the last alternative, "sight posting", the evidence is conflicting but sufficient to indicate it is not clear this alternative was so obviously superior as to be mandated under these circumstances. There were differing estimates as to the time required, and it was indicated such a procedure would upset and delay the eventual computer bookkeeping required to return the bank to current status. And as in the consideration of the previous alternatives, it was not clearly demonstrated that this procedure would have allowed American National to meet its deadlines even if it had been adopted.

Appellant asserts two other grounds for reversal that merit some discussion here. First, they assert that if the first check was only for $72.00, then it was not insufficient and thus the appellee is liable. This argument ignores the fact that the check had been encoded for $72,000 and thus had to be returned before proper credits could be advanced. Additionally, Oklahoma statutes and case law provide that a check is not an assignment of funds held by the drawee and fixes no liability on the drawee until it accepts or pays an instrument.

Next appellant asserts that appellee adopted an order of payment that ignored first-in-first-out, and argues that appellee should be liable as a result. However, as appellant indicates in its brief, there is no case law or statute establishing such a procedure as mandatory. We find no merit in such a contention.

Lastly, the parties have asserted several contentions concerning the proper face amount of the first check and the measure of damages under the applicable provisions of the code. However, as we affirm the trial court's holding denying liability, the discussion of these contentions is unnecessary.

Affirmed.

GEORGIA RAILROAD BANK & TRUST COMPANY v. THE FIRST NATIONAL BANK AND TRUST CO.

Court of Appeals of Georgia, 1976.
139 Ga.App. 683, 229 S.E.2d 482, aff'd 238 Ga. 693, 235 S.E.2d 1 (1977).

SMITH, JUDGE.

Georgia Railroad Bank & Trust Company (plaintiff) brought an action against The First National Bank & Trust Company of Augusta (defendant) to recover $22,500. The defendant filed a third party complaint against William W. Jones and Bill Jones Dodge City, Inc. The plaintiff moved for a judgment on the pleadings and for summary judgment. The defendant also made a motion for summary judgment. The trial court overruled plaintiff's motion for judgment on the pleadings and its motion for summary judgment and granted defendant's motion for summary judgment against the plaintiff. The plaintiff appeals the order of the trial court granting summary judgment in favor of the defendant.

The record shows the following undisputed facts. Both plaintiff and defendant utilize electronic equipment in the handling and processing of checks. When the plaintiff processes a check, it marks the check with magnetic coding ink. The check is subsequently handled by each bank in the chain of collection by electronic equipment which reads the magnetic coding ink. The amount of the check which has been encoded thereon is considered the amount of the check throughout the chain of collection.

On or about September 12, 1974, Charles Freeman deposited into his checking account with plaintiff bank a check in the amount of $25,000.00. The check was drawn on the defendant bank by William W. Jones. The plaintiff under-encoded the check as being $2,500; thus Freeman's account was incorrectly credited with a deposit of $2,500 rather than $25,000.

Jones' check was presented to the defendant through the Augusta Clearing House on or about September 13, 1974. It was processed by the defendant as a $2,500 item. The plaintiff was paid $2,500 as of the date of receipt, and Jones' account was debited in the amount of $2,500 rather than $25,000.

On September 26, 1974, the plaintiff notified Freeman that his account had been overdrawn. Plaintiff's encoding error was then discovered, and the plaintiff credited Freeman's account in the amount of $22,500. On September 27, the plaintiff notified the defendant of its encoding error and requested payment from the defendant in the amount of $22,500. The defendant contacted Mr. Jones and informed him regarding what had happened. Jones' canceled check had already been returned in his monthly statement. Jones told the defendant not to "bother" his account. The defendant then informed plaintiff that it was unable to pay the requested amount even though there were sufficient funds in Jones' account to comply with the demand for payment.

The issue presented is whether the collecting bank can recover the amount of the deficiency from the drawee bank where the latter pays the encoded amount of an under-encoded check. This issue is one of first impression in this state and, as far as we can determine, in any state. Although no court has dealt with this particular problem, various articles and treatises have discussed this specific situation. See B. Clark, The Law of Bank Deposits, Collections and Credit Cards 217 (1970); Brady, The Law of Bank Checks 326–328 (1969); J. Clarke, *Mechanized Check Collection,* The Business Law 994–1000 (July 1959).

No particular provision of the Uniform Commercial Code controls the present situation; however, several of its provisions are applicable to the ultimate resolution of the problem. Code § 109A–4–213(1) provides: "An item is finally paid by a payor bank when the bank has done any of the following, whichever happens first: * * * (c) completed the process of posting the item to the indicated account of the drawer, maker or other person to be charged therewith. * * * Upon a final payment under subparagraphs (b), (c) or (d) the payor bank shall be accountable for the amount of the item." The final sentence of the above section would create liability on the part of the drawee bank for the amount of the check when any "final payment" had been made. In the present case, the check had been marked "paid" and returned to the drawer; thus, the item had been posted to the account of the drawer. We find that the posting of the item, although in a smaller amount than the true amount of the item, was sufficient to constitute final payment within the meaning of the statute. Therefore, the item had been "finally paid" under the provision of subparagraph (c) above; and the payor bank became accountable for the amount of the item.

Further, Code § 109A–4–302 provides in pertinent part: "* * * if an item is presented on and received by a payor bank the bank is accountable for the amount of (a) a demand item * * * if the bank * * * retains the item beyond midnight of the banking day of receipt without settling for it or * * * does not pay or return the item * * * until after its midnight deadline * * *." In this case, the payor bank retained the item past the midnight deadline without completely settling for it; thus, under Section 4–302, the payor bank would be accountable for the amount of the retained check.

The payor bank contends that the drawer stopped payment on the check when he told the payor bank not to "touch" his account. The drawer of a check has the right to stop payment of it at any time *before it has been certified or paid by the drawee.* See *Tidwell v. Bank of Tifton,* 115 Ga.App. 555, 155 S.E.2d 451. As discussed above, the item had been "finally paid" by the drawee prior to the drawer's attempted revocation. Once the item was finally paid, the right to revoke settlement was lost.

We conclude that the drawer is responsible for the amount of the check according to its tenor. Since only the encoded amount has been paid, the drawee is accountable to the collecting bank for the deficiency. Accordingly, the trial court erred in granting summary judgment for the defendant. Summary judgment should have been granted in favor of the plaintiff against the defendant in the amount of the deficiency.

We are not here concerned with a situation wherein the drawee cannot recover from the drawer the amount of the deficiency. In such a situation there would possibly exist a defense or counterclaim in favor of the drawee bank against the collecting bank which had under-encoded the check. See *J. Clarke, Mechanized Check Collection,* supra at 1004. The record in the present case shows that the drawer's account contained sufficient funds, as of the date payment was demanded by plaintiff, to cover the deficiency.

Judgment reversed.

BISBEY v. D.C. NATIONAL BANK

United States Court of Appeals, District of Columbia Circuit, 1986.
793 F.2d 315.

HARRY T. EDWARDS, CIRCUIT JUDGE:

Sandra Bisbey challenges the refusal of the District Court to hold the District of Columbia National Bank ("the Bank") liable for a violation of the Electronic Fund Transfer Act of 1984 ("the Act"). The District Court found that the Bank, in its resolution of Ms. Bisbey's inquiry about her account, erroneously failed to deliver or mail to her an explanation of its investigative findings. However, the trial court concluded that the Act did not contemplate a finding of civil liability for this type of procedural mistake.

We reverse the District Court. Although there is no evidence of bad faith in this case, it is nonetheless clear that Bank officials failed to comply with provisions of the Act. Therefore, the case must be remanded for a determination of civil liability and attorney's fees.

I. BACKGROUND

A. Facts

Ms. Bisbey opened a checking account with the defendant Bank in January 1981. Subsequently, she authorized the Bank to debit her checking account for fund transfer directives submitted monthly by the New York Life Insurance Company ("NYLIC") for payment for her insurance premiums.

In September 1981, Ms. Bisbey's account lacked sufficient funds to cover the NYLIC directive, and no transfer was made. Thus, the September request was resubmitted by NYLIC in October, along with the latter month's directive. Appellant's funds were insufficient to satisfy either submission, both of which were covered by the Bank. As a result, two overdraft notices were sent to Ms. Bisbey, each in the amount of her monthly insurance premium. The appellant, having forgotten her nonpayment in September, believed that the Bank had erroneously made two payments in October.

At this point, Ms. Bisbey informed a customer representative of the Bank that she believed that an error had occurred with regard to these preauthorized transfers. Upon request by the Bank, she confirmed her inquiry by letter. Approximately ten days later, an official of the Bank telephoned appellant and orally explained that there had been no improper duplication of her premium payments. Ms. Bisbey, however, still considered the matter unresolved, and she filed suit under the EFTA.

B. Procedural History

In her complaint, plaintiff alleged that the Bank unlawfully failed to properly inform her about the result of its investigation into the alleged duplication error in her checking account.[2] She sought compensatory, treble and liquidated damages; the Bank filed a counterclaim for costs and attorney's fees, alleging that the plaintiff had brought suit in bad faith.

In relevant part, the opinion of the District Court held that the Bank had failed to comply with its statutory obligation to provide written notice of its findings when it concluded that no electronic funds transfer error had occurred. However, the trial court determined that section 915 of the Act,[3] which provides for civil liability and attorney's fees for certain violations, was, by its own terms, not applicable to the mistake at issue. Finally, neither party was deemed to have acted in bad faith; thus, the District Court found that an award of attorney's fees was unwarranted.

II. ANALYSIS

Section 908(d) of the Act provides:

> If [a] financial institution determines after its investigation * * * that an error did not occur, it shall *deliver or mail to consumer an explanation of its findings within 3 business days* after the conclusion of its investigation, and upon request of the consumer promptly deliver or mail to the consumer reproductions of all documents which the financial institution relied on to conclude that such error did not occur. *The financial institution shall include notice of the right to request reproductions with the explanation of its findings.*[4]

This section imposed a duty upon the Bank to "deliver or mail" the results of its investigation to Ms. Bisbey and to advise her of her right to request reproductions of all documents which it relied upon to

2. She also claimed that the Bank impermissibly failed to provisionally credit her checking account in the disputed amount pending resolution of her inquiry; however, that claim was decided adversely to her by the trial court and is not before us on appeal.

3. 15 U.S.C. § 1693m (Supp.II 1984).

4. *Id.* § 1693f(d) (emphasis added).

conclude that no error occurred.[5] The oral notice given to appellant was insufficient with respect to the required "explanation," and it did not even purport to give "notice of the right to request reproductions" as required by the statute.

The Bank's foregoing failures to comply with the statute give rise to civil liability under section 915 of the Act. That section provides that "any person who fails to comply with any provision of [the Act] with respect to any consumer, except for an error resolved in accordance with section 908, is liable to such consumer" for actual damages or for a symbolic award. Thus, under the plain terms of the Act, civil liability attaches to *all* failures of compliance with respect to *any* provision of the Act, including section 908.

An examination of other provisions of the Act supports this analysis. We note, for example, that section 908(e) specifies certain egregious *violations of section 908* which would result in an award of treble damages, such as a failure to provisionally recredit a consumer's account while simultaneously failing to perform a good faith investigation. The singling out of these particular violations and their focus on willful unlawfulness for an award of treble damages suggests that other failures to comply with the statute in the application of section 908 give rise to standard civil liability.

The Bank contends that the only "fail[ure]s to comply" to which civil liability should adhere are those which *may be* cured by the error resolution process of section 908. And, appellee maintains, it is unlikely that such procedural mistakes as occur in the course of an attempt to utilize the error resolution process would, in turn, be resolved by that same process.

This argument is patently flawed. There are "fail[ure]s of compliance" with the Act which cannot be or are unlikely to be resolved under section 908—such as a violation of section 908 itself—and which nonetheless give rise to civil liability. For example, section 910 sets forth the liability of financial institutions for damages caused by certain acts and omissions with regard to electronic fund transfers. These acts and omissions plainly constitute "fail[ure]s to comply" with the Act, yet they do not fall within the statutory definition of "error" for purposes of utilizing the error resolution procedures set forth in section 908.[6] But surely a financial institution cannot escape civil

5. Although it did not cross-appeal the decision against it on this issue, the Bank suggests that the phrase "deliver or mail" encompasses oral delivery of the results of an investigation and argues that this theory provides an alternative ground for dismissal of the case. We disagree. This section also requires that, at the customer's request, reproductions of documents be delivered or mailed, obviously requiring a physical transfer of documents by mail or by hand. We find it highly improbable that these phrases would possess different meanings when used so closely in conjunction.

In any event, the Bank has no explanation for its failure to give appellant "notice of the right to request reproductions," as required by the last sentence in the cited section.

6. For example, under certain circumstances, a failure to make an electronic fund transfer is a violation of section 910,

liability for a breach of section 910 merely because the breach cannot be resolved under section 908 pursuant to the "error" correction procedures. Civil liability attaches due to the "fail[ure] to comply" with the law.

Section 915 provides for an exception to civil liability for "an error resolved in accordance with section 908." Plainly, this exception has no play in this case. The Bank's failures to comply (*i.e.* the failure to "deliver or mail * * * an explanation" *and* the failure to give "notice of the right to request reproductions") were never cured. Therefore, these failures cannot be viewed as "errors resolved in accordance with section 908" within the exception to civil liability enunciated in section 915. The District Court's ruling to the contrary is simply wrong as a matter of law.

If the Bank had made a mistake in transferring funds from appellant's account and then had redressed the error pursuant to section 908 (without otherwise failing to comply with section 908), then the exception to section 915 would have to come into play. In such a case, the Bank could not be charged with civil liability for the mistaken transfer of funds because the "error" would have been fully cured pursuant to section 908. In this case, however, there is no problem with mistaken fund transfers; rather, the problem here has arisen because the Bank failed to comply with provisions in the Act when addressing a lawful inquiry about *possible* mistaken fund transfers.

It may seem odd that the Bank is held liable for a transaction that benefited the plaintiff. Ms. Bisbey's account contained insufficient funds to cover either of the premium requests submitted by NYLIC. Though she had no overdraft agreement, the Bank did not charge an overdraft fee. Thus, the effect of the Bank's payments was to provide her, at no cost, with insurance coverage she would not have had otherwise. Upon Bisbey's inquiry, the Bank gave her a correct report but neglected to send it in writing, as the statute requires. Ms. Bisbey conceded below that she had suffered no damage and the District Court's surmise that she may have been benefited [7] seems correct. Despite this, the litigation has continued for nearly three years, and the statute compels a finding that the Bank is liable. Doubtless the discretion given the District Court to award only nominal damages and a "reasonable" attorney's fee [8] was designed to mitigate the results of strict liability in cases such as this, involving a technical and non-damaging violation.

but that omission does not conform to any of the definitions of "error" in section 908.

7. *See Bisbey v. D.C. National Bank,* Civ. Action No. 83–3566, mem. op. at 8 (D.D.C. July 17, 1985).

8. *See Hensley v. Eckerhart,* 461 U.S. 424, 430, 103 S.Ct. 1933, 1938, 76 L.Ed.2d 40 (1983) (the district court may consider the amounts involved and the results obtained in determining the amount of fees to be awarded); *Johnson v. Georgia Highway Express, Inc.,* 488 F.2d 714, 718 (5th Cir.1974).

III. Conclusion

The "fail[ure]s to comply" with the EFTA in the instant case are plain; moreover, they are failures to which civil liability attaches for they have not been resolved in accordance with section 908. We therefore remand this case to the District Court for a determination of civil liability and attorney's fees pursuant to section 915.

So ordered.

B. EXPORT CONTROLS

Since the early 1900s, Congress has imposed various forms of export controls for security and foreign policy reasons. In 1949, Congress adopted the first regulated licensing process under the Export Control Act. The 1949 Act prohibited exports that would significantly benefit the Soviet Union economically, even if the items were not of military significance. The government issued export licenses depending upon the military, economic, and political significance of the item and its destination. In 1969, Congress adopted the Export Administration Act, which allowed United States firms to trade with communist countries. The Act is the enabling statute for the 1983 Export Administration Regulations which provide the actual licensing procedures.

Until the passage of the Act in 1969, the law permitted almost no exports to Communist countries. The basic policies of the 1969 Act were to allow export of goods and technologies that did not add to the military strength of non-allies, to promote trade with allies, and to prevent shortages in the United States. The Act attempted to remove unnecessary barriers to East–West trade. Pursuant to the Act, the United States was instrumental in forming the International Coordinating Committee on Strategic Trade with Communist Countries (CoCom). Other members included JAPAN and the NATO countries. The purpose of CoCom was to coordinate trade restrictions with Communist countries, by preventing competition in liberalization of national export policies. (American companies had long complained that they suffered under a stricter export control policy than their foreign competitors.) A 1977 Amendment to the Act changed the focus from end use critical technologies. The Act provided for a Commodity Control List of these technologies. The Department of Commerce was required to use this List and the Military Critical List in dealing with export license requests. Congress amended the Act in 1985 to streamline licensing procedures.

The Act gives the authority to the President to control export of technology and commodities if the national security is endangered. The Act allows the President to:

> add any country * * * or remove any country from such list of controlled countries if he determines that the export of goods or

> technology to such country would or would not * * * make a significant contribution to the military potential of such country or a combination of countries which would prove detrimental to the national security of the United States.

These concerns are rather obvious. If our enemies obtain technology that is crucial to our national defense, the United States pays twice: (1) for the development of the technology and (2) for the additional research to offset the use of the initial technology by a potential military opponent. A computer-industry example is the Toshiba–Kongsberg incident. Toshiba and Kongsberg sold machine tools with high precision computerized controls to a Soviet buyer. The buyer was a front for the Soviet military, which used the machine tools to produce much quieter submarine propellers. The United States had to spend large sums on improved detection systems. After a Japanese court imposed only a token fine and a suspended sentence against Toshiba, the United States Congress decided to take action. The Omnibus Trade and Competitiveness Act of 1988 imposed severe sanctions against Toshiba Machine Company and Kongsberg Trading Company.

The President can also restrict exports for foreign policy reasons. An example is the prohibition on export of computer technology for use by the South African police in enforcing racial discrimination. The President:

> may prohibit or curtail the exportation of any goods, technology, or other information subject to the jurisdiction of the United States, to the extent necessary to further significantly the foreign policy of the United States or to fulfill its declared international obligations.

Before restricting exports for foreign policy purposes, the President must:

> determine that reasonable efforts have been made to achieve the purposes of the controls through negotiations or other alternative means.

The President must also consider: (1) the effectiveness of the control in light of availability; (2) the compatibility with general and country-specific foreign policies; (3) the reaction of other countries; (4) the effect on United States exports and United States suppliers; (5) the enforcement capabilities; and (6) the foreign policy consequences of not imposing controls.

The problem of indirect export through third countries is a serious one. If the United States only controlled exports to the Soviet Union, exporters could send products to France, for instance, and the Soviet military could buy them there. The establishment of uniform export restrictions through CoCom is one solution to this problem. If exporters ship high-technology goods to countries that enforce CoCom restrictions, there is little worry that the goods will reach the Soviet Union. There are also international agreements allowing government guarantees against reexports of particular commodities. Nevertheless, the export control system is a major burden for United States exporters in the computer industry.

The licensing procedures under the Regulations are complicated and must be followed to avoid unnecessary delay or disapproval. The Commerce Department issues licenses based on the country of destination, the nature of the commodity or technical data, the critical technology, and the foreign availability of the technology. Computer exporters face separate procedures for exporting technical data and hardware. There are generally two types of licenses for the export of computers—the general license and the validated license. The general license procedure covers exports that pose no threat to the United States security. A general license requires no application, but export carriers must report exports made under general license. Most microcomputer exports, even to the Soviet Union, fall under general license provisions.

Export of critical technology, for instance a supercomputer, requires a validated license. To apply for a validated license, the exporter must submit a detailed application to the Department of Commerce. Depending upon the goods and destination, the Department may deny a license, issue a license for a single export transaction, or issue a license for multiple transactions.

Software is governed by the technical data provisions. Like hardware, technical data is exported under either a general license or a validated license. There are two types of general licenses relevant to computers. The GTDA allows export of technical data that is publicly available free or for the cost of copying. An example is a copy of a patent. The GTDR allows export of most microcomputer software and of technical manuals for equipment exportable under general license.

The Omnibus Trade and Competitiveness Act of 1988 amended the Export Administration Act to liberalize and to simplify general export control procedures to improve controls on strategic products.

The major changes included liberalization of reexport controls to CoCom countries and allowing low technology to be exported under a "GFW" general license. The 1988 Act mandates an annual review of computer products. Products are added to or deleted from the Commodities Control List on the basis of this review. Goods freely available in the foreign market no longer require a validated license even for export to controlled countries. Goods containing microprocessors no longer automatically require validated licenses. The focus has shifted to what is the function of the goods. A newly-added section allows the President to impose sanctions from two to five years against any foreign violator of CoCom regulations who adversely affected United States strategic defense.

Violations of the Export Administration Act can result in both criminal and civil penalties. These include imprisonment for up to 10 years, fines of up to five times the value of the exports, and suspension of export privileges.

WEST-WEST DECONTROL OF CERTAIN LOW CAPACITY HARD DISK DRIVES

Department of Commerce.
Bureau of Export Administration, 15 CFR Part 799.

Summary: This final rule removes the validated export licensing requirements from exports to noncontrolled countries of certain low capacity hard disk drives controlled under Export Control Commodity Number (ECCN) 1565A in the Commodity Control List (Supplement No. 1 to § 799.1 of the Export Administration Regulations). This action is in accordance with a positive determination of foreign availability under section 5(f) of the Export Administration Act of 1979, as amended. Notice of the determination was published in the Federal Register on January 3, 1990 (55 FR 163). The net effect of this rule will be to reduce the number of export license applications submitted for this equipment.

Effective Date: This rule is effective April 5, 1990.

For Further Information Contact: Randolph Williams, Office of Technology and Policy Analysis, Bureau of Export Administration, U.S. Department of Commerce, Washington, DC 20230, Telephone: (202) 377–0708.

SUPPLEMENTARY INFORMATION:

Background

The Bureau of Export Administration maintains the Commodity Control List (CCL), which identifies those items subject to Department of Commerce export controls. This final rule amends the validated license controls on certain hard disks described in ECCN 1565A of the CCL.

As a result of this regulatory action, exports of hard disk drives no longer require a validated license to any destination in Country Group T or V (except the People's Republic of China and Afghanistan), provided that they do not exceed any of the following technical performance characteristics described in the *Validated License Required* paragraph for ECCN 1565A:

(1) A "gross capacity" of 440 million bits (55 Megabytes, unformatted);

(2) A "maximum bit transfer rate" of 5.2 million bits per second; or

(3) An "access rate" of 40 accesses per second.

A validated license continues to be required for national security reasons for exports of these disk drives to destinations in Country Groups Q, S, W, Y, and Z, the People's Republic of China, and Afghanistan.

The Bureau of Export Administration has initiated action to implement a West–East decontrol of the hard disk drives affected by this rule.

* * *

DECISION; COMPUTECH ISPAT LIMITED AND COMPUTECH INTERNATIONAL; BARIN NATH CHATTERJEE, SANTOSH K. RATERIA AND E. ERMAN

BUREAU OF EXPORT ADMINISTRATION, 1990.
55 Fed.Reg. 3758

DECISION AND ORDER

On June 6, 1989, the Department issued a Charging Letter against Barin Nath Chatterjee (Chatterjee), individually and doing business as Computech Ispat Limited and Computech International, and on June 14, 1989 issued separate Charging Letters against Santosh K. Rateria (Rateria) and E. Erman (Erman), individually and both doing business as Computech Ispat Limited and Computech International (referred to collectively as respondents). The three separate Charging Letters alleged that respondents violated the provisions of §§ 787.3(b), 787.4, 787.5, and 787.6 of the Export Administration Regulations (codified at 15 CFR parts 768–799 (1989)) (the Regulations), issued pursuant to the Export Administration Act of 1979, as amended (50 U.S.C.A. app. 2401–2420 (Supp.1989)) (the Act), by reexporting a VAX 11/780 computer from Singapore to India without the reexport authorization which they knew or had reason to know was required by § 774.1 of the Regulations, and by submitting an ITA Form 629P Statement by Ultimate Consignee and Purchaser in connection with an application for an export license to the Department, wherein they made false or misleading statements and representations of material fact to the Department.

Respondents filed answers to the Charging Letters. After the respondents filed their answers, the Department and the respondents entered into a Consent Agreement whereby they agreed to settle the matters by Chatterjee's paying to the Department a civil penalty of $100,000 and by a denial of respondents' export privileges for 5 years, portions of which are suspended as set forth below.

The parties thereupon submitted a Consent Agreement to the Administrative Law Judge, that he approved, and recommended that I approve it as well. The Administrative Law Judge submitted a Decision and Order approving the Consent Agreement. Because the Decision and Order included a discussion not relevant to the approval of the Consent Agreement by the Administrative Law Judge, the Decision and Order of the Administrative Law Judge is modified by striking all that appears before the Order itself.

I hereby approve the Consent Agreement.

Therefore, it is ordered:

First, (1) Barin Nath Chatterjee, individually and doing business as Computech Ispat Limited and Computech International, with addresses at 507 Jodhpur Park, Calcutta 68, India, 77/2A Hazra Road, Fourth Floor, Calcutta, India, and 72 rue Pierre Curie, 91420 Morangis, France;

(2) Santosh K. Rateria, individually and doing business as Computech Ispat Limited and Computech International, with addresses at 507 Jodhpur Park, Calcutta 68, India, 77/2A Hazra Road, Fourth Floor, Calcutta, India, and 105 Southern Avenue, Calcutta, India; and

(3) E. Erman, individually and doing business as Computech Ispat Limited and Computech International, with addresses at 507 Jodhpur Park, Calcutta 68, India, 77/2A Hazra Road, Fourth Floor, Calcutta, India, and J.L. Pawiyaten No. 9, Surabaya, Indonesia; collectively referred to herein as respondents, and all their successors, assignees, officers, partners, representatives, agents and employees, shall be denied, for a period of five years from the date of this Order, all privileges of participating, directly or indirectly, in any manner or capacity, in any transaction involving the export of U.S.-origin commodities or technical data from the United States or abroad.

A. All outstanding individual validated export licenses in which any respondent appears or participates, in any manner or capacity, are hereby revoked and shall be returned forthwith to the Office of Export Licensing for cancellation. Further, all of respondents' privileges of participating, in any manner or capacity, in any special licensing procedure including, but not limited to, distribution licenses, are hereby revoked.

B. Without limiting the generality of the foregoing, participation prohibited in any such transaction, either in the United States or abroad, shall include, but is not limited to, participation: (i) As a party or as a representative of a party to any export license application submitted to the Department; (ii) in preparing or filing with the Department any export license application or request for reexport authorization, or any document to be submitted therewith; (iii) in obtaining from the Department or using any validated or general export license or other export control document; (iv) in carrying on negotiations with respect to, or in receiving, ordering, buying, selling, delivering, storing, using, or disposing of any commodities or technical data, in whole or in part, exported or to be exported from the United States and subject to the Regulations; and (v) in financing, forwarding, transporting, or other servicing of such commodities or technical data. Such denial of export privileges shall extend only to those commodities and technical data which are subject to the Act and the Regulations.

C. After notice and opportunity for comment, such denial may be made applicable to any person, firm, corporation, or business organization with which any respondent is now or hereafter may be related by affiliation, ownership, control, position of responsibility, or other connection in the conduct of trade or related services.

D. No person, firm, corporation, partnership or other business organization, whether in the United States or elsewhere, without prior disclosure to and specific authorization from the Office of Export Licensing shall, with respect to U.S.-origin commodities and technical data, do any of the following acts, directly or indirectly, or carry on negotiations with respect thereto, in any manner or capacity, on behalf of or in any association with any respondent or any related person, or whereby any respondent or any related person may obtain any benefit therefrom or have any interest or participation therein, directly or indirectly: (a) Apply for, obtain, transfer, or use any license, Shipper's Export Declaration, bill of lading, or other export control document relating to any export, reexport, transshipment, or diversion of any commodity or technical data exported, in whole or in part, or to be exported by, to, or for any respondent or any related person denied export privileges; or (b) order, buy, receive, use, sell, deliver, store, dispose of, forward, transport, finance, or otherwise service or participate in any export, reexport, transshipment, or diversion of any commodity or technical data exported or to be exported from the United States. These prohibitions apply only to those commodities and technical data which are subject to the Act and the Regulations.

E. As authorized by Section 788.16(c) of the Regulations, the denial period herein provided for against respondents shall be suspended as to each respondent as follows:

(1) Chatterjee—for a period of four years and six months, beginning six months from the date of entry of this Order;

(2) Rateria and Erman—for a period of five years beginning from the date of entry of this Order;

(3) Computech Ispat Limited and Computech International—for a period of four years and nine months, beginning three months from the date of entry of this Order and shall thereafter be waived provided that, during the period of applicable suspension, (a) respondents have committed no violation of the Act or any regulation, order or license issued under the Act, and (b) Computech Ispat Limited, the owner and operator of the computer that is the subject of the administrative proceedings, allows routine inspections of the computer by United States authorities on its premises in India, provided that such inspections do not disturb computer operations.

Second, a civil penalty in the amount of $100,000 is assessed against Barin Nath Chatterjee. Chatterjee shall pay to the Department the sum of $50,000 within 30 days from the date of the entry of this Order. Within one year after the date of entry of this Order, Chatterjee will make a second payment to the Department of $50,000. Each payment shall be made in the manner specified in the attached instructions.

Third, that the Charging Letters, the Consent Agreement and this Order shall be made available to the public. A copy of this Order shall be served upon each respondent and published in the Federal Register.

This constitutes final agency action in this matter.

Dated: January 29, 1990.

Dennis Kloske,

Under Secretary for Export Administration.

DECISION AND ORDER

Appearance for Respondent: Byron Keith Huffman, Jr., Esq., Webster & Sheffield, 2000 Pennsylvania Avenue NW., Suite 7400, Washington, DC 20006.

Appearance for Agency: Louis K. Rothberg, Attorney–Advisor, Office of Chief Counsel for Export Administration, U.S. Department of Commerce, Room H–3837, 14th & Constitution Avenue NW., Washington, DC 20230.

PRELIMINARY STATEMENT [1]

This proceeding against Respondent Barin Nath Chatterjee (Chatterjee), individually and doing business as Computech Ispat Limited and Computech International, was initiated with the issuance of a charging letter on June 6, 1989. On June 14, 1989, two similar charging letters were also issued against Respondent Santosh K. Rateria (Rateria) and Respondent E. Erman (Erman), individually and doing business as Computech Ispat Limited and Computech International (referred to collectively as Respondents). The violations alleged in all three letters assert a conspiracy relating to the same events, resulting in the consolidation of these cases. These letters were issued under the authority of the Export Administration Act of 1979 (50 U.S.C.A. app. 2401–2420), as amended (the Act), and the Export Administration Regulations (the Regulations).

The letters alleged that from November 1985 to July 1987, Respondents violated §§ 787.3(b), 787.4, 787.5, and 787.6 of the Regulations by reexporting a VAX 11/780 computer from Singapore to India without the reexport authorization which they know or had reason to know was required by § 774.1 of the Regulations, and by submitting an ITA Form 629P Statement by Ultimate Consignee and Purchaser in connection with an application for an export license to the Agency, wherein they made false or misleading statements and representations of material fact to the Agency.

1. Pursuant to the Secretary's order *In the Matter of A.M.Y. Enterprises,* 54 FR 47801 (November 17, 1989) the Order here does not provide findings of facts, conclusions of law, nor findings of violation. Citing *In the Matter of Bernardus Johannes Jozef Smit,* 54 FR 39027 (Sept. 22, 1989) where it was held:

That "neither the Act nor the Regulations require that a finding of violation be made in order to impose sanctions under a consent agreement" (54 FR at 39028). [T]here is no requirement for a finding of violation to impose a civil penalty in consent proceedings brought pursuant to § 788.17(a)(2).

Respondents filed answers to the charging letters. After the Respondents filed their answers, the Agency and the Respondents entered into a Consent Agreement. To settle the admitted violation of §§ 787.-3(b), 787.4, 787.5, and 787.6 of the Regulations, as alleged in the charging letter, Chatterjee consented to pay a civil penalty of $100,000 and each of the Respondents consented to a denial of export privileges for 5 years, portions of which are suspended as set forth below.

Beginning on the date of final Agency action, the denial of export privileges set forth above is to be suspended, as authorized by § 788.-16(c) of the Regulations, and as stated in the following Order provided that Respondents commit no further violations of the Export Administration Act, the Regulations, or the Final Order issued in this proceeding.

Discussion

Upon examination of the record in these cases, following submission of the Consent Agreement, it appeared that the $100,000 civil penalty was unusually high. A comparison with other cases adjudicated since the Act was amended in 1985 reflected that the amount was approximately three times the average of consent settlement cases during the same period. The parties were ordered to show cause for approval of the proposed settlement. The submissions represent that the settlement proposed was reached after intense negotiations and reflect substantial compromise. The individual respondents are in Europe and India, making communication difficult and costly. A plea bargained criminal conviction of Computech Ispat Limited, in settlement of proceedings initiated in the United States District Court in Houston, Texas against all of these Respondents, some or all of whom had been initially incarcerated and later released on bond, resulted in a guilty plea by the Computech Ispat Limited and a fine against that company only, of $17,500. As a result the criminal charges against the individuals were dropped. Agency Counsel asserts that the holding of the United States Supreme Court in *United States v. Halper* 109 S.Ct. 1892 (1989) is not applicable here because the individuals were not convicted in the criminal proceeding. I note, however, that they were charged here individually and doing business as Computech Ispat Limited. Therefore the conviction clearly relates to the company aspect of their individual activities. That the criminal plea was *sub nomine* by the corporation through which they are charged here, that does not exculpate them here. I do not see the situation as significantly different than that in a pending penalty case where the conviction of an officer is asserted by Agency Counsel as binding upon and chargeable against a Corporate Respondent.

The show cause submission provides some additional details on the incidents, but also raises further questions.

The most significant of these remains the appropriateness of the proposed civil penalty. Agency Counsel's representations, which are not new, to the effect that each of these export compliance cases is unique and therefore there need be no standard, is preposterous. For almost five decades export control was shrouded in secrecy and immune from judicial review. Some vestiges still remain, principally in the Agency and Counsel attitudes. These cases are as routine and run of the mill as any group processed administratively or judicially. The adamant attitude of Counsel—attributable to the client agency, as well, is simply at variance with elemental fairness. Each Agency Counsel appears to pull out of the air whatever number he or she considers on a given day, and that is the rule. That cannot be.

This subject has been addressed before. The Administrative Conference of the United States in its Reports and Recommendations, which have been adopted by this Department, lay out the Government policy as well as the legal requirement for standards. Agency Counsel's assertions that these cases are unique and that there need be no standards provide no basis for evaluating sanctions proposed, leaving nothing for this office to adjudicate.

This particular case is also significant in that Agency Counsel's representation to the effect that the unlicensed export of a sophisticated VAX 11/780 Computer which can be used in nuclear testing, to India via Singapore, appears to conflict with the Congressionally defined purpose for civil penalties. From the outset of their statutory authorization in 1962 civil penalties were to be imposed in minor matters not involving national security. Nuclear proliferation is hardly a matter outside national security interests. The emphasis on a substantial civil penalty with almost totally suspended revocation of export privileges, is an exceptional approach.

Nevertheless, there is a representation by Agency Counsel in the response to the Order to Show Cause which provides some support for approval of the $100,000 civil penalty. The comment "* * * that the settlement amount of $100,000 approximates the profit realized by the Respondents on the deal", provides such link. Taking the profit out of the transaction has been a legitimate consideration in arriving at civil penalty assessments, although it is usually a part of the criminal sanction when such process is present as it was here. With some residual concern that this may be a Pontius Pilate washing of the hands, I nevertheless approve and pass the matter to the delegated Secretarial official for final determination.[2]

ORDER

I. For a period of 5 years from the date of the final Agency action, Respondents:

Barin Nath Chatterjee, 72 rue Pierre Curie, 91420 Morangis, France, and,

2. A notice is being transmitted removing this office from the approval of settlements in these matters. Since no factual determination remains, there is no adjudication. Rather a policy determination, not within the limited statutory function of Administrative Law Judges appears to be involved.

Santosh K. Rateria, 105 Southern Avenue, Calcutta, India, and,

E. Erman, J.L. Pawiyaten No. 9, Surabaya, Indonesia,

individually and doing business as

Computech Ispat Limited and Computech International, 507 Jodhpur Park, Calcutta 68, India, 77/2A Hazra Road, 4th Floor, Calcutta, India

and all successors, assignees, officers, partners, representatives, agents, and employees hereby are denied all privileges of participating, directly or indirectly, in any manner or capacity, in any transaction involving commodities or technical data exported from the United States in whole or in part, or to be exported, or that are otherwise subject to [the Act] and the Regulations.

II. Commencing on the date of the final Agency action, the denial of export privileges set forth in Paragraph I, above, shall be suspended, in accordance with Section 788.16 of the Regulations, to each Respondent as follows:

Chatterjee—for a period of 4 years, 6 months beginning six months from the date of entry of this Order;

Rateria and Erman—for a period of 5 years beginning from the date of entry of this Order;

Computech Ispat Limited and Computech International—for a period of 4 years, 9 months beginning three months from the date of entry of this Order;

and shall thereafter be terminated, provided that Respondent has committed no further violation of the Act, the Regulations, or the final order in this proceeding; further, during the applicable suspension period, Computech Ispat Limited, the owner and operator of the computer that is the subject of the administrative proceedings, allows routine inspections of the computer by United States authorities on its premises in India, provided that such inspections do not disturb computer operations.

A civil penalty in the amount of $100,000 is assessed against Barin Nath Chatterjee. Chatterjee shall pay to the Agency the sum of $50,000 within 30 days of the date of the entry of this Order. Within one year after the date of entry of this Order, Chatterjee will make a second payment to the Agency of $50,000. Each payment shall be made in the manner specified in the attached instructions.

The charging letters, the Consent Agreement, and this Order shall be made available to the public. A copy of this Order shall be served upon each Respondent and published in the Federal Register.

III. Participation prohibited in any such transaction, either in the United States or abroad, shall include, but is not limited to, participation:

(i) As a party or as a representative of a party to a validated or general export license application;

(ii) In preparing or filing any export license application or request for reexport authorization, or any document to be submitted therewith;

(iii) In obtaining or using any validated or general export license or other export control document;

(iv) In carrying on negotiations with respect to, or in receiving, ordering, buying, selling, deliverying, storing, using, or disposing of, in whole or in part, any commodities or technical data exported from the United States, or to be exported; and

(v) In the financing, forwarding, transporting, or other servicing of such commodities or technical data.

Such denial of export privileges shall extend to those commodities and technical data which are subject to the Act and the Regulations.

IV. After notice and opportunity for comment, such denial of export privileges may be made applicable to any person, firm, corporation, or business organization with which the Respondent is now or hereafter may be related by affiliation, ownership, control, position of responsibility, or other connection in the conduct of trade or related services.

V. All outstanding individual validated export licenses in which Respondent(s) appears or participates, in any manner or capacity, are hereby revoked and shall be returned forthwith to the Office of Export Licensing for cancellation. Further, all of Respondents' privileges of participating, in any manner or capacity, in any special licensing procedure, including, but not limited to, distribution licenses, are hereby revoked.

VI. No person, firm, corporation, partnership, or other business organization, whether in the United States or elsewhere, without prior disclosure to and specific authorization from the Office of Export Licensing, shall, with respect to commodities and technical data, do any of the following acts, directly or indirectly, or carry on negotiations with respect thereto, in any manner or capacity, on behalf of or in any association with any Respondent or any related person, or whereby any Respondent or any related person may obtain any benefit therefrom or have any interest or participation therein, directly or indirectly;

(i) Apply for, obtain, transfer, or use any license, Shipper's Export Declaration, bill of lading, or other export control document relating to any export, reexport, transshipment, or diversion of any commodity or technical data exported in whole or in part, or to be exported by, to, or for any Respondent or related person denied export privileges, or

(ii) Order, buy, receive, use, sell, deliver, store, dispose of, forward, transport, finance or otherwise service or participate in any export, reexport, transshipment or diversion of any commodity or technical data exported or to be exported from the United States.

VII. This Order as affirmed or modified shall become effective upon entry of the Secretary's final action in this proceeding pursuant to the Act (50 U.S.C. app. 2412(c)(1)).

Dated: December 29, 1989.

Hugh J. Dolan,

Administrative Law Judge.

Chapter XIII

ANTITRUST CONSIDERATIONS

A. MONOPOLIZATION

The computer industry has witnessed a plethora of antitrust suits. The need for product compatibility helped companies keep and expand their market shares. The term "computer" frequently is used to refer to one unit, but in fact, a computer consists of interconnected components, all of which are necessary to process information. An understanding of the functions of these components shows why the computer industry has been a breeding ground for antitrust litigation. Companies can secretly develop new products that are compatible with their previous products, but incompatible with competitors' related products. For instance a large computer manufacturer could supply new computers with disk drive interfaces that worked only with its disk drives. When customers "upgrade" to such new products, competitors are cut out of competition to supply related products.

Developments during the 1980s drastically changed the nature of the computer market. Industry-wide standards are coming to dominate the computer industry. Computer magazines and data banks are providing information about detailed objective tests of competing products. Many companies compete in the markets for personal computers and work stations. The result is something much closer to the theoretical economist's perfect market than was the IBM-dominated computer industry of the 1960s and 1970s. Thus, we may see less antitrust litigation in the 1990s.

TELEX CORPORATION v. INTERNATIONAL BUSINESS MACHINES CORPORATION

United States Court of Appeals, Tenth Circuit, 1975.
510 F.2d 894, cert. dismissed 423 U.S. 802, 96 S.Ct. 8, 46 L.Ed.2d 244 (1975).

* * *

Telex has alleged in the complaint that IBM violated sections 1 and 2 of the Sherman Act, 15 U.S.C. §§ 1, 2, and section 2 of the Clayton

Act, 15 U.S.C. § 13, in that IBM had monopolized and attempted to monopolize the manufacture, distribution, sale, and leasing of electronic data processing equipment. The complaint was later amended to charge IBM in more specific terms with monopolization in the manufacture, distribution, sale, and leasing of plug compatible peripheral products which are attached to IBM central processing units.

* * *

A supplemental complaint was filed by Telex. This charged that IBM had violated section 2 of the Sherman Act by announcing its "Fixed Term Plan" and "Extended Term Plan" for the leasing of IBM equipment.

Still other supplemental claims were filed by Telex alleging other violations and seeking an injunction to prohibit IBM from integrating memory and disk control circuitry as well as from lowering its prices on memories.

The court in Minnesota issued a temporary restraining order enjoining IBM from announcing its new central processing units. However, this order was dissolved by the Court of Appeals for the Eighth Circuit. Following the completion of discovery, the instant case was remanded to the United States District Court for the Northern District of Oklahoma for trial.

* * *

VII.

Consideration of the Issues

1. The Relevant Market

The threshold issue is whether the court erred in its findings as to the scope and extent of the relevant product market for determination whether there existed power to control prices or to exclude competition, that is, whether there was monopoly power. As heretofore pointed out, the court determined that the relevant product market was limited to peripheral devices plug compatible with IBM central processing units together with particular product submarkets; magnetic tape products, direct access storage products, memory products, impact printer products and communication controllers, all of which were plug compatible with an IBM CPU. IBM had sought a determination that the relevant product market consisted of electronic data processing systems together with the products which are part of such systems or at least that the relevant product market should consist of all peripheral products and not be limited to those currently attached to IBM systems.

The trial court's initial approach to the problem was restricted to consideration of whether the market "may be realistically subdivided in the time frame 1969–1972 to focus on and encompass only those parts of current product lines which are respectively attached to IBM systems rather than all those products which actually have similar uses in connection with other systems." The court recognized that inasmuch as every manufacturer, originally at least, has 100 per cent of its own product, including the peripherals, the likelihood of finding monopolization in this area increases as the circumscribing products market is more circumscribed.

The trial court also recognized that the cost of adaptation of peripherals to the CPUs of other systems is roughly the same with respect to every system, that is, the cost of the interface, the attachment which allows the use of peripherals manufactured by one system to be used on another central processing unit is generally about the same. But these practical interchange possibilities did not deter the court in reaching a conclusion that the products market was practically restricted. A factor which influenced the trial court was the commitment of Telex to supplying peripherals plug compatible with IBM systems. The court appeared to disregard the interchangeability aspect of the peripherals manufactured by companies other than IBM, giving emphasis to the fact that Telex, for example, had not chosen to manufacture such peripheral products of the kind and character manufactured by companies other than IBM.[14] The trial court did, however, recognize the presence of interchangeability of use and the presence of cross-elasticity of demand. The court thought, however, that the presence of these factors were not sufficiently immediate.

We recognize that market definition is generally treated as a matter of fact and that findings on this subject are not to be overturned unless clearly erroneous. Our question is, therefore, whether it was clearly erroneous for the court to exclude peripheral products of systems other than IBM such as Honeywell, Univac, Burroughs, Control Data Corp. and others, together with peripheral products plug compatible with the systems and, indeed, whether the systems themselves manufactured by the companies are to be taken into account. It is significant, of course, that peripheral products constitute a large percentage of the entire data processing system, somewhere between 50 and 75 per cent.

14. Findings 52 and 53 are as follows:

"F52. The court finds that the peripheral devices plug compatible with the CPU's of IBM may be considered the relevant market for the purposes of this case, and that relevant submarkets existed for plug compatible tapes, disks, memories, and printers with their respective controllers, and communications controllers.

"F53. CPU's are not reasonably includable within this market and these submarkets, nor are software as such, but the peripheral equipment plug compatible to IBM CPU's which are separately leased by leasing companies to end-users are. Alternate sources of computer time such as service bureaus, time-sharing companies, data centers, users selling excess time and the like are not reasonably includable in the relevant market or submarkets with which we are concerned in this case, since their competitive relationships are tangential and indirect, and do not supply a real or substantial competitive force in the relevant markets mentioned. It is true that a large part of the competition in the industry takes place on a systems basis, but the relationship of this competition to the relevant markets with which we are concerned against is tangential and practically indiscernible. Certainly in another context the competition between systems manufacturers would constitute, or be a part of, a relevant market, but such relevant market is not material under the facts of this case since the competition involved here is not between systems manufacturers but between IBM and plug compatible manufacturers and suppliers.

Inasmuch as IBM's share of the data processing industry as a whole is insufficient to justify any inference or conclusion of market power [17] in IBM, the exclusion from the defined market of those products which are not plug compatible with IBM central processing units has a significant impact on the court's decision that IBM possessed monopoly power.

We then must inquire whether this market definition was correct in light of the following factors:

1. Should peripheral products not plug compatible with IBM systems be considered part of the relevant market in view of the existence of easy and practicable interchange of these products by use of interfaces designed for this purpose?

2. Should not the peripheral products plug compatible with systems other than IBM be considered part of the relevant market because of the admitted competition existing as between system manufacturers on a system by system basis in which the peripherals are a significant part of the system?

In dealing with the issue whether peripheral products non-compatible with IBM systems ought to be considered, the court said in Finding 47 that as a *practical* matter there is no direct competition between IBM peripherals and the peripherals of other systems manufacturers. However, this finding is out of harmony with other findings which the court made. *See,* for example, Finding 38, wherein the court said that "It cannot be gainsaid that indirectly at least and to some degree the peripheral products attached to non-IBM systems necessarily compete with and constrain IBM's power with respect to peripherals attached to IBM systems." The court also stated in Finding 38 that:

> "* * * [S]uppliers of peripherals plug compatible with non-IBM systems could in various instances shift to the production of IBM plug compatible peripherals, and vice versa, should the economic rewards in the realities of the market become sufficiently attractive and if predatory practices of others did not dissuade them. In the absence of defensive tactics on the part of manufacturers of CPU's, the cost of developing an interface for a peripheral device would generally be about the same regardless of the system to which it would be attached, and such cost has not constituted a substantial portion of the development cost of the peripheral device."

The factor of ease of designing interfaces to allow interchange of peripherals was obviously troublesome to the court and this trouble continued after the court had rendered its decision. He was still treating the issue on October 17, 1973, in the posttrial hearing. *See* Court Papers, 445–446. The court's final words on the subject were:

17. *See* Finding 61. For example, according to the U.S. Bureau of the Census figures, IBM's share of the value of 1971 equipment of "electronic computers and peripheral equipment, except parts," was only 36.7 per cent.

"I'm down to the edge lawn, and I think the best service I can do is to speed the matter to that final determination. If I'm wrong on my market definition, then you did what you had a right to do."

In essence, this witness said that the engineering costs of developing interfaces was minimal and that he had advocated modifying interfaces so that Telex products could be used with systems other than IBM. Another example of ease of interface design is shown by the fact that following RCA's decision to abandon the computer systems business and turn it over to Univac, Telex recognized a marketing opportunity and it began marketing its 6420 tape unit, the plug compatible equivalent of IBM's 3420 Aspen tape unit, as a plug compatible unit with RCA CPUs. The documents sought to emphasize the ease of use in the RCA system of this peripheral equipment designed for IBM equipment originally.

Still another exhibit in the record recognizing the practicability of interface change on peripheral equipment is a February 4, 1972, memorandum of R.M. Wheeler, Chairman of the Board of Telex, requesting a letter or his signature which could be sent to systems manufacturers. This letter was to be sent to systems manufacturers. It offered to sell peripheral equipment plug compatible with the central processing units of the manufacturers. Specific reference was made to the 6420 tape unit, among others, which would normally be compatible to IBM's central processing unit. The Wheeler letter stated that Telex would be willing to interface their equipment at no cost to the purchaser.

Manufacturers of peripherals were not limited to those which were plug compatible with IBM CPUs. These manufacturers were free to adapt their products through interface changes to plug into non-IBM systems. It also followed that systems manufacturers could modify interfaces so that their own peripheral products could plug into IBM CPUs. Factually, then, there existed peripheral products of other CPU manufacturers which were competitive with IBM peripherals and unquestionably other IBM peripherals were capable of having their interfaces modified so that their peripheral products would plug into non-IBM's CPU.

The fact that Telex had substantially devoted itself to the manufacture of peripheral products which were used in IBM CPUs and which competed with IBM peripheral products cannot control in determining product market since the legal standard is whether the product is reasonably interchangeable.

This standard was laid down by the Supreme Court in the famous case of *United States v. E.I. DuPont de Nemours & Co.*, 351 U.S. 377, 76 S.Ct. 994, 100 L.Ed. 1264 (1956). In this case, as in the case at bar, the scope of the products market was crucial. The Supreme Court determined that if one product may substitute for another in the market it is "reasonably interchangeable." It was applied there even though DuPont largely controlled the production of cellophane. It was held to be not guilty of monopolization simply because the relevant market included cellophane as well as other flexible wrapping materials. On this the Court stated:

> "[W]here there are market alternatives that buyers may readily use for their purposes, illegal monopoly does not exist merely because the product said to be monopolized differs from others. If it were not so, only physically identical products would be a part of the market." 351 U.S. at 394, 76 S.Ct. at 1006–1007.

One evidence of cross-elasticity is the responsiveness of sales of one product to price changes of another. But a finding of actual fungibility is not necessary to a conclusion that products have potential substitutability. In this respect the Court said:

> "Every manufacturer is the sole producer of the particular commodity it makes but its control in the above sense of the relevant market depends upon the availability of alternative commodities for buyers: i.e., whether there is a cross-elasticity of demand between cellophane and the other wrappings. This interchangeability is largely gauged by the purchase of competing products for similar uses considering the price, characteristics and adaptability of the competing commodities." 351 U.S. at 380, 76 S.Ct. at 999.

The Court's further rendition of examples clarified its ruling:

> "Determination of the competitive market for commodities depends on how different from one another are the offered commodities in character or use, how far buyers will go to substitute one commodity for another."

* * *

It is helpful to consider the rulings of lower courts based on the *DuPont* decision. An example is United States v. Charles Pfizer & Co., 246 F.Supp. 464 (D.C.N.Y.1965), where the court applied the ruling of *DuPont* that complete identity of use is not a prerequisite to a finding of interchangeability. The Government had argued that the defendant had a monopoly in the citric acid market. The record, however, disclosed that citric acid was in competition with lactic acid, tartaric acid, phosphoric acid and fumaric acid in its uses in the food and beverage industry. Since these different products were functionally interchangeable, the court decided that the relevant market included all such acidic products, and on that account the Government was held to have not proven that the relevant market was solely the citric acid market.

In still another case, Advance Business Systems & Supply Co. v. SCM Corp., 287 F.Supp. 143 (D.C.Md.1968), the plaintiff sought to establish that the relevant market was restricted to the paper used in SCM machines, but the court delineated the product market in much broader terms:

> "When SCM introduced its first machine it had a natural monopoly for a few months of the sale of paper and other supplies for use with that machine. But competition quickly developed for the sale of paper,

and by 1965 for replenisher. The evidence shows that SCM has attempted by various means to keep for itself the sale of paper for use in its own machines. If paper for use in SCM machines is a relevant market, which one may attempt to monopolize in violation of section 2 of the Sherman Act, SCM has made such an attempt. But the facts in this case do not show that the relevant market should be defined in such unrealistically narrow terms. The relevant submarket is the sale of coated *paper for use in SCM and other machines* which employ the direct electrostatic process." 287 F.Supp. at 153–154. (Emphasis added).

So here again the relevant product market included not only SCM's paper but also paper manufactured for use in other machines inasmuch as these products were reasonably interchangeable within the meaning of the *DuPont* case.

In South End Oil Co. v. Texaco, Inc., 237 F.Supp. 650 (D.C.Ill.1965), the court found that there was no monopolization and again on the basis that the product market as defined by the plaintiff was too limited. The court said that where commodities are competitive and reasonably interchangeable, the relevant market is not to be confined to the products of one manufacturer.

One of the most significant decisions of all is that of the Supreme Court in United States v. Grinnell Corp., 384 U.S. 563, 86 S.Ct. 1698, 16 L.Ed.2d 778 (1966). In the opinion of Mr. Justice Douglas who had dissented in *DuPont,* the *DuPont* case is cited approvingly. The opinion recognizes that substitute products are to be included within the definition of relevant market "since customers may turn to them if there is a slight increase in the price of the main product." 384 U.S. at 571, 86 S.Ct. at 1704. The relevant market in *Grinnell* was broadly defined and included the entire accredited central station service business involving such systems as automatic burglar alarms, automatic fire alarms, sprinkler supervisory service, and watch signal service. The basis for combining these various products was that all of them provided protection of property.

The consequences of the Court's holding are very clear; there can be no ruling of monopolization where the issue is judged on the basis of the entire market rather than a small segment of it. * * *

* * *

It seems clear that reasonable interchangeability is proven in the case at bar and hence the market should include not only peripheral products plug compatible with IBM CPUs, but all peripheral products, those compatible not only with IBM CPUs but those compatible with non-IBM systems. This is wholly justifiable because the record shows that these products, although not fungible, are fully interchangeable and may be interchanged with minimal financial outlay, and so cross-elasticity exists within meaning of the *DuPont* decision.

The court's very restrictive definition of the product market in the face of evidence which established the interchangeable quality of the products in question, together with the existence of cross-elasticity of demand, must be regarded as plain error.

* * *

2. *The "Acts" of IBM.*

If it be assumed that IBM had monopoly power during the period under consideration, which we do not decide, but the trial court so found, and further, that this position had been lawfully attained, also as the trial court found, were the changes in marketing methods under such conditions made by IBM lawful? The trial court found they were not. These changes were price reductions and leasing of equipment under fixed term leases and extended term leases.

* * *

It is necessary to briefly consider the characterization of the above considered marketing changes as "predatory" by the trial court. The term probably does not have a well-defined meaning in the context it was used, but it certainly bears a sinister connotation.

The "predatory" conclusion was expressed after the trial court had given extended consideration to the creation of "task forces" by IBM, and the direction of their attention and study to Telex especially and other corporations in the business. The consequences of repricing and the pricing of new products upon competitors was also considered by the trial court to have legal consequences adverse to IBM. The record demonstrates that these acts of IBM are again part of the competitive scene in this volatile business inhabited by aggressive, skillful businessmen seeking to market a product cheaper and better than that of their competitors. To do this, the record shows it was customary for them to study their competitors, all their capabilities, and what may be expected of them when a new product appears on the market. It is IBM's participation in this marketing that the trial court termed "predatory," but the record shows this was no more than engaging in the type of competition prevalent throughout the industry. It would not seem necessary to discuss this point at length as it is another manifestation of the conclusions the trial court derived from the "acts" which we have considered above. This aspect of the case is, for all practical purposes, governed by the opinion in Times–Picayune Pub. Co. v. United States, 345 U.S. 594, 73 S.Ct. 872, 97 L.Ed. 1277.

The "attempt to monopolize" aspect need not be separately considered.

* * *

Disposition of the Case

The judgment of the trial court against IBM must be reversed because it is based upon an erroneous determination of a fundamental element in the case. This element is the "market" as the term is used in the antitrust laws, and in which the competition, the market shares, the acts, and the identity of the competitors may be evaluated and compared. The trial court's definition of this "market" was in error as described above.

The judgment against IBM must also be reversed because, as stated above, the findings of fact as to the "acts" of IBM made by the trial court when evaluated under the Sherman Act and when set in the context of the prevailing court opinions do not constitute a violation of law.

* * *

B. VERTICAL RESTRAINTS

BUSINESS ELECTRONICS v. SHARP ELECTRONICS

United States Supreme Court, 1988.
485 U.S. 717, 108 S.Ct. 1515, 99 L.Ed.2d 808.

JUSTICE SCALIA delivered the opinion of the Court.

Petitioner Business Electronics Corporation seeks review of a decision of the United States Court of Appeals for the Fifth Circuit holding that a vertical restraint is *per se* illegal under § 1 of the Sherman Act, 26 Stat. 209, as amended, 15 U.S.C. § 1, only if there is an express or implied agreement to set resale prices at some level. 780 F.2d 1212, 1215–1218 (1986). We granted certiorari, 482 U.S. ___, 107 S.Ct. 3182, 96 L.Ed.2d 671 (1987), to resolve a conflict in the Courts of Appeals regarding the proper dividing line between the rule that vertical price restraints are illegal *per se* and the rule that vertical nonprice restraints are to be judged under the rule of reason.

I

In 1968, petitioner became the exclusive retailer in the Houston, Texas area of electronic calculators manufactured by respondent Sharp Electronics Corporation. In 1972, respondent appointed Gilbert Hartwell as a second retailer in the Houston area. During the relevant period, electronic calculators were primarily sold to business customers for prices up to $1000. While much of the evidence in this case was conflicting—in particular, concerning whether petitioner was "free riding" on Hartwell's provision of presale educational and promotional services by providing inadequate services itself—a few facts are undisputed. Respondent published a list of suggested minimum retail prices, but its written dealership agreements with petitioner and Hartwell did not obligate either to observe them, or to charge any other specific price. Petitioner's retail prices were often below respondent's suggested retail prices and generally below Hartwell's retail prices, even though Hartwell too sometimes priced below respondent's suggested retail prices. Hartwell complained to respondent on a number of occasions about petitioner's prices. In June 1973, Hartwell gave respondent the ultimatum that Hartwell would terminate his dealership unless respondent ended its relationship with petitioner within 30 days. Respondent terminated petitioner's dealership in July 1973.

Petitioner brought suit in the United States District Court for the Southern District of Texas, alleging that respondent and Hartwell had conspired to terminate petitioner and that such conspiracy was illegal *per se* under § 1 of the Sherman Act. The case was tried to a jury. The District Court submitted a liability interrogatory to the jury that asked whether "there was an agreement or understanding between Sharp Electronics Corporation and Hartwell to terminate Business Electronics as a Sharp dealer because of Business Electronics' price cutting." Record, Doc. No. 241. The District Court instructed the jury at length about this question:

> "The Sherman Act is violated when a seller enters into an agreement or understanding with one of its dealers to terminate another dealer because of the other dealer's price cutting. Plaintiff contends that Sharp terminated Business Electronics in furtherance of Hartwell's desire to eliminate Business Electronics as a price-cutting rival.
>
> "If you find that there was an agreement between Sharp and Hartwell to terminate Business Electronics because of Business Electronics' price cutting, you should answer yes to Question Number 1.
>
> * * *
>
> "A combination, agreement or understanding to terminate a dealer because of his price cutting unreasonably restrains trade and cannot be justified for any reason. Therefore, even though the combination, agreement or understanding may have been formed or engaged in . . . to eliminate any alleged evils of price cutting, it is still unlawful.
> * * *
>
> "If a dealer demands that a manufacturer terminate a price cutting dealer, and the manufacturer agrees to do so, the agreement is illegal if the manufacturer's purpose is to eliminate the price cutting." App. 18–19.

The jury answered Question 1 affirmatively and awarded $600,000 in damages. The District Court * * * entered judgment for petitioner for treble damages plus attorney's fees.

The Fifth Circuit reversed, holding that the jury interrogatory and instructions were erroneous, and remanded for a new trial. It held that, to render illegal *per se* a vertical agreement between a manufacturer and a dealer to terminate a second dealer, the first dealer "must expressly or impliedly agree to set its prices at some level, though not a specific one. The distributor cannot retain complete freedom to set whatever price it chooses." 780 F.2d, at 1218.

II

A

Section 1 of the Sherman Act provides that "[e]very contract, combination in the form of trust or otherwise, or conspiracy, in restraint of trade or commerce among the several States, or with foreign nations, is declared to be illegal." 15 U.S.C. § 1. Since the earliest decisions of this Court interpreting this provision, we have recognized that it was intended to prohibit only unreasonable restraints of trade. Ordinarily, whether particular concerted action violates § 1 of the Sherman Act is determined through case-by-case application of the so-called rule of reason—that is, "the factfinder weighs all of the circumstances of a case in deciding whether a restrictive practice should be prohibited as imposing an unreasonable restraint on competition." *Continental T.V., Inc. v. GTE Sylvania Inc.,* 433 U.S. 36, 49, 97 S.Ct. 2549, 2557, 53 L.Ed.2d 568 (1977). Certain categories of agreements, however, have been held to be *per se* illegal, dispensing with the need for case-by-case evaluation. We have said that *per se* rules are appropriate only for "conduct that is manifestly anticompetitive," *id.,* at 50, 97 S.Ct., at 2557, that is, conduct " 'that would always or almost always tend to restrict competition and decrease output.' "

Although vertical agreements on resale prices have been illegal *per se* since *Dr. Miles Medical Co. v. John D. Park & Sons Co.,* 220 U.S. 373, 31 S.Ct. 376, 55 L.Ed. 502 (1911), we have recognized that the scope of *per se* illegality should be narrow in the context of vertical restraints. In *Continental T.V., Inc. v. GTE Sylvania Inc., supra,* we refused to extend *per se* illegality to vertical nonprice restraints, specifically to a manufacturer's termination of one dealer pursuant to an exclusive territory agreement with another. We noted that especially in the vertical restraint context "departure from the rule-of-reason standard must be based on demonstrable economic effect rather than * * * upon formalistic line drawing." We concluded that vertical nonprice restraints had not been shown to have such a " 'pernicious effect on competition' " and to be so " 'lack[ing] [in] * * * redeeming value' " as to justify *per se* illegality. Rather, we found, they had real potential to stimulate interbrand competition, "the primary concern of antitrust law".

* * *

Moreover, we observed that a rule of *per se* illegality for vertical nonprice restraints was not needed or effective to protect *intra* brand competition. First, so long as interbrand competition existed, that would provide a "significant check" on any attempt to exploit intrabrand market power. In fact, in order to meet that interbrand competition, a manufacturer's dominant incentive is to lower resale prices. *Id.,* at 56, and n. 24, 97 S.Ct., at 2560 and n. 24. Second, the *per se* illegality of vertical restraints would create a perverse incentive for manufacturers to integrate vertically into distribution, an outcome hardly conducive to fostering the creation and maintenance of small businesses.

Finally, our opinion in *GTE Sylvania* noted a significant distinction between vertical nonprice and vertical price restraints. That is, there was support for the proposition that vertical price restraints reduce *inter* brand price competition because they " 'facilitate cartelizing.' " The authorities cited by the Court suggested how vertical price agreements might assist horizontal price fixing at the manufacturer level (by reducing the manufacturer's incentive to cheat on a cartel, since its retailers could not pass on lower prices to consumers) or might be used to organize cartels at the retailer level. Similar support for the cartel-facilitating effect of vertical non-price restraints was and remains lacking.

We have been solicitous to assure that the market-freeing effect of our decision in *GTE Sylvania* is not frustrated by related legal rules. In *Monsanto Co. v. Spray–Rite Service Corp.,* 465 U.S. 752, 763, 104 S.Ct. 1464, 1470, 79 L.Ed.2d 775 (1984), which addressed the evidentiary showing necessary to establish vertical concerted action, we expressed concern that "[i]f an inference of such an agreement may be drawn from highly ambiguous evidence, there is considerable danger that the doctrin[e] enunciated in *Sylvania* * * * will be seriously eroded." We eschewed adoption of an evidentiary standard that "could deter or penalize perfectly legitimate conduct" or "would create an irrational dislocation in the market" by preventing legitimate communication between a manufacturer and its distributors.

Our approach to the question presented in the present case is guided by the premises of *GTE Sylvania* and *Monsanto:* that there is a presumption in favor of a rule-of-reason standard; that departure from that standard must be justified by demonstrable economic effect, such as the facilitation of cartelizing, rather than formalistic distinctions; that interbrand competition is the primary concern of the antitrust laws; and that rules in this area should be formulated with a view towards protecting the doctrine of *GTE Sylvania.* These premises lead us to conclude that the line drawn by the Fifth Circuit is the most appropriate one.

There has been no showing here that an agreement between a manufacturer and a dealer to terminate a "price cutter," without a further agreement on the price or price levels to be charged by the remaining dealer, almost always tends to restrict competition and reduce output. Any assistance to cartelizing that such an agreement might provide cannot be distinguished from the sort of minimal assistance that might be provided by vertical nonprice agreements like the exclusive territory agreement in *GTE Sylvania,* and is insufficient to justify a *per se* rule. Cartels are neither easy to form nor easy to maintain. Uncertainty over the terms of the cartel, particularly the prices to be charged in the future, obstructs both formation and adherence by making cheating easier. Without an agreement with the remaining dealer on price, the manufacturer both retains its incentive to cheat on any manufacturer-level cartel (since lower prices can still be passed on to consumers) and cannot as easily be used to organize and hold together a retailer-level cartel.

The District Court's rule on the scope of *per se* illegality for vertical restraints would threaten to dismantle the doctrine of *GTE Sylvania.* Any agreement between a manufacturer and a dealer to terminate another dealer who happens to have charged lower prices can be alleged to have been directed against the terminated dealer's "price cutting." In the vast majority of cases, it will be extremely difficult for the manufacturer to convince a jury that its motivation was to ensure adequate services, since price cutting and some measure of service cutting usually go hand in hand. Accordingly, a manufacturer that agrees to give one dealer an exclusive territory and terminates another dealer pursuant to that agreement, or even a manufacturer that agrees with one dealer to terminate another for failure to provide contractually-obligated services, exposes itself to the highly plausible claim that its real motivation was to terminate a price cutter. Moreover, even vertical restraints that do not result in dealer termination, such as the initial granting of an exclusive territory or the requirement that certain services be provided, can be attacked as designed to allow existing dealers to charge higher prices. Manufacturers would be likely to forgo legitimate and competitively useful conduct rather than risk treble damages and perhaps even criminal penalties.

We cannot avoid this difficulty by invalidating as illegal *per se* only those agreements imposing vertical restraints that contain the word "price," or that affect the "prices" charged by dealers. Such formalism was explicitly rejected in *GTE Sylvania.* As the above discussion indicates, all vertical restraints, including the exclusive territory agreement held not to be *per se* illegal in *GTE Sylvania,* have the potential to allow dealers to increase "prices" and can be characterized as intended to achieve just that. In fact, vertical nonprice restraints only accomplish the benefits identified in *GTE Sylvania* because they reduce intrabrand price competition to the point where the dealer's profit margin permits provision of the desired services. As we described it in *Monsanto:* "The manufacturer often will want to ensure that its distributors earn sufficient profit to pay for programs such as hiring and training additional salesmen or demonstrating the technical features of the product, and will want to see that 'free-riders' do not interfere."

* * *

Finally, we do not agree with petitioner's contention that an agreement on the remaining dealer's price or price levels will so often follow from terminating another dealer "because of [its] price cutting" that prophylaxis against resale price maintenance warrants the District Court's *per se* rule. Petitioner has provided no support for the proposition that vertical price agreements generally underlie agreements to terminate a price cutter. That proposition is simply incompatible with the conclusion of *GTE Sylvania* and *Monsanto* that manufacturers are often motivated by a legitimate desire to have dealers provide services, combined with the reality that price cutting is frequently made possible by "free riding" on the services provided by other dealers. The District Court's *per se* rule would therefore discourage conduct recognized by *GTE Sylvania* and *Monsanto* as beneficial to consumers.

B

In resting our decision upon the foregoing economic analysis, we do not ignore common-law precedent concerning what constituted "restraint of trade" at the time the Sherman Act was adopted. But neither do we give that pre–1890 precedent the dispositive effect some would. The term "restraint of trade" in the statute, like the term at common law, refers not to a particular list of agreements, but to a particular economic consequence, which may be produced by quite different sorts of agreements in varying times and circumstances. The changing content of the term "restraint of trade" was well recognized at the time the Sherman Act was enacted.

The Sherman Act adopted the term "restraint of trade" along with its dynamic potential. It invokes the common law itself, and not merely the static content that the common law had assigned to the term in 1890. * * * If it were otherwise, not only would the line of *per se* illegality have to be drawn today precisely where it was in 1890, but also case-by-case evaluation of legality (conducted where *per se* rules do not apply) would have to be governed by 19th–century notions of reasonableness. It would make no sense to create out of the single term "restraint of trade" a chronologically schizoid statute, in which a "rule of reason" evolves with new circumstances and new wisdom, but a line of *per se* illegality remains forever fixed where it was.

Of course the common law, both in general and as embodied in the Sherman Act, does not lightly assume that the economic realities underlying earlier decisions have changed, or that earlier judicial perceptions of those realities were in error. It is relevant, therefore, whether the common law of restraint of trade ever prohibited as illegal *per se* an agreement of the sort made here, and whether our decisions under § 1 of the Sherman Act have ever expressed or necessarily implied such a prohibition.

With respect to this Court's understanding of pre-Sherman Act common law, petitioner refers to our decision in *Dr. Miles Medical Co. v. John D. Park & Sons Co., supra.* Though that was an early Sherman Act case, its holding that a resale price maintenance agreement was *per se* illegal was based largely on the perception that such an agreement was categorically impermissible at common law. As the opinion made plain, however, the basis for that common-law judgment was that the resale restriction was an unlawful restraint on alienation. * * * "*Dr. Miles* * * * decided that under the general law the owner of movables ... could not sell the movables and lawfully by contract fix a price at which the product should afterwards be sold, because to do so would be at one and the same time to sell and retain, to part with and yet to hold, to project the will of the seller so as to cause it to control the movable parted with when it was not subject to his will because owned by another." In the present case, of course, no agreement on resale price or price level, and hence no restraint on alienation, was found by the jury, so the common-law rationale of *Dr. Miles* does not apply.

Petitioner's principal contention has been that the District Court's rule on *per se* illegality is compelled not by the old common law, but by our more recent Sherman Act precedents. First, petitioner contends that since certain horizontal agreements have been held to constitute price fixing (and thus to be *per se* illegal) though they did not set prices or price levels, see, *e.g., Catalano, Inc. v. Target Sales, Inc.,* 446 U.S. 643, 647–650, 100 S.Ct. 1925, 1927–29, 64 L.Ed.2d 580 (1980) (*per curiam*), it is improper to require that a vertical agreement set prices or price levels before it can suffer the same fate. This notion of equivalence between the scope of horizontal *per se* illegality and that of vertical *per se* illegality was explicitly rejected in *GTE Sylvania,* as it had to be, since a horizontal agreement to divide territories is *per se* illegal, held that a vertical agreement to do so is not.

Second, petitioner contends that *per se* illegality here follows from our two cases holding *per se* illegal a group boycott of a dealer because of its price cutting. This second contention is merely a restatement of the first, since both cases involved horizontal combinations. * * *

Third, petitioner contends, relying on *Albrecht v. Herald Co.,* 390 U.S. 145, 88 S.Ct. 869, 19 L.Ed.2d 998 (1968), and *United States v. Parke, Davis & Co.,* 362 U.S. 29, 80 S.Ct. 503, 4 L.Ed.2d 505 (1960), that our vertical price-fixing cases have already rejected the proposition that *per se* illegality requires setting a price or a price level. We disagree. In *Albrecht,* the maker of the product formed a combination to force a retailer to charge the maker's advertised retail price. This combination had two aspects. Initially, the maker hired a third party to solicit customers away from the noncomplying retailer. This solicitor "was aware that the aim of the solicitation campaign was to force [the noncomplying retailer] to lower his price" to the suggested retail price. Next, the maker engaged another retailer who "undertook to deliver [products] at the suggested price" to the noncomplying retailer's customers obtained by the solicitor. *Ibid.* This combination of maker, solicitor, and new retailer was held to be *per se* illegal. It is plain that the combination involved both an explicit agreement on resale price and an agreement to force another to adhere to the specified price.

In *Parke, Davis,* a manufacturer combined first with wholesalers and then with retailers in order to gain "the retailers' adherence to its suggested minimum retail prices." The manufacturer also brokered an agreement among its retailers not to advertise prices below its suggested retail prices, which agreement was held to be part of the *per se* illegal combination. This holding also does not support a rule that an agreement on price or price level is not required for a vertical restraint to be *per se* illegal—first, because the agreement not to advertise prices was part and parcel of the combination that contained the price agreement, *id.,* at 35–36, 80 S.Ct., at 507, and second because the agreement among retailers that the manufacturer organized was a *horizontal* conspiracy among competitors.

* * *

In sum, economic analysis supports the view, and no precedent opposes it, that a vertical restraint is not illegal *per se* unless it includes some agreement on price or price levels. Accordingly, the judgment of the Fifth Circuit is affirmed.

* * *

Note

Note that in *Sharp* the Court required direct evidence of an agreement between manufacturer/developer and remaining distributor to raise prices, for the terminated distributor to succeed in a Section 1 complaint.

C. HORIZONTAL RESTRAINTS

Successful operation of a price-fixing cartel in any industry requires regular communication of price information among members of the cartel and "punishment" for "cheaters" who undercut cartel prices. Government investigators can detect such communications more easily than intra-firm communications. Therefore, government antitrust enforcers often focus on such communications. In the past conspirators talked by telephone or met in smoke-filled rooms. Today they may communicate by computer. See Edwin McDowell, "9 Airlines Face Suit on Prices," *New York Times*, August 8, 1991, p. C1; Asra Q. Nomani, "Fare Game: Airlines May Be Using a Price-Data Network to Lessen Competition; Coding of Tariffs/Can Tell Rivals of One's Intentions; U.S. Begins Investigation; Signaling an Attack on a Hub," *Wall Street Journal,* June 28, 1990, p. 1, col. 6.

D. TIE–INS

INNOVATION DATA PROCESSING, INC. v. INTERNATIONAL BUSINESS MACHINES CORP.

United States District Court, District of New Jersey, 1984.
585 F.Supp. 1470.

HAROLD A. ACKERMAN, DISTRICT JUDGE.

This is an antitrust action commenced by plaintiff Innovation Data Processing, Inc. (Innovation) on April 22, 1983. On that date, Innovation filed its complaint accompanied by an order to show cause seeking to enjoin defendant International Business Machine Corporation (IBM) from marketing and shipping to its customers a new piece of computer software called Multiple Virtual System/System Product System Installation Productivity Option Release 3.8J ("IPO"J" "). In its complaint, plaintiff Innovation alleges that IPO"J" constitutes a "tie-in" in violation of Section 1 of the Sherman Act, 15 U.S.C. Section 1, and Section 3 of the Clayton Act, 15 U.S.C. Section 14. Innovation asserts that the "tying" product is the IPO"J," and the "tie-in" product is an IBM software program product known as Data Facilities Data Set Services (DFDSS or Data Set Services program). Innovation claims that the alleged tie was implemented by IBM for the purpose of impeding

Innovation's ability to market its own program product, called Fast Dump Restore, (FDR) which competes with IBM's DFDSS program.

Plaintiff's application for a temporary restraining order was heard by my colleague, Judge Sarokin, on April 26, 1983. After hearing oral argument on the application, Judge Sarokin denied the requested relief, ruling in part as follows: "Insofar as the application for a temporary restraining order is concerned, pending a hearing on the preliminary injunction I am going to deny that application. I cannot, based on what is presently before me, conclude that the plaintiff has a likelihood of success on the merits. There is a serious question in my mind, and I think it is evidenced in the discussion we have had—we have all had today, as to whether or not this is indeed a condition imposed by IBM, or whether as (IBM counsel) Mr. Mullen just suggested, that customers are acquiring this license out of choice because they find it to be essential and beneficial to their own operations. But I cannot possibly resolve that factual issue on the record that is now before me.

"I am satisfied that in this interim period, assuming that within a month or possibly two months, at the most, I'll be able to resolve the matter, that plaintiff is not entitled to injunctive relief on the ground that it can prove irreparable injury. There is no substantial evidence before me of any irreparable injury * * * "

Following this ruling, the parties commenced discovery of each other in anticipation of a hearing on plaintiff's motion for a preliminary injunction. No such hearing was held, however, because after taking all of the discovery it had requested from IBM, plaintiff voluntarily withdrew its motion for a preliminary injunction on April 30, 1983. This matter is presently before me on plaintiff's motion to strike defendant IBM's third affirmative defense of release, and defendant IBM's motion for summary judgment.

I turn first to consider IBM's summary judgment motion. Rule 56 of the Federal Rules of Civil Procedure provides that summary judgment is not to be granted unless after all reasonable inferences have been drawn in favor of the non-moving party, there is no genuine issue of material fact, and the moving party is entitled to judgment as a matter of law. *See DeLong Corp. v. Raymond International,* 622 F.2d 1135 (3d Cir.1980). On a motion for summary judgment supported by affidavits and depositions, "an adverse party may not rest upon the mere allegations or denials, of his pleadings, but must set forth specific facts showing that there is a genuine issue for trial." *First National Bank of Arizona v. Cities Service Co.,* 391 U.S. 253 at 288, 88 S.Ct. 1575 at 1592, 20 L.Ed.2d 569 (1968). While "summary procedures should be used sparingly in complex anti-trust litigation," *Poller v. Columbia Broadcasting System,* 368 U.S. 464, 473, 82 S.Ct. 486, 491, 7 L.Ed.2d 458 (1962), this does not rule out the granting of a Rule 56 motion under appropriate circumstances. * * *

Applying these standards to the matter before me I have determined to grant IBM's motion for summary judgment as, the plaintiff's per se tying claim, but to deny it as to the plaintiff's claim that the general standards of the Acts have been violated.

The undisputed facts relevant to this motion are as follows: IBM produces and markets a wide range of computer products, including hardware, such as central processing units and disk and tape storage devices and software, such as operating system programs. It is the latter that is involved in this action.

An "operating system" is a set of computer programs which guide and control the basic function of a computer. These operating system programs also provide the necessary link between the physical "hardware" and the various applications programs "software", designed to perform specific tasks, such as accounting, word-processing, payroll or even video games.

The IBM operating system involved in this lawsuit is called the Multiple Virtual System, or "MVS," and is IBM's largest and most complex system of operating system programs. It is designed for use with very large or "high-end" IBM or IBM plug-compatible (PCM) computers, and the various programs which together constitute the MVS. The MVS collectively contain more than five million lines of computer instructions. IBM does not license MVS or any other operating system, at a single-price, aggregated fee. Rather, a customer must separately license the various separate underlying operating system programs which would together make up that particular user's MVS.

It is undisputed that IBM's customers are not required to license all or any particular combination of these programs. Instead, they may choose to license any one or more of them at their option, and may even order operating system programs designed by IBM competitors in place of, or in addition to, IBM's programs. Plaintiff Innovation's FDR offering and its optional enhancement COMPAKTOR and Automatic Backup and Recovery constitute such an alternative or supplemental program.

The specific operating system program at issue in this case is IBM's competitive equivalent to the FDR, the DFDSS program, which was introduced in 1980. Both DFDSS and FDR are known as "dump-restore" programs, which enable a computer user to transfer information to (the "dump" function) and from (the "restore" function) computer disks and tapes. DFDSS is also capable of the process of loading other MVS operating system programs into a computer system for the first time.

This process, along with that of loading new or revised versions of MVS into a computer program is very complex and delicate. Generally, such installation entails the transfer of the MVS programs from the source computer tapes on to data storage disks, which are housed within the user's computers system in storage devices known as disk drives. In the past, defendant IBM has supplied its customers with an operating system for which IBM did not charge and which could be used in that installation process.

More recently, IBM customers were given the option of licensing from IBM at a fee the DFDSS program which represented an improvement over the program which IBM had provided at no fee, or of licensing at a fee some other version of an IBM dump/restore program to perform the "restore" function necessary to install MVS.

IBM produces improvements to existing operating system installation programs at irregular intervals which have historically been about 6 to 18 months. These improvements have been marketed to users since 1976 as Installation Productivity Options, or "IPO"s, and consist of optionally available packages of basic operating system programs and detailed sets of written in instructions.

IBM has offered about 61 IPO's for various operating systems, including 17 for MVS. At the time this suit was commenced, IBM's newest and most advanced MVS Installation Productivity Option was IPO"J", which became generally available on April 19, 1983. As with former Installation Productivity Options, IPO"J", was and is available in two packaged formats; an "integrated" format and a "segmented" format. The integrated version consists of a preselected group of components that correspond to an underlying group of operating system programs. The integrated IPO"J" was denied to facilitate the installation of the MVS operating system, and the "dramatic" time efficiencies achieved through its use in this regard have saved IBM itself an estimated 13 and $15 million, or roughly 200 employee years in labor which would otherwise have been expended in installing MVS.

Among the changes which IBM instituted was the introduction of IPO"J" was in the formatting of computer instructions and data on the computer tape which the user would receive from IBM for transfer or "loading" onto the user's computer disk. Prior to the introduction of IPO"J", IBM had offered users the choice or ability to load earlier IPO's onto disks through the use of other formats such as IEHDASDR (IBM's cost-free dump and restore computer program) or another such program, IEBCOPY. With the release of IPO"J" IBM instituted a change of format which now requires new users to license IBM's DFDSS program for which a fee is charged in order to load the system. IEHDASDR and IEBCOPY may no longer be used to achieve this function. As a further aspect of this change, IBM has chosen to incorporate into the integrated version of IPO"J" the DFDSS program which such new customers must use for the load function. The DFDSS program is, as I have previously stated, the allegedly "tied" product in this case.

The loading function of dump/restore programs such as IBM's DFDSS program, and Innovation's FDR is only a very small part of the installation of an IPO. Innovation's FDR in fact has never been able to load an IPO tape. The real importance of a dump/restore program lies in its ability to "back up" data which is located on disks to magnetic tape, and in recovering the information when necessary. These two functions are a critical part of the operation of a computer center, since such back up copies of data and programs are needed as security for such disasters as fire, flood and equipment failure and accidental erasure. In the past, Innovation has depended upon receiving orders from FDR after customers had restored their computer systems, given that FDR is not offered by the computer manufacturers to purchasers of larger IBM and IBM-compatable computers. These purchasers would have the freedom to use, as I have indicated, IBM's free dump/restore program which is IEHDASDR, or they could obtain a license for a priced program to accomplish that task such as IBM's DFDSS program, or Innovation's FDR, by requiring new customers to license DFDSS to load new IPO's. Plaintiff contends that IBM has eliminated this freedom of choice as a practical matter forcing the customer to hold onto the DFDSS program. And use it as a dump/restore program in anticipation of the need to use it to load future IPO's and to avoid the technical and administrative problems associated with a decision to license a competing product such as Innovation's FDR.

Plaintiff thus argues that IBM's inclusion of the DFDSS program in the integrated IPO format constitutes a per se tying arrangement and a violation of the Sherman and Clayton Acts.

IBM responds by stating that it added the DFDSS program to the integrated IPO"J" for several legitimate business and technological reasons. First, many IBM customers had reportedly indicated that they wanted the program to be incorporated into any new Installation Productivity Option offering. Second, it is undisputed that, at present, the DFDSS is the only program product available from any source which is technologically capable of loading the MVS operating system from tape onto IBM's technologically-advanced model 3375 disk drives without the assistance of a pre-existing operating system. While plaintiff's expert John Iannantuoni disputes the underlying technical rationale or basis for this fact, and suggests that as an alternative IBM could have modified its other dump/restore programs such as IEHDASDR or IEBCOPY to be able to work with the model 3375's, the fact remains that IBM has not chosen to do so—nor, of course, has plaintiff chosen to modify FDR so as to be able to perform the load function for these or about other disk drives.

Finally, DFDSS is the only currently maintained dump/restore program capable of loading the integrated IPO"J" into *any* disk drive without the assistance of a pre-existing operating system—although this, of course, is the result of a format decision by IBM. Which plaintiff might characterize as self-serving.

The IPO"J" is also available in a segmented version, which is composed, at the customer's option, of various components of the integrated version. A segmented IPO"J" may or may not include the DFDSS program, depending on the customer's choice. While the integrated version of IPO"J" is particularly suited to new users of MVS, who do not yet have an MVS operating system, "up" and functioning in their computer systems, the segmented version is more suited for existing users of MVS who may wish to use only specific components of IPO"J" or who may wish to install only certain new programs. In either version, the customer does not pay for or license the IPO"J" materials as such, but must separately license the underlying programs selected.

I note that if a customer orders either the integrated version of IPO"J" or includes that DFDSS program as part of the segmented version, he or she may cancel the DFDSS program license at any time. If this cancellation occurs within 30 days, the customer incurs no charge for the license. If the cancellation occurs later we understand there is, as of April there is a $67.00 per month charge.

Thus, it is possible for a customer to order the integrated IPO"J" and use the DFDSS program only to provide the installation or loading function and thereafter cancel the DFDSS license—even achieving that load function for free if the cancellation is within the 30-day period.

IBM points to its undisputed marketing experience record to highlight the nonillusory nature of these options which are offered to its customers. Through the end of 1983, 781 customers in the United States had ordered and received IPO"J". New MVS users ordering the integrated version accounted for 227 of that total. Of the remainder, 304 users order the integrated version and 250 ordered a segmented version. Of that 250, roughly half ordered a segment that did not include the DFDSS program. Thus, while nearly 85 percent of these orders included the DFDSS program, the option to exclude it was exercised by some. Defendant IBM thus contends there is no tying arrangement in these circumstances and that it has not violated the Sherman or Clayton Acts.

To prove a per se illegal tie-in, a plaintiff must establish three distinct elements: "First, he must establish that the conduct in question was a tie-in: 'an agreement by a party to sell one product but only on the condition that the buyer also purchases a different (or tied) product'. *Northern Pacific Railway v. United States,* 356 U.S. 1, 5, 78 S.Ct. 514, 518, 2 L.Ed.2d 545 (1958). Second, he must establish that the seller 'has sufficient economic power with respect to the tying product to appreciably restrain free competition in the market for the tied product.' See Page 6, page 518, 78 S.Ct. of the Northern Pacific decision. Third, he must establish that 'a "not insubstantial" amount of interstate commerce is affected'." * * *

The Supreme Court in the *Northern Pacific Railway* case which was referred to by Judge Aldisert in Dunkin' Donuts as "perhaps the fountainhead of tying law under Section 1 of the Sherman Act," explained the marketplace rationale for forbidding tying arrangements. The Court stated that where such arrangements "are successfully and exacted, competition on the merits with respect to the tied product is inevitably curbed.... They deny competitor's free access to the market for the tied product, not because the party imposing the tying requirements has a better product or a lower price, but because of his power or leverage in another market. At the same time buyers are forced to forego their free choice between competing products." See *Northern Pacific Railway v. United States,* 356 U.S. at Pages 5 and 6, 78 S.Ct. at Page 518. Finally, as Justice Black noted in the *Northern Pacific* case, "(*o*)f course where the buyer is free to take either product by itself, there is no tying problem even though the seller may also offer the two items as a unit at a single price." 356 U.S., page 6 at note 4, 78 S.Ct., page 518 at note 4.

I conclude that here IBM customers are for the purposes of the Sherman and Clayton Acts free to take either the DFDSS program or the IPO"J" by itself and that on this basics alone there is no illegal tying arrangement. Three uncontradicted facts confirm this conclusion. First, any IBM customer is free to license the DFDSS program at any time by itself. Second, any IBM customer can order IPO"J" in a segmented version which does not include the DFDSS program. And, third, any IBM customer who orders the DFDSS program, whether by itself or together with either a segmented or integrated version of IPO"J", is free to cancel the license for the program at any time, paying the license fee only for the period of usage. While plaintiff argues that users may be dissuaded from such a cancellation by the technical and administrative burdens associated therewith, it admits that the terms and procedure for such a cancellation are the same as those for any other IBM license. Thus, as a matter of law, in the absence of evidence that the purchase of the alleged tied product was required as a condition of sale of the alleged tying product—rather than merely as a prerequisite for practical and effective use of the tying product—Innovation has failed to show the requisite coercion necessary to establish a per se illegal tying arrangement.

There is, in addition, another basis for granting IBM's motion for summary judgment as to plaintiff's per se tying claim, and that is that the integrated IPO"J" rather than constituting an illegal tying arrangement, instead constitutes—on this undisputed record—a lawful package of technologically interrelated components. Even if the components of IPO"J" were not priced separately and available individually, there would still be no unlawful "tie." As the Ninth Circuit has stated, "it is not an unlawful tying arrangement for a seller to include several items in a single mandatory package when the items may be reasonably considered to constitute parts of a single distinct product." See *International Manufacturing Company v. Landon, Inc.,* 336 F.2d 723 at 730 (9th Cir.1964). Further, as Judge Wallace has recently stated, "as a general rule * * * we hold that the development in introduction of a system of technologically interrelated products is not sufficient alone to establish a per se unlawful tying arrangement even if the new products are incompatable with the products then offered by the competition and effective use of any one of the new products necessitates purchase of some or all of the others." See *Foremost Pro Color v. Eastman Kodak, Inc.,* 703 F.2d at pages 542 and 43.

IBM has sufficient justification to offer the DFDSS program as part of the integrated Installation Productivity Option "J". In addition, to the reported sentiments or preferences of its customers, the DFDSS program is the only IBM dump/restore program that is currently capable of loading an integrated format tape onto a disk without the assistance of a pre-existing operating system, typical of the situation facing a new MVS customer, and it is admittedly the only program available anywhere which can thus load an IBM model 3375 disk drive absent a pre-existing operating system. Under these circumstances IBM would have been justified in offering only an integrated version of IPO"J"—as a single product and at a single price.

Thus, because IBM, under these circumstances, could have properly chosen to offer IPO"J" without giving its customers the option of licensing its components separately, it is clear that IBM's actual conduct here cannot constitute an unlawful tying arrangement. For both this reason and because of the lack of any legally sufficient showing of coercion, I conclude that plaintiff has failed to demonstrate the existence of a per se unlawful tying arrangement. I will therefore grant defendant's motion for summary judgment as to this claim.

Plaintiff, however notes that even if it fails on its *per se* illegal tying arrangement theory, it must still be entitled to proceed under its claim that defendant IBM's practices violate the general standards of the Sherman and Clayton Acts. As Justice Black noted in *Fortner Enterprises v. U.S. Steel,* 394 U.S. 495 at page 500, 89 S.Ct. 1252 at page 1257, 22 L.Ed.2d 495 (1959), (Fortner) "(a) plaintiff can still prevail on the merits (if it) can prove, on the basis of a more thorough examination of the purposes and effects of the practices involved, that the general standards of the Sherman Act have been violated." The standards guiding such an inquiry are, of course, known as the "rule of reason." *U.S. Steel Corp. v. Fortner Enterprises,* 429 U.S. 610 at 612 note 1, 97 S.Ct. 861 at 863–64 note 1, 51 L.Ed.2d 80 (1977) (Fortner II). This more generalized claim presents genuine issues of material fact which preclude my granting summary judgment at this time. These issues include *inter alia* defendant IBM's intent, motive or purpose in linking the DFDSS program to the IPO"J"; its practical effect on competition; its practical effect both beneficial and detrimental—in use by customers and the nature and circumstances of the business the parties are engaged in.

Therefore, I must deny defendant's motion for summary judgment as to plaintiff's claim that defendant IBM violated the general rule of reason standards in introducing the integrated version of IPO"J" which included the DFDSS program as one of its components.

* * *

In sum, I have determined to grant a partial—defendant a partial summary judgment as to plaintiff's *per se* tying claim but to deny summary judgment as to plaintiff's general "rule of reason" claims. I have also decided to grant plaintiff's motion to strike IBM's Third Affirmative Defense of release.

DIGIDYNE CORP. v. DATA GENERAL CORP.

United States Court of Appeals, Ninth Circuit, 1984.
734 F.2d 1336.

BROWNING, CHIEF JUDGE:

The issue presented for review is whether Data General's refusal to license its NOVA operating system software except to purchasers of its NOVA central processing units (CPUs) is an unlawful tying arrangement under section 1 of the Sherman Act, 15 U.S.C. § 1 (1976) and section 3 of the Clayton Act, 15 U.S.C. § 14 (1976). We conclude that it is.

I.

Defendant Data General manufactures a computer system known as NOVA. The system consists of a NOVA CPU designed to perform a particular "instruction set" or group of tasks, and a copyrighted NOVA operating system called RDOS containing the basic commands for operation of the system. Not all operating systems work with all CPUs. Plaintiffs produce emulator NOVA CPUs designed to perform the NOVA instruction set and thus to make use of defendant's RDOS.

Data General refuses to license its RDOS to anyone who does not also purchase its NOVA CPU. Plaintiffs allege that this constitutes an unlawful tying arrangement; the defendant's RDOS being the tying product, the NOVA instruction set CPU being the tied product.

Plaintiffs filed a number of actions alleging violations of section 1 of the Sherman Act and section 3 of the Clayton Act. The actions were consolidated. The issues of liability and damages were segregated for trial. This appeal is from a judgment on liability.

After extensive discovery, the parties filed cross-motions for summary judgment. The district court denied the motions, but found certain facts to be uncontroverted under Fed.R.Civ.P. 56(d). Trial, limited to the issue of defendant's economic power, resulted in a jury verdict for plaintiffs. Defendant's motion for judgment n.o.v. or for a new trial was granted. Plaintiffs appealed.

II.

A tying arrangement is illegal if it is shown to restrain competition unreasonably or is illegal *per se,* without such a showing, if certain prerequisites are met. The prerequisites of *per se* illegality are: (1) separate products, the purchase of one (tying product) being conditioned on purchase of the other (tied product); (2) sufficient economic power with respect to the tying product to restrain competition appreciably in the tied product; and (3) an effect upon a substantial amount of commerce in the tied product. These prerequisites were satisfied in this case. We therefore do not consider whether competition was in fact unreasonably restrained.

The district court properly granted summary judgment on the first and third of the required elements of a *per se* violation, holding that on the undisputed facts the NOVA instruction set CPU and defendant's RDOS are separate products and the volume of commerce in NOVA instruction set CPUs tied to the purchase of defendant's RDOS is substantial. *In re Data General Corp. Antitrust Litigation,* 490 F.Supp. 1089, 1104–07, 1116–17 (N.D.Cal.1980).

We adopt the district court's reasoning on these issues, adding that the court's analysis of defendant's "single product" claim is supported by the Supreme Court's recent discussion in *Jefferson Parish Hospital District No. 2 v. Hyde,* ___ U.S. ___, 104 S.Ct. 1551, 1561–65, 80 L.Ed.2d 2 (1984). The undisputed facts summarized in the district court's opinion establish that a demand existed for NOVA instruction set CPUs separate from defendant's RDOS, and that each element of the NOVA computer system could have been provided separately and selected separately by customers if defendant had not compelled purchasers to take both.

The remaining element necessary to establish a *per se* violation—defendant's possession of sufficient economic power with respect to the tying product, defendant's RDOS—was tried to a jury and resolved in plaintiffs' favor. The district court erred in setting aside this verdict or, alternatively, ordering a new trial.

III.

One of the purposes of a *per se* rule is to avoid an "incredibly complicated and prolonged economic investigation * * * to determine at large whether a particular restraint has been unreasonable." *Northern Pacific Railway Co. v. United States,* 356 U.S. 1, 5, 78 S.Ct. 514, 518, 2 L.Ed.2d 545 (1958). *See also Jefferson Parish Hospital,* 104 S.Ct. at 1560 n. 25. Although not requiring as extensive an inquiry as would be necessary to determine whether the tie-in violated the general standard of reasonableness, the district court held that plaintiffs "could not recover on the alleged tie-ins unless they identified and proved the relevant market for the tying and tied products." *In re Data General Corp. Antitrust Litigation,* 529 F.Supp. 801, 809 (N.D.Cal.1981). The trial that followed "focused upon the definition of the relevant markets" for the two products, which the Court characterized as the "critical issue," (*id.* at 806) and consumed forty-five days. *Id.* at 804.

The district court recognized that detailed market analysis was not required in a *per se* tying case prior to *United States Steel Corp. v. Fortner Enterprises, Inc.,* 429 U.S. 610, 97 S.Ct. 861, 51 L.Ed.2d 80 (1977) (*Fortner II*), but read that opinion as rejecting this approach in favor of a requirement of "some degree of market analysis even in a per se case." 529 F.Supp. at 808. The court relied particularly upon language in *Fortner II,* which states the question to be:

> whether the seller has the power, within the market for the tying product, to raise prices or to require purchasers to accept burdensome terms that could not be exacted in a completely competitive market. In short, the question is whether the seller has some advantage not shared by his competitors in the market for the tying product.

429 U.S. at 620, 97 S.Ct. at 867.

From the district court's analysis of the asserted deficiencies in plaintiffs' proof, it appears the court read this statement as requiring proof of power to fix the price of the tying product in the whole of the relevant market as defined by the inquiry described in *United States v. E.I. du Pont de Nemours & Co.,* 351 U.S. 377, 76 S.Ct. 994, 100 L.Ed. 1264 (1956), a monopolization case. In this the district court erred. Possession by the seller of such monopoly power is sufficient to establish *per se* illegality, but it is not required.

As the Supreme Court said in *United States v. Loew's, Inc.,* 371 U.S. 38, 45, 83 S.Ct. 97, 102, 9 L.Ed.2d 11 (1962):

> Market dominance—some power to control price and to exclude competition—is by no means the only test of whether the seller has the requisite economic power. Even absent a showing of market dominance, the crucial economic power may be inferred from the tying product's desirability to consumers or from uniqueness in its attributes.[4]

4. Since the requisite economic power may be found on the basis of either uniqueness or consumer appeal, and since market dominance in the present context does not necessitate a demonstration of market power in the sense of § 2 of the Sherman Act, it should seldom be necessary in a tie-in sale case to embark upon a full-scale factual inquiry into the scope of the relevant market for the tying product and into the corollary problem of the seller's percentage share in that market. This is even more obviously true when the tying product is patented or copyrighted, in which case, as appears in greater detail below, sufficiency of economic power is presumed.

This position was re-affirmed in the *Fortner* cases. In *Fortner I:*

> The standard of "sufficient economic power" does not, as the District Court held, require that the defendant have a monopoly or even a dominant position throughout the market for the tying product. Our tie-in cases have made unmistakably clear that the economic power over the tying product can be sufficient even though the power falls far short of dominance and *even though the power exists only with respect to some of the buyers in the market.* * * *
>
> * * * [T]he presence of any appreciable restraint on competition provides a sufficient reason for invalidating the tie. Such appreciable restraint results *whenever the seller can exert some power over some of the buyers in the market, even if his power is not complete over them and over all other buyers in the market.* * * * [D]espite the freedom of some or many buyers from the seller's power, other buyers—whether few or many, whether scattered throughout the market or part of some group within the market—can be forced to accept the higher price because of their stronger preferences for the product, and the seller

> could therefore choose instead to force them to accept a tying arrangement that would prevent free competition for their patronage in the market for the tied product. Accordingly, the proper focus of concern is whether the seller has the power to raise prices, or impose other burdensome terms such as a tie-in, *with respect to any appreciable number of buyers within the market.*

394 U.S. at 502–04, 89 S.Ct. at 1258–59 (emphasis added).

In *Fortner II* the Court reiterated that its prior decisions "do not require that the defendant have a monopoly or even a dominant position throughout the market for a tying product," 429 U.S. at 620, 97 S.Ct. at 867, and approved a commentator's summary of the holding in *Fortner I:* "Whenever there are *some* buyers who find a seller's product uniquely attractive, and are therefore willing to pay a premium above the price of its nearest substitute, the seller has the opportunity to impose a tie to some other good." 429 U.S. at 620 n. 14, 97 S.Ct. at 868, n. 14. (quoting Note, *The Logic of Foreclosure: Tie–In Doctrine after Fortner v. U.S. Steel,* 79 Yale L.J. 86, 93–94 (1969) (emphasis added). The language from *Fortner II* relied upon by the district court is not inconsistent with this interpretation; it required only "power, within the market for the tying product, to raise prices or to require purchasers to accept burdensome terms that could not be exacted in a *completely* competitive market." 429 U.S. at 620, 97 S.Ct. at 867 (emphasis added).

In its most recent decision on the question (filed after the ruling of the district court in this case) the Supreme Court again made it clear that a tying arrangement is illegal *per se* if the seller of the tying product has the capacity to force some buyers to purchase a tied product they do not want or would have preferred to purchase elsewhere. When such forcing occurs "competition on the merits in the market for the tied item is restrained." *Jefferson Parish Hospital,* ___ U.S. ___, 104 S.Ct. at 1558 (1984). Thus, what is required in a *per se* case is not power over the whole market for the tying product, but only, as the Court said, a "type of market power [that] has sometimes been referred to as 'leverage * * * defined here as a supplier's ability to induce his customers for one product to buy a second product from him that would not be purchased solely on the merit of that second product.'" *Id.* at 1559 n. 20 quoting V.P. Areeda & D. Turner, *Antitrust Law,* ¶ 1134a at 202 (1980). "[W]e have condemned tying arrangements," the Court said, "when the seller has some special ability—usually called 'market power'—to force a purchaser to do something that he would not do in a competitive market." *Id.* at 1559.

Nor is a restraint on competition that is substantial in terms of the entire market for the tied product required. "If only a single purchaser were 'forced' with respect to the purchase of a tied item, the resultant impact on competition would not be sufficient to warrant the concern of antitrust law." *Id.* at 1560. Beyond that, however, it need only appear that "a substantial volume of commerce is foreclosed," *id.,* which the court earlier defined as "substantial enough in terms of dollar-volume so as not to be merely *de minimis.* " *Fortner I* at 501, 89 S.Ct. at 1258. *See also Moore v. Jas. H. Matthews & Co.*, 550 F.2d at 1216.

In accordance with these holdings, we review the record not for what it may reveal as to defendant's position in a defined market in which defendant's RDOS was sold, but only to determine whether the jury reasonably could have concluded defendant's RDOS was sufficiently unique and desirable to an appreciable number of buyers to enable defendant to force those buyers also to buy a substantial volume of defendant's NOVA instruction set CPUs they would have preferred not to buy.

IV.

There was abundant evidence that defendant's RDOS was distinctive and particularly desirable to a substantial number of buyers, and could not be readily produced by other sellers. There was also substantial evidence that defendant's insistence upon licensing its RDOS only to purchasers of defendant's NOVA instruction set CPU, led buyers to purchase defendant's NOVA CPUs who would not have bought them or would have bought them elsewhere absent the tying requirement.

Although expressing some doubt as to the sufficiency of the evidence, the district court assumed defendant's RDOS was superior to competing operating systems and was viewed as uniquely desirable by buyers. 529 F.Supp. at 816. We do not share the court's hesitancy about the adequacy of the proof of the strong preference of many customers for RDOS. It was a most popular product. Experts, customers, and even competitors testified to its many advantages over competitive products.[2] Defendant's own officials expressed the same opinion in pre-litigation documents.

Defendant's RDOS has copyright protection. Defendant also claimed the production of RDOS required use of defendant's trade secrets. The RDOS copyright established both the distinctiveness of RDOS and a legal bar to its reproduction by competitors. "The requisite economic power is presumed when the tying product is patented or copyrighted." *United States v. Loew's, Inc.*, 371 U.S. at 45, 83 S.Ct. at 102. The copyright confers upon defendant "some advantages not shared by his competitors in the market for the tying product." *Fortner II,* 429 U.S. at 620, 97 S.Ct. at 868. "[T]he copyright monopolies in *United States v. Paramount Pictures, Inc.*, 334 U.S. 131 [68 S.Ct. 915, 92 L.Ed. 1260] and *United States v. Loew's Inc.*, 371 U.S. 38 [83 S.Ct. 97, 9 L.Ed.2d 11] * * * represented tying products that the Court regarded as sufficiently unique to give rise to a presumption of economic power." 429 U.S. at 619, 97 S.Ct. at 867. "[P]er se prohibition is appropriate if anticompetitive forcing is likely. For example, if the government has

2. There was documentary and oral testimony that RDOS was the best in the industry, the most comprehensive, compatible, field proven, and rapid. One customer testified, for example, that tests showed RDOS ran approximately four times faster than any similarly-priced system. Another witness called it "the only full service operating system available for the NOVA."

granted the seller a patent or similar monopoly over a product, it is fair to presume that the inability to buy the product elsewhere gives the seller market power." *Jefferson Parish Hospital,* 104 S.Ct. at 1560. *See also Moore v. Jas. H. Matthews & Co.,* 550 F.2d at 1215–16.

There is abundant evidence, including testimony of defendant's own executives, customers, and plaintiffs' expert witnesses, that defendant's RDOS could not be reproduced without infringing defendant's copyright and utilizing defendant's trade secrets.[3] Defendant vigorously pursued those who assertedly violated defendant's proprietary rights. Additionally, there was evidence that creating and testing a compatible system would require millions of dollars and years of effort. One of defendant's officers testified that the passage of the time required to reproduce RDOS would render the completed software obsolete.

The power to coerce that RDOS gave the defendant was enhanced by the fact that many of defendant's customers were "locked in" to the use of RDOS. Briefly, defendant sells RDOS and NOVA CPUs primarily to original equipment manufacturers (OEMs) who combine them with application software (a set of instructions that allows the system to accomplish a particular task) to create a complete computer system for resale. Application system software for particular uses is developed by OEMs at substantial expense. Once developed, application software for a particular use may be used by an OEM in producing any number of computer systems for that use for resale to different customers. However, application software is designed to function only with a particular operating system. OEMs who construct their application software to function with defendant's RDOS therefore must purchase an RDOS for each computer system they assemble using that application software. Because of the tying condition, they also must purchase one of defendant's NOVA instruction set CPUs for each such computer system they sell.

An OEM can free itself from this "lock in" only by abandoning its application software compatible with defendant's RDOS, in which it has a substantial investment, or converting the software so that it may be used with another operating system. There was abundant testimony that conversion was not economically feasible.[4]

The defendant argues that "lock-in" is irrelevant in determining its market power because OEMs are aware of the tie when they select an

3. One of defendant's officers admitted it would be impossible to develop operating system software performing all the functions of defendant's RDOS without violating defendant's copyright and utilizing its trade secrets.

4. Defendant's former marketing manager could recall no instance in which an existing OEM customer had abandoned defendant's equipment and switched to a new supplier. Competitors and customers of defendant testified that conversion was virtually impossible without a complete rewriting of application software. One OEM estimated the cost of conversion to be 90 percent of the original development costs. Another ruled out the possibility of changing operating systems because "it would simply take too long to change all the software that we have, all the software on hand. We can't shut down the operation we have going. * * * " And another, "it is just not possible to do in our environment because it would just take forever."

operating system for the computer system they are assembling. At that point, defendant argues, the OEM has made no investment in application software and, as a result, chooses freely among competing systems. 529 F.Supp. at 821. This characterization of the market is not accurate. As the evidence in this case establishes, the initial choice is not free of forcing. Defendant's operating system has been shown to be unique as a matter of law and distinctively attractive as a matter of fact. Defendant's initial leverage is magnified by the lock-in. By 1979, 93 percent of defendant's NOVA CPU sales were made to locked-in customers. These buyers were not only forced to buy defendant's CPUs initially to acquire the operating system they found most attractive, they were thereafter forced to buy defendant's CPUs for their subsequent needs in order to acquire the only operating system they could economically use. Not even a decision by CPU manufacturers to broaden their base and compete in the operating system market would have alleviated the problem, for the locked-in customers were not free to choose among competing operating systems. RDOS was the only operating system that would allow them to realize the benefit of their investment in application software, an investment that in some cases totalled millions of dollars.

OEM testimony confirmed defendant's potential power to coerce arising from the lock-in. For example, one OEM witness testified "[w]ithout [the RDOS operating system] I can't operate"; and another: "economically I was in a position where I had to use RDOS. I had no choice at that point."

The power arising from the special attraction of RDOS, coupled with the copyright protection, the trade secret barrier, and the lock-in, was evidenced by defendant's minimum equipment configuration (MEC) program. To obtain defendant's RDOS all licensees were required to purchase not only defendant's CPU but also a set quantity of other peripheral hardware, or pay a program license charge. Defendant's national accounts manager accurately referred to the charge as a "penalty." Customers testified they were forced to buy peripherals from defendant they otherwise would not have purchased. An OEM testified he purchased defendant's fixed disc because he "had to * * * or pay a $5,000 fine." He also testified he could have bought a superior disc drive for his purposes from another source at half the price. Another customer testified "we've had to take equipment that we either couldn't use, or equipment that, for one reason or another, might, in our opinion, have been best—best obtained from another source." Still another OEM called the MEC "arbitrary" because it required the purchase of "items of hardware specified in the Minimum Equipment Configuration for certain products that have no functional bearing or are not required, or not used necessarily by the programs themselves." Defendant's senior vice-president testified the complaints were received from customers about the MEC program "all the time."

Defendant retained the MEC program despite buyer resistance because, as defendant's president testified, if required to forgo the program defendant would have suffered a loss in revenues. The tie-in of RDOS to defendant's NOVA instruction set CPU was an equally conscious exercise of economic power in one market to gain an advantage in others. As one of defendant's managers wrote in an intra-company memorandum, "[p]rotection from knock-off products still lies in software licensing restrictions."

The district court properly rejected defendant's argument, vigorously renewed in this court, "that it must bundle its software together with its CPUs in order to recover its substantial investment in software research and development," (490 F.Supp. at 1121), and that "it would be unfair to permit emulator-CPU manufacturers to reap the benefits of [defendant's] software [research and development] when they sell their competing CPUs for use with [defendant's] software." 490 F.Supp. at 1121–22.

Defendant's president testified the tie was devised to ensure recovery of RDOS development costs. He testified the decision to tie was made after a competitive manufacturer of NOVA emulator CPUs requested permission to use RDOS. Rather than sell the software separately at a price that would reflect research and development, defendant chose to restrict availability to its own CPU customers, thus restricting competition for the tied product. As the district court said, "Recovery of investment costs has been explicitly excluded from the narrowly-construed exceptions to the *per se* rule against tie-ins." *Id.* at 1122. Defendant "has not shown, nor has it raised a genuine issue of fact with respect to its ability to show at trial, that it is any less capable than was Jerrold Electronics [*United States v. Jerrold Electronics Corp.*, 187 F.Supp. 545 (E.D.Pa.1960), *aff'd per curiam,* 365 U.S. 567, 81 S.Ct. 755, 5 L.Ed.2d 806 (1961)] of adopting the less restrictive alternative of restructured prices in order to recoup its investment costs and maintain its incentive for further innovation." 490 F.Supp. at 1122.

If the tie were allowed, competing manufacturers of CPUs would be forced

> not only to match existing sellers of the tied product in price and quality, but to offset the attraction of the tying product itself. Even if this is possible through simultaneous entry into production of the tying product, entry into both markets is significantly more expensive than simply entry into the tied market. * * *

Jefferson Parish Hospital, 104 S.Ct. at 1558 n. 19 (quoting *Fortner I,* 394 U.S. at 513, 89 S.Ct. at 1263 (White, J., dissenting)). In short, defendant must recover the cost of RDOS development by pricing RDOS appropriately, not by tying it to a separate product.

Evidence regarding the potential sources of power with respect to RDOS (copyright, trade secret, and "lock-in"), was submitted to the jury under appropriate instructions. The jury found as a fact that defendant possessed and used the power by means of the tying arrangement to appreciably restrain competition in the market for NOVA instruction set CPUs. The evidence outlined above fully supported the jury's verdict.

V.

Most, although not all, of the trial court's reasons for setting aside the verdict are traceable to the court's view that the legality of a tying arrangement must be tested by the seller's economic power throughout the market for the tying product, and by the relative substantiality of the restraint on competition in the tied product market considered as a whole.

As we have said, the trial court assumed customers regarded RDOS as "uniquely desirable and that it in fact possesses various features which render it superior to other software," but concluded that plaintiffs had failed to prove that defendant's "competitors were prevented from developing functionally equivalent software." 529 F.Supp. at 816. Conceding that the copyright on RDOS and the trade secrets involved in its creation precluded development by defendant's competitors of "compatible" software, the court held plaintiffs had failed to prove the effect of defendant's copyright and secrets on the development of software "comparable" to RDOS. *Id.* at 816–17.

The court erroneously imposed the burden of proof on plaintiffs. The RDOS copyright created a presumption of economic power sufficient to render the tying arrangement illegal *per se.*[5] The burden to rebut the presumption shifted to defendant.

More basically, the court was misled by its conception that power throughout the product market for the tying product was required. Earlier in its opinion the court indicated the relevant market must be defined to permit the jury to determine whether defendant's competitors "were prevented from developing competitive software." *Id.* at 809. The court continued:

> The focus in defining a relevant product market must be upon recognizing those firms and products which present relevant alternatives to the defendant's product, to the extent that they are "reasonably interchangeable" for the same or similar uses, and thus restrict the defendant's power to raise prices. *See United States v. E.I. du Pont de Nemours & Co.,* 351 U.S. 377 [76 S.Ct. 994, 100 L.Ed. 1264] (1956).

Id. Thus the court's concern was whether there were reasonably interchangeable substitutes for RDOS in the operating systems market as a whole, a question of critical importance if the question were whether that market had been monopolized.

5. The district court suggested that "the presumption of economic power may be inappropriate in the computer software context because copyright notices do not necessarily prevent others from copying the material embodiment of the source program." 529 F.Supp. at 816. The premise of this position was laid to rest in *Apple Computer, Inc. v. Formula Int'l., Inc.,* 725 F.2d 521 (9th Cir.1984); and *Apple Computer, Inc. v. Franklin Computer Corp.,* 714 F.2d 1240, 1249–54 (3d Cir.1983), decided after the district court's opinion in this case was filed.

As the authorities cited earlier establish, the focus of the prohibition against tying arrangements is quite different. The concern is not with the restraint on competition in the tying product but on competition in the market for the tied product. What is required is not monopoly power in the tying product market, but only sufficient power to enable the seller to restrict competition in the tied product. If a seller's product is distinctive, not available from other sources, and sufficiently attractive to some buyers to enable the seller by tying arrangements to foreclose a part of the market for a tied product, the adverse impact on competition in the tied product is not diminished by the fact that other sellers may be selling products similar to the tying product.

* * *

The law was succinctly summarized in *Carpa, Inc. v. Ward Foods, Inc.*, 536 F.2d 39, 48 (5th Cir.1976), a trademark tying case, in a manner particularly pertinent here:

> What is required is a factual assessment of the tying product's uniqueness and desirability, not its market power in the sense of a Section 2 Sherman Act violation. *United States v. Loew's, Inc.*, 371 U.S. 38, 45, 83 S.Ct. 97 [102], 9 L.Ed.2d 11 (1962). Uniqueness, of course, presupposes that competitors are in some way foreclosed from offering the distinctive product. *Fortner* points out at 505, 89 S.Ct. 1252, note 2, that such barriers may be legal, as in the cases of patented or copyrighted products. Trademarks surely may be included in the list of such legal restraints, and, as with copyrighted material, *the mere presence of competing substitutes is insufficient to destroy the legal, and more importantly the economic, distinctiveness of the trademark.* See *Loew's,* 371 U.S. at 49, 83 S.Ct. 97.

(emphasis added).

Fortner II is not to the contrary, as the district court thought. There must, of course be power to coerce. *Fortner II* holds only that a seller lacks such power if buyers may choose between fungible products offered by different sellers. In *Fortner II* the tying item was favorable credit terms, the tied product U.S. Steel's prefabricated homes. U.S. Steel's credit was not unique; money is fungible. Anyone willing to accept less profit could have offered credit terms similar to those offered by U.S. Steel. As the Supreme Court said, "The unusual credit bargain offered to Fortner proves nothing more than a willingness to provide cheap financing in order to sell expensive houses." *Fortner II,* 429 U.S. at 622, 97 S.Ct. at 868. In contrast, no one but defendant could offer RDOS. It was not fungible, but rather in many ways unique.

The question is not whether other operating systems with which RDOS competed were as good as RDOS or better in the eyes of some buyers, but rather whether RDOS, available only from defendant, was sufficiently attractive to some customers to enable defendant to require those who wished to obtain it also to buy from defendant NOVA instruction set CPUs they might otherwise have purchased from others.[6] As we have seen, evidence of the defendant's possession of such power was ample.

Clearly the availability of "comparable" or "functionally equivalent" operating systems would not have freed "locked-in" OEMs of the pressure, imposed by their investment in application software "compatible" only with RDOS, that compelled them to accede to defendant's condition that they purchase defendant's NOVA CPU in order to obtain RDOS.

The district court held that the "lock-in" did not confer upon defendant any "legally cognizable power over price" because OEMs who purchased RDOS and defendant's NOVA instruction set CPUs for use in assembling computer systems for resale were constrained by competition in the resale market from paying non-competitive prices for components of their systems, and that, in fact, defendant's prices to OEMs were fully competitive. 529 F.Supp. at 814–15, 817–18. There are several answers. Some OEMs are insulated from strict price sensitivity. As defendant's marketing manual stated: "[M]any OEM's have an effective monopoly or near-monopoly for their product, because of patent position, market share dominance, control of distribution channels, or whatever. This guy isn't forced to go the lowest possible unit cost." Moreover, to the extent that end-users considered defendant's RDOS to be superior to other operating system software, the OEM's price to the end-user and thus defendant's price of hardware to the OEM, could exceed that of other suppliers. Most important, the passage in *Fortner II* to which defendant refers ("whether the seller has the power, within the market for the tying product, to raise prices *or to require purchasers to accept burdensome terms* that could not be exacted in a completely competitive market" (429 U.S. at 620, 97 S.Ct. at 867) (emphasis added), recognizes that a seller's power to impose an onerous tying arrangement is sufficient to invoke *per se* condemnation. Even assuming defendant's package of RDOS and defendant's NOVA instruction set CPU was competitively priced, the record establishes that defendant could, and did, force that package upon some buyers who, if free to choose, would have bought RDOS from defendant but NOVA instruction set CPUs from others.

"Fundamentally," the district court held, "plaintiffs have not presented evidence demonstrating that their alleged inability to compete with [defendant's] NOVA CPUs is attributable to the software licensing restrictions rather than this failure to meet" defendant's standards of quality and service. Even from the brief summary

6. One of defendant's customers stated the Fairchild NOVA instruction set CPU was ahead of its time technologically but he had to eliminate it from consideration because Fairchild "did not have an operating system available." Another customer testified the SCI Mercury 3 emulator was superior to Data General's NOVA CPU. The record is rich in testimony from customers who stated the tie prevented them from purchasing any CPU other than Data General's.

presented here, it is evident there was ample direct and circumstantial evidence to support the jury's verdict to the contrary.

VI.

The district court also concluded that plaintiffs failed to prove an appreciable restraint in the market for the tied product, the NOVA instruction set CPU. The court noted that the general market for CPUs was highly competitive, "characterized by a wide range of competitive hardware offerings, intense price competition, ease of entry, and rapid growth." 529 F.Supp. at 818. The court noted many competitors had entered the CPU market after the introduction of defendant's RDOS tied to defendant's CPU. *Id.* Even assuming the tie-in appreciably restrained competition "in the NOVA instruction set sub-market," the court said, "the portion of the broad market conceivably affected by this phenomenon is so small that it cannot be characterized as indicative of power 'appreciably to restrain competition' in the general market." *Id.*

But as we have already seen, a detailed analysis of competitive conditions in the tied product market is inappropriate in a *per se* case. Indeed as the district court held in its first opinion, *see* 490 F.Supp. at 1116–17, all that is required in respect to the extent of the restraint in the market for the tied product is that a "substantial *volume* of commerce be foreclosed," *Jefferson Parish Hospital District No. 2 v. Hyde,* 104 S.Ct. at 1560 (emphasis added); and "substantial volume" in this context means only an amount greater than *de minimis,* a requirement clearly satisfied here. *See* 490 F.Supp. at 1117.

* * *

Reversed on the appeal, affirmed on the cross-appeal, and remanded for further proceedings consistent with this opinion.

Note

Data General has led firms that produce both hardware and software to market them separately rather than selling them only as a combined package. Manufacturers of mainframes and minicomputers usually sell the computers and lease or license the software. IBM and Apple are the only major microcomputer manufacturers that produce both hardware and software. IBM markets its hardware and software separately. For software, IBM uses a "shrink wrap contract" that purports to create only a license in the customer. Both Apple and IBM cooperate extensively with outside software makers, since a personal computer is only as attractive as the available software. However Apple, unlike IBM, sues any hardware manufacturer who produces a computer compatible with its own products. So far Apple has succeeded in preventing the sale of "clones" of its successful Macintosh line. In addition it has sued the leading microcomputer software company, Microsoft, claiming that Microsoft Windows infringes Apple's Macintosh user interface.

XETA, INC. v. ATEX, INC.

United States Court of Appeals, Federal Circuit, 1988.
852 F.2d 1280.

PAULINE NEWMAN, CIRCUIT JUDGE.

Xeta, Inc. appeals the decision of the United States District Court for the District of New Hampshire, denying Xeta's motion to enjoin Atex, Inc. and its parent Eastman Kodak Company, *pendente lite,* from conducting certain activities asserted to be in violation of Section 1 of the Sherman Act, 15 U.S.C. § 1; Section 3 of the Clayton Act, 15 U.S.C. § 14; Section 2(a) of the Clayton Act as amended by the Robinson–Patman Act, 15 U.S.C. § 13(a); and New Hampshire laws R.S.A. 356:2 and 358–A:2; and certain actions asserted to be in tortious interference with Xeta's contractual relations, business relations, and prospective advantage, in violation of New Hampshire state law.

* * *

THE PRODUCTS

Atex has since 1974 manufactured and sold text-processing computer systems for use by newspapers, magazines, and other businesses such as law firms that publish large amounts of text. The systems are designed to meet the customer's particular requirements, and comprise Atex proprietary software, a central processing mini-computer unit, disc drives, terminals (which consist of video display units and keyboards), and an output device such as a printer or typesetter. Atex warrants its systems and provides technical and debugging services to its customers.

Xeta produces and sells terminals (video display units and keyboards) that are designed to be used with or as a substitute for Atex terminals in the Atex systems. Xeta's introduction of these terminals in 1985 stimulated the commercial responses from Atex that are the subject of this action.

THE PRELIMINARY INJUNCTION

The district court denied Xeta's motion for injunction *pendente lite.* The sole issue is whether this denial was an abuse of the district court's discretionary authority.

* * *

I

The principal antitrust claim asserted by Xeta is that Atex imposed on its customers an illegal tying arrangement, in violation of Section 1 of the Sherman Act, Section 3 of the Clayton Act, and corresponding New Hampshire law N.H. R.S.A. 356:2.

To show an illegal tie three elements must be demonstrated: first, the purchase of one product (the tying product) must be conditioned on the purchase of another product (the tied product); second, the defendant must have "sufficient economic power with respect to the tying product to appreciably restrain free competition in the market for the tied product"; and third, the amount of commerce affected must be "not insubstantial".

Xeta states that Atex conditions the sale of its proprietary software on the customer's purchase of Atex hardware, and enforces this tie with its announced disclaimer of warranty and technical service obligations when Atex components are used in "foreign" systems. Xeta also states that Atex made illegal and prejudicial changes in its pricing practices in response to Xeta's entry: specifically, the imposition of a software license fee. According to Xeta, this fee is charged to Xeta's customers but not to Atex's customers, and implements the tie between Atex software and hardware.

Atex responds that its system consists of interrelated components designed to be used as an integrated system for the specialized purpose of text processing, that the major components are not interchangeable with those of other systems, and that neither the software nor the specialized hardware has an independent market. Atex states that its warranty practice is common in the computer industry and is not a tool of coercion, and in any event that it has never withheld warranty services of its components in such circumstances.

Atex states that the software license fee is charged to all, and that it had merely "unbundled" the fee which, until 1986, had not been separately charged. Atex states that the license fee has been contemplated in its Sales Agreements since 1982, well before the appearance of Xeta in this field. Atex argues that its separate fee for the software license actually emphasizes the absence of a coerced tie among components, since each aspect of the system carries its independent price. Xeta conceded at oral argument that the license fee of $1000 per terminal was not inordinately high in view of the total cost of these systems, ranging to millions of dollars.

Xeta did not show likelihood of success in proving the asserted tie. Xeta presented no evidence to show that Atex's warranty and servicing practices were unreasonable under the circumstances, and showed no illegality in the software licensing practice. Xeta did not support its allegation that the fee is not being charged to all, at least after the "grace period" described by Atex.

On the record before it, the district court did not abuse its discretion in declining to grant a preliminary injunction on these bases. The antitrust laws do not prohibit Atex from changing its sales and pricing practices, or from responding to competition.

II

The district court focussed primarily on the tying claim, which was the principal claim developed by Xeta. Xeta had raised additional issues and arguments, and asserts that the district court erred in failing to grant a preliminary injunction on these additional bases and in not making express findings of fact on all issues.

A

We turn first to Xeta's assertion that it lost a sale to Lockheed and is experiencing serious commercial difficulties because Atex lowered its prices in response to Xeta's low prices.

Price competition is not itself an antitrust violation. Whether Atex's pricing policies show the requisite predatory intent requires proof beyond that adduced by Xeta. *See Barry Wright Corp. v. ITT Grinnell Corp.,* 724 F.2d 227, 236 (1st Cir.1983) (requiring consideration of the seller's incremental and average total cost); *Kartell v. Blue Shield of Massachusetts, Inc.,* 749 F.2d 922, 927–28 (1st Cir.1984), *cert. denied,* 471 U.S. 1029–30, 105 S.Ct. 2040, 2049, 85 L.Ed.2d 322 (1985). Xeta's charge in its complaint that Atex was selling below cost was contravened by Xeta's admission, on argument before the district court, that Atex was selling at a substantial markup.

The law that prohibits predatory pricing practices does not routinely bar a seller from lowering its prices to compete with a competitor's lower prices.

Xeta also charges that Atex violated provisions of the Robinson–Patman Act, 15 U.S.C. § 13(a), and corresponding N.H. R.S.A. 358–A:2. Violation of the Robinson–Patman Act requires, inter alia, that the same commodity be sold to separate customers at different prices during the same time period. *Bruce's Juices, Inc. v. American Can Co.,* 330 U.S. 743, 755, 67 S.Ct. 1015, 1020, 91 L.Ed. 1219 (1947) ("no single sale can violate the Robinson–Patman Act"). Xeta relies on Atex's reduced price negotiated with Lockheed as compared with Atex's higher list prices. Xeta showed no sale at a different price during this period, thus failing to show likelihood of success on the threshold burden of a Robinson–Patman violation.

B

Xeta states that Atex threatened it with legal action as to patent infringement and also with respect to Atex's assertion that William West, the founder and president of Xeta, misappropriated trade secrets learned while he was an employee of Atex. Xeta also asks that Atex be enjoined from threatening Xeta's customers. Atex responds that Xeta had engaged in commercial fraud, a separate matter the details of which we need not discuss, but which prompted the response about which Xeta complains. On this record of argument without development of factual support, we discern no abuse of the district court's discretion.

C

The premise of the New Hampshire state action for tortious interference with contractual relations is that the wrongdoer intentionally induced or otherwise caused a third party not to enter into or continue a business relation with the plaintiff. *See Baker v. Dennis Brown Realty, Inc.*, 121 N.H. 640, 433 A.2d 1271, 1274 (1981). Xeta offered as evidence the affidavit of Mrs. West, Xeta Vice President, that Xeta had an agreement with Lockheed, supported by a price quotation from Xeta to Lockheed. The record contains no acceptance by Lockheed, no purchase order, no exchange of correspondence, and no testimony from Lockheed. Atex testified that Lockheed requested reduced prices from Atex after Lockheed had Xeta's offer, but did not tell Atex the prices offered by Xeta.

We take note that customers are wont to negotiate for the most favorable terms, and that a potential customer is not barred from negotiating with more than one supplier. On this record Xeta has not shown a likelihood of success on the merits of these tort claims. *See Restatement of Torts (Second)* § 768(1) (1979) (no wrong if the action concerns proper competition between the parties).

III

The burden is on the requester of preliminary relief to show likelihood of success on the merits of its claim and, if this requirement is met, to show the other necessary elements of entitlement to an injunction. Although Xeta impugns Atex's motives, Xeta did not present evidence sufficient to support a ruling of likelihood of success on these asserted violations of antitrust and tort law.

* * *

Affirmed.

PATENT ACT

§ 271. Infringement of patent

* * *

(d) No patent owner otherwise entitled to relief for infringement or contributory infringement of a patent shall be denied relief or deemed guilty of misuse or illegal extension of the patent right by reason of his having done one or more of the following: (1) derived revenue from acts which if performed by another without his consent would constitute contributory infringement of the patent; (2) licensed or authorized another to perform acts which if performed without his consent would constitute contributory infringement of the patent; (3) sought to enforce his patent rights against infringement or contributory infringement; (4) refused to license or use any rights to the patent; or (5) conditioned the license of any rights to the patent or the sale of the patented product on the acquisition of a license to rights in another patent or purchase of a separate product, unless, in view of the circumstances, the patent owner has market power in the relevant market for the patent or patented product on which the license or sale is conditioned.

Note

Subsections 4 and 5 of § 271(d) were added by Public Law 100–703, the Patent and Trademark Authorization Act, approved Nov. 19, 1988.

Chapter XIV

TRADEMARK LAW, COMPUTER STANDARDIZATION, AND COMPETITION

Is there "computer trademark law" that differs from ordinary trademark law? This chapter argues that there is a difference, related to the issue of software and hardware compatibility. Ordinarily, trademarks serve two purposes: identifying the manufacturer of goods and guaranteeing quality. The buyer of a bottle of "Coca–Cola" knows which company makes it and knows that it will have a uniform taste and quality. The buyer of "7–UP" will get a product with a different taste from a different manufacturer. 7–UP competes by being different, advertising itself as the "Un–Cola". Likewise, Apple Computer Company has competed in the personal computer market with IBM by emphasizing the difference between the Macintosh and the IBM personal computers. Apple's use of Macintosh for this purpose does not raise any unique trademark issues.

Computer-related trademarks, however, are not used just to show differences. Often a competitor will want to show that its product is not different from, but compatible with a nationally-advertised product. A new spreadsheet maker will want users to know that its spreadsheet will process spreadsheets created with Lotus 1–2–3. A modem manufacturer will want users to know that its modems will plug inside Toshiba portable computers. It is virtually impossible to convey this sort of knowledge without mentioning the competing organization's trademark. Computer-related trademark litigation has centered on defining the exact ways in which software and hardware companies can use their competitors' trademarks. Too much restriction could harm competition; too little could discourage marketing of new and better products.

APPLE COMPUTER, INC. v. FORMULA INTERNATIONAL, INC.

United States District Court, Central District of California, 1983.
562 F.Supp. 775.

IRVING HILL, DISTRICT JUDGE.

Before the Court is Plaintiff's motion for preliminary injunction filed September 27, 1982. The motion was argued on December 20, 1982.

In announcing its decision on the motion, the Court is making certain findings of fact and formulating certain conclusions of law. These are based only on the evidence now before the Court in connection with the motion and the Points and Authorities that have been submitted up to this time. These findings and conclusions are made without prejudice to those which the Court will be required to make on the same issues after the trial of the matter on the merits.

I. THE PARTIES AND THE PRODUCTS THEY MAKE AND SELL

Plaintiff Apple Computer, Inc., manufactures and sells computers and related peripheral equipment, including computer programs and other software for computers. Though established only in 1976, Apple has become a giant concern selling its products worldwide. Its gross sales are in the hundreds of millions of dollars annually. Among Apple's principal products is the Apple II computer, a small computer designed primarily for personal use in the home or in the office of a small business. Apple also makes a wide variety of peripheral equipment for compatible use with the Apple II computer. Among such items are diskettes.

The Apple II computer contains a number of computer programs embodied in ROMs. The Apple diskettes also contain computer programs embodied therein. Five Apple computer programs are in issue in this case. Two of these, "Autostart" and "Applesoft" are embodied in ROMs. The other three programs, "HELLO", "DOS 3.3" and "Apple Integer BASIC" are embodied in diskettes. All five programs have been registered under the Federal Copyright Act.

The ROMs in issue in this case have a copyright notice either printed on the ROM itself or printed immediately next to the ROM on the circuit board to which the ROM is affixed. Each diskette in issue in this case bears a copyright notice on its face.

The terms ROMs, diskettes and some of the other terms which have been used will shortly be defined.

The Defendant, Formula International, Inc., operates a single large electronics supply store selling at retail and wholesale. Its major business is the sale of electrical components of various kinds. Formula apparently does not itself manufacture any of the components it sells.

To this point, Formula's revenues from the sale of computer products constitute only a small percentage of its total sales.

Up to now, Formula has sold no assembled computers. In May of 1982, Formula commenced the sale of a computer kit under the trade mark "Pineapple". When assembled, the materials contained in the kit make up a computer which is, like the Apple II, designed for personal use in the home or in small businesses. The assembled Pineapple computer in external appearance is virtually indistinguishable from the appearance of the Apple II counterpart and its uses and capacities are very similar if not identical. Formula, in addition, sells equipment for personal computers, some of which is identical to that which Apple sells.

Apple has presented evidence that Formula's kit and its peripheral equipment contain computer programs embodied in ROMs and diskettes which are virtually identical copies of the above mentioned computer programs embodied in Apple's ROMs and diskettes. This factual claim is not disputed. Formula claims no copyright on any of its computer programs. Formula's kits are assembled by apparently independent concerns in Taiwan and Hong Kong. Formula acknowledges that at least some of these concerns make the kits and components according to Formula's instructions and specifications.

As of the time Formula filed its response to Apple's motion for a preliminary injunction, Formula had sold only 49 Pineapple kits. The sale of these kits has now been discontinued. Formula, however, is advertising and offering for sale, a new type of Pineapple kit. From it, there can be assembled a personal computer with the same capacities and computer programs as are found in its previous model and in the Apple II. But its exterior is somewhat less like the present Apple II exterior.

II. The Complaint

Apple sues Formula on three separate theories, copyright infringement, trademark infringement and unfair competition. Apple charges that Formula violates its copyrights on the various computer programs embodied in the Apple ROMs and diskettes.

Apple has five trademarks embodying the "Apple" name as used on various computers, computer equipment and computer programs. Apple accuses Formula of infringing each of its registered trademarks by adoption of the "Pineapple" name. Formula does not claim any federal trademark registration of its "Pineapple" name.

The unfair competition charge is centered on (1) alleged misappropriation of the fruit of Apple's efforts in developing an integral computer component called a "Mother Board" and (2) alleged palming off resulting from the use of similar names in marketing.

* * *

III. The Requested Preliminary Injunction

Apple's motion asks the Court, pending trial of the case, to enjoin Formula from:

(1) Manufacturing, importing, distributing or selling the Pineapple computer either in assembled or kit form,

(2) Using a case which copies or imitates the configuration of the Apple II computer case,

(3) Using the mark or name Pineapple or any other colorable imitation of the Apple trademark or trade name and

(4) Distributing or selling any items which are, or include, copies of the computer programs copyrighted by Apple including the Autostart, Applesoft, HELLO, DOS 3.3 and Apple Integer BASIC.

* * *

The Court will enjoin Defendant, pending trial, from using as a trademark or trade name, the name "Pineapple" or any other name embodying the word or term "Apple" or otherwise confusingly similar to the trademarks of Plaintiff. However, the said injunction will not include a restraint on the Defendant as to the shape or configuration of the container or box in which its computer, or a computer made from its kit parts, is contained.

* * *

VII. Trademark Matters

As mentioned above, the Court has decided to issue a preliminary injunction as to the trademarks involved.

Certain essential findings and conclusions underlie that decision in accordance with the Ninth Circuit standards. The Court finds that Apple has shown a reasonable probability of success on the merits. The Court further finds that use by the Defendant of the names "Apple" or "Pineapple" would be confusingly similar to the Plaintiff's use of its Apple trademark and trade name when used on related goods.

Under the Ninth Circuit test, the Court also finds that Plaintiff has demonstrated a strong possibility of irreparable injury to itself and that the balance of hardships tips sharply in its favor.

VIII. Unfair Competition

The Court expresses no views and makes no findings on Plaintiff's alternative theory of unfair competition. The relief which has already been granted should be totally adequate to the Plaintiff's requirements and objectives *pendente lite.* Thus it is unnecessary to base relief, even alternatively, on any unfair competition theory.

* * *

Notes and Questions

1. Obviously the most direct way for a competitor to convince the public that a computer was Apple-compatible would be for the competitor to copy the Apple trademark as well as the hardware and software. There is a good reason why this casebook does not have a case involving direct mislabeling of software or hardware with the trademark of another company. The fly-by-night outfits that engage in this sort of counterfeiting do not bother to show up in court to contest trademark claims. Judges rarely write full opinions in such cases because of the lack of interesting legal issues. So there is a dearth of reported cases of direct trademark copying.

2. Why did Formula International choose the name "Pineapple" for its computers?

3. Why did Formula International originally shape its computers to look like Apple computers?

4. Because of the generic meaning of the words and the existence of prior trademarks, it is almost impossible to obtain protection for marks using terms such as "micro," "bit," and "byte."

5. Users of new product designations have found that they often become the generic terms for various types of compatability before they obtain trademark protection. Generic terms cannot be protected by trademarks. Trademarks that become generic lose their protection. The Trademark Act now allows reservation of a trademark by registration of intent to use it. Will this provision help against the danger of marks becoming generic?

SIERRA ON-LINE, INC. v. PHOENIX SOFTWARE, INC.

United States Court of Appeals, Ninth Circuit, 1984.
739 F.2d 1415.

WISDOM, SENIOR CIRCUIT JUDGE:

This appeal arises out of a dispute over the right to use the term "Hi-Res Adventure" to identify home computer strategy games with high-resolution (hi-res) graphic displays.[1] The defendant, Phoenix Software, Inc. (Phoenix), appeals from an order denying reconsideration of a preliminary injunction, and also denying its motion for summary judgment. We affirm the preliminary injunction in favor of the plaintiff, Sierra On-Line, Inc. (Sierra), and dismiss the remainder of the appeal for lack of jurisdiction.

I.

Sierra is a manufacturer of computer software. Since 1980 it has used "Hi-Res Adventure" (for which federal registration is pending) in

1. John Curtis Williams, a Sierra employee, explained that "high resolution graphics" are "pen line graphics, basically, using single pixel draw, which means one dot on the screen would be one pixel, and a high resolution graphic would be made up of numerous lines of one pixel". A game with high resolution graphics has illustrations that are more realistic or detailed than low-resolution, or block, graphics will permit. 3 Record at 32–33.

connection with a number of computer games. In October 1982 Sierra sued to stop Phoenix from using the term in connection with Phoenix games. The district court issued a temporary restraining order on October 28, 1982, and a preliminary injunction on February 3, 1983. In granting the injunction, the court held that "Hi–Res Adventure" is a "descriptive" term, that such a term can be a protected trademark only if it has acquired secondary meaning, and that Sierra had shown "a fair chance of success on the merits". Although the court found that Sierra had not yet produced sufficient evidence to support an ultimate finding of secondary meaning, the court granted the injunction because the balance of hardships strongly favored Sierra. Phoenix had voluntarily stopped using the term and would therefore not be injured by the injunction. The court did not explicitly discuss Phoenix's principal contentions: that "Hi–Res Adventure" was a generic term incapable of trademark protection, and that Phoenix was protected by a "fair use" defense.

On February 14 Phoenix filed a motion for reconsideration and a memorandum of points and authorities in support of this motion, but did not file a formal "Notice of Motion", setting a date for hearing, until February 23. The motion for reconsideration did not assert any new grounds, but rather reasserted the "generic" and "fair use" defenses. The district court denied the motion for reconsideration on May 31. At that time the court also denied Phoenix's motion for summary judgment. On June 30 Phoenix filed its notice of appeal "from the Order denying the Motion for Reconsideration of Preliminary Injunction and the Motion for Summary Judgment entered in this action on the 31st day of May, 1983".

II

* * *

In this case, Phoenix had voluntarily stopped using the disputed term "Hi–Res Adventure"; Sierra, on the other hand, stood to suffer from consumer confusion if Phoenix resumed use of the term. Phoenix has not challenged, either in its motion for reconsideration or in this appeal, the trial court's finding that the balance of hardships strongly favored Sierra. We must therefore determine whether the trial judge abused his discretion in concluding that Sierra had a "fair chance of success on the merits".

Phoenix contends that "Hi–Res Adventure" is a generic phrase and therefore unprotectible. The trial judge held that the phrase is descriptive and that to prevail on the merits Sierra will therefore have to show that the mark had acquired secondary meaning, that is, that the purchasing public generally believes that a product bearing the mark is in some way connected with Sierra or its products. The court stated that Sierra had a fair chance of establishing secondary meaning, but would have to produce more evidence at trial to meet its burden of proof. Phoenix, asserting that a descriptive mark may not be protected unless secondary meaning is shown, now argues that the trial judge cannot grant an injunction unless he first makes a finding of secondary meaning. This argument misperceives the purpose of a *preliminary* injunction. As pointed out earlier, the injunction is not a preliminary adjudication on the ultimate merits: it is an equitable device for preserving rights pending final resolution of the dispute. The district court is not required to make any binding findings of fact; it need only find probabilities that the necessary facts can be proved. In this case the trial court could reasonably conclude that Sierra had shown enough to support a preliminary injunction. Sierra produced correspondence from consumers stating that they understood "Hi–Res Adventure" to identify Sierra's products, and also produced trade publications that referred to Sierra's products only as "Hi–Res Adventures". The court could reasonably assume that more evidence in the same vein could be produced at trial. Accordingly, it could properly find that Sierra had a fair chance of success in proving that the mark was descriptive, not generic, and that the mark had acquired secondary meaning.

Phoenix also argues that it has an absolute "fair use" defense, making a preliminary injunction inappropriate. Phoenix bases this defense on section 33 of the Lanham Act, which provides that an incontestable registered trademark is not infringed if

> "the use of the name, term, or device charged to be an infringement is a use, otherwise than as a trade or service mark * * * of a term or device which is descriptive of and used fairly and in good faith only to describe to users the goods or services of such party, or their geographic origin. * * *"

15 U.S.C. § 1115(b)(4) (1982). By its terms this statutory defense applies only to registered trademarks that have become incontestable through passage of time. "Hi–Res Adventure" is not such a trademark. Assuming, as Phoenix argues, that a common-law fair use defense exists, the defense is neither absolute nor so clearly applicable to this case as to make a preliminary injunction inappropriate. Phoenix must show that it "is making good faith *non-trademark use* " of the phrase "Hi–Res Adventure". 1 J. Gilson, Trademark Protection and Practice § 4.03[3][c], at 4–27 (1984). It is not obvious that Phoenix's use was a non-trademark use, that is, that the term was used only to describe the product rather than to associate it with a manufacturer. Furthermore, Phoenix's good faith is in issue: its choice of the phrase "Hi–Res Adventure" when other phrases were available could indicate an intent to trade on Sierra's good will and product identity. The fair use defense, therefore, is not so obvious as to deny Sierra a fair chance of success.

In the absence of any suggestion that the preliminary injunction will harm Phoenix, the district court did not abuse its discretion. The order granting the preliminary injunction is affirmed. In all other respects the appeal is dismissed.

Note and Question

This is the "look and feel" problem revisited. Customers like Sierra On–Line's "Hi–Res Adventure" games. Assuming that Phoenix Software has avoided copyright violations, shouldn't it have some way to tell customers they will be getting the kind of games they like so much?

UNITED STATES GOLF ASSOCIATION v. ST. ANDREWS SYSTEMS, DATA–MAX, INC.

United States Court of Appeals, Third Circuit, 1984.
749 F.2d 1028.

BECKER, CIRCUIT JUDGE.

This appeal presents two interesting questions in the law of intellectual property. It arises from a lawsuit brought by appellant, the United States Golf Association ("U.S.G.A."), the governing body of amateur golf in the United States. The U.S.G.A. has developed a system for deriving the "handicaps" of amateur golfers, the core of which is a mathematical formula. Appellee Data–Max, Inc., d/b/a St. Andrews Systems, markets small computers that are programmed to calculate a golfer's handicap based on the U.S.G.A. formula. The U.S.G.A. brought this suit to enjoin Data–Max from using its formula as the basis for its computerized handicap system.

The U.S.G.A. bases its claim for an injunction on two theories. The first is that the use of the U.S.G.A. formula by Data–Max amounts to a "false designation of origin," and thus violates both section 43(a) of the Lanham Act, 15 U.S.C. § 1125(a), and the New Jersey common law against unfair competition. * * *

We conclude that the U.S.G.A. handicap formula is "functional," and thus that the U.S.G.A. cannot enjoin the use of the formula either under section 43(a) of the Lanham Act or under state law on the basis of any association in the public mind between the formula and the U.S.G.A. * * *

I. FACTS AND PROCEDURAL HISTORY

The U.S.G.A. has been the governing body of amateur golf in the United States since 1894. It seeks to promote the game of golf by numerous means, including the establishment of rules and regulations for play, the promotion of amateur tournaments, and the regulation of its member golf clubs. Among the services that the U.S.G.A. provides to amateur golfers is a "handicap" formula that allows golfers of different skill levels to compete with each other on an equal basis. The U.S.G.A. handicap system takes account of the difficulty of the course on which a round is played and provides "safeguards" against the inflation of handicaps by excluding particularly bad holes and by counting only the best ten of a golfer's last twenty rounds.[1]

1. The U.S.G.A. brief outlines the critical elements of the U.S.G.A. handicap formula:

The U.S.G.A. has developed the handicap formula over a period of eighty years. The first version of the system was published in 1897. A system based on a golfer's best three scores, first devised in 1904, was adopted by the U.S.G.A. in 1911. In later years, the basic formula was altered by the addition of several features: a "course rating system" and "net score" (score adjusted for course difficulty) method of handicapping; a "current ability" approach, in which only a golfer's most recent scores are counted; a system of "equitable stroke control" which disallows very high scores for individual holes; an upper limit on handicaps; and a "discounting" approach, in which a handicap is calculated based on a percentage, currently 96%, of the differentials between the player's score and the course difficulty. A single, nationwide system was prescribed by the U.S.G.A. in 1958. The most recent change of significance took place on January 1, 1976.

Data–Max was incorporated in 1980 for the purpose of providing golfers, primarily those who do not belong to U.S.G.A.-member clubs, with "instant handicaps." A computer program to calculate a handicap based on the U.S.G.A. formula is central to the products and services that Data–Max offers. Data–Max has sold or leased its computer to U.S.G.A.-member golf clubs, which use the computer in calculating handicaps.[2] Data–Max also markets a subscription telephone handicap service, which enables a golfer to call in a new score and immediately receive an updated handicap, and a computer that enables a golfer to directly enter a new score and receive an updated handicap.[3]

The U.S.G.A. filed a three count complaint in the United States District Court for the District of New Jersey, seeking relief for service mark infringement under the Lanham Act, 15 U.S.C. §§ 1051 *et seq.;* for service mark infringement, unfair competition, and misappropriation under the common law of New Jersey; and for unfair competition under Section 43(a) of the Lanham Act, 15 U.S.C. § 1125(a). Data–Max responded with a seven-count counterclaim. The two primary counterclaims sought declaratory judgments on the two critical issues in the

The U.S.G.A. Handicap Formula uses a golfer's ten best adjusted scores out of his most recent twenty adjusted scores.* The U.S.G.A. Handicap Formula also reflects the difficulty of the golf course on which each score was achieved. The Formula averages the lowest ten handicap "differentials" ** among the golfer's last twenty scores, multiplies the total by 96 percent, and then rounds off to the nearest whole number.

* A golfer's adjusted score reflects certain adjustments which are designed to eliminate aberrations caused by an unusually high score on a single hole.

** A differential represents the difference between a golfer's adjusted score and the course rating of the golf course on which the golfer achieved that score.

2. The U.S.G.A. has no objection to this aspect of Data–Max's business, since the handicap is ultimately provided by a member golf club. The U.S.G.A. objects to an unauthorized organization, such as Data–Max, providing handicaps derived by means of the U.S.G.A. formula directly to golfers.

3. This service operates on the same principle as electronic teller machines: a golfer puts his or her plastic "score card" into the machine and types in the new score. The machine then tells the golfer the new handicap.

case: Data–Max's right to use the U.S.G.A. formula in providing handicaps, and its right to advertise that use.

The district court considered these issues on Data–Max's motion for summary judgment on the counterclaims. The district court granted the motion on the first counterclaim mentioned above. The court held * * * that, because the formula was "functional," it was not subject to protection under either federal or state law as a service mark. The court denied the summary judgment motion on the second counterclaim, holding that material issues of fact existed as to the "likelihood of confusion" if Data–Max continued to advertise that its handicaps were calculated by use of the U.S.G.A. formula. Having granted summary judgment on the first counterclaim, the court then entered a final judgment as to that claim under Rule 54(b). The U.S.G.A. appeals from that judgment.

II. Discussion

A. Contentions of the Parties

The U.S.G.A. advances two distinct legal theories to support its claim to an injunction. The first, which can be broadly characterized as "false designation of origin," is based on a branch of the law of unfair competition closely related to trademark law. The U.S.G.A. asserts that Data–Max, by using the U.S.G.A. formula, is misleading the golfing public into thinking that the U.S.G.A. endorses Data–Max's products and services. * * *

On appeal, the U.S.G.A. argues that the district court erred in both its conclusions. On the first theory, the U.S.G.A. argues that, on summary judgment, the district court was obligated to presume that the public associated the formula with the U.S.G.A., since the evidence would support such a conclusion. In addressing the district court's conclusion that the formula was functional, the U.S.G.A. argues that "even though a product or feature performs a function (*i.e.,* is useful), it can nevertheless acquire secondary meaning," and that other handicap formulas could easily be devised. From these two premises, the U.S.G.A. argues that the "functionality" doctrine was inapplicable. Alternatively, the U.S.G.A. argues that "the functionality doctrine * * * covers only matters of physical or visual design." * * *

In response, Data–Max raises two basic arguments with respect to the false designation of origin question. The first is that the formula can have no secondary meaning because it is neither "an object in commerce" nor an "identification for an object in commerce." Their second point is that the "use of the formula to compute does not exhibit it, and therefore [the formula] *could not be a designation of origin,*" (emphasis in original) and hence could not be a *false* designation of origin. * * *

Although we reach the result advocated by Data–Max, our reasoning differs substantially from that advanced by the parties. On the false designation of origin point, our reasoning parallels that of the district court. * * *

B. *The "False Designation of Origin" Claim*

Under both New Jersey law and federal law, the functional aspects of a product or service may not be protected under trademark law, or under the related unfair competition doctrines based on possible confusion as to the source of origin of the products or services.[6] This rule reflects a balancing of divergent social interests. The use of "non-functional" features of a product or service to identify its source is legally protected against limitation by competitors, because the value of such features in identifying the source of the goods or services outweighs the social interest in allowing competitors to copy them. Functional features, on the other hand, may not be legally protected methods of identification, regardless of their association with the original manufacturer, because their usefulness in identifying the source of the product or service is outweighed by the social interest in competition and improvements, which are advanced by giving competitors free access to those features.

The "functionality" of a feature of a product or service cannot be determined by the application of a mechanical test. Although various forms of the inquiry have been articulated,[7] the essence of the question

6. The New Jersey and Lanham Act requirements for a finding of unfair competition are substantively similar. *See SK & F Co.,* 625 F.2d at 1065–66. To establish "unprivileged imitation" of a competitor's product, under either the Lanham Act or New Jersey law, a plaintiff must establish both "non-functionality" and "secondary meaning." *Id.* at 1063 (New Jersey law).

A preliminary requirement of § 43(a) of the Lanham Act is that plaintiff establish a likelihood of damages. *Johnson & Johnson v. Carter–Wallace, Inc.,* 631 F.2d 186, 190 (2d Cir.1980); *Ames Publ. Co. v. Walker–Davis Publ.,* 372 F.Supp. 1, 13 (E.D.Pa. 1974). There must be "more than a mere subjective belief" that the plaintiff is likely to be harmed. *Coca–Cola Co. v. Tropicana Products, Inc.,* 690 F.2d 312, 316–17 (2d Cir.1982). It is not clear on the record developed thus far whether the handicap formula at issue had any commercial value for the U.S.G.A., and therefore, whether U.S.G.A. is likely to be injured by defendant's use of the formula. However, since none of the parties raised this issue at trial or on appeal, we will not hinge our result on this requirement. At all events, it has not been suggested that the U.S.G.A.'s interest in its formula is insufficient to create a "case or controversy" within the meaning of Article III.

7. Section 742 of the Restatement of Torts provides the most commonly cited definition of functionality. That section defines functionality as follows:

> A feature of goods is functional, under the rule stated in § 741, if it affects their purpose, action or performance, or the facility or economy of processing, handling or using them; it is non-functional if it does not have any of such effects.

Comment a further elaborates on that definition:

> a. A feature of goods, or of their wrappers or containers, may be functional because it contributes to efficiency or economy in manufacturing them or in handling them through the marketing process. It may be functional, also, because it contributes to their utility, to their durability or to the effectiveness or ease with which they serve their function or are handled by users. When goods are bought largely for their aesthetic value, their features may be functional because they definitely contribute to that value and thus aid the performance of an object for which the goods are intended. Thus, the shape of a bottle or other container may be functional though a different bottle or container may hold the goods equally well. A candy box in the shape of a heart may be functional, because of its significance as a gift to a beloved one, while a box of a

is whether a particular feature of a product or service is substantially related to its value *as a product or service, i.e.,* if the feature is part of the "function" served, or whether the primary value of a particular feature is the identification of the provider. *See In re Morton–Norwich Products, Inc.,* 671 F.2d 1332, 1337–40 (C.C.P.A.1982); Restatement of Torts § 742 comment a (1938). Several courts have noted that the key policy served by barring the use of functional features for identification is the policy favoring competition, and that the "functionality" inquiry must be addressed in light of this policy. *See Morton–Norwich Products,* 671 F.2d at 1339.

The question of the "functionality" of the U.S.G.A. formula is not difficult. Its simple mathematical formula is the basic tool for deriving a handicap from a golfer's raw scores; as such, the formula is central to the "function" performed by the Data–Max products and services. The U.S.G.A., relying on *Ideal Toy Corp. v. Plawner Toy Manufacturing Corp.,* 685 F.2d 78 (3d Cir.1982), argues that the availability of numerous alternative methods of designing a particular feature of a product or service defeats the functionality of any single method. This argument proceeds from an overly broad reading of *Plawner.* Although other formulas could be developed to serve the function of handicapping golfers, a particular method of serving that function may be superior to others. The feature at issue in *Plawner,* the color scheme of the Rubik's Cube, was held to be non-functional because the choice of colors was essentially arbitrary. If another aspect of the cube had been in issue, for instance, the internal design or the number of squares per side, a different result would probably have been reached. The manufacturer could not have asserted that these features were "non-functional" simply on the ground that other designs were conceivable because granting a monopoly over the "best" design of those features would have effectively excluded competition for the basic product—six-sided puzzles requiring that nine independent panels on each side be aligned in a single particular configuration.

different shape or the form in which a ribbon is tied around the box may not be functional. Or a distinctive printing type face may be functional though the print from a different type may be read equally well. The determination of whether or not such features are functional depends upon the question of fact whether prohibition of imitation by others will deprive the others of something which will substantially hinder them in competition.

A feature is non-functional if, when omitted, nothing of substantial value in the goods is lost. A feature which merely associates goods with a particular source may be, like a trade-mark or trade name, a substantial factor in increasing the marketability of the goods. But if that is the entire significance of the feature, it is non-functional; for its value then lies only in the demand for goods associated with a particular source rather than for goods of a particular design.

As to the significance of the distinction between functional and non-functional features, *see* § 741, Comment j.

The Restatement (Second) of Torts did not deal with these questions, because its drafters felt that this area had become a separate area of law. Courts continue to cite the First Restatement on the definition of functionality. *E.g., In re Hollaender Mfg. Co.,* 511 F.2d 1186 (C.C.P.A.1975). *See also* 4A R. Callmann, The Law of Unfair Competition, Trademarks and Monopolies, § 25.29 n. 11 (4th ed. 1983).

When products or services of different providers are close substitutes for one another, the development of "industry standards" for certain aspects of the products or services will benefit consumers by facilitating comparability between and interchangeability among alternative products. The fact that any number of standards may be feasible and useful does not mean that the preferred standard is not "functional," since use of that standard promotes comparability and interchangeability. The U.S.G.A. formula is like an "industry standard": it allows the handicaps calculated by different providers to be compared with one another, much as the standard gauge of railroad track allows a locomotive of one company to run on the track of another. Allowing one provider to obtain exclusive rights in such a standard would enable it to exclude competitors desiring to provide the same product or service, particularly if the original provider, such as the U.S.G.A. in this case, starts with a virtual monopoly. To allow a monopoly over such a standard would defeat the policy of fostering competition that underlies the functionality doctrine.

The U.S.G.A. has raised no factual issues that would call into question a conclusion that the formula is "functional." Accordingly, we hold that the district court's entry of summary judgment on this aspect of the U.S.G.A.'s claim was appropriate.

* * * To the extent that the approval of the U.S.G.A. would enhance the value of "instant handicaps," the U.S.G.A. has an opportunity, if it wishes to exercise it, of offering either Data–Max or other companies the use of the U.S.G.A. name in marketing its products and services.

III. Conclusion

We hold that the U.S.G.A. has no legally protectible interest in its formula, and thus is not entitled to an injunction in this case. The U.S.G.A. formula is a functional aspect of its handicap system, and thus may not be protected as an identifying characteristic under either federal or New Jersey law. The false designation of origin claims are therefore legally insufficient. * * *

Accordingly, the judgment of the district court will be affirmed.

Notes and Questions

1. Consider again *Apple Computer, Inc. v. Formula International Inc.,* 562 F.Supp. 775. If Formula International changed the name of its computer from "Pineapple" to "Pinecone" and avoided violating Apple's copyrights and patents, would Apple have any claim against it?

2. Nutek Computers says it will be licensing technology to manufacturers who then will be able to produce legal "clones" of the Apple Macintosh computer. Andrew Pollack, Small Company in Effort to Clone an Apple Computer, New York Times, Jan. 24, 1991, p. D1. If a manufacturer makes such "clones" without violating Apple's patents or copyrights, it will want to advertise its success by stating, "Our Computers will run software designed for Apple's Macintosh Computers." Since this will be a

true statement, the manufacturer probably has a First Amendment right to make it. Must it add a disclaimer, "Macintosh is a Registered Trademark of Apple Computer, with which Nutek has no connection?"

3. Makers of "clone" computers may find the law of other countries more restrictive. In a leading case, *Bismag v. Amblins Ltd.*, [1940] Ch. 667, a British court, interpreting an English trademark statute of "fuliginous obscurity," held that Amblins, a competitor, could not use the Bismag trademark in the truthful statement that its pharmaceutical product was the chemical equivalent of Bismag.

4. Obviously St. Andrews Systems must do more than use the United States Golf Association formula to be successful. It must somehow convey to golfers that the St. Andrews Systems computer will use the same formula as that used by the United States Golf Association. It must, however, avoid a false implication of sponsorship by the United States Golf Association.

5. The United States Golf Association can exploit its name by making or endorsing a computer as "The Only Computer Officially Approved by the United States Golf Association."

Chapter XV

RESTRICTION OF COMPETITION IN THE COMPUTER INDUSTRY

A. RESTRICTIONS ON TELEPHONE COMPANY COMPETITION

For decades, the Federal government has restricted telecommunications companies from offering computer services. Because computer services are closely related to telecommunications, the government feared that these companies would use their regulated monopoly powers in telecommunications to extract unregulated monopoly profits from computers. The telephone companies attack these restrictions, arguing that only they can offer vigorous competition in a field dominated by huge American companies such as IBM and Japanese-government-supported electronics conglomerates.

Paradoxically, the year 1956 saw both a successful attack on the AT&T monopoly of telephone services and a consent decree based upon the assumption of the continued existence of the monopoly. The attack came in *Hush–A–Phone Corp. v. United States,* 238 F.2d 266 (D.C.Cir. 1956), which tested the legality of a tariff prohibiting all "foreign attachments" to the AT&T phone system. The Federal Communications Commission (FCC) had determined that the use of devices such as Hush-a-Phone was "deleterious to the telephone system" and would result in a general degradation of the quality of service. The Court of Appeals for the District of Columbia reversed, holding that the tariff was an unwarranted interference with the right of the telephone subscriber to reasonably use the telephone in ways that are privately beneficial without being publicly detrimental. On remand, the FCC invalidated the tariff prohibiting foreign attachments, but only as to Hush–a–Phones. Many other cases followed, in which the AT&T end-to-end service was challenged. In the 1970s and 1980s, the FCC gradually permitted competition against AT&T. A 1956 antitrust consent decree prohibited AT&T from offering, even through a separate subsidiary, any device that possessed the capability to perform any data processing function. The purpose of this decree was to prevent AT&T from using its communications monopoly to secure monopoly powers over data processing.

In 1974, the Department of Justice filed another antitrust case against AT&T. The suit was brought under Section Two of the Sherman Act and relied initially on a novel "triple-bottleneck" theory. The Justice Department alleged, in essence, that AT&T had illegally manipulated its dominant position in three sets of telecommunications markets—equipment, local exchange, and long-distance, in order to monopolize the entire domestic telecommunications industry. In January 1982, the parties agreed to a settlement. In return for spinning off regional telephone companies, and other concessions, AT&T emerged with the right to manufacture computer systems and provide computer services, thus escaping from the 1956 consent decree. The spun-off regional companies, however, remained subject to a ban on providing computerized information services. The final agreement between the Justice Department and AT&T is called the Modified Final Judgment.

The Modified Final Judgment seeks to achieve three objectives: (1) the promotion of true and fair competition in the telecommunications long distance and equipment markets, (2) the preservation of AT&T as a dynamic force, capable of research, manufacturing, and marketing in technologically advanced fields, and (3) the protection of the principle of universal telephone service, accessible to all segments of the population regardless of income.

The Regional Operating Companies suffer more severe restrictions than AT&T under the Modified Final Judgment. Not surprisingly, they have asked for interpretations of and changes in the Modified Final Judgment on several occasions. In particular, they have found the restrictions on entering computerized information services and other communications-related businesses to be increasingly burdensome. They have repeatedly asked for "waivers" to enter more business banned by Modified Final Judgment. The following decision shows the complexity of the issues.

UNITED STATES v. WESTERN ELECTRIC COMPANY

United States Court of Appeals, District of Columbia Circuit, 1990.
900 F.2d 283.

Before MIKVA, EDWARDS and SILBERMAN, CIRCUIT JUDGES.

Opinion for the Court filed PER CURIAM.

PER CURIAM:

As part of the 1982 consent decree that severed the seven Regional Bell Operating Companies ("BOCs") from AT & T, the parties agreed that the BOCs, which inherited AT & T's local exchange monopoly, would be prohibited from providing interexchange (long distance) or information services, manufacturing telephone equipment, and participating in any non-telecommunications industry. The district judge retained jurisdiction over the case, and the Department of Justice ("DOJ") pledged to report to the court every three years as to the continuing need for these "line of business" restrictions. In the first such "Triennial Review," after considering the DOJ's report, as well as the comments of the other parties and dozens of other individuals and organizations, the district judge issued two opinions lifting the restriction against BOC participation in non-telecommunication businesses, modifying the restriction against their entering the information services market, and leaving intact the interexchange and manufacturing restrictions. *See United States v. Western Elec. Co.,* 673 F.Supp. 525 (D.D.C.1987); *United States v. Western Elec. Co.,* 714 F.Supp. 1 (D.D.C.1988). With the exception of the district judge's ruling dealing with information services—which we reverse and remand—we affirm.

I.

A. The 1982 Consent Decree

In 1974, the DOJ filed this antitrust suit against AT & T. After seven years of pretrial proceedings, the case was tried in district court for eleven months but did not culminate in a verdict. Instead, the parties submitted a proposed consent decree to the court for review according to the "public interest" standard prescribed by the Antitrust Procedures and Penalties Act, 15 U.S.C. § 16(b)–(h) ("Tunney Act"). After extensive Tunney Act proceedings, and after the parties agreed to certain modifications added by the district judge, the district court approved the decree. *See United States v. American Tel. & Tel. Co.,* 552 F.Supp. 131 (D.D.C.1982), *aff'd sub nom. Maryland v. United States,* 460 U.S. 1001, 103 S.Ct. 1240, 75 L.Ed.2d 472 (1983).

Although the district court made no explicit findings of liability in the course of the Tunney Act proceedings, it did examine whether the evidence was sufficient to warrant antitrust relief. The evidence indicated that AT & T or the "Bell System" was, at the time of the trial, a massive, vertically-integrated enterprise which enjoyed a monopoly in local exchange services, provided long distance service, designed and developed telephone equipment (through Bell Laboratories), and manufactured that equipment at its wholly-owned subsidiary, Western Electric. AT & T used its local exchange monopoly—the so-called "bottleneck"—in a number of ways to promote its own affiliated operations in the long distance and equipment fields. In the interexchange field, other providers such as MCI were dependent on AT & T's local exchange facilities since there was no other way to reach the ultimate consumer. AT & T therefore had a strong incentive to provide more expensive or inferior quality local exchange access to its long distance competitors than it provided to itself. According to the DOJ, despite vigilant FCC attempts to prevent it, AT & T was able to discriminate against its interexchange competitors and, in that way, to stave off significant interexchange competition. *See* 552 F.Supp. at 160–63.

* * *

Under the consent decree, AT & T retained its long distance and equipment manufacturing operations but agreed to divest itself of its local exchange monopoly, transferring those operations to the BOCs which were to become totally separate from AT & T. In turn, the BOCs were to be limited to the provision of local exchange services and precluded from participating in the markets for interexchange (long distance) services, equipment manufacturing, information services,[5] and all other non-telecommunications businesses. *See* 552 F.Supp. at 227–28. The BOCs were, however, permitted to provide—but not manufacture—customer premises equipment and also to produce, publish, and distribute "Yellow Pages" directories. *See* 552 F.Supp. at 231. These line of business restrictions were premised on the notion that, because the BOCs still controlled the local exchange bottlenecks, there was a risk that they would engage in the same sort of anticompetitive abuses that AT & T had. *See* 552 F.Supp. at 187–91.

Before approving the restrictions, the district judge scrutinized them carefully to ensure "that they will not actually limit competition by unnecessarily barring a competitor from a market." 552 F.Supp. at 186. He rejected as overly simplistic the DOJ's equation of the post-divestiture BOCs with the pre-divestiture Bell System based simply on the proposition that they both possessed a monopoly in local telecommunications. The separated BOCs, the district judge recognized, would be far more manageable monopolists for regulators to oversee than AT & T had been because they would be regional rather than national in scope, they would not be vertically integrated, and, if permitted to enter competitive markets, they would face "the most potent conceivable competitor: AT & T itself." 552 F.Supp. at 187. He therefore ruled that the Tunney Act's public interest standard would permit banning the BOCs from a market only if there was a substantial possibility that the BOCs would use monopoly power to impede competition in that market. 552 F.Supp. at 187. As part of that "public interest" analysis, the district judge undertook a two-part inquiry to determine for each market barred to the BOCs whether (1) the BOCs would actually have the incentive and opportunity to act anticompetitively and (2) whether the participation of the BOCs would contribute to the creation of a competitive market. *See* 552 F.Supp. at 187, 188–94. In addition, the district judge examined the effect of the restrictions on "important

5. Section IV(J) of the decree defines "information services" as:

> the offering of a capability for generating, acquiring, storing, transforming, processing, retrieving, utilizing, or making available information which may be conveyed via telecommunications, except that such service does not include any use of any such capability for the management, control, or operation of a telecommunications system or the management of a telecommunications service.

552 F.Supp. at 229.

public policies." 552 F.Supp. at 187. The district judge ultimately determined that the proposed restrictions were indeed warranted.

The line of business restrictions were not meant necessarily to be permanent, however. The district judge retained jurisdiction [6] and insisted that a mechanism be inserted into the decree for removing them at a later date. Rejecting the DOJ's view that mere monopoly power in local exchange services warranted the restrictions, the district judge thought that removal of the restrictions should be governed by a standard that allows a petitioning BOC to prove that there is no substantial possibility that the BOC could use its monopoly power to impede competition in the relevant market. *See* 552 F.Supp. at 195. The district judge therefore drafted, and the parties agreed to, section VIII(C) of the decree, which reads:

> The restrictions imposed upon the separated BOCs by virtue of section II(D) [the line of business restrictions] shall be removed upon a showing by the petitioning BOC that there is no substantial possibility that it could use its monopoly power to impede competition in the market it seeks to enter.

552 F.Supp. at 231. This removal standard was intended to supplant the "test usually applied to a contested modification of a consent decree," set out in *United States v. Swift & Co.* that asks whether " 'unforeseen conditions' " make modification appropriate. *See* 552 F.Supp. at 195 n. 266 (quoting *United States v. Swift & Co.*, 286 U.S. 106, 119, 52 S.Ct. 460, 464, 76 L.Ed. 999 (1932)). Whether section VIII(C) would also apply to *uncontested* modifications is a question upon which the district court was silent in 1982.

B. *The Triennial Review*

When the decree was entered, the DOJ pledged to report to the court on the third anniversary of divestiture and every three years thereafter on the continuing need for the line of business restrictions. Since divestiture was not actually accomplished until 1984, the first such Triennial Review was held in 1987. The DOJ hired an independent consultant, Peter Huber, to conduct in-depth research on the telecommunications industry as a whole as well as on each of the relevant sub-markets. The *Huber Report* provided the factual basis for the DOJ's preliminary submission, filed with the district court in February 1987, in which it recommended the complete removal of the manufacturing, non-telecommunications, and information restrictions as well as the modification of the interexchange restriction. Quite clearly, the DOJ's position—which conceded the continued existence of

6. Section VII of the decree is entitled "Retention of Jurisdiction" and reads:

> Jurisdiction is retained by this Court for the purpose of enabling any of the parties to this Modification of Final Judgment, or, after the reorganization specified in section I, a BOC to apply to this Court at any time for such further orders or directions as may be necessary or appropriate for the construction or carrying out of this Modification of Final Judgment, for the modification of any of the provisions hereof, for the enforcement of compliance herewith, and for the punishment of any violation hereof.

552 F.Supp. at 231.

the BOCs' local exchange monopoly—represented a significant change from its position when the decree was entered that mere monopoly power in local exchange services necessitated the restrictions.

After studying the comments of the parties and intervenors on its recommendations, the DOJ formally moved the court—apparently under section VIII(C) of the decree—for the removal of all the line of business restrictions, with the exception of the interexchange restriction. The DOJ was evidently persuaded to alter its position on interexchange services, and it instead asked the court to leave the restriction intact but to grant waivers as soon as local regulation in a given area is lifted. The Department believes that the BOCs' bottleneck monopolies persist primarily because of local regulation which, if removed, would allow potentially competitive access alternatives to be made available by new technology. The seven BOCs also filed motions under section VIII(C) of the decree asking for complete removal of all the line of business restrictions.

The district court held proceedings in which interested persons were invited to comment and respond to the report and the motions. With respect to the non-telecommunications and information services restrictions, all of the parties to the original decree—AT & T, the BOCs, and the DOJ—as well as the FCC agreed that the restrictions should be removed.[7] AT & T opposed any modification of the other restrictions, thus making those BOC motions undeniably "contested." Not surprisingly, numerous existing participants in the markets that the BOCs sought to enter intervened and vigorously opposed each of the proposed modifications. And, as noted above, the DOJ opposed the complete removal of the interexchange restriction.

After discussing the standard for removal of restrictions under section VIII(C) of the decree, the district judge determined that the BOCs still possessed a bottleneck monopoly over local exchange service. *See* 673 F.Supp. at 536–40. The court then analyzed each line of business restriction to decide whether the BOCs had nevertheless met their burden under section VIII(C) to warrant removal. In reviewing the restriction concerning nontelecommunications businesses, the court noted that it had routinely reviewed and granted requests to waive this restriction since the decree became operational in 1984. Despite losing the safeguards that the waiver process afforded by virtue of the conditions imposed whenever a waiver was granted,[8] the district court removed the restriction entirely because potential competitors did not

7. AT & T stated that it did not oppose information services relief for the BOCs but argued that any modification of that restriction should be made pursuant to section VII of the decree, not under section VIII(C).

8. The court normally required the BOCs to operate the competitive business through a separate subsidiary that would obtain its own debt financing. Furthermore, the total net revenues for all non-telecommunications activities engaged in by a single BOC were limited to ten percent of that company's total net revenues. These conditions were designed to minimize the risk of cross-subsidization and to guarantee that the BOCs would not neglect their primary responsibility of providing local telephone service. *See* 673 F.Supp. at 598.

actively oppose the removal and because cross-subsidization is more difficult in enterprises unrelated to telecommunications. *See* 673 F.Supp. at 599. In addition, the court asserted that lifting the restriction would eliminate a significant burden on BOCs' business planning and free the court from unnecessary and detailed oversight of BOC decisions. *See id.*

The district judge left largely intact the decree's so-called "core" restrictions—those regarding interexchange services, manufacturing, and information services. The manufacturing and interexchange restrictions remained completely unchanged since the district court rejected arguments that circumstances had changed since the issuance of the decree so as to justify the BOCs' entrance into those markets under the standard imposed by section VIII(C). The district judge did grant partial relief to the BOCs on the information services provision but rejected the request of the DOJ and the BOCs to remove the restriction entirely for much the same reasons as he left the manufacturing and interexchange restrictions in place. The court asserted that information services are vulnerable even to slight manipulation and discrimination in access or transmission quality, thereby making it especially easy for the BOCs to use their bottleneck monopolies anticompetitively if they entered the market. *See* 673 F.Supp. at 566. Nevertheless, the information restriction was lifted insofar as it prevented the BOCs from providing transmission of information services generated by others. *See* 673 F.Supp. at 587–97. The district judge described the economic and social advantages of making information services more widely available and noted that the telephone system was perhaps the only means of accomplishing that goal, because it uniquely offers providers a means "to reach large, dispersed audiences over reasonably priced, interactive facilities." 673 F.Supp. at 564. So long as the BOCs do not compete with the companies that *generate* the information services, the district judge reasoned, they would have an incentive to afford the widest, fastest, and highest quality access and transmission to all information providers, thereby maximizing their own revenues. This determination was further explained and substantially reaffirmed by the district judge following a separate proceeding held to work out the details of the information services restriction. *See* 714 F.Supp. at 1. All of these rulings have been appealed.

II.

A. Standard of Review

We have repeatedly held that the construction of a consent decree (indeed of this particular consent decree) is subject to *de novo* appellate review. * * *

* * *

B. Applicability of Section VIII(C)

Except for some BOC petitions regarding information services, the BOCs and the DOJ brought, and the district court analyzed, all of the motions to lift the line of business restriction under the standard set out in section VIII(C) of the decree. It is unclear to us, however, that section VIII(C) applies at all to some of those motions. In the first place, section VIII(C) refers to "a showing by the *petitioning BOC,*" and thus on its face contemplates only petitions brought by BOCs. The DOJ's hard-line position in favor of the restrictions in 1982 further indicates that when the parties agreed to the decree, none of them contemplated that the DOJ would seek to invoke section VIII(C). We do not see, therefore, how the DOJ can petition for removal of restrictions under section VIII(C). That is not to suggest that if section VIII(C) is not available to the DOJ no avenue for requesting modification would be open to it. Section VII explicitly provides for modifications of the decree, and the district court would possess equitable power to modify the decree even if section VII were not included, *see United States v. Swift & Co.,* 286 U.S. 106, 114–15, 52 S.Ct. 460, 462–63, 76 L.Ed. 999 (1932). Furthermore, as a party to the decree, the DOJ's position on any BOC petition would be considered by the district court in much the same way as is an intervenor's views—whether it supports or opposes the petition. Strictly speaking, however, only the BOCs can be petitioners under section VIII(C).

We also believe that section VIII(C) does not apply to proposed modifications that are agreed to by all the parties to the decree, such as the motions for removal of the restrictions on BOC entry into the information services field. Section VIII(C) speaks of a "*showing* by the *petitioning* BOC," thereby indicating that it applies only to contested motions for removal—and this reading comports with the intent of the parties as expressed to the district court in 1982. *See infra* Part III.C.1. As we explain more fully in Part III of this opinion, uncontested motions for modification—those involving the information services and non-telecommunications businesses restrictions—should be treated by the district judge under section VII of the decree, and should be approved so long as the modifications satisfy the "public interest" standard embodied in the Tunney Act. Thus, while both the district judge and the parties treated the removal of the line of business restrictions as though it were governed entirely by section VIII(C), that section was really the appropriate standard only for the BOC petitions for removal of the manufacturing and interexchange restrictions—the former opposed by AT & T and the latter by both AT & T and the DOJ.

* * *

C. Information Services

The BOCs and the DOJ also appeal from the district court's decision not to lift the restriction on "information services" under section II(D)(1), as that restriction is applied to the *generation* of information.[25] The district court found that there had "been no signifi-

25. Under the Decree, "Information service" means the offering of a capability for generating, acquiring,

cant, relevant change in" market conditions justifying removal of this restraint under section VIII(C). 673 F.Supp. at 564. Noting that neither the DOJ nor AT & T opposed lifting the information services ban, the BOCs contend that the district court should have reviewed this question under a more flexible "public interest" standard pursuant to section VII. *See supra* note 6. We agree, and hold that the district court erred in applying section VIII(C) to the uncontested motion to remove the line-of-business restriction on information services. And because we are unable to say that the district court would have reached the same result had it applied the proper legal standard, we are constrained to remand the case for further consideration of the BOCs' motion to remove the information services ban in its entirety.

1. The Applicability of Section VII to Uncontested Motions to Modify a Line-of-Business Restriction Under the Decree

* * *

2. Application of the Public Interest Test to the Motion to Remove the Restriction on Information Services

Having determined that section VII's public interest test governs uncontested proposals to modify the decree's line-of-business restrictions, we must next examine whether the district court's erroneous reliance on section VIII(C) affected the court's decision to deny the BOCs' unopposed motion to remove the decree's restriction on information services. We conclude that it did, and, consequently, we reverse.

As we have indicated, section VII and section VIII(C) involve different inquiries. Section VII's public interest test directs the district court to approve an uncontested modification so long as the resulting array of rights and obligations is within the *zone of settlements* consonant with the public interest *today*. *Cf. Bechtel Corp.*, 648 F.2d at 666. Section VIII(C) requires the district court to determine whether the petitioning BOC has shown that it could not impede competition in the relevant market as it was believed it could *when the decree was approved;* applying this standard, Judge Greene denied the BOCs' motion to remove the information-services restriction because he found that "[t]here has been no change whatever in" the information services market. 673 F.Supp. at 565.

Under only two circumstances could we discount the possibility that the district court would have reached a different result had it applied section VII rather than section VIII(C). The first would be if the inclusion of the information services restriction was mandatory, not merely permissible, at the time that the decree was adopted. If market conditions or assumptions in 1982 so constrained the range of permissi-

storing, transforming, processing, retrieving, utilizing, or making available information which may be conveyed via telecommunications, except that such service does not include any use of any such capability for the management, control, or operation of a telecommunications service.

Decree § IV(J), *reprinted in* 552 F.Supp. at 229.

ble settlements that *only* a decree incorporating this restriction could have been approved as consistent with the public interest *then*, it would follow that the parties would need to show that those conditions had abated before the court could approve removal of the restriction *today*.

We cannot say, on the record before us at least, that this condition is met. The Government's case in the *AT & T* antitrust litigation centered exclusively on AT & T's activities in the interexchange-service and equipment-manufacturing markets. *See, e.g.*, COMPETITIVE IMPACT STATEMENT IN CONNECTION WITH PROPOSED MODIFICATION OF FINAL JUDGMENT, 47 Fed.Reg. 7172 (1982). Indeed, because the 1956 consent decree enjoined AT & T "from engaging * * * in any business other than the furnishing of common carrier communications services," *United States v. Western Elec. Co.*, 1956 Trade Cas. (CCH) ¶ 68,246, at 71,138 (D.N.J.1956), and because relatively few information services were provided to the public before the DOJ moved to reopen that decree in 1974, there really was no record to speak of concerning AT & T's activities in the information services market. The parties agreed to the information services restriction as a precautionary measure in light of uncertainty about how divestiture of AT & T would affect the development of this embryonic market. Under these circumstances, it would not have been legal error for the district court to approve the decree had the parties *not* agreed on their own to include the restriction on information services. Consequently, the district court's bare finding that the BOCs failed to show a *change* in market conditions does not suffice to show that the decree, absent the information services restriction, would no longer be " 'within the reaches of the public interest.' " *Bechtel Corp.*, 648 F.2d at 666 (quoting *Gillette Co.*, 406 F.Supp. at 716).

The second condition under which we could disregard the district court's reliance on section VIII(C) would be if the record conclusively showed that, regardless of whether the parties were *obliged* to include the information services restriction in 1982, removing it would be against the public interest now. Because the "public interest" test must take its meaning from the nation's antitrust laws, *see American Cyanamid Co.*, 719 F.2d at 565, the appropriate question under section VII is whether the proposed modification would be certain to lessen competition in the relevant market. *See generally* 2 P. AREEDA & D. TURNER, ANTITRUST LAW ¶ 330, at 141–42 (1978) ("To remain consistent with antitrust policy, the court should revise the decree that is shown to lessen competition substantially in present circumstances."). Purporting to find that the BOCs would have both the incentive and the ability to cross-subsidize the information-service operations of unregulated affiliates and to discriminate against information-service competitors, the district court concluded that removal of section II(D)(1)'s restriction on information services would be *anticompetitive* under current market conditions. 673 F.Supp. at 565–67.

But because we cannot be certain that these findings were not infected by the court's legal error concerning the proper standard of review, we may not rely on them to support the district court's denial of the BOCs' motion. *See Pullman–Standard v. Swint,* 456 U.S. 273, 292, 102 S.Ct. 1781, 1792, 72 L.Ed.2d 66 (1982). The district court's analysis of the contemporary risk of anticompetitive behavior repeatedly incorporates the failure of the BOCs to show a change in market conditions from those existing when the decree became effective:

> There still has been no *significant, relevant change* in the situation.

673 F.Supp. at 564 (emphasis added).

> It is necessary next to determine whether, with respect to the provision of information services, the incentive and ability of the Regional Companies to engage in anticompetitive conduct *remains the same* as it was when the decree was entered. The answer is plain. *There has been no change whatever* in this respect since 1984. * * *

Id. at 565 (emphasis added).

> In short, the reasons cited by the Court in 1982 and in 1984 *are as valid today as they were then.*

Id. at 567 (emphasis added). Consequently, we cannot be sure whether the district court's findings of anticompetitive risk stemmed from its *de novo* assessment of the evidence.

Nor can we say that "the record permits only one resolution of the factual issue[s]" pertinent to determining whether lifting the information-services prohibition would be pro- or anticompetitive. *Pullman–Standard,* 456 U.S. at 292, 102 S.Ct. at 1792. To be sure, the district court had before it evidence to support its findings on the risk of discrimination and cross-subsidization. But the record also contains considerable evidence cutting the other way. The *Huber Report,* in particular, discounts the prospect of anticompetitive behavior, citing the ability of competing information-service providers to bypass the BOCs' local-exchange networks, *see Huber Report* at 6.8, 6.17–6.21, the existence of nontelecommunications substitutes for information services, *see id.* at 6.21–6.23, and the lack of common costs between local-exchange services and *the generation of information, see id.* at 6.35. Because resolving these disputed factual issues "would be wholly inconsistent with the function of an appellate court," *Southern Pacific Communications Co. v. American Tel. & Tel. Co.,* 740 F.2d 980, 984 (D.C.Cir.1984), *cert. denied,* 470 U.S. 1005, 105 S.Ct. 1359, 84 L.Ed.2d 380 (1985), we are constrained to remand the case for further factfinding, pursuant to the proper legal standard. *See Pullman–Standard,* 456 U.S. at 292, 102 S.Ct. at 1792.

In sum, we find that the district court erred in applying section VIII(C) rather than section VII's public interest standard to the BOCs' unopposed motion to lift the decree's information-services restriction in its entirety. And because we are unable to say that the district court would have reached the same result had it applied the proper legal standard, we reverse the court's decision and remand the case for further proceedings. In reconsidering the BOCs' motion, the district court should determine whether removal of the information-services restriction as applied to the generation of information would be anticompetitive under *present* market conditions.[29] The court should also bear in mind the *flexibility* of the public interest inquiry: the court's function is not to determine whether the resulting array of rights and liabilities "is the one that will *best* serve society," but only to confirm that the resulting "settlement is 'within the *reaches* of the public interest.'" *Bechtel Corp.*, 648 F.2d at 666 (quoting *Gillette Co.*, 406 F.Supp. at 716) (emphasis added).

IV.

* * *

V.

With the exception of the district judge's ruling dealing with information services—which we reverse and remand—we affirm.

So ordered.

Note

On remand, Judge Greene wrote a bitter opinion attacking the holding of the Court of Appeals and staying its effect. *United States v. Western Electric Co.*, 767 F.Supp. 308 (D.D.C.1991). The Court of Appeals reversed one stay. *New York Times*, Oct. 8, 1991, Sec. C, p. 1.

B. RESTRICTIONS ON GOVERNMENT COMPETITION

COMPUTERWARE, INC. v. KNOTTS

United States District Court, Eastern District of North Carolina, 1986.
626 F.Supp. 956.

BRITT, CHIEF JUDGE.

In this action questions of sovereign immunity and jurisdiction have put this case in an interesting legal posture. Plaintiff is a North Carolina corporation which maintains computer stores in Jacksonville and Havelock, North Carolina. Both stores are full-service dealerships for Apple Computer, Inc. The defendants are officers at the Marine Corps Bases at Camp Lejeune and Cherry Point, North Carolina. Plaintiff contends that (a) the list of approved items for sale at Post Exchanges was improperly amended to include home computers, and (b) even if the list of approved items was properly amended, the defendants have exceeded their authority by selling business computers and computers manufactured outside the United States. On 6 December 1985

29. We are also concerned with the practical difficulty of enforcing a merely *partial* repeal of the information-services ban; as the trial court recognized, significant disputes can be expected to arise concerning whether the BOCs are using their right to transmit the information of others as a cover for generating their own. *See* 673 F.Supp. at 596. Because it is clearly in the public interest to minimize the district court's oversight responsibilities under the decree, *see id.* at 599, the district court on remand should also consider whether the residual anticompetitive risks associated with lifting the restriction on generation of information are sufficiently great to outweigh the administrative burdens on the court of policing this limited prohibition.

plaintiff filed its complaint and motion for preliminary injunctive relief, to which the defendants responded and filed a motion to dismiss. On 12 December 1985 a hearing was held on plaintiff's preliminary injunction motion. By order dated 16 December 1985 the court denied plaintiff's preliminary injunction motion on the basis that plaintiff had failed to establish a reasonable probability of success on the jurisdiction question. The court gave plaintiff ten days to file a response to the defendants' motion to dismiss. Plaintiff submitted a response to the defendants' motion to dismiss and renewed its motion for preliminary injunctive relief, to which the defendants have submitted a reply. This matter is now ripe for ruling.

As an initial matter the court will grant the defendants' motion to dismiss plaintiff's claim that the list of approved items was improperly amended to include home computers. The amendments to the list of approved items was made by the House of Representatives' Committee on Armed Services, not by the Department of Defense or the defendant officials. Therefore, this claim is dismissed. The court finds, however, that it does have jurisdiction over plaintiff's claim that the defendants have exceeded their authority by selling business computers and computers manufactured outside the United States.

The initial roadblock for plaintiff in bringing this action was to frame the complaint in such a way as to confer jurisdiction on this court yet avoid the federal government's sovereign immunity. Plaintiff chose to rely on a string of cases which stood for the proposition that federal officials could not hide behind the government's sovereign immunity if they acted in excess of their statutory authority. *See Colorado v. Toll,* 268 U.S. 228, 45 S.Ct. 505, 69 L.Ed. 927 (1925). The problem with this approach is that a showing that the defendants' acts are wrongful or erroneous is not sufficient to demonstrate that they are outside the scope of their authority. *See* 14 C. Wright, A. Miller, & E. Cooper, Federal Practice and Procedure § 3655 at 226 (1985). In this case the defendants are authorized by the Armed Services Committee to sell items of merchandise at Post Exchanges. The defendants may be acting "erroneously" by selling certain items that are not on the "approved list," but they are acting well within the scope of their authority. Moreover, the defendants' decision to sell the items at issue in this case has been approved by the defendants' superior officials.

Plaintiff now contends that the sale of computers at Post Exchanges in violation of Armed Services Exchange Regulations (ASER) is agency action reviewable pursuant to the Administrative Procedure Act, 5 U.S.C. §§ 551 *et seq.,* and 28 U.S.C. § 1331. The court agrees. Prior to 1976 28 U.S.C. § 1331 could not be used as a jurisdictional basis to review administrative action where no monetary relief was sought. In order to avoid the inequities which often resulted seven circuits, including the Fourth Circuit, held that the Administrative Procedure Act was an independent grant of jurisdiction to review agency action. *See, e.g., Deering Milliken, Inc. v. Johnston,* 295 F.2d 856 (4th Cir.1961). In 1976 Congress amended 28 U.S.C. § 1331 to eliminate the $10,000 amount in controversy requirement. The effect of this amendment was to confer jurisdiction on federal courts to review agency action, thus undercutting the rationale for interpreting the Administrative Procedure Act as an independent grant of jurisdiction. One year later the Supreme Court specifically held that the Administrative Procedure Act was not an independent grant of jurisdiction. *See Califano v. Sanders,* 430 U.S. 99, 97 S.Ct. 980, 51 L.Ed.2d 192 (1977).

The next question is whether this suit is barred by the government's sovereign immunity. The first circuit to address the question held that the Administrative Procedure Act "did not remove the defense of sovereign immunity in actions under § 1331." *See Watson v. Blumenthal,* 586 F.2d 925, 932 (2d Cir.1978). Every other circuit to address the question has held that the Administrative Procedure Act does waive the government's sovereign immunity. *See, e.g., Jaffee v. United States,* 592 F.2d 712 (3d Cir.), *cert. denied,* 441 U.S. 961, 99 S.Ct. 2406, 60 L.Ed.2d 1066 (1979). The court agrees with this majority view. As the House Report shows, Congress amended 5 U.S.C. § 702 with the specific purpose of waiving sovereign immunity in "non-statutory" review of agency action under section 1331. *See* H.R.Rep. No. 94–1656, 94th Cong., 2d Sess. 5, *reprinted in* 1976 U.S.Code Cong. & Admin.News 6121, 6125 (hereinafter House Report). These suits are called "non-statutory" because they are not brought under statutes that specifically provide for review of agency action. The House Report notes that the acts of the older executive departments, such as the Department of Defense, are subject to judicial review only through "non-statutory" suits under section 1331. *Id.*

The defendants argue that the Administrative Procedure Act is inapplicable because (a) there has been no "agency action," and (b) this is a suit against individuals, not a federal agency. This argument lacks merit for several reasons. First, Marine Corps Post Exchanges are "agencies" within the meaning of the Administrative Procedure Act. *See Ellsworth Bottling Co. v. United States,* 408 F.Supp. 280, 282 (W.D.Okla.1975). Second, the regulations at issue in this case are sufficiently formal to provide a proper basis for a suit in federal court. *See Chasse v. Chasen,* 595 F.2d 59, 61 (1st Cir.1979). Third, plaintiff has standing to obtain judicial review of the defendants' action. The challenged action has caused an identifiable injury and plaintiff is a "local dealer" within the class of persons the Exchange Regulations are designed to protect. *See Ellsworth Bottling Co. v. United States,* 408 F.Supp. at 282. Fourth, plaintiff has exhausted its administrative remedies to the extent that it may do so. There is no formal procedure for plaintiff to contest the defendants' alleged abuse of discretion under the Exchange Regulations, but the president of the plaintiff corporation has written letters to Marine Corps officials who have made it clear that the Post Exchanges will continue selling the items complained about by plaintiff.

Finally, plaintiff has brought suit against the appropriate officials. Section 703 of the Administrative Procedure Act was amended in 1976 to remove any uncertainty as to who may be named as a defendant when the United States is sued. *See* 5 U.S.C. § 703. "When an instrumentality of the United States is the real defendant, the plaintiff should have the option of naming as defendant the United States, the agency by its official title, appropriate officers, or any combination of them. The outcome of the case should not turn on the plaintiff's choice." *See* House Report at 6138. Therefore, this action has been properly brought under the Administrative Procedure Act, and the defendants' motion to dismiss must be denied.

In ruling on the plaintiff's renewed motion for preliminary injunctive relief the court must examine the factors set forth in *Blackwelder Furniture Co. v. Seilig Manufacturing Co.,* 550 F.2d 189, 193 (4th Cir.1977). A party seeking injunctive relief must establish: (1) that there is a substantial likelihood that it will prevail on the merits; (2) that, in the absence of the requested relief, there is a substantial threat that it will suffer irreparable injury; (3) that the threatened injury to the moving party outweighs the threatened harm to the non-moving party; and (4) that the requested relief will not disserve the public interest. *Id.*

The court finds that there is a substantial likelihood that plaintiff will prevail on the merits of at least part of its complaint. The court will just briefly summarize the factual findings set forth in the 16 December 1985 order. The "approved list" of merchandise that may be sold at Post Exchanges, as amended, specifically excludes computers "oriented toward the office or business environment," and "computers produced and/or manufactured" by other than "U.S. sources." In selling the Macintosh computer system the defendants appear to be violating the first of these limitations. Plaintiff has submitted several brochures and advertisements by Apple Computer, Inc., which indicate that the Macintosh computer system is "oriented toward the office or business environment." The defendants have responded with affidavits to the effect that there is an informal agreement between Department of Defense officials and the Armed Services Committee that all computers which sell for less than $5,000 are to be considered "home computers." There is no such interpretation set forth in the Exchange Regulations or in any correspondence from the Armed Services Committee submitted to the court. Thus, the court must rely on the brochures and advertisements of Apple Computer, Inc., which indicate the Macintosh computer system is "oriented toward the office or business environment."

The second limitation, that computers "produced and/or manufactured of U.S. sources are to be used to meet the demand for these products," is extremely vague. It is unclear what distinction can be made between the terms "produced" and "manufactured." More importantly, plaintiff has not convinced the court that "U.S. sources" refers to manufacturing facilities located within the United States, rather than to domestic companies which may have manufacturing facilities in foreign countries. For example, the Apple IIe computer is manufactured in Singapore by a subsidiary of Apple Computer, Inc., and is then shipped to the United States for sale in this country. The court concludes that the "U.S. sources" limitation does not prohibit the sale of computers and accessories which are manufactured abroad by domestic companies or their subsidiaries. The "U.S. sources" limitation does, of course, prohibit the sale of computers and accessories manufactured outside the United States by companies which are not subsidiaries of domestic companies.

The court is aware of the fact that the Armed Services Committee may at any time amend the "approved list" to allow Post Exchanges to sell computers which are (a) "oriented toward the office or business environment," and (b) produced and manufactured by foreign companies. Likewise, it is within the discretion of the Secretaries of the Military Departments to authorize deviations from the "approved list." *See* ASER 1–102. That discretion must be exercised, however, within the bounds of the applicable regulations. ASER 1–102 specifies that "[d]eviations shall be authorized only after judicious review and granted primarily on the basis of geographical isolation of the installation concerned." *Id.*

The three remaining *Blackwelder* factors weigh in plaintiff's favor. First, with regard to the threat of irreparable injury to plaintiff the court notes that the busy Christmas season has ended. Nevertheless, whatever damage plaintiff continues to suffer is irreparable due to the government's immunity to a subsequent damages award. Second, the potential harm to the defendants is minimal. Third, the public interest lies in favor of plaintiff.

In summary, the defendants' motion to dismiss is granted as to the plaintiff's claim that (a) the list of approved items for sale at Post Exchanges was improperly amended to include home computers, and denied as to plaintiff's claim that (b) defendants have exceeded their authority to selling business computers and computers manufactured outside the United States. Plaintiff's renewed motion for preliminary injunctive relief is granted in part and denied in part. The defendants and all those in active concert and participation with them are hereby enjoined, pending further orders of this court, from authorizing or permitting the sale of the following items at the Marine Corps Post Exchanges at Camp Lejeune and Cherry Point, North Carolina: (a) The Macintosh computer system and all other computers and accessories "oriented toward the office or business environment;" and (b) all computers and accessories which are manufactured outside the United States by companies which are not subsidiaries of United States companies.

The plaintiff is hereby ordered to post a bond in the amount of $10,000 within five days from the date of this order.

C. ANTIDUMPING RESTRICTIONS ON FOREIGN COMPETITION

Dumping, under United States law, occurs when a foreign producer sells in the United States market at a price less than its price in the home market. Antidumping legislation provides relief for United States manufacturers faced with dumping by foreign competitors. United States manufacturers naturally attempt to stretch the definition of dumping to keep out as much foreign competition as possible. There is thus a great risk that legislation aimed at "unfair competition" can be enforced so as to ban competition that would be highly beneficial to American consumers. See William N. Eskridge, "Dynamic Interpretation of Economic Regulatory Legislation (Countervailing Duty Law)," *Law and Policy in International Business* 663 (1990). Dumping is particularly likely to occur where there are high fixed costs. The making of computer components, particularly memory chips requires huge investments in research and equipment. Once an assembly line is producing chips, the marginal cost of producing a few million more is very small. If the manufacturer, perhaps because of import restrictions or existence of a domestic cartel, can charge high domestic prices, it can increase its profits still further by raising production and exporting the surplus for whatever it can get. There are two laws that protect the computer industry from dumping: (1) the Revenue Act of 1916 and (2) the Trade Agreement Act of 1979.

The Revenue Act of 1916 (1916 Act) is basically an antitrust law against foreign price discrimination rather than an import relief law. The Federal Trade Commission stated that the 1916 Act classifies dumping as unfair competition. If there is a restraint of trade, in addition to dumping, the antitrust laws also apply. The 1916 Act allows individuals injured by dumping to sue the offending manufacturer in a private suit and provides for recovery of treble damages by a successful plaintiff. The 1916 Act also makes it unlawful for a manufacturer "commonly and systematically to import, sell, or cause to be sold" products in the United States at a price substantially below actual market price (wholesale) in the country of origin, with the intent to destroy, injure, or prevent an industry from being established in the United States. The 1916 Act has not been extensively used. Perhaps one reason for its limited use is the low success rate of suits brought under the 1916 Act.

Matsushita Electric v. Zenith (475 U.S. 574, 1986) was the first in many years. Zenith alleged that Japanese manufacturers were dumping televisions, radios, phonographs, and tape and cassette recorders and subsidizing this dumping by higher prices in Japan. The Court found that it was implausible that firms would, over many years, subsidize low prices in the U.S. with high prices and profits in the Japanese market and thus affirmed the dismissal of the case.

The Trade Agreement Act of 1979 (1979 Act) is the primary form of relief from foreign dumping, and prevents pricing at "less than fair value." Antidumping actions are conducted by the Department of Commerce. It institutes investigations and determines if goods are sold at "less than fair value." In comparing the foreign price and the United States price, the Department makes numerous adjustments. These adjustments are based on highly technical rules, which often have little relation to business reality. This means that a foreign firm accused of dumping must spend hugh sums paying Washington lawyers and experts in economics and accounting. Thus, even the threat of an antidumping suit can deter competition. If dumping has occurred and has caused injury to a U.S. industry, the International Trade Commission can direct the imposition of antidumping duties.

Note on the 64K and 256K DRAM Cases

In the 1980s the United States took a series of legal actions aimed at the Japanese semiconductor memory chip industry.

The Japanese government precipitated the conflict in the Japanese semiconductor industry. The case began in 1971 when Japanese legislation authorized the Japanese Ministry of International Trade and Industry (MITI) to plan for the development of strategic industries. Semiconductor memory chip manufacturing was one of those strategic industries. The plan developed by MITI, under a grant of immunity from Japanese antitrust laws, consisted of five general steps: (1) Japanese import quotas, (2) specialization in limited, high-volume product lines, (3) investment in the requisite production equipment to ensure minimal production costs at the predicted high volumes, (4) entry into the export market and aggressive pricing in the export market, (5) diversification into the full range of related product lines once market domination in the initial product was achieved.

In early 1972, MITI directed the formation of a cartel to carry out the targeting of semiconductors. The cartel performed basic research which was financed by the Japanese government and disseminated the findings among the participants. Sharing research resulted in substantial savings in the rapidly developing semiconductor area. In 1982, American semiconductor memory manufacturing firms charged Japanese semiconductor manufacturers with dumping. The charges were a result of a massive drop in the U.S. price of 64K Dynamic Random Access Memory (DRAM) chips during 1981. In response to the charges, the Japanese manufacturers agreed to limit their exports of DRAM chips to the United States. Price cuts initiated by Japanese manufacturers in late 1984 and early 1985 set off another round of protests by U.S. manufacturers. Acting pursuant to Section 301 of the Trade Act of 1974, the Semiconductor Industry Association requested that the President enforce the General Agreements on Tariffs and Trade and compel Japan to open its markets to the U.S. semiconductor industry. A formal dumping action against the Japanese was also brought by Micron Technology, Inc. in June 1985. This action culminated in a finding by the International Trade Administration of the Commerce Department that the Japanese had dumped 64K DRAM chips in the United States. The International Trade Commission then determined that the dumping had caused material injury to a United States industry and directed the imposition of antidumping duties on the Japanese 64K DRAM chips.

The Commerce Department also made preliminary findings that the Japanese had dumped both 256K DRAMs and Erasable Programmable Read Only Memories (EPROMs) in the United States.

Portions of the ITA decision follow:

64K DYNAMIC RANDOM ACCESS MEMORY COMPONENTS (64K DRAM'S) FROM JAPAN: FINAL DETERMINATION OF SALES AT LESS THAN FAIR VALUE

51 Fed.Reg. 15943

Agency: International Trade Administration/Import Administration/Commerce.

Action: Notice.

Summary: We have determined that 64K DRAMs from Japan are being, or are likely to be, sold in the United States at less than fair value, and have notified the U.S. International Trade Commission (ITC) of our determination. We have also directed the U.S. Customs Service to continue to suspend the liquidation of all entries of 64K DRAMs from Japan that are entered, or withdrawn from warehouse, for consumption, on or after December 11, 1985 and to require a cash deposit or bond for each entry in an amount equal to the estimated dumping margin as described in the "Suspension of Liquidation" section of this notice.

Effective date: April 29, 1986.

Final Determination

We have determined that 64K DRAMs from Japan are being, or are likely to be, sold in the United States at less than fair value, as provided in section 735(a) of the Tariff Act of 1930, as amended (19 U.S.C. 1673(a)) (the Act). We made fair value comparisons on almost all sales of the class or kind of merchandise to the United States by the respondents during the period of investigation. We excluded from our fair value comparisons U.S. sales of certain 64K DRAMs sold in insignificant quantities. The weighted-average margins are shown in the "Suspension of Liquidation" section of this notice.

Case History

On June 24, 1985, we received a petition from Micron Technology, Inc. on behalf of the domestic merchant manufacturers of 64K DRAMs. In compliance with the filing requirements of § 353.36 of the Commerce Regulations (19 CFR 353.36), the petition alleged that imports of 64K DRAMs from Japan are being, or are likely to be, sold in the

United States at less than fair value within the meaning of section 731 of the Act, and that these imports are materially injuring, or are threatening material injury to a United States industry. The petition also alleged that sales of the subject merchandise were being made in the home market at less than the cost of production. After reviewing the petition, we determined that it contained sufficient grounds upon which to initiate an antidumping duty investigation. We notified the ITC of our action and initiated such an investigation on July 15, 1985 (50 FE 29458). On August 8, 1985, the ITC determined that there is a reasonable indication that imports of 64K DRAMs from Japan are materially injuring, or are threatening material injury to, a U.S. industry (50 FR 32778).

* * *

Products Under Investigation

The products covered by this investigation are all 64K dynamic random access memory components of the N-channel metal oxide semiconductor type (64K DRAMs) from Japan. This merchandise is currently provided for in item 687.7441 of the *Tariff Schedules of the United States Annotated.* We investigated sales of 64K DRAMs during the period January 1 through June 30, 1985.

Fair Value Comparisons

To determine whether sales of the subject merchandise in the United States were made at less than fair value, we compared the United States price to the foreign market value for all companies. We used data provided in their responses, as explained in the "Foreign Market Value" section of this notice, except where otherwise noted.

We used date of shipment as the date of sale as that was the first date on which a binding commitment to sell the subject merchandise can be said to have occurred, as explained more fully in the comment section of this notice. All companies provided shipment dates for U.S. sales. Hitachi, Mitsubishi, and Oki provided shipment dates for home market sales as well. NEC provided only order dates for its home market sales. However, examination of individual NEC home market sales showed that the average length of time between order and shipment in the home market was substantially less than 30 days. Therefore, we determined that NEC's home market order date was a reasonable indication of shipment date, and we used that as best information available.

United States Price

For certain Hitachi sales we used the purchase price of the subject merchandise to represent United States price, as provided in section 772(b) of the Act, since the merchandise was sold to unrelated purchasers prior to its importation into the United States. For other Hitachi sales and sales by all other respondents, we used exporter's sales price (ESP) to represent United States price, in accordance with section

772(c) of the Act, as the merchandise was sold after the time of importation.

We calculated purchase price and ESP based on the packed, duty paid, C.I.F. prices to unrelated purchasers in the United States.

For purchase price, we made deductions for foreign inland freight and insurance, air freight, marine insurance, brokerage charges in Japan and the United States, and U.S. duty. For ESP, where appropriate, we made deductions for brokerage charges in Japan and the United States, foreign inland freight and insurance, air freight and insurance, U.S. duty, U.S. freight and insurance, commissions to unrelated parties, U.S. selling expenses incurred in the U.S. and Japan, credit expenses, warranties, advertising, royalties, and post-shipment price adjustments in the U.S. market. As Oki had no U.S. short-term borrowing, we used the U.S. prime rate for the first and second quarter of 1985 as the best information available in calculating Oki's U.S. credit expense.

Foreign Market Value

The petitioner alleged that sales in the home market by all the respondents were at prices below the cost of producing the merchandise.

In accordance with section 773(a) of the Act, for all companies, we calculated foreign market value based on home market prices where there were sufficient home market sales at or above the cost of production to determine foreign market value. We used constructed value as the basis for calculation foreign market value where there were no sales of such or similar merchandise in the home market or where there were insufficient sales above the cost of production, as defined in section 773(b) of the Act.

Where foreign market value was based on home market prices, we calculated a foreign market value for each product group for each month of the period of investigation, due to sharp declines in monthly prices. Where foreign market value was based on constructed value, we used a quarterly constructed value for each product group.

Since the production of 64K DRAMs was not at the developmental stage but rather at a mature stage of production, the Department used quarterly costs as the basis for the constructed value. The Department considered the significant changes in cost from quarter to quarter, the length of time for production, and the average inventory level of 64K DRAMs in order to appropriately match the sales data to the cost data. We concluded that the average costs of manufacturing incurred in the quarter proceding the sale most accurately reflected the costs of the product sold. Accordingly, the Department based its cost of production on the average manufacturing cost for the prior quarter and general expenses for the quarter in which the sale took place.

Cost of Production

In determining the cost of production for the respondents, the Department relied on the submissions, when verified and appropriately valued, and adjusted such data when certain costs necessary for the production of 64K DRAMs were not verified, not included, or not appropriately quantified or valued.

The Department analyzed industry practices of accounting for the equipment used to produce 64K DRAMs and concluded that the accelerated method of depreciation based on a five-year useful life was appropriate. In reaching this conclusion, the Department considered the characteristics of the industry which show rapid changes in manufacturing technology and a relatively brief market life for the 64K DRAM integrated circuits.

The Department included, as part of the depreciation expense, additional depreciation which was expensed when a company utilized the equipment in excess of normal production hours and when such expense was reflected on its records.

The Department's method of accounting for research and development (R & D) expenses encompassed the historic R & D for 64K DRAMs allocated over the market life of the product, which was considered part of the cost of manufacturing, and a proportional share of the current product line R & D and general R & D, which were considered to be part of the general expenses.

* * *

PRICE TO PRICE COMPARISONS

For each company examined, we found sufficient sales above the cost of production for certain product groups to allow use of home market prices to determine foreign market value in accordance with section 773(a)(1)(A) of the Act. We used home market prices for identical merchandise sold in the United States as the basis for foreign market value. We calculated the home market price on the basis of the F.O.B. price to unrelated purchasers. When we compared purchase price to foreign market value, we made deductions, where appropriate, for foreign inland freight and insurance, discounts and rebates. We also made adjustments, where appropriate, for differences in circumstances of sale for credit terms, in accordance with § 353.15 of our regulations. On purchase price sales by Hitachi, we offset commissions paid on U.S. sales with indirect selling expenses in the home market, in accordance with § 353.15(c) of our regulations.

When we compared ESP with foreign market value, we made deductions, where appropriate, for foreign inland freight and insurance, advertising, credit expenses, direct selling expenses, discounts, rebates, and commissions. We also used indirect selling expenses in the home market to offset United States selling expenses, in accordance with § 353.15(c) of our regulations.

For both purchase price and ESP, in order to adjust for differences in packing between the two markets, we deducted home market packing costs and added U.S. packing costs to the home market prices.

We disallowed deductions for inland freight between Hitachi and its subsidiaries, because we considered this expense an intra-company transfer and included it in the cost of production. We also disallowed technical servicing expenses incurred by Hitachi since these could not be tied to particular sales during the period of investigation.

Constructed Value

In accordance with section 773(e) of the Act, we calculated foreign market value based on constructed value when there were not sufficient home market sales above the cost of production of such or similar merchandise for the purpose of comparison. For constructed value, the Department used the cost of all materials, fabrication, general expenses, and profit based on the respondents submissions, revised, as detailed under the "Cost of Production" section of this notice. Actual general expenses were used, since in all cases, such expenses exceeded the statutory minimum of 10 percent of materials and fabrication. Only one respondent provided verifiable profit data. This figure exceeded the eight percent statutory minimum for profit. Since the other respondents were unable to provide verifiable profit data, we used the best information available for them, which was the verified profit of the one firm which provided an adequate profit submission. We made adjustments under § 353.15 of the regulations for differences in credit and royalties between the two markets.

Where there were commissions in one market and not in the other, we offset the commissions with indirect selling expenses in the other market. We also used indirect selling expenses in the home market to offset United States selling expenses, in accordance with § 353.15(c) of our regulations.

Currency Conversion

In calculating foreign market value, we made currency conversions from Japanese yen to U.S. dollars in accordance with § 353.56(a) of our regulations, using the certified daily exchange rates for comparisons involving purchase price. For ESP comparisons, we used the official exchange rate for the date of sale, which we determined was the date of shipment, since the use of that exchange rate is consistent with section 615 of the Trade and Tariff Act of 1984 (1984 Act). We followed section 615 of the 1984 Act rather than § 353.56(a)(2) of our regulations because the later law supersedes that section of the regulations.

* * *

Suspension of Liquidation

In accordance with section 733(d)(2) of the Act, we are directing the United States Customs Service to continue to suspend liquidation of all entries of 64K DRAMs from Japan that are entered, or withdrawn from warehouse, for consumption, on or after December 11, 1985. The United States Customs Service shall require a cash deposit or the posting of a bond equal to the estimated weighted-average amount by which the foreign market value of the merchandise subject to this investigation exceeds the United States price as shown in the table below. This suspension of liquidation will remain in effect until further notice.

Manufacturer/producer/exporter	Margin percentage
NEC Corporation	22.76
Hitachi Ltd.	11.87
Oki Electric Industry Co. Ltd.	35.34
Mitsubishi Electric Corporation	13.43
All other manufacturers/producers/cxporters	20.75

ITC Notification

In accordance with section 735(d) of the Act, we will notify the ITC of our determination. In addition, we are making available to the ITC all non-privileged and non-confidential information relating to this investigation. We will allow the ITC access to all privileged and confidential information in our files, provided the ITC confirms that it will not disclose such information either publicly or under an administrative protective order without the consent of the Deputy Assistant Secretary for Import Administration. The ITC will determine whether these imports materially injure, or threaten material injury to, a U.S. industry within 45 days after we make our final determination. If the ITC determines that material injury or threat of material injury does not exist, this proceeding will be terminated and all securities posted as a result of the suspension of liquidation will be refunded or cancelled. However, if the ITC determines that such injury does exist, we will issue an antidumping duty order on 64K DRAMs from Japan entered, or withdrawn from warehouse, for consumption after the suspension of liquidation, equal to the amount by which the foreign market value exceeds the United States price.

This determination is published pursuant to section 735(d) of the Act (19 U.S.C. 1673d(d)).

April 23, 1986.

Index

References are to Pages

References are to Pages

†

0-314-92197-4
90000
9 780314 921970